SHOWCASE PRESENTS

Wonder Woman

VOLUME ONE

WONDER WOMAN CREATED BY WILLIAM MOULTON MARSTON.

Dan DiDio Senior VP-Executive Editor

Whitney Ellsworth, Robert Kanigher Editors-original series

Peter Hamboussi Editor-collected edition

Robbin Brosterman Senior Art Director

Paul Levitz President & Publisher

Georg Brewer VP-Design & DC Direct Creative

Richard Bruning Senior VP-Creative Director

Patrick Caldon Executive VP-Finance & Operations

Chris Caramalis VP-Finance

John Cunningham VP-Marketing

Terri Cunningham VP-Managing Editor

Alison Gill VP-Manufacturing

Hank Kanalz VP-General Manager, WildStorm

Jim Lee Editorial Director-WildStorm

Paula Lowitt Senior VP-Business & Legal Affairs

MaryEllen McLaughlin VP-Advertising & Custom Publishing

John Nee VP-Business Development

Gregory Noveck Senior VP-Creative Affairs

Sue Pohja VP-Book Trade Sales

Cheryl Rubin Senior VP-Brand Management

Jeff Trojan VP-Business Development, DC Direct

Bob Wayne VP-Sales

Cover illustration by Ross Andru and Mike Esposito.
Front cover colored by Richard and Tanya Horie.

SHOWCASE PRESENTS: WONDER WOMAN VOLUME ONE
Published by DC Comics. Cover and compilation
copyright © 2007 DC Comics. All Rights Reserved.

Originally published in single magazine form in WONDER WOMAN 98-117
Copyright © 1958-1960 DC Comics. All Rights Reserved. All characters, their
distinctive likenesses and related elements featured in this publication
are trademarks of DC Comics.

Special thanks to Mike Tiefenbacher for loan of source material.

DC Comics, 1700 Broadway, New York, NY 10019
A Warner Bros. Entertainment Company
Printed in Canada. First Printing.
ISBN: 1-4012-1373-1
ISBN 13: 978-1-4012-1373-2

PART I
"THE SECRET
AMAZON TRIALS!"

TABLE OF CONTENTS

ALL STORIES WRITTEN BY **ROBERT KANIGHER**.
ALL STORIES AND COVERS PENCILLED BY **ROSS ANDRU** AND INKED BY **MIKE ESPOSITO**, UNLESS OTHERWISE NOTED.

UNTIL THE 1970S IT WAS NOT COMMON PRACTICE IN THE COMIC BOOK INDUSTRY TO CREDIT ALL STORIES. IN THE PREPARATION OF THIS COLLECTION WE HAVE USED OUR BEST EFFORTS TO REVIEW ANY SURVIVING RECORDS AND CONSULT ANY AVAILABLE DATABASES AND KNOWLEDGEABLE PARTIES. WE REGRET THE INNATE LIMITATIONS OF THIS PROCESS AND ANY MISSING OR MISASSIGNED ATTRIBUTIONS THAT MAY OCCUR. ANY ADDITIONAL INFORMATION ON CREDITS SHOULD BE DIRECTED TO: EDITOR, COLLECTED EDITIONS, C/O DC COMICS.

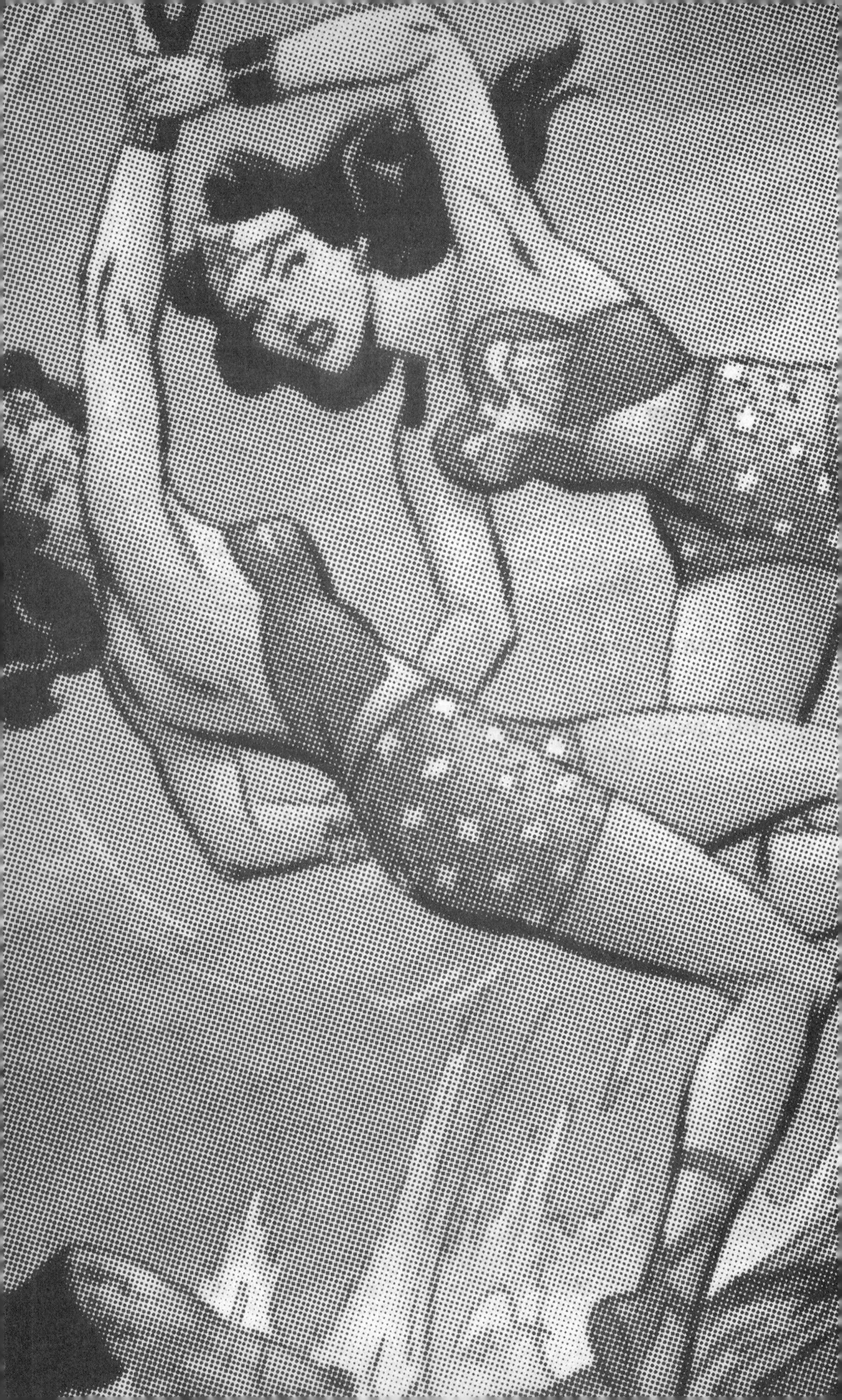

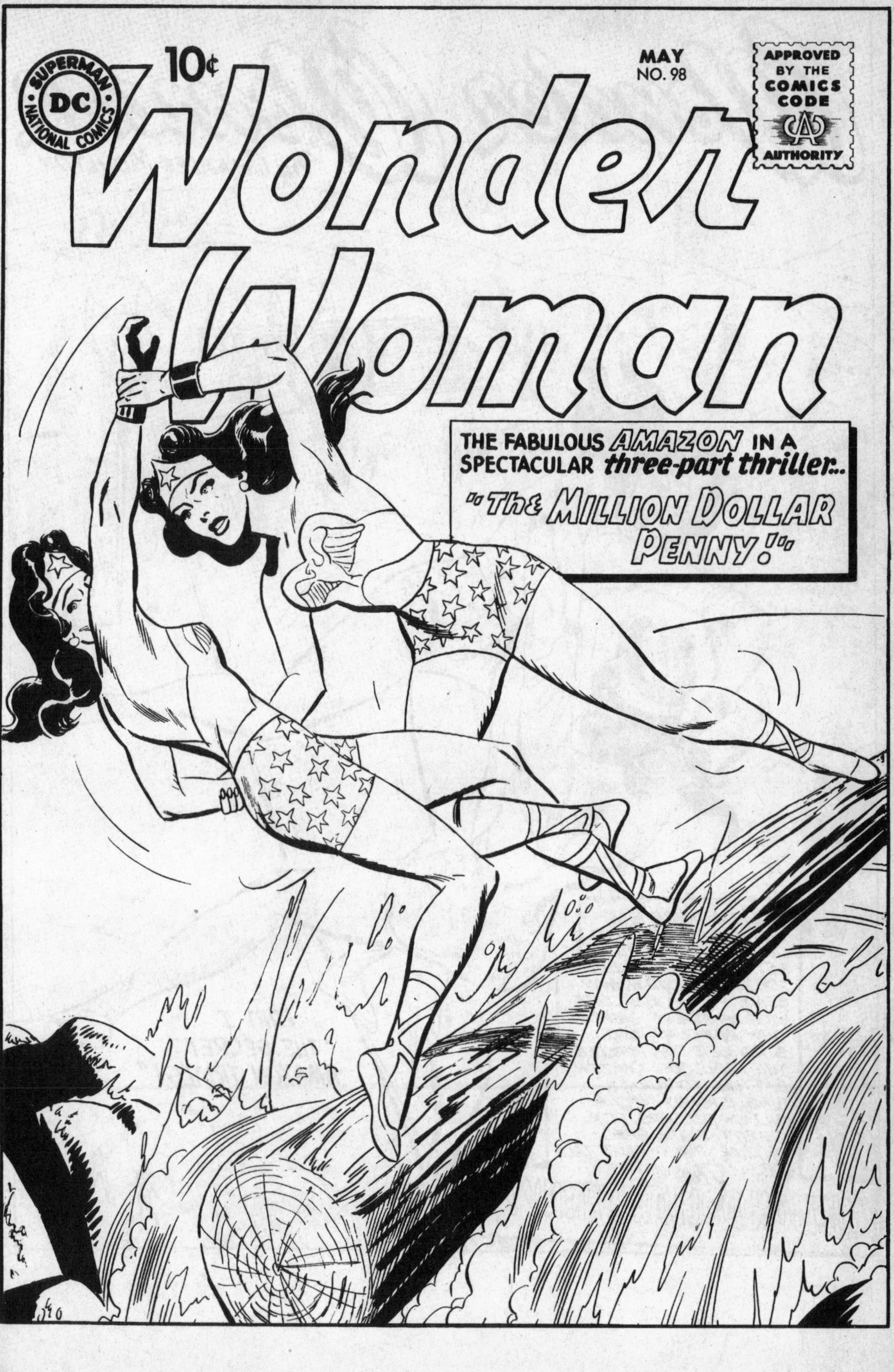
SUPERMAN DC NATIONAL COMICS
10¢
MAY
NO. 98
APPROVED BY THE COMICS CODE AUTHORITY
Wonder Woman
THE FABULOUS AMAZON IN A SPECTACULAR three-part thriller...
"The MILLION DOLLAR PENNY!"

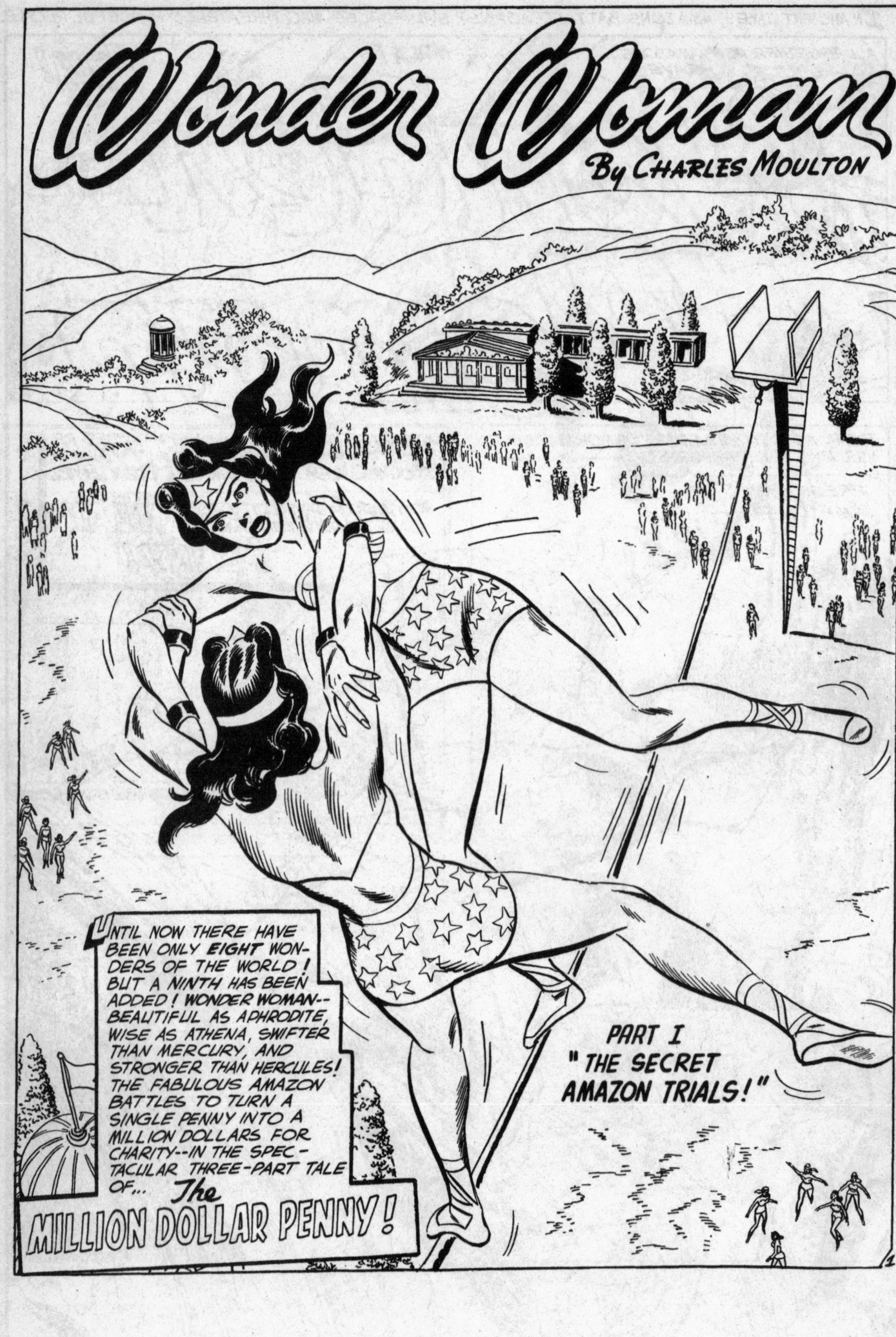
Wonder Woman
By CHARLES MOULTON
UNTIL NOW THERE HAVE BEEN ONLY EIGHT WONDERS OF THE WORLD! BUT A NINTH HAS BEEN ADDED! WONDER WOMAN--BEAUTIFUL AS APHRODITE, WISE AS ATHENA, SWIFTER THAN MERCURY, AND STRONGER THAN HERCULES! THE FABULOUS AMAZON BATTLES TO TURN A SINGLE PENNY INTO A MILLION DOLLARS FOR CHARITY--IN THE SPECTACULAR THREE-PART TALE OF... The
MILLION DOLLAR PENNY!
PART I
"THE SECRET AMAZON TRIALS!"
1

IN ANCIENT TIMES, AMAZONS BATTLED AGAINST EVIL FORCES WHO THREATENED PEACEFUL PEOPLE.

ALL TOGETHER NOW, AMAZONS... HEAVE!

HOLA!

HOLA!

THEIR ASTOUNDING FEATS DEMORALIZED VILLAINS EVERYWHERE...

PRESS ON, AMAZONS!

WHEN ALL WAS PEACEFUL, THE AMAZONS RETIRED TO THEIR SECRET ISLAND HOME IN THE PACIFIC...REIGNED OVER BY QUEEN HIPPOLYTA...

YOU SING AS SWEETLY AS A LARK, DAUGHTER DIANA!

THE AMAZONS WERE INCREDIBLY DARING..

DOES NOT PRINCESS DIANA SOAR GRACEFULLY AS ANY BIRD!

AT THE ATHLETIC GAMES WHICH KEPT THE AMAZONS IN PERFECT PHYSICAL CONDITION...

MY DAUGHTER BOUNDS LIGHTLY AS A FEATHER!

BEHOLD! DIANA'S AGILITY IS INCREDIBLE!

ONE DAY, PALLAS-ATHENA, PATRON GODDESS OF THE AMAZONS APPEARED TO THE QUEEN...

HIPPOLYTA!...THE TIME HAS COME FOR YOU TO CHOOSE THE GREATEST OF THE AMAZONS! YOU MUST SEND HER ON A MISSION TO MAN'S WORLD TO BATTLE CRIME AND INJUSTICE-- AND HELP PEOPLE IN DISTRESS! ONLY WHEN HER SERVICES ARE NO LONGER NEEDED-- CAN SHE THINK OF HERSELF!

THE NEXT DAY... BY PALLAS-ATHENA'S COMMAND, I AM TO HOLD A COMPETITION TO SELECT THE GREATEST AMAZON AMONG YOU, TO LIVE IN MAN'S WORLD, TO HELP THE NEEDY, AND TO BATTLE CRIME AND INJUSTICE EVERYWHERE!

NOBLE QUEEN! ALL OF US WANT TO SERVE! THAT IS WHY I MUST POINT OUT THAT YOU ARE NOT ONLY A QUEEN--BUT A MOTHER! YOU ARE ONLY HUMAN! HOW CAN YOU PREVENT YOUR HEART FROM FAVORING YOUR OWN DAUGHTER, PRINCESS DIANA?

ORANA IS RIGHT, MOTHER!

AFTER A FEW LIGHTNING MOMENTS OF DEEP THOUGHT...

I HAVE A PLAN THAT WILL POSITIVELY GUARANTEE THAT NO FAVORITISM CAN POSSIBLY BE USED IN MY BEHALF... HERE IT IS...

THE NEXT DAY, AT THE VAST ISLAND SPORTS FIELD...

GREAT HERA! EVERYWHERE I LOOK--I SEE MY DAUGHTER'S FACE!

AYE! WITH THESE **COMPLETE** DISGUISES, **EVERY** COMPETING AMAZON LOOKS LIKE **ME**! UNABLE TO TELL ONE DIANA FROM ANOTHER--YOU CANNOT POSSIBLY FAVOR ME--EVEN INNOCENTLY!

SHORTLY, A HUGE AIRSHIP IS WHEELED ONTO THE FIELD...

THE FIRST CONTEST IS A TUG OF WAR! WHICHEVER GROUP OF AMAZONS TUGS THE OTHER OVER THE CENTER LINE--IS THE WINNER! **BEGIN**!

FIRST ONE WAY...AND THEN THE OTHER, THE MASSIVE OBJECT IS TUGGED...

HOLD, SISTER AMAZONS!

PULL BACK-- OR WE LOSE!

BACK AND FORTH ACROSS THE FIELD THE MAMMOTH STRUGGLE CONTINUES...

AMAZONS-- DON'T YIELD!

HOLD YOUR GROUND!

WE MUST NOT LOSE!

FINALLY, WITH A TREMENDOUS SURGE, THE CONTEST IS SUDDENLY DECIDED...

THE LOSING AMAZONS WILL REMOVE THEIR MASKS!

ANXIOUSLY, THE QUEEN STARES AT THE FACES OF THE LOSING CONTESTANTS...

THANK HERA! DIANA IS STILL WITH THE WINNERS! SHE IS *STILL* ELIGIBLE!

THE REMAINING GROUP OF AMAZONS THEN MARCH TO RAPID RIVER WHERE...

THE NEXT CONTEST IS TO RIDE THOSE LOGS OVER *HURRICANE FALLS!* BEGIN!

AMAZON AFTER AMAZON LOSES HER FOOTING -- IN THE TURBULENT RIDE -- TOWARD THE RUSHING WATERFALLS...

I CANNOT HOLD ON -- ANY LONGER!

SPLASH!

THIS RACE -- HAS BESTED ME!

SHADES OF PLUTO -- I LOSE!

OVER THE CRASHING FALLS STILL MORE AMAZONS TUMBLE OFF THEIR WHIRLING MOUNTS...

MY BALANCE-- GONE !

I CAN'T CONTINUE !

MY SKILL IS OVERTAXED !

STILL MORE TOPPLE WHEN THE LOGS HURTLE TO THE FOAMING POOL AT THE BOTTOM...

THE RACE ENDS FOR ME HERE !

I HAVE LOST !

UNTIL... OF ALL THE AMAZONS WHO HAD STARTED...

ONLY WE TWO ARE LEFT !

AYE !

AGAIN THE LOSERS REMOVE THEIR MASKS BEFORE THE BREATHLESS QUEEN...

THANK HERA ! MY DAUGHTER IS STILL IN THE COMPETITION !

AS THE TWO REMAINING CONTESTANTS RE- CEIVE THEIR FINAL INSTRUCTION FROM THE AMAZON QUEEN...

ONE OF THESE IS DIANA !... BUT WHICH ONE ?-- WHICH ONE --?

THE FINAL CONTEST FINDS THE TWO CONTESTANTS FACING EACH OTHER ON A SLENDER HIGH WIRE...

THE WINNER OF THIS WRESTLING MATCH -- WILL BE CHOSEN TO GO TO MAN'S WORLD! READY? BEGIN!

ON THE SWAYING HIGH WIRE...

THE ASTONISHING CONTEST...

REACHES A BREATHLESS CONCLUSION ... WHEN...

AS THE AMAZON HURTLES TOWARD THE GROUND...

SUFFERING SAPPHO! SHE FAILED TO SEIZE HOLD OF THE WIRE TO STOP HER FALL! IS SHE -- MY DAUGHTER?

INSTANTLY... THE REMAINING AMAZON DIVES DOWN AFTER THE OTHER...

BEFORE THE BREATHLESS GAZE OF THE SPECTATORS...

HOLA!

WHAT A CATCH!

THE SUSPENSE IS UNBEARABLE AS...

WHICH ONE... IS MY DAUGHTER?

THE NEXT MOMENT AMIDST THUNDEROUS CHEERS...

HOLA!

PRINCESS DIANA WON!

SHE IS A WONDER WOMAN!

AYE--A WONDER WOMAN INDEED!

AND THEN... DIANA--YOU WILL HAVE TO PERFORM WONDERS INDEED-- IN MAN'S WORLD! FOR YOUR FIRST MISSION IS TO DONATE A SUMMER CAMP TO THE CHILDREN'S CHARITIES! IT WILL COST A MILLION DOLLARS!

A MILLION DOLLARS? BUT, MOTHER! YOU KNOW I DON'T HAVE ANY MONEY!

8

BY PALLAS-ATHENA'S COMMAND... YOU ARE TO TURN THIS PENNY INTO A MILLION DOLLARS IN 24 HOURS!

THE AMAZON'S TASK SEEMS IMPOSSIBLE TO PERFORM--UNLESS SHE IS A WONDER WOMAN! WE SHALL SEE IN PART TWO!

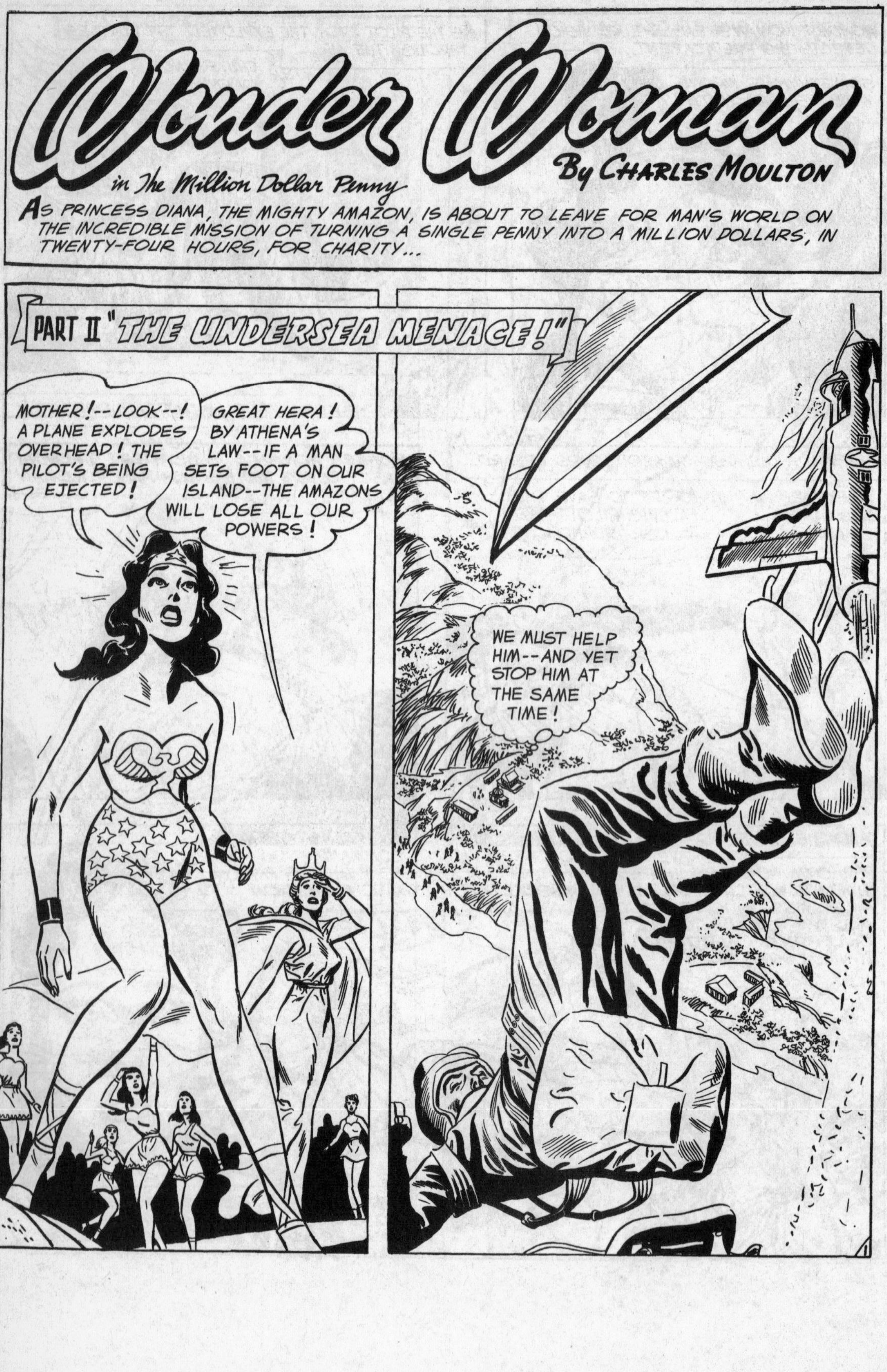
Wonder Woman
in The Million Dollar Penny
By CHARLES MOULTON
AS PRINCESS DIANA, THE MIGHTY AMAZON, IS ABOUT TO LEAVE FOR MAN'S WORLD ON THE INCREDIBLE MISSION OF TURNING A SINGLE PENNY INTO A MILLION DOLLARS, IN TWENTY-FOUR HOURS, FOR CHARITY...
PART II "THE UNDERSEA MENACE!"
MOTHER!--LOOK--! A PLANE EXPLODES OVERHEAD! THE PILOT'S BEING EJECTED!
GREAT HERA! BY ATHENA'S LAW--IF A MAN SETS FOOT ON OUR ISLAND--THE AMAZONS WILL LOSE ALL OUR POWERS!
WE MUST HELP HIM--AND YET STOP HIM AT THE SAME TIME!

WONDER WOMAN'S EAGLE-LIKE VISION DETECTS HIS PREDICAMENT...

SOMETHING'S WRONG WITH HIS PARACHUTE!

AS THE PILOT FROM THE EXPLODED JET HURTLES THROUGH THE AIR...

CHUTE--NOT OPENING--!

INSTANTLY, THE AGILE AMAZON LEAPS UPWARD...

WHERE ARE YOU GOING, DIANA?

TO TRY TO SAVE THE FALLING PILOT--AND OUR ISLAND!

WONDER WOMAN'S MAGNIFICENT STRENGTH EASILY BENDS THE SPRINGY FLAGPOLE ALMOST IN TWO...

CREEEEEK!

LIKE A HUMAN CANNONBALL--THE DARING AMAZON CATAPULTS HERSELF INTO SPACE...

BRRRNNNGG!

HERA HELP ME TO SAVE HIM!

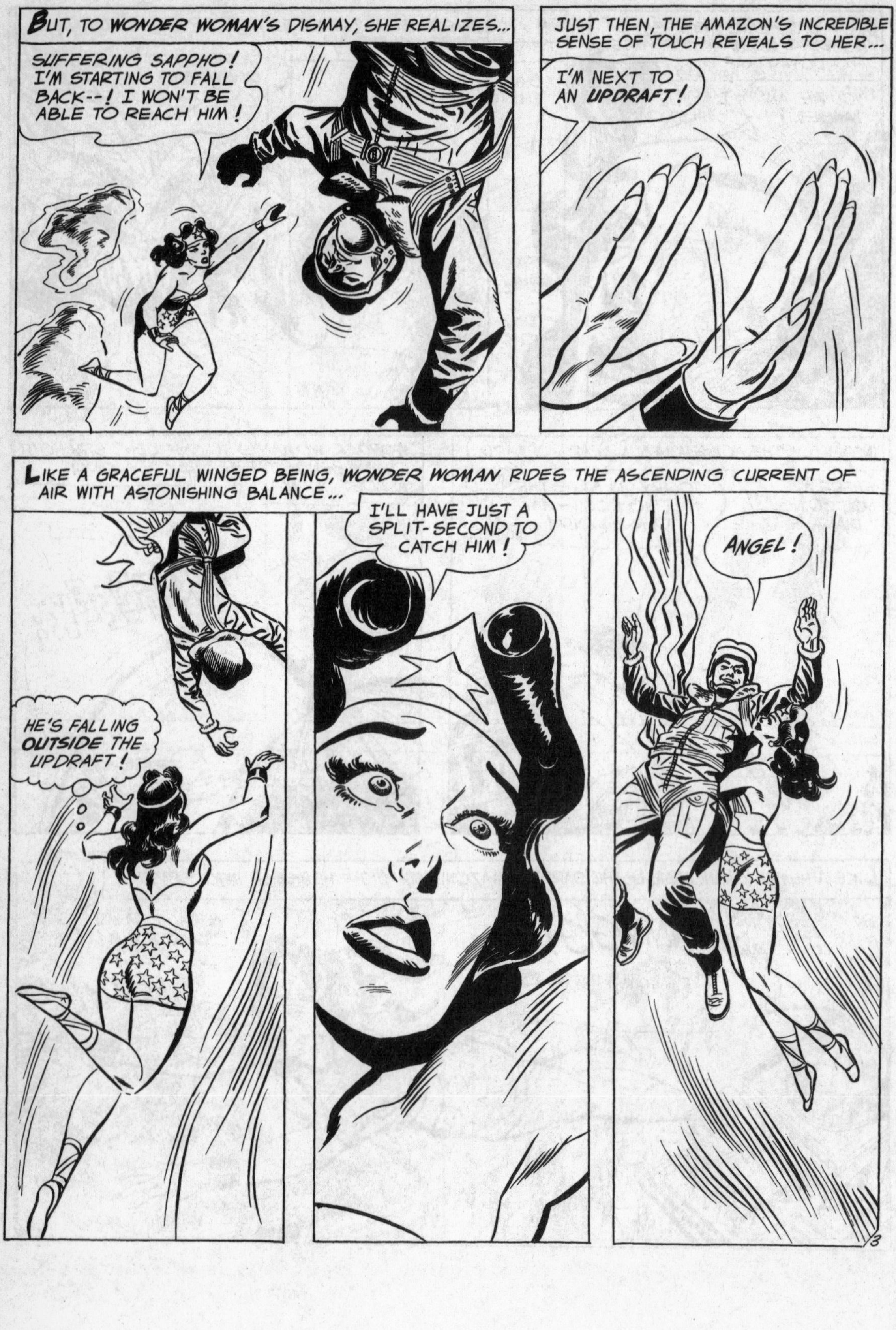
BUT, TO WONDER WOMAN'S DISMAY, SHE REALIZES...
SUFFERING SAPPHO! I'M STARTING TO FALL BACK--! I WON'T BE ABLE TO REACH HIM!
JUST THEN, THE AMAZON'S INCREDIBLE SENSE OF TOUCH REVEALS TO HER...
I'M NEXT TO AN UPDRAFT!
LIKE A GRACEFUL WINGED BEING, WONDER WOMAN RIDES THE ASCENDING CURRENT OF AIR WITH ASTONISHING BALANCE...
HE'S FALLING OUTSIDE THE UPDRAFT!
I'LL HAVE JUST A SPLIT-SECOND TO CATCH HIM!
ANGEL!
3

WITH DAZZLING AGILITY, WONDER WOMAN UPDRAFTS... AND DOWNDRAFTS...

YOU'RE AN ANGEL!

I'M JUST AN AMAZON!

IN A DESPERATE ATTEMPT TO AVOID LANDING ON PARADISE ISLAND...

SAME THING!

YOU'RE BEAUTIFUL-- AND YOU SAVED MY LIFE!

FINALLY...

YOUR DAUGHTER IS A WONDER WOMAN, NOBLE QUEEN! SHE MANAGED TO KEEP THE MAN FROM SETTING FOOT ON OUR ISLAND! OUR POWERS ARE SAVED!

AYE! BUT HER MIGHTY TASKS-- MERELY BEGIN! NOW, SHE MUST HELP THE PILOT REACH SAFETY-- AND TURN THE PENNY SHE HAS INTO A MILLION DOLLARS IN A SINGLE DAY!

AT THAT MOMENT...

SHARKS BELOW! SORRY I GOT YOU INTO THIS MESS, BEAUTIFUL! THE MOMENT WE HIT THE WATER--I'LL TRY TO KEEP THEM OCCUPIED-- WHILE YOU SWIM AWAY!

YOU WOULDN'T LAST TEN SECONDS WITH THOSE KILLERS! THERE MUST BE SOME OTHER WAY OF ESCAPING THEM!

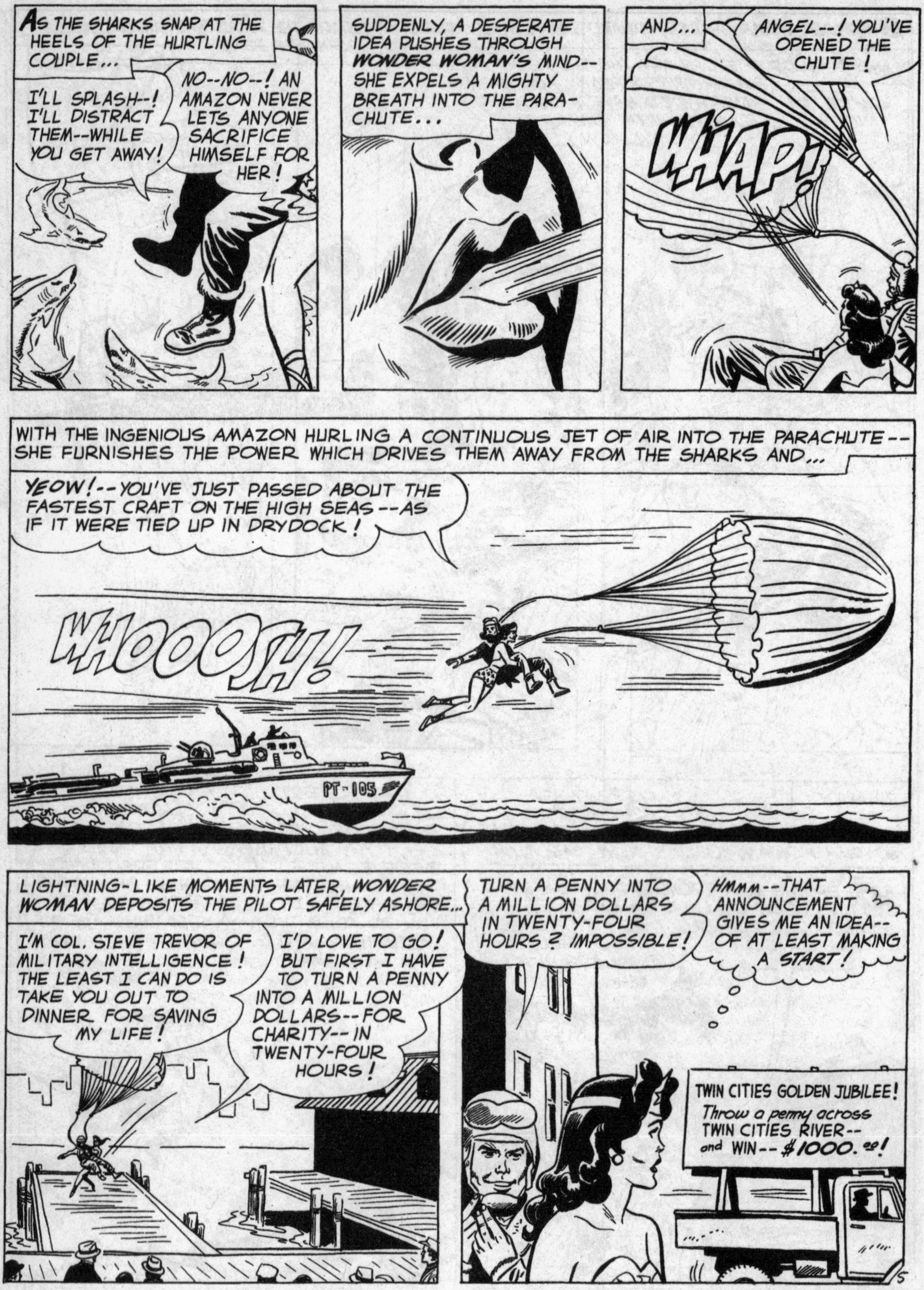
AS THE SHARKS SNAP AT THE HEELS OF THE HURTLING COUPLE...
I'LL SPLASH--! I'LL DISTRACT THEM--WHILE YOU GET AWAY!
NO--NO--! AN AMAZON NEVER LETS ANYONE SACRIFICE HIMSELF FOR HER!
SUDDENLY, A DESPERATE IDEA PUSHES THROUGH WONDER WOMAN'S MIND--SHE EXPELS A MIGHTY BREATH INTO THE PARACHUTE...
AND...
ANGEL--! YOU'VE OPENED THE CHUTE!
WHAP!
WITH THE INGENIOUS AMAZON HURLING A CONTINUOUS JET OF AIR INTO THE PARACHUTE--SHE FURNISHES THE POWER WHICH DRIVES THEM AWAY FROM THE SHARKS AND...
YEOW!--YOU'VE JUST PASSED ABOUT THE FASTEST CRAFT ON THE HIGH SEAS--AS IF IT WERE TIED UP IN DRYDOCK!
WHOOOSH!
PT-105
LIGHTNING-LIKE MOMENTS LATER, WONDER WOMAN DEPOSITS THE PILOT SAFELY ASHORE...
I'M COL. STEVE TREVOR OF MILITARY INTELLIGENCE! THE LEAST I CAN DO IS TAKE YOU OUT TO DINNER FOR SAVING MY LIFE!
I'D LOVE TO GO! BUT FIRST I HAVE TO TURN A PENNY INTO A MILLION DOLLARS--FOR CHARITY--IN TWENTY-FOUR HOURS!
TURN A PENNY INTO A MILLION DOLLARS IN TWENTY-FOUR HOURS? IMPOSSIBLE!
HMMM--THAT ANNOUNCEMENT GIVES ME AN IDEA--OF AT LEAST MAKING A START!
TWIN CITIES GOLDEN JUBILEE!
Throw a penny across TWIN CITIES RIVER--
and WIN--$1000.00!
5

As WONDER WOMAN RACES TOWARD TWIN CITIES RIVER..

IF I CAN WIN THE THOUSAND DOLLARS BY THROWING A PENNY ACROSS THE RIVER--I'LL HAVE A GOOD SUM TO WORK WITH TOWARD THAT MILLION!

GUM

BUT...IN THE AMAZON'S HASTE...SHE DROPS THE PENNY...

PLINK!

IT ROLLS DOWN THE STREET...

TIC! TIC! TIC! TIC!

UNTIL...

TING!

A PENNY! WHAT LUCK!

AT THAT MOMENT, FRANTICALLY RETRACING HER FOOTSTEPS...

THAT BOY--HE'S FOUND THE PENNY! THANK HERA! IF THAT PENNY WERE LOST--MY MISSION WOULD BE A FAILURE-- BECAUSE I HAVE TO MAKE THE MILLION WITH THAT PARTICULAR PENNY--AND NO OTHER!

BUT THEN...

MERCIFUL MINERVA! HE PLACED THE PENNY IN THAT CHEWING GUM MACHINE! ONCE THAT PENNY IS SPENT--I'VE LOST--FAILED THE CHARITY--DISGRACED MYSELF AND ALL THE AMAZONS!

COIN RETURN

TUNG!

IN HORROR *WONDER WOMAN* WATCHES HER PENNY VANISHING...AND THEN... UNEXPECTEDLY. SHE SIGHS WITH RELIEF AS...

WHRRRRR!

CLICK!

AW--THE MACHINE'S EMPTY-- I GOT MY PENNY BACK!

BUT, WHEN THE AMAZON ASKS FOR HER PENNY!

NO! HOW DO I KNOW YOU'RE TELLING THE TRUTH UNLESS YOU CAN PROVE YOU'RE AN AMAZON--? DO AN AMAZON TRICK! SOMETHING THAT NO ONE ELSE IN THE WORLD CAN! HERE--LET'S SEE YOU SKIP THE ROPE AROUND YOU TEN--NO--A *HUNDRED TIMES*-- *BEFORE* YOUR FEET TOUCH THE GROUND!

WONDER WOMAN SKIPS OFF THE GROUND AND WHIRLS THE ROPE AROUND HER WITH DAZZLING SPEED WHILE...

ONE--TWO-- THREE...

SIXTY-NINE SEVENTY-- SEVENTY- ONE...

NINETY-EIGHT... NINETY-NINE... ONE HUNDRED!

YOU PROVED YOU'RE AN AMAZON ALL RIGHT! GOSH--YOU'RE A *WONDER WOMAN*! HERE'S THE PENNY!

THANK YOU-- YOU'RE A GOOD BOY!

WITH A SPEED NO HUMAN EYE CAN FOLLOW, *WONDER WOMAN* RACES ON TO TWIN CITIES RIVER WHERE...

IT'S NO USE! NO ONE CAN PERFORM THIS FEAT! WITHDRAW THE OFFER!

NO--WAIT!

N CITIES GOLDEN JUBILEE! Throw a penny across TWIN CITIES RIVER WIN-- $1000.ºº!

WONDER WOMAN PLEADS WITH THE OFFICIALS TO ALLOW HER TO MAKE THE ATTEMPT...

OH, ALL RIGHT, AMAZON! BUT IT'S A WASTE OF TIME! YOU'LL FAIL--JUST LIKE EVERYONE ELSE!

THANK YOU-- THANK YOU!

HERA HELP ME SUCCEED--SO THE CHILDREN CAN GET THEIR SUMMER CAMP--AND I DON'T DISGRACE THE AMAZONS!

UP... UP... UP... FLASHES THE COIN INTO THE AIR...

VROOSH!

UNTIL THE GLEAMING COIN ATTRACTS THE ATTENTION OF A GREAT HAWK WHOSE POINTED BEAK CLAMPS DOWN...

CLICK!

FRANTICALLY, WONDER WOMAN HURLS HER GOLDEN LASSO AT THE WINGED CREATURE...

THAT HAWK'S FLYING AWAY WITH YOUR PENNY! YOU'VE LOST!

NO--WAIT--PLEASE GIVE ME A CHANCE TO GET THE PENNY BACK--SO I CAN TRY AGAIN!

BUT AS THE LASSO TIGHTENS, THE POWERFUL BIRD DOES NOT TOPPLE DOWN TO EARTH-- INSTEAD...

LET GO, AMAZON! NEVER MIND THAT PENNY!

SAVE YOURSELF!

NO! I MUST RECOVER THAT PENNY-- NO MATTER WHAT HAPPENS!

WONDER WOMAN'S ASTOUNDING ADVENTURES REACH GREATER HEIGHTS IN THE CONCLUDING CHAPTER!...

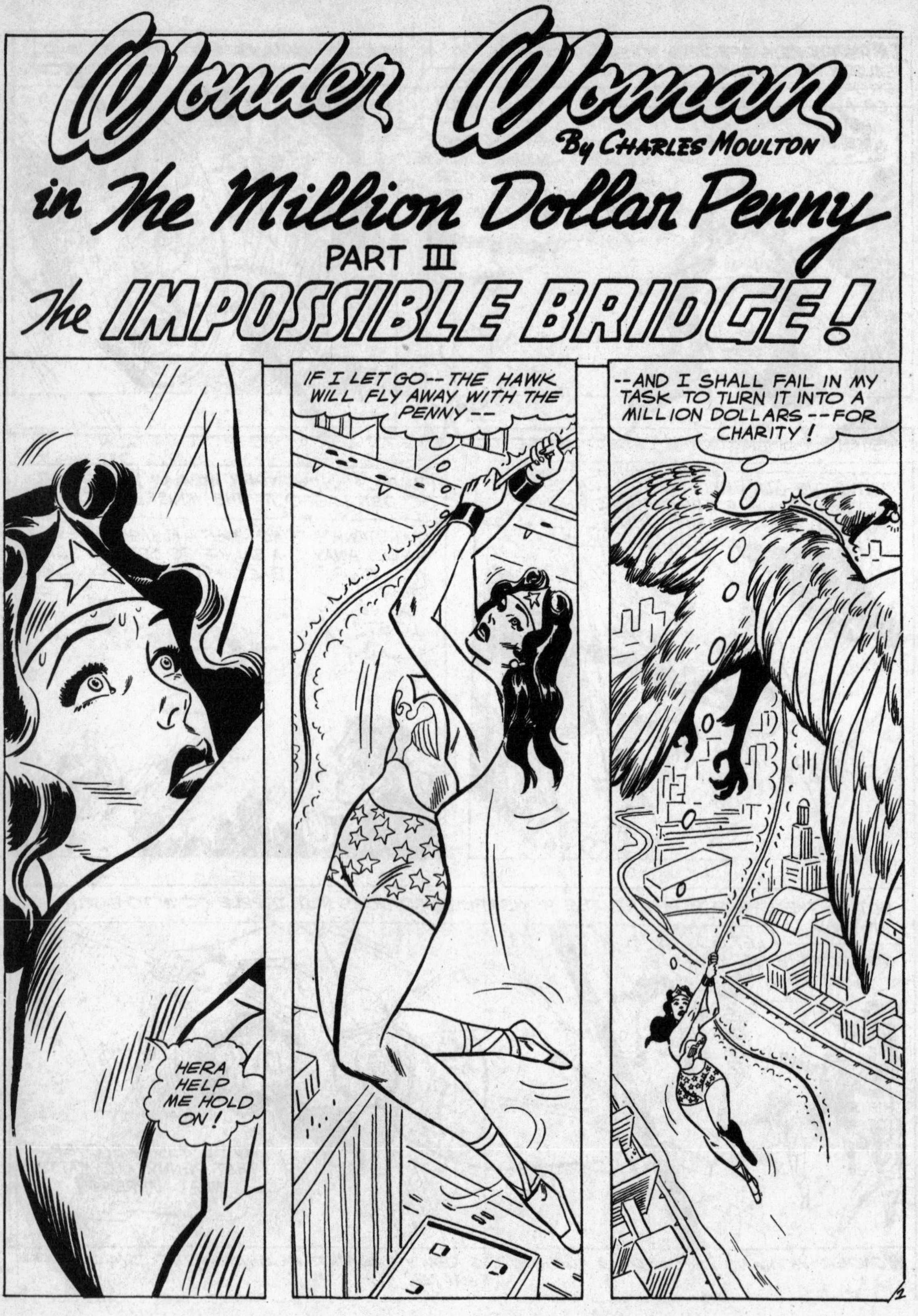
Wonder Woman
By Charles Moulton
in The Million Dollar Penny
PART III
The IMPOSSIBLE BRIDGE!
HERA HELP ME HOLD ON!
IF I LET GO--THE HAWK WILL FLY AWAY WITH THE PENNY--
--AND I SHALL FAIL IN MY TASK TO TURN IT INTO A MILLION DOLLARS--FOR CHARITY!
2

IN HIS FURIOUS EFFORTS TO SHAKE OFF THE STUBBORN CLINGING FIGURE, THE GIANT HAWK DROPS THE UNIQUE PENNY...

WONDER WOMAN'S EYES FOLLOW THE GLEAMING OBJECT AS IT HURTLES DOWN..

SUFFERING SAPPHO -- IF THAT COIN IS LOST --?!

INSTANTLY SHAKING THE LASSO LOOSE...

THE PENNY'S DROPPING INTO THE RIVER!

LIKE AN ARROW THE LITHE AMAZON CLEAVES THROUGH THE MURKY DEPTHS OF THE RIVER UNTIL...

THE PENNY -- IT FELL ON THAT STRANGE SUB!

BEFORE **WONDER WOMAN** CAN RETRIEVE THE PRECIOUS PENNY LYING ON THE STRANGE SUB'S DECK...

THUNDERBOLTS OF JOVE! THAT SUB-- BELONGS TO THE ENEMY! IT JUST FIRED A TORPEDO-- WITH AN ATOMIC WARHEAD!

WHOOOSH!

I HAVE NO CHOICE--BUT TO LEAVE THE PENNY--AND TRY TO STOP THE DEADLY MISSILE--BEFORE IT EXPLODES IN THE CITY!

INSTANTLY, THE DAUNTLESS AMAZON FLIPS TOWARD THE TORPEDO...

PERHAPS I CAN PROPEL IT FAR OUT TO SEA--WHERE IT WILL EXPLODE WITHOUT HARM TO ANYONE!

BUT, THE MECHANICAL STEED LEAPS OUT OF THE WATER...

SHADES OF PLUTO! SOME DEVICE HAS MADE IT AIRBORNE-- SO IT WILL GO OFF-- **ABOVE** THE CITY!

WHOOOSH!

BUT, THE INGENIOUS AMAZON QUICKLY FASHIONS A PROPELLER OUT OF HER GOLDEN LASSO...

THANK HERA-- I CAN NOW DIRECT THE TORPEDO!

WHRRRRRRR...!

WITH INFINITE CAUTION, **WONDER WOMAN** MANEUVERS THE TITANIC EXPLOSIVE TOWARD A DESERTED BEACH...

I DON'T KNOW HOW LONG BEFORE THE TORPEDO WILL EXPLODE! I'LL HAVE TO RENDER IT HARMLESS IMMEDIATELY!

HOLDING HER BREATH, THE DAUNTLESS AMAZON LANDS LIGHTLY AS A FEATHER...

IT DIDN'T GO OFF ON CONTACT--BUT IT MAY AT ANY MOMENT!

SUDDENLY, TO **WONDER WOMAN'S** HORROR...

ANGEL!--KIDS--THERE'S THE BRAVE AMAZON I TOLD YOU ABOUT! GOSH-- WE JUST WENT ON A PICNIC-- AND HERE WE MET HER! AREN'T WE LUCKY?

NO--**NO**--DON'T GO NEAR ME!

NOW--OF ALL TIMES--I NEED A STEADY HAND! HERA HELP ME!

4

BEFORE THE ASTOUNDED GAZE OF HER AUDIENCE...

IT CAN'T BE DONE-- *IT CAN'T BE DONE!*

WONDER WOMAN WHIRLS THE TORPEDO AROUND IN THE SAND WITH SUCH FLASHING SPEED...

SCREEE!

THAT...

ANGEL--ANGEL-- YOU DID IT-- *YOU DID IT!* FUSED SAND--AND TORPEDO INTO A HARMLESS MOLTEN MASS!

AND THEN ...

ANGEL-- YOU'RE TREMBLING! IT'S ALL OVER--YOU SAVED US ALL!

BUT IF I HADN'T--? OH-- IT MAKES ME SHIVER TO--TO THINK OF IT--!

THE KIDS HAVE NO PLAYGROUND--SO I TAKE THEM ON PICNICS AND HIKES-- WHENEVER I HAVE TIME! IF WE COULD ONLY BUILD THEM A CAMP--

SUFFERING SAPPHO-- I ALMOST FORGOT!

BACK INTO THE WATERY DEPTHS DIVES WONDER WOMAN...

THE PENNY--WHICH I'M TO TURN INTO A MILLION DOLLARS BEFORE THE DAY IS OVER-- IT'S STILL ON THAT ENEMY SUB'S DECK!

BUT, BEFORE THE AMAZON CAN REACH THE PRECIOUS COIN...

THUNDERBOLTS OF JOVE! THEY MUST HAVE SEEN ME! THEY JUST FIRED A TORPEDO AT ME!

VROOSH!

EASILY, WONDER WOMAN TWISTS OUT OF THE WAY OF THE MISSILE...

THANK HERA--IT'S AN ORDINARY TORPEDO-- AND ALL I HAVE TO WORRY ABOUT IS ELUDING IT-- MYSELF! AND THAT SEEMS TO BE A SIMPLE JOB!

WHOOOSH

TO THE AMAZON'S DIS-MAY, HOWEVER...

SUFFERING SAPPHO--IT'S TURNED WITH ME! IT MUST BE MAGNETICALLY CON-TROLLED--TO FOLLOW ME--EVERYWHERE!

WHOOOSH

FASTER AND FASTER SHE WHIRLS...

THE MORE SPEED I PUT ON--THE NEARER IT GETS--!

WITH ONE LAST FINAL BLINDING EFFORT, **WONDER WOMAN** ROCKETS UNDER THE SUB— AS BEHIND HER...

THE TORPEDO-- HURTLED INTO ITS OWN SUB!

EXHAUSTIVELY, THE AMAZON SEARCHES EVERY INCH OF RIVER BED...BUT FINALLY...

CAN'T FIND THE PENNY-- IT MUST HAVE BEEN BLOWN TO COPPER DUST--I'VE...FAILED...

WHEN SHE EMERGES, **WONDER WOMAN** IS MADE EVEN SADDER WHEN...

HURRAY FOR WONDER WOMAN!

THEY DON'T KNOW... I FAILED THEM--!

IF WE EVER GET A PLAYGROUND-- WILL YOU COME-- AND VISIT US?

MAYBE-- YOU'LL STAY AND PLAY WITH US?

I CAN'T FACE THEM--I HAVE TO TELL THEM THE TRUTH!

A HUSH FALLS UPON THE CHILDREN... AS THE DEJECTED AMAZON REVEALS...

...AND NOW YOU KNOW! IF YOU HAVEN'T A CAMP TO PLAY IN--IT'S ALL MY FAULT!

LOOK AT THEIR FACES -- THEY'LL NEVER FORGIVE ME!

BUT THE SILENCE IS BROKEN AS...

IT DOESN'T MATTER, **WONDER WOMAN!**

WE KNOW YOU TRIED YOUR BEST!

WE'VE DONE WITHOUT A CAMP SO LONG--WE CAN WAIT!

AND THEN--A STUNNING SURPRISE...

LOOK WHAT I FOUND IN MY NET--WHEN I WAS LOOKING FOR SEA-SHELLS!

IT'S--**THE PENNY!!**

INSTANTLY, **WONDER WOMAN** TAKES THE UNIQUE PENNY AND...

THE DAY ISN'T OVER YET! I STILL HAVE TIME TO TRY TO TURN THIS INTO A MILLION DOLLARS!

ALL THAT DAY THE INDOMITABLE AMAZON RACES ABOUT THE CITY ON HER STUPENDOUS TASK WHILE THE PRECIOUS HOURS GO BY...UNTIL...

NOTHING...

NOTHING...

I STILL HAVE THE SAME PENNY...

I'M AS FAR FROM TURNING IT INTO A MILLION DOLLARS AS...

AND THEN, WITH THE DAY ALMOST GONE, THE DESPERATE **WONDER WOMAN** PASSES TWIN CITIES HIGHWAY AND TRANSPORTATION OFFICE WHERE...

WHO'S GOING TO BUILD THE BRIDGE?

NO ONE! THEY CAN'T DO IT FOR ONLY A MILLION DOLLARS--AND WE DON'T HAVE MORE MONEY TO OFFER!

TWIN CITIES BRIDGE BID...MUST NOT EXCEED $1,000,000.00 CLOSING DATE:

WAIT--GIVE ME THE CHANCE!

YOU? YOU'RE ONLY A WOMAN--A GIRL--NOT A WHOLE CONSTRUCTION COMPANY! IMPOSSIBLE! FORGET ABOUT IT!

8

EXERTING IMMEASURABLE PRESSURE AGAINST THE COPPER PENNY...

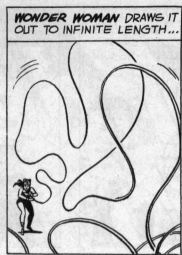

WONDER WOMAN DRAWS IT OUT TO INFINITE LENGTH...

WEAVING IT INTO A NETWORK OF INDESTRUCTIBLE LINES...

AND THEN, BEFORE THE ASTOUNDED GAZE OF THE MULTITUDES ASSEMBLED TO WATCH HER--SHE SPINS A BRIDGE ACROSS THE RIVER...

I DON'T BELIEVE IT!

BUT YOU'RE SEEING IT!

AMAZING-- SHE'S A *WONDER WOMAN!*

LATER...IN THE MAYOR'S OFFICE...

A CHECK FOR ONE MILLION DOLLARS, *WONDER WOMAN*-- FOR BUILDING A BRIDGE!

PLEASE USE IT FOR A SUMMER CAMP FOR UNDERPRIVILEGED CHILDREN!

AND SO, THE AMAZING AMAZON COMPLETES HER FABULOUS MISSION... AND REMAINS IN MAN'S WORLD... FOR WHAT FUTURE SENSATIONAL ADVENTURES-- WE SHALL SEE...

ANY AMAZON COULD HAVE DONE THE SAME THING, STEVE!

ONLY YOU COULD. BECAUSE YOU'RE AN ANGEL!

The End

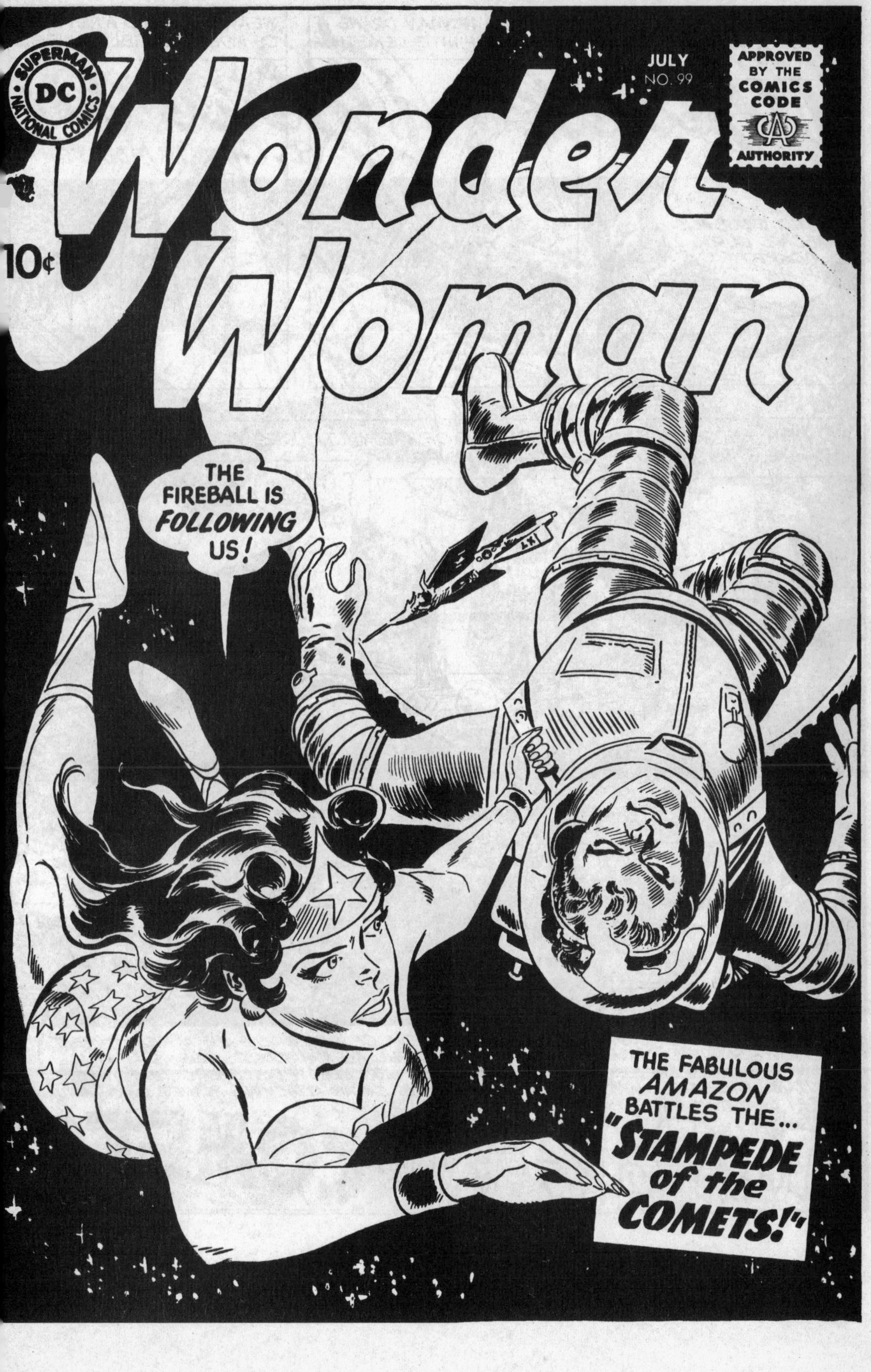
SUPERMAN DC NATIONAL COMICS
Wonder Woman
10¢
JULY NO. 99
APPROVED BY THE COMICS CODE AUTHORITY
THE FIREBALL IS FOLLOWING US!
THE FABULOUS AMAZON BATTLES THE... "STAMPEDE of the COMETS!"

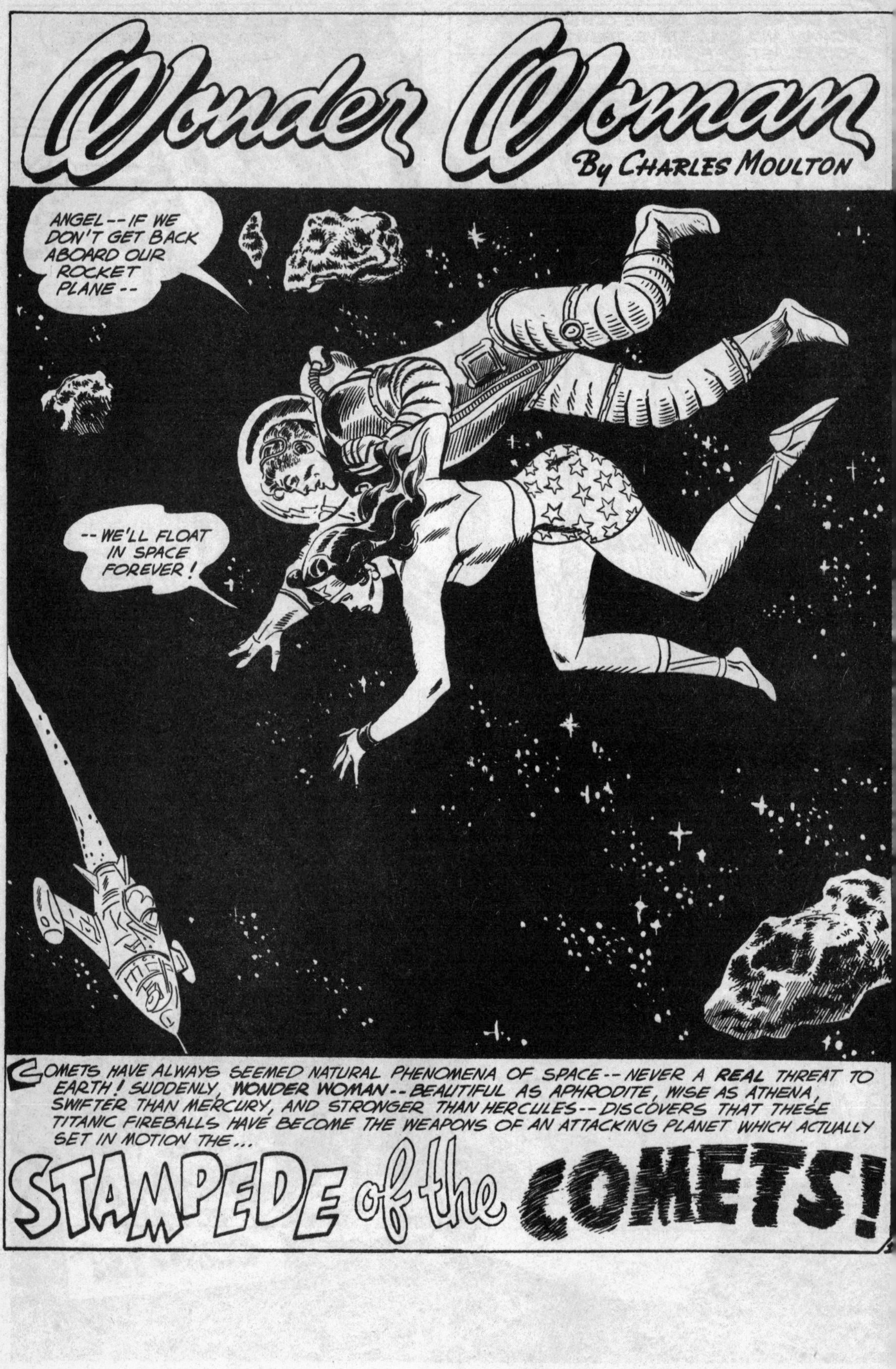
Wonder Woman
By Charles Moulton
ANGEL--IF WE DON'T GET BACK ABOARD OUR ROCKET PLANE--
--WE'LL FLOAT IN SPACE FOREVER!
COMETS HAVE ALWAYS SEEMED NATURAL PHENOMENA OF SPACE--NEVER A REAL THREAT TO EARTH! SUDDENLY, WONDER WOMAN--BEAUTIFUL AS APHRODITE, WISE AS ATHENA, SWIFTER THAN MERCURY, AND STRONGER THAN HERCULES--DISCOVERS THAT THESE TITANIC FIREBALLS HAVE BECOME THE WEAPONS OF AN ATTACKING PLANET WHICH ACTUALLY SET IN MOTION THE...
STAMPEDE of the COMETS!

AT A SECRET BASE ON THE COAST, *WONDER WOMAN* AND COL. STEVE TREVOR WAIT FOR BLAST-OFF TIME...

I WISH I WERE GOING ALONG WITH YOU, STEVE!

THE INSIDE OF A ROCKET PLANE -- ASSIGNED TO TRACK A ROCKET THROUGH SPACE -- IS HARDLY THE PLACE FOR A BEAUTIFUL YOUNG GIRL -- EVEN IF SHE IS AN *AMAZON!*

PLEASE BE CAREFUL, STEVE!

I'LL BE BACK IN TIME FOR OUR DINNER DATE, ANGEL!

A HUMAN EYE-WITNESS TO HOW A ROCKET BEHAVES IN FLIGHT WILL GIVE US ADDITIONAL DATA -- WHICH EVEN INSTRUMENTS CANNOT!

YES, GENERAL DARTWELL!

TENSE MOMENTS GO BY IN THE CONTROL ROOM ...AND THEN... WITH A FLAMING ROAR...

GOOD LUCK, DARLING!

THERE GOES THE FIRST ROCKET-HUNTER IN HISTORY!

ON THE INTRICATE *TRACKING-SCREEN*, THE LOVELY AMAZON TENSELY WATCHES THE UNIQUE FLIGHT...

STEVE IS HAVING A HARD TIME--BUT HE IS KEEPING THE ROCKET IN VIEW, WONDER WOMAN!

WE SHOULD BE HEARING REPORTS FROM HIM SOON, GEN. DARTWELL!

ROCKET

X-1

CONTROL

SUDDENLY, THE PILOT'S VOICE CRACKLES OVER THE INTERCOM--AT THE SAME MOMENT THAT AN ASTOUNDING SIGHT IS SEEN...

X-ONE CALLING BLUE BASE!... CONTROLS NOT RESPONDING!... ONLY THING I CAN THINK OF IS THAT--

ROCKET

THE NEXT MOMENT...

IMPOSSIBLE! THE PLANE IS SLOWER THAN THE ROCKET!

BUT IT'S TRUE, GENERAL! STEVE LEFT THE ROCKET BEHIND--AS IF IT WERE STANDING STILL!

EVERY OBSERVATORY IN THE WORLD IS ALERTED TO SCAN THE SKIES FOR THE MISSING PILOT... BUT...

NO WORD FROM ANYONE!...THEY THINK IT'S HOPELESS-- BUT I'M GOING TO LOOK FOR HIM MYSELF!

3

WONDER WOMAN RACES TO THE AMAZON SPACE LABORATORY... ON PARADISE ISLAND...

I AM GOING TO HUNT FOR COL. STEVE TREVOR-- MISSING IN SPACE! I NEED AN OUTFIT THAT WILL ENABLE ME TO EXIST ON ANY SOLAR SYSTEM!

OUR NEW CONTACT SPACE SUIT MEETS YOUR RE- QUIREMENTS, PRINCESS! BUT IT'S STILL IN THE EX- PERIMENTAL STAGE! NO HUMAN HAS TESTED IT YET!

I WILL TEST IT!

THE INTREPID AMAZON IS PLACED IN A PRESSURE CHAMBER WHERE...

AIR-PRESSURE IS PUTTING THE CONTACT SPACE SUIT ON YOU, PRINCESS! IT IS INVISIBLE --LIKE A CONTACT LENS OVER A HUMAN EYE!

PRESSURE CHAMBER

YOU ARE NOW BEING SUB- JECTED TO THE COLD OF SPACE --ALMOST ABSOLUTE ZERO! ANY REACTIONS, PRINCESS?

NONE!

NOW YOU ARE BEING SUB- JECTED TO 10,000 DEGREES FARENHEIT-- THE HEAT OF THE SUN'S SURFACE -- ANY REACTIONS?

NONE!

PRINCESS-- I CANNOT SUB- JECT YOU TO THE FINAL TEST--TO BOMBARD YOU WITH COSMIC RAYS!

YOU MUST, PAULA! THERE'S NO OTHER WAY FOR ME TO FIND OUT WHAT HAP- PENED TO COL. TREVOR! I COM- MAND YOU TO BOMBARD ME!

THE AMAZON SCIENTIST FALTERINGLY OBEYS THE COMMAND OF *WONDER WOMAN*...

PRINCESS--YOU ARE NOW BEING SUBJECTED TO A BOMBARDMENT OF COSMIC RAYS! HAVE YOU--HAVE YOU-- ANY REACTIONS? PRINCESS? PRINCESS-- CAN YOU ANSWER?

THE CONTACT SPACE SUIT IS WORKING PERFECTLY! CONGRATULATIONS!

AT *WONDER WOMAN'S* INSTRUCTIONS, BOTH A ROCKET AND A ROCKET PLANE ARE PREPARED FOR LAUNCHING...

WE HAVE NOW DUPLICATED THE EXACT CONDITIONS THAT PREVAILED BEFORE-- EXCEPT *THIS* TIME-- I AM GOING TO TRY TO TRACK A ROCKET! I AM READY FOR BLAST-OFF!

ONCE AGAIN THE DUAL LAUNCHING TAKES PLACE-- AS THE DAUNTLESS *AMAZON* SETS OFF ON HER INCREDIBLE QUEST...

WHOOOOOOOO

CAN EVEN THE MIGHTY AMAZON FIND A LONE HUMAN MISSING IN THE VASTNESS OF SPACE?

5

AWAY FROM EARTH AND ITS SATELLITE MOON HURTLE THE *ROCKET* AND THE *DARING AMAZON*...

NO QUESTION ABOUT IT! MY SHIP'S SLOWER THAN THE *ROCKET*! I CAN JUST ABOUT KEEP IT IN SIGHT!

SUDDENLY...

SOMETHING'S HAPPENING TO MY CONTROLS-- THEY'RE NOT RE-SPONDING AT ALL!

GREAT HERA! I'VE JUST *PASSED* THE ROCKET!

AND THEN--WITH THE FLEETNESS OF THOUGHT--AN EFFORTLESS SURGE OF POWER CATAPULTS *WONDER WOMAN'S* SHIP FORWARD...

MERCIFUL MINERVA-- I'M BEING PROPELLED INTO OUTER SPACE! NOW-- I'VE JUST PASSED MARS!

HELPLESS TO CONTROL HER SHIP, WHICH IS BEING PROPELLED BY A MYSTERIOUS FORCE AT INDESCRIBABLE SPEED, WONDER WOMAN IS STARTLED TO SEE...

STEVE'S ROCKET-PLANE-- WRECKED-- EMPTY!

STEVE STEVE DARLING-- WHAT HAS HAPPENED TO YOU? AM I... TOO LATE?

AND THEN, AHEAD OF HER, AN AMAZING SIGHT...

GREAT HERA!--THERE'S STEVE! EVIDENTLY HAVING BEEN THROWN OUT OF HIS SHIP--FLOATING HELPLESSLY IN SPACE!

INSTANTLY, THE FEARLESS AMAZON DIVES OUT INTO SPACE...

WILL THE SPEED OF MY DIVE--ADDED TO THE SPEED OF MY SHIP--GIVE ME ENOUGH MOMENTUM TO REACH STEVE?

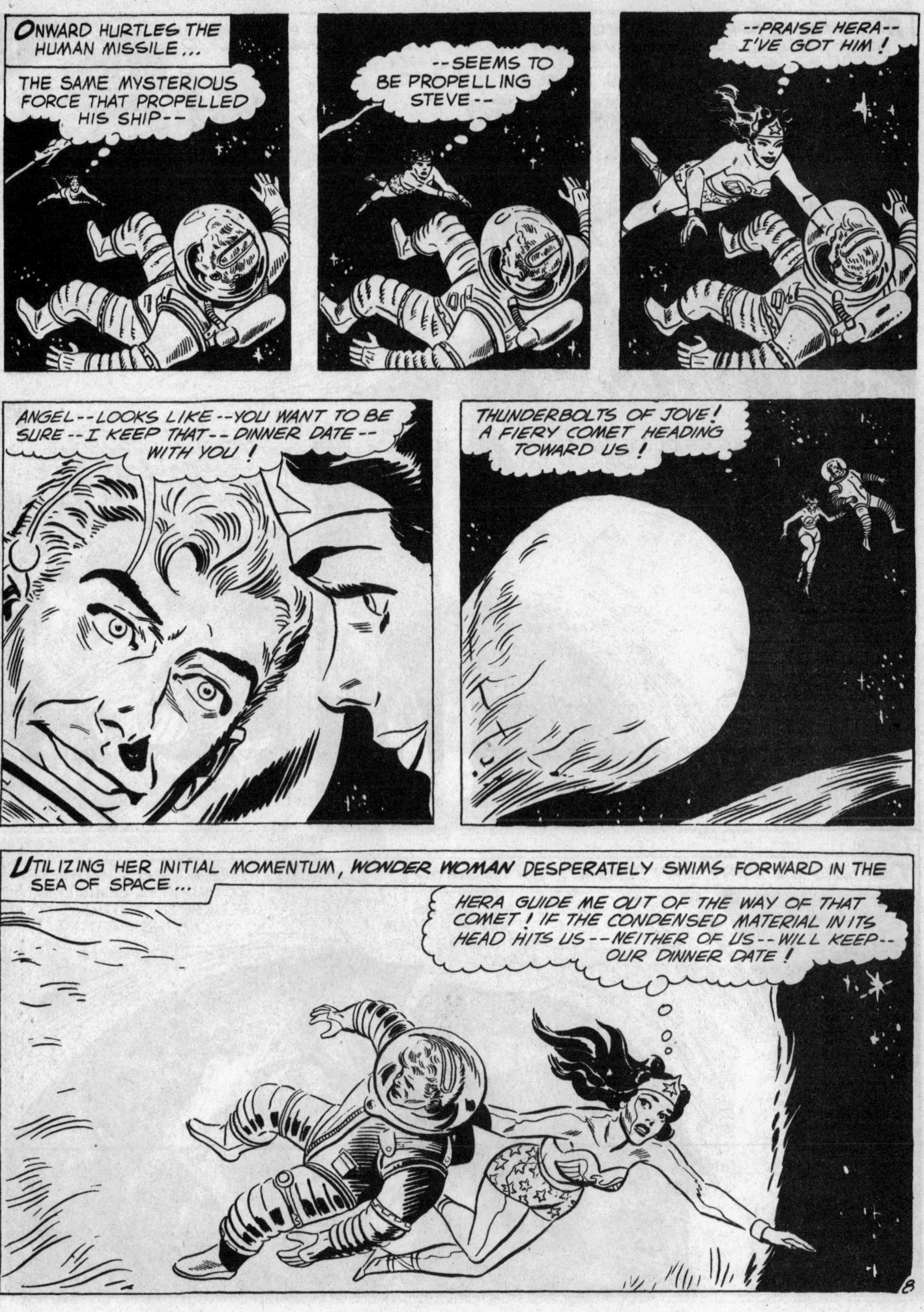
ONWARD HURTLES THE HUMAN MISSILE...
THE SAME MYSTERIOUS FORCE THAT PROPELLED HIS SHIP--
--SEEMS TO BE PROPELLING STEVE--
--PRAISE HERA-- I'VE GOT HIM!
ANGEL--LOOKS LIKE--YOU WANT TO BE SURE--I KEEP THAT--DINNER DATE--WITH YOU!
THUNDERBOLTS OF JOVE! A FIERY COMET HEADING TOWARD US!
UTILIZING HER INITIAL MOMENTUM, WONDER WOMAN DESPERATELY SWIMS FORWARD IN THE SEA OF SPACE...
HERA GUIDE ME OUT OF THE WAY OF THAT COMET! IF THE CONDENSED MATERIAL IN ITS HEAD HITS US--NEITHER OF US--WILL KEEP--OUR DINNER DATE!
8

BY A SUPREME EFFORT, *WONDER WOMAN* TOWS THE HELPLESS PILOT AND HERSELF AWAY FROM THE HEAD OF THE FIERY COMET... BUT...

YOU'VE DONE IT, ANGEL! DODGED A COMET!

ONLY ITS HEAD, STEVE! WE CAN'T AVOID ITS TAIL! HERE IT COMES!

LIKE HUMAN SPECKS OF DUST, THE TRAVELERS IN SPACE ARE WHIRLED INSIDE THE HUNDRED THOUSAND MILE LENGTH OF THE COMET'S TAIL...

SOMETHING ODD ABOUT THIS COMET?-- IT'S THE FIRST ONE I'VE EVER SEEN WHOSE TAIL POINTS *TOWARD* THE SUN!

THEN... AS THE FIERY STAR FLASHES ON ITS WAY...

ANGEL! WILL WE BE ABLE TO WRITE A BOOK! I'LL BET WE'RE THE FIRST--

GREAT HERA! STEVE-- LOOK! THE COMET IS PLUMMETING STRAIGHT FOR THE EARTH!

BEFORE THE HORRIFIED GAZE OF THE SPACE TRAVELERS, THE TITANIC COMET HURTLES HEAD-ON INTO THE PLANET...

THE EARTH--

--IS GONE!

OUR PLANET... OUR HOME... OUR LOVED ONES... OUR FRIENDS... GONE-- WE'RE DOOMED TO FLOAT IN SPACE UNTIL--!

ALL THE FAMILIAR THINGS WE'VE ALWAYS KNOWN-- GONE! SKY-SCRAPERS... PICNICS... SWEETHEARTS WATCHING THE MOON...

THE MOON?-- STEVE-- THIS EARTH HAD NO MOON! IT'S PROBABLY A DUPLICATE EARTH STATIONED HERE BY THAT SAME MYSTERIOUS POWER THAT PROPELLED US HERE! AND THAT COMET-- IT'S AN ARTIFICIAL ONE! LOOK-- ITS TAIL IS POINTING TOWARD THE SUN!

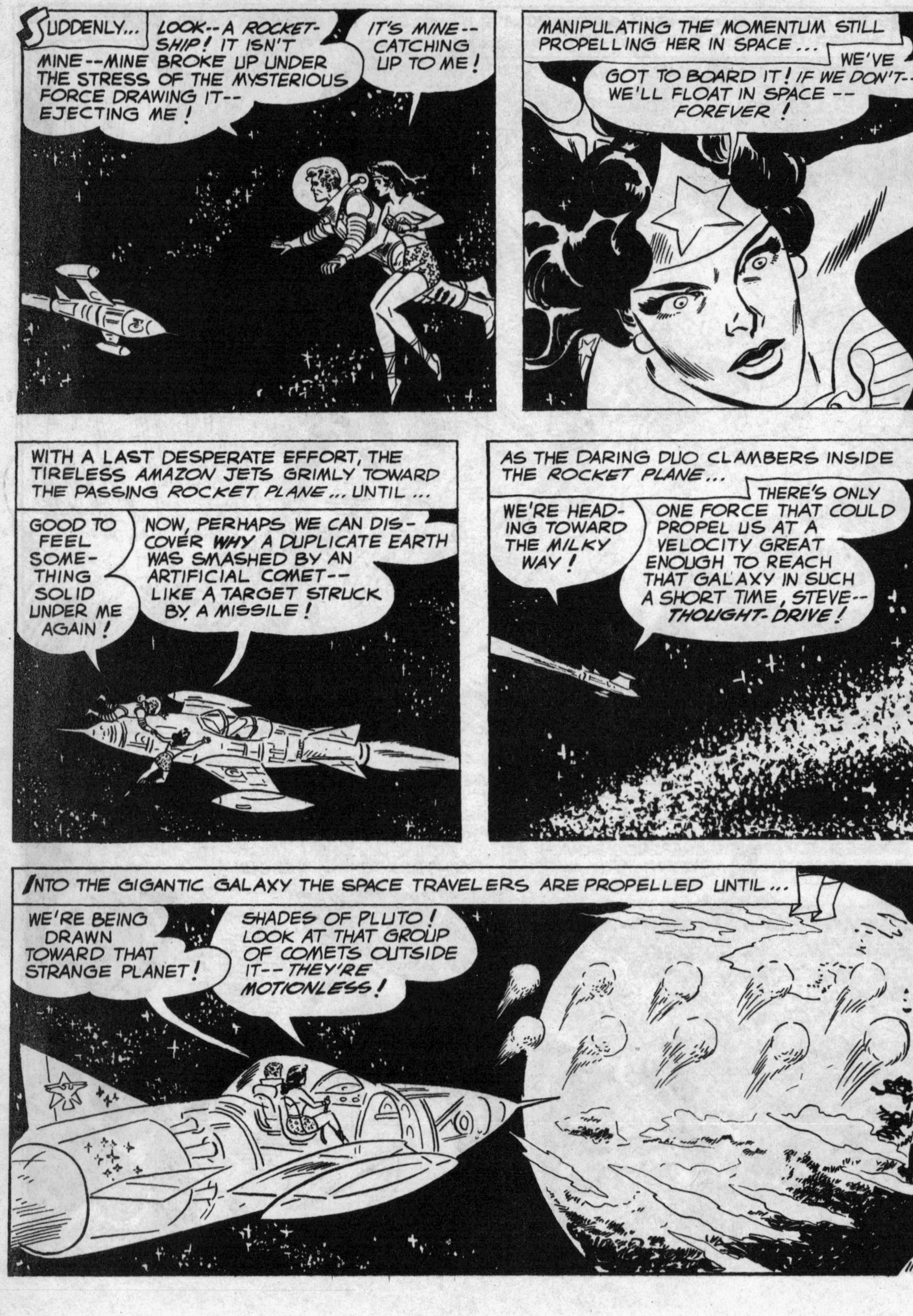
SUDDENLY...
LOOK--A ROCKET-SHIP! IT ISN'T MINE--MINE BROKE UP UNDER THE STRESS OF THE MYSTERIOUS FORCE DRAWING IT--EJECTING ME!
IT'S MINE--CATCHING UP TO ME!
MANIPULATING THE MOMENTUM STILL PROPELLING HER IN SPACE...
WE'VE GOT TO BOARD IT! IF WE DON'T--WE'LL FLOAT IN SPACE--FOREVER!
WITH A LAST DESPERATE EFFORT, THE TIRELESS AMAZON JETS GRIMLY TOWARD THE PASSING ROCKET PLANE... UNTIL...
GOOD TO FEEL SOME-THING SOLID UNDER ME AGAIN!
NOW, PERHAPS WE CAN DIS-COVER WHY A DUPLICATE EARTH WAS SMASHED BY AN ARTIFICIAL COMET--LIKE A TARGET STRUCK BY A MISSILE!
AS THE DARING DUO CLAMBERS INSIDE THE ROCKET PLANE...
WE'RE HEAD-ING TOWARD THE MILKY WAY!
THERE'S ONLY ONE FORCE THAT COULD PROPEL US AT A VELOCITY GREAT ENOUGH TO REACH THAT GALAXY IN SUCH A SHORT TIME, STEVE--THOUGHT-DRIVE!
INTO THE GIGANTIC GALAXY THE SPACE TRAVELERS ARE PROPELLED UNTIL...
WE'RE BEING DRAWN TOWARD THAT STRANGE PLANET!
SHADES OF PLUTO! LOOK AT THAT GROUP OF COMETS OUTSIDE IT--THEY'RE MOTIONLESS!
11

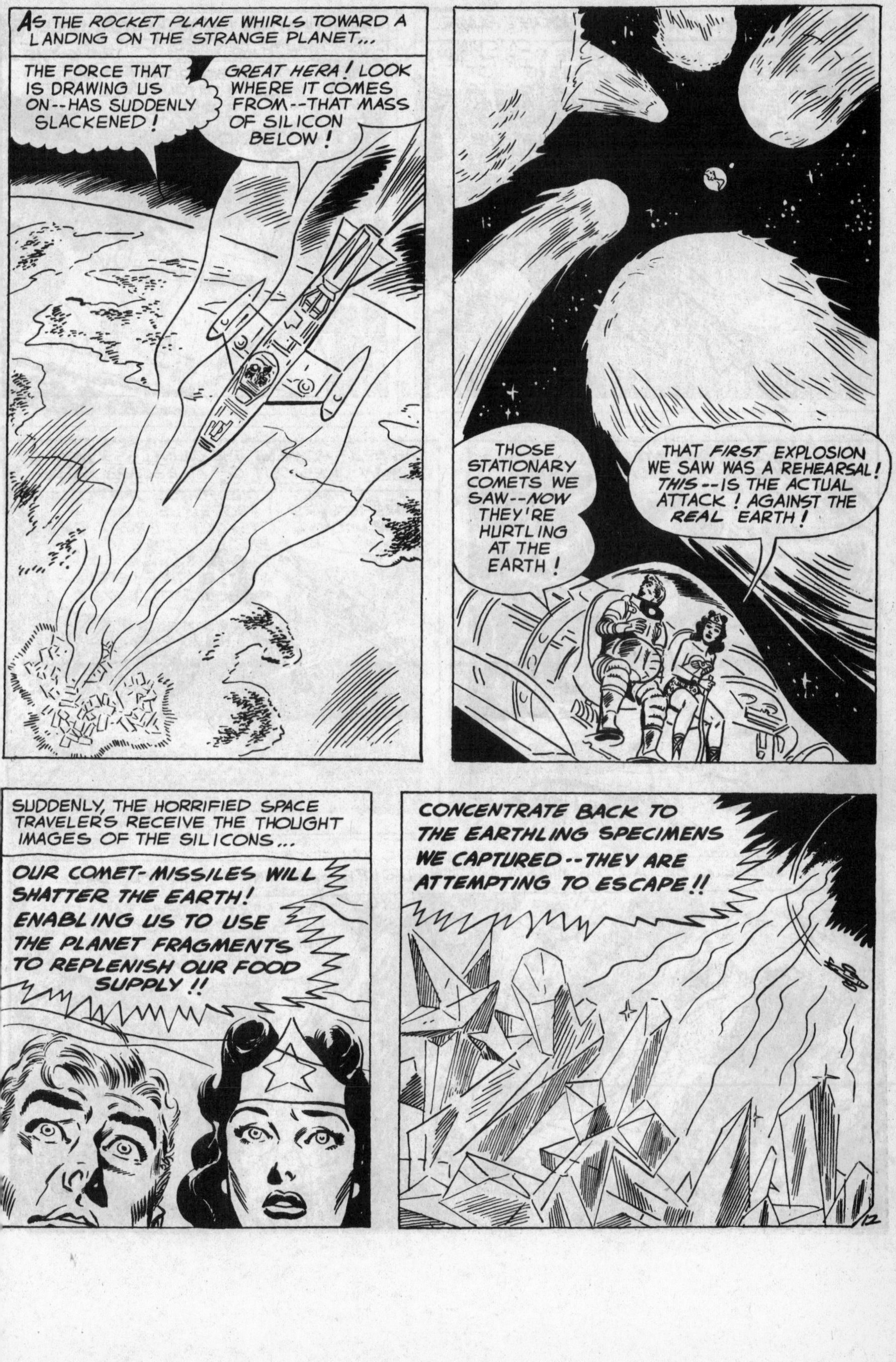
AS THE ROCKET PLANE WHIRLS TOWARD A LANDING ON THE STRANGE PLANET...
THE FORCE THAT IS DRAWING US ON--HAS SUDDENLY SLACKENED!
GREAT HERA! LOOK WHERE IT COMES FROM--THAT MASS OF SILICON BELOW!
THOSE STATIONARY COMETS WE SAW--NOW THEY'RE HURTLING AT THE EARTH!
THAT FIRST EXPLOSION WE SAW WAS A REHEARSAL! THIS--IS THE ACTUAL ATTACK! AGAINST THE REAL EARTH!
SUDDENLY, THE HORRIFIED SPACE TRAVELERS RECEIVE THE THOUGHT IMAGES OF THE SILICONS...
OUR COMET-MISSILES WILL SHATTER THE EARTH! ENABLING US TO USE THE PLANET FRAGMENTS TO REPLENISH OUR FOOD SUPPLY!!
CONCENTRATE BACK TO THE EARTHLING SPECIMENS WE CAPTURED--THEY ARE ATTEMPTING TO ESCAPE!!
12

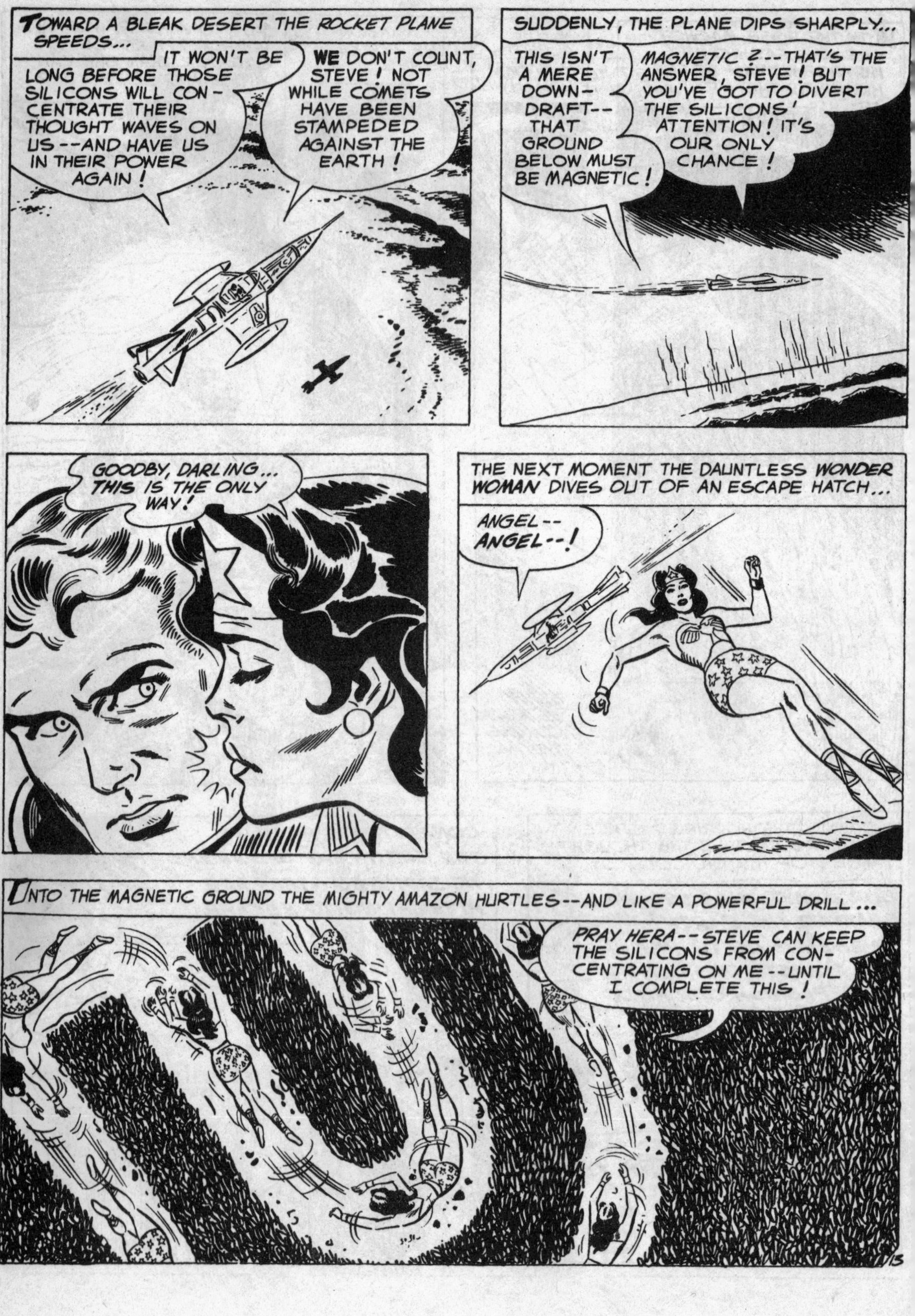
TOWARD A BLEAK DESERT THE ROCKET PLANE SPEEDS...
IT WON'T BE LONG BEFORE THOSE SILICONS WILL CONCENTRATE THEIR THOUGHT WAVES ON US--AND HAVE US IN THEIR POWER AGAIN!
WE DON'T COUNT, STEVE! NOT WHILE COMETS HAVE BEEN STAMPEDED AGAINST THE EARTH!
SUDDENLY, THE PLANE DIPS SHARPLY...
THIS ISN'T A MERE DOWN-DRAFT--THAT GROUND BELOW MUST BE MAGNETIC!
MAGNETIC?--THAT'S THE ANSWER, STEVE! BUT YOU'VE GOT TO DIVERT THE SILICONS' ATTENTION! IT'S OUR ONLY CHANCE!
GOODBY, DARLING... THIS IS THE ONLY WAY!
THE NEXT MOMENT THE DAUNTLESS WONDER WOMAN DIVES OUT OF AN ESCAPE HATCH...
ANGEL-- ANGEL--!
UNTO THE MAGNETIC GROUND THE MIGHTY AMAZON HURTLES--AND LIKE A POWERFUL DRILL...
PRAY HERA--STEVE CAN KEEP THE SILICONS FROM CONCENTRATING ON ME--UNTIL I COMPLETE THIS!
13

WITH THE HUGE MAGNET SHE HAS FASHIONED, *WONDER WOMAN* LEAPS HIGH INTO THE AIR JUST AS...

STEVE'S CIRCLED AGAIN!

AS THE MIGHTY AMAZON ALIGHTS ON THE *ROCKET PLANE* IT FLASHES EARTHWARD...

STEVE IS STEERING US TOWARD THE COMETS! *THANK HERA--* THE MAGNET IS ATTRACTING THE CONDENSED MATERIAL IN THE COMETS!

BUT TO *WONDER WOMAN'S* HORROR... A FORCE GREATER THAN SHE CAN WITHSTAND SEIZES HER AGAIN...

THE SILICONS ARE CONCENTRATING THEIR THOUGHT WAVES ON US-- AND ARE PROPELLING US BACK TO THEIR PLANET AGAIN-- COMETS AND ALL!

BACK...BACK...BACK TOWARD THE SILICON PLANET WONDER WOMAN IS DRAWN UNTIL...

THEY'VE WRENCHED MAGNET-- AND COMETS --FROM MY GRIP!

THE NEXT INSTANT, THE AMAZING ROCKET PLANE IS VIOLENTLY HURLED INTO SPACE AS BEHIND THEM-- A TITANIC ERUPTION...

SHADES OF PLUTO! THE SILICONS WERE UNABLE TO HALT THEIR OWN COMET MISSILES --IN TIME!

BACK INTO THE ROCKET PLANE CLIMBS THE SOLEMN AMAZON...

ANGEL --DO YOU KNOW WHAT I'M THINKING? THE SILICONS BROUGHT US HERE WITH THOUGHT-DRIVE!--

EVEN IF WE COULD TRAVEL AT THE SPEED OF LIGHT-- WE'RE MORE THAN 200 LIGHT YEARS AWAY FROM EARTH!

WE'RE DOOMED TO ORBIT IN SPACE FOREVER...FOR THE REST... OF OUR LIVES...

THE CASTAWAYS IN SPACE ORBIT HOPE-LESSLY UNTIL...

ANGEL-- LOOK!

A GIANT METEOR-- HURTLING STRAIGHT AT US! WE HAVE NO CHANCE TO GET OUT OF THE WAY!

BUT AT THAT MOMENT WHEN AN ANNIHILATING CRASH SEEMS IMMINENT...

THE METEOR-- JUST DIS-APPEARED!

SOMETHING MADE IT VANISH! LET'S FIND OUT!

AS *WONDER WOMAN* STEERS THE ROCKET PLANE TOWARDS THE AREA...

SOMETHING STRANGE ABOUT THIS PLACE-- THE PLANE'S PITCHING AND TOSSING AS IF THIS PART OF SPACE IS AN ANGRY SEA! GET AWAY!

NO, STEVE! THIS MAY BE OUR ONLY CHANCE OF ESCAPE BACK TO EARTH!

IF THIS IS A WARP IN SPACE-- IT WILL BE LIKE A CRACK THROUGH WHICH WE CAN SLIP BACK TO OUR SOLAR SYSTEM! IF IT ISN'T-- WE MAY SEAL OUR DOOM IMMEDIATELY IF WE GO THROUGH IT!

WHAT-EVER HAPPENS, WE'LL BE TOGETHER, ANGEL! LET'S GO!

INTO THE CENTER OF THE VIOLENT TUR-BULENCE ITSELF .THE DARING *WONDER WOMAN* HURLS HER ROCKET PLANE...

AND THEN...

ANGEL-- YOU'VE DONE IT! IT *WAS* A WARP IN SPACE! WE SLIPPED THROUGH IT TO MARS-- AND THERE'S *EARTH!*

WE'RE ON OUR WAY HOME!

The End 16

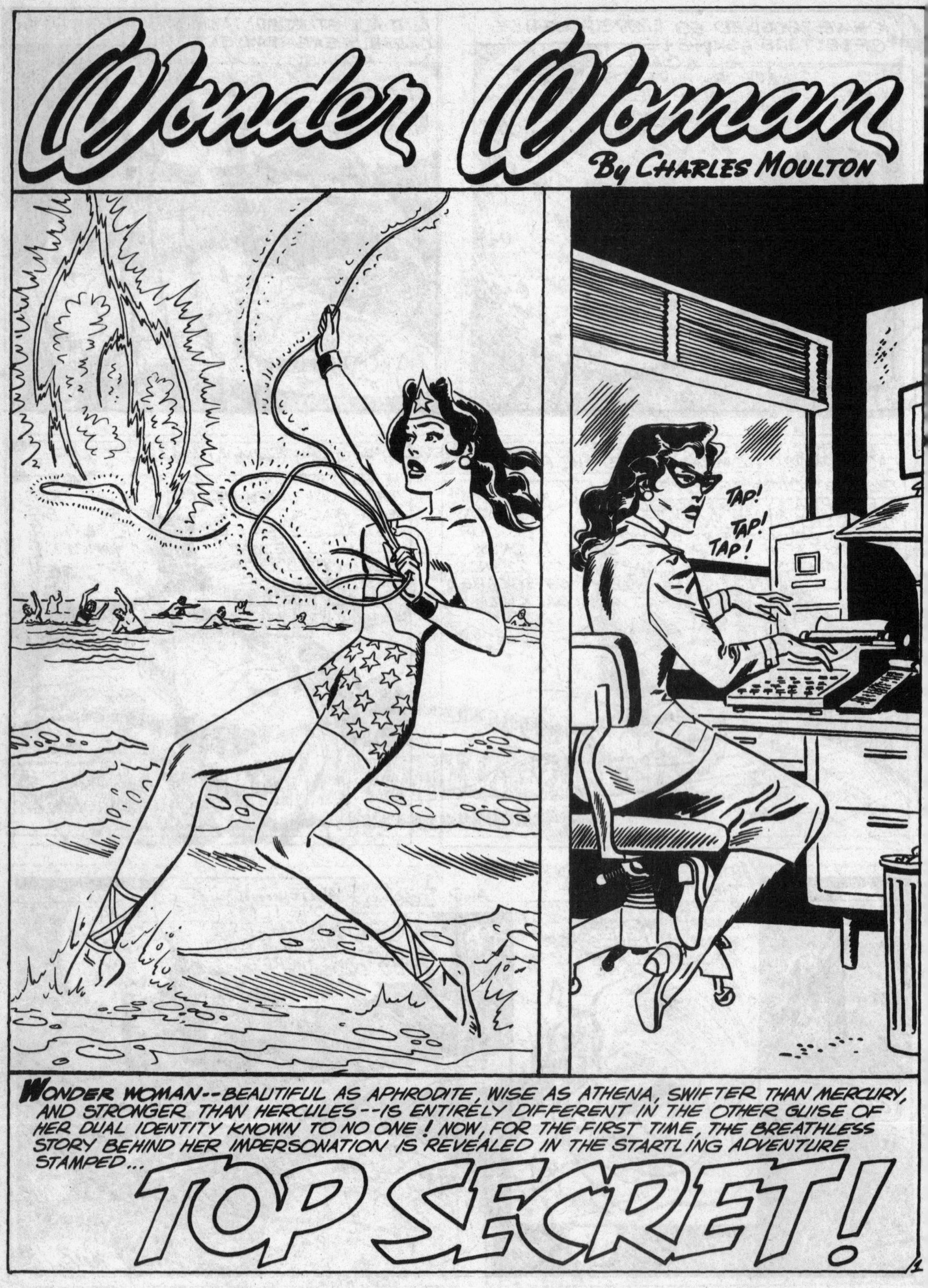
Wonder Woman
By CHARLES MOULTON
TAP! TAP! TAP!
WONDER WOMAN--BEAUTIFUL AS APHRODITE, WISE AS ATHENA, SWIFTER THAN MERCURY, AND STRONGER THAN HERCULES--IS ENTIRELY DIFFERENT IN THE OTHER GUISE OF HER DUAL IDENTITY KNOWN TO NO ONE! NOW, FOR THE FIRST TIME, THE BREATHLESS STORY BEHIND HER IMPERSONATION IS REVEALED IN THE STARTLING ADVENTURE STAMPED...
TOP SECRET!
1

WE HAVE RECEIVED SO MANY THOUSANDS OF LETTERS ASKING US...

How did Wonder Woman assume her DUAL identity?

Can please that on

What made the Fighting Amazon create a single identity?

What is the story behind Wonder Woman's self which nobody knows?

IT ALL STARTED EARLY SATURDAY MORNING WHEN...

"...COL. STEVE TREVOR OF MILITARY INTELLIGENCE PERFORMED AN AMAZING STUNT..."

THUNDERBOLTS OF JOVE! STEVE REALLY PERFORMED THE STUNT OF PLUCKING MY SCARF OFF THAT POLE!

3

4

"AS THE INTREPID PILOT ZOOMED UP..."

SHADES OF PLUTO! A WING IS BREAKING OFF STEVE'S PLANE!

CRACK!

"INSTANTLY, THE FEARLESS WONDER WOMAN LEAPED HIGH INTO THE AIR..."

IF I DON'T FIND SOME WAY OF HELPING HIM-- HE'LL SURELY CRASH!

3

2

"*THE STARTLED SPECTATORS ON THE FIELD WITNESSED AN AMAZING SIGHT...*"

LOOK! WONDER WOMAN'S CAUGHT THE RIPPED-OFF WING!

WHAT CAN SHE HOPE TO DO WITH IT?

"*A GASP AROSE AS THE MIGHTY AMAZON, WITH PERFECT TIMING...*"

ANGEL--I CAN'T BELIEVE WHAT I SEE--YOU'VE STUCK THE WING BACK INTO PLACE!

I DON'T KNOW HOW LONG I CAN HOLD IT-- HURRY AND LAND--HURRY--!

THUD!

"*BREATHLESSLY THE PILOT HEADED DOWN FOR A LANDING...*"

LET GO, ANGEL! BEFORE YOU'RE CRUSHED AGAINST THE GROUND!

NO--YOU'LL CRASH IF I LET THE WING DROP! COMPLETE YOUR LANDING--I'LL TAKE CARE OF MYSELF!

"*WITH HAIRBREADTH TIMING, WONDER WOMAN LET GO OF THE WRECKED WING THE PRECISE MOMENT STEVE SAFELY LANDED...*"

SHE DID IT-- **SHE DID IT**-- I CAN'T BELIEVE MY EYES!

YOU'LL BELIEVE THE PICTURES CAMERAS ARE TAKING OF THIS IMPOSSIBLE STUNT!

THUD!

"*A MOMENT LATER...*"

YOU **MUST** LOVE ME TO RISK YOUR LIFE FOR ME LIKE THAT, ANGEL! WHEN ARE YOU GOING TO MARRY ME? YOU KNOW HOW I FEEL ABOUT YOU!

I DO, STEVE, BUT I **CAN'T** MARRY YOU-- UNTIL MY SERVICES ARE NO LONGER NEEDED TO BATTLE CRIME AND INJUSTICE! ONLY **THEN** CAN I THINK ABOUT MYSELF!

IT'S NOT FAIR! I CAN'T LIVE WITHOUT YOU, ANGEL! WHY--EVEN WHEN I'M SURROUNDED BY AN ARMY OF PEOPLE-- ALL I SEE IS YOU! WHY--I COULD PICK YOU OUT IF YOU WERE JUST A SINGLE GRAIN OF SAND ON A BEACH--OR ONE STAR IN THE SKY!

THAT WAS A VERY PRETTY SPEECH, STEVE! BUT YOU KNOW YOU **REALLY** COULDN'T PICK ME OUT IF I WERE IN A HUGE CROWD--OR DISGUISED!

PROMISE TO MARRY ME IF I CAN PROVE IT?

ALL RIGHT, STEVE! I'LL TELL YOU WHERE I'LL BE--AND IF YOU CAN PICK ME OUT THREE TIMES IN TWENTY FOUR HOURS--I'LL MARRY YOU!

WONDER WOMAN DOESN'T KNOW IT-- BUT I CAN'T LOSE--!

"THE NEXT DAY..." SINCE WE'RE PRACTICALLY MARRIED, ANGEL--YOU MIGHT AS WELL SLIP ON THIS ENGAGEMENT RING!

YOU HAVEN'T WON **YET**, STEVE! SO PLEASE TAKE BACK YOUR RING UNTIL YOU DO!

"AN HOUR LATER ... ENGULFED AMONG THE MILLIONS OF SUNDAY BATHERS ON THE BEACH ... "

STEVE SAID HE'D FIND ME IF I WERE BUT A SINGLE GRAIN OF SAND ON A BEACH! WELL--THAT'S JUST WHY I AM **HERE**-- HE'LL **NEVER** FIND ME!

HE'S LOST IN THE JUNGLE OF PEOPLE--!

HE CAN'T POSSIBLY--!

HE CAN'T--!

"TO WONDER WOMAN'S AMAZEMENT..."

IT'S A TRICK--A TRICK--THERE'S NO OTHER WAY YOU COULD HAVE DONE IT--YOU WENT STRAIGHT TOWARD ME--AS IF BY A COMPASS!

I TOLD YOU I'D FIND YOU IN A CROWD, ANGEL! READY TO GIVE UP? READY TO WEAR MY ENGAGEMENT RING?

"IN ANSWER--WONDER WOMAN SUDDENLY LEAPED INTO THE WATER AS HIGH ABOVE HER..."

CRASH!

"WITH INCREDIBLE SKILL THE INGENIOUS AMAZON STARTED WEAVING TRACKS WITH HER UNIQUE LASSO, AT FLASHING SPEED..."

HERA HELP ME!

RROAR!

"AND THEN, A SENSATIONAL SPECTACLE, AS THE MIGHTY WONDER WOMAN SKILLFULLY GUIDED THE RUNAWAY ROLLERCOASTER DOWN THE TRACKS OF UNBREAKABLE LINKS..."

THE AMAZON SAVED OUR LIVES!

THANK GOODNESS FOR WONDER WOMAN!

RRUMBLE!

"LATER..." DON'T YOU SEE *NOW* WHY I MUST THINK ONLY OF OTHERS--TO PERFORM MY TASKS TO THE BEST OF MY ABILITY, STEVE?

A BET'S A BET, ANGEL! READY TO PUT ON MY ENGAGEMENT RING?

I HAVEN'T LOST! YOU HAVE TO PICK ME OUT *TWICE* MORE WITHIN TWENTY FOUR HOURS!

YOU HAVEN'T A CHANCE, ANGEL! YOU MIGHT AS WELL GIVE UP! I CAN PICK YOU OUT EVEN IF YOU ARE DISGUISED!

"A FEW HOURS LATER..."

STEVE WILL NEVER FIND ME IN *THIS* DISGUISE!

EVEN IF HE IS A JUDGE AT THIS VERY CONTEST FOR THE BEST COSTUME!

"BUT TO THE DISGUISED AMAZON'S UTTER AMAZEMENT..."

READY TO WEAR MY ENGAGEMENT RING *NOW*, ANGEL?

NO--BUT I DON'T KNOW HOW YOU DO IT?

"*AT THAT MOMENT, AN OMINOUS CRACKLING SOUNDED AS...*"

MERCIFUL MINERVA-- LIGHTNING HEADING STRAIGHT FOR THOSE BATHERS IN THE WATER!

CRAACK!

"*AGAIN, WONDER WOMAN'S BREATHLESS PROWESS WITH HER AMAZON LASSO IS DISPLAYED AS...*"

SHE'S SAVING THE PEOPLE-- BY ATTRACTING THE LIGHTNING TO **HERSELF**!

CRANNGG!

"*BUT AT THE LAST MOMENT, THE FEARLESS AMAZON WHIPPED THE LIGHTNING INTO THE SEA...*"

THANK HERA-- THE LIGHTNING IS GROUNDING ITSELF AWAY FROM ANYBODY!

"*AGAINST **WONDER WOMAN'S** PLEAS...*"

HOW CAN I HELP PEOPLE IN TROUBLE IF I'M WITH YOU, STEVE?

IF I PICK YOU OUT ONCE MORE--YOU'LL MARRY ME? OR ARE YOU READY TO GIVE·UP **NOW**, ANGEL--AND WEAR MY ENGAGEMENT RING?

"LATER... AS FIREWORKS SHOWERED THE SKIES IN ALL THEIR COLORFUL BRILLIANCE..."

WHOOOSH!

YOU'VE GOT UNTIL TO-MORROW NOON TO OUTWIT ME, ANGEL--OR BE MY BRIDE!

WHAT MAKES HIM ABLE TO PICK ME OUT ANYWHERE AS IF I'M MARKED?

"AND THEN, SUDDENLY REVEALED IN THE MULTI-COLORED RAYS..."

A GLOWING CIRCULAR MARK ON MY RING FINGER--! GREAT HERA! STEVE MUST HAVE PUT IT ON THE RING--AND THEN ON MY FINGER WHEN HE SLIPPED THE RING ON ME! BUT HOW CAN HE SEE IT?

"NOW, WONDER WOMAN'S AMAZON GAZE DETECTED..."

SPECIAL CONTACT LENSES! HE'S CERTAINLY OUT-WITTED ME!

"ON THE WAY HOME..."

YOU MIGHT AS WELL GIVE UP, ANGEL!

WHERE CAN I HIDE-- SO HE'LL NEVER THINK OF FINDING ME? I'VE ONLY ONE MORE CHANCE!

"THE NEXT MORNING AS THE PERPLEXED AMAZON IDLY GLANCED AT THE PAPER..."

HMMM--! THIS AD GIVES ME AN IDEA! IT MIGHT-- JUST--WORK!

"SHORTLY, AT MILITARY INTELLIGENCE..."

LADIES--ONLY **ONE** AMONG YOU WILL BE ABLE TO PASS THE DIFFICULT MENTAL AND PHYSICAL COMPETITIONS AHEAD OF YOU FOR THE POSITION! *GOOD LUCK!*

"AFTER THE WRITTEN EXAMINATION..."

ONLY YOU FIVE STILL QUALIFY FOR THE POSITION, LADIES! NOW FOR THE ORAL EXAMINATION!

"EXHAUSTIVE QUESTIONING REDUCED THE NUMBER OF CANDIDATES STILL FURTHER.."

NOW, FOR THE LAST SERIES OF TESTS-- WHICH ONLY **ONE** OF YOU CAN FINALLY COMPLETE! WHICH ONE SHALL IT BE?

"ONE GRUELING TEST FOLLOWED ANOTHER UNTIL..."

HERE IS YOUR COMMISSION, LIEUTENANT! THE OTHER APPLICANT DROPPED OUT OF THE RACE! CONGRATULATIONS!

"LATER, BACK AT MILITARY INTELLIGENCE.."

YOUR NEW ASSISTANT, LT. DIANA PRINCE, STEVE!

EXCUSE ME! I HAVE UNTIL NOON TO LOOK FOR SOMEONE!

"AND THAT'S THE STORY OF *WONDER WOMAN'S* DUAL IDENTITY!"

WHAT BETTER PLACE TO CONCEAL MYSELF FROM STEVE-- AFTER THE STAIN WORE OFF -- THAN RIGHT UNDER HIS NOSE?

The End /10

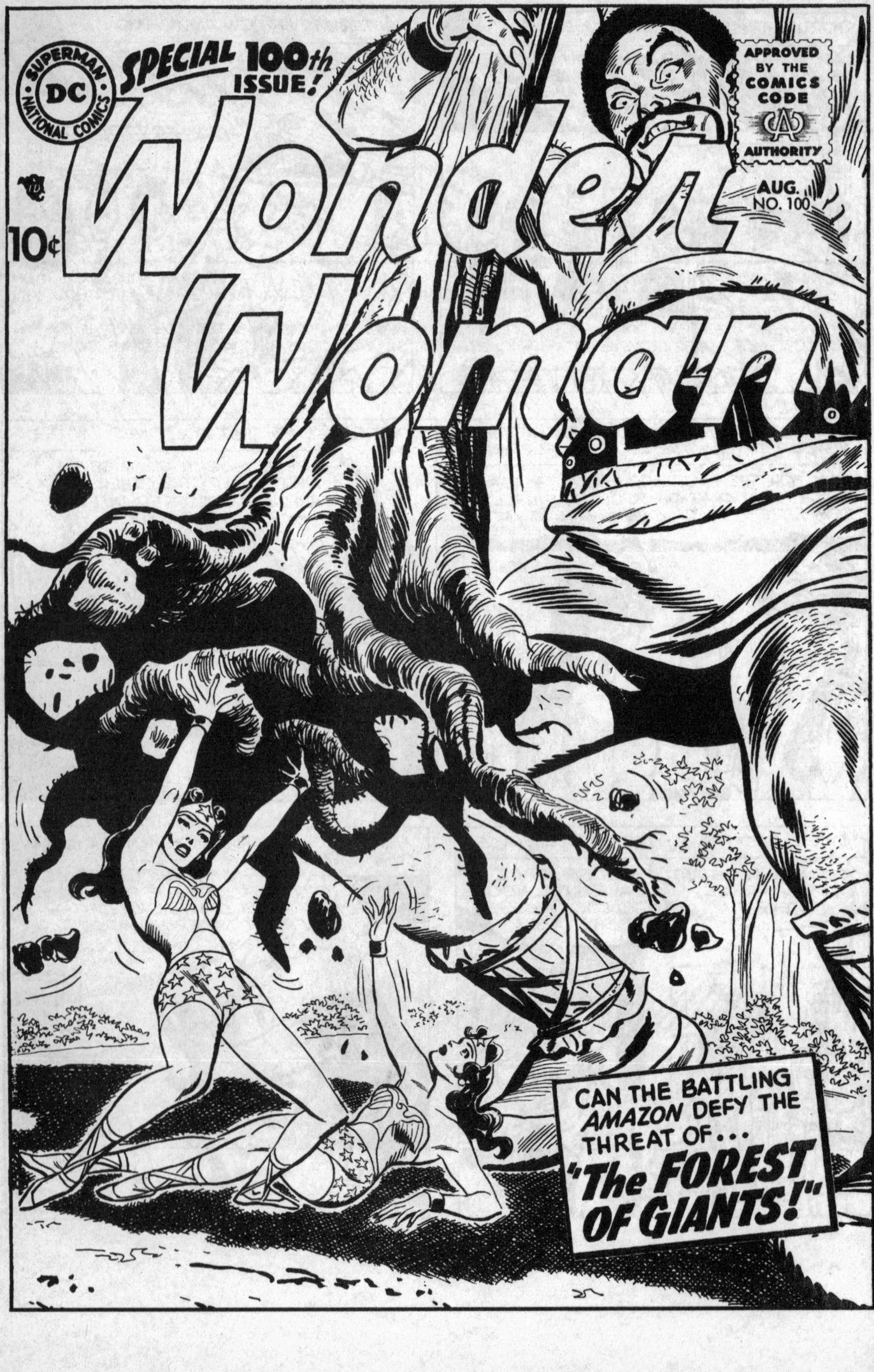
SUPERMAN DC NATIONAL COMICS
SPECIAL 100th ISSUE!
APPROVED BY THE COMICS CODE AUTHORITY
Wonder Woman
AUG. NO. 100
10¢
CAN THE BATTLING AMAZON DEFY THE THREAT OF... "The FOREST OF GIANTS!"

Wonder Woman

By Charles Moulton

The FOREST OF GIANTS!

A PRIZE TWO-PART Story

WONDER WOMAN--BEAUTIFUL AS APHRODITE, WISE AS ATHENA, SWIFTER THAN MERCURY, AND STRONGER THAN HERCULES--HAS MET THE CHALLENGE OF EVERY CONCEIVABLE OPPONENT FROM EVERY POSSIBLE WORLD!

NOW--FOR THE FIRST TIME, SHE ENCOUNTERS A MIGHTY ANTAGONIST UNIQUE ENOUGH TO DEFEAT HER--HER DOUBLE IN EVERY RESPECT...IN THE CONSTANTLY SURPRISING TALE...

The CHALLENGE of DIMENSION X!

PART I

AT THE ALL-CHAMPIONS STADIUM, *WONDER WOMAN* AND HER SWEETHEART COL. STEVE TREVOR, WATCH A STRANGE CONTEST...

SO HE'S THE WORLD'S CHAMPION SPRINT RUNNER?

YES, ANGEL! HE HAS NO COMPETITION!

--THAT'S WHY HE'S COMPETING AGAINST *HIMSELF* -- TO SET A NEW RECORD!

AS THE NEXT UNIQUE CONTEST STARTS...

AND THERE'S ANOTHER CHAMPION WHO HAS NO RIVALS!

EXCEPT HIMSELF!

YOU'RE THE WORLD'S GREATEST ALL-AROUND ATHLETE! WHAT A SIGHT IT WOULD BE TO SEE *YOU* COMPETING AGAINST YOURSELF, ANGEL!

SORRY, STEVE! YOU KNOW I ONLY USE WHATEVER SKILLS I HAVE TO BATTLE CRIME AND INJUSTICE-- NOT TO GIVE EXHIBITIONS!

AT THAT MOMENT, THE MINIATURE *SOS* SYSTEM IN *WONDER WOMAN'S* AMAZON BRACELET SIGNALS HER....

QUEEN HIPPOLYTA CALLING *WONDER WOMAN!*... COME TO PARADISE ISLAND IMMEDIATELY, DIANA!

I'LL LEAVE AT ONCE, MOTHER!

STEVE ACCOMPANIES *WONDER WOMAN* TO HER PARKED AMAZON PLANE WHERE ...

CAN'T I GO WITH YOU, ANGEL?

I'D LOVE YOU TO, STEVE! BUT NO MAN MAY SET FOOT ON PARADISE ISLAND, HOME OF THE AMAZONS!

AS THE UNIQUE PLANE LITERALLY BOLTS INTO THE AIR ...

SOMEDAY I'LL MARRY THAT ANGEL! IF I CAN ONLY GET HER TO STOP IN ONE SPOT LONG ENOUGH-- WITHOUT HER HAVING TO ANSWER SOME *SOS* OR ANOTHER!

VROOOSH!

AT INDESCRIBABLE SPEED, *WONDER WOMAN* FLASHES TOWARDS THE SECRET ISLAND HOME OF HER SISTER AMAZONS...

VROOOOSH!

WONDER WHAT MOTHER WANTED? THE ISLAND'S NOT UNDER ATTACK ... EVERYTHING SEEMS PEACEFUL ENOUGH?

SIGHTING THE *QUEEN OF THE AMAZONS*, THE IMPATIENT *WONDER WOMAN* LEAPS FROM HER ROBOT PLANE...

HOLA, MOTHER! WHY HAVE YOU SUMMONED ME AWAY FROM MY DUTIES IN MAN'S WORLD?

EVIDENTLY YOU'VE BEEN SO OCCUPIED BATTLING CRIME AND INJUSTICE-- THAT YOU'VE FORGOTTEN THAT ANNUALLY--YOU HAVE TO COMPETE AGAINST ANY CHALLENGER FOR THAT HONOR, DAUGHTER!

SHORTLY, THE AMAZON PRINCESS FACES HER CHALLENGERS IN THE OUTDOOR ARENA ...

AS IS OUR CUSTOM, THE CHAMPION DEFENDS HER CROWN UNDER A HANDICAP! START THE RACE

FOR A MOMENT, THE GALLOPING HORSES LEAVE *WONDER WOMAN* GASPING IN THE DUST...

I CAN'T CATCH THEM BY RUNNING--!

HERA HELP ME *LEAP* AFTER THEM!

ENCASED THOUGH SHE IS...

LIKE A BOLT OF TWISTED LIGHTNING...

THE *LITHE AMAZON* WHIRLS TO THE FINISH LINE...

WONDER WOMAN WINS!

FINISH

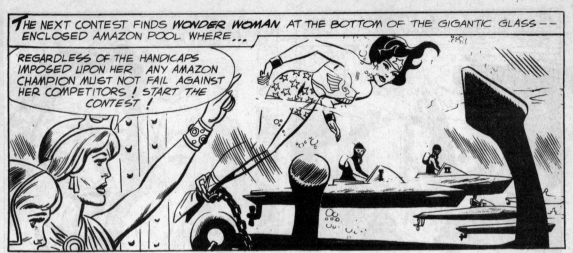

THE NEXT CONTEST FINDS *WONDER WOMAN* AT THE BOTTOM OF THE GIGANTIC GLASS—— ENCLOSED AMAZON POOL WHERE...

REGARDLESS OF THE HANDICAPS IMPOSED UPON HER ANY AMAZON CHAMPION MUST NOT FAIL AGAINST HER COMPETITORS! START THE CONTEST!

HELD BY THE MASSIVE ANCHOR, THE AMAZON PRINCESS IS ENVELOPED IN THE FROTH OF THE DEPARTING UNDERWATER SPEEDBOATS..

I CANNOT BEAT MY COMPETITORS BY SWIMMING!

WHIRLING THE HUGE ANCHOR AROUND HER...

NEPTUNE HELP ME FIND SOME OTHER WAY!

LIKE A HUMAN SHOT-PUT *WONDER WOMAN* FLASHES THROUGH THE WATER——PASSING THE OTHER SPEEDSTERS IN A BLINDING INSTANT...

SWIISH!

WONDER WOMAN WINS AGAIN!

FINISH

AFTER THE RACES... QUEEN HIPPOLYTA CONGRATULATES THE CHAMPION

ONCE AGAIN, PRINCESS DIANA YOU HAVE EARNED THE RIGHT TO REPRESENT **ALL** THE AMAZONS IN BATTLING CRIME AND INJUSTICE IN MAN'S WORLD!

HOLA!

CONGRATULATIONS... DAUGHTER... I'M PROUD OF YOU--!

THANKS, MOTHER!

SUDDENLY, ON THE QUEEN'S BRACELET-RECEIVER...

QUEEN HIPPOLYTA! ALPHA REPORTING FROM THE EXPERIMENTAL LAB! I HAVE JUST FINISHED BUILDING THE X DIMENSION MACHINE!

I SHALL COME TO YOU AT ONCE, ALPHA!

HURRYING TO THE AMAZON EXPERIMENTAL LABORATORY.

IT HASN'T BEEN TESTED YET, O'QUEEN! BUT I BELIEVE THE X-DIMENSION MACHINE WILL TRANSPORT THE USER TO A DIMENSION **BEYOND** ANY YET KNOWN TO US!

BY JUPITER-- THERE'S ONLY ONE WAY TO FIND OUT! I SHALL TEST IT!

THE DAUNTLESS AMAZON STEPS IN FRONT OF THE UNTESTED MACHINE...

BZRRRR

AND AMIDST THE STRANGE HUMMING...

SEEMS TO MERGE WITH HER SURROUNDINGS...

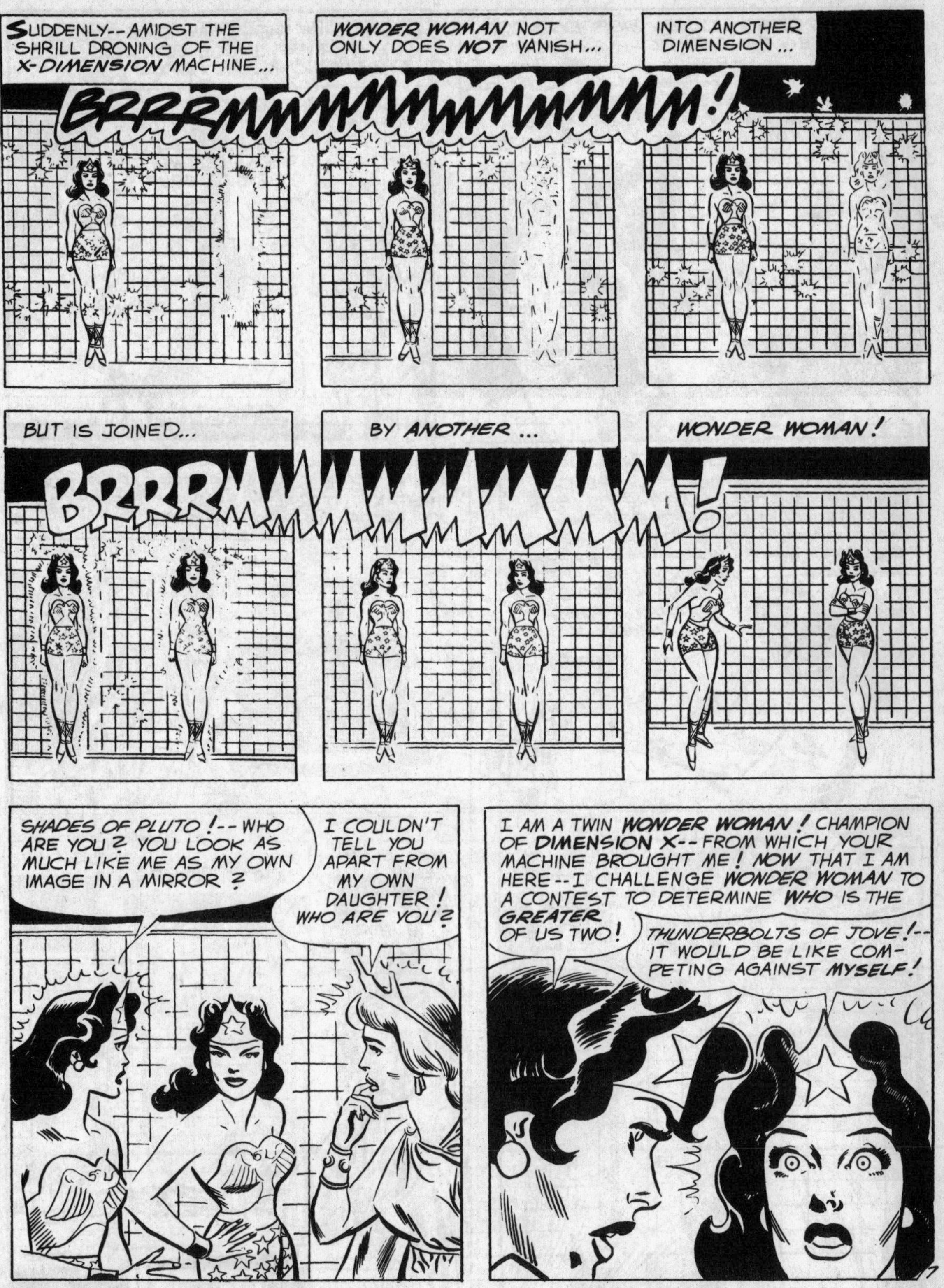
SUDDENLY--AMIDST THE SHRILL DRONING OF THE X-DIMENSION MACHINE...
BRRRMMMMMMMMMMMMMMM!
WONDER WOMAN NOT ONLY DOES NOT VANISH...
INTO ANOTHER DIMENSION...
BUT IS JOINED...
BY ANOTHER...
WONDER WOMAN!
BRRRMMMMMMMMMM!
SHADES OF PLUTO!--WHO ARE YOU? YOU LOOK AS MUCH LIKE ME AS MY OWN IMAGE IN A MIRROR?
I COULDN'T TELL YOU APART FROM MY OWN DAUGHTER! WHO ARE YOU?
I AM A TWIN WONDER WOMAN! CHAMPION OF DIMENSION X--FROM WHICH YOUR MACHINE BROUGHT ME! NOW THAT I AM HERE--I CHALLENGE WONDER WOMAN TO A CONTEST TO DETERMINE WHO IS THE GREATER OF US TWO!
THUNDERBOLTS OF JOVE!--IT WOULD BE LIKE COMPETING AGAINST MYSELF!
7

BUT, *WONDER WOMAN* IS HONOR-BOUND TO ANSWER ANY CHALLENGE--EVEN FROM A DUPLICATE OF HERSELF...

SANDS OF MORPHEUS! I FEEL AS IF I'M IN A DREAM!

YOU WON'T FOR LONG, AMAZON-- AS SOON AS I DEFEAT YOU!

BECAUSE OF THE REMARKABLE CONTEST-ANTS INVOLVED, UNIQUE CONTESTS HAVE TO BE IMPROVISED... FINALLY...

WHO PER-FORMS FIRST, REGA'?

I DON'T KNOW, O'QUEEN! THE COMPETITORS WILL DE-CIDE BETWEEN THEMSELVES THE NEXT TIME THE GEYSER ERUPTS!

MOMENTS OF BREATHLESS SUSPENSE FOLLOW... AND THEN... AS THE GEYSER HURTLES INTO THE AIR--ONE OF THE TENSE FIGURES AGILELY LEAPS UPON THE FOAMING CREST...

WHICH ONE IS IT? DIANA--OR THE CHAMPION FROM DIMENSION X?

WITH INCREDIBLE BALANCE, THE DARING CON-TESTANT LITERALLY "RIDES" THE PILLAR OF WATER TO DIZZY HEIGHTS!

WHO IS UP THERE? WONDER WOMAN--? OR HER CHALLENGER?

END OF PART ONE ...

B

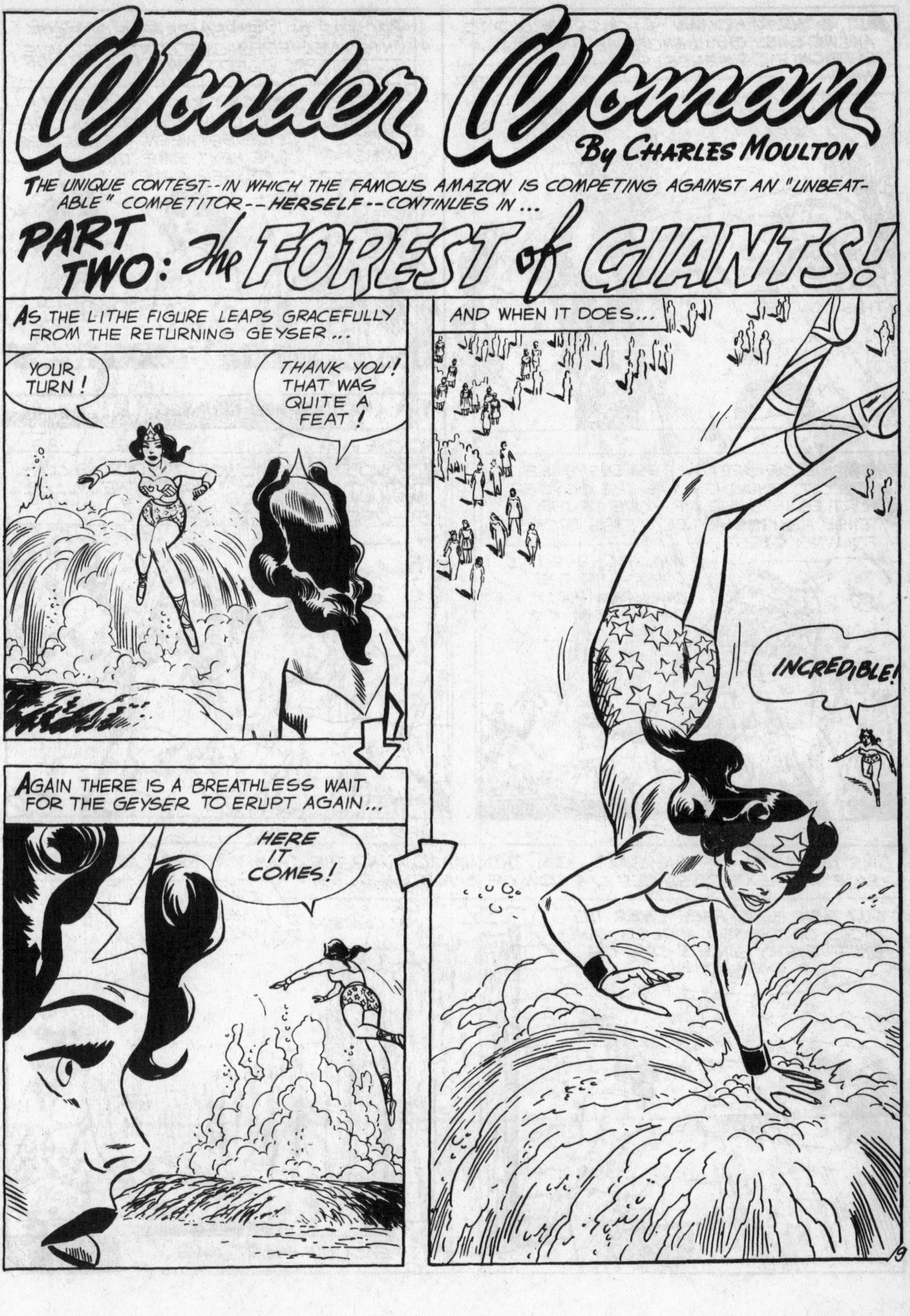
Wonder Woman
By Charles Moulton
THE UNIQUE CONTEST--IN WHICH THE FAMOUS AMAZON IS COMPETING AGAINST AN "UNBEATABLE" COMPETITOR--HERSELF--CONTINUES IN ...
PART TWO: The FOREST of GIANTS!
AS THE LITHE FIGURE LEAPS GRACEFULLY FROM THE RETURNING GEYSER...
YOUR TURN!
THANK YOU! THAT WAS QUITE A FEAT!
AGAIN THERE IS A BREATHLESS WAIT FOR THE GEYSER TO ERUPT AGAIN...
HERE IT COMES!
AND WHEN IT DOES...
INCREDIBLE!
9

BUT TO THE AMAZEMENT OF ALL, THE SLIM FIGURE SUCCESSFULLY BALANCES HERSELF ON THE WHIRLING COLUMN OF WATER...

SHE'S BALANCING HERSELF--ON ONE HAND! NO QUESTION ABOUT IT! SHE WINS THIS CONTEST!

AND WHEN THE IDENTICAL FIGURES STAND BEFORE THE QUEEN...

WHICH ONE OF YOU IS WONDER WOMAN?... WHICH ONE OF YOU... BALANCED HERSELF ON ONE HAND?

SHE DID, MOTHER! SHE BEAT ME FAIRLY!

THE AMAZONS ARE STUNNED...

NO ONE HAS EVER DEFEATED WONDER WOMAN BEFORE!

THE NEXT CONTEST WILL DECIDE IT!

IF SHE DOESN'T WIN IT-- IT'S ALL OVER!

WHAT WILL BE THE OUTCOME?

LIKE TWO SIDES OF THE SAME COIN, THE AMAZON AND THE CHAMPION FROM DIMENSION X FACE THE NEXT OBSTACLE... A ROW OF GIANT CANDLES!

OUR TASK IS TO RACE OVER THE WICKS OF THESE CANDLES--AND SNUFF EVERY SINGLE ONE OF THEM OUT!

I'M READY-- WHENEVER YOU ARE!

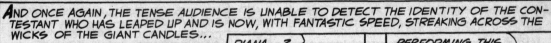

AND ONCE AGAIN, THE TENSE AUDIENCE IS UNABLE TO DETECT THE IDENTITY OF THE CONTESTANT WHO HAS LEAPED UP AND IS NOW, WITH FANTASTIC SPEED, STREAKING ACROSS THE WICKS OF THE GIANT CANDLES...

WHO IS IT?

DIANA -- 2 OR THE OTHER...

PERFORMING THIS AMAZING FEAT?

AND THEN...

YOU DID IT, WONDER WOMAN! SNUFFED OUT EVERY SINGLE LIGHT! IT *MUST* BE YOU! ONLY YOU COULD HAVE DONE THIS!

EVERYONE THINKS THE FIRST CONTESTANT MUST HAVE BEEN MY DAUGHTER!... BUT THERE IS NO WAY OF REALLY TELLING -- THERE GOES THE OTHER GIRL -- WHAT IS SHE DOING?

BEFORE THE GASPING AUDIENCE, THE INCREDIBLE ACROBAT ROCKETS ACROSS THE WICKS OF THE GIANT CANDLES ON HER *HANDS*!

ONCE AGAIN, THE IDENTICAL *WONDER WOMEN* STAND BEFORE THE FLABBERGASTED QUEEN...

WHICHEVER ONE OF YOU RACED ACROSS THOSE CANDLES ON YOUR HANDS -- WON! WHO -- WHO WAS IT?

YOUR DAUGHTER, QUEEN! WE'RE NOW EVEN! WHOEVER WINS THE NEXT CONTEST WILL BE THE REAL CHAMPION *WONDER WOMAN*! BUT SINCE I'VE RACED AGAINST HER TWICE IN *HER* DIMENSION -- I THINK IT NO MORE THAN FAIR THAT *SHE* MEET ME IN THE FINAL CONTEST -- IN *MY* DIMENSION X!

WONDER WOMAN ACCEPTS THE AMAZING CHALLENGE...AND SHORTLY...SHE AND HER "TWIN" STAND IN FRONT OF THE *X-DIMENSION* MACHINE...

GOOD LUCK... TO BOTH OF YOU!

BRRMMMMMMM!

AMIDST THE STRANGE DRONING OF THE MACHINE..., THE IDENTICAL FIGURES MELT INTO NOTHINGNESS...

THEY'RE GONE O' QUEEN!

I WONDER WHAT WILL BE THE OUTCOME? WHAT WILL HAPPEN TO MY DAUGHTER IN *DIMENSION X*?

LIKE A PICTURE SUDDENLY FLASHED ON A GIANT SCREEN, *WONDER WOMAN* VIEWS THE STRANGE YET FAMILIAR LANDSCAPE IN WHICH SHE HAS *ARRIVED*...

GREAT HERA! THIS LOOKS LIKE A SCENE OUT OF A FAIRY TALE!

NATURALLY, *WONDER WOMAN*! THAT'S WHAT *DIMENSION X* IS -- AND THERE'S MY CASTLE -- WHERE WE'LL HOLD OUR LAST AND DECIDING CONTEST!

12

SUDDENLY, A MASSIVE SHADOW FALLS UPON THE STARTLED DUO AND...

SHADES OF PLUTO!

THE GIANTS OF THE FOREST HAVE COME OUT AGAIN! IT TOOK US YEARS TO DRIVE THEM BACK! Ohh-- MY FOOT'S CAUGHT!

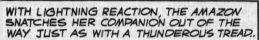

WITH LIGHTNING REACTION, THE AMAZON SNATCHES HER COMPANION OUT OF THE WAY JUST AS WITH A THUNDEROUS TREAD.

YOU SAVED MY LIFE, WONDER WOMAN! LET'S RUN TO MY CASTLE--SO WE CAN GET HELP!

THUD!

BUT, AS THE TWO ATHLETES RACE TOWARDS THE CASTLE... A FOREST OF TREES SPRING UP AMONGST THEM AS...

THE GIANTS... ARE TRYING TO THROW A BARRICADE--OF TREES-- AROUND US!

THUD! THUD! THUD!

Suddenly, amidst the newly-sprung forest of trees, Wonder Woman finds...

SUFFERING SAPPHO! MY DOUBLE -- IS GONE!

Unhesitatingly, the dauntless Amazon retraces her steps...

I RAN SO FAST -- I MUST HAVE LOST HER -- BACK THERE!

Into the clearing Wonder Woman bursts with blinding speed...

THE GIANTS ARE WAITING -- CERTAIN I'LL COME BACK TO LOOK FOR MY COMPANION!

Instantly, the Amazon Princess whips her unbreakable lasso through the air -- like a bolt of golden lightning..

THEY'RE RIGHT! BUT WHAT THEY DON'T KNOW -- IS THAT I HAVE GUESSED WHERE SHE IS!

Wonder Woman's intuition is correct -- for as she snatches the giant's hat from under his fumbling hands...

AMAZON -- YOU'VE SAVED ME AGAIN!

WE STILL HAVE A FIGHT TO WIN!

NO SOONER ARE THE TWO WONDER WOMEN TOGETHER AGAIN...

ANOTHER GIANT--PINNING US TO THE GROUND!

LEAPING UP, THE DEFIANT AMAZON HURLS HERSELF AGAINST THE TREE HELD BY THE STARTLED GIANT...

THUD!

YOU'VE SAVED ME FOR THE THIRD TIME, WONDER WOMAN-- I AM INDEBTED TO YOU FOREVER!

THE NEXT INSTANT, THE GROUND SHAKES UNDER A THUNDEROUS TREAD AS...

THEY'RE RUSHING US ALL TOGETHER-- THEY'RE LIKE A FOREST OF TREES ON THE MOVE!

TREES--Hmmm-- THAT GIVES ME AN IDEA!

WITH A SURGE OF POWER, WONDER WOMAN BENDS THE TREE INTO A CERTAIN SHAPE...

WHAT ARE YOU DOING, AMAZON?

SHAPING THE TREE INTO A BOOMERANG!

LIKE A GIGANTIC CATAPULT, *WONDER WOMAN* HURLS THE TREE-SIZED BOOMERANG INTO THE ADVANCING GIANTS...

THEY'RE FALLING LIKE TEN-PINS! YOU'VE SAVED US ALL FROM THE MENACE OF THE GIANTS! WE'LL CELEBRATE!

VROOOOSH!

AS THE BOOMERANG RETURNS TO ITS POWER-FUL HURLER...

--AND AS FOR THAT THIRD CONTEST...

LOOK OUT-- OR THERE WON'T BE A THIRD CONTEST!

SHORTLY, IN THE EXPERIMENTAL LAB ON *PARADISE ISLAND*...

I CAN'T STAND THE SUSPENSE, ALPHA! WHAT HAS HAPPENED TO MY DAUGHTER? WHO WON?

I HAVE JUST MANAGED TO TUNE IN ON *DIMENSION X*, O'QUEEN-- YOU CAN SEE FOR YOURSELF!

TO THE *ONLY* WONDER WOMAN-- NO MATTER IN *WHAT* DIMENSION-- *PRINCESS DIANA* OF *PARADISE ISLAND!*

The End 16

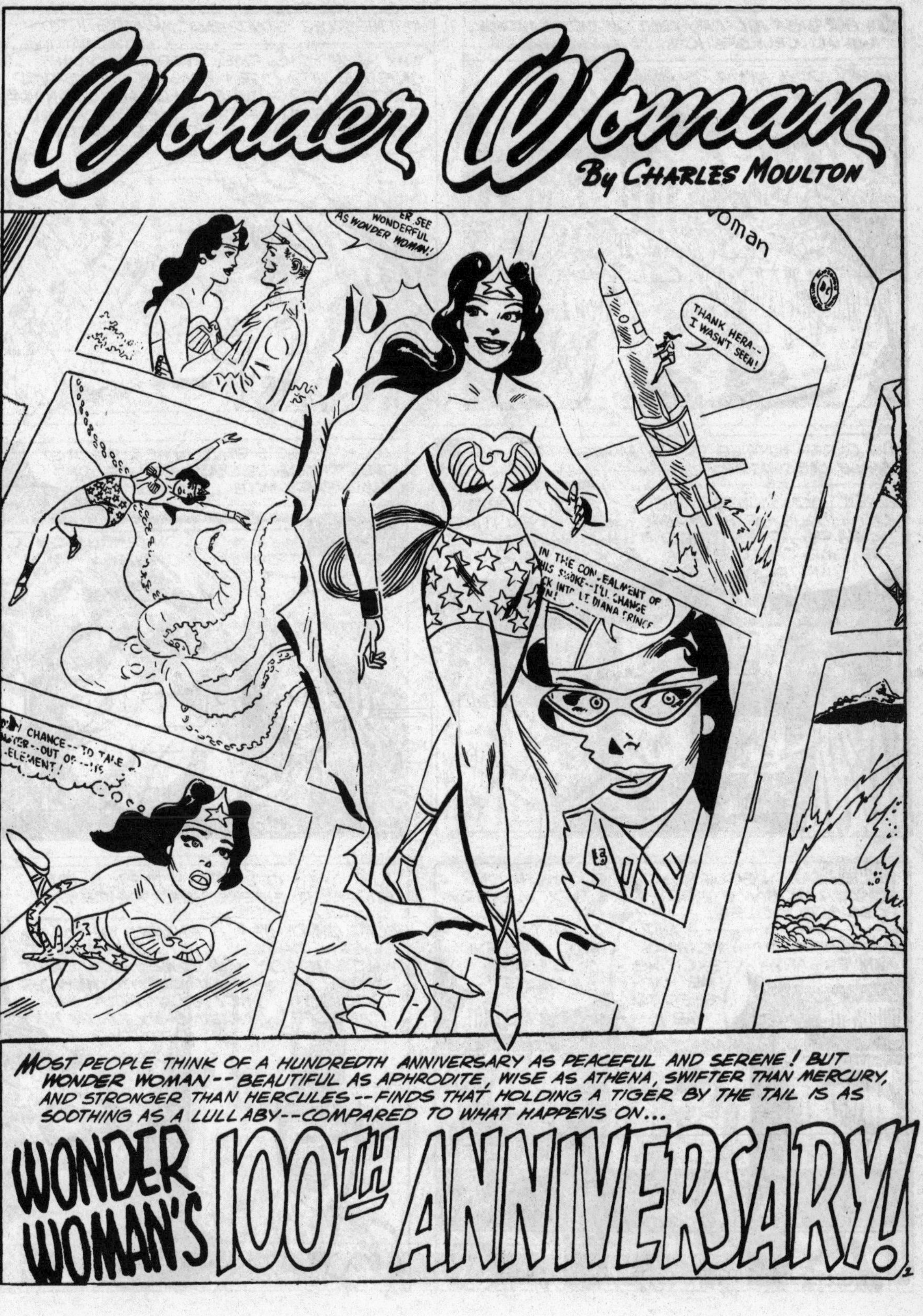
Wonder Woman
By CHARLES MOULTON
THANK HERA-- I WASN'T SEEN!
MOST PEOPLE THINK OF A HUNDREDTH ANNIVERSARY AS PEACEFUL AND SERENE! BUT WONDER WOMAN--BEAUTIFUL AS APHRODITE, WISE AS ATHENA, SWIFTER THAN MERCURY, AND STRONGER THAN HERCULES--FINDS THAT HOLDING A TIGER BY THE TAIL IS AS SOOTHING AS A LULLABY--COMPARED TO WHAT HAPPENS ON...
WONDER WOMAN'S 100TH ANNIVERSARY!

ON *PARADISE ISLAND*, HOME OF THE AMAZONS.. A GREAT CELEBRATION... IS IN PROGRESS...

HAPPY 100th ANNIVERSARY, QUEEN HIPPOLYTA!

HAPPY 100th TO ALL OF YOU!

AT THE GROVE OF ATHENA...

WHY HASN'T THE TIME CAPSULE WITH OUR RECORDS FOR FUTURE AGES TO STUDY-- BEEN CLOSED YET?

WE'RE WAITING FOR THE 100th ISSUE OF *WONDER WOMAN'S* ADVENTURES TO BE DELIVERED TO US, NOBLE QUEEN?

THE QUEEN HURRIES TO THE *AMAZON TIME AND SPACE LABORATORY*...

HAVEN'T YOU PRINTED THE 100th ISSUE OF *WONDER WOMAN'S* ADVENTURES? THE TIME CAPSULE IS WAITING!

WHY SEE FOR YOUR-SELF, O' QUEEN! NOTHING EXCITING HAS HAPPENED TO YOUR DAUGHTER!

LOOK--! SHE'S **STILL** IN HER SECRET IDENTITY OF LT. DIANA PRINCE OF MILITARY INTELLIGENCE!

WHILE AMAZON EQUIPMENT IS FOCUSED ON *WONDER WOMAN'S* EVERY MOVE --FROM EVERY POSSIBLE ANGLE...

OUR HUNDREDTH ANNIVERSARY--

AND NOTHING EXCITING HAS HAP-PENED TO ME!

I CAN'T FAIL MOTHER...AND MY SISTER AMAZONS!

JUST THEN, COL. STEVE TREVOR, DIAN SUPERIOR, ENTERS HER OFFICE...

COME ON, DIANA! GENERAL DARNELL WANTS US TO WATCH A ROCKET TAKEOFF!

SHADES OF PLUTO WITH STEVE NEXT TO ME... HOW CAN I CHANGE INTO *WONDER WOMAN* WITHOUT RE-VEALING MY SECRET IDENTITY?

AT THE ROCKET TESTING GROUNDS, DIANA WATCHES THE COUNT DOWN FROM A CONCRETE SHELTER ... AND THEN...

SOMETHING'S GONE WRONG--THE ROCKET'S JUST *HOVERING* THERE !

IT'S GOING TO CRASH ANY MOMENT !

WITH EVERYONE'S EYES GLUED TO THE DOOMED ROCKET...

NOW IS MY CHANCE TO CHANGE INTO WONDER WOMAN !

IN FRONT OF THE VIEW SLIT--A STARTLING DRAMA UNFOLDS...

LOOK AT WONDER WOMAN !

WHAT CAN EVEN SHE HOPE TO DO ?

LIKE A SHADOW, WONDER WOMAN STREAKS FROM THE SHELTER...

THANK HERA-- I WASN'T SEEN !

BEFORE *WONDER WOMAN'S* IRRESISTABLE SURGE UPWARDS, AIR PRESSURE OF UN-DREAMED OF POWER SENDS THE ROCKET HURTLING AWAY...

WILL THE ROCKET ATTAIN THE SPEED OF FIVE MILES PER SECOND NECESSARY FOR IT TO FREE ITSELF OF THE GRAVITATIONAL PULL OF THE EARTH?

WHOOOOSH!!

IN THE CONTROL ROOM, JUBILATION REIGNS AS...

WONDER WOMAN'S DONE IT--! SHE FURNISHED THE THRUST NEEDED TO SEND THE ROCKET INTO ORBIT!

THAT'S *MY* GIRL!

THE DARING AMAZON ALIGHTS GRACEFULLY BACK TO THE GROUND...

IN THE CONCEAL-MENT OF THIS SMOKE--I'LL CHANGE BACK INTO LT. DIANA PRINCE AGAIN! BUT--HAS STEVE NOTICED MY DISAPPEARANCE?

AND AS SHE FLASHES BACK INTO THE SHELTER AGAIN...

DID YOU EVER SEE ANYTHING AS WONDERFUL AS *WONDER WOMAN* IN ACTION, DIANA?

N-NO--!

THANK HERA-- I WAS UNOBSERVED IN MY DUAL IDENTITY! NOW, I CAN RE-LAX! THIS ACTION WILL COMPLETE THE HUNDREDTH ISSUE OF *WONDER WOMAN!*

BUT AT THE AMAZON TIME AND SPACE LABORATORY, CONSTERNATION REIGNS

THE SMOKE AND FLAME SHOWERED BY THE ROCKET COMPLETELY CONCEALED WONDER WOMAN'S ACTIONS FROM OUR CAMERAS!

SUFFERING SAPPHO! INFORM HER THAT THE HUNDREDTH ISSUE OF HER ADVENTURES IS BEING HELD UP!

AND SO, LATER IN DIANA'S APARTMENT...

SORRY, DAUGHTER! WE'RE WITHOUT A 100th ISSUE OF YOUR ADVENTURES FOR THE TIME CAPSULE!

IT COULDN'T BE HELPED, MOTHER! BUT, AT LEAST WHEN SOMETHING DOES HAPPEN, I WON'T HAVE TO WORRY ABOUT STEVE DISCOVERING MY DUAL IDENTITY!

WHEN HER DOORBELL RINGS A FEW MOMENTS LATER, HOWEVER...

SORRY TO DISTURB YOU! BUT THE GENERAL WANTS US TO INSPECT A NEW EXPERIMENTAL JET PLANE ABOARD THE AIRCRAFT CARRIER IN THE HARBOR!

SUFFERING SAPPHO! HOW CAN I CHANGE INTO WONDER WOMAN WITH STEVE AROUND?

IN THE MOTORBOAT TAKING THE TWO TOWARD THE AIRCRAFT CARRIER SHORTLY...

HELP--!

A SKIN DIVER IN TROUBLE! I'M GOING TO HELP HIM! TAKE OVER THE WHEEL, ANGEL, WHILE I GO TO HIS HELP!

ANXIOUS MOMENTS PASS...

THEY'RE BOTH GONE!

5

LEAVING THE *MOTORBOAT* ANCHORED

AT LEAST-- STEVE HASN'T SEEN THE CHANGE INTO MY SECRET IDENTITY OF *WONDER WOMAN!*

INTO THE MURKY DEPTHS THE AMAZON DIVES-- WHILE BACK ON *PARADISE ISLAND...*

WE'VE GOT OUR CAMERAS TRAINED DIRECTLY ON *WONDER WOMAN!*

GOOD! THERE'S NOTHING TO PREVENT OUR GETTING EXCITING PICTURES OF HER IN ACTION FOR THE *100th* ISSUE OF HER ADVENTURES FOR THE TIME CAPSULE!

MEANWHILE, ON THE TRAIL OF STEVE AND THE SKIN DIVER, *WONDER WOMAN* SEES...

SHADES OF PLUTO! STEVE AND THE SKIN DIVER -- IMPRISONED BY A MONSTER OCTOPUS!

AS THE DAUNTLESS AMAZON UNHESITATINGLY DIVES TOWARD THEIR RESCUE...

THUNDERBOLTS OF JOVE! THE OCTOPUS IS DISCHARGING A VAST QUANTITY OF INKY FLUID TO HIDE HIS CAPTIVES FROM VIEW!

WITH A SKILLFUL CAST OF HER LASSO--WONDER WOMAN ENCIRCLES THE CAPTIVES.

THANK HERA--I WAS ABLE TO YANK THEM OUT OF THE CLUTCHES OF THAT OCTOPUS!

AND THEN, WITH A POWERFUL FLIP OF HER MIGHTY ARM, THE TIRELESS AMAZON HURLS THEM TOWARDS THE SURFACE...

THEY MUST BE ALMOST OUT OF OXYGEN BY THIS TIME!

SAVING THE OTHERS, PLACES WONDER WOMAN WITHIN REACH OF THE ENRAGED UNDERSEA BEAST...

I'M--CAUGHT--!

UNSUCCESSFUL IN HER GRIM ATTEMPTS TO FREE HERSELF FROM THE IMMOBILE TENTACLES... THE MIGHTY AMAZON HURLS HERSELF UPWARDS...

ONLY CHANCE--TO TAKE MONSTER-- OUT OF--ITS ELEMENT!

LIKE A TORPEDO, WONDER WOMAN THUNDERS OUT OF THE WATERY DEPTHS --INTO THE AIR ...

THANK HERA--IT'S LET GO OF ME!--NOW--I CAN CHANGE BACK TO DIANA-- AND RETURN TO THE BOAT! AND THIS ADVENTURE WILL CLOSE THE 100th ISSUE!

BUT UPON HER RETURN HOME, DIANA IS STARTLED BY ANOTHER MESSAGE..

OUR CAMERAS COULD NOT PIERCE THE INKY BLACK LIQUID THROWN OUT BY THE OCTOPUS, DIANA! WE *STILL* HAVE NO *100th* ISSUE FOR THE TIME CAPSULE!

IMMEDIATELY, *WONDER WOMAN* RACES BACK TO *PARADISE ISLAND* IN HER UNIQUE AMAZON PLANE...

NO ONE IS BLAMING ME-- BUT IT IS MY FAULT! AND IT DOESN'T LOOK AS IF ANYTHING EXCITING WILL HAPPEN IN TIME FOR OUR *100th* ANNIVERSARY!

AT THAT MOMENT, THE VERY SEA WRITHES -- AND FROM THE CLIFF SHE IS SITTING ON IN HER LONELINESS, *WONDER WOMAN* IS HORRIFIED BY...

MERCIFUL MINERVA! A GIGANTIC TIDAL WAVE THUNDERING AT OUR ISLAND!

RRRROAR!

LASSOING A NEARBY PEAK WITH HER RARE LASSO OF UNBREAKABLE LINKS...

HERA HELP THIS TO HOLD!-- IF IT DOESN'T-- THE ISLAND WILL BE ENGULFED!

CALLING HER ROBOT PLANE, *WONDER WOMAN* SEIZES A WING...

PLANE-- CLIMB-- AT MAXIMUM SPEED!

AS THE MOUNTAINOUS WAVE CRASHES BY UNDERNEATH, THE MIGHTY *WONDER WOMAN* HOLDS UP THE ISLAND OF THE AMAZONS

THANK HERA! THE ISLAND IS SAFE--AND THE TIDAL WAVE WILL DISSIPATE ITSELF LONG BEFORE IT REACHES THE MAINLAND!

AS THE LOVELY AMAZON SAFELY LOWERS THE ISLAND BACK INTO PLACE...

SUFFERING SAPPHO! DID THE CAMERAS CATCH ANY OF THIS?

THE ANSWER IS IN THE TIME CAPSULE...

WONDER WOMAN SAVES PARADISE ISLAND FROM DESTRUCTION BY TIDAL WAVE ON 100th ANNIVERSARY!

The End

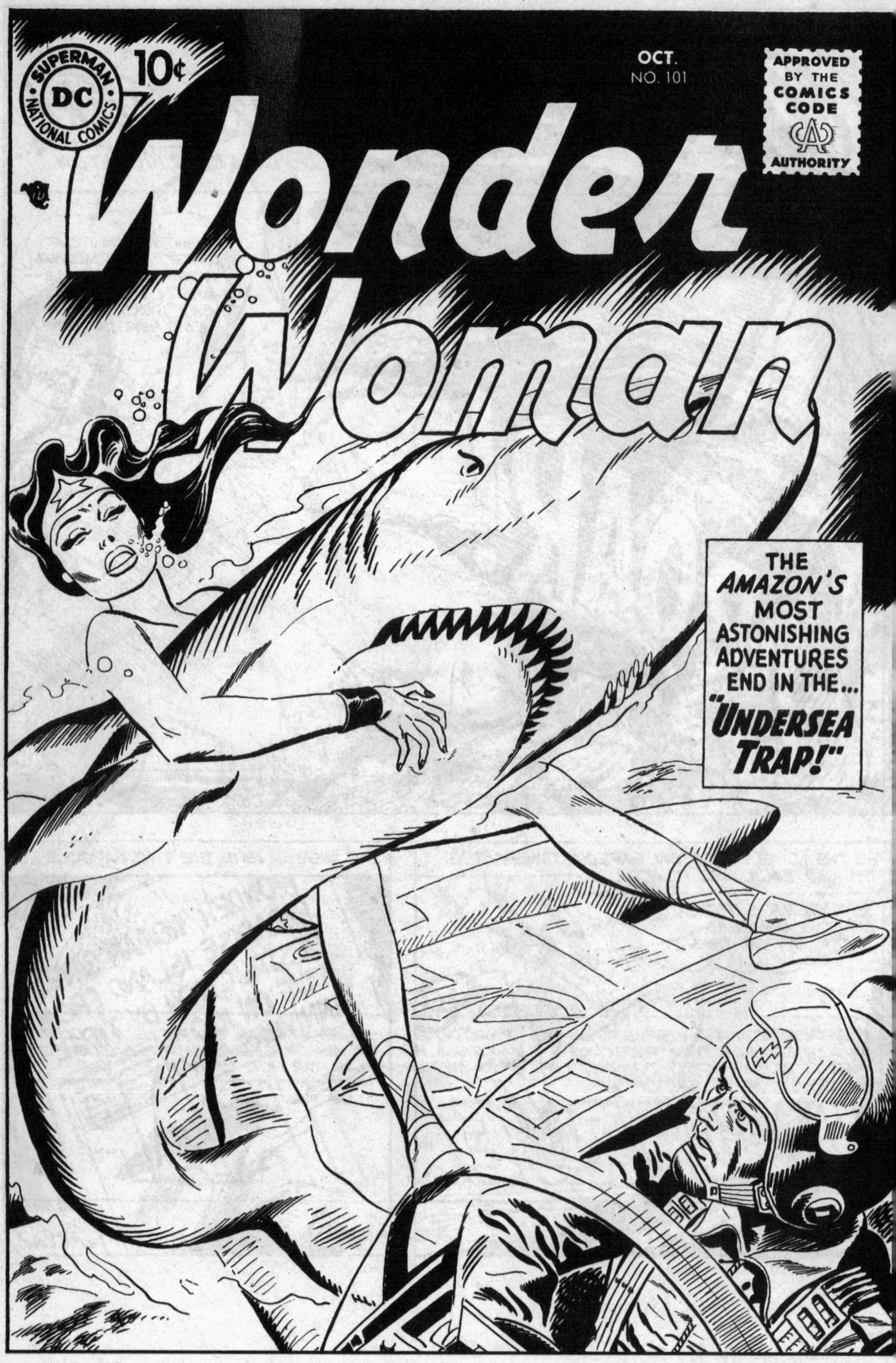
SUPERMAN DC NATIONAL COMICS
10¢
OCT.
NO. 101
APPROVED BY THE COMICS CODE AUTHORITY
Wonder Woman
THE AMAZON'S MOST ASTONISHING ADVENTURES END IN THE... "UNDERSEA TRAP!"

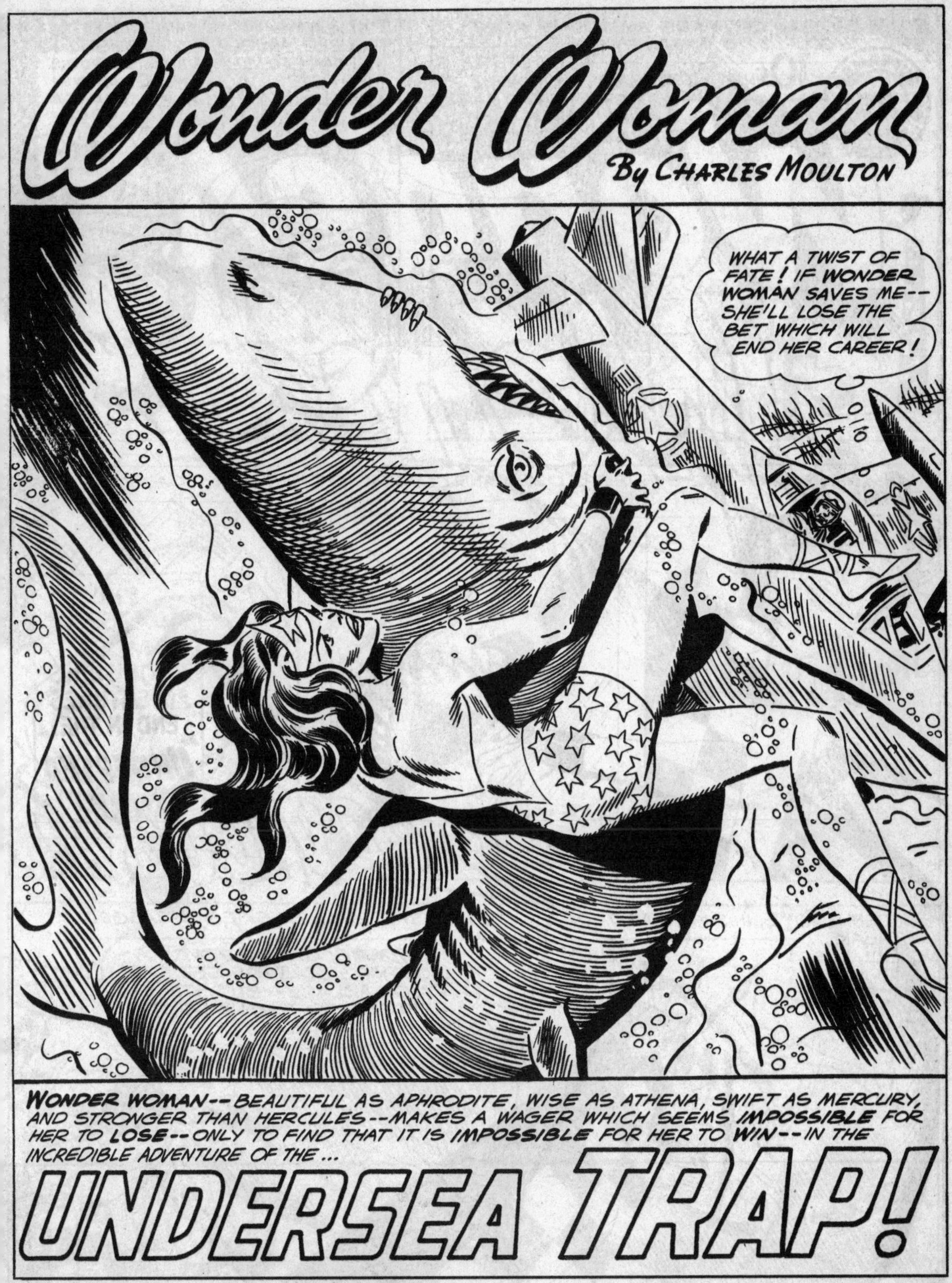
Wonder Woman
By Charles Moulton
WHAT A TWIST OF FATE! IF WONDER WOMAN SAVES ME-- SHE'LL LOSE THE BET WHICH WILL END HER CAREER!
WONDER WOMAN-- BEAUTIFUL AS APHRODITE, WISE AS ATHENA, SWIFT AS MERCURY, AND STRONGER THAN HERCULES--MAKES A WAGER WHICH SEEMS IMPOSSIBLE FOR HER TO LOSE--ONLY TO FIND THAT IT IS IMPOSSIBLE FOR HER TO WIN--IN THE INCREDIBLE ADVENTURE OF THE ...
UNDERSEA TRAP!

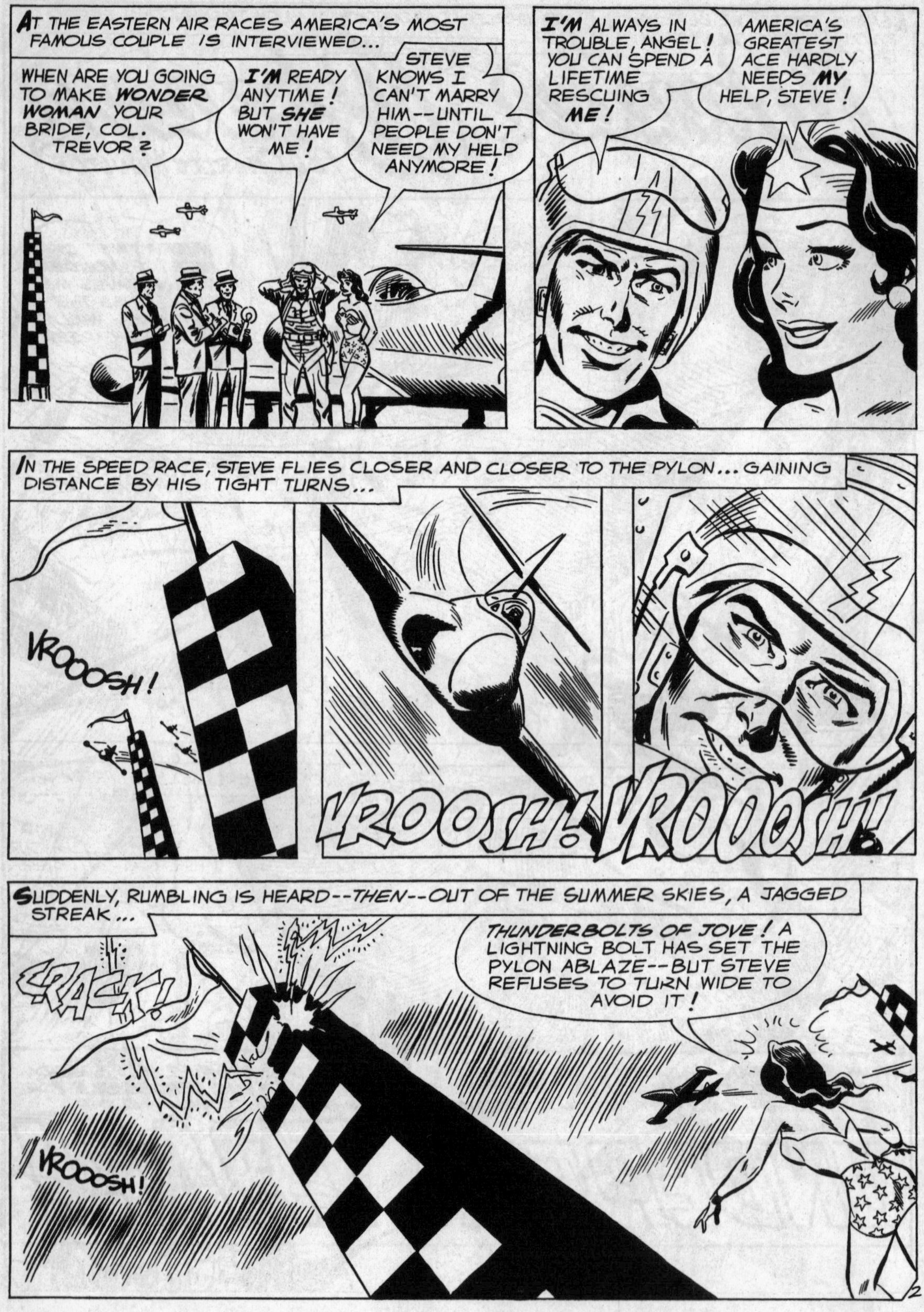
AT THE EASTERN AIR RACES AMERICA'S MOST FAMOUS COUPLE IS INTERVIEWED...
WHEN ARE YOU GOING TO MAKE WONDER WOMAN YOUR BRIDE, COL. TREVOR?
I'M READY ANYTIME! BUT SHE WON'T HAVE ME!
STEVE KNOWS I CAN'T MARRY HIM--UNTIL PEOPLE DON'T NEED MY HELP ANYMORE!
I'M ALWAYS IN TROUBLE, ANGEL! YOU CAN SPEND A LIFETIME RESCUING ME!
AMERICA'S GREATEST ACE HARDLY NEEDS MY HELP, STEVE!
IN THE SPEED RACE, STEVE FLIES CLOSER AND CLOSER TO THE PYLON... GAINING DISTANCE BY HIS TIGHT TURNS...
VROOOSH!
VROOSH!
VROOOSH!
SUDDENLY, RUMBLING IS HEARD--THEN--OUT OF THE SUMMER SKIES, A JAGGED STREAK...
CRACK!
THUNDERBOLTS OF JOVE! A LIGHTNING BOLT HAS SET THE PYLON ABLAZE--BUT STEVE REFUSES TO TURN WIDE TO AVOID IT!
VROOOSH!
2

LEAPING TOWARD THE BLAZING PYLON--THE MIGHTY AMAZON UPROOTS IT--

AND WHIRLS IT AROUND WITH SUCH TREMENDOUS SPEED THAT...

SWIIISH!

THANK HERA-- THE FIRE IS OUT!

ABOVE, THE DAUNTLESS SPEED PILOT ROARS THROUGH THE SMOKE TO WIN THE RACE...

VROOOSH!

STEVE WINS THE TROPHY!

LATER... ON THE GROUND... AT THE VICTORY DANCE...

TODAY-- STEVE GAVE A GOOD EXAMPLE-- HOW LITTLE HE NEEDED MY HELP!

BUT WHAT IF I DID, ANGEL? WHAT IF I NEEDED YOUR HELP--SAY--THREE TIMES IN A SINGLE DAY-- WOULD YOU MARRY ME?

AT STEVE'S URGING, *WONDER WOMAN* AGREES TO HIS PLEA...

ALL RIGHT, STEVE! IF YOU NEED MY HELP--*THREE TIMES*--DURING THE NEXT TWENTY FOUR HOURS-- I'LL MARRY YOU!

YOU'VE LOST, ANGEL!

SHE IS STARTLED BY...

I'VE GOT SO MUCH TESTING TO DO IN EXPERIMENTAL PLANES TOMORROW--THAT I'M SURE TO NEED YOUR HELP THIRTY TIMES--*NOT JUST THREE!*

THAT'S NOT FAIR, STEVE! YOU DIDN'T TELL ME OF THIS!

ALL'S FAIR IN LOVE AND WAR, ANGEL!

JUST THEN, IT IS STEVE WHO IS SURPRISED WHEN *GENERAL DARNELL* ANNOUNCES...

COL. TREVOR--YOU'VE BEEN FLYING TOO MUCH! FOR THE NEXT DAY--THE ONLY THING YOU'LL FLY--IS YOUR DESK! THAT'S AN ORDER!

ALL'S FAIR IN LOVE AND WAR?

AWWW-- WHAT CHANCE DO I HAVE OF NEEDING YOUR HELP--SITTING BEHIND A DESK?

AT *MILITARY INTELLIGENCE, WONDER WOMAN* CHANGES INTO HER SECRET IDENTITY OF LT. DIANA PRINCE...

IT WILL BE FUN-- WATCHING STEVE!

LATER, STEVE AND DIANA LUNCH ON THE ROOF OF THE *MILITARY INTELLIGENCE* BUILDING..

WONDER WOMAN MUST BE LAUGHING AT ME--KNOWING THAT I HAVEN'T THE SLIGHTEST CHANCE OF RUNNING INTO ANY PERIL AROUND HERE!

THE ONLY DANGER TO ME HERE--IS IF I FALL ASLEEP-- AND GET A SUNBURN...

WELL...I'LL HAVE TO LEAVE... I HAVE WORK TO DO!

JUST THEN... A SOUND HEARD BY NO ORDINARY EAR--ATTRACTS DIANA'S ATTENTION ...

MERCIFUL MINERVA!

THE NEXT MOMENT, THE *MILITARY INTELLI-GENCE* OFFICER MAKES A LIGHTNING CHANGE INTO HER SECRET IDENTITY ...

THIS CALLS FOR WONDER WOMAN!

EX

UNHESITATINGLY, THE ALERT AMAZON LEAPS BACK TOWARDS THE DOZING STEVE...

THE GIANT CONE OF A ROCKET-- IS HURTLING STRAIGHT AT HIM!

VROOOSH!!

5

WHIPPING UP HER AMAZON LASSO, *WONDER WOMAN* HALTS THE HUGE ROCKET CONE -- PERILOUSLY NEAR STEVE'S HEAD...

WELL--MY PRAYERS HAVE BEEN ANSWERED! ANGEL--YOU SAVED MY LIFE!

AS THE MIGHTY AMAZON LOWERS THE MASSIVE OBJECT TO THE ROOF...

THAT'S *ONCE* YOU'VE SAVED ME FROM PERIL, ANGEL! TWICE MORE --AND YOU'LL MARRY ME!

HOURS PASS... AND AT A DANCE IN THE RECREATION HALL ...

WHY SO GLUM, STEVE?

WHAT CHANCE DO I HAVE OF NEEDING YOUR HELP AT A DANCE?

BUT, DURING INTERMISSION...

HANDS UP, EVERYONE! THIS IS A STICKUP! JUST TOSS YOUR VALUABLES ON THE FLOOR!

IMMEDIATELY...

DROP YOUR GUNS, YOU BUZZARDS!

THE ONLY THING AROUND HERE THAT WILL DROP-- IS YOU, PIGEON!

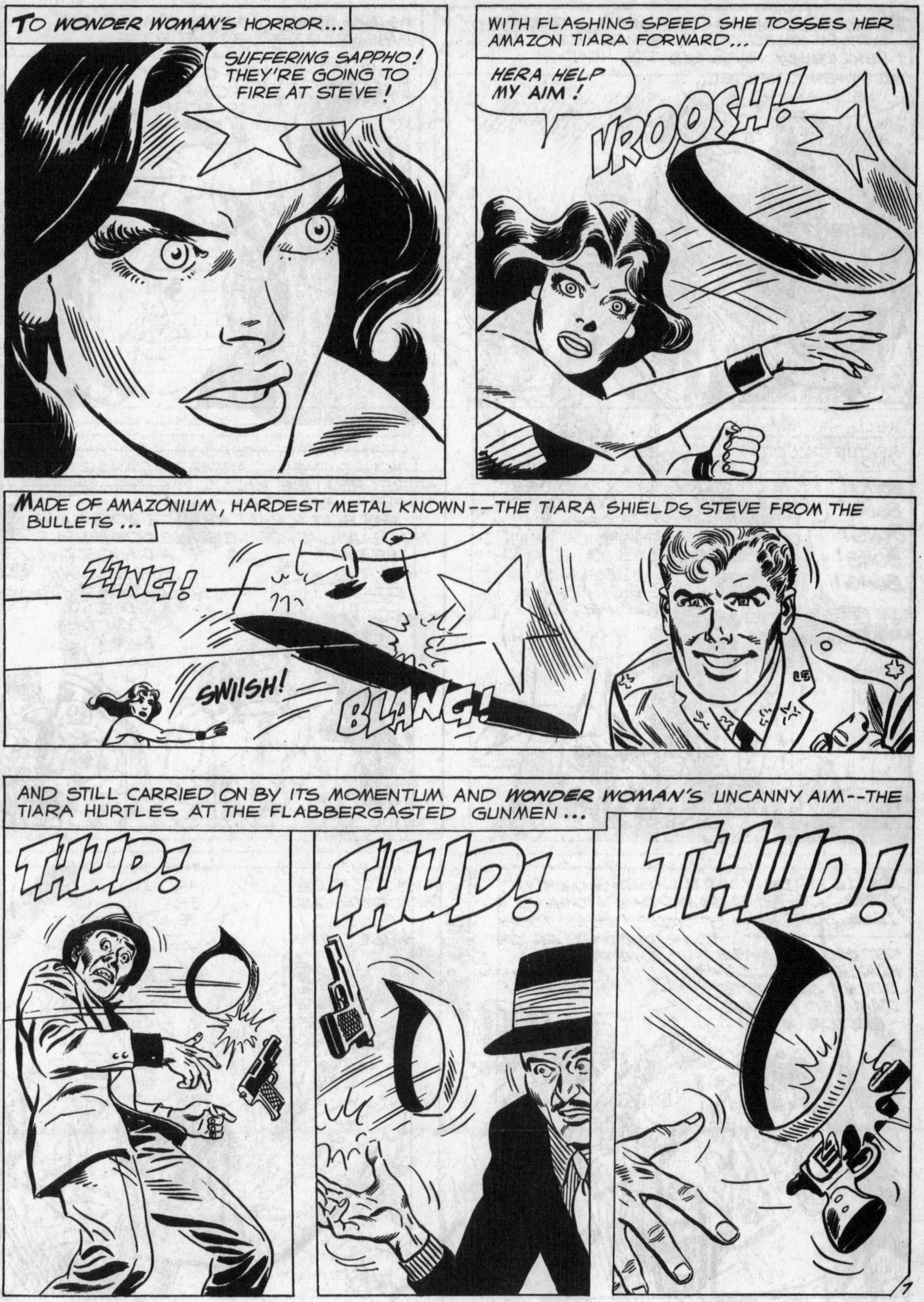
TO WONDER WOMAN'S HORROR...
SUFFERING SAPPHO! THEY'RE GOING TO FIRE AT STEVE!
WITH FLASHING SPEED SHE TOSSES HER AMAZON TIARA FORWARD...
HERA HELP MY AIM!
VROOSH!
MADE OF AMAZONIUM, HARDEST METAL KNOWN--THE TIARA SHIELDS STEVE FROM THE BULLETS...
ZING!
SWIISH!
BLANG!
AND STILL CARRIED ON BY ITS MOMENTUM AND WONDER WOMAN'S UNCANNY AIM--THE TIARA HURTLES AT THE FLABBERGASTED GUNMEN...
THUD!
THUD!
THUD!
7

THE DISARMED GUNMEN ARE QUICKLY SUBDUED...

THAT'S *TWICE* YOU SAVED ME--WHEN I NEEDED HELP--ANGEL!

ONCE MORE MAKES THREE --AND YOU MARRY ME!

AS THE DAY DRAWS TO A CLOSE...

BONG! BONG! BONG! BONG! BONG!

FIVE O'CLOCK! ONE MORE HOUR TO SIX! IF I DON'T NEED HELP BEFORE THEN--I LOSE!

BUT IN A GOOD CAUSE, STEVE! DON'T FORGET MY MISSION HERE IS TO HELP PEOPLE IN DISTRESS-- ALL PEOPLE!

JUST THEN...THE *INTERCOM* SOUNDS...

STEVE--I'D LIKE YOU TO FERRY ME OVER TO THE FLATTOP THAT'S ANCHORED IN THE EAST RIVER!

YES, GEN. DARNELL!

I MIGHT AS WELL BE A TAXICAB DRIVER-- FOR ALL THE DANGER I'M GOING TO RUN INTO ON THIS TRIP!

MINUTE AFTER MINUTE PASSES... AND THEN ...ON *WONDER WOMAN'S* OMNI- TELE SCREEN...

CST CALLING BASE!... FLAME-OUT!...CAN'T DITCH! CANOPY'S JAMMED! OVER SECTOR 4Y7G--!

MERCIFUL MINERVA! IT'S STEVE-- IN TROUBLE!

HAVE TO RIDE THIS ONE OUT--

SPLASH!

8

CALLING HER ROBOT PLANE... *WONDER WOMAN* BOARDS IT ON THE WING...

PLANE...BANK...AND HEAD EAST...AT MAXIMUM SPEED!

OVER THE AREA OF THE CRASH THE DAUNTLESS AMAZON DIVES FROM THE PLANE...

I NEVER THOUGHT WHEN I MADE THE WAGER WITH STEVE-- THAT HE WOULD NEED MY HELP THREE TIMES--IN THE SAME DAY!

PLUMMETING TOWARD THE BOTTOM, *WONDER WOMAN* IS STARTLED TO BEHOLD...

WITH *THIS* RESCUE--I WILL HAVE TO MARRY STEVE AND--SHADES OF PLUTO! A SHARK-- BATTERING STEVE'S COCKPIT!

THUD!

UNHESITATINGLY, THE FEARLESS AMAZON HURTLES AT THE SHARK...

I NEVER DREAMED I'D NEED MY ANGEL'S HELP FOR THE THIRD TIME!

BUT--HELPING ME THIS THIRD TIME--MEANS SHE LOSES HER WAGER WITH ME!

9

WITH A FINAL SURGE, THE MIGHTY AMAZON HURLS THE FIERCE SHARK FROM THE PLANE...

I'LL HAVE TO GET STEVE OUT--BEFORE THIS BRUTE SWIMS BACK!

SMASHING THE CANOPY IN--*WONDER WOMAN* LIFTS OUT THE TRAPPED PILOT AND...

I HAVE TIME ENOUGH TO SWIM TOWARD SHORE-- BEFORE STEVE'S BREATH GIVES OUT!

IN FLASHING SECONDS, THE FLEET AMAZON REACHES SHORE WITH STEVE...

YOU HELPED ME THREE TIMES *BEFORE* 6 O'CLOCK, ANGEL! THOSE ARE OUR WEDDING BELLS YOU HEAR!

LOOK AGAIN, STEVE!

BONG! BONG!

BLAZES--! IT'S 6:15! THE THIRD TIME YOU HELPED ME WAS *AFTER* SIX! I LOSE--!

DON'T FEEL TOO BADLY, STEVE! DON'T FORGET-- MY MISSION HERE IS TO HELP ALL PEOPLE IN DISTRESS!

The End

Wonder Woman

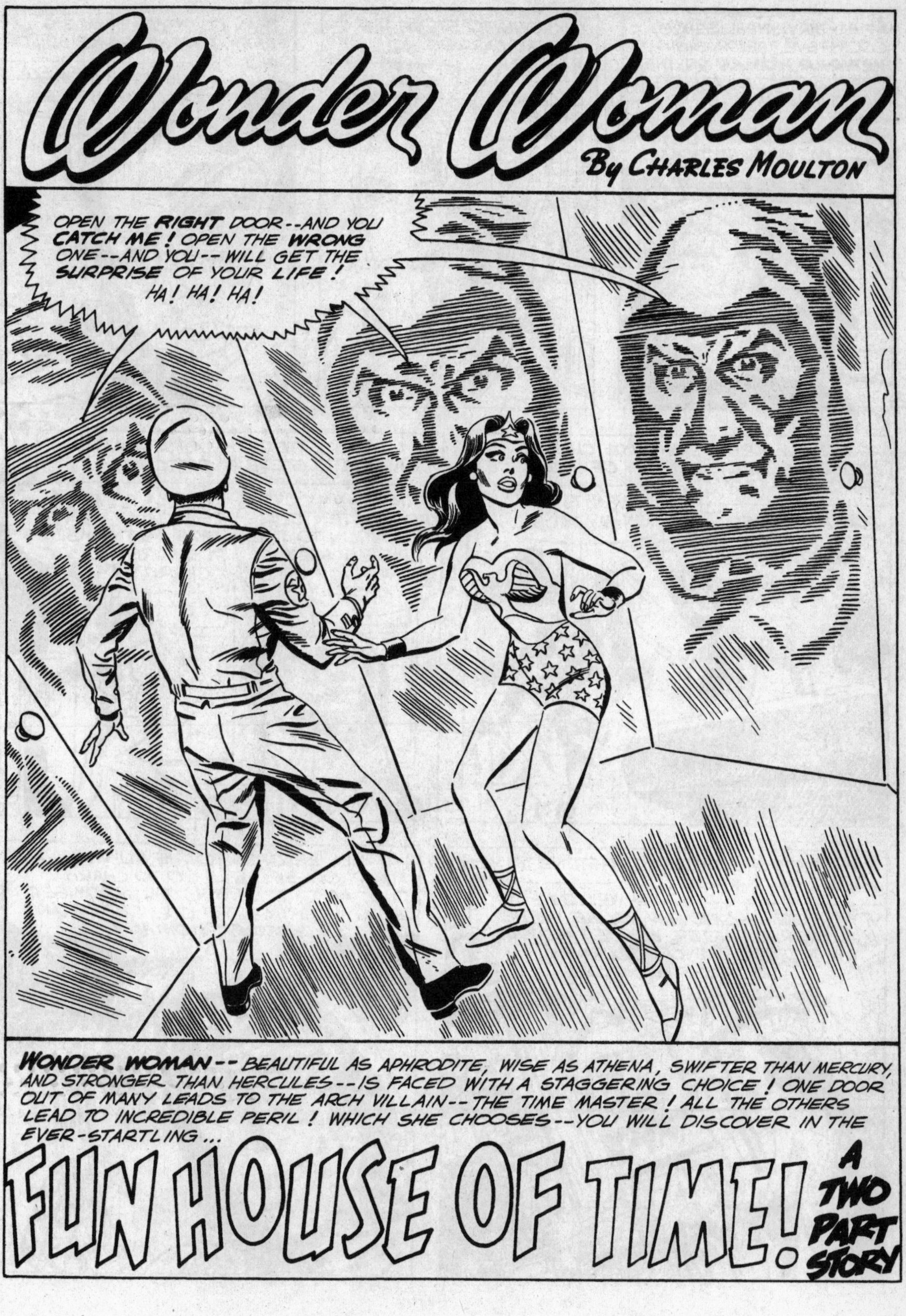
Wonder Woman
By CHARLES MOULTON
OPEN THE RIGHT DOOR--AND YOU CATCH ME! OPEN THE WRONG ONE--AND YOU--WILL GET THE SURPRISE OF YOUR LIFE! HA! HA! HA!
WONDER WOMAN--BEAUTIFUL AS APHRODITE, WISE AS ATHENA, SWIFTER THAN MERCURY, AND STRONGER THAN HERCULES--IS FACED WITH A STAGGERING CHOICE! ONE DOOR OUT OF MANY LEADS TO THE ARCH VILLAIN--THE TIME MASTER! ALL THE OTHERS LEAD TO INCREDIBLE PERIL! WHICH SHE CHOOSES--YOU WILL DISCOVER IN THE EVER-STARTLING...
FUN HOUSE OF TIME!
A TWO PART STORY

AT MILITARY INTELLIGENCE, COL. STEVE TREVOR SIGNALS *WONDER WOMAN* ON THE SPECIAL AMAZON RADIO SHE HAS GIVEN HIM...

CALLING WONDER WOMAN... CALLING WONDER WOMAN...

UNKNOWN TO STEVE, HIS SIGNAL CARRIES NO FURTHER...

CALLING WONDER WOMAN...

CALLING WONDER WOMAN...

THAN LT. DIANA PRINCE'S OFFICE IN THE *SAME* BUILD-ING...

WONDER WOMAN CALLING STEVE...

AS DIANA MAKES A LIGHTNING CHANGE INTO HER SECRET IDENTITY OF THE CELE-BRATED AMAZON...

DON'T FORGET OUR DATE, ANGEL...

I HAVEN'T... I'M ON MY WAY...

A MOMENT LATER, THE AGILE AMAZON LEAPS INTO STEVE'S OFFICE...

I THOUGHT YOU'D FORGOTTEN OUR INVITATION TO THE NEW FUN HOUSE IN FROLIC PARK, ANGEL!

OF COURSE NOT! ESPECIALLY--SINCE THIS VISIT COMBINES PLEASURE AND CHARITY!

THE CELEBRATED COUPLE HASTENS TO FROLIC PARK WHERE...

WELCOME TO THE MOST UNIQUE *FUN HOUSE* IN THE WORLD! AFTER *WONDER WOMAN* AND COL. TREVOR JOURNEY THROUGH THE HOUSE...

FUN H

--IT WILL BE OPEN TO THE PUBLIC--AND ALL PROCEEDS WILL GO TO CHARITY JUST AS I, *TY. M. MASTER*, PROMISED IN MY INVITATION TO COL. TREVOR AND *WONDER WOMAN!*

INSIDE THE **FUN HOUSE**, THE AMAZON AND THE COLONEL FIND...

WE'RE SURROUNDED BY DOORS! THIS IS EXCITING! WHICH ONE SHALL WE OPEN?

YOU CHOOSE, STEVE!

LET'S TRY THIS ONE!

I WONDER WHAT'S ON THE OTHER SIDE?

MERCIFUL MINERVA-- WE--WE'RE IN THE TIME OF THE DINOSAURS!-- AND THAT--THAT'S A GIANT PTERODACTYL SWOOPING DOWN AT US!

IMPOSSIBLE! THEY LIVED MILLIONS OF YEARS AGO! THIS IS AN ILLUSION! A TRICK OF THE **FUN HOUSE**! A DECEPTION MR. TY M. MASTER, THE PRO- PRIETOR, IS PLAYING ON US!

EVEN AS STEVE REFUSES TO BELIEVE WHAT HE SEES, A HUGE CLAW DARTS OUT AND...

NOW-- DO YOU BELIEVE WHAT YOU SEE?

NO--NO! IT'S A TRICK! WE'RE JUST IMAGINING THIS!

BUT AS THE GIGANTIC BIRD WINGS OVER THE PREHISTORIC JUNGLE...

WHEN WILL YOU BELIEVE THAT SOMEHOW-- WE HAVE BEEN TRICKED--TRANS-PORTED INTO ANOTHER TIME-- BY ENTERING THAT DOOR?

I--I'M CONVINCED, ANGEL! I-I'LL SLOW UP THIS BEAST WITH A BULLET!

BUT, AS THE COLONEL SQUEEZES THE TRIGGER...

IT--IT WON'T FIRE--! IT'S FULLY LOADED-- IT'S NOT JAMMED-- WHY DOESN'T IT FIRE?

BECAUSE THE PISTOL HASN'T BEEN INVENTED YET, STEVE!

VROOSH!

AS IF WE'RE NOT IN ENOUGH TROUBLE--A FLAMING METEOR'S FALLING THIS WAY!

HMM--THAT GIVES ME AN IDEA!

WITH HER AMAZON LASSO, THE INDOMITABLE *WONDER WOMAN* ENCIRCLES THE FLAMING METEORITE...

VROOOSH!

ZZZZING!

HERA HELP MY PLAN TO SUCCEED...

THE MIGHTY AMAZON WHIRLS THE FLAMING METEORITE AROUND THE GREAT PTERODACTYL UNTIL...

YOU'VE DONE IT, ANGEL -- COUGH-COUGH THE SMOKE IS MAKING -- THE BIG BUZZARD LOOSEN HIS GRIP ON US!

WHOOOSH!

THE NEXT MOMENT...

WE'RE FREE--! BUT THE WEIGHT OF THE METEORITE --IS PULLING US DOWN!

BUT WITH A DEXTROUS FLIP OF HER LASSO, *WONDER WOMAN* RELEASES THE HURTLING METEORITE AND...

YOU SAVED US, ANGEL--BUT WHAT HAPPENS NEXT?

TO THE FAMOUS COUPLE'S AMAZEMENT, THEY FIND THEM— SELVES...

WE--WE'RE BACK IN THE *FUN HOUSE* -- IN THE ROOM WITH DOORS!

BUT--HOW DID WE GET HERE?

BY DEFEATING WHATEVER IMPERILS YOU IN ANOTHER TIME!

TY. M. MASTER-- THE OWNER OF THIS PLACE!

TY. M. MASTER IS MY LITTLE JOKE! REPEAT MY NAME ALOUD AND YOU WILL REALIZE I AM THE *TIME MASTER*! FROM THE TIME DIMENSION I LIVE IN-- I HAVE SEEN YOU DEFEAT EVERY THREAT TO THE EARTH! HENCE I HAVE DEVISED THIS TIME-TRAP HOUSE TO DESTROY YOU!

WITH FLASHING SPEED, *WONDER WOMAN* LUNGES FOR THE UNIQUE VILLAIN – BUT...

SHADES OF PLUTO-- I--I CAN'T REACH YOU!

NATURALLY--SINCE I APPEAR TO YOU AS I *WAS*--A SECOND AGO! SINCE TIME NEVER STANDS STILL--THAT SECOND MIGHT AS WELL BE AN HOUR TO YOU!

SUDDENLY, THE *TIME MASTER* VANISHES...

TO MAKE THIS GAME INTEREST- ING--

--I'VE GIVEN YOU A CHANCE TO CATCH ME!

I AM BE- HIND ONE OF THESE DOORS!

BUT WHICH ONE?

OPEN AND SEE!

WE MUST FIND THE *TIME MASTER* BEFORE HE MENACES EARTH ITSELF!

YES--BUT WHICH DOOR DO WE HAVE TO OPEN TO FIND HIM? WHICH ONE?

*T*ENSE MOMENTS TICK BY WHILE THE TRAPPED PAIR STARE AT EACH DOOR...

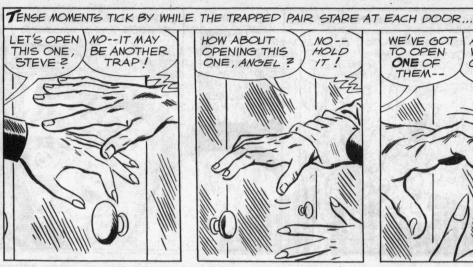

LET'S OPEN THIS ONE, STEVE?

NO--IT MAY BE ANOTHER TRAP!

HOW ABOUT OPENING THIS ONE, ANGEL?

NO-- HOLD IT!

WE'VE GOT TO OPEN **ONE** OF THEM--

OKAY, ANGEL! WE'LL BOTH OPEN THIS ONE!

*O*N THE OTHER SIDE OF THE OPENED DOOR, *WONDER WOMAN* AND STEVE FIND THEMSELVES WHIRLING IN A FROTHING SEA...

WE'RE ON THE EDGE OF A GIGANTIC WHIRLPOOL--!

BUT AT LEAST-- THAT DOOR OPENED ON THE PRESENT!

*A*T THAT VERY MOMENT, A FAMILIAR SHIP APPEARS...

SHADES OF PLUTO, STEVE! DID YOU SAY WE'RE IN THE PRESENT?--LOOK AT THAT SHIP!

IT'S THE SANTA MARIA OF COLUMBUS AND IT'S BEING DRAWN INTO THE WHIRLPOOL!

WITH A SWEEP OF HER POWERFUL ARM, *WONDER WOMAN* HURLS STEVE TO SAFETY OUT OF THE PULL OF THE WHIRLPOOL...

SAVE THAT SHIP--!

SPLASH!

A LIGHTNING CAST OF HER LASSO, AND THE MIGHTY AMAZON LASSOES THE DOOMED SHIP..

COLUMBUS' SHIP MUST HAVE BECOME SEPARATED FROM THE *NINA* AND THE *PINTO*! IF IT SINKS-- HE WILL NOT DIS- COVER AMERICA!

DESPERATELY, *WONDER WOMAN* STRAINS AGAINST THE IRRESISTIBLE PULL OF THE WHIRLPOOL -- BUT...

THE SHIP'S --DRIFTING --INTO THE WHIRLPOOL -- DESPITE --ALL MY EFFORTS --!

MERCIFUL MINERVA--

PART TWO OF WONDER WOMAN'S ASTONISHING ADVENTURES IN THE FUN HOUSE OF TIME CONTINUES...

Wonder Woman

By Charles Moulton

in THE FUN HOUSE OF TIME! PART TWO

OPENING ANOTHER DOOR IN THE FUN HOUSE OF TIME TRANSPORTS WONDER WOMAN TO THE EDGE OF A GIGANTIC WHIRLPOOL IN THE SEA -- WHERE SHE GRIMLY STRUGGLES TO SAVE NONE OTHER THAN COLUMBUS' OWN FLAGSHIP FROM FOUNDERING !

CAN'T--TOW--THE--SHIP--TO--SAFETY--HAVE--TO--FIND--ANOTHER--WAY--!

SUMMONING THE LAST IOTA OF HER AMAZON POWER, WONDER WOMAN SNAPS THE FAMOUS SHIP THROUGH THE AIR ...

THANK HERA! COLUMBUS' SHIP IS FREE OF THE WHIRLPOOL!

THE TIRELESS AMAZON SWIMS TOWARD STEVE AND TOGETHER...

THERE -- COLUMBUS' SHIP IS CATCHING UP TO THE REST OF HIS FLEET!

THANKS TO YOU-- HE CAN GO ON TO DISCOVER AMERICA! BUT-- WHAT WILL HAPPEN TO US?

AND IT SEEMS IN THE SAME INSTANT...

WE'RE BACK IN THE FUN HOUSE OF TIME!

HOUSE OF TRAPS--IS MORE LIKE IT! WONDER WHERE THE TIME MASTER IS?

AGAIN THE TAUNTING FACE OF THE TIME MASTER APPEARS...

OPEN ANOTHER DOOR! EITHER YOU'LL CATCH ME BEHIND ONE--IF YOU OPEN THE RIGHT DOOR ...

...OR YOU'LL MEET YOUR DOOM SOONER OR LATER-- BY CONTINUING TO OPEN THE WRONG DOOR!

HE'S GONE AGAIN-- WHICH DOOR DO WE HAVE TO OPEN TO FIND HIM?

HE DIDN'T KNOW IT, ANGEL--BUT HE GAVE US A CLUE! HE SAID WE HAVE TO OPEN THE RIGHT DOOR TO FIND HIM! THIS IS THE FIRST DOOR ON OUR RIGHT!

THE TIME MASTER TRAPPED HIMSELF! HE MUST BE BEHIND THIS DOOR!

BUT--JUST AS STEVE IS ABOUT TO STEP THROUGH THE OPEN DOOR...

ANGEL--WH-WHAT ARE YOU DOING?

FORGIVE ME, STEVE--BUT I'LL FEEL BETTER IF I KNOW YOU'RE BACK HERE--OUT OF HARM'S WAY!

SHUTTING THE DOOR BEHIND HER...

THANK HERA-- STEVE'S NOT WITH ME!

THIS TIME, BY OPENING THE DOOR, **WONDER WOMAN** NOT ONLY HAS NOT FOUND THE **TIME MASTER**--BUT DISCOVERS HERSELF IN A MIND-STAGGERING PREDICAMENT...

THUNDERBOLTS OF JOVE! THIS TIME I HAVE BEEN TRANSPORTED TO SOME TIME IN THE FUTURE--WHEN EARTH IS UNDER INTERPLANETARY ATTACK! AND I'M RIDING ON THE VERY WEAPON OF DESTRUCTION!

THE GRIM AMAZON'S EFFORTS TO FIND AN OPENING INTO THE INVADING CRAFT MEET WITH FAILURE...

I CAN'T MAKE A DENT IN IT-- IT'S MADE OF SOME UNKNOWN SUBSTANCE THAT DEFIES MY EVERY EFFORT! IF I CAN'T HALT IT--EARTH IS DOOMED!

SUDDENLY...

BUT--THERE MUST BE A WAY--THERE MUST BE-- HMMM--LIGHTNING STRIKING THAT SKYSCRAPER--GIVES ME AN IDEA!

CRACK!

LOOPING THE ATTACKING SHIP AROUND, *WONDER WOMAN* HURLS THE OTHER END TOWARDS THE LOFTY SKYSCRAPER...

THAT BUILDING HAS ALWAYS ATTRACTED LIGHTNING!

HURRIEDLY, THE AGILE AMAZON SLIDES DOWN THE LASSO CONNECTING THE TWO OBJECTS...

PERHAPS--

--I CAN USE LIGHTNING..

--TO SAVE THE EARTH!

SUDDENLY, LIGHTNING STRIKES THE HUGE SKYSCRAPER AGAIN...

THE DANGLING AMAZON IS SHAKEN TO HER INNERMOST BEING AS THE MASSIVE ELECTRICAL CHARGE RACES ALONG THE LASSO PAST HER...

THE DARING **WONDER WOMAN'S** PLAN SUCCEEDS AS THE LIGHTNING BOOMERANGS INTO THE SPACE INVADER AND...

IN AN INSTANT SHE IS BACK IN THE SINISTER *FUN HOUSE*...

I CAN SEE BY YOUR FACE, DARLING -- WE OPENED THE **WRONG** DOOR!

WE CERTAINLY DID OPEN THE WRONG DOOR! IT SEEMS AS IF EVERY ONE WE **OPEN** --

STEVE! *THAT* MIGHT BE THE ANSWER! OUR MISTAKE MIGHT BE IN *OPENING* THE DOORS!

ANGEL-- I DON'T KNOW WHAT YOU MEAN!

WITHOUT EXPLAINING, *WONDER WOMAN* WHIRLS AT SUCH FLASHING SPEED THAT...

SHE'S VIBRATING IN AND OUT OF EVERY DOOR...

--WITHOUT...

--OPENING ANY!

AND THEN...THE INGENIOUS AMAZON RE-APPEARS WITH THE VILLAIN...

HIS PLAN WAS DIABOLICAL! EVERY TIME I *OPENED* A DOOR-- I FELL INTO A TRAP!

I THOUGHT I COULD OUTWIT YOU BY HIDING BE-HIND A DOOR **HERE** ALL THE TIME--!

--GAMBLING YOU WOULDN'T GUESS YOU HAD TO PASS THROUGH **WITHOUT** **OPENING** THE DOOR TO FIND ME! YOU SUCCEEDED -- I FAILED!

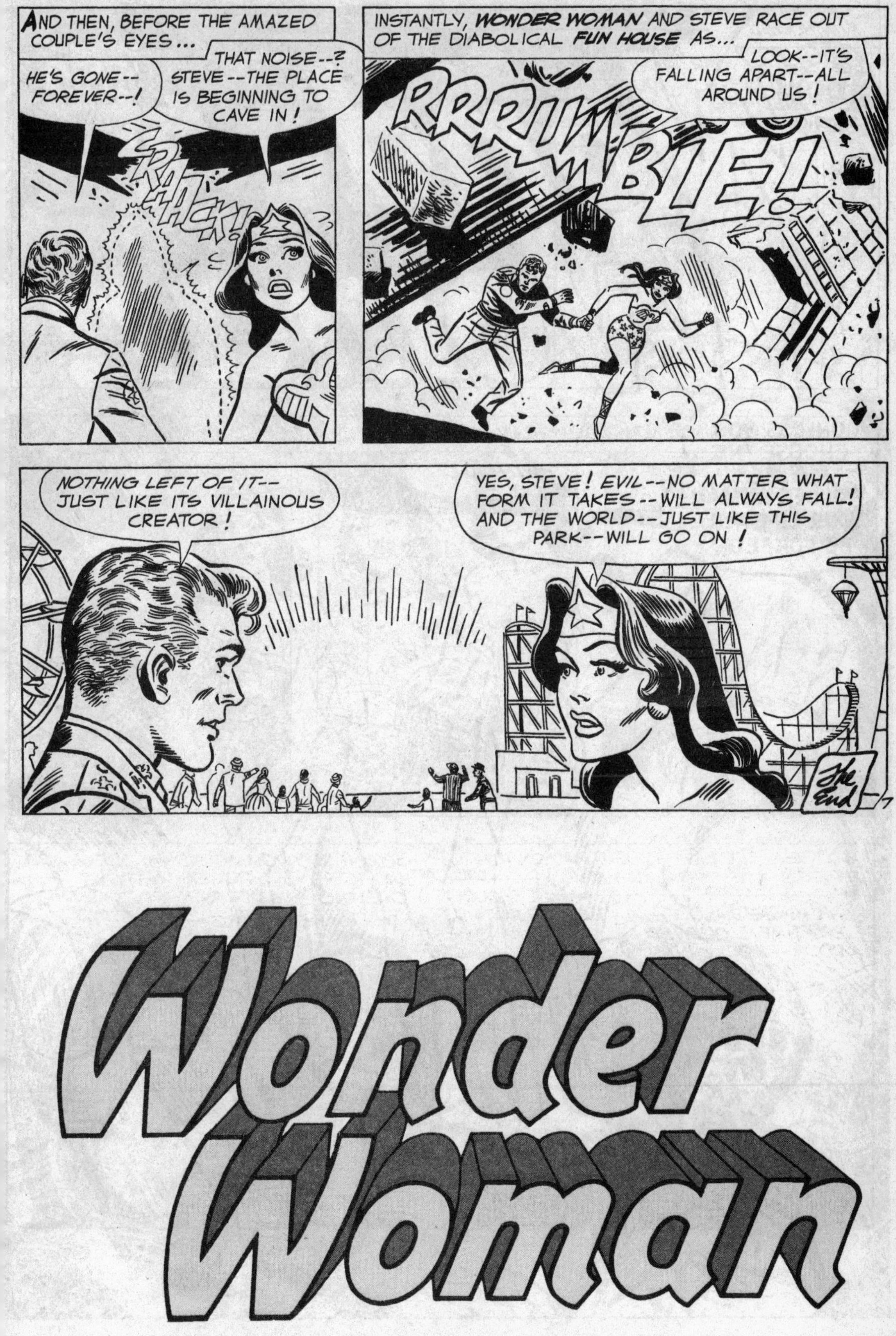
AND THEN, BEFORE THE AMAZED COUPLE'S EYES ...
HE'S GONE -- FOREVER--!
THAT NOISE--? STEVE--THE PLACE IS BEGINNING TO CAVE IN!
SRAACK!
INSTANTLY, WONDER WOMAN AND STEVE RACE OUT OF THE DIABOLICAL FUN HOUSE AS...
LOOK--IT'S FALLING APART--ALL AROUND US!
RRRUMBLE!
NOTHING LEFT OF IT-- JUST LIKE ITS VILLAINOUS CREATOR!
YES, STEVE! EVIL--NO MATTER WHAT FORM IT TAKES--WILL ALWAYS FALL! AND THE WORLD--JUST LIKE THIS PARK--WILL GO ON!
The End
7

Wonder Woman

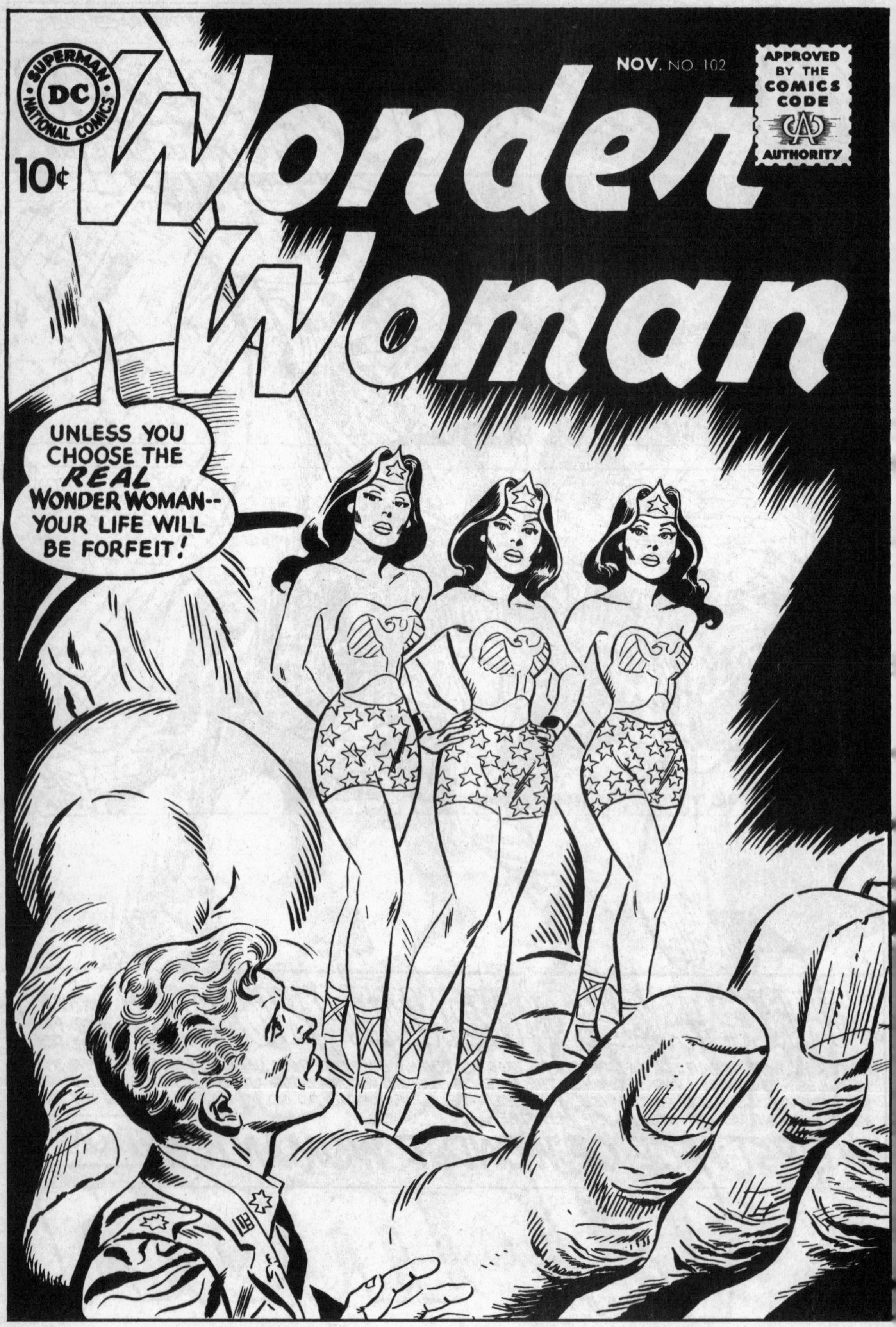

SUPERMAN DC NATIONAL COMICS
10¢
Wonder Woman
NOV. NO. 102
APPROVED BY THE COMICS CODE AUTHORITY
UNLESS YOU CHOOSE THE *REAL* WONDER WOMAN-- YOUR LIFE WILL BE FORFEIT!

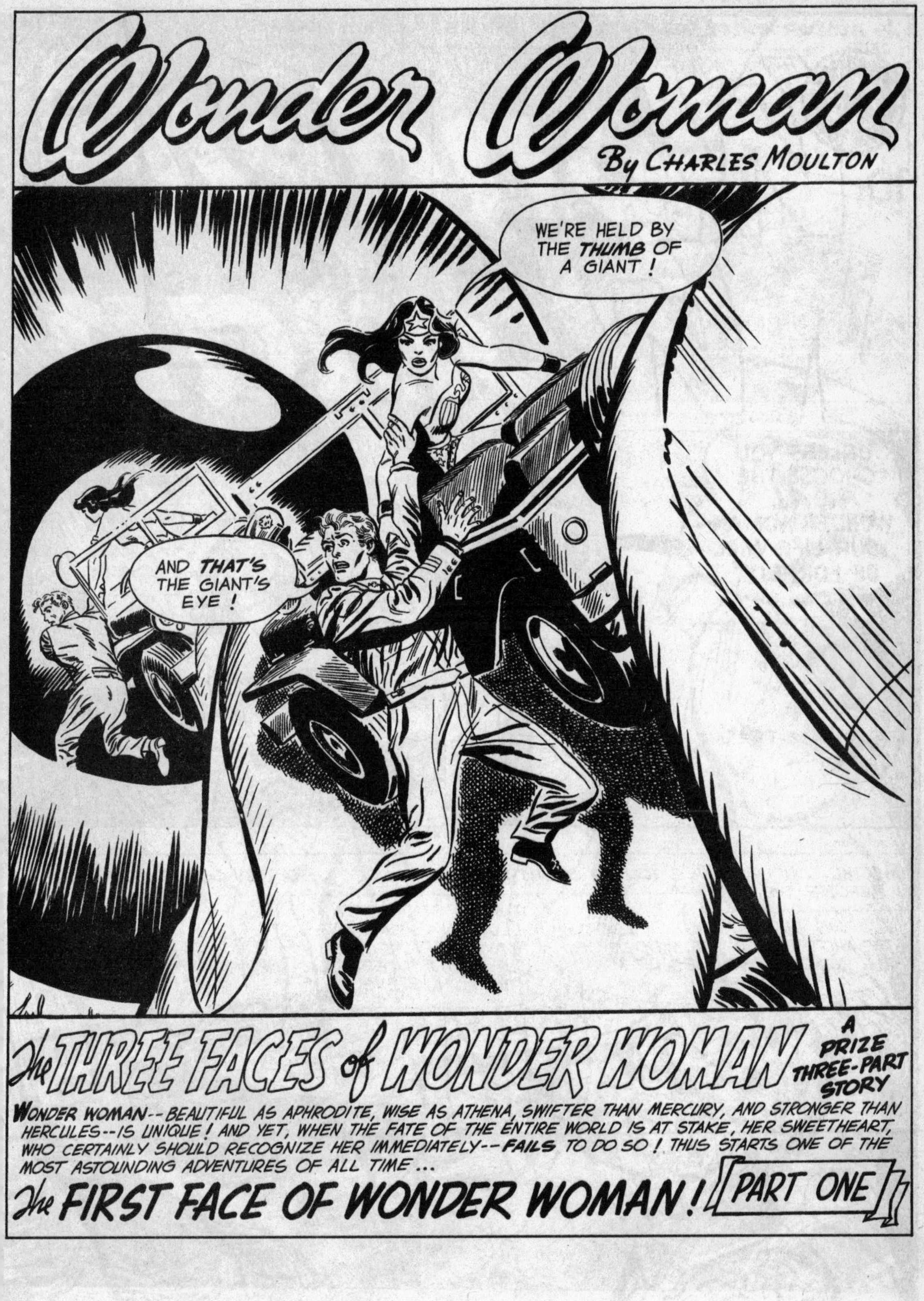
Wonder Woman
By Charles Moulton
WE'RE HELD BY THE THUMB OF A GIANT!
AND THAT'S THE GIANT'S EYE!
The THREE FACES of WONDER WOMAN
A PRIZE THREE-PART STORY
WONDER WOMAN--BEAUTIFUL AS APHRODITE, WISE AS ATHENA, SWIFTER THAN MERCURY, AND STRONGER THAN HERCULES--IS UNIQUE! AND YET, WHEN THE FATE OF THE ENTIRE WORLD IS AT STAKE, HER SWEETHEART, WHO CERTAINLY SHOULD RECOGNIZE HER IMMEDIATELY--FAILS TO DO SO! THUS STARTS ONE OF THE MOST ASTOUNDING ADVENTURES OF ALL TIME...
The FIRST FACE OF WONDER WOMAN!
PART ONE

As *WONDER WOMAN* STEPS INTO STEVE TREVOR'S JEEP...

HAPPY BIRTHDAY, ANGEL!

PERFUME!

YOU DARLING-- HOW SWEET!

NOT AS SWEET AND WARM AS YOUR LIPS, ANGEL--I'D KNOW THEM IN A MILLION!

SO YOU'D KNOW MY KISS IF IT WAS ONE IN A MILLION, STEVE? I HOPE YOU WON'T BE PUT TO THE TEST! YOU'D LOSE, YOU KNOW!

THERE ISN'T A CHANCE IN THE WORLD OF ME MISTAKING ANY- ONE ELSE'S FOR YOURS ANGEL! NOT A CHANCE IN THE WORLD!

As THE COUPLE DRIVES TO THE COUNTRY FOR A PICNIC, A STARTLING SCENE UNFOLDS BEFORE THEM...

JUMPING JUPITER, ANGEL! LOOK--! THE WHITE LINE IN THE MIDDLE OF THE ROAD--**CONTINUES UP TO THE SKY!**

IT MUST BE AN OPTICAL ILLUSION--HEAT WAVES PLAYING TRICKS WITH OUR SIGHT! KEEP RIGHT ON, STEVE!

2

ON RIDES THE COUPLE TO WHERE THE ROAD MARKER BENDS INTO THE SKY...

WONDER WHEN THIS OPTICAL ILLUSION WILL END?

AS SOON AS WE'VE PASSED THIS SECTION OF THE ROAD, PROBABLY!

HOW MANY TIMES HAVE YOU SEEN A ROAD SHIMMY IN THE S--???

WH-WHAT DID YOU SAY?

WITH BREATHTAKING SUDDENNESS...

ANGEL--WE'RE SPEEDING UP INTO THE AIR LIKE A--LIKE A--FLY GOING UP A WALL!

FROM GIDDY HEIGHTS, THE TWO STARE DOWN...

LOOK--OTHER CARS ARE STAYING RIGHT ON THE GROUND!

GREAT HERA--WE'VE RIDDEN INTO A TRAP! BUT WHO IS RESPONSIBLE FOR THIS-- AND WHY--AND WHERE WILL IT LEAD TO?

SUDDENLY, THE AMAZING MARKER IN THE SKY LIES FLAT AGAIN ...

THOSE MILITARY AIRCRAFT--THEY DON'T SEE US! AND WHY DON'T WE NEED OXYGEN? WE'RE HIGH ENOUGH!

THIS COULD ONLY MEAN THAT WE'RE IN A PARALLEL DIMENSION TO THE EARTH'S--WHERE *WE* CAN SEE ANYTHING HAPPENING ON IT--BUT EARTH *CANNOT* SEE THIS DIMENSION!

THIS ROAD LEADS RIGHT THROUGH THAT CLOUD--I'D BETTER TURN--I WOULDN'T BE ABLE TO SEE A THING ONCE WE'RE IN IT!

ANGEL--I CAN'T TURN THIS WHEEL--IT'S AS IF THE CAR'S ON AUTOMATIC PILOT!

WHOEVER PLANNED THIS, STEVE--DIDN'T INTEND US TO ESCAPE!

THROUGH THE BLANKET OF CLOUD THE TWO HURTLE LIKE A METEOR ... AND THEN ...

SPINNING SATURN! WE'VE FINALLY ARRIVED IN THIS PARALLEL DIMENSION! BUT--THERE DOESN'T SEEM TO BE ANYONE AROUND! WHAT'S THAT AHEAD--LOOKS LIKE SHIPS IN A STREET--OR SOMETHING!

LET'S GO CLOSER... AND FIND OUT!

WONDER WOMAN AND STEVE RIDE UP TO ONE OF THE STRANGE OBJECTS--TO RECEIVE THE GREATEST SHOCK OF THEIR LIVES...

I SEE IT--*I SEE IT*--BUT I CAN'T BELIEVE IT! ANGEL--I SIMPLY CAN'T BELIEVE WHAT I SEE!

SHADES OF PLUTO--WE *BOTH* CAN'T BE HAVING THE SAME HALLUCINATION, STEVE--IT IS TRUE!

THIS IS--A DIMENSION OF GIANTS--GIANTS SO BIG--THEIR FACES ARE OUT OF SIGHT! LOOK! THERE'S ONE OF THEIR BOOTS!

SUDDENLY...

WHAT'S THAT PICKING US UP? LOOKS LIKE THE CLAW OF A STEAM SHOVEL!

MERCIFUL MINERVA-- IT'S ONE OF THE GIANT'S FINGERS!

THE GIANT'S LIFTING US UP TOWARDS HIM!

LIKE A ROCKET SENT INTO SPACE -- *WONDER WOMAN* AND STEVE ARE LIFTED TOWARD THE GIANT'S EYE ... WHERE THE AMAZON BOLDLY CHALLENGES THEIR CAPTOR...

WHAT DO YOU WANT WITH US?

WE HEARD YOU SAY YOU'D RECOGNIZE YOUR SWEETHEART IF SHE WERE ONE IN A MILLION! IF YOU REALLY ARE CLEVER ENOUGH TO DO SO -- THEN WE'LL HALT OUR PLANS OF INVADING EARTH!

WITH PARALYZING SWIFTNESS STEVE FINDS HIMSELF BEING LOWERED TO THE GROUND ALONE AS...

WONDER WOMAN--! HE'S KEPT HER!

LIKE A TOY, THE JEEP IS OVERTURNED...TOSSING STEVE OUT AS IF HE WERE A LITTLE RUBBER BALL...

WHAT DOES HE INTEND DOING WITH HER?

6

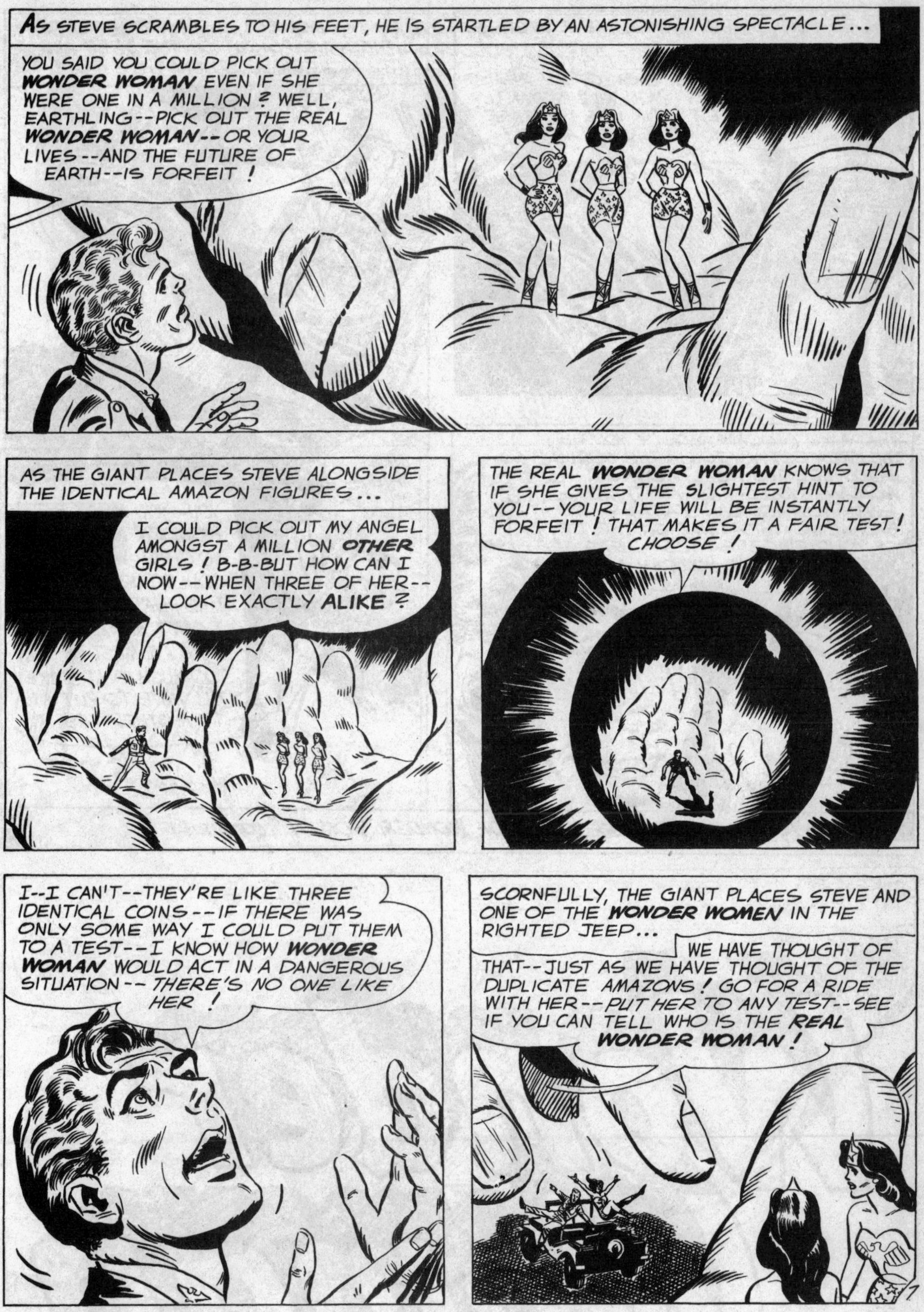
AS STEVE SCRAMBLES TO HIS FEET, HE IS STARTLED BY AN ASTONISHING SPECTACLE...
YOU SAID YOU COULD PICK OUT WONDER WOMAN EVEN IF SHE WERE ONE IN A MILLION? WELL, EARTHLING--PICK OUT THE REAL WONDER WOMAN--OR YOUR LIVES--AND THE FUTURE OF EARTH--IS FORFEIT!
AS THE GIANT PLACES STEVE ALONGSIDE THE IDENTICAL AMAZON FIGURES...
I COULD PICK OUT MY ANGEL AMONGST A MILLION OTHER GIRLS! B-B-BUT HOW CAN I NOW--WHEN THREE OF HER--LOOK EXACTLY ALIKE?
THE REAL WONDER WOMAN KNOWS THAT IF SHE GIVES THE SLIGHTEST HINT TO YOU--YOUR LIFE WILL BE INSTANTLY FORFEIT! THAT MAKES IT A FAIR TEST! CHOOSE!
I--I CAN'T--THEY'RE LIKE THREE IDENTICAL COINS--IF THERE WAS ONLY SOME WAY I COULD PUT THEM TO A TEST--I KNOW HOW WONDER WOMAN WOULD ACT IN A DANGEROUS SITUATION--THERE'S NO ONE LIKE HER!
SCORNFULLY, THE GIANT PLACES STEVE AND ONE OF THE WONDER WOMEN IN THE RIGHTED JEEP...
WE HAVE THOUGHT OF THAT--JUST AS WE HAVE THOUGHT OF THE DUPLICATE AMAZONS! GO FOR A RIDE WITH HER--PUT HER TO ANY TEST--SEE IF YOU CAN TELL WHO IS THE REAL WONDER WOMAN!
7

PAST THE FEET OF THE GIANTS, STEVE STEERS..

ARE YOU MY ANGEL?

YOU HEARD! IF I GIVE YOU THE SLIGHTEST SIGN OF MY REAL IDENTITY--YOU WILL INSTANTLY FORFEIT YOUR LIFE! PLEASE DON'T ASK ME AGAIN!

THE NEXT MOMENT, THE AMAZON FIGURE LITHELY LEAPS OUT OF THE JEEP AND WITH INCREDIBLE STRENGTH...

LIKE-- THIS?

YOU--YOU MUST BE **WONDER WOMAN!** NO OTHER WOMAN COULD DUPLICATE THIS FEAT! BUT--WAIT--! I CAN'T MAKE A MIS-TAKE! I MUST BE SURE, TOO MUCH IS AT STAKE! I'LL HAVE TO PUT YOU TO ANOTHER TEST!

WHAT AM I GLOOMY ABOUT? YOU'RE THE GREATEST AMAZON IN THE WORLD! IF YOU ARE THE **REAL WONDER WOMAN**-- YOU CAN DO ANYTHING-- ANYTHING! YOU CAN START BY--BY-- BALANCING THIS JEEP ON THE TIP OF YOUR FINGERS! YES--LET'S SEE YOU DO THAT--**IF** YOU CAN!

The second part of "THE THREE FACES OF WONDER WOMAN" continues...

/8

Wonder Woman

By Charles Moulton

PART TWO
The SECOND FACE of Wonder Woman

FACED WITH A CHOICE ON WHICH THE FATE OF THE EARTH, AND HIS OWN LIFE DEPENDS, STEVE TREVOR MUST PICK THE REAL WONDER WOMAN, OUT OF THREE IDENTICAL AMAZONS! CAN HE SUCCEED?

I'VE GOT TO PUT THIS WONDER WOMAN TO AN IMPOSSIBLE TASK--ONE WHICH ONLY THE REAL WONDER WOMAN COULD ACCOMPLISH!

∘∘ IF YOU REALLY ARE WONDER WOMAN-- THROW ME OVER THAT MOUNTAINTOP--AND TUNNEL A WAY THROUGH-- BEFORE I LAND ON THE OTHER SIDE!

INSTANTLY, THE AMAZON FIGURE CATAPULTS THE JEEP AND ITS OCCUPANT TOWARDS THE DISTANT MOUNTAINTOP...

VROOOSH!

CLINGING TO HIS HURTLING JEEP, STEVE STARES DOWN THROUGH THE GIDDY HEIGHTS ...

THERE SHE GOES--HITTING THE MOUNTAINSIDE LIKE A HUMAN DRILL!

WHRRRR!

WHIRLING OVER THE MOUNTAINTOP...

NO SIGN OF HER YET!

IT LOOKS AS IF SHE ISN'T THE REAL WONDER WOMAN--EVEN IF SHE LOOKS EXACTLY LIKE HER!

BUT, AT THE VERY LAST MOMENT, THE AMAZON FIGURE TUNNELS THROUGH THE MOUNTAIN, AND CATCHES THE FALLING VEHICLE ...

YOU MUST BE WONDER WOMAN! NO ONE ELSE IN THE WORLD COULD HAVE DONE THIS, ANGEL!

CRRRACK!

ON THE WAY BACK TO THE WAITING GIANTS OF THE PARALLEL DIMENSION ...

I KNOW MY ANGEL WHEN I SEE HER! YOU'RE *WONDER WOMAN*-- YOU--AND NO ONE ELSE!

IF YOU SAY SO!

WHAT DO YOU MEAN IF "*I*" SAY SO? YOU ARE *WONDER WOMAN*, AREN'T YOU?

YOU WERE ALREADY WARNED THAT THE SLIGHTEST HINT FROM ME WOULD PLACE YOUR LIFE IN JEOPARDY!

THUS, BY THE TIME STEVE RETURNS, DOUBT ASSAILS HIM AS HE STARES AT THE THREE IDENTICAL FIGURES ...

WELL, EARTHLING! WHICH ONE IS THE *REAL* WONDER WOMAN?

I--I'M NOT SURE ... NOW-- PERHAPS I'D BETTER TEST THE NEXT ONE--JUST TO MAKE *TRIPLY* CERTAIN!

IF YOU'RE AN EXAMPLE OF THE INGENUITY OF EARTHLINGS, THEN IT WON'T BE DIFFICULT TO INVADE YOUR PLANET! ALL RIGHT--PROCEED!

AND SO, STEVE SETS OUT AGAIN WITH THE SECOND "*WONDER WOMAN*" ...

I'VE GOT TO MAKE SURE! AND THE ONLY WAY I CAN--IS TO THINK UP SOMETHING SO IMPOSSIBLE--THAT ONLY THE *REAL* WONDER WOMAN COULD POSSIBLY ACCOMPLISH IT!

THROUGH A GIGANTIC FOREST STEVE WALKS WITH THE AMAZON FIGURE...

LOOK AT THOSE REDWOODS!

THEY'RE NOT REDWOODS--THEY'RE JUST BUSHES! REMEMBER, IN THIS PARALLEL DIMENSION--EVERYTHING IS INFINITELY HUGER THAN IT IS ON EARTH!

HOW WOULD SHE KNOW THIS--IF SHE WERE WONDER WOMAN?

THAT BOULDER IS BIGGER THAN A BUILDING!

THAT'S NOT A BOULDER-- IT'S JUST A PEBBLE! YOU FORGET EVERYTHING GROWS ON A TREMENDOUS SCALE IN THIS DIMENSION!

THIS PROVES IT! HOW CAN SHE POSSIBLY KNOW ALL THESE THINGS ABOUT THIS DIMENSION UNLESS SHE WERE PART OF IT! SHE CAN'T BE WONDER WOMAN! I'LL TURN BACK!

AT THAT MOMENT, THE LIGHT IS BLOTTED OUT OF THE SKY AS...

NO--NO! I'M SEEING THINGS!

IT IS TRUE-- YOU'RE SEEING EXACTLY WHAT I AM!

AN AWESOME SPECTACLE HURTLES TOWARD THE TWO FIGURES...

IT'S A TREMENDOUS METEOR--MILES IN CIRCUMFERENCE! NO ONE IN THE WORLD BUT WONDER WOMAN COULD EVER POSSIBLY SAVE US FROM DESTRUCTION!

IF YOU'RE WONDER WOMAN--NOW IS YOUR CHANCE TO PROVE IT!

INSTANTLY, THE AMAZON FIGURE LEAPS BACK TOWARDS THE FOREST AND...

SHE'S UPROOTED ONE OF THE GIANT RED-WOODS--AS IF IT WERE JUST A MERE TOOTHPICK!

SKKRRUNCH!

THE NEXT MOMENT, BEFORE THE WATCHER'S INCREDULOUS GAZE...

THUD!

NOW--SHE'S DRIVEN THE TREE RIGHT THROUGH THAT SOLID ROCK! BUT-- WHAT DOES SHE HOPE TO ACCOMPLISH?

5

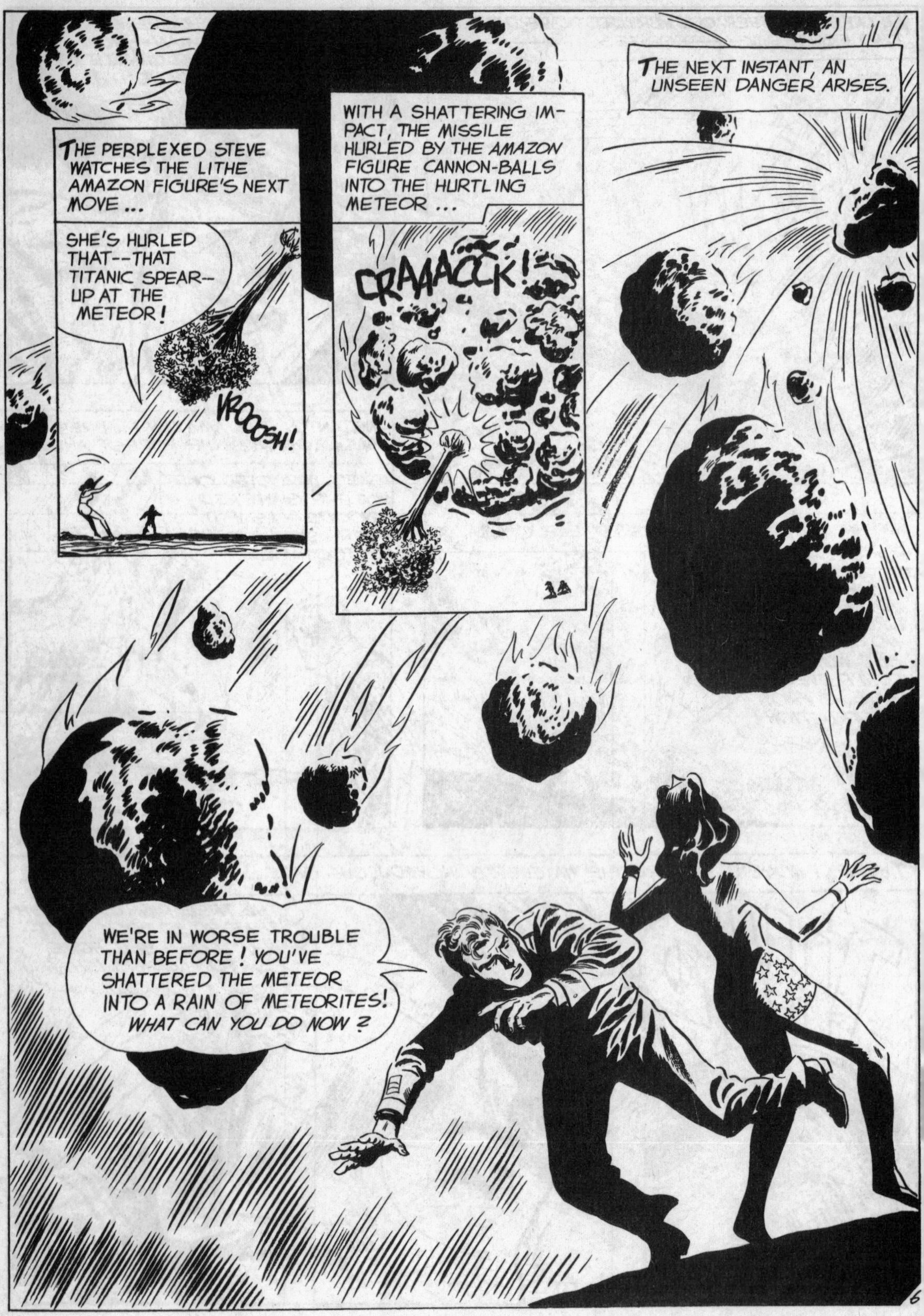
THE PERPLEXED STEVE WATCHES THE LITHE AMAZON FIGURE'S NEXT MOVE ...
SHE'S HURLED THAT--THAT TITANIC SPEAR--UP AT THE METEOR!
VROOOSH!
WITH A SHATTERING IMPACT, THE MISSILE HURLED BY THE AMAZON FIGURE CANNON-BALLS INTO THE HURTLING METEOR ...
CRAAACCK!
THE NEXT INSTANT, AN UNSEEN DANGER ARISES.
WE'RE IN WORSE TROUBLE THAN BEFORE! YOU'VE SHATTERED THE METEOR INTO A RAIN OF METEORITES! WHAT CAN YOU DO NOW?
6

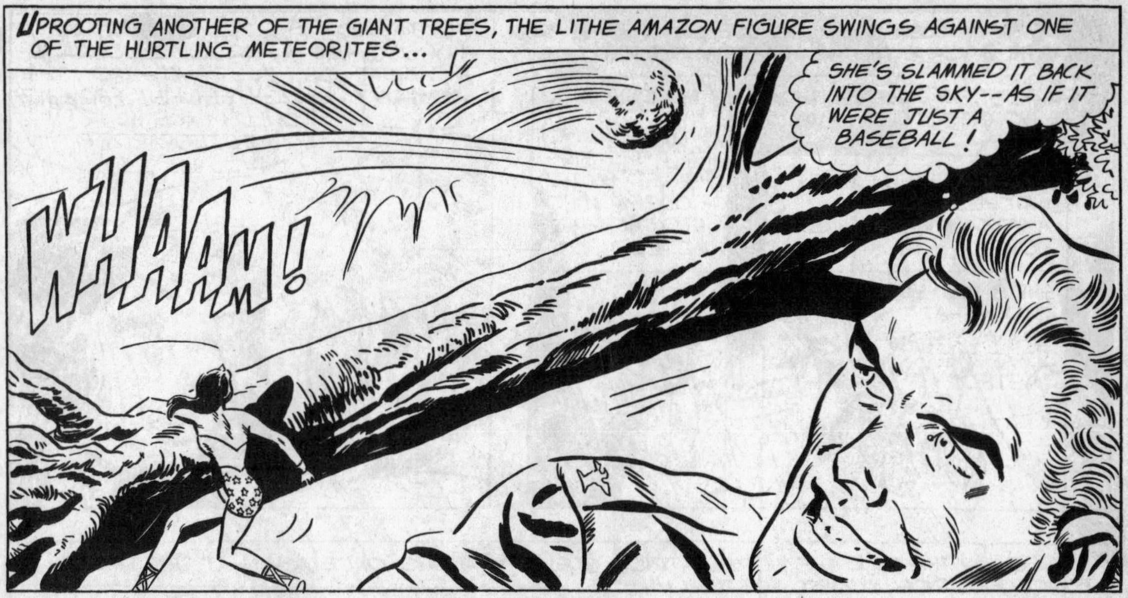
UPROOTING ANOTHER OF THE GIANT TREES, THE LITHE AMAZON FIGURE SWINGS AGAINST ONE OF THE HURTLING METEORITES...
SHE'S SLAMMED IT BACK INTO THE SKY--AS IF IT WERE JUST A BASEBALL!
WHAAM!

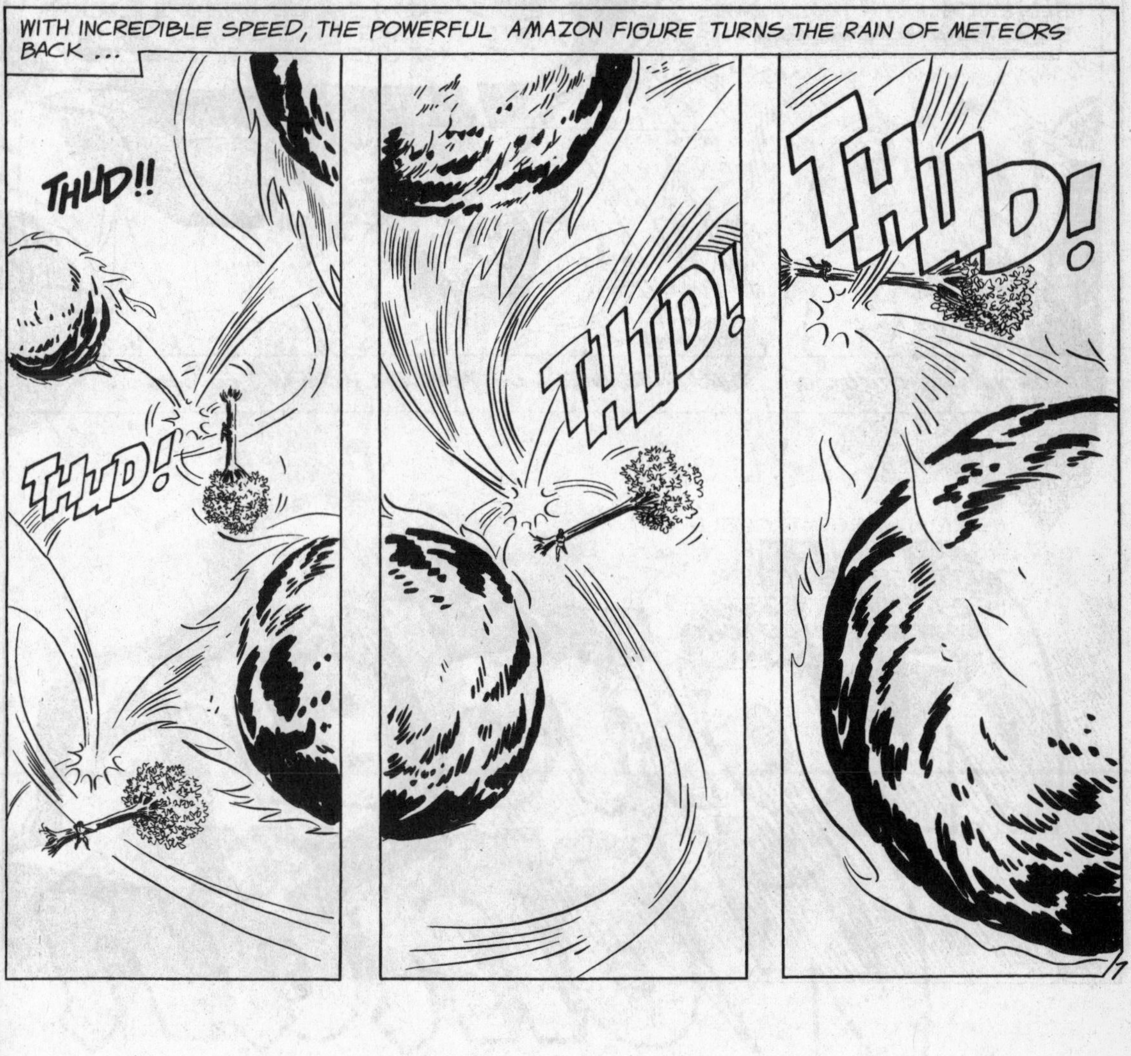
WITH INCREDIBLE SPEED, THE POWERFUL AMAZON FIGURE TURNS THE RAIN OF METEORS BACK...
THUD!!
THUD!
THUD!
THUD!

WITH THE PERIL AVERTED, THE JUBILANT STEVE STARTS BACK WITH THE AMAZON FIGURE...

YOU MUST BE *WONDER WOMAN* ! NO ONE IN THE WORLD COULD HAVE DONE THIS -- BUT YOU, ANGEL --!

IF YOU SAY SO !

IF I SAY SO ? WHY--YOU *ARE* WONDER WOMAN !

DON'T LOOK TO ME FOR ANY ENCOURAGE-MENT ! YOU KNOW THE SLIGHTEST HINT FROM ME WOULD PLACE YOUR LIFE IN JEOPARDY !

AND SO, BY THE TIME THE SORELY-TRIED STEVE GLANCES ONCE AGAIN AT THE THREE EXACT FIGURES, DOUBT ASSAILS HIM ...

WELL, EARTHLING ? WHICH ONE IS THE *REAL* WONDER WOMAN ?

THEY'RE ALL SO IDENTICAL ! ... HOW--HOW CAN I TAKE A CHANCE WITH THE WORLD'S FATE AT STAKE ? ... I-I'D BETTER TEST THIS *LAST* ONE -- BEFORE I DECIDE !

The astounding climax of " *THE THREE FACES OF WONDER WOMAN* " follows ...

18

Wonder Woman

By Charles Moulton

PART THREE
The THIRD FACE of Wonder Woman

HAVING TESTED TWO IDENTICAL WONDER WOMEN OUT OF THREE, STEVE TREVOR STILL FINDS HIMSELF UNABLE TO PICK THE REAL AMAZON! THUS, HE STARTS ON HIS FINAL TEST--ON WHICH THE FATE OF THE WORLD DEPENDS...

THAT'S WHY I MUST BE SURE! THAT'S WHY I MUST THINK UP SOME REALLY IMPOSSIBLE FEAT--THAT ONLY THE REAL WONDER WOMAN COULD PERFORM! BUT WHAT--WHAT?

EARTHLING--FAIL AGAIN-- AND YOU AND YOUR WORLD ARE FINISHED! FOR YOU ARE PROVING HOW PUNY WOULD BE YOUR DEFENSE AGAINST OUR INVASION!

GRIMLY, STEVE DISCOUNTS COUNTLESS IDEAS WHIRLING THROUGH HIS MIND...

IT'S GOT TO BE DIFFERENT--REALLY DIFFERENT! A FANTASTIC FEAT--THAT ONLY *WONDER WOMAN* CAN MAKE HAPPEN!

FINALLY HE SEIZES THE THIRD AMAZON FIGURE'S HAND AND...

LET'S GO! I'VE SUDDENLY THOUGHT OF A WAY OF PROVING WHETHER YOU REALLY ARE *WONDER WOMAN*-- THAT'S A SHEER STROKE OF GENIUS!

WHAT IS IT?

I'M NOT GIVING AWAY MY IDEA IN ADVANCE! I'LL LET YOU KNOW WHEN THE TIME COMES!

AS THE TWO WALK ON, HEAT LIGHTNING FORKS ACROSS THE SKIES--AND THEN--SUDDENLY...

CRACK!

A LIGHTNING BOLT-- HEADING STRAIGHT FOR US! ONLY *WONDER WOMAN* COULD STOP IT!

AND LIKE A WARNING FROM A TALKING MAN-MOUNTAIN...

YOU BETTER NOT MAKE ANY MISTAKES, EARTHMAN! THIS IS YOUR *LAST* CHANCE!

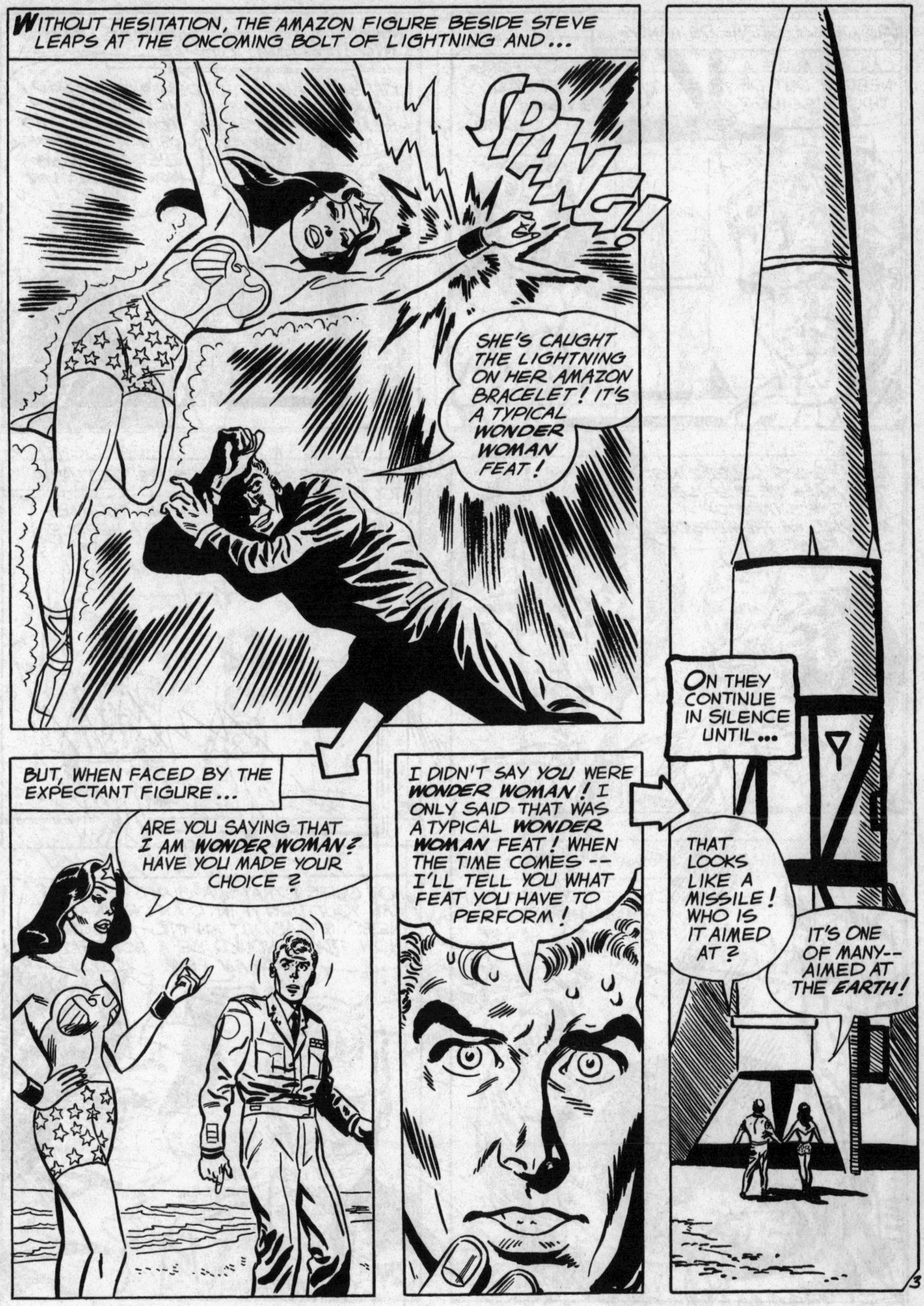
WITHOUT HESITATION, THE AMAZON FIGURE BESIDE STEVE LEAPS AT THE ONCOMING BOLT OF LIGHTNING AND...
SPANG!
SHE'S CAUGHT THE LIGHTNING ON HER AMAZON BRACELET! IT'S A TYPICAL WONDER WOMAN FEAT!
ON THEY CONTINUE IN SILENCE UNTIL...
BUT, WHEN FACED BY THE EXPECTANT FIGURE...
ARE YOU SAYING THAT I AM WONDER WOMAN? HAVE YOU MADE YOUR CHOICE?
I DIDN'T SAY YOU WERE WONDER WOMAN! I ONLY SAID THAT WAS A TYPICAL WONDER WOMAN FEAT! WHEN THE TIME COMES -- I'LL TELL YOU WHAT FEAT YOU HAVE TO PERFORM!
THAT LOOKS LIKE A MISSILE! WHO IS IT AIMED AT?
IT'S ONE OF MANY-- AIMED AT THE EARTH!
3

SUDDENLY, STEVE DEMANDS...

CAN YOU MAKE A NEEDLE OUT OF THAT MISSILE?

I'M READY FOR ANY TEST YOU DEVISE!

INSTANTLY, THE AMAZON FIGURE LEAPS ONTO THE GIANT MISSILE...

WHAM!

SHE'S PUNCHED A HOLE THROUGH THAT METAL -- AS IF IT WERE PAPER-- JUST THE THING WONDER WOMAN CAN DO!

NOW-- SHE'S SQUEEZING THAT MASSIVE MISSILE INTO THE SHAPE OF A NEEDLE -- A TREMENDOUS FEAT!

WHEN THE AMAZON FIGURE RETURNS TO STEVE'S SIDE...

DID TURNING THAT MISSILE INTO A NEEDLE CONVINCE YOU THAT I AM WONDER WOMAN?

NOT QUITE! THAT'S A GIANT NEEDLE! CAN YOU TURN IT INTO AN ORDINARY NEEDLE -- ABOUT AN INCH IN SIZE? NOW THAT-- WOULD BE A WONDER WOMAN FEAT!

WITHOUT HESITATION, THE AMAZON FIGURE STARTS EXERTING SUCH TREMENDOUS PRESSURE ON THE MASSIVE METALLIC OBJECT--THAT SHE TURNS IT INTO LIQUID...

FINALLY, OUT OF A FEW DROPS OF THE SMOKING LIQUID... SHE SHAPES AN ORDINARY—SIZED NEEDLE...

INCREDIBLE--*INCREDIBLE*-- JUST THE THING *WONDER WOMAN* COULD DO!

DOES THAT MEAN YOU HAVE CHOSEN ME?

I WILL--AFTER THE FEAT I THOUGHT OF WHEN WE FIRST STARTED OUT! CAN YOU PASS *ME* THROUGH THE EYE OF THAT NEEDLE?

AGAIN, THE AMAZON FIGURE EXERTS TREMENDOUS PRESSURE...

AND WITH INFINITE DELICACY...

SSSSSSSSS!

STRETCHES THE PLIABLE METAL...

FINALLY, WITH THE NEEDLE STRETCHED TO THE NECESSARY SIZE...

YOU'VE DONE IT -- DONE WHAT ONLY *WONDER WOMAN* COULD DO! PASSED ME THROUGH THE EYE OF A NEEDLE! YOU'RE MY ANGEL! YOU'RE MY *WONDER WOMAN*!

IF YOU SAY SO!

IF I SAY SO? DO YOU MEAN TO TELL ME YOU'RE *NOT* WONDER WOMAN?

I CAN'T TELL YOU *ANYTHING!* *YOU* HAVE TO MAKE THE DECISION!

THUS, BY THE TIME STEVE RETURNS, HE IS AGAIN ASSAILED BY DOUBT...

HOW DO I KNOW WHETHER THE FIRST TWO COULDN'T *ALSO* PASS ME THROUGH THE EYE OF A NEEDLE? AFTER ALL -- *THEY* DID WHAT I THOUGHT ONLY *WONDER WOMAN* COULD DO!

OMINOUSLY, THE MOUNTAIN-LIKE CREATURES OF THE PARALLEL DIMENSION DEMAND..

CHOOSE THE REAL *WONDER WOMAN*, EARTHLING! OR YOU LOSE YOUR LIFE BY DEFAULT--AND THE INVASION OF EARTH WILL BE ON!

FRANTICALLY STEVE STARES AT THE THREE IDENTICAL *WONDER WOMEN*...

YOU'D THINK I'D BE ABLE TO RECOGNIZE MY ANGEL JUST BY LOOKING AT HER -- WHY -- DIDN'T SHE KISS ME FOR THAT BIRTHDAY GIFT ONLY A SHORT TIME -- WAIT -- *WAIT* -- THAT'S IT -- THAT'S THE TEST -- *THE ONLY REAL TEST!*

SNAP!

AND THEN -- STEVE ADDRESSES THE CLOUD-HIGH FIGURES...

I HAVE ONE MORE FINAL TEST TO MAKE! IT WILL ONLY TAKE A MOMENT! I CAN DO IT RIGHT HERE!

GRANTED -- BUT IF YOU HAVE FAILED UP TO NOW -- I CANNOT SEE WHAT YOU HOPE TO ACCOMPLISH!

IF YOU'RE MY ONE AND ONLY *WONDER WOMAN* --

--THIS WILL PROVE IT!

THE PERPLEXED OTHER DIMENSIONAL BEINGS STARE DOWN...

WHAT IS HE DOING? THE EARTHLING HAS LOST HIS WITS!

BUT STEVE CONTINUES WITH THE SECOND AMAZON FIGURE...

I SHOULD HAVE THOUGHT OF THIS IN THE FIRST PLACE!

--THIS IS THE ONLY TRUE TEST!

WELL?

JUST ONE MORE!

IF I'M WRONG ABOUT THIS--BUT I CAN'T BE WRONG--I CAN'T BE--THE FATE OF THE WORLD DEPENDS ON THIS KISS!

8

AND THEN--FOR THE FIRST TIME, STEVE ANNOUNCES WITHOUT HESITATION...

THIS IS *WONDER WOMAN*-- THE REAL *WONDER WOMAN*-- MY ONE AND ONLY AMAZON!

IMMEDIATELY...

I WAS RIGHT--*I WAS RIGHT*-- SEE--THE OTHERS ARE BEING DESTROYED--THEY WERE ONLY ROBOTS!

MHRRRRRRR!

YOU HAVE PROVEN YOU HAVE A POWER UNKNOWN TO US! INVASION WILL BE TOO MUCH OF A RISK! WE WILL THEREFORE--SEND YOU BACK TO YOUR OWN DIMENSION!

LATER, AS *WONDER WOMAN* AND STEVE ARE RE-TURNED TO THEIR OWN WORLD...

I CAN'T UNDERSTAND WHY YOU'RE MAD AT ME, ANGEL? I THOUGHT YOU'D BE PROUD OF ME FOR RECOGNIZING THE TOUCH OF YOUR WARM LIPS--IN CONTRAST TO THE OTHERS?

BUT DID YOU HAVE TO KISS THOSE--THOSE ROBOTS FIRST? WHY COULDN'T YOU HAVE *STARTED* WITH ME? HOW MANY OTHER GIRLS HAVE YOU KISSED? DOZENS, I SUPPOSE...

The End

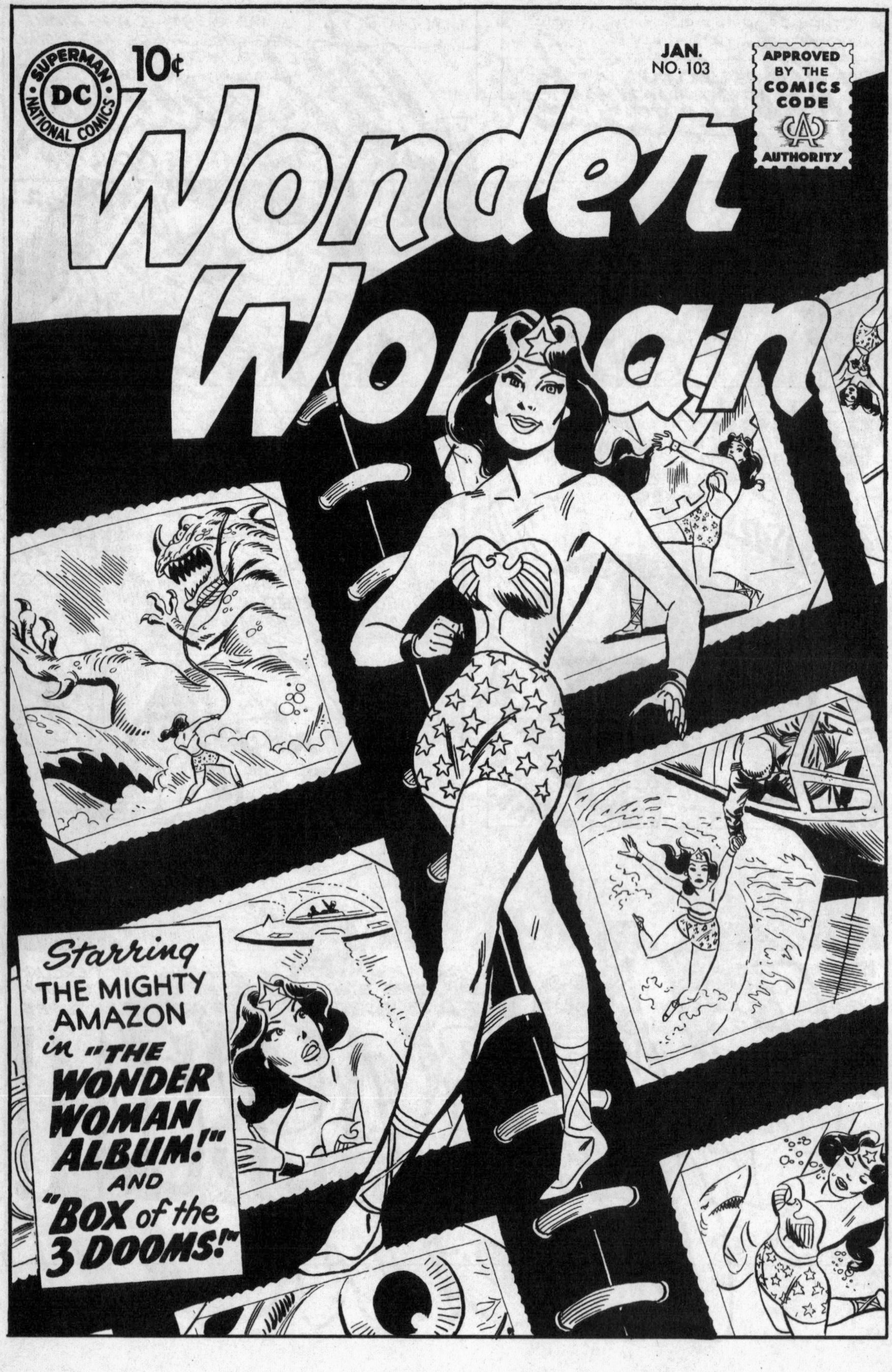
SUPERMAN DC NATIONAL COMICS
10¢
JAN. NO. 103
APPROVED BY THE COMICS CODE AUTHORITY
Wonder Woman
Starring THE MIGHTY AMAZON in "THE WONDER WOMAN ALBUM!" AND "BOX of the 3 DOOMS!"

WONDER WOMAN -- BEAUTIFUL AS APHRODITE, WISE AS ATHENA, SWIFTER THAN MERCURY, AND STRONGER THAN HERCULES -- HAS HAD MORE STARTLING ADVENTURES THAN ANY-ONE ON THE FACE OF THIS EARTH! BUT EVEN MORE INCREDIBLE ARE THE PICTURES OF HER AMAZING FEATS IN...

The WONDER WOMAN ALBUM!

IN THE AMAZONIAN INSTITUTE ON PARADISE ISLAND, SECRET HOME OF THE FAMOUS AMAZONS, ARE MANY SOUVENIRS OF THEIR STARTLING ADVENTURES ...

BUT NOTHING IS MORE AMAZING THAN THIS -- A SIMPLE BLACK BOOK WITH A SIMPLE TITLE...

THIS -- IS THE WONDER WOMAN ALBUM!

WONDER WOMAN ALBUM

THE ALBUM NEVER FAILS TO STARTLE VISITORS WHO SEE IT FOR THE FIRST TIME ...

WONDER WOMAN VS THE TIDAL WAVE

GREAT HERA-- THE PAGE IS BLANK!

WHAT HAP- PENED?

WHERE'S THE PHOTO SHOWING WONDER WOMAN FIGHTING THE TIDAL WAVE?

I MIGHT AS WELL TELL YOU THE STORY FROM THE BEGINNING! I WAS THERE! IN FACT, I WAS THE PHOTOGRAPHER! IT ALL STARTED WHEN ...

"WONDER WOMAN WAS INVITED TO ATTEND THE NEW MOON DANCES ON PEARL ISLAND IN THE PACIFIC ... "

LET ME TAKE A PICTURE OF YOU AT THE CONTROLS OF YOUR AMAZON PLANE, PRINCESS!

SAVE YOUR FILM FOR SOMETHING UNUSUAL, TARA! COME ON! I DON'T WANT TO BE LATE!

"AFTER WE LANDED ON PEARL ISLAND, I WANTED TO TAKE PICTURES OF *WONDER WOMAN* WHIRLING THROUGH A SERIES OF MOONS--BUT..."

HOLD IT, TARA! ARE YOU FORGETTING YOU'RE AN AMAZON?

WAIT UNTIL SOMETHING *REALLY* UNUSUAL HAPPENS!

"JUST THEN A TREMENDOUS WIND AROSE..."

PRINCESS--I'VE NEVER FELT--A WIND LIKE THIS--BEFORE!

WHREEEE!

"A FEW MOMENTS LATER WE KNEW THE REASON FOR THE GREAT WIND--AS THE SEA SEEMED TO RISE HIGHER THAN THE TOPS OF HOUSES..."

TIDAL WAVE! IT WILL SWEEP THE PEOPLE OFF THE ISLAND!

RRRRRRRRUMMMBLE!

3

"WITH EYE-BLURRING SPEED, *WONDER WOMAN* UPROOTED A GIANT PALM WHICH HAD BEEN STANDING NEXT TO ANOTHER ONE..."

SHE'S MOVING TOO FAST--I CAN'T FOCUS ON HER!

RRRRJIIP!

"AS IF IT WERE MERELY A LIGHTWEIGHT SPEAR, PRINCESS DIANA HURLED A PALM TREE INTO THE GROUND A MILE AWAY...."

THUD!

"NOW I SAW THE REASON FOR THIS FEAT, AS *WONDER WOMAN* MADE THE PEOPLE FORM A HUMAN CHAIN STRETCHING FROM ONE TREE TO ANOTHER..."

WHIRRREEEEEEE!!

AS LONG AS THE TREES HOLD--THEY WON'T BE BLOWN AWAY--BUT WHAT WILL HAPPEN WHEN THE TIDAL WAVE WASHES OVER THE ISLAND?

"*WONDER WOMAN* RACED PAST ME..."

YOU WANTED A PICTURE WORTHY OF AN AMAZON COLLECTION, TARA--GET READY TO TAKE THIS ONE!

"I COULD HARDLY KEEP MY EYE-LIDS OPEN AGAINST THE TREMENDOUS TUG OF THE WIND AS ..."

MERCIFUL MINERVA! *WONDER WOMAN*-- HAS LEAPED INTO THE BOILING SEA!

"WONDER WOMAN DOVE BENEATH THE ISLAND TO THE CORAL REEF..."

THIS IS THE ONLY THING I CAN USE!

"WITH HER TIARA, MADE OF AMAZONIUM, HARDEST METAL KNOWN, SHE SHEARED OFF AN IMMENSE SLAB OF THE REEF..."

HERA HELP MY PLAN SUCCEED TO FORM A WIND-BREAK WITH THIS REEF WALL!

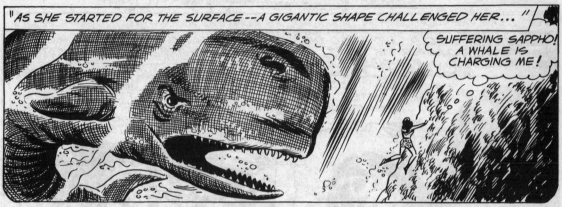

"AS SHE STARTED FOR THE SURFACE--A GIGANTIC SHAPE CHALLENGED HER..."

SUFFERING SAPPHO! A WHALE IS CHARGING ME!

"DEFENDING HERSELF AGAINST THE MIGHTY SEA BEAST, WONDER WOMAN WAS FORCED TO..."

THUNDERBOLTS OF JOVE! I'VE SPLIT THE REEF IN TWO--THE REEF I NEED TO PROTECT THE PEOPLE ON THE ISLAND AGAINST THE TIDAL WAVE!

CRRACK!

"RACING BACK ONTO THE ISLAND, *WONDER WOMAN* PRESSED TOGETHER THE TWO HALVES OF THE REEF-WALL, AND DAUNTLESS STOOD IN THE PATH OF THE IMMENSE TIDAL WAVE.."

WHAAAMMMM!

HERA-- HELP ME HOLD!

"*WONDER WOMAN* HELD... AND SAVED THE ISLANDERS... AND AS FOR THE GREAT PICTURE I SHOULD HAVE TAKEN ..."

COULDN'T GET A THING--WATER DRENCHED EVERYTHING!

BACK ON PARADISE ISLAND, THE YOUNG AMAZONS PLY THE GUIDE WITH QUESTIONS...

YOU'RE ENTITLED TO ONE MISTAKE!

YOU MUST HAVE GOTTEN SEN- SATIONAL PICTURES OF *WONDER WOMAN* DOING OTHER FEATS!

TURN THE PAGE, TARA-- LET'S SEE THE REST OF THE BOOK?

THE NEXT PAGE OF THE *WONDER WOMAN* ALBUM IS TURNED TO REVEAL..

WONDER WOMAN vs THE GIANT GLACIER!

AGAIN THE STARTLED VISITORS INTERROGATE THE AMAZON GUIDE ...

WHAT HAPPENED *THIS* TIME, TARA?

WELL-- TO BEGIN AT THE BEGINNING-- I ACCOMPANIED *WONDER WOMAN* TO THE NORTH POLE ...

6

"SHE WAS COLLECTING SPECIMENS OF ARCTIC FLORA FOR A SCIENTIFIC CONVENTION... AND WHEN I WANTED TO TAKE A PICTURE OF HER..."

OH, TARA... DON'T WASTE PRECIOUS FILM ON ANYTHING AS TAME AS THIS! WAIT UNTIL SOMETHING REALLY EXCITING HAPPENS!

"AND WHEN SHE WRESTED A GIANT SAVAGE POLAR BEAR AWAY FROM A DOOMED ESKIMO FAMILY..."

HOLD IT, TARA! A PICTURE LIKE THIS SIMPLY ISN'T EXCITING ENOUGH FOR THE AMAZON MUSEUM! WAIT! SOMETHING BIG IS BOUND TO HAPPEN!

"I FOLLOWED **WONDER WOMAN** AROUND LIKE A FROZEN SHADOW... BUT..."

NOTHING'S HAPPENING!

NOTHING'S HAPPENING!

NOTHING'S HAPPENING!

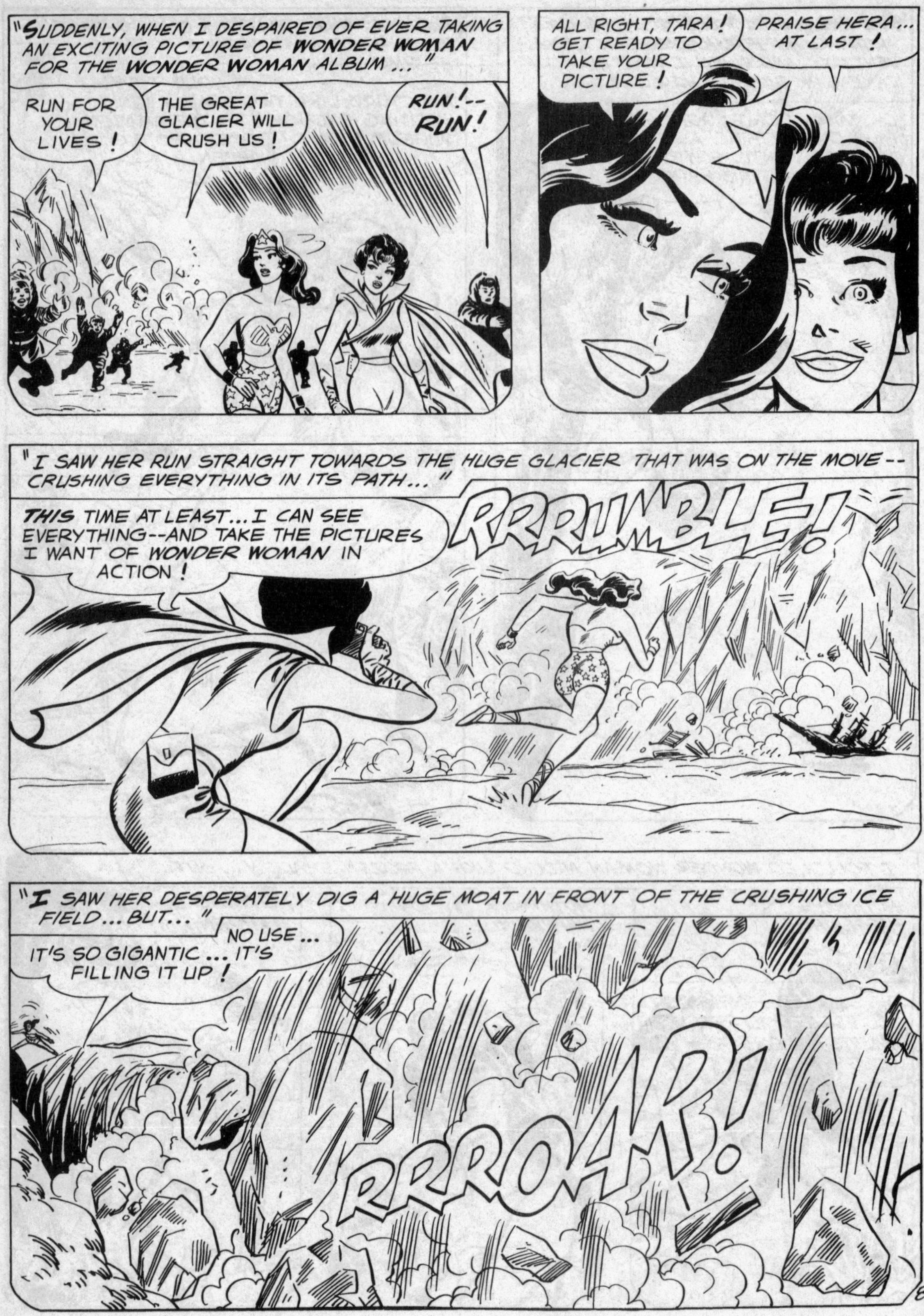
"SUDDENLY, WHEN I DESPAIRED OF EVER TAKING AN EXCITING PICTURE OF WONDER WOMAN FOR THE WONDER WOMAN ALBUM ..."
RUN FOR YOUR LIVES!
THE GREAT GLACIER WILL CRUSH US!
RUN!-- RUN!
ALL RIGHT, TARA! GET READY TO TAKE YOUR PICTURE!
PRAISE HERA... AT LAST!
"I SAW HER RUN STRAIGHT TOWARDS THE HUGE GLACIER THAT WAS ON THE MOVE-- CRUSHING EVERYTHING IN ITS PATH..."
THIS TIME AT LEAST... I CAN SEE EVERYTHING--AND TAKE THE PICTURES I WANT OF WONDER WOMAN IN ACTION!
RRRUMBLE!
"I SAW HER DESPERATELY DIG A HUGE MOAT IN FRONT OF THE CRUSHING ICE FIELD... BUT..."
NO USE... IT'S SO GIGANTIC... IT'S FILLING IT UP!
RRROAR!
8

"*AND THEN, WITH A SURGE OF HER EXTRAORDINARY POWER, WONDER WOMAN BEGAN RIPPING HUGE CHUNKS OFF THE ADVANCING GLACIER ...*"

HERA HELP ME IN THIS PLAN--OR ALL WILL BE LOST!

CR A ACK!

"*HIGH INTO THE SKY SHE HURLED THOSE MASSIVE SLABS OF THE GLACIER -- WITH SUCH DAZZLING SPEED...THAT FRICTION BURNED THEM UP...*"

"*THE MIGHTY AMAZON HAD TURNED THE GREAT GLACIER INTO HARMLESS RAIN-- AND I HAD GOTTEN IT ALL OR THOUGHT I HAD UNTIL ...*"

THE SHUTTER--*THE SHUTTER*--I WAS TOO EXCITED TO REALIZE THAT THE SHUTTER WAS FROZEN STIFF BY THE COLD--AND HADN'T SNAPPED A SINGLE PICTURE!

AND AS THE AMAZON GUIDE FINISHES HER TALE...

WONDER WOMAN--VISITING US!

WHAT LUCK! WE CAN TAKE A PICTURE OF HER FOR *OUR* ALBUMS!

As WONDER WOMAN poses for her picture...

TARA WAS TELLING US HOW DIFFICULT IT IS TO TAKE YOUR PICTURE, PRINCESS!

NONSENSE -- I'M THE EASIEST SUBJECT IN THE WORLD!

SUDDENLY, ON WONDER WOMAN'S UNIQUE BRACELET -- AN SOS SOUNDS...

SOS! SHIP ON FIRE! SOS!

IN THAT SAME INSTANT, DISAPPEARING IN A DAZZLING FLASH OF SPEED...

I MUST HELP THEM!

WONDER WOMAN LEFT BEFORE WE COULD SNAP HER PICTURE!

SHE'S JUST TOO FAST!

NOW YOU KNOW WHY THE WONDER WOMAN ALBUM IS EMPTY!

The End

10

IT LOOKED LIKE AN ORDINARY BOX UNTIL *WONDER WOMAN*—BEAUTIFUL AS APHRODITE, WISE AS ATHENA, SWIFTER THAN MERCURY, AND STRONGER THAN HERCULES—OPENED IT!
THEN—SURPRISE AFTER SURPRISE LEAPED OUT AT THE MIGHTY AMAZON FROM...

The BOX of THREE DOOMS!

AT A SECRET HIDEOUT FILLED WITH FANTASTIC GADGETS OF EVERY DESCRIPTION...THE INFAMOUS *GADGET-MAKER* LABORS...

THE *GADGET-MAKER* IGNORES HIS PUPPET TIGER THAT CAN SLAY LIKE A REAL ONE...

ROWR!

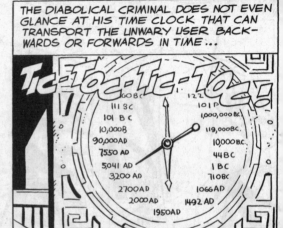

THE DIABOLICAL CRIMINAL DOES NOT EVEN GLANCE AT HIS TIME CLOCK THAT CAN TRANSPORT THE UNWARY USER BACK- WARDS OR FORWARDS IN TIME...

Tic-Toc-Tic-Toc!

INSTEAD, HE STARES AT AN INNOCENT- LOOKING BOX...

MY MASTERPIECE! DESIGNED TO DESTROY *WONDER WOMAN*!

THIS IS THE *BOX OF DOOM*--FOR *WONDER WOMAN*!

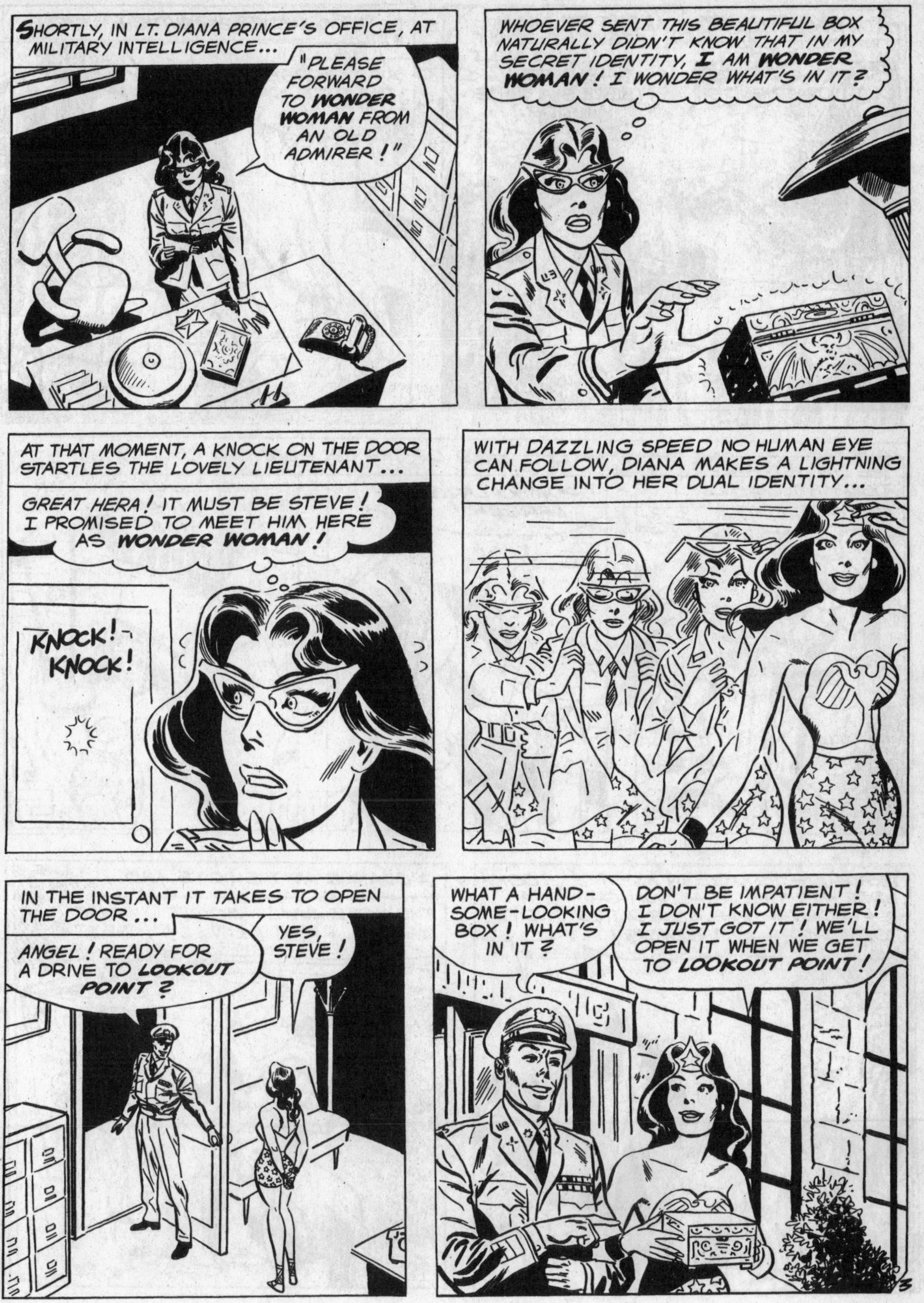
SHORTLY, IN LT. DIANA PRINCE'S OFFICE, AT MILITARY INTELLIGENCE...
"PLEASE FORWARD TO WONDER WOMAN FROM AN OLD ADMIRER!"
WHOEVER SENT THIS BEAUTIFUL BOX NATURALLY DIDN'T KNOW THAT IN MY SECRET IDENTITY, I AM WONDER WOMAN! I WONDER WHAT'S IN IT?
AT THAT MOMENT, A KNOCK ON THE DOOR STARTLES THE LOVELY LIEUTENANT...
GREAT HERA! IT MUST BE STEVE! I PROMISED TO MEET HIM HERE AS WONDER WOMAN!
KNOCK! KNOCK!
WITH DAZZLING SPEED NO HUMAN EYE CAN FOLLOW, DIANA MAKES A LIGHTNING CHANGE INTO HER DUAL IDENTITY...
IN THE INSTANT IT TAKES TO OPEN THE DOOR...
ANGEL! READY FOR A DRIVE TO LOOKOUT POINT?
YES, STEVE!
WHAT A HAND-SOME-LOOKING BOX! WHAT'S IN IT?
DON'T BE IMPATIENT! I DON'T KNOW EITHER! I JUST GOT IT! WE'LL OPEN IT WHEN WE GET TO LOOKOUT POINT!

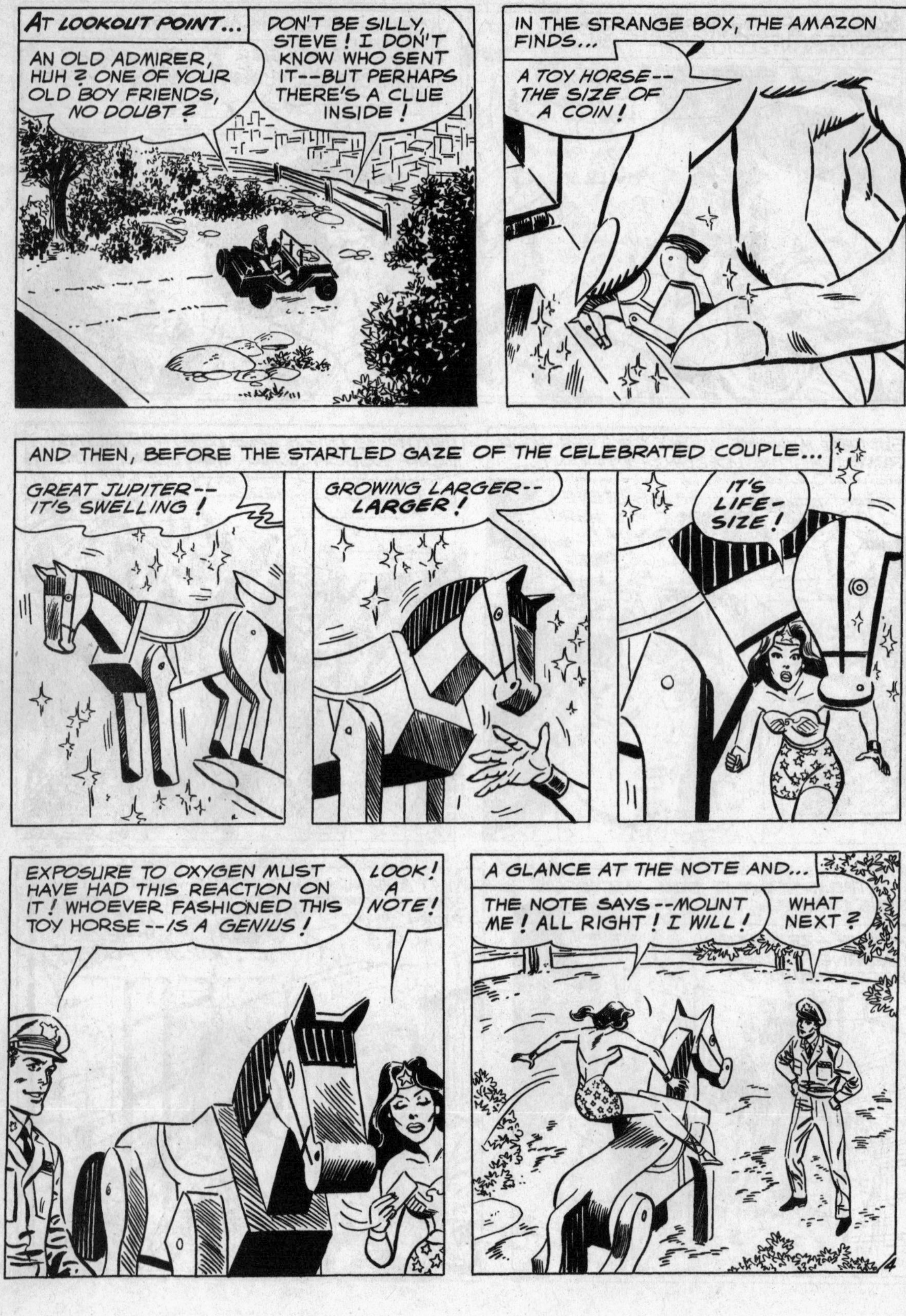
AT LOOKOUT POINT...
AN OLD ADMIRER, HUH ? ONE OF YOUR OLD BOY FRIENDS, NO DOUBT ?
DON'T BE SILLY, STEVE ! I DON'T KNOW WHO SENT IT--BUT PERHAPS THERE'S A CLUE INSIDE !
IN THE STRANGE BOX, THE AMAZON FINDS...
A TOY HORSE--THE SIZE OF A COIN !
AND THEN, BEFORE THE STARTLED GAZE OF THE CELEBRATED COUPLE...
GREAT JUPITER--IT'S SWELLING !
GROWING LARGER--LARGER !
IT'S LIFE-SIZE !
EXPOSURE TO OXYGEN MUST HAVE HAD THIS REACTION ON IT ! WHOEVER FASHIONED THIS TOY HORSE--IS A GENIUS !
LOOK ! A NOTE !
A GLANCE AT THE NOTE AND...
THE NOTE SAYS--MOUNT ME ! ALL RIGHT ! I WILL !
WHAT NEXT ?
4

NO SOONER HAS **WONDER WOMAN** MOUNTED THE TOY HORSE THAN...

SHADES OF PLUTO-- IT'S MOVING!

WAIT FOR ME!

AS THE MECHANICAL HORSE RACES ON...

I WONDER WHAT'S FURNISHING ITS POWER OF LOCOMOTION?

SOME SOLAR ENERGY FORCE, PROBABLY!

SUDDENLY, IN THE MIDST OF THEIR REVELRY, THE AMAZON'S ACUTE HEARING DETECTS...

THAT SOUND--?

TIC-TOC-TIC!

STEVE--! THIS HORSE IS A TIME BOMB! HERA ALONE KNOWS WHEN IT MIGHT GO OFF!

IF IT EXPLODES HERE-- IT WILL CAUSE TERRIBLE DAMAGE!

INSTANTLY, **WONDER WOMAN** SUMMONS HER ROBOT PLANE AND, MAKING THE TOY TIME BOMB FAST TO HER LASSO...

PLANE--CLIMB! STEVE--GET OFF BEFORE IT'S TOO LATE!

WHEREVER YOU GO, ANGEL-- I GO! WHATEVER CHANCES YOU TAKE--I'LL TAKE!

TIC TIC TIC

5

AS THE PLANE CLIMBS TO A HIGH ALTITUDE...

YOU'VE SAVED THE CITY FROM HARM, ANGEL!

BUT WE'RE STILL TIED TO A TIME BOMB, STEVE! HURRY UP--CLIMB INTO THE PLANE!

TIC-TOC!

A MOMENT LATER, AT THE CONTROLS...

HANG ON! I'M GOING TO TRY TO SNAP THAT DREADFUL TOY HORSE LOOSE!

AS WONDER WOMAN HURLS HER UNIQUE PLANE INTO A SLAP TURN, WHICH WHIPS THE TIME BOMB LOOSE...

WHAM!

DESPERATELY, THE MIGHTY AMAZON BATTLES TO RIGHT HER SPINNING PLANE...

FINALLY, WHEN THE PLANE IS FLYING A STABLE COURSE AGAIN...

WHOEVER SENT THAT BOX TO YOU--WANTS TO DESTROY YOU, ANGEL! GET RID OF IT!

NO, STEVE! I CAN'T!

ANGEL--GET RID OF THIS INFERNAL BOX!

IF I DO--THE VILLAIN WHO SENT IT WILL BE FREE TO CONTINUE HIS VILLAINY! THE PATH TO HIM LIES IN THIS BOX! I MUST FOLLOW IT TO HIM!

TENSELY, THE AMAZON LIFTS OUT...

IT'S A TOY BIRD!

A HAWK -- NO BIGGER THAN A CHARM!

INSTANTLY, A STARTLING TRANSFORMATION TAKES PLACE...

IT'S GROWING BIGGER!

JUST LIKE THE OTHERS!

IT'S IMMENSE!

AND THEN...

WONDER WOMAN MANIPULATES THE CONTROLS AT LIGHTNING SPEED AND...

THAT'S QUICK THINKING, ANGEL! YOU'VE TOSSED THAT BOOBY TRAP AWAY FROM THE SHIP!

ZOOOOOOM!

BUT, TO WONDER WOMAN'S HORROR, SHE DISCOVERS...

SUFFERING SAPPHO! THAT EXPLOSIVE TOY IS FLYING BACK TOWARD US!

INSTANTLY, THE ALERT AMAZON SENDS HER PLANE INTO A HURTLING DIVE...

IT'S CHANGED DIRECTION TO FOLLOW US!

WHAT IS THE NEXT INSIDIOUS DOOM THAT HAS BEEN PREPARED FOR THE DAUNTLESS AMAZON?

TURN TO THE PAGE FOLLOWING FOR THE EXCITING CONCLUSION TO THIS STORY!

DESPITE THE AMAZON'S FRENZIED ACROBATICS...

NO USE!

YOU CAN'T SHAKE IT!

I'VE GOT TO!

AGAIN, THE SORELY-PRESSED AMAZON SENDS HER PLANE INTO A DIVE...

ANGEL--YOU'VE CROSSED YOUR CONTROLS!

IT'S OUR ONLY CHANCE, STEVE! THERE'S NO TELLING WHEN THE FLYING TIME BOMB MAY EXPLODE!

DEEP INTO THE NARROWING SIDES OF THE VOLCANO, **WONDER WOMAN** FLIES WITH INCREDIBLE DARING...

THAT INFERNAL EXPLOSIVE TOY MUST OPERATE ON SOME GYROSCOPIC, MAGNETIC FORCE-- IT'S STILL FOLLOWING US!

THAT'S WHAT I'M DEPENDING ON!

JUST AS SHE REACHES THE BED OF BOILING LAVA, THE KEEN-EYED AMAZON SWITCHES HER CONTROLS WITH LIGHTNING RAPIDITY...

HOLD ON, STEVE! I'M GOING TO -- REVERSE!

I CAN FEEL THE Gs -- PULLING AT ME -- ALREADY!

PAST THE REVERSING PLANE THE IMPLACABLE TRACKER HURTLES...

WHOOOSH!

AND THEN... WITH A THUNDEROUS ROAR...

YOU PULLED US OUT OF THAT ONE, ANGEL! THAT FLYING TIME BOMB EXPLODED WHEN IT CRASHED AGAINST THE SIDES OF THE MOUNTAIN -- TRYING TO TURN BACK AFTER YOU!

WHAMM!

AS WONDER WOMAN FLIES OUT TOWARD SAFETY AGAIN...

GET RID OF THAT DIABOLICAL BOX, ANGEL!

AND LOSE THE ONLY LINK TO THE RUTHLESS CRIMINAL BEHIND ALL THIS? NO, STEVE! FOR THE SAFETY OF THE WORLD -- HE MUST BE FOUND AND CAPTURED -- AND THIS IS THE ONLY WAY!

WHAT ELSE IS THERE?

A FISH -- A TINY FISH!

BUT IN AN INSTANT...

IT'S A SHARK!

THE TINY FISH SWELLS IN SIZE...

IT'S GETTING BIGGER-- *BIGGER!*

UNTIL... ANOTHER BOOBY TRAP! WHAT WILL WE DO WITH THIS?

PLACING HER UNIQUE PLANE ON ROBOT CONTROL, *WONDER WOMAN* UNHESITATINGLY DIVES OUT INTO SPACE...

I HAVE AN IDEA THAT THESE EXPLOSIVE TRAPS ARE NOT MAGNETIZED TO THE PLANE-- I'LL KNOW IN A MOMENT!

AS SHE HURTLES THROUGH THE AIR TOWARDS THE SEA BELOW...

I WAS RIGHT! THE SHARK IS FOLLOWING ME!

INTO THE DEPTHS THE DAUNTLESS AMAZON PLUNGES...

NEPTUNE HELP ME DIVERT IT FROM ITS TASK OF DE-STRUCTION--THAT GIANT CLAM DOWN THERE--MAY HELP ME--IF I'M SWIFT ENOUGH!

PAST THE CLUTCHING JAWS OF THE IMMENSE CLAM *WONDER WOMAN* ROCKETS WITH DESPERATE SPEED...

I CANNOT-- SWIM--ANY FASTER!

BY A HAIR'S-BREADTH, THE MIGHTY AMAZON ESCAPES--WHILE BEHIND HER...

CLAM--IMPRISONED-- THE TIME BOMB SHARK!

THUMP!

EVEN AS SHE GRIMLY CLAWS FOR THE SURFACE, THE SEA HEAVES...

THANK HERA--THE CLAM CONTAINED THE EXPLOSION!

WHOOSH!

WITH INCREDIBLE AGILITY, *WONDER WOMAN* BOARDS HER ROBOT PLANE IN FLIGHT...

WELL, ANGEL--IT'S ALL OVER--I LOOKED INSIDE THE BOX-- AND IT'S EMPTY--NO MORE CLUES! YOU'LL HAVE TO GET RID OF IT *NOW!*

BUT, THE UNPREDICTABLE AMAZON AGAIN STARTLES STEVE...

NO, STEVE! THIS BOX STILL REMAINS THE ONLY CLUE TO A DIABOLICAL VILLAIN WHO MUST BE FOUND! AND THE ONLY WAY TO HIM--IS INSIDE THIS BOX!

BUT ANGEL-- THERE'S NOTHING MORE IN IT! WHAT CAN YOU DO?

12

BACK TO MILITARY INTELLIGENCE THE ADVENTUROUS COUPLE RETURNS AT THE AMAZON'S SUGGESTION...

I DON'T SEE HOW YOU CAN TRACE THE VILLAIN WHO SENT THIS!

SO FAR-- EVERYTHING WE TOOK *OUT* OF THE BOX-- *INCREASED* IN SIZE! WHAT IF WE *REVERSED* THE PROCESS? WHAT IF WE PUT SOMETHING *INTO* THE BOX?

WHAT?! WHAT ARE YOU GOING TO PUT INSIDE?

ME!

BEFORE STEVE'S UTTERLY DUMBFOUNDED STARE...

SHE'S GETTING SMALLER--!

AN AMAZING PHENOMENON TAKES PLACE...

smaller--!

AS... SHE'S INSIDE!

13

THE NEXT MOMENT...

THE BOX--IT'S FLYING OFF -- TAKING *WONDER WOMAN* AWAY WITH IT!

WITH *ROCKET-LIKE* SPEED THE UNIQUE BOX ARRIVES AT THE *GADGET-MAKER'S* SECRET HIDEOUT...

AND SO--MY LITTLE BOX OF TRAPS RETURNS TO ME-- PROOF THAT IT HAS DISPOSED OF THE ENEMY OF CRIME EVERYWHERE-- *WONDER WOMAN!*

THUMP!

INSIDE THE BOX, *WONDER WOMAN* WAITS TENSELY AS...

I WONDER *WHICH* OF MY TRAPS WAS SUCCESSFUL-- THE HORSE? THE HAWK-- OR THE SHARK?

AS THE VILLAIN'S HAND RESTS ON THE EDGE OF THE DIABOLICAL BOX--THE SILENT AMAZON CASTS HER GOLDEN LASSO...

WH-WHAT IS THIS--?

THE NEXT MOMENT, *WONDER WOMAN* SPRINGS PAST THE MOLECULAR FILTER WHICH RESTORES HER TO HER FORMER SIZE AND...

IT--IT CAN'T BE--?

IT CAN'T BE--?

WONDER WOMAN--!

14

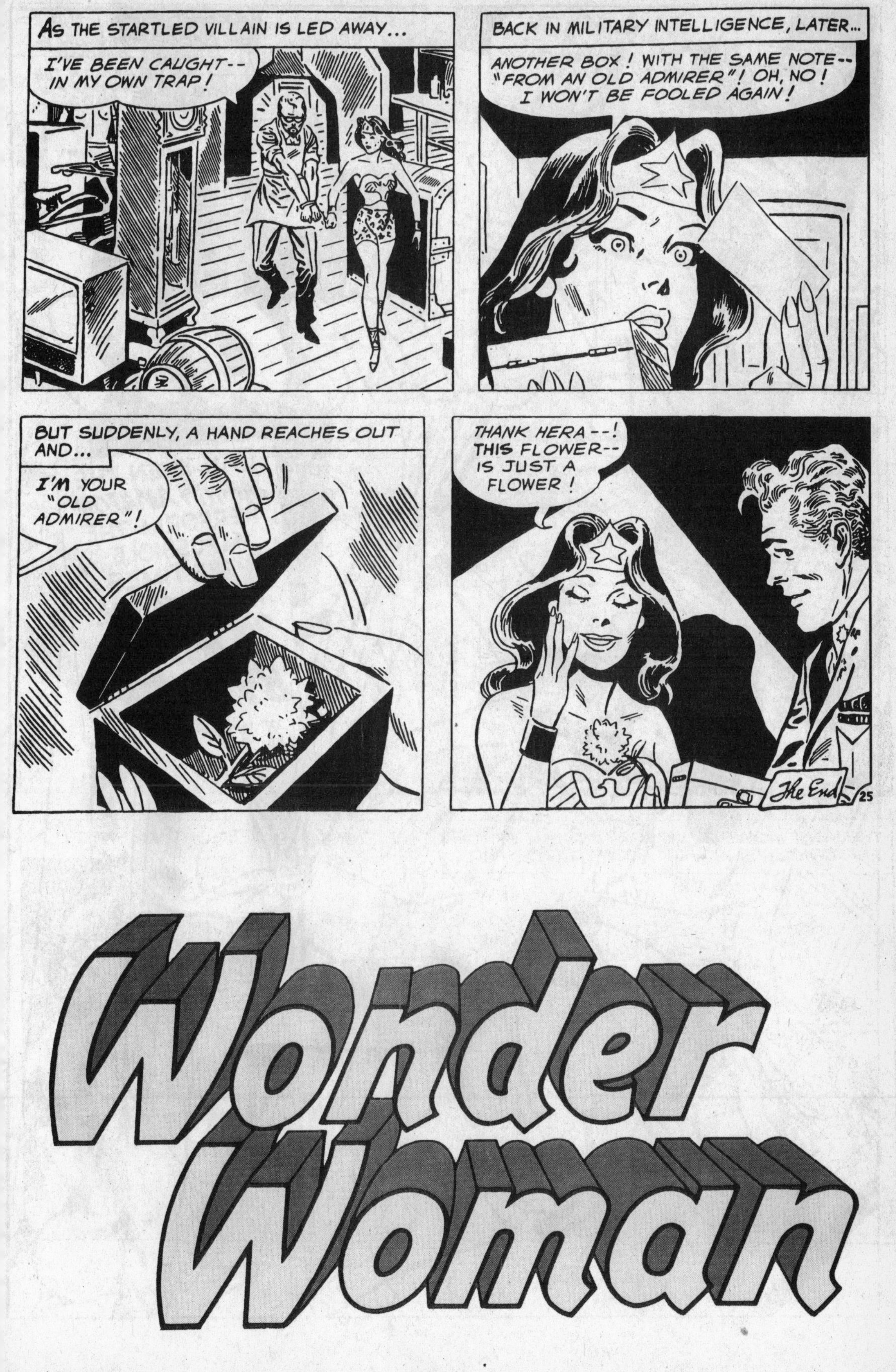
AS THE STARTLED VILLAIN IS LED AWAY...
I'VE BEEN CAUGHT-- IN MY OWN TRAP!
BACK IN MILITARY INTELLIGENCE, LATER...
ANOTHER BOX! WITH THE SAME NOTE-- "FROM AN OLD ADMIRER"! OH, NO! I WON'T BE FOOLED AGAIN!
BUT SUDDENLY, A HAND REACHES OUT AND...
I'M YOUR "OLD ADMIRER"!
THANK HERA--! THIS FLOWER-- IS JUST A FLOWER!
The End
25

Wonder Woman

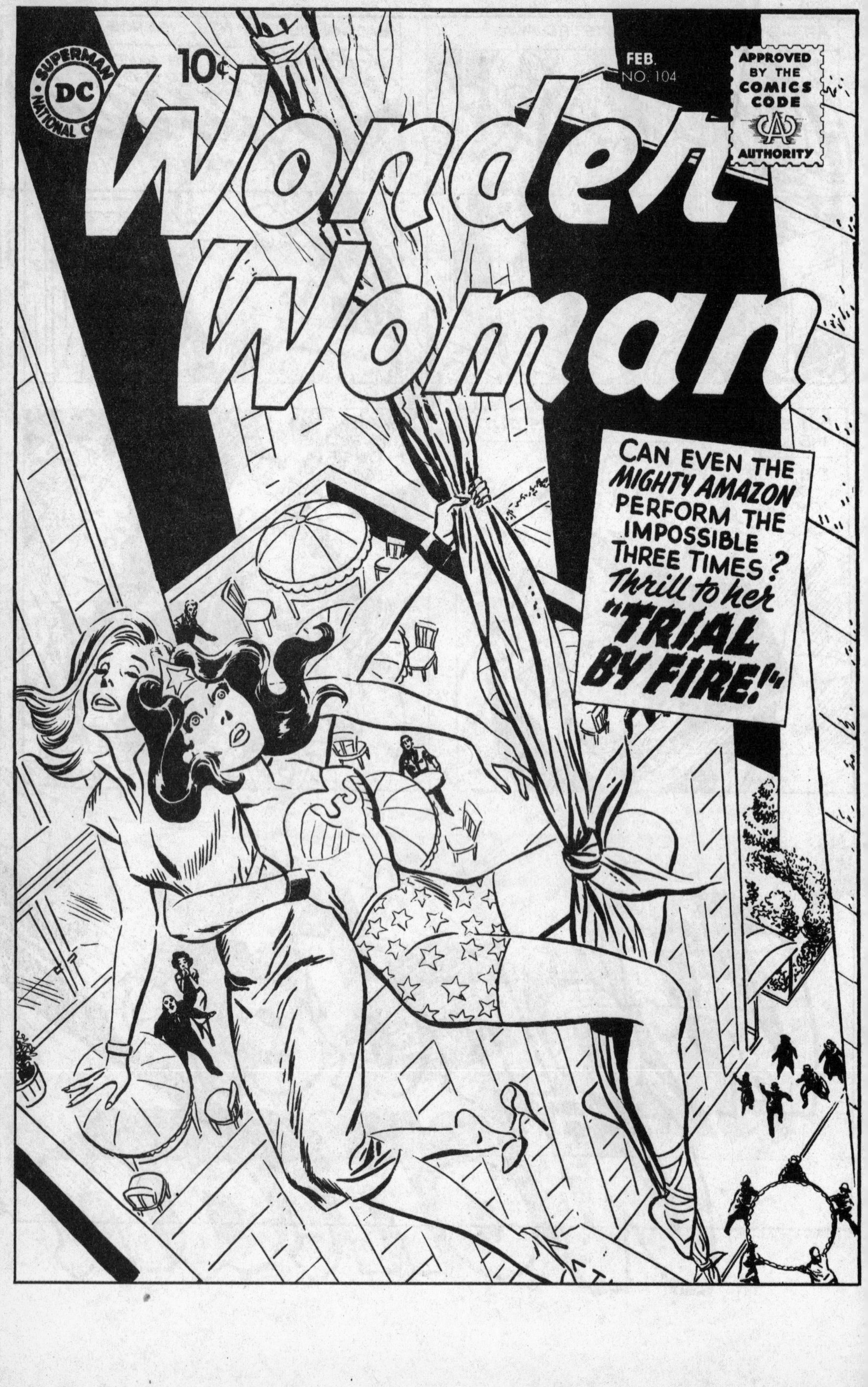

SUPERMAN DC NATIONAL COMICS
10¢
FEB.
NO. 104
APPROVED BY THE COMICS CODE AUTHORITY
Wonder Woman
CAN EVEN THE MIGHTY AMAZON PERFORM THE IMPOSSIBLE THREE TIMES? Thrill to her "TRIAL BY FIRE!"

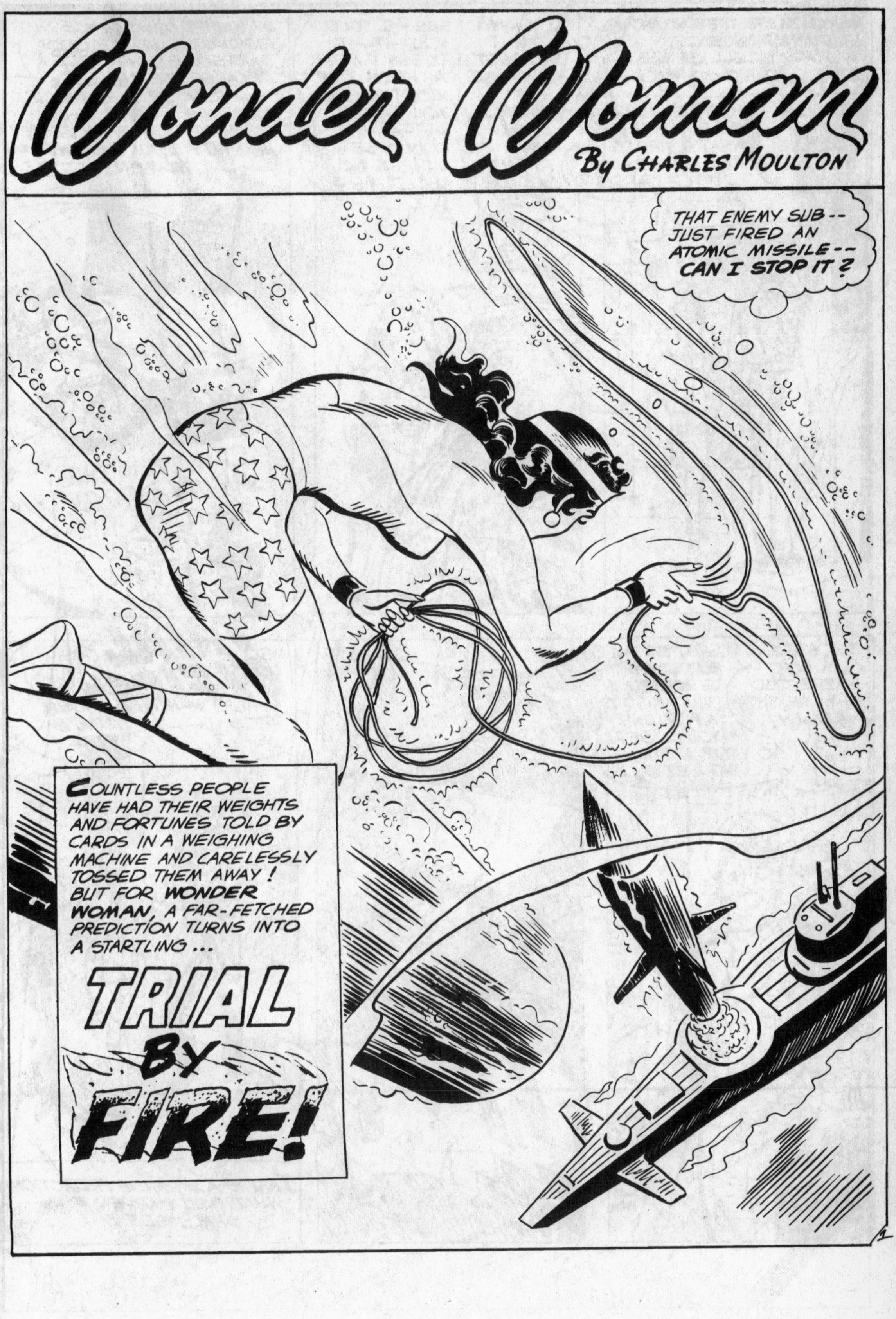
Wonder Woman
By CHARLES MOULTON
THAT ENEMY SUB-- JUST FIRED AN ATOMIC MISSILE-- CAN I STOP IT?
COUNTLESS PEOPLE HAVE HAD THEIR WEIGHTS AND FORTUNES TOLD BY CARDS IN A WEIGHING MACHINE AND CARELESSLY TOSSED THEM AWAY! BUT FOR WONDER WOMAN, A FAR-FETCHED PREDICTION TURNS INTO A STARTLING ...
TRIAL BY FIRE!

As COL. STEVE TREVOR AND LT. DIANA PRINCE OF MILITARY INTELLIGENCE STOP AT A WEIGHING MACHINE...

WONDER WHAT MY FORTUNE WILL BE?

OH, STEVE--SURELY YOU DON'T BELIEVE WHAT'S WRITTEN ON THESE SILLY LITTLE CARDS?

IT SAYS: THE BIGGEST SURPRISE OF YOUR LIFE IS RIGHT BESIDE YOU!

SEE? I TOLD YOU--IT--IT DOESN'T MEAN A THING! I'M RIGHT BESIDE YOU--AND WHAT--WHAT COULD BE SURPRISING ABOUT ME?

BY SHEER COINCIDENCE THAT RIDICULOUS LITTLE CARD SAID SOMETHING TRUE! BECAUSE THE BIGGEST SURPRISE OF STEVE'S LIFE IS AT HIS SIDE IF HE DISCOVERED THAT IN MY SECRET IDENTITY I AM WONDER WOMAN!

BUT, STEVE-- I'M NOT INTERESTED IN MY WEIGHT-- REALLY!

NEITHER AM I! BUT I AM INTERESTED IN WHAT KIND OF A FORTUNE YOU'LL GET! SO STOP ARGUING AND GET ON!

ZZING!

WELL-- DON'T KEEP ME IN SUSPENSE! WHAT DOES IT SAY?

OH--SOMETHING SILLY! TODAY WILL BE YOUR TRIAL BY FIRE!

THAT IS A STRANGE PREDICTION! WHAT WILL HAPPEN? WE SHALL SEE...

2

As THE COUPLE JEEPS BACK TOWARDS MILITARY INTELLIGENCE...

MAYBE A *FIRE* WILL BREAK OUT IN ONE OF THOSE BUILDINGS AND YOU'LL RESCUE SOME-ONE, DI ? THAT WILL BE YOUR *TRIAL BY FIRE!*

DON'T BE RIDICULOUS, STEVE ! I'M NOT A *FIREMAN!* AND THERE'S NO FIRE BREAKING OUT ANYWHERE !

LOOK ! A *FIRE SALE!* MAYBE *THAT'S* WHERE YOU'RE GOING TO HAVE YOUR TRIAL ? PICKING UP A BARGAIN !

VERY FUNNY, STEVE ! REMIND ME TO LAUGH !

FIRE SALE

JUST THEN, SHOTS ARE HEARD FROM INSIDE THE STORE AND...

GUNMEN--! GET OUT OF THE JEEP, DI ! I'M GOING TO TACKLE THEM !

POW! POW! POW!

SALE

FIRE SA

AS STEVE HEADS FOR THE GUNMEN, DIANA LIGHTLY LEAPS OUT OF THE JEEP, AND WHIRLING AROUND WITH SUCH INCREDIBLE SPEED THAT VIBRATIONS CONCEAL HER AS IF BY A SCREEN ...

STEVE CAN'T TACKLE THOSE THREE ARMORED KILLERS BY HIMSELF--!

VROOSH!

LIKE A HUMAN ROCKET, DI CHANGES INTO *WONDER WOMAN* JUST AS ...

SUFFERING SAPPHO ! ALL THREE HAVE JUST FIRED AT STEVE !

POW! POW!

CAN STEVE ESCAPE THE BULLETS HURT-LING AT HIM ?

3

BUT FASTER EVEN THAN THE HURTLING LEAD, *WONDER WOMAN* RACES IN FRONT OF THE BULLETS AND WITH HER BRACELETS MADE OF AMAZONIUM, HARDEST METAL KNOWN...

SHE'S BOUNCED OUR GUNS OUT'VE OUR HANDS!

SPANG!

BLANG!

WITH OUR OWN BULLETS!

SPAANG!

W-W-WE-- S-SURRENDER!

AS THE FLABBERGASTED GUNMEN ARE LED AWAY...

THIS *IS* A SURPRISE, ANGEL! ONE THAT PROBABLY SAVED MY LIFE! WONDER WHAT HAPPENED TO DI? PROBABLY WENT FOR HELP!

THE *REAL* SURPRISE WOULD BE IF HE KNEW WHO I *REALLY* AM!

OH, THIS WAS JUST A COINCIDENCE! AND I'D HARDLY CALL CAPTURING GUNMEN AT A *FIRE SALE*-- A TRIAL BY FIRE!

AS STEVE LOOKS FOR DIANA... *WONDER WOMAN* SEIZES THE OPPORTUNITY TO CHANGE BACK INTO HER OTHER IDENTITY AGAIN... AND...

OH, THERE YOU ARE, DI! I GUESS *WONDER WOMAN* MUST HAVE TOLD YOU WHAT HAPPENED-- BEFORE SHE WENT ON HER WAY AGAIN!

THE COUPLE CONTINUES TO ITS DESTINATION AGAIN...

WELL, DI-- MAYBE THAT WASN'T YOUR *TRIAL BY FIRE*-- BUT SOMETHING ELSE MIGHT BE!

NONSENSE, STEVE! ANYMORE THAN THE *BIGGEST SURPRISE* OF YOUR LIFE IS *RIGHT BESIDE YOU!*

What will happen next?

4

SHORTLY PASSING THE YARD OF AN EXPLOSIVES WORKS, THE TWO ARE STARTLED BY...

LOOK AT THAT GIANT FIRECRACKER!

IT MUST BE FOR EXPERIMENTAL PURPOSES!

JUST THEN...

THAT FIRECRACKER IS GOING TO GO OFF ANY SECOND--!

SOMETHING'S GONE WRONG WITH THE FUSE!

MAYBE I CAN HELP! I KNOW SOMETHING OF ANTI-DEMOLITIONS! BETTER STAY BACK HERE, DI!

EVEN AS STEVE DISAPPEARS, DIANA MAKES A LIGHTNING CHANGE BACK INTO WONDER WOMAN...

I'D BETTER GO ALONG--JUST IN CASE MY HELP'S NEEDED!

GREAT HERA! THAT GIANT FIRECRACKER IS GOING TO EXPLODE BEFORE STEVE HAS HAD A CHANCE TO DISMANTLE IT!

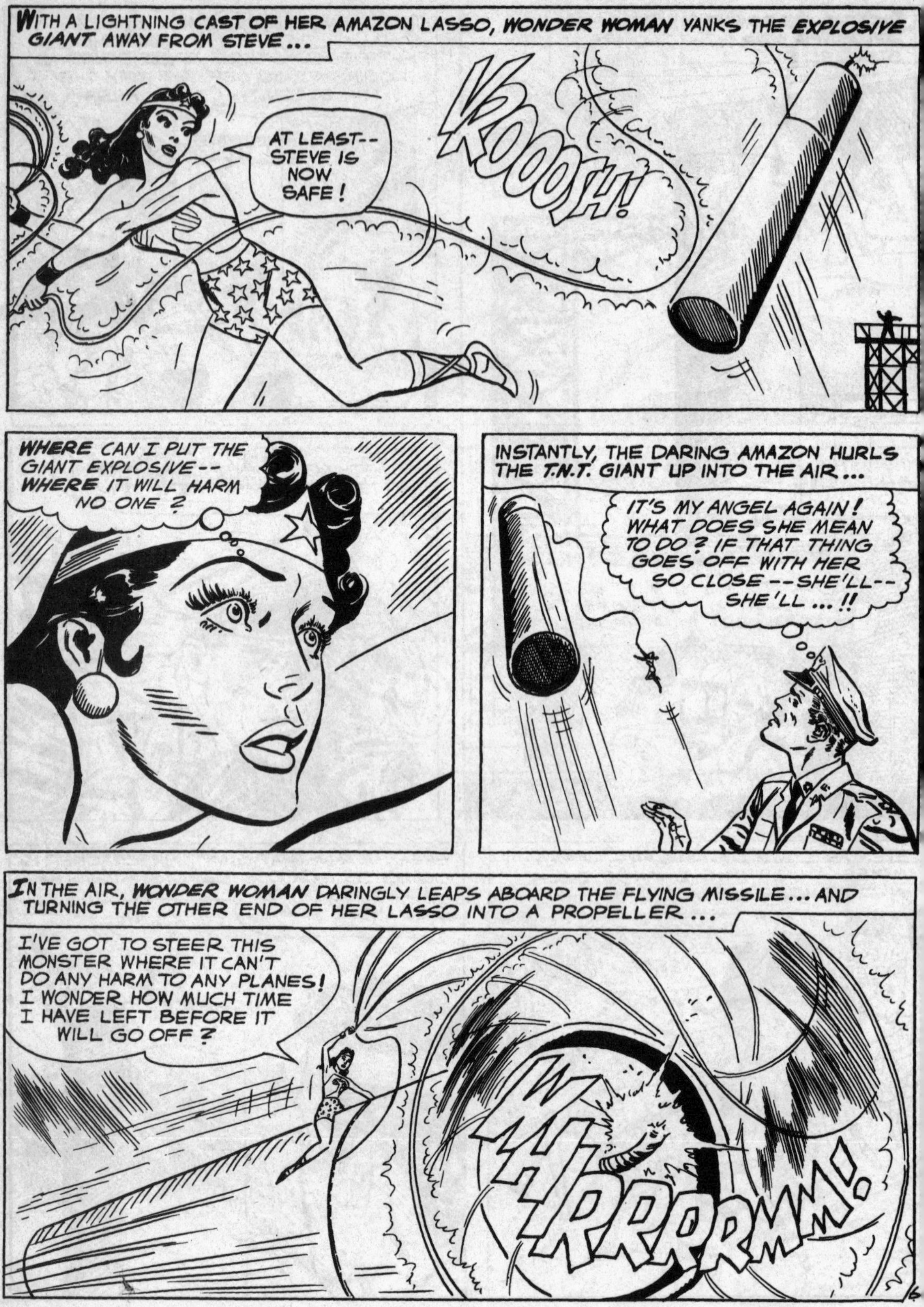
WITH A LIGHTNING CAST OF HER AMAZON LASSO, WONDER WOMAN YANKS THE EXPLOSIVE GIANT AWAY FROM STEVE...
AT LEAST-- STEVE IS NOW SAFE!
KOOOSH!
WHERE CAN I PUT THE GIANT EXPLOSIVE-- WHERE IT WILL HARM NO ONE?
INSTANTLY, THE DARING AMAZON HURLS THE T.N.T. GIANT UP INTO THE AIR...
IT'S MY ANGEL AGAIN! WHAT DOES SHE MEAN TO DO? IF THAT THING GOES OFF WITH HER SO CLOSE--SHE'LL-- SHE'LL...!!
IN THE AIR, WONDER WOMAN DARINGLY LEAPS ABOARD THE FLYING MISSILE... AND TURNING THE OTHER END OF HER LASSO INTO A PROPELLER...
I'VE GOT TO STEER THIS MONSTER WHERE IT CAN'T DO ANY HARM TO ANY PLANES! I WONDER HOW MUCH TIME I HAVE LEFT BEFORE IT WILL GO OFF?
WHRRRRMM!
6

JUST THEN...LOOMING AHEAD OF HER...

MERCIFUL MINERVA! PLANE COMING! HAVE TO GET OUT OF THE WAY!

BRRRRMMM!

205

INSTANTLY, THE DAUNTLESS AMAZON MANEUVERS HER "FLYING STEED" DOWNWARD...

I'LL LET IT EXPLODE IN THE WATER--

INGENIOUSLY, SHE TURNS THE FLYING MISSILE INTO AN UNDERSEA ONE...

--WHERE IT WON'T HARM ANYONE!

SPLASH!

BUT A MOCKING FATE HAS NOT DONE WITH WONDER WOMAN... BECAUSE IN THE DEPTHS AHEAD OF HER...A SUB!

I'VE GOT TO KEEP STEERING OUT OF ITS WAY TOO!

BUT THE NEXT MOMENT, TO *WONDER WOMAN'S* HORROR.

THUNDERBOLTS OF JOVE! THAT'S AN *ENEMY* SUB! IT JUST FIRED AN ATOMIC MISSILE UP TOWARDS THE SURFACE!

WHOOOSH!

WITH A DESPERATE LUNGE, THE MIGHTY AMAZON HURLS THE DYNAMITE-LADEN STEED SHE IS RIDING--TOWARDS THE ONCOMING PROJECTILE ...

WILL I BE IN TIME TO STOP IT-- *BEFORE* IT UNLEASHES DESTRUCTION?

The unexpected *T.N.T.* thrills of *"TRIAL BY FIRE"* continues on the page following...

Wonder Woman

Wonder Woman
By Charles Moulton
TRIAL BY FIRE!

PART II -- THE SINISTER CARNIVAL!

A SIMPLE LITTLE FORTUNE-TELLING CARD IN A WEIGHING MACHINE HAS STARTED WONDER WOMAN OFF ON ONE STARTLING ADVENTURE AFTER ANOTHER--AND AT THIS VERY MOMENT..

WAS I TOO LATE--

TO-- STOP--

THE ATOMIC MISSILE. THE ENEMY SUB HAD FIRED--?

THE THUNDERING ROAR WHEN THE GIANT FIRECRACKER THE MIGHTY AMAZON HAD HURLED AT THE ENEMY ATOMIC MISSILE--IS THE ANSWER ...

KROOOM!

THE TIRELESS AMAZON MAKES HER WAY TO THE SURFACE...

HOW IRONICAL! THE ENEMY SUB WAS DESTROYED BEFORE IT COULD CAUSE HARM TO INNOCENT PEOPLE-- BY THE PREMATURE EXPLOSION OF ITS OWN ATOMIC MISSILE!

ANYWAY-- AT LEAST THAT'S THE LAST OF MY HAVING ANYTHING THE SLIGHTEST TO DO WITH ANY *TRIALS BY FIRE!*

BUT, AS SHE LOOKS OUT TOWARDS SEA, *WONDER WOMAN'S* PIERCING AMAZON VISION DETECTS ...

SHADES OF PLUTO! TWO *FIREBOATS* ARE STARTING TO BLAZE FROM THE SHIP FIRE THEY'RE TRYING TO PUT OUT! GUESS THEY SIMPLY CAN'T PUMP ENOUGH WATER FAST ENOUGH TO PUT OUT THE FIRE!

THOSE CLOUDS MIGHT PROVIDE THE ANSWER-- IF I CAN GET ENOUGH SILVER IODIDE!

AT INDESCRIBABLE SPEED, THE MIGHTY AMAZON WHIRLS AROUND IN THE WATER UNTIL SHE CREATES AN IRRESISTIBLE SUCTION ...

I'M PULLING THE SEAWATER UP *AFTER* ME-- AT LEAST THE FIRST PART OF MY TASK IS FINISHED! NOW-- FOR THE SECOND!

WROOOSH!

WHAT DOES *WONDER WOMAN* HOPE TO ACCOMPLISH?

DRAWING THE HUGE FUNNEL OF SEA-WATER AFTER HER, *WONDER WOMAN* PIERCES THE CLOUDS...

I'VE SEEDED THE CLOUDS WITH THE SILVER IODIDE IN THE SEAWATER-- WILL MY PLAN WORK?

INSTANTLY, THE AMAZING TRANSFORMATION TAKES PLACE, AND FROM THE DESPERATE CREWS BELOW IN THE BURNING FIRE-BOATS...A CHEER ARISES AS...

RAIN! A CLOUDBURST OF IT--JUST WHAT WE NEEDED TO BLANKET THIS BLAZE!

FUNNY-- A MOMENT AGO--IT DIDN'T SEEM LIKE IT WOULD RAIN FOR A YEAR!

MEANWHILE, OUT OF SIGHT AND SOUND, THE TIRELESS AMAZON CONTINUES ON HER WAY...

FIRE SALES--*FIRECRACKER--FIREBOATS--*THAT SHOULD BE THE LAST!

CHANGING BACK TO HER OTHER IDENTITY, DIANA SETS OUT TO MEET STEVE AGAIN...

NOW-- ALL I HAVE TO DO IS KEEP STEVE FROM FINDING OUT MY DUAL IDENTITY!

BUT IS THAT ALL? HAS THE AMAZON'S TRIAL BY FIRE ENDED?

3

PICKING UP STEVE AGAIN AT THE EXPLOSIVES FACTORY...

YOU SHOULD HAVE SEEN *WONDER WOMAN* IN ACTION, DI !

HOW COULD I--IF YOU ALWAYS SEND ME OUT OF HARM'S WAY EVERY TIME SOMETHING DANGEROUS THREATENS !

WELL, DI--AFTER ALL-- YOU ARE NO *WONDER WOMAN*, NOW, ARE YOU ?

EVEN THOUGH *WONDER WOMAN* IS MY FRIEND, STEVE--LET'S STOP TALKING ABOUT HER !

LET'S TALK ABOUT WHAT KIND OF *TRIAL BY FIRE*-- YOU'RE GOING TO HAVE NEXT ?

STOP TALKING NON-- SENSE, STEVE ! THERE'S NOTHING IN THOSE CARDS !... OH, LOOK--A FLEA CIRCUS ! LET'S GO IN !

FLEA CIRCUS

Tickets

GO RIGHT ON IN, FOLKS ! I'LL PUT ON A SPECIAL SHOW--JUST FOR THE TWO OF YOU !

FLE

AS THE COUPLE PASSES THROUGH THE STRANGE LIGHT SHINING DOWN AT THEM...

WHAT'S HAPPENING ?

WE'RE SHRINKING !

THAT LIGHT-- HAS REDUCED US TO A-- A--FRACTION OF AN INCH !

THE NEXT MOMENT, THE MINIATURE FIGURES ARE PICKED UP BY THE GIANT HAND OF THE TICKET SELLER...

NOW--AT LAST-- I WILL HAVE AN ACT-- THE GREATEST IN THE WORLD!

MY REDUCING RAY HAS CHANGED YOU INTO A SIZE FAR SMALLER THAN YOUR OPPONENT-- WHO WILL COME OUT TO MEET YOU IN ONE SECOND!

AND THEN--DWARFING THEM--BLINDING THEM WITH ITS LIGHT...

A FIREFLY! GET BACK, DI--MAYBE I CAN HOLD IT OFF--WHILE YOU CLIMB OUT OF THIS BOX!

SWIFTER THAN A HUMAN EYE CAN FOLLOW, DI MAKES A LIGHTNING CHANGE INTO HER AMAZON IDENTITY...

ANOTHER UNEXPECTED TRIAL BY FIRE -- THE STRANGEST ONE YET!

DI--DI-- SAVE YOUR-SELF--!

MERCIFUL MINERVA-- THE MONSTER HAS KNOCKED STEVE OFF HIS FEET!

WITH AN UNERRING CAST OF HER AMAZON LASSO, **WONDER WOMAN** PULLS THE GIANT FIREFLY AWAY FROM STEVE ...

THANK HERA-- STEVE IS OUT OF DANGER!

BOUNDING ONTO THE BLINKING GIANT...

THIS IS THE STRANGEST STEED I'VE EVER TRIED TO RIDE!

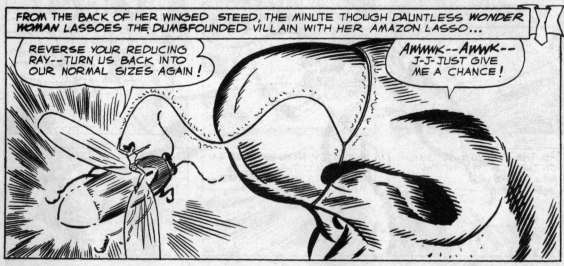

FROM THE BACK OF HER WINGED STEED, THE MINUTE THOUGH DAUNTLESS **WONDER WOMAN** LASSOES THE DUMBFOUNDED VILLAIN WITH HER AMAZON LASSO...

REVERSE YOUR REDUCING RAY--TURN US BACK INTO OUR NORMAL SIZES AGAIN!

AWWWK--AWWK-- J-J-JUST GIVE ME A CHANCE!

A MOMENT LATER...THE RAY IS REVERSED AND...

WE'RE BEING CHANGED BACK TO OUR OWN SIZES AGAIN!

NOW--I'VE GOT TO CHANGE BACK TO **DIANA**...

--BEFORE STEVE BECOMES SUSPICIOUS!

WITH THE VILLAIN HANDED OVER TO THE POLICE, STEVE AND DI CONTINUE ON THEIR WAY...

WELL--THE DAY IS ALMOST DONE! GUESS THAT FORTUNE-TELLING CARD WAS WRONG AFTER ALL-- SAYING YOU WERE GOING TO HAVE A *TRIAL BY FIRE*, DI!

I TOLD YOU IT WAS NONSENSE!

BUT, UPON ROUNDING THE NEXT CORNER...

HELP!

FIRE-- I'D BETTER HELP!

BEFORE STEVE HAS GONE FAR...DIANA HAS MADE A LIGHTNING SWITCH INTO HER SECRET IDENTITY OF *WONDER WOMAN*, EVEN AS SHE LEAPS STRAIGHT FOR THE BURNING APARTMENT...

HERE'S MY *TRIAL BY FIRE* AT LAST! BUT IT DOESN'T LOOK LIKE MUCH OF A TRIAL--BUT A SIMPLE RESCUE--WITH MY AMAZON LASSO!

AS THE AMAZON ALIGHTS ON THE LOFTY WINDOW SILL HOWEVER...

MY LASSO-- FALLEN!

INSTANTLY, *WONDER WOMAN* KNOTS ALL THE SHEETS SHE FINDS IN THE APARTMENT...

THIS IS THE ONLY WAY TO GET DOWN-- THE STAIRWAY IS BLOCKED!

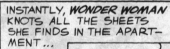

FLAMES GREEDILY LICK AT THE SHEETS AND...

THANK HERA! THE GIRL HAS FAINTED-- SHE DOESN'T KNOW WHAT HAS HAPPENED!

BUT FIREMEN HAVE COME UP WITH THEIR EQUIPMENT, AND THEY HOLD OUT THE LIFE-NET JUST IN TIME AS...

I KNEW I COULD COUNT ON THE FIRE DEPARTMENT!

SHORTLY, AS THE FIRE IS BROUGHT UNDER CONTROL...

FUNNY-- *YOU'RE* ALWAYS PERFORMING THE *TRIAL BY FIRE* THAT DIANA PRINCE IS SUPPOSED TO BE DOING TODAY! I WONDER WHAT THAT MEANS?

GREAT HERA! HE'S BEGINNING TO PUT TWO AND TWO TOGETHER-- AND GUESS MY DUAL IDENTITY! UNLESS I CAN DIVERT HIM SOME-HOW!

316

WHY-- WHAT *ELSE* CAN IT MEAN BUT THAT *THAT'S* THE BIGGEST SURPRISE AT YOUR SIDE--THAT *I'M* DOING IT INSTEAD OF DI!

OF COURSE-- OF COURSE, ANGEL--TRUST YOU TO THINK UP THE RIGHT ANSWER!

The End 8

Wonder Woman

By Charles Moulton

THERE WAS ONLY ONE MIGHTY BEING WHO CONSTANTLY THWARTED THE MARTIAN MASTER OF MENACE'S INVASION PLANS AGAINST THE EARTH -- *WONDER WOMAN!* AND SO, WONDER WOMAN -- BEAUTIFUL AS APHRODITE, WISE AS ATHENA, SWIFTER THAN MERCURY, AND STRONGER THAN HERCULES -- FOUND HERSELF IN THE MOST STARTLING TRAP OF HER CAREER, WITH THE FUTURE OF EARTH AT STAKE THE MOMENT SHE TURNED THE...

KEY OF DECEPTION!

ON THE PLANET MARS, A TREMENDOUS SPACESHIP POINTS LIKE AN ARROW OF DOOM AT THE UNSUSPECTING EARTH...

I WILL COMMAND THE SHIP!

NO--*I* WILL!

I AM BETTER FITTED THAN ALL OF YOU--AM I NOT, *DUKE DECEPTION*?

THE MARTIAN VILLAIN GRINS DIABOLICALLY...

THE ONE WHO SHOULD *LEAD* THIS INVASION AGAINST THE EARTH -- SHOULD BE THE ONLY ONE WHO UNTIL NOW--HAS *STOPPED* US-- *WONDER WOMAN!*

HOW IS THAT POSSIBLE, DUKE? EVEN YOU --WITH ALL YOUR MIGHTY POWERS OF DECEPTION COULDN'T ACCOMPLISH THAT STAGGERING FEAT!

NO--? WE SHALL SEE! MY SCHEME IS ALREADY IN MOTION! *WONDER WOMAN* IS WALKING INTO MY TRAP AT THIS VERY MOMENT!

MEANWHILE, ON EARTH, *WONDER WOMAN* AND STEVE OBSERVE...

THERE'S THE BIGGEST EARTH SATELLITE WE'VE LAUNCHED YET!

AT 18,000 MILES PER HOUR--IT WOULD GO THROUGH ANYTHING IN ITS PATH!

LATER, AN UNWARY *WONDER WOMAN* STOPS AT A CHARITY BOOTH WITH HER SWEETHEART, COL. STEVE TREVOR...

THANK YOU, *WONDER WOMAN!* EVERYONE WHO HAS CONTRIBUTED TO THIS CHARITY RECEIVES A KEY! ONLY *ONE* FITS THAT TREASURE CHEST! OPEN IT--AND THE FORTUNE INSIDE IS YOURS!

THAT PERSON'S KEY DIDN'T WORK!

I HOPE MINE DOES--SO I CAN GIVE THE TREASURE RIGHT BACK TO CHARITY!

KEY AFTER KEY IS TRIED... AND NONE FITS ... AND THEN...

TURN THE KEY WITH ME, STEVE-- FOR GOOD LUCK!

HOLDING YOUR HAND IS GOOD ENOUGH LUCK FOR ME, ANGEL!

SLOWLY THE KEY IS IN- SERTED...AND AS THE LOVELY AMAZON HOLDS HER BREATH...

STEVE--IT'S--IT'S TURNING THE LOCK-- THE KEY FITS-- *THE KEY FITS!*

AND THEN--BEFORE THE HORRIFIED EYES OF THE SPECTATORS...

LOOK-- THEY-- THEY'RE-- *WONDER WOMAN* AND STEVE!

GONE-- VANISHED!

IN THE NEXT INSTANT... ANOTHER ASTONISHING SURPRISE ...

THE TICKET BOOTH-- AND THE SELLER--!

GONE TOO! IT WAS ALL A DECEPTION!

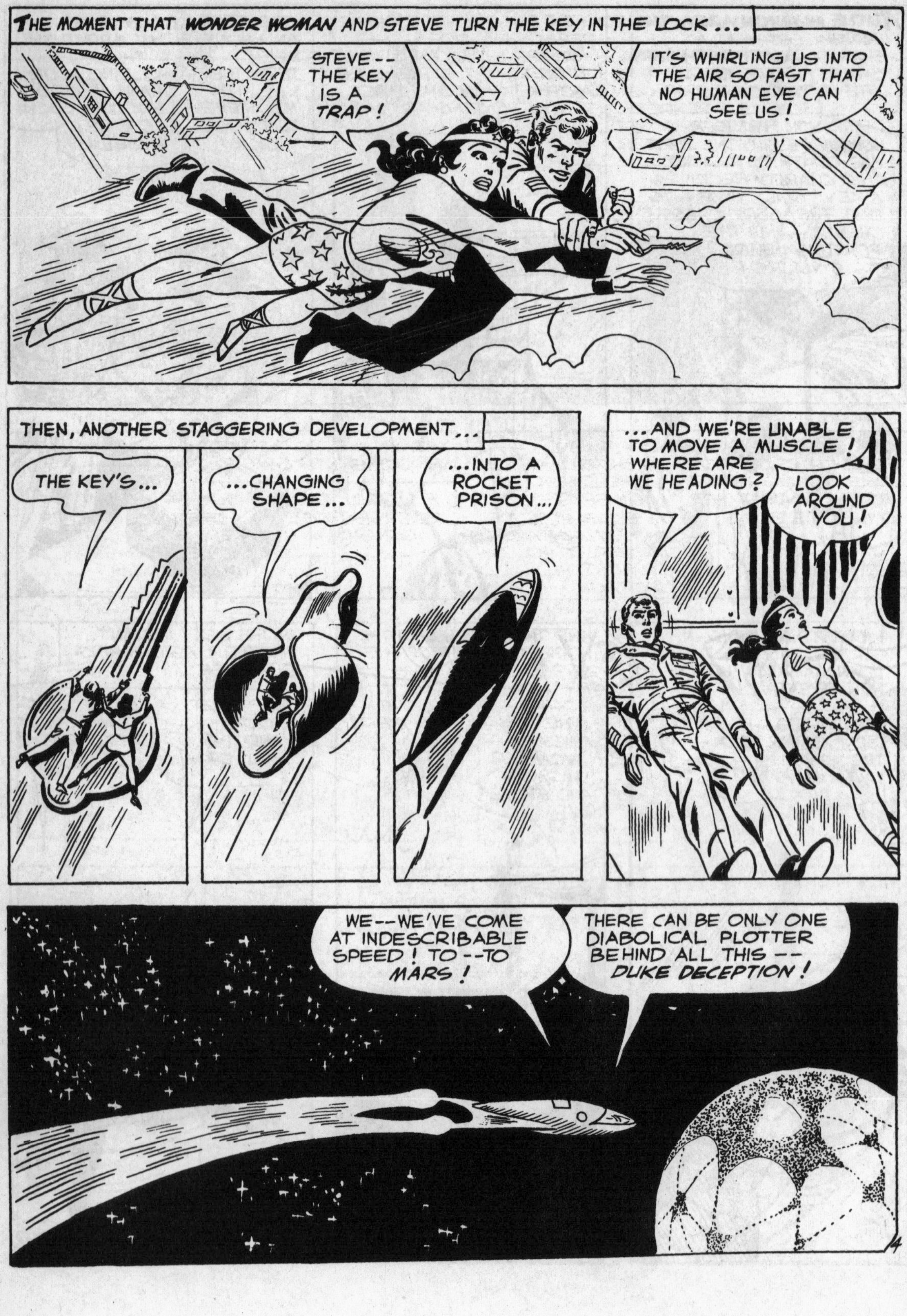
THE MOMENT THAT WONDER WOMAN AND STEVE TURN THE KEY IN THE LOCK...
STEVE-- THE KEY IS A TRAP!
IT'S WHIRLING US INTO THE AIR SO FAST THAT NO HUMAN EYE CAN SEE US!
THEN, ANOTHER STAGGERING DEVELOPMENT...
THE KEY'S...
...CHANGING SHAPE...
...INTO A ROCKET PRISON...
...AND WE'RE UNABLE TO MOVE A MUSCLE! WHERE ARE WE HEADING?
LOOK AROUND YOU!
WE--WE'VE COME AT INDESCRIBABLE SPEED! TO--TO MARS!
THERE CAN BE ONLY ONE DIABOLICAL PLOTTER BEHIND ALL THIS -- DUKE DECEPTION!
4

AT THE INVASION AREA, THE ROCKET PRISON LANDS...

WONDER WOMAN -- YOU ARE GOING TO LEAD OUR INVASION FLEET AGAINST YOUR OWN EARTH -- WHILE I RENDEZVOUS WITH FLEETS FROM SATURN AND JUPITER!

THE NEXT MOMENT...

WE'VE BEEN SENT OFF!

HOW CAN WE STOP THIS?

YOUR GREATEST MASTER-PIECE OF DECEPTION, DUKE -- USING WONDER WOMAN AGAINST HER OWN HOME PLANET!

AYE! AND SHORTLY, WE'LL RENDEZVOUS IN SPACE WITH THE FLEETS OF SATURN AND JUPITER TO FOLLOW HER FOR THE ATTACK!

MEANWHILE, AS THE ANGUISHED PAIR ROCKETS INTO SPACE ...

IF I COULD ONLY REVERSE THOSE CONTROLS--!

BUT HOW, WONDER WOMAN? SOMETHING IN THOSE VERY SAME CONTROLS IS KEEPING US IMMOBILIZED!

WITH ALL HER STRENGTH...

MY ONLY CHANCE--

THE MIGHTY AMAZON SQUEEZES HER WRISTS...

--IS TO CON-TRACT MY WRISTS--

-- UNTIL MY BRACELETS ARE LOOSE!

5

WONDER WOMAN'S ASTONISHING AGILITY ENABLES HER TO FLIP HER BRACELETS OFF HER CONTRACTED WRISTS -- AT THE CONTROLS...

SPLANG!

THE NEXT MOMENT...

YOU'VE DONE IT, ANGEL! RELEASED THE CONTROLS WHICH IMMOBILIZED US!

BUT OUR JOB HAS ONLY *JUST* BEGUN, STEVE!

NOW WE HAVE TO STOP THE INVASION FLEETS! FIRST-- TO PLUTO!

THE MARTIAN PRISON ROCKET BECOMES A BLUR OF SPEED THROUGH SPACE UNTIL WITH MIND-STAGGERING SPEED...

PLUTO!

THEIR INVASION FLEET HAS ALREADY STARTED OUT!

THE NEXT MOMENT, THE TWO ARE RINGED WITH FLASHING RAYS...

THEY'VE OPENED FIRE!

THEY'VE SPOTTED US!

OUT THROUGH A HATCH INTO OUTER SPACE THE DAUNTLESS AMAZON CLIMBS...

ONLY A QUESTION OF TIME BEFORE ONE OF THOSE RAYS SMASHES THIS SHIP!

WITH A LIGHTNING CAST OF HER UNIQUE LASSO...

CAN'T AFFORD TO MISS!

AROUND AND AROUND *WONDER WOMAN* WHIRLS THE CAPTURED INVASION CRAFT--AND THEN--LIKE A GIGANTIC BOLO ...

BACK INTO HER SPACE CRAFT, THE INDOMITABLE AMAZON RETURNS...

YOU'VE STOPPED THEM!

BUT THEY'RE ONLY ONE-THIRD OF THE INVASION FLEETS! SATURN AND MARS *STILL* MENACE THE EARTH!

ANOTHER FLASHING RACE THROUGH SPACE BY THE TENSE PAIR ... UNTIL ...

THERE'S SATURN!

THEIR FLEET HAS ALREADY LEFT TO RENDEZVOUS WITH THE MARTIANS!

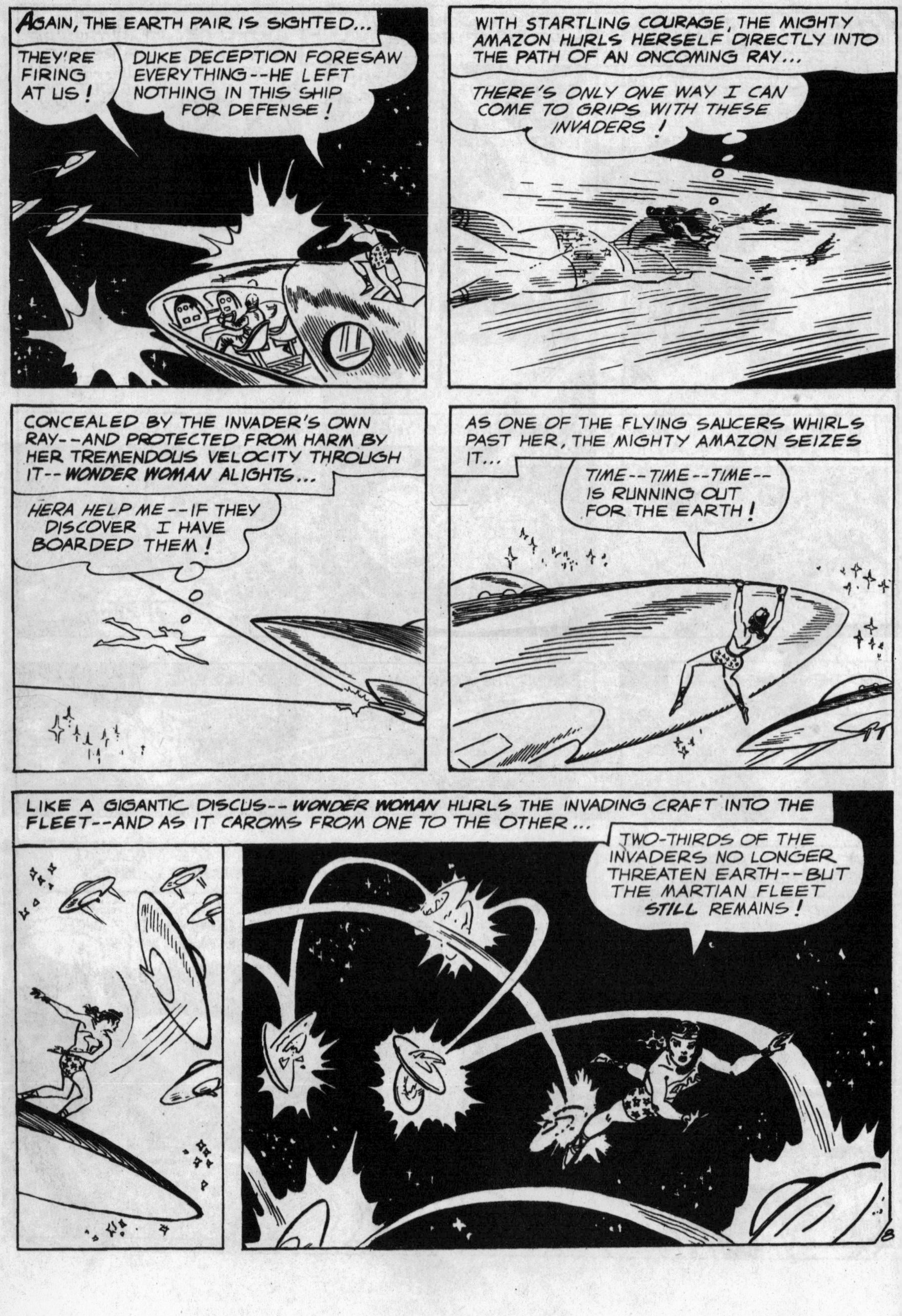
AGAIN, THE EARTH PAIR IS SIGHTED...
THEY'RE FIRING AT US!
DUKE DECEPTION FORESAW EVERYTHING--HE LEFT NOTHING IN THIS SHIP FOR DEFENSE!
WITH STARTLING COURAGE, THE MIGHTY AMAZON HURLS HERSELF DIRECTLY INTO THE PATH OF AN ONCOMING RAY...
THERE'S ONLY ONE WAY I CAN COME TO GRIPS WITH THESE INVADERS!
CONCEALED BY THE INVADER'S OWN RAY--AND PROTECTED FROM HARM BY HER TREMENDOUS VELOCITY THROUGH IT--WONDER WOMAN ALIGHTS...
HERA HELP ME--IF THEY DISCOVER I HAVE BOARDED THEM!
AS ONE OF THE FLYING SAUCERS WHIRLS PAST HER, THE MIGHTY AMAZON SEIZES IT...
TIME--TIME--TIME--IS RUNNING OUT FOR THE EARTH!
LIKE A GIGANTIC DISCUS--WONDER WOMAN HURLS THE INVADING CRAFT INTO THE FLEET--AND AS IT CAROMS FROM ONE TO THE OTHER...
TWO-THIRDS OF THE INVADERS NO LONGER THREATEN EARTH--BUT THE MARTIAN FLEET STILL REMAINS!
8

MEANWHILE, AT HIS SPACE RENDEZVOUS, AN ENRAGED DUKE DECEPTION SEES *WONDER WOMAN'S* SMALL CRAFT SPEED ACROSS HIS VISION LIKE A TINY GADFLY...

IT'S THE AMAZON! SOMEHOW SHE REVERSED THE CONTROLS! NO NEED TO KNOW NOW WHY THE OTHER INVASION FLEETS DIDN'T APPEAR! SHE MUST HAVE STOPPED THEM!

THE STUPENDOUS SHIP HURTLES AFTER THE TINY ONE...

WE'LL SMASH IT OUT OF THE WAY-- AND THEN CONTINUE ON TO DESTROY THE EARTH OURSELVES!

THEY'RE AFTER US-- NOW WHAT, ANGEL?

AS LONG AS THEY'RE PURSUING US--EARTH IS OUT OF DANGER!

AND THEN--AHEAD--A DREAD SIGHT...

A METEOR STORM--IF A SINGLE ONE OF THOSE HITS US--?!

THIS SHIP ISN'T EQUIPPED WITH METEOR BUMPERS-- I'LL HAVE TO **DODGE** THE METEORS!

BEHIND THE FRANTICALLY-- DODGING LITTLE CRAFT-- THE PURSUIT CONTINUES...

OUR BUMPERS TURN AWAY THE METEORS--BUT THE AMAZON HAS TO MIS-CALCULATE JUST *ONCE*--

--AND SHE IS FINISHED!

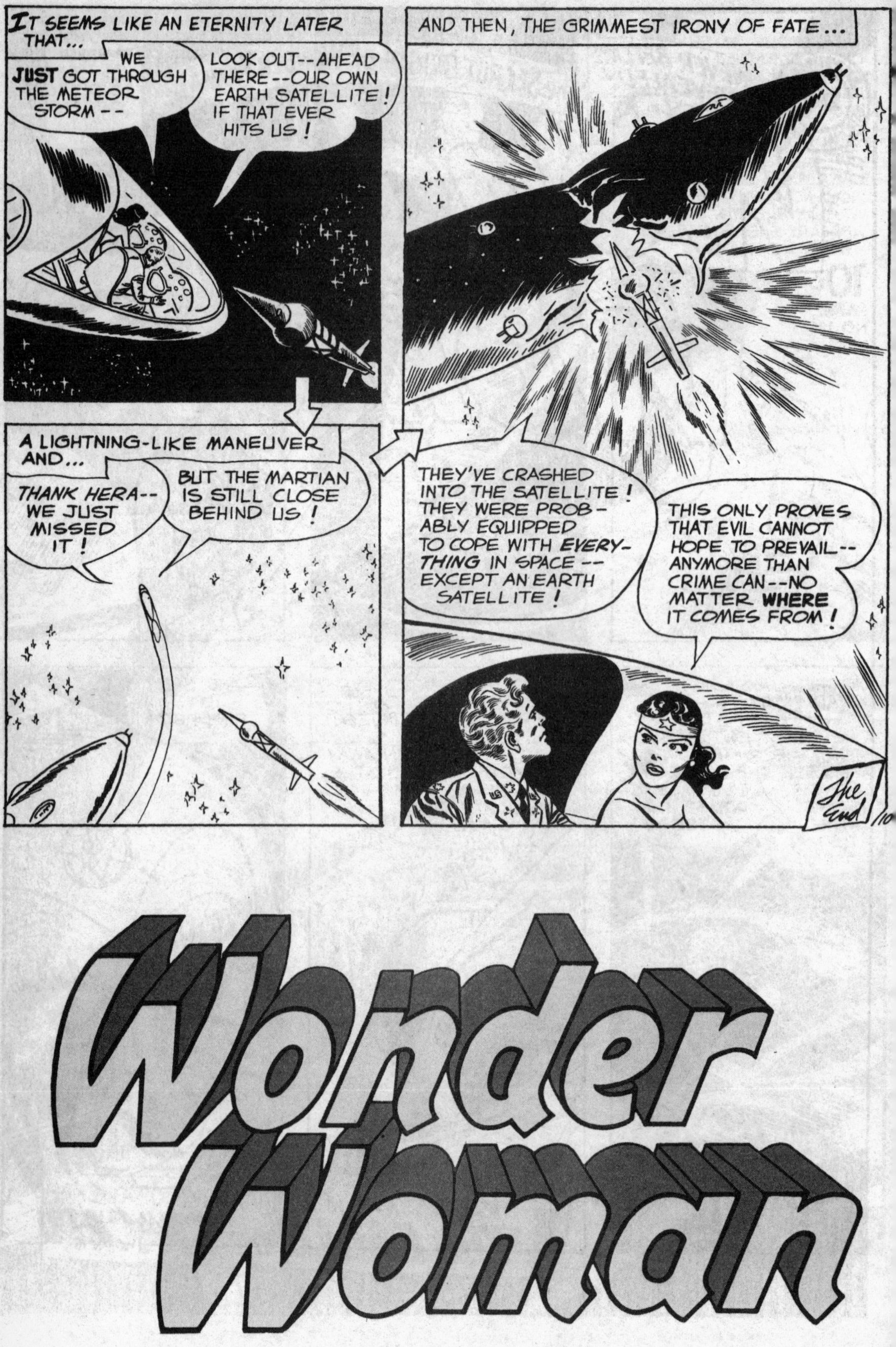
IT SEEMS LIKE AN ETERNITY LATER THAT...
WE JUST GOT THROUGH THE METEOR STORM --
LOOK OUT--AHEAD THERE--OUR OWN EARTH SATELLITE! IF THAT EVER HITS US!
AND THEN, THE GRIMMEST IRONY OF FATE...
A LIGHTNING-LIKE MANEUVER AND...
THANK HERA-- WE JUST MISSED IT!
BUT THE MARTIAN IS STILL CLOSE BEHIND US!
THEY'VE CRASHED INTO THE SATELLITE! THEY WERE PROBABLY EQUIPPED TO COPE WITH EVERYTHING IN SPACE -- EXCEPT AN EARTH SATELLITE!
THIS ONLY PROVES THAT EVIL CANNOT HOPE TO PREVAIL-- ANYMORE THAN CRIME CAN--NO MATTER WHERE IT COMES FROM!
The End
10

Wonder Woman

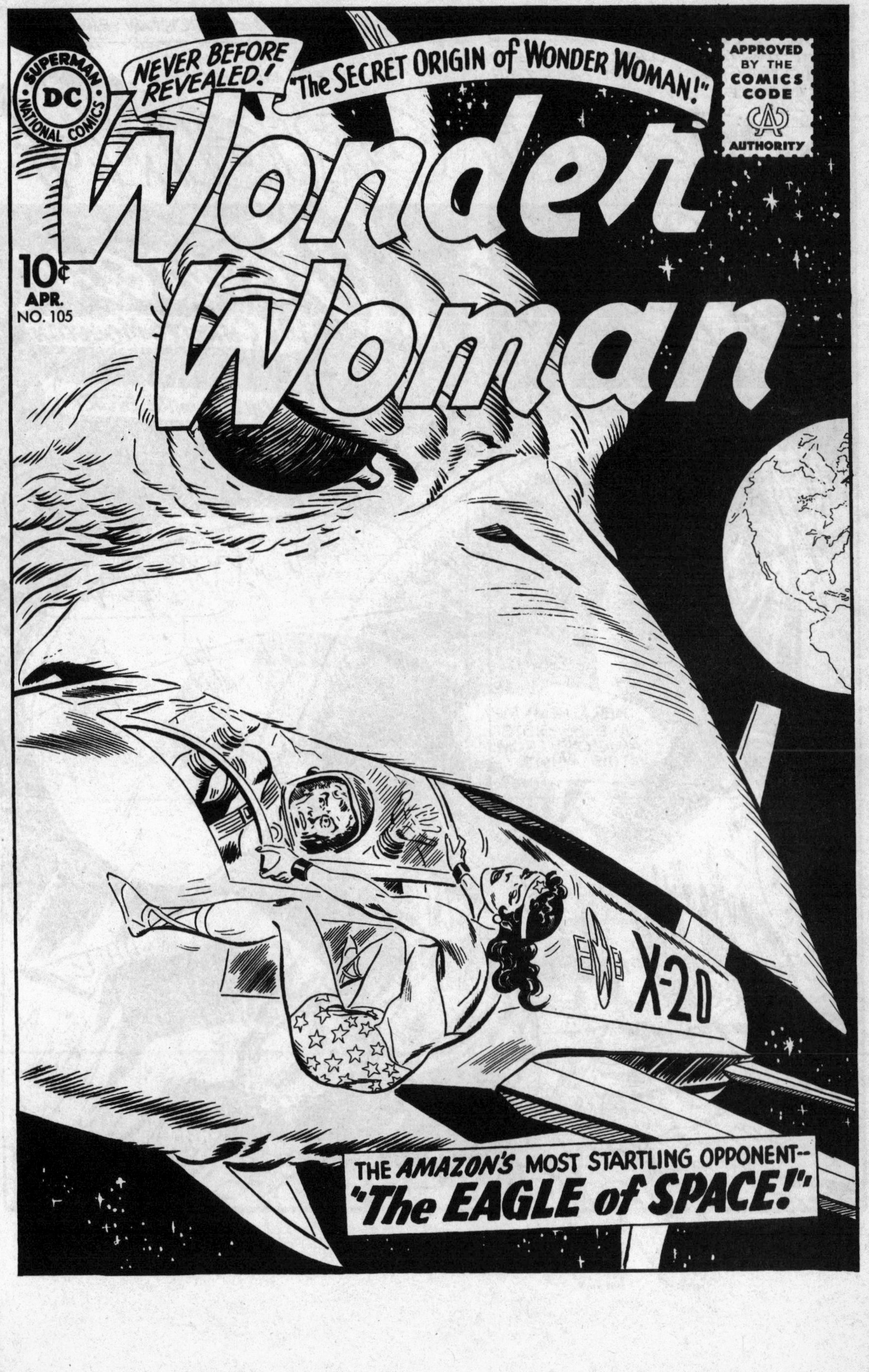
SUPERMAN DC NATIONAL COMICS
NEVER BEFORE REVEALED!
"The SECRET ORIGIN of WONDER WOMAN!"
APPROVED BY THE COMICS CODE AUTHORITY
Wonder Woman
10¢
APR.
NO. 105
X-20
THE AMAZON'S MOST STARTLING OPPONENT--
"The EAGLE of SPACE!"

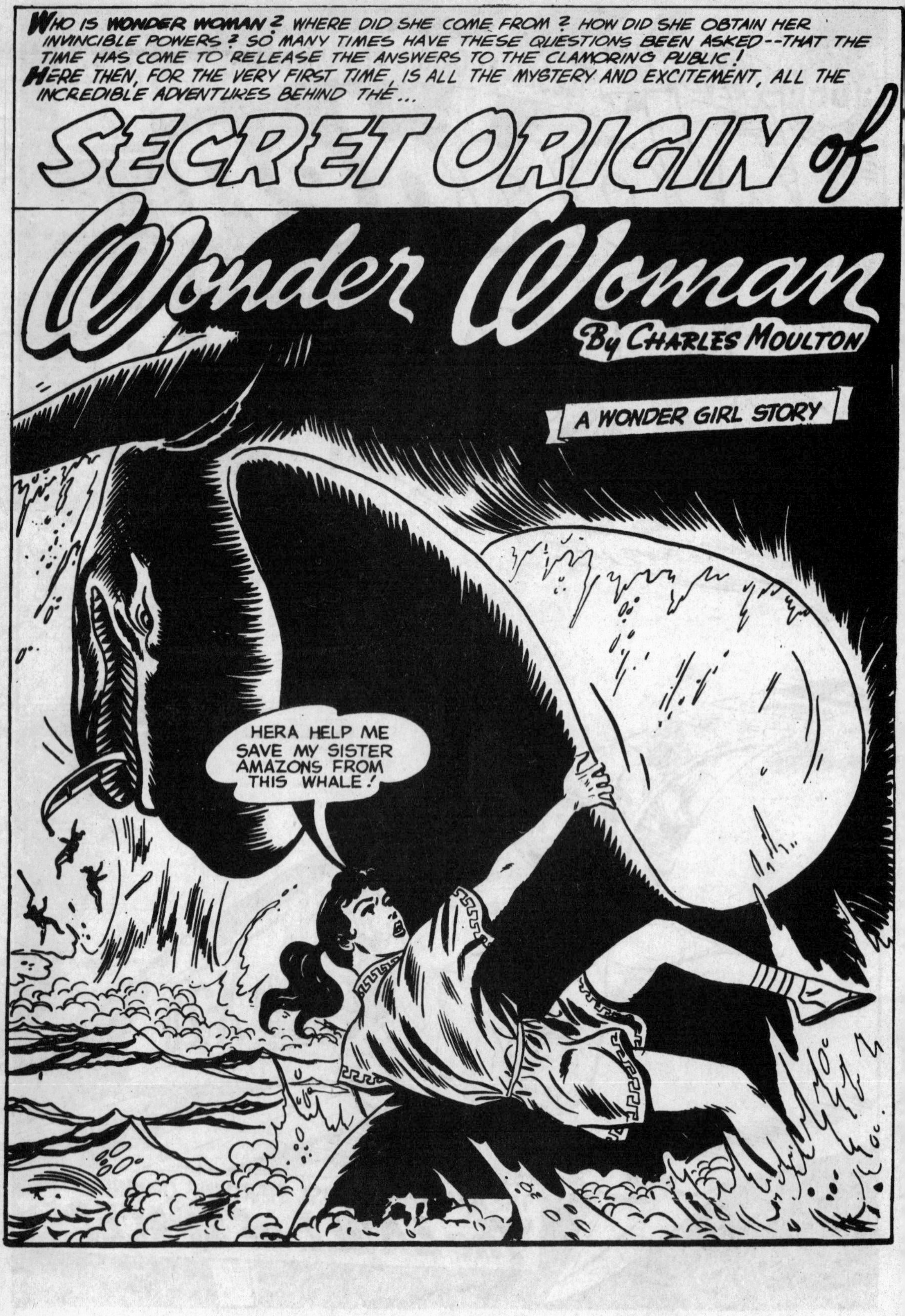
WHO IS WONDER WOMAN? WHERE DID SHE COME FROM? HOW DID SHE OBTAIN HER INVINCIBLE POWERS? SO MANY TIMES HAVE THESE QUESTIONS BEEN ASKED--THAT THE TIME HAS COME TO RELEASE THE ANSWERS TO THE CLAMORING PUBLIC!
HERE THEN, FOR THE VERY FIRST TIME, IS ALL THE MYSTERY AND EXCITEMENT, ALL THE INCREDIBLE ADVENTURES BEHIND THE...
SECRET ORIGIN of Wonder Woman
By CHARLES MOULTON
A WONDER GIRL STORY
HERA HELP ME SAVE MY SISTER AMAZONS FROM THIS WHALE!

CENTURIES AGO--TO THE ROYAL CHAMBER OF HIPPOLYTA, QUEEN OF THE AMAZONS, COMES A LEGENDARY VISITOR...

APHRODITE, GODDESS OF LOVE AND BEAUTY!

FOR YOUR MANY DEEDS OF JUSTICE, NOBLE QUEEN--I BRING A GIFT FOR YOUR INFANT DAUGHTER!

I BEQUEATH TO YOU, PRINCESS DIANA, ALL THE BEAUTY OF GOODNESS! SO THAT YOU MAY BE ONE OF THE FAIREST OF MAIDS THROUGHOUT THE WORLD!

AND THEN, ANOTHER PRESENCE IS FELT...

WISE ATHENA!

DID YOU THINK I WOULD ALLOW MY SISTER GODDESS APHRODITE TO BEAR A GIFT-- WHILE I COME EMPTYHANDED?

I BEQUEATH TO YOU, PRINCESS DIANA, ALL THE WISDOM OF THE PLANETS!

AND THEN, MORE SILENT THAN A SHADOW AND SWIFTER THAN THE WIND... A FOURTH VISITOR TO THE ROYAL CHAMBER...

FLEET MERCURY!

MY COUSINS DID NOT INFORM ME OF THEIR VISIT--BUT NO MATTER--I CAN ALWAYS CATCH UP TO THEM! AND WHAT SHALL I BEQUEATH TO THE LITTLE PRINCESS?

HMMM-- LET ME SEE? --Ohh-- I DROPPED MY HELMET!

SWIFTER THAN THOUGHT, A TINY HAND DARTS OUT...

BY JOVE'S THUNDERBOLT--DID YOU SEE THE SPEED WITH WHICH SHE CAUGHT MY HELMET? I BEQUEATH TO HER EVEN GREATER SPEED THAN I MYSELF POSSESS!

JUST THEN, BELLOWING WITH THE VOICE OF A LION...

MIGHTY HERCULES!

AYE--DID YOU THINK I WOULD ALLOW ANY FEMALE TO OUT-DO ME IN GIFTS? NOW-- WHAT SHALL I BEQUEATH TO THIS YOUNG PRINCESS?

AS THE POWERFUL HERCULES BENDS OVER THE CRADLE, A TINY HAND REACHES OUT AND...

AIEEE--! TWEAKED MY BEARD, DID SHE? AS IF I WERE A MERE MORTAL! AYE, PRINCESS DIANA--AYE-- WHAT BETTER GIFT CAN I DEED YOU--THAN STRENGTH EVEN GREATER THAN MINE!

AS THE IMMORTAL VISITORS DEPART, THE QUEEN BENDS OVER THE ROYAL CRADLE...

BEAUTIFUL AS APHRODITE, WISE AS ATHENA, SWIFTER THAN MERCURY, AND STRONGER THAN HERCULES--YOU WILL GROW INTO A WONDER, LITTLE ONE! A WONDER GIRL! AND YOU MUST ALWAYS USE YOUR POWERS FOR JUSTICE!

THEN, ONE BLEAK DAY, YEARS LATER, TERRIBLE NEWS...

ALL THE MEN... WIPED OUT... IN THE WARS...!

WOE IS US... WE ARE... ALONE... NOW--!

YOU MUST BE...BRAVE... DIANA... AS BEFITTING... A...PRINCESS--!

Y-Y-YES... MOTHER...!

QUEEN HIPPOLYTA GATHERS ALL THE AMAZONS TOGETHER..

TOMORROW, WE WILL START BUILDING A STOUT SHIP, THAT WILL TAKE US FAR AWAY FROM THESE TERRIBLE WARS!

DURING THE NIGHT, THE QUEEN AWAKENS AND IS STARTLED TO BEHOLD...

DIANA--GONE! GREAT HERA--WH-WHAT COULD HAVE HAPPENED TO HER?

FEARFULLY, THE QUEEN, ACCOMPANIED BY OTHER AMAZONS STARTS SEARCHING FOR THE LITTLE PRINCESS--WHEN...

NOISE--FROM THE BEACH, NOBLE QUEEN!

PERHAPS--INVADERS ARE LANDING!

HURRY-HURRY-PERHAPS THEY HAVE ALREADY TAKEN LITTLE DIANA!

BUT, A STARTLING SIGHT CONFRONTS THE SEARCHERS..

SHE IS...

AS WITH LIGHTNING SPEED, ASTOUNDING STRENGTH, AND DAZZLING SKILL...

A...

THEY SEE THE YOUNG AMAZON PRINCESS FASHION A MIGHTY SHIP SINGLE--HANDEDLY IN ONE NIGHT!

WONDER GIRL!

THE NEXT DAY, THE AMAZON SHIP SETS FORTH...

WE SHALL SAIL UNTIL WE FIND SOME ISLAND FAR FROM THE COURSE OF SHIPS -- AND MAKE THAT THE SECRET ISLAND HOME OF THE AMAZONS!

HOLA! HOLA! HOLA!

DAY AFTER DAY THE LONE SHIP SAILS ON UNCHARTED SEAS UNTIL...

A HUGE WHIRLPOOL DRAGS OUR SHIP TO DOOM!

INSTANTLY, A LITHE FIGURE DIVES OFF THE SIDE OF THE STRICKEN SHIP...

MIGHTY HERCULES -- NOW WE SHALL PUT *YOUR* GIFT TO THE TEST!

FROM THE DOOMED SHIP, AN ANXIOUS MOTHER, AND BREATHLESS AMAZONS WATCH THE TINY FIGURE...

MY DAUGHTER... MY DAUGHTER...

WITH ALL THE STRENGTH THAT MIGHTY *HERCULES* HAD BEQUEATHED TO HER, THE *WONDER GIRL* STRUGGLES TO TOW THE SHIP PAST THE TITANIC CLUTCHES OF THE FROTHING VORTEX...

FINALLY, THE FEARFUL STRUGGLE IS WON, AND A GREAT CHEER GOES UP AS THE YOUNG PRINCESS RETURNS...

WELL DONE, DAUGHTER!

HAIL, PRINCESS DIANA!

THE AMAZON SHIP SAILS IN BETWEEN TWO PEAKS COVERED WITH SNOW...

NEVER BEFORE HAVE I SEEN SUCH A SIGHT AS THIS!

FAR INDEED ARE WE FROM THE HAUNTS OF WARRING MEN!

AND THEN, SMOKE CURLING ALL ABOUT THE SHIP...

SUFFERING SAPPHO! BURNING SEAS ARE UNDER US NOW!

THE SHIP IS CATCHING FIRE!

AGAIN THE TIRELESS WONDER GIRL DIVES OVERBOARD...

THEY ARE USING THE LAST OF THEIR DRINKING WATER -- BUT IT IS NOT ENOUGH TO PUT OUT THE BLAZE!

WITH THE INCREDIBLE SPEED BEQUEATHED HER BY MERCURY, THE WONDER GIRL STREAKS THROUGH THE WATER SO FAST... THAT SHE IS UNHARMED...

I CANNOT USE SEAWATER TO PUT OUT THE BLAZE -- IT IS LIQUID FIRE ITSELF!

IN FLASHING MOMENTS, THE YOUNG AMAZON REACHES ONE OF THE PEAKS...

HERA HELP ME -- OR MY MOTHER AND MY SISTER AMAZONS ARE DOOMED! I MUST GATHER ALL THE SNOW I CAN -- AND THEN --!

AT THE TOP OF THE PEAK, THE *WONDER GIRL* HURLS THE HUGE SNOWBALL SHE HAS FASHIONED IN HER RACE UP THE PEAK...

WISE ATHENA GUIDE MY ARM !

WITH FLASHING SPEED THE TREMENDOUS SNOWBALL BURSTS AGAINST THE FLAMES ENGULFING THE SHIP AND IN A TWINKLING...

HOLA-- WE HAVE BEEN SAVED BY SNOW FALLING FROM THE SKY !

SNOW--IN THIS WEATHER WHENCE COULD IT HAVE COME FROM ?

THE ANSWER IS SOON APPARENT...

I SHOULD HAVE KNOWN IT WAS MY WONDER GIRL !

HOLA-- PRINCESS DIANA !

BUT THE AMAZON SHIP IS NOT OUT OF PERIL YET... FOR SHORTLY AFTER...

WE SAIL-- OVER A SEA--OF... GASES--!

HOW LONG-- CAN WE LAST--?

ONE BY ONE...THE AMAZONS DROP OFF TO SLEEP...OVERCOME BY THE FUMES...

FINALLY, EVEN THE QUEEN HERSELF FALTERS...

DAUGHTER... MY HANDS...CAN NO LONGER... HOLD...THE...TILLER...

HERA HELP ME...KEEP...AWAKE...AND THE SHIP...ON COURSE...LEST IT... CRASH...AGAINST...SOME... UNKNOWN...REEF --!

ON SAILS THE DOOMED SHIP...HER DESTINY AND THAT OF ALL ABOARD HER IN THE HANDS OF THE *WONDER GIRL*...

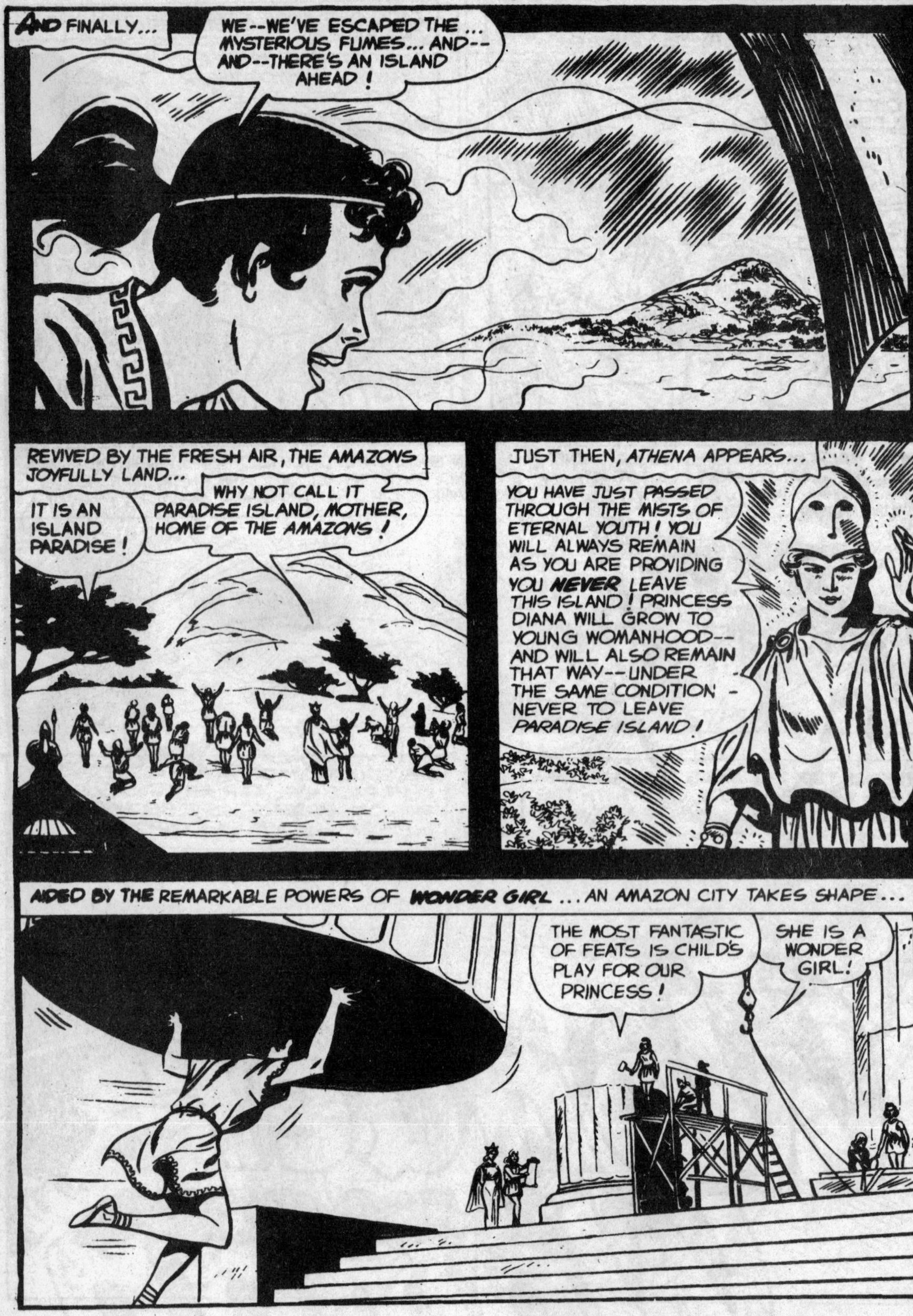
AND FINALLY...
WE--WE'VE ESCAPED THE ... MYSTERIOUS FUMES... AND--AND--THERE'S AN ISLAND AHEAD!
REVIVED BY THE FRESH AIR, THE AMAZONS JOYFULLY LAND...
IT IS AN ISLAND PARADISE!
WHY NOT CALL IT PARADISE ISLAND, MOTHER, HOME OF THE AMAZONS!
JUST THEN, ATHENA APPEARS...
YOU HAVE JUST PASSED THROUGH THE MISTS OF ETERNAL YOUTH! YOU WILL ALWAYS REMAIN AS YOU ARE PROVIDING YOU NEVER LEAVE THIS ISLAND! PRINCESS DIANA WILL GROW TO YOUNG WOMANHOOD--AND WILL ALSO REMAIN THAT WAY--UNDER THE SAME CONDITION--NEVER TO LEAVE PARADISE ISLAND!
AIDED BY THE REMARKABLE POWERS OF WONDER GIRL ... AN AMAZON CITY TAKES SHAPE...
THE MOST FANTASTIC OF FEATS IS CHILD'S PLAY FOR OUR PRINCESS!
SHE IS A WONDER GIRL!

MANY WERE THE ASTOUNDING FEATS PERFORMED BY THE *WONDER GIRL* ... OF WHICH WE CAN ONLY SHOW A FEW ...

LOOK, NOBLE QUEEN!

SHE'S SWIMMING *UP* THE WATERFALL!

EACH ONE MORE STARTLING THAN THE ONE BEFORE ...

DIANA! TIME FOR LUNCH! STOP RIDING ON THAT ROC!

UNDAUNTED, THE AGILE *WONDER GIRL* LETS *HERSELF* DROP ... AND WITH THE *GRACE OF A FALLING LEAF* ...

I GOT THIS COLORED FEATHER FOR YOU, MOTHER!

OH, DIANA, HOW SWEET!

THE EDUCATION OF THE AMAZON PRINCESS KEPT PACE WITH HER REMARKABLE PHYSICAL POWERS ... SHE BECAME VERSED IN EVERY LANGUAGE EVER SPOKEN ...

AND HOW DO YOU SAY "I AM A FRIEND" IN CAVEMAN DIALECT?

OORNGH LLN RHGGGN!

EVERY SCIENCE IS MADE KNOWN TO THE GIRL WONDER...

EVERYONE KNOWS THAT LIGHT TRAVELS 186,000 MILES PER SECOND! HOW FAR DOES IT TRAVEL IN ONE YEAR, PRINCESS?

5,880,000,000,000 MILES!

WATER COVERS 71% OF THE ENTIRE EARTH'S SURFACE! HOW MUCH IS THAT IN MILES?

350,000,000 CUBIC MILES!

WHAT'S THE MELTING POINT OF BENZOIC ACID?

122 DEGREES CENTIGRADE!

ONE DAY, WHILE THE AMAZONS ARE BATHING NEAR THEIR ISLAND...

A WHALE! SWIM FOR YOUR LIVES!

BUT THE GREAT THRASHING TAIL HURLS THE SWIMMERS IN ALL DIRECTIONS...

FROM A DIVING PLATFORM, THE *WONDER GIRL* SEES THE DANGER, AND WITHOUT A MOMENT'S HESITATION...

HERA HELP ME PROTECT MY SISTER AMAZONS!

BUT, THE WILY SEA BEAST BLOWS OUT A HUGE WATER SPOUT WHEN HE SEES THE LITHE DIVER AND...

SUFFERING SAPPHO— I'M CAUGHT!

THE GIANT WHALE JUGGLES THE *WONDER GIRL* ...

AS IF SHE WERE A TOY BALL...

HELD ALOFT BY A SPOUT OF WATER...

THEN -- SHE FINALLY BREAKS LOOSE ...

LUCKILY HE STOPPED SPOUTING -- FOR A -- MOMENT!

ONTO THE HUGE TAIL SHE DROPS...

I HAVE TO DISCOURAGE HIM FROM EVER APPROACHING THE ISLAND AGAIN!

NOW INDEED DOES THE UNIQUE *WONDER GIRL* DISPLAY HER PROWESS AS WITH A FANTASTIC BURST OF STRENGTH ...

BY NEPTUNE'S TRIDENT -- DIANA IS DRAGGING THE WHALE **BACKWARDS** THROUGH THE WATER -- AWAY FROM US!

AS THE THOROUGHLY DEMORALIZED SEA BEAST LUMBERS AWAY...

THANK HERA -- MY SISTER AMAZONS ARE SAFE!

THE OVERJOYED AMAZONS CARRY THE *WONDER GIRL* BACK TO THE ISLAND IN AN AQUATIC PARADE...

HURRAY!

HURRAY FOR THE WONDER GIRL!

HER EXPLOIT IS PLACED IN A SCRAP BOOK...

ONE OF THE AMAZON PHOTOGRAPHERS TOOK IT WITH A *TELEPHOTO LENS*, DIANA! I'LL WAGER IT WILL BE SOON FILLED WITH OTHER THRILLING EXPLOITS!

THUS BEGINS ONE OF THE MOST LEGENDARY CAREERS OF ALL TIME!

The End

AND FROM TIME TO TIME, WE SHALL INVITE YOU ON OTHER BREATHLESS TALES OF ADVENTURE WITH THE UNIQUE *WONDER GIRL*!

Wonder Woman
By Charles Moulton

THE DINOSAUR AGE ENDED ON EARTH MILLIONS OF YEARS AGO! AND YET, *WONDER WOMAN*-- BEAUTIFUL AS APHRODITE, WISE AS ATHENA, SWIFTER THAN MERCURY, AND STRONGER THAN HERCULES--FINDS HERSELF IN THE MOST ASTOUNDING ADVENTURE OF HER ACTION-STUDDED CAREER WHEN SHE DISCOVERS THAT OUR WORLD MAY HAVE TO COPE WITH A DINOSAUR INVASION FROM ANOTHER PLANET! HOW THIS STARTLING TALE ENDS YOU WILL READ IN THE SPECTACULAR ... *EAGLE OF SPACE!*

AT MILITARY INTELLIGENCE COL. STEVE TREVOR HURRIES TO HIS ASSOCIATE, LOVELY LT. DIANA PRINCE...

THIS IS THE FILM WE'VE RECOVERED FROM A PHOTOGRAPHIC SECTION OF ONE OF THE ROCKETS WE LOST! ONE OF THE SERIES WE SHOT TOWARD MARS, DIANA!

PERHAPS IT WILL GIVE US A CLUE TO THE DISAPPEARANCE OF THE **WHOLE** SERIES OF ROCKETS, STEVE!

BEFORE THE INCREDULOUS EYES OF THE TWO IN THE DARK ROOM, A STARTLING SCENE IS REVEALED...

A PTERODACTYL! A PREHISTORIC MONSTER OF THE DINOSAUR AGE -- IN SPACE! SOMEONE MUST BE PLAYING A JOKE ON US!

THERE'S ONLY **ONE** WAY TO FIND OUT, STEVE!

WE SHOULD GET AN EYE-WITNESS CONFIRMATION OF WHAT ACTUALLY HAPPENS ON ONE OF THOSE MARTIAN SHOOTS!

NOT "WE"! I! I'M GOING MYSELF, DIANA! THIS IS A MAN'S JOB!

AND SO, DESPITE LT. PRINCE'S PROTESTS...

THERE HE GOES! BUT IF HE THINKS I'M GOING TO REMAIN BEHIND -- HE'S MISTAKEN!

VROOSH!

UNOBSERVED, THE LOVELY OFFICER WHISPERS AN ORDER SO SOFTLY THAT NO HUMAN EAR CAN HEAR IT..

PLANE -- DIVE -- AND BANK... AT MAXIMUM SPEED!

NO HUMAN EAR -- BUT THE SUPERSONIC TRANSMISSION OF HER ROBOT PLANE ANSWERS AND THEN, WITH A SPEED NO HUMAN EYE CAN DETECT, LT. PRINCE HURLS HERSELF ON AN UPDRAFT TOWARD HER ROBOT PLANE..

STEVE DOESN'T HAVE TO KNOW IT -- BUT I'M GOING TO TRACK HIM!

2

INSIDE HER ROBOT PLANE, THE DARING GIRL MAKES A LIGHTNING CHANGE INTO HER SECRET IDENTITY OF *WONDER WOMAN*...

I'LL TUNE INTO MY OMNI-WAVE SET AND KEEP STEVE'S SHIP ON MY SCREEN!

TRACKING STEVE'S PLANE ON HER OMNI-SCREEN AS SHE SOARS INTO SPACE, *WONDER WOMAN* IS HORRIFIED TO BEHOLD..

MERCIFUL MINERVA! IT IS TRUE! SOMEHOW THERE *ARE* CREATURES OF THE DINOSAUR AGE IN SPACE! AND AT THIS VERY MOMENT, STEVE IS BEING PURSUED BY A PTERO-DACTYL -- A FLYING MONSTER! BUT-- THERE'S NO AIR IN SPACE AGAINST WHICH TO BEAT ITS WINGS! HOW CAN IT FLY?

IN FLASHING MOMENTS *WONDER WOMAN* REACHES THE SCENE -- BUT, TO THE HEROIC AMAZON'S DISMAY, DESPITE THE FORCE WITH WHICH SHE DIVES AT THE SPACE PTERODACTYL..

THUNDERBOLTS OF JOVE! THE MONSTER HURLED ME AWAY WITH A LASH OF ITS TAIL!

NOW, THE DARING *WONDER WOMAN* ATTEMPTS A NEW MANEUVER...

IT'S MY AMAZON ANGEL! TRYING TO HELP ME OUT OF THIS SPOT! BUT HOW--?

MY ONLY CHANCE TO RESCUE STEVE IS TO DISTRACT THE MONSTER'S ATTENTION WITH MY SHIP-- WHILE I TRY TO REMOVE HIM FROM HIS PLANE!

WITH ALL HER STRENGTH, THE POWERFUL AMAZON TUGS AT STEVE'S JAMMED CANOPY..

MIGHTY HERCULES-- WILL THE STRENGTH YOU ENDOWED ME WITH--BE SUFFICIENT FOR THIS TASK?

THE NEXT INSTANT...EVEN AS SHE WRENCHES OPEN THE CANOPY...

THE MONSTER HAS TILTED THE SHIP-- STEVE IS FALLING OUT!

UNHESITATINGLY, THE ACROBATIC **WONDER WOMAN** DIVES AFTER THE HURTLING PILOT..

PLANE--DIVE AT MAXIMUM SPEED!

AND, WITH MATCHLESS PRECISION, CATCHES THE FALLING STEVE AND BOARDS THE PLANE IN ONE LIGHTNING-LIKE MOVEMENT...

STEVE-- ARE YOU ALL RIGHT?

EVEN AS THE PILOT'S EYES OPEN...AN IMMENSE SHADOW FALLS OVER THE ROBOT PLANE ...

LOOK AT IT--! A PREHISTORIC MONSTER-- ONE THAT CEASED TO EXIST ON EARTH 100 MILLION YEARS AGO-- ALIVE TODAY IN SPACE!

SHADES OF PLUTO! IT'S CAPTURED MY SHIP NOW!

A BREATHLESSLY DARING PLAN IS AGREED UPON...

THERE'S ONLY ONE WAY WE CAN FIND OUT WHERE IT COMES FROM --LET IT TAKE US TO ITS LAIR!

AGREED!

4

TO THE ENTRAPPED PAIR'S ASTONISHMENT, AN INCREDIBLE FLIGHT BEGINS...

WE'RE PASSING MARS!

NOW-- JUPITER!

LOOK-- WE'RE APPROACHING SATURN! HOW COULD THIS MONSTER POSSIBLY FLY SO FAST?

SATURN'S BIGGEST MOON LOOMS UP BEFORE THE CAPTIVES...

THERE'S THE ANSWER, STEVE! SOMEHOW, THEY'VE DISCOVERED COSMIC JET STREAMS WHICH CARRY THEM AT IMMEASURABLE SPEEDS ALMOST ANYWHERE THEY WANT TO GO!

DO YOU REALIZE WHAT THIS MEANS? EARTH CAN BE THREATENED-- BY CREATURES WHICH DON'T EXIST!

BUT THEY DO EXIST, STEVE! LOOK AHEAD THERE!

THE DINOSAUR AGE LIVES AGAIN-- ON TITAN-- SATURN'S MOON!

AS THE *PTERODACTYL* NEARS THE GROUND OF *TITAN*, AN AWESOME SHAPE ARISES, AND WITH A FEARSOME GROWL LIKE HISSING STEAM ...

A TYRANNOSAURUS REX -- THE MOST FEARSOME DINOSAUR THAT EVER LIVED!

IT'S GRABBED US FROM THE PTERODACTYL'S CLUTCHES!

THE FEARSOME MONSTERS CLASH ...

THEY'RE FIGHTING FOR POSSESSION OF US!

NOW'S OUR CHANCE TO GET AWAY!

THE NEXT MOMENT, AS THE MIGHTY BATTLERS TWIST AND TURN ...

I'VE BEEN CATAPULTED OUT!

IN VAIN DOES THE AGILE *WONDER WOMAN* ATTEMPT TO SOAR BACK...

NO AIR DRAFTS --

I CAN UTILIZE --

-- TO GET BACK TO STEVE AND THE SHIP!

THEN, AS THE SATURNIAN LAKE CLOSES OVER HER... THE PLUMMETING AMAZON SEES WAITING BELOW FOR HER--ANOTHER NIGHTMARE FORM...

BY NEPTUNE'S TRIDENT-- A PLESIOSAUR-- IS WAITING FOR ME!

EVEN AS SHE WHIRLS HER UNIQUE LASSO AT THE UNDERWATER MONSTER, *WONDER WOMAN* HAS BUT ONE THOUGHT...

STEVE--STEVE-- I MUST GET BACK TO STEVE!

WITH A TREMENDOUS SPURT, THE POWERFUL AMAZON ELUDES THE SUPPOSEDLY EXTINCT PLESIOSAUR --BY KICKING UP A CURTAIN OF FOAM...

EVERY MOMENT I DELAY MEANS MORE PERIL FOR STEVE!

FINALLY LEAPING BACK ONTO SHORE, AN ENTIRELY DIFFERENT SCENE GREETS *WONDER WOMAN*...

THE MONSTER IS GONE--AND STEVE--STEVE-- WITH THEM! HE'S--HE'S A PRISONER!

WH-WHEN WILL I EVER--SEE HIM-- AGAIN?

AND THEN, A HAPPY THOUGHT STRIKES THE LOVELY AMAZON..

MY ROBOT PLANE IS SUPER-SONICALLY EQUIPPED! IT ANSWERS TO THE SOUND OF MY VOICE! I'LL SUMMON IT FROM WHEREVER IT IS--IT WILL RETURN WITH STEVE! PLANE--ZOOM AT MAXIMUM SPEED!

IN FLASHING MOMENTS, THE ROBOT PLANE WINGS TOWARD *WONDER WOMAN*...

WHICHEVER MONSTER HAD IT IN ITS CLUTCHES--MUST HAVE LAID IT DOWN FOR A MOMENT--ENABLING IT TO FLY BACK!

BUT THEN, THE AMAZON'S EAGLE-LIKE VISION MAKES A STARTLING DISCOVERY LONG BEFORE THE PLANE LANDS...

EMPTY-- STEVE'S GONE -- !

SUDDENLY, THE LOVELY GIRL IS SURROUNDED...

CAVE PEOPLE! JUST LIKE THOSE WHO LIVED ON EARTH DURING THE *STONE AGE*! BUT-- THE EARTH CAVE PEOPLE PROGRESSED-- WHILE THESE HAVE NOT-- WHY?

IGN NUU KRRRRR LNGH!

AND *WONDER WOMAN*, WHO AS AN AMAZON KNOWS EVERY LANGUAGE...

LLBD NNNGH TTYU LIIPODD

UNLIKE EARTH--WHERE INCESSANT FIGHTING, FAMINE, AND THE ICE AGE DESTROYED THE DINOSAURS-- HERE THE BEASTS HAVE PROSPERED! THEY'VE KEPT THE PEOPLE IN CONSTANT TERROR--DESTROYING EVERY ATTEMPT THEY HAVE MADE TO ADVANCE THEIR CIVILIZATION!

JUST THEN, WITH EAR-SHATTERING ROARS--A FRIGHTENING CAVALCADE STARTS TO APPEAR..

RRROAR!

NNGH JLLYTT WNMH....!

WHAT? THIS ATTACK BY THE WATER DINOSAURS IS A FREQUENT HAPPENING? NO WONDER YOU HAVEN'T HAD A CHANCE TO ADVANCE YOUR-SELVES!

INSTANTLY, **WONDER WOMAN** TURNS HER AMAZON LASSO INTO A WHIRLING DRILL...

LLNV FFYYL...

I'VE GOT TO STOP THOSE BEASTS SOMEHOW!

WHRRRRR!

AND THEN, ROCKETING OFF WITH FLASHING SPEED...

AND THIS IS ONE WAY OF DOING IT!

WHIRRRRR!

BEFORE THE STARTLED EYES OF THE CAVE BOY, THE MIGHTY AMAZON DIGS A HUGE MOAT AROUND THE LAKE...

THERE! THEY'RE STOPPED BY THE MOAT! IT'S TOO DEEP AND WIDE FOR THEM TO CROSS OVER!

AND SO THE INGENIOUS **WONDER WOMAN** BUILDS THE FIRST DINOSAUR AQUARIUM IN THE HISTORY OF THE UNIVERSE...

THE ONLY CLUE THAT MIGHT LEAD ME TO STEVE -- IS THE PLANE THAT RETURNED WITHOUT HIM! IF IT COULD ONLY TALK?

CAREFULLY, EXHAUSTIVELY, THE AMAZON EXAMINES EVERY INCH OF THE PLANE... AND THEN, REVEALED BY HER UNIQUE VISION...

Hmmm -- A PHOSPHORESCENT SMEAR ON THE UNDERSIDE OF THE PLANE -- IT MUST HAVE BRUSHED UP AGAINST SOME KIND OF FOLIAGE THAT EMITS THIS KIND OF RED GLOW!

9

A MOMENT LATER, *WONDER WOMAN* AND THE CAVE BOY ARE IN HER PLANE...

LLNK..?

YES! SOME-WHERE DOWN THERE--I'VE GOT TO FIND THAT RED GLOW! IT'S WHERE THE PLANE CAME FROM! IT'S MY ONLY CHANCE TO FIND STEVE!

AFTER A TENSE SEARCH, HER EXTRAOR-DINARY AMAZON VISION LEADS *WONDER WOMAN* TO...

LOOK--THERE--THE RED GLOW! THAT'S WHERE THE PLANE CAME FROM!

THROUGH THE PHOSPHORESCENT FOLIAGE THE DAUNTLESS AMAZON DIVES--TO DISCOVER A HAIR-RAISING SCENE...

SNAP

IT'S STEVE! IN THE NEST OF A TYRANNO-SAURUS REX!--THUNDER-BOLTS OF JOVE--THE BEAST'S GRABBED MY PLANE!

OUT OF THE PLANE *WONDER WOMAN* IMMEDIATELY LEAPS...

ANGEL--I FIGURED YOU WERE TRYING TO FIND ME WHEN THE PLANE TOOK OFF!

THE DINOSAUR'S JUST DISCOVERED WE'RE NO LONGER IN THE PLANE!

HE'S COMING AFTER US!

INSTANTLY ATTRACTED BY THE BELLOWING OF THE PURSUING DINOSAUR...

RRRONKR!

HE MUST BE THE KING OF THE DINOSAURS -- EVERYONE IS FOLLOWING HIM!

AND THEY'RE ALL FOLLOWING US! BUILDING A MOAT AROUND THESE BEASTS WON'T STOP THEM! I'LL HAVE TO TRY SOMETHING ELSE!

AND THEN, WITHOUT HESITATION...THE AMAZON UPROOTS A TREE...

WHAT ARE YOU DOING, WONDER WOMAN?

YOU AND THE CAVE BOY KEEP RUNNING -- AND YOU WILL SEE!

LLLKNH?

I DON'T UNDERSTAND YOU, BOY! BUT IF YOU'RE WONDERING WHAT SHE'S DOING -- SO AM I! SHE'S SCOOPING OUT A HOLLOW IN THAT TREE -- THAT'S ALL!

BUT, THE INGENIOUS WONDER WOMAN SOON PUTS THE IMPROVISED MUSICAL INSTRUMENT TO GOOD USE WHEN ...

THE MUSICAL NOTES I'M PLAYING ARE JARRING THEM TO A STANDSTILL!

AND WHILE THE ONRUSH OF THE DINOSAURS IS HALTED BY VIBRATION, THE POWERFUL AMAZON UPROOTS ONE HUGE TREE AFTER ANOTHER AND...

ZZVVHHHH

I COULD ALMOST UNDERSTAND YOU SAYING THAT WONDER WOMAN HAS BUILT A ZOO AROUND THOSE DINOSAURS -- SO THAT THEY'LL NEVER BOTHER YOU!

BEFORE *WONDER WOMAN* LEAVES, BY MENTAL TELEPATHY... SHE TRANSMITS...

WITH THE KNOWLEDGE I AM GIVING YOU OF OUR CIVILIZATION, IT WON'T BE TOO LONG BEFORE YOU CATCH UP TO US--!

IN ANSWER TO HER COMMAND, THE ROBOT PLANE RETURNS...

WE... HOPE... VISIT... YOU... SOON--!

LISTEN TO HIM! HE'S PICKED UP OUR LANGUAGE ALREADY!

INTO THE COSMIC JET STREAM *WONDER WOMAN* MANEUVERS HER PLANE...

WHAT NEXT, WONDER WOMAN?

HOME!

AFTER THE TWO LAND AND MAKE THEIR REPORT TO MILITARY INTELLIGENCE...

I'D LIKE YOU TO MEET MY ASSOCIATE, LT. DIANA PRINCE! SHE WANTED TO COME ALONG-- BUT--I OVERRULED HER! SHE WON'T FEEL SO BAD IF SHE HEARS ABOUT OUR ADVENTURES FIRSTHAND!

SOME OTHER TIME, STEVE!

The End / 12

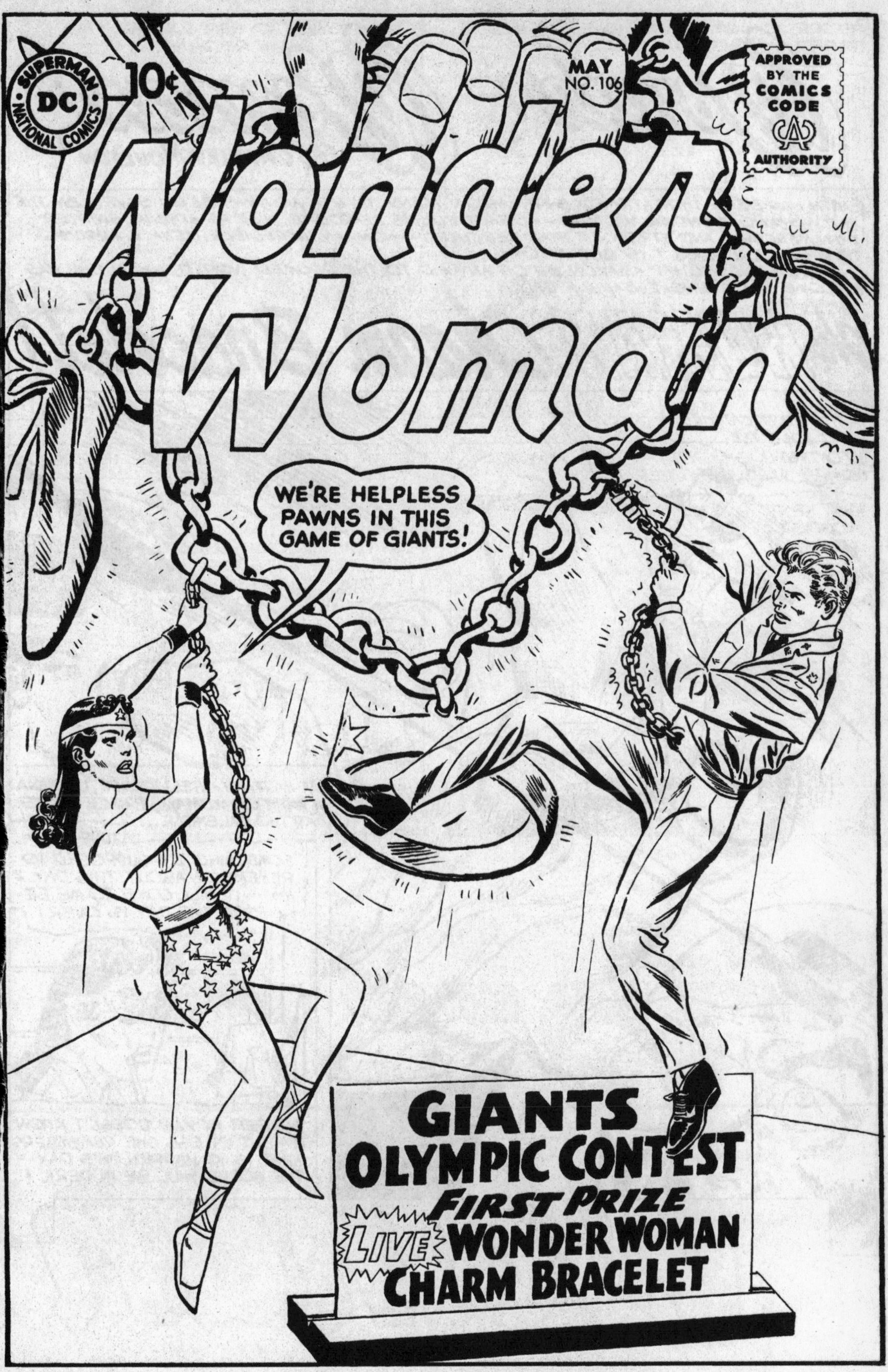
SUPERMAN
DC
NATIONAL COMICS
10¢
MAY
NO. 106
APPROVED BY THE COMICS CODE AUTHORITY
Wonder Woman
WE'RE HELPLESS PAWNS IN THIS GAME OF GIANTS!
GIANTS
OLYMPIC CONTEST
FIRST PRIZE
LIVE
WONDER WOMAN
CHARM BRACELET

Wonder Woman

By Charles Moulton

EARTH HAS BEEN THREATENED BY INVASION MANY TIMES, AND HAS BEEN SAVED BY THE ASTONISHING **WONDER WOMAN**--BEAUTIFUL AS APHRODITE, WISE AS ATHENA, SWIFTER THAN MERCURY, AND STRONGER THAN HERCULES--NOW, AN INCREDIBLE MENACE ARRIVES-TO WHOM OUR PLANET IS BUT A TOY! CAN EVEN THE MIGHTY AMAZON BE OF ANY AID TO THE DOOMED WORLD, WHEN SHE HAS BECOME BUT A SINGLE BAUBLE ON...

The HUMAN Charm Bracelet!

IF THE GIANT CATCHES ME--I LOSE THE CONTEST!

AT MILITARY INTELLIGENCE, LT. DIANA (WONDER WOMAN) PRINCE LOOKS AT THE CALENDAR... JUNE 19th...

SOMETHING I'M SUPPOSED TO REMEMBER ABOUT THIS DAY..? Hmm--IT WILL COME TO ME BEFORE THE DAY IS OVER!

WONDER WOMAN DOESN'T KNOW IT--BUT UNLESS SHE REMEMBERS WHAT IS TO HAPPEN THIS DAY-- THE WORLD WILL BE IN PERIL!

ON PLANET G, HOME OF THE SPACE GIANTS, A GIANT OLYMPICS IS BEING HELD...

HO-HO-HO!

I'M THE ONLY ONE TO RIDE A WHALE -- *WITHOUT* FALLING OFF!

I WIN!

AND IN THE DECIDING CONTEST... OF THE GIANTS OLYMPICS...

SWISH!

AND I'VE REELED IN A SUBMARINE! I WIN THIS CONTEST TOO! *HO! HO!*

THUNDEROUS APPLAUSE GREETS THE WINNER ...

TOOROO WINS!

TOOROO IS THE CHAMPION OF ALL THE SPACE GIANTS!

THUD!

THUD!

THUD!

TOOROO! AS IS OUR CUSTOM, YOU MAY ASK ANY PRIZE FOR WINNING THE OLYMPICS!

I WANT THE PLANET EARTH!

EARTH IS YOURS FOR A PLAYTHING! DO WITH IT AS YOU WISH! BUT RE- MEMBER--ONLY ONE OPPONENT MAY STAND IN YOUR WAY--THE MIGHTY *WONDER WOMAN!*

JUST BEFORE THE SPACE GIANT TAKES OFF...HE BIDS FAREWELL TO A GIANTESS...

DON'T FORGET TO BRING ME BACK A NICE PRESENT FROM THE EARTH, *TOOROO*! SOMETHING FOR MY CHARM BRACELET! NOT THE EMPIRE STATE BUILDING BUT SOMETHING REALLY NOVEL--*UNUSUAL--UNIQUE*!

LEAVE IT TO ME, *RIKKAA*!

AND SO, AT COSMIC SPEED, THE SPACE GIANT SOON HURTLES TOWARDS THE UNSUSPECTING EARTH...

NOW--WHAT CAN I GET RIKKAA? A BRIDGE--?

MEANWHILE, AT *MILITARY INTELLIGENCE,* LT. DIANA PRINCE IS BEING VISITED BY COL. STEVE TREVOR WHEN ...

SHOTS COMING FROM THE YARD!

YOU'D BETTER STAY HERE OUT OF TROUBLE, DIANA--I'LL RUN DOWN AND SEE IF I CAN HELP!

POW! POW!

BUT, EVEN BEFORE THE DOOR HAS CLOSED BEHIND STEVE--DIANA MAKES A LIGHTNING CHANGE INTO HER SECRET IDENTITY...

I'D BETTER CHANGE INTO *WONDER WOMAN* IN CASE MY HELP IS NEEDED!

BELOW HER, *WONDER WOMAN* SEES A STARTLING SCENE...

MERCIFUL MINERVA! THE TWO SPIES WE CAUGHT ARE BEING RESCUED BY HELICOPTER! A GUARD IS ALREADY WOUNDED--AND STEVE IS IN PERIL!

BAM! BAM!

THE DARING WONDER WOMAN ALIGHTS ON THE WHIRLING HELICOPTER PROPELLER...

THE CRIMINALS WON'T THINK OF LOOKING UP HERE!

WHOOOOSH!

WITH UNCANNY AGILITY, THE AMAZON KEEPS HER BALANCE.

MERCIFUL MINERVA! STEVE IS RUSHING UNARMED RIGHT INTO THE FIRE OF THE SPIES!

WONDER WOMAN HURLS HER AMAZON TIARA AT THE GUNMEN WITH LIGHTNING SPEED...

HERA HELP MY AIM!

THE UNIQUE TIARA BOUNDS LIKE A STRANGE BOOMERANG FROM GUNMAN TO GUNMAN...

THAT TIARA DISARMING THOSE SPIES -- CAN ONLY MEAN WONDER WOMAN IS ON THE SCENE!

SPANG!

SPANG!

INSTANTLY, THE DARING PILOT HURLS HIMSELF AT THE SPIES...

THIS IS WHERE YOUR ESCAPE ENDS!

AT THAT MOMENT, INSIDE THE GET AWAY HELICOPTER...

THAT OFFICER IS TRYING TO STOP OUR MEN FROM GETTING AWAY WITH THE INFORMATION THEY STOLE!

THIS WILL STOP HIM!

RATTAT!

BUT WITHOUT HESITATION, *WONDER WOMAN* LEANS DOWN FROM THE WHIRLING HELICOPTER BLADE AND WITH HER UNIQUE AMAZON BRACELET...

YEOWWW--SOMETHIN' IS MAKIN' MY SLUGS BOUNCE RIGHT BACK AT ME AGAIN!

STOP FIRIN'-- *STOP FIRIN'*-- YOU'RE FILLIN' THE INSIDE OF THE CABIN WITH LEAD!

BWEEE!

ZING

BWEEE!

WITH AN AGILE LEAP BACKWARD, *WONDER WOMAN* CASTS HER UNIQUE AMAZON LASSO AROUND THE WHIRLING PROPELLER AND...

THAT ENDS THE ESCAPE OF THE SPIES AND THEIR WOULD-BE RESCUERS!

RRRRIP

WITH THE CRIMINALS CAPTURED...

WE'RE A WINNING COMBINATION, ANGEL! THIS ESCAPE IS STOPPED COLD! THANKS TO YOU!

I ♥ YOU WERE WONDERFUL, STEVE! REMEMBER, I HAVE MY TIARA, BRACELETS, AND LASSO TO HELP ME!

MEANWHILE, ON *PARADISE ISLAND,* WONDER WOMAN'S MOTHER IS WATCHING HER ON THE OMNI-SCREEN...

TEN MINUTES TO TEN--AND DIANA *STILL* HASN'T REMEMBERED WHAT IS GOING TO HAPPEN TO HER AND THE WORLD--AT TEN O'CLOCK!

AT THAT MOMENT, IN THE HARBOR...

WHAT WAS THAT-- LIGHTNING?

I'M NOT SURE-- IT PASSED SO SWIFTLY?

WHOOOSH!

32

BUT THEN... BELOW THE WATER...THE SPACE GIANT EMERGES...

I'VE SPECIAL EQUIPMENT TO LIVE ANYWHERE ON EARTH! NOW, I'LL LEAVE MY ROCKETSHIP HERE--AND LOOK FOR PRESENTS FOR *RIKKAA'S* CHARM BRACELET!

SUDDENLY, A DRIPPING HAND ARISES FROM THE DEPTHS...

IT'S AN INVASION OF SOME KIND! RADIO A SPECIAL ALARM!

A PATROL PLANE SPEEDS TO THE SCENE... BUT IT IS SNATCHED OUT OF THE AIR AS IF IT WERE A TOY...

I WONDER IF *RIKKAA* WILL BE SATISFIED WITH THESE TO WEAR ON HER CHARM BRACELET!

MEANWHILE, IN ANSWER TO THE ALARMS, WONDER WOMAN SPEEDS TO THE SCENE WITH STEVE IN HER UNIQUE AMAZON PLANE...

THOSE REPORTS WERE NOT WILD! THERE'S THE GIANT!

MY SPECIAL LASSO WILL TAME HIM!

BUT, TO THE FEARLESS AMAZON'S SURPRISE...

GREAT HERA! HE PULLED IT RIGHT OUT OF MY HAND! SOMETHING'S GONE WRONG! MY LASSO HAS **LOST** ITS SPECIAL POWER!

IN A STARTLING MOMENT...

PLANE ZOOM AT MAXIMUM SPEED!... SUFFERING SAPPHO-- MY ROBOT PLANE HAS ALSO LOST *ITS* POWER!

AND THEN, *WONDER WOMAN* REALIZES...

MERCIFUL MINERVA! IT'S JUNE 19TH! IT MUST BE 10 O'CLOCK! FOR THE NEXT 24 HOURS--ALL MY UNIQUE WEAPONS AGAINST CRIME--HAVE LOST THEIR SPECIAL POWERS! AND WE'RE PRISONERS OF THIS GIANT!

HO! HO! HO! I'VE CAPTURED *WONDER WOMAN!* THE ONLY ONE WHO COULD CHALLENGE MY PLAYING WITH THE EARTH AS IF IT WERE A TOY!

INSTANTLY THE GIANT FROM OUTER SPACE PLUNGES INTO THE RIVER ...

WHAT MORE NOVEL GIFT CAN I BRING RIKKAA THAN WONDER WOMAN--AND ALL HER UNIQUE WEAPONS!

ON THE RIVER BED THE GIANT PLACES WONDER WOMAN'S PLANE INTO HIS ROCKETSHIP...

LOOK AT THE SIZE OF HIM!

THE FAMOUS COUPLE STARES AT EACH OTHER...

THAT GIANT COULD MAKE MATCH-WOOD OF EARTH! WHAT A TERRIBLE TIME FOR YOU TO LOSE YOUR UNIQUE POWERS!

EVEN SO, WE MUST FIND OUT WHERE HE CAME FROM! IF THERE ARE OTHERS--THERE'S NO TELLING WHEN EARTH WILL BE SMASHED!

AT THE CONTROLS, THE SPACE GIANT SENDS HIS ROCKETSHIP HURTLING UP FROM THE WATER...

VROOSH!

SOMEHOW-- I MUST STOP THESE GIANTS!

BUT YOUR WEAPONS ARE NOW USELESS, WONDER WOMAN!

PART TWO OF THIS ASTONISHING ADVENTURE IN WHICH THE FUTURE OF OUR WORLD IS AT STAKE CONTINUES...ON NEXT PAGE FOLLOWING!

Wonder Woman

Part Two of "THE HUMAN CHARM BRACELET!"

INTO SPACE THE ROCKETSHIP FLASHES WITH ITS UNARMED CAPTIVES...

SOMEHOW-- I MUST SAVE THE EARTH DESPITE THIS HANDI-CAP! EVEN THOUGH-- RIGHT NOW-- I HAVEN'T THE FAINTEST IDEA HOW!

AND THEN, INSIDIOUS FUMES DRIFT INTO THE CAPTIVE AMAZON PLANE...

LOSING... CONSCIOUS...

GOT TO...HOLD ON... AS LONG... AS I--

THE CAPTIVES RECOVER CONSCIOUSNESS TO FIND THEMSELVES IN THE MOST FANTASTIC SITUATION OF THEIR AMAZING CAREERS...

THUNDER-BOLTS OF JOVE! WE'RE FASTENED TO A CHARM BRACELET!

AND YOUR PLANE, LASSO, TIARA AND BRACELET-- ARE ALL CHARMS ON THE BRACELET!

SUDDENLY THE DAZED COUPLE BE-COMES AWARE THAT...

SHADES OF PLUTO! THE SPACE GIANT HAS MADE A LIVE CHARM BRACELET OF US... AND HE'S MAKING A PRESENT OF US!

I DON'T KNOW HOW LONG IT TOOK US TO GET HERE OR WHETHER BY THIS PLANET'S TIME DIMENSION-- 24 EARTH HOURS HAVE ELAPSED--AND MY WEAPONS HAVE HAD THEIR POWER RESTORED! BUT--EVEN IF THEY ARE USELESS --I MUST CHALLENGE THIS MENACE TO EARTH!

AND SO THE FEARLESS WONDER WOMAN VERSED IN ALL CUSTOMS BOLDLY DEFIES THE GIANT...

I CHALLENGE YOU TO AN OLYMPICS CONTEST! THE WINNER TO CLAIM HIS OWN PRIZE ACCORDING TO THE CUSTOM OF YOUR PLANET!

THUNDEROUS LAUGHTER ARISES AT THE INTREPID AMAZON'S CHALLENGE ...

HO HO HO HO HO

YOU FOOL! I THOUGHT YOU SAID YOU HAD BEATEN WONDER WOMAN!

YOU'LL HAVE TO ANSWER THE AMAZON'S CHALLENGE, TOOROO! THAT'S THE CUSTOM OF OUR PLANET!

WHY YOU--YOU EARTHLING MOSQUITO! YOU WOULDN'T STAND A CHANCE AGAINST ME! I WON THE PLANET OLYMPICS!

THEN YOU WON'T OBJECT TO RETURNING MY PLANE, TIARA,-- LASSO, AND BRACELETS SO I CAN USE THEM IN THE CONTEST?

AGAIN MOCKING LAUGHTER ARISES-- AND AS THE GIANT IS FORCED TO AGREE...

YOU'D BETTER WIN MY WONDER WOMAN CHARMS BACK!

HOW CAN I POSSIBLY FAIL 2 ESPECIALLY SINCE, AS THE CHALLENGED PARTY, I CAN NAME THE CONTESTS MYSELF!

HO HO!

BEFORE THE ASSEMBLED SPACE GIANTS IN THE PLANET ARENA SHORTLY...

THE CAPTURE OF A "MOUSE"-- BEGINS THE FIRST OF THREE CONTESTS BETWEEN *TOOROO* AND *WONDER WOMAN*! WINNER TO NAME HIS OWN PRIZE!

THE PLANET "MOUSE" IS RELEASED...AND A FEW MOMENTS LATER...

THERE! I'VE CAUGHT IT! BUT *WONDER WOMAN* WILL FAIL!

IS IT POSSIBLE THAT THE MIGHTY AMAZON CANNOT CAPTURE A MOUSE?

ANOTHER "MOUSE" IS RELEASED... BUT IN COMPARISON TO *WONDER WOMAN'S* SIZE...

AGAINST THIS GIANT UNICORN-- I'M MORE LIKE A MOUSE! BUT-- MY LASSO SHOULD CAPTURE IT-- IF THE 24 HOURS ARE UP-- AND ITS UNIQUE POWERS HAVE RETURNED!

TO THE AMAZON'S DISMAY...

THE *UNICORN* EASILY TOSSED IT OFF! THIS MEANS THE LASSO'S POWERS HAVE NOT YET RETURNED.

BARELY KEEPING AHEAD OF THE ENRAGED ANIMAL...

I'VE GOT TO CAPTURE THE *UNICORN* WITHOUT THE USE OF ANY OF MY SPECIAL POWERS!

LIKE A MINIATURE MATADOR... THE DARING AMAZON NARROWLY AVOIDS...

THE THRUSTING HORN...

FINALLY, WITH UNCANNY AGILITY, WONDER WOMAN LEAPS OUT OF THE WAY AS THE GIANT UNICORN THRUSTS AT HER...

THANK HERA! I'VE MADE THE UNICORN CAPTURE ITSELF!

THUD

AS THE GIANT SPECTATORS LAUGH AT THE AMAZON'S SUCCESS...

SO--YOU CAN'T FAIL!

THIS IS ONLY THE FIRST CONTEST! WONDER WOMAN CAN'T POSSIBLY SUCCEED IN THE NEXT ONE I'VE PLANNED!

HO! HO!

IN THE SECOND CONTEST...

CATCH THIS BIRD-- AND BRING IT BACK TO THE GROUND!

INSTANTLY, THE GIANT INHALES SHARPLY...

AND DESPITE THE BIRD'S STRUGGLES...

DRAWS IT DOWN TO THE GROUND WITH HIS INHALED BREATH...

GOT IT! I WIN! THE AMAZON CANNOT POSSIBLY SUCCEED!

WILL WONDER WOMAN FAIL TO CAPTURE A MERE BIRD?

12

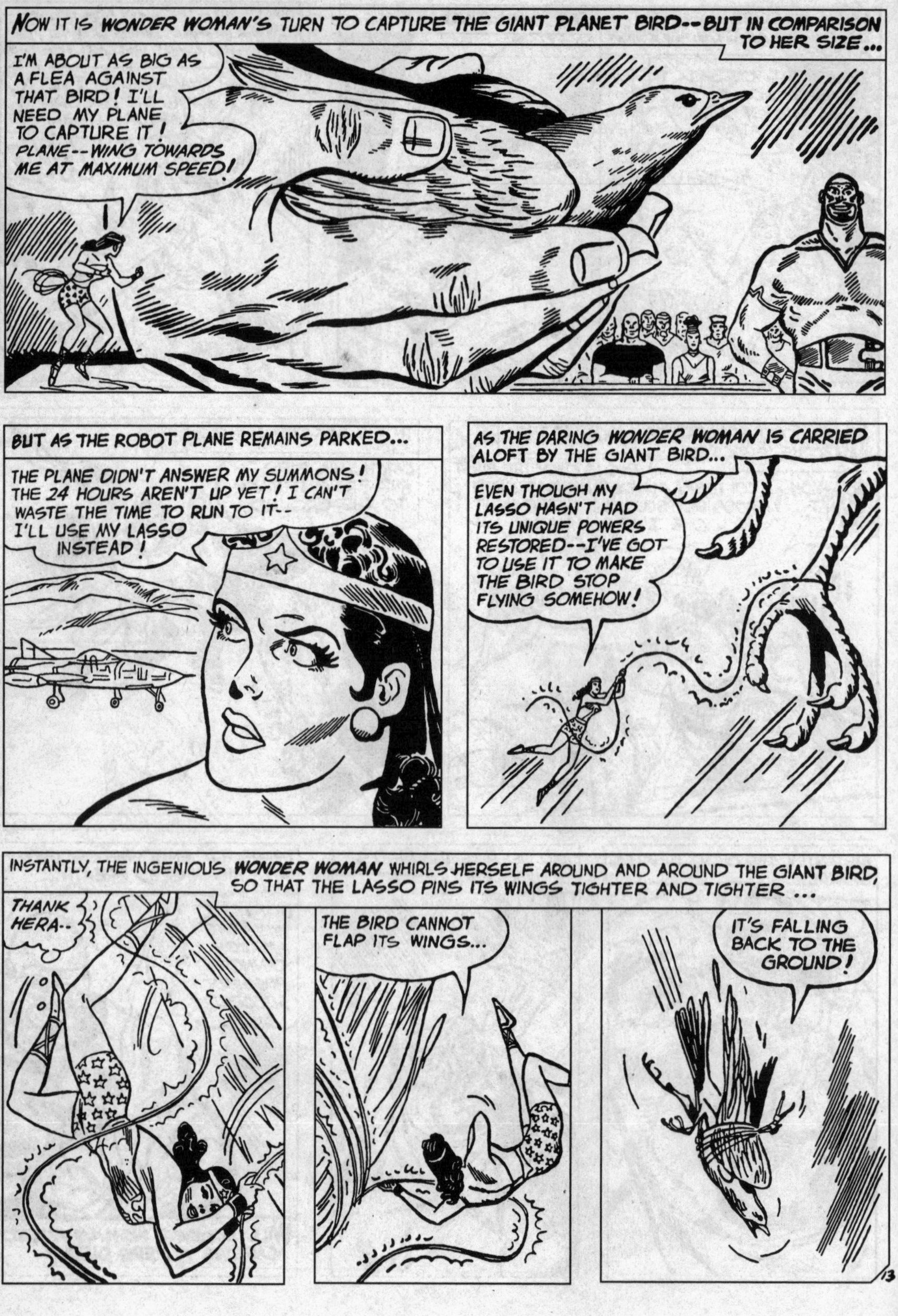
NOW IT IS WONDER WOMAN'S TURN TO CAPTURE THE GIANT PLANET BIRD--BUT IN COMPARISON TO HER SIZE...
I'M ABOUT AS BIG AS A FLEA AGAINST THAT BIRD! I'LL NEED MY PLANE TO CAPTURE IT! PLANE--WING TOWARDS ME AT MAXIMUM SPEED!
BUT AS THE ROBOT PLANE REMAINS PARKED...
THE PLANE DIDN'T ANSWER MY SUMMONS! THE 24 HOURS AREN'T UP YET! I CAN'T WASTE THE TIME TO RUN TO IT-- I'LL USE MY LASSO INSTEAD!
AS THE DARING WONDER WOMAN IS CARRIED ALOFT BY THE GIANT BIRD...
EVEN THOUGH MY LASSO HASN'T HAD ITS UNIQUE POWERS RESTORED--I'VE GOT TO USE IT TO MAKE THE BIRD STOP FLYING SOMEHOW!
INSTANTLY, THE INGENIOUS WONDER WOMAN WHIRLS HERSELF AROUND AND AROUND THE GIANT BIRD, SO THAT THE LASSO PINS ITS WINGS TIGHTER AND TIGHTER ...
THANK HERA--
THE BIRD CANNOT FLAP ITS WINGS...
IT'S FALLING BACK TO THE GROUND!
13

DESPITE THEMSELVES, THE GIGANTIC SPECTATORS HAVE TO CHEER THE AMAZING AMAZON'S FEAT...

I THOUGHT YOU SAID *WONDER WOMAN* COULDN'T PERFORM THESE FEATS!

I GUARANTEE YOU SHE POSITIVELY WILL BE ABSOLUTELY HELPLESS TO EVEN *START* IN THE LAST CONTEST! AND I *MUST* WIN!

HOORAY! HOORAY!

EACH OF YOU MUST FIND AN ARROW I'M SHOOTING INTO THE AIR--AND BRING IT BACK!

I'LL BE RIGHT BACK WITH IT-- TO WIN THE CONTEST! HO! HO! HO!

TWAANG!

AS *WONDER WOMAN'S* ARROW IS RELEASED, SHE MAKES A DARING LEAP ONTO THE HUGE ARROW...

I'VE GOT TO BOARD THIS ARROW!

WHOOSH!

THROUGH THE AIR THE FEARLESS AMAZON IS BORNE...

IN COMPARISON TO MY SIZE, IT'S NOT TRAVELING FEET... BUT *MILES!*

WHOOSH!

IT'S DOUBTFUL IF I COULD HAVE FOUND IT IN TIME TO BRING IT BACK IF I SEARCHED FOR IT ON FOOT!

I MUST BE 1000 MILES FROM THE FINISH LINE! I'LL NEED THE PLANE TO BRING IT BACK IN TIME! ARE THE 24 HOURS UP *NOW*? ARE ITS POWERS RESTORED? WILL IT ANSWER? *PLANE--FLY DUE EAST AT MAXIMUM SPEED...*

AFTER ANXIOUS MOMENTS, A FAMILIAR SHAPE FLASHES THROUGH THE AIR...

HERE IT COMES! *THANK HERA!* THIS MUST MEAN THE 24 HOURS ARE UP! MY ARMS MUST HAVE RECOVERED THEIR UNIQUE POWERS!

AS THE ROBOT PLANE SWOOPS PAST, *WONDER WOMAN* LASSOES IT ON THE WING...

THE LASSO IS WORKING TOO!

BACK FLASHES THE UNIQUE PLANE AT INDESCRIBABLE SPEED AS THE MIGHTY AMAZON HOLDS THE ARROW IN PLACE...

IF MY OPPONENT HAS REACHED THE FINISH LINE AHEAD OF ME WITH HIS ARROW--I WILL HAVE FAILED! WILL I BE IN TIME?

BUT AS THE DYNAMIC *WONDER WOMAN* HURTLES TOWARDS THE FINISH LINE...

GALLOPING GALAXIES! THERE COMES THE AMAZON! SHE'LL PASS ME WITH THAT PLANE! BUT I'LL FIX HER!

THE TREACHEROUS GIANT'S COWARDLY BLOW STARTLES THE AMAZON...

NOW--LET'S SEE YOU CARRY THAT ARROW TO THE FINISH LINE? *HO, HO!*

IT APPEARS AS IF THE KNAVISH GIANT WINS... BUT *WONDER WOMAN* BATTLES TO THE LAST AS SHE HURLS HER BODY BACKWARD...

HERA HELP ME TURN THE ARROW OVER!

I CAN TAKE MY TIME **WALKING** TO THE FINISH LINE! HO! HO!

WHAT DESPERATE PLAN DOES THE AMAZON HAVE IN MIND?

15.

WONDER WOMAN'S AMAZING EFFORT BRINGS THE FEATHERS OF THE ARROW UNDER THE GIANT'S NOSE...

AHHHH-

WHICH TICKLES HIM INTO A GARGANTUAN SNEEZE...

CHOOOO!

HE BLEW ME OVER THE FINISH LINE -- I WIN!

FINISH

ONCE AGAIN, THE INCREDIBLE AMAZON WINS OVER SEEMINGLY UNSURMOUNTABLE ODDS... AND WHEN SHE IS ASKED WHAT PRIZE SHE WANTS...

I WANT YOUR PLANET! JUST AS YOU GAVE EARTH TO THAT SCOUNDREL THERE!

IT--IT IS YOURS! Y-YOU WON IT! TH-THAT IS OUR CUSTOM--AND WE MUST OBEY! B-BUT WHAT WILL YOU DO WITH US?

WONDER WOMAN DISPENSES THE KIND OF JUSTICE SHE IS FAMOUS FOR--AS SHE AND STEVE PREPARE TO DEPART BACK TO EARTH...

JUST BECAUSE YOU ARE BIG, DOESN'T MEAN YOU CAN DISREGARD THE RIGHTS OF THOSE WHO ARE SMALLER THAN YOU! IT IS MY COMMAND THAT YOU RESPECT THE RIGHTS OF OTHERS AND LIVE IN PEACE!

YOU HAVE TAUGHT US A LESSON WE SHALL NEVER FORGET! ALL OF US WISH YOU A SAFE TRIP HOME!

The End

Wonder Woman

By Charles Moulton

THERE ARE MANY STARTLING TALES OF *WONDER WOMAN*--BEAUTIFUL AS APHRODITE, WISE AS ATHENA, SWIFTER THAN MERCURY, AND STRONGER THAN HERCULES--BUT NONE MORE REMARKABLE THAN HER UNTOLD ADVENTURES AS A TEEN-AGER!
HERE IS THE FIRST OF MANY SENSATIONAL STORIES OF THE YOUTHFUL AMAZON, NEVER BEFORE TOLD! HERE IS THE MYSTERY OF...

The INVISIBLE WONDER GIRL!

ON *PARADISE ISLAND*, SECRET ISLAND HOME OF THE AMAZONS, THE QUEEN POSES FOR A GROUP PICTURE WITH HER DAUGHTER, *WONDER GIRL*, AND OTHER AMAZONS...

FINE--! I'LL DEVELOP THE FILM IMMEDIATELY!

CLICK!

BUT, AFTER THE FILM HAS BEEN DEVELOPED...

THAT'S ODD! EVERYONE *BUT* WONDER GIRL APPEARS!

AFTER EXPLAINING TO THE MYSTIFIED QUEEN...

THERE MIGHT HAVE BEEN SOMETHING WRONG WITH THE FILM! I'M NOW USING FILM I'VE TESTED AND FOUND PERFECT! THERE -- I'VE GOT THE PICTURE!

CLICK!

AGAIN THE UNEXPECTED HAPPENS...

LOOK-- *WONDER GIRL* IS THE *ONLY* ONE NOT APPEARING ON THE FILM!

PERHAPS IT'S MY LENS, O QUEEN! I'LL RE-PLACE MY CAMERA AND TAKE ANOTHER PICTURE IMMEDIATELY!

THERE--! I'M SURE *THIS* ONE WILL BE ALL RIGHT! NOTHING COULD GO WRONG! EVERY PIECE OF EQUIPMENT HAS BEEN TESTED! THERE'S NO REASON WHY *WONDER GIRL* SHOULDN'T APPEAR!

CLICK!

FOR THE THIRD TIME, HOWEVER, THE STARTLING PHENOMENON OCCURS...

DAUGHTER--IS THERE ANY REASON *YOU* CAN THINK OF THAT WOULD MAKE IT IMPOSSIBLE TO PHOTO-GRAPH YOU?

N-N-NO!

WHAT IS THE EXPLANATION FOR THIS AMAZING SITUATION?

2

AS THE WHOLE ISLAND BUZZES WITH NEWS OF THE UNIQUE HAPPENING...

THERE'S SOMETHING STRANGE ABOUT *WONDER GIRL!* SHE'S NOT ACTING LIKE HERSELF! SOMETHING'S BOTHERING HER!

SHE WAS ALL RIGHT UNTIL NOW, NOBLE QUEEN! I'VE BEEN TAKING PICTURES OF HER UNTIL TODAY-- AND EVERY ONE TURNED OUT ALL RIGHT! REMEMBER THE ONE I TOOK OF HER YESTERDAY...?

"*THE NORTHEASTERN TIP OF OUR ISLAND HAD SUFFERED A SLIGHT QUAKE...*"

RRRRUMBLE!

"*THE QUAKE SHATTERED A HUGE PILLAR WE HAD ERECTED FOR A NEW TEMPLE...*"

AMAZONS-- SCATTER! THE PILLAR IS FALLING!

SAVE YOURSELF, DIANA-- I'M TRIPPING--!

CRAACK!

"*BUT, DISREGARDING THE PERIL TO HERSELF, WONDER GIRL THRUST HER BODY IN FRONT OF HER MOTHER, AND WITH THE MIGHTY POWER DEEDED TO HER BY THE GREAT HERCULES...*"

DIANA SAVED THE QUEEN!

AND I'VE GOT THE *PICTURE!*

CLICK!

THE AMAZON PHOTOGRAPHER CONCLUDES HER STORY BY SHOWING THE PICTURE AGAIN..

THERE'S THE PICTURE OF THE RESCUE ALL RIGHT! BUT-- WHAT COULD HAVE HAPPENED BETWEEN YESTERDAY AND TODAY TO ACCOUNT FOR DIANA *NOT* BEING ABLE TO BE PHOTOGRAPHED *NOW?*

I DON'T KNOW, O QUEEN!

THE TROUBLED QUEEN QUESTIONS THE *WONDER GIRL* ...

IS ANYTHING WRONG, DIANA? ARE YOU SURE THERE'S NOTHING YOU WANT TO TELL ME? I'M YOUR MOTHER--YOU SHOULD FEEL FREE TO TELL ME ANYTHING THAT MIGHT BE BOTHERING YOU!

N-NO...NOTHING IS... IS...BOTHERING ME...

SOMETHING IS WRONG--BUT WHAT? I'LL REMAIN NEARBY-- IN CASE DIANA CHANGES HER MIND--AND WANTS TO CON- FIDE IN ME!

SUDDENLY...ABOVE...

SOMETHING HAS GONE WRONG WITH THAT EXPER- IMENTAL PLANE--THE AMAZON PILOT IS BEING EJECTED!

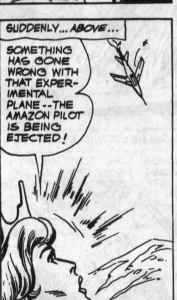

AND THEN--TO THE QUEEN'S HORROR...

DIANA--! LOOK OUT FOR THAT PLANE--IT'S HEADING STRAIGHT FOR YOU! THANK HERA--YOUR UNIQUE SPEED WILL EASILY BE ABLE TO GET YOU OUT OF HARM'S WAY!

BUT, AS THE *WONDER GIRL* SEEMS ROOTED TO THE SPOT...

WHAT HAS HAPPENED TO YOU, DIANA--? *LOOK OUT--!*

CRASH!

AMAZONS HURRY TO THE SCENE OF THE ACCIDENT AND STARE ACCUSINGLY AT THE *WONDER GIRL*...

YOU HAVE THE SPEED OF MERCURY-- AND THE STRENGTH OF HERCULES-- WHY DIDN'T YOU USE THEM TO SAVE THE QUEEN FROM HARM?

AND THEN--A STARTLING CONFESSION...

I--I'M *NOT* REALLY *WONDER GIRL!* I'M *RRARA*, A CHAMELEON GIRL! I-- T--TOOK HER PLACE! AND WHEN I D--DID... SHE WAS AUTOMATICALLY TRANSPORTED TO M--MY WORLD--THE *CHAMELEON PLANET*-- WHERE ALL WE CHAMELEONS HAVE THE POWER TO CHANGE OUR SHAPES! WHEN WE DO-- IT'S ONLY AN *ILLUSION*--THAT'S WHY I DIDN'T APPEAR ON THE PHOTO- GRAPHS!

"*I'D* BEEN WATCHING *WONDER GIRL* ON OUR *CHAMEOSCOPE*... AND I THOUGHT HOW WONDERFUL IT WOULD BE TO TAKE HER PLACE FOR 24 HOURS... I DIDN'T MEAN ANY HARM..."

SUDDENLY, AN AWESOME SHAPE LOOMS IN THE SKIES --AND A RAY THUNDERBOLTS DOWN ...

WE'RE BEING INVADED!

WITH THE QUEEN UNCONSCIOUS -- WE NEED *WONDER GIRL* DESPERATELY NOW TO BEAT BACK THIS ATTACK! CHAMELEON-- BRING HER BACK!

VROOOSH!

ZZZIP!

BUT TO THE CHAMELEON'S DISMAY...

WHAT'S HAPPENING? WHY ISN'T *WONDER GIRL* BACK? WHY ARE *YOU* STILL HERE?

I--I DON'T KNOW! SOMETHING IS STOPPING HER! I *CAN'T* BRING HER *BACK!*

ZZZIIlp!

ZZZIIlp!

WHAT CAN HAVE HAPPENED AT THIS CRUCIAL MOMENT ON THE CHAMELEON PLANET?

AT THAT MOMENT, ON THE CHAMELEON PLANET, THE REAL *WONDER GIRL* STARES ABOUT HER BEWILDEREDLY...

CHAMELEONS-- CHANGE YOUR SHAPES! AVOID THE DANGER OF THE RAIN OF COSMIC DUST!

HOW DID I GET HERE? WHO ARE THESE PEOPLE WHO CAN CHANGE THEIR SHAPES AT WILL TO PROTECT THEMSELVES? WHAT IS THREATENING THEM?

NOW WE KNOW! IT IS THE COSMIC DUST WHICH ACTS AS A SHIELD--PREVENTING WONDER GIRL FROM BEING TRANSPORTED BACK TO PARADISE ISLAND IN ITS GREAT MOMENT OF PERIL!

SUDDENLY... THUNDERBOLTS OF JOVE! THAT FALLING METEOR IS RAINING COSMIC DUST! HERA HELP ME TO STOP THIS SHOWER OF DOOM!

WITH THE POWER GIVEN HER BY THE IMMORTAL HERCULES, WONDER GIRL HURLS A TREMENDOUS BLAST OF AIR...

WHOOSH!

THE NEXT MOMENT, THE MASSIVE MENACE IS BLOWN BACK INTO SPACE...

HURRAY FOR THE AMAZON GIRL! SHE HAS SAVED US! IT'S SAFE TO RETURN TO OUR REAL SHAPES!

WHREEE!

16

MEANWHILE ON *PARADISE ISLAND*, AS THE INTERPLANETARY INVADER HOVERS OVERHEAD...

CHAMELEON--YOU *MUST* TRANSPORT *WONDER GIRL* BACK!

I'M TRYING-- I'M TRYING--!

AND THEN, WITH THE SUDDENNESS WITH WHICH SHE HAS DISAPPEARED...

LOOK--THE *REAL* WONDER GIRL IS BACK!

B-B-BUT SOMETHING'S WRONG! I SHOULD HAVE BEEN TRANSPORTED *BACK* TO THE CHAMELEON PLANET!

PERHAPS THE RAIN OF COSMIC DUST I WAS IN--HAS DESTROYED YOUR POWER TO RETURN! SUFFERING *SAPPHO!* WHAT A DILEMMA! THERE *CAN'T* BE TWO *WONDER GIRLS*--THINK WHAT CHAOS THAT WOULD CAUSE!

MOTHER--! WHAT'S HAPPENED TO HER?

SHE WAS HURT TRYING TO SAVE THE CHAMELEON GIRL--THINKING SHE WAS *YOU!* BUT WE'RE STILL FACED WITH A THREAT! LOOK UP *WONDER GIRL!* WE'RE BEING INVADED!

INSTANTLY, *WONDER GIRL* LEAPS UPWARD...

THAT INVASION CRAFT IS REMAINING WHERE IT IS--FIRING DOWN AT THE ISLAND! I'LL USE RISING CURRENTS OF AIR TO REACH IT!

ZZZZZT!

ZZZZZT!

ZZZZT!

WITH UNCANNY AGILITY...

WONDER GIRL RIDES THE AIR CURRENTS...

NARROWLY AVOIDING THE RAYS SHOT AT HER...

AND THEN, LIGHTLY POISED ON AN UPDRAFT, THE *WONDER GIRL* DELIVERS A HERCULEAN BLOW...

I MUST TRY TO KEEP THEM FROM GETTING SET TO FIRE AT US AGAIN!

WITH THE GRIM JUSTICE WHICH OVERTAKES RUTHLESS INVADERS--THE ATTACKING SPACE CRAFT REELS INTO ITS OWN BLAZING RAYS AND...

LIGHTLY, *WONDER GIRL* RIDES A DOWNDRAFT TOWARDS THE ISLAND...

THERE'S STILL THE PROBLEM OF *TWO WONDER GIRLS!* WHAT'S GOING TO HAPPEN WITH THE CHAMELEON GIRL AND MYSELF BEING IDENTICAL?

BUT, AS THE AMAZON LANDS...

PLEASE FORGIVE ME, QUEEN-- I MEANT NO HARM!

FORGIVE YOU FOR WHAT?

SUFFERING SAPPHO--EVEN MY OWN MOTHER *CAN'T* TELL US APART!

BUT THEN...

YOU'RE CHANGING SHAPE?

IT MUST HAVE BEEN A DELAYED REACTION!

FINALLY, A BEAUTIFUL YOUNG GIRL RETURNS...

MOTHER--AS LONG AS SHE CAN'T GO BACK TO HER OWN PLANET--LET'S MAKE HER AN HONORARY AMAZON AND TEACH HER EVERYTHING WE KNOW!

IT SHALL BE DONE, DIANA--AND *YOU* SHALL TEACH HER!

MORE *WONDER GIRL* ADVENTURES IN FUTURE ISSUES OF *WONDER WOMAN!* *The End*

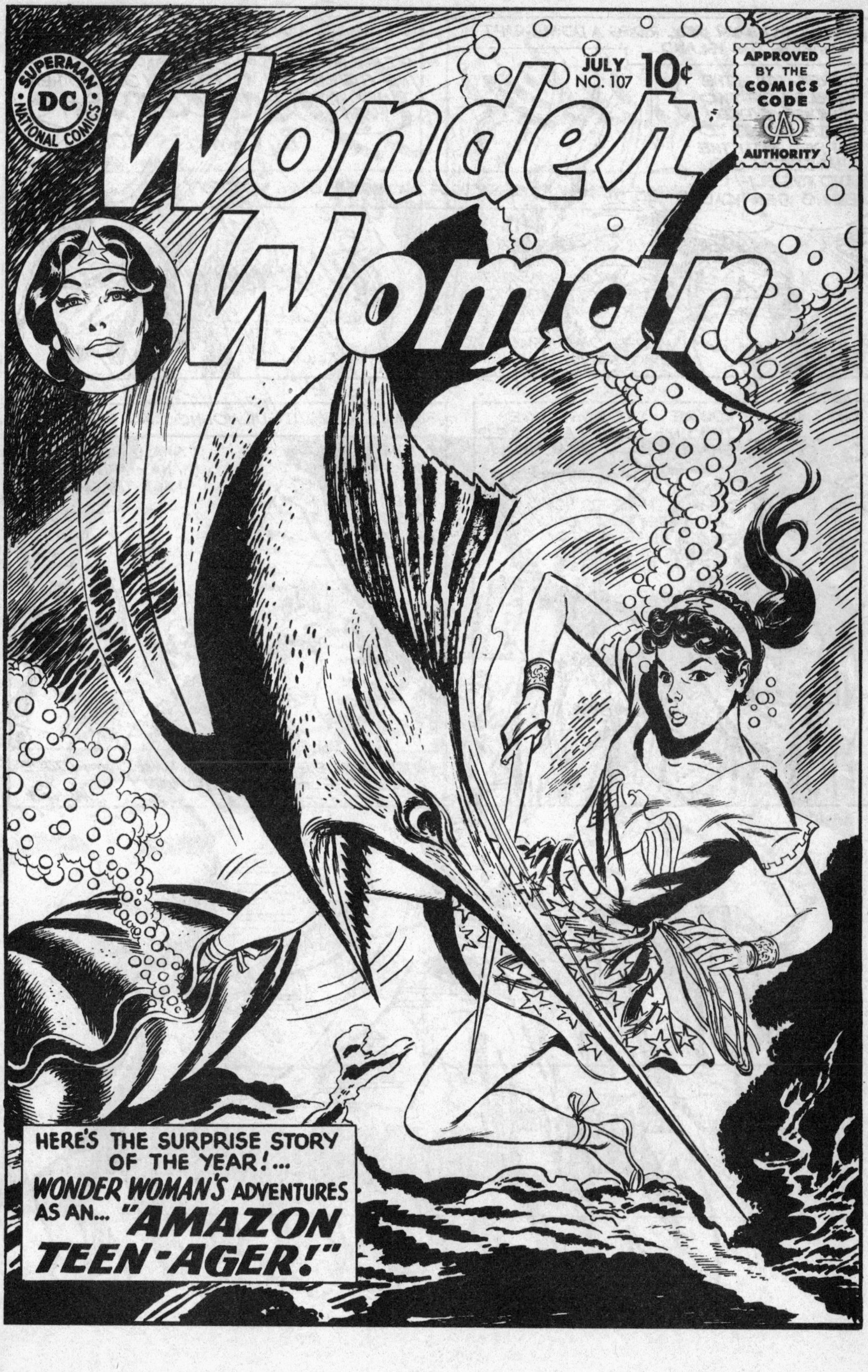
SUPERMAN
DC
NATIONAL COMICS
Wonder Woman
JULY
NO. 107
10¢
APPROVED BY THE COMICS CODE AUTHORITY
HERE'S THE SURPRISE STORY OF THE YEAR!... WONDER WOMAN'S ADVENTURES AS AN... "AMAZON TEEN-AGER!"

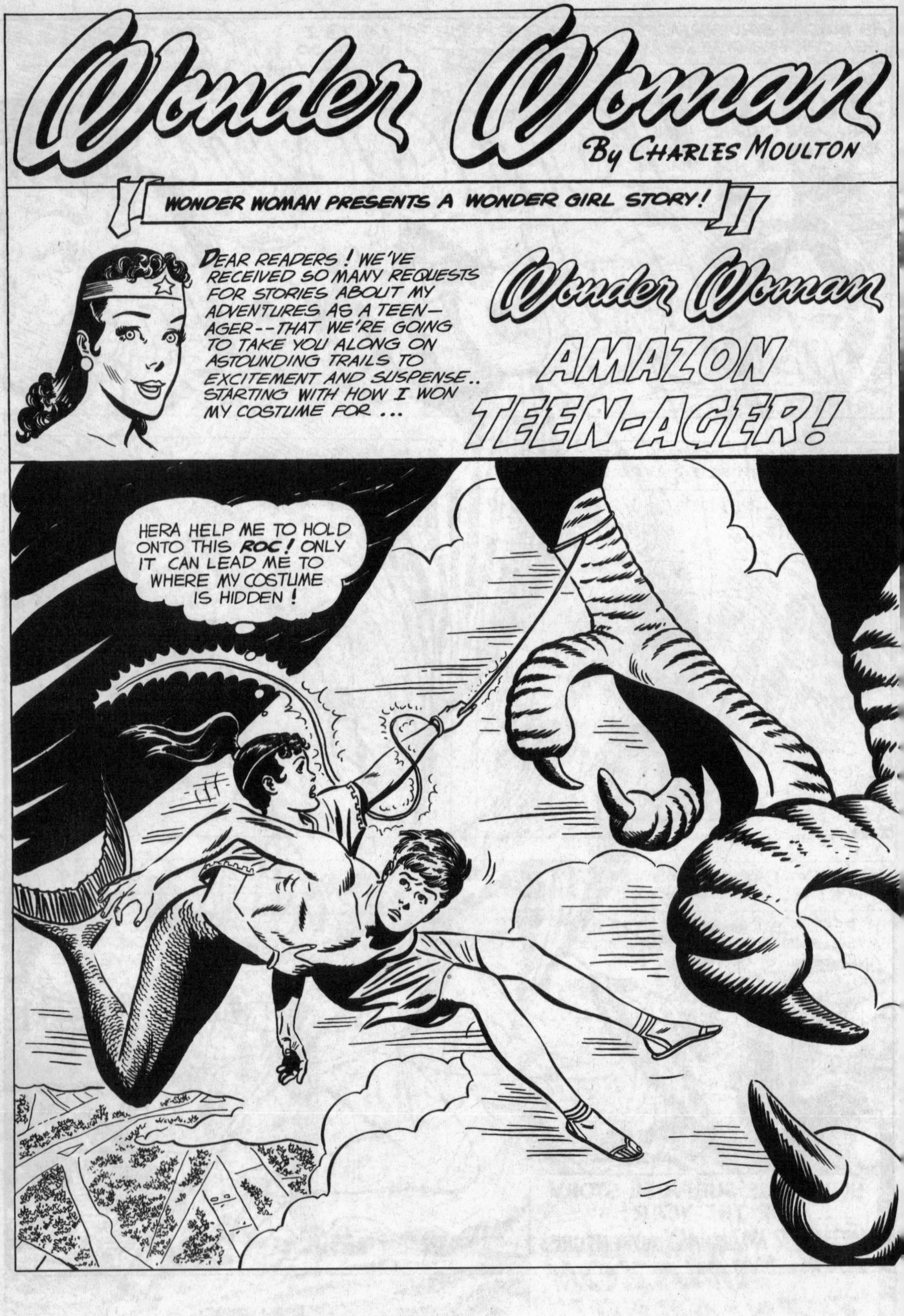
Wonder Woman
By CHARLES MOULTON
WONDER WOMAN PRESENTS A WONDER GIRL STORY!
DEAR READERS! WE'VE RECEIVED SO MANY REQUESTS FOR STORIES ABOUT MY ADVENTURES AS A TEEN-AGER--THAT WE'RE GOING TO TAKE YOU ALONG ON ASTOUNDING TRAILS TO EXCITEMENT AND SUSPENSE.. STARTING WITH HOW I WON MY COSTUME FOR ...
Wonder Woman
AMAZON TEEN-AGER!
HERA HELP ME TO HOLD ONTO THIS ROC! ONLY IT CAN LEAD ME TO WHERE MY COSTUME IS HIDDEN!

AS *WONDER GIRL* SURFACES AFTER A DIVE IN THE SEA OFF *PARADISE ISLAND*...

SHADES OF PLUTO! WH-WHERE DID *YOU* COME FROM? WE'RE THOUSANDS OF MILES FROM LAND! EXCEPT FOR PARADISE ISLAND! AND YOU CAN'T GO ASHORE! ATHENA'S LAW FORBIDS ALL MALES!

LAND? I NEVER GO ASHORE! HAHAHA!

GREAT HERA! H-H-H-HE'S A MERBOY!

SPLASH!

PLAYFULLY AS A DOLPHIN, THE MERBOY LEAPS OVER *WONDER GIRL'S* HEAD...

YOU ARE THE PRETTIEST FISH I HAVE EVER SEEN!

I'M AN AMAZON! NOT A FISH!

MY NAME IS RONNO, *WONDER GIRL!* FAREWELL! IF EVER YOU SHOULD NEED ME -- I WILL BE NEARBY!

THE NEXT DAY, *WONDER GIRL* AND THE QUEEN ARE IN THE AMAZON LABORATORY, VIEWING THE TIME AND SPACE TELEVISOR...

IT FEELS STRANGE -- WATCHING MYSELF IN THIS TIME MACHINE -- AND SEEING HOW I'LL LOOK WHEN I'M OLDER!

YOUR MISSION WILL BE TO HELP ANYONE IN DISTRESS -- ANYWHERE IN THE UNIVERSE! I WONDER HOW YOU'RE GOING TO SAVE THE CREW IN THAT BURNING PLANE?

2

THE RAPT AUDIENCE WATCHES *WONDER WOMAN* DIVE HER ROBOT PLANE AT SUCH FLASH-ING SPEED--THAT SHE WHIPS THE FLAMES AWAY FROM THE PLANE IN DISTRESS...

WHOOSH!

AT THE END OF THE PREVIEW INTO *WONDER GIRL'S* FUTURE CAREER AS *WONDER WOMAN...*

MOTHER! I WAS THINKING ABOUT THE COSTUME I'M GOING TO WEAR WHEN I'M OLDER! IT'S BEAUTIFUL! CAN'T I START WEARING IT NOW?

WONDER WOMAN HAD TO **WIN** THE RIGHT TO **WEAR** THAT COSTUME-- BY PERFORMING INCREDIBLE FEATS! ARE YOU PREPARED TO DO THE SAME?

WHEN *WONDER GIRL* EAGERLY AGREES TO THE TRIALS...ALL THE AMAZONS ON THE ISLAND ARE TOLD TO SEND IN SUGGESTIONS ABOUT WHAT *WONDER GIRL'S* COSTUME SHOULD LOOK LIKE...

AND THEN, WHEN ONE IS FINALLY SELECTED...

OH, MOTHER! AREN'T YOU GOING TO LET ME SEE THE WINNING SKETCH?

IT'S A SECRET, DIANA! YOU'LL HAVE TO WIN IT FIRST--BEFORE YOU CAN SEE IT! BUT I **CAN** TELL YOU IT'S COMPOSED OF THREE PARTS! AND NOW, WE MUST SELECT THE FEATS YOU WILL PERFORM!

TO REMOVE ANY POSSIBILITY OF FAVORITISM, *ALL* THE AMAZONS SUBMIT THEIR IDEAS OF DIFFICULT TASKS... WITHOUT THEIR SIGNATURES...

3

FINALLY, AN IMPARTIAL BOARD OF AMAZONS MAKES THE SELECTIONS FROM ALL THE ENTRIES...

WE CHOSE THESE THREE FEATS AS THE MOST DIFFICULT SUBMITTED! THEY WERE UNSIGNED SO WE DON'T KNOW WHO THOUGHT THEM UP, NOBLE QUEEN!

THE MOMENT THE QUEEN GLANCES AT THEM...

GREAT HERA! IT'S DIANA'S HAND-WRITING! *YOU* SELECTED THE MOST DIFFICULT TASKS ANYONE THOUGHT OF!

I WANTED TO BE WORTHY OF THE COSTUME, MOTHER! JUST AS *WONDER WOMAN* IS WORTHY OF HERS!

A HUSH FALLS UPON THE ASSEMBLED AMAZONS AS THE QUEEN ANNOUNCES...

AS YOU ALL KNOW-- *WONDER GIRL'S* COSTUME CONSISTS OF *THREE* SEPARATE PARTS! SHE WILL FIND OUT *WHAT* THESE PARTS ARE--*ONLY* IF SHE SUCCEEDS IN WINNING THEM! IT WILL TAKE DAYS FOR US TO PLACE THEM WHERE SHE WILL HAVE TO BE A *REAL WONDER GIRL*-- TO RECOVER THEM!

DAYS LATER *WONDER GIRL* EAGERLY READS THE FIRST COMMAND...

YOU MAY PERFORM THESE IN ANY ORDER! ONE OF THE THREE PARTS ON YOUR COSTUME IS *INSIDE* THE CANNIBAL CLAM!

INSTANTLY, THE TEEN-AGE AMAZON BEGINS THE FIRST OF HER STARTLING MISSIONS WITH THE BENDING OF A TREE OVERLOOK-ING THE SEA...

THIS WILL HELP ME GET TO MY DESTINATION QUICKER!

TWAAANG!

AS *WONDER GIRL* DIVES INTO THE SEA, SHE IS UNAWARE THAT BELOW HER...

Ahh! 'TIS MY *WONDER GIRL*! I SHALL KEEP MY EYE ON HER IN CASE SHE NEEDS MY HELP!

FAR BELOW, THE TEEN-AGE AMAZON CLEAVES THE WATER LIKE A LIGHTNING BOLT...

THERE'S THE CANNIBAL CLAM! THE FIRST PART OF MY COSTUME IS INSIDE IT!

As *WONDER GIRL* NEARS THE GIANT CLAM...

HOW BEAUTIFUL! STARS FOR MY COSTUME--JUST LIKE *WONDER WOMAN'S!* AMAZONS MUST HAVE PLACED THEM INSIDE!

BUT THE PRESENCE OF THE DARING GIRL CAUSES THE SINISTER CLAM TO OPEN AND CLOSE ITS MASSIVE JAWS...

IF I GO INSIDE THE CLAM FOR THE STARS--I'LL BE-COME A PRISONER--HOW CAN I GET THEM OUT?

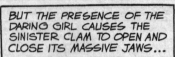

CLUMP!

SEEING A CORAL FORMATION NEARBY, *WONDER GIRL* GETS AN INGENIOUS IDEA...

I'LL FASHION A PIECE IN THE SHAPE OF A SWORD!

A MOMENT LATER, THRUSTING THE SWORD OF CORAL BETWEEN THE CLASHING JAWS OF THE GIANT CLAM...

THANK HERA! THIS WILL KEEP THE CLAM OPEN LONG ENOUGH FOR ME TO TAKE OUT THE STARS FOR MY COSTUME!

EAGERLY, THE TEEN-AGE AMAZON FULFILLS HER FIRST TASK...

I'VE WON THE FIRST PART OF MY COSTUME!

WITH GIRLISH ENTHUSIASM SHE PLACES THEM ON HER TOGA...

THERE'S A SPECIAL ADHESIVE ON THEM--SO I CAN PUT THEM ON WITHOUT SEWING THEM ON!

5

BUT, AS SHE STEPS OUTSIDE, *WONDER GIRL* IS CONFRONTED BY AN OMINOUS SIGHT...

IT'S THE MERBOY! COME TO WARN ME ABOUT THIS GIANT SWORDFISH! ONLY TO FALL INTO DEADLY PERIL HIMSELF!

THE ONLY WEAPON I HAVE AGAINST THIS MONSTER -- IS THIS SWORD!

BUT NO SOONER HAS SHE SNATCHED THE SWORD FROM BETWEEN THE GIANT CLAM'S JAWS THAN...

SHADES OF PLUTO! MY FOOT IS CAUGHT!

PART TWO OF THIS EXCITING STORY CONTINUES..

76

WONDER GIRL -- TEEN-AGE AMAZON... PART TWO

SUCCESSFULLY COMPLETING THE FIRST OF HER THREE TASKS TO WIN THE RIGHT TO A UNIQUE COSTUME ALL HER OWN -- WONDER GIRL IS MENACED BY A GIANT SWORDFISH...

EVEN THOUGH SHE IS A PRISONER OF THE GIANT CLAM, WONDER GIRL BEGINS THE MOST AMAZING DUEL IN HISTORY... BATTLING A HUGE SWORDFISH WITH A SWORD OF CORAL...

HERA HELP ME WIN THIS BATTLE!

KLUNK!

KLUNK

THANK HERA! HE'S HAD ENOUGH!

THEN, WITH A MIGHTY BLOW OF HER SWORD...

CRAACK!

HOW GOOD IT IS TO BE FREE AGAIN!

NEXT, THE AMAZON TEEN-AGER TENDS TO THE PROSTRATE MERBOY...

A LITTLE FRESH AIR WILL DO US BOTH GOOD!

ON THE SURFACE, THE MERBOY RECOVERS AND...

WHEN I SAW YOU IN DEADLY PERIL FROM THE SWORDFISH-- ALL I COULD THINK OF -- WAS TO SAVE YOU--NO MATTER WHAT THE COST!

THANK YOU! IT WAS VERY BRAVE OF YOU!

AS SOON AS WONDER GIRL IS SURE THAT THE MERBOY IS RECOVERED...

I MUST BE OFF ON MY NEXT QUEST! FAREWELL!

FAREWELL! BUT IF YOU SHOULD NEED ANY HELP--I SHALL BE AROUND!

THE SECOND FEAT WONDER GIRL MUST PERFORM DIRECTS HER TO...

ANOTHER PART OF MY COSTUME IS ON THE GIANT ROC'S NEST--ON TOP OF THAT CLIFF!

BUT AS THE TEEN-AGE AMAZON ATTEMPTS TO CLIMB UP...

THE ROCK IS COATED WITH A SLIPPERY SUBSTANCE--I CAN'T GET A HOLD--ANYWHERE!

WONDER GIRL NEXT TRIES TO RIDE THE UP AND DOWN DRAFTS...BUT AGAIN...

AIR CURRENTS--

NOT STRONG ENOUGH--

--TO CARRY ME U--

THE YOUNG AMAZON TURNS TO THE THIRD AND LAST DIRECTIVE ...

I CAN TAKE THESE FEATS IN ANY ORDER! I'LL COME BACK TO THE ROC'S NEST LAST! I'LL TRY THIS ONE INSTEAD! ANOTHER PART OF YOUR COSTUME IS IN THE CRATER OF VOLCANO ISLAND!

AT FLASHING SPEED, THE TIRELESS TEEN-AGER SWIMS TOWARDS THE MYSTERIOUS ISLAND ...

VOLCANO ISLAND! NOW TO FIND A PART OF MY COSTUME IN THE CRATER!

UP TO THE EDGE OF THE BOILING CRATER WONDER GIRL RUNS ...

THERE'S THE SECOND PART OF MY COSTUME! A LASSO--JUST LIKE THE ONE I'LL USE WHEN I'M OLDER!

DARINGLY, THE AMAZON TEEN-AGER LEAPS DOWN...

IT'S A GOOD THING WE AMAZONS WERE TRAINED TO WITHSTAND TREMENDOUS HEAT AND COLD! NO ORDINARY PERSON WOULD BE SAFE TRYING THIS!

AS SHE FLASHES BY...

I'VE GOT THE LASSO!

AND THEN, WITHIN SIGHT OF THE YAWNING LAVA, WONDER GIRL'S PLUNGE IS HALTED WHEN ...

JUST AS I HOPED! THE TREMENDOUS UPDRAFTS CREATED BY THE HOT AIR--ARE STOPPING ME!

19

WITH HER UNCANNY SKILL, THE AMAZON *TEEN-AGER* "RIDES" THE UPDRAFTS TO SAFETY...

I'M OUT AT LAST! NOW--TO GET BACK TO THE *ROC'S* NEST ON TOP OF THE CLIFF!

AT THE BASE OF THE SLIPPERY CLIFF, **WONDER GIRL** HURLS HER LASSO UP...BUT...

GREAT HERA! THE CLIFF IS SO SLIPPERY THAT EVEN THE LASSO CAN'T TIGHTEN ON ANYTHING!

AND THEN... AN OUTCRY...

LOOK OUT! **WONDER GIRL!**

THE **MERBOY** HAS FALLEN INTO THE CLUTCHES OF THE GIANT *ROC* HIMSELF!

INSTANTLY, THE YOUNG AMAZON HURLS HER GLEAMING LASSO UPWARDS...

DON'T WORRY--I'LL SAVE YOU!

THANK HERA! THE LASSO WILL HELP ME TO SAVE THE MERBOY!

AGILELY **WONDER GIRL** CLIMBS UP THE LASSO..

WHEN I SAW THE *ROC* FLY TOWARDS YOU--I TRIED TO FRIGHTEN HIM OFF!

THAT WAS VERY COURAGEOUS OF YOU!

10

ABOVE ITS NEST, THE HUGE WINGED-MONSTER RELEASES THE MERBOY...

THUNDERBOLTS OF JOVE! THERE'S THE LAST PART OF MY NEW COSTUME IN THE *ROC'S* NEST--THE EAGLE EMBLEM I WEAR AS *WONDER WOMAN!*

DANGLING FROM THE LASSO, *WONDER GIRL* SEIZES THE EAGLE EMBLEM IN ONE HAND...

THE LAST PART OF MY COSTUME!

INSTANTLY, THE SPECIAL ADHESIVE QUALITY OF THE EMBLEM ENABLES THE *TEEN-AGER* TO FASTEN IT ON ...

YOU LOOK-- BEAUTIFUL!

BUT--THEN--AN UNEXPECTED DEVELOPMENT...

SUFFERING SAPPHO! THE *ROC!* HE'S FLYING AWAY WITH MY LASSO! IF I DON'T RECOVER IT--ALL MY EFFORTS WILL BE FOR NOTHING!

SEIZING THE MERBOY, *WONDER GIRL* HURLS HERSELF DESPERATELY AFTER THE GREAT BIRD...

IF I DON'T RECOVER THE LASSO--MY COSTUME WILL BE INCOMPLETE --AND I SHALL HAVE FAILED!

HER PRODIGIOUS LEAP PLACES THE AMAZON TEEN-AGER WITHIN REACH OF THE LASSO...

BY PLUTO! YOU'VE YANKED YOUR LASSO FREE!

BUT THEN, THE ENRAGED GIANT TURNS UPON THE FALLING COUPLE...

HERA HELP ME ELUDE HIM!

FINDING AIR CURRENTS...

SNAP!

WONDER GIRL TWISTS AND TURNS ON THEM...

SNAP!

GRIMLY ELUDING THE WINGED PURSUER'S CLUTCHES...

UNTIL SHE COMES WITHIN REACH OF THE HOLE IN THE ROCK SHE USES TO ESCAPE INTO...

THANK HERA--THE ROC CAN NO LONGER FOLLOW US!

WHEN THE AMAZON GIRL AND THE MERBOY FINALLY SURFACE, THE WINGED FURY IS GONE...

I TOLD YOU I WOULD BE AROUND IN CASE YOU EVER NEEDED ME!

I CAN'T THANK YOU ENOUGH!

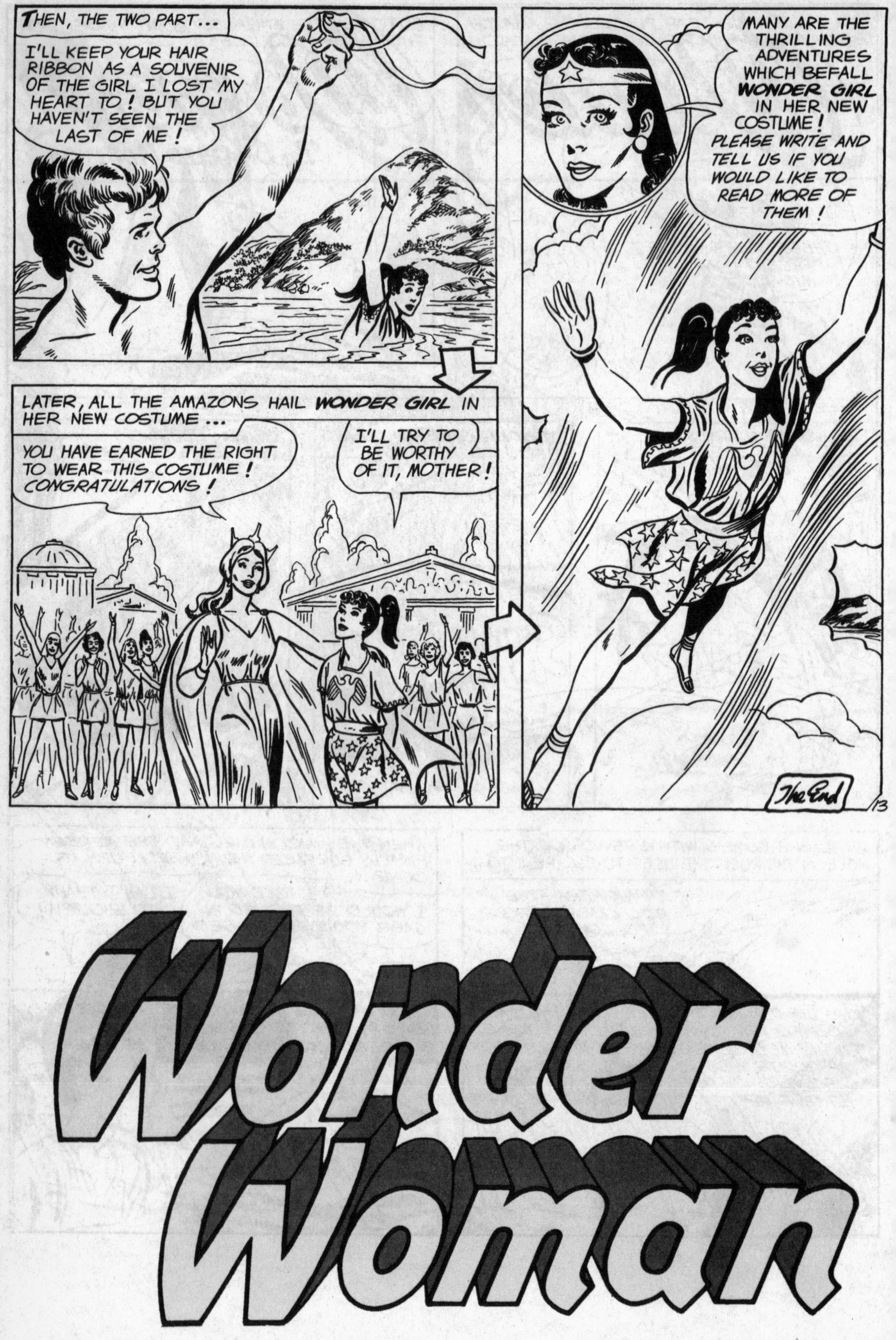
THEN, THE TWO PART...
I'LL KEEP YOUR HAIR RIBBON AS A SOUVENIR OF THE GIRL I LOST MY HEART TO! BUT YOU HAVEN'T SEEN THE LAST OF ME!
LATER, ALL THE AMAZONS HAIL WONDER GIRL IN HER NEW COSTUME...
YOU HAVE EARNED THE RIGHT TO WEAR THIS COSTUME! CONGRATULATIONS!
I'LL TRY TO BE WORTHY OF IT, MOTHER!
MANY ARE THE THRILLING ADVENTURES WHICH BEFALL WONDER GIRL IN HER NEW COSTUME! PLEASE WRITE AND TELL US IF YOU WOULD LIKE TO READ MORE OF THEM!
The End
13

Wonder Woman

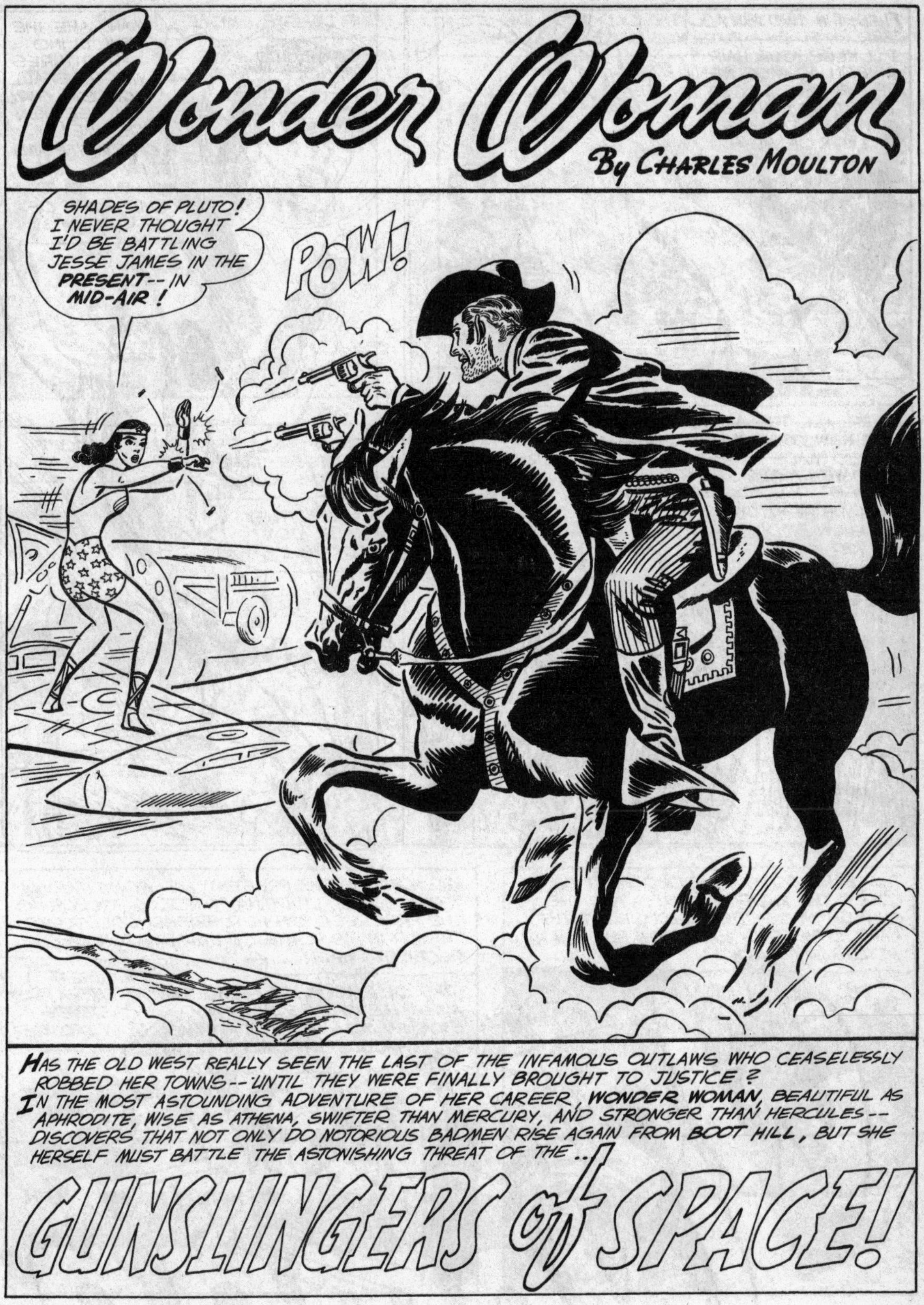
Wonder Woman
By CHARLES MOULTON
SHADES OF PLUTO! I NEVER THOUGHT I'D BE BATTLING JESSE JAMES IN THE PRESENT-- IN MID-AIR!
POW!
HAS THE OLD WEST REALLY SEEN THE LAST OF THE INFAMOUS OUTLAWS WHO CEASELESSLY ROBBED HER TOWNS--UNTIL THEY WERE FINALLY BROUGHT TO JUSTICE ?
IN THE MOST ASTOUNDING ADVENTURE OF HER CAREER, WONDER WOMAN, BEAUTIFUL AS APHRODITE, WISE AS ATHENA, SWIFTER THAN MERCURY, AND STRONGER THAN HERCULES-- DISCOVERS THAT NOT ONLY DO NOTORIOUS BADMEN RISE AGAIN FROM BOOT HILL, BUT SHE HERSELF MUST BATTLE THE ASTONISHING THREAT OF THE..
GUNSLINGERS of SPACE!

ALMOST A CENTURY AGO, THE OLD WEST WAS TERRORIZED BY A RUTHLESS GANG OF OUTLAWS...

RUN! IT'S THE JESSE JAMES GANG!

POW! POW!

THEIR LEADER SEEMED INVINCIBLE...

NEXT TIME YOU WON'T TRY TUH TANGLE WITH JESSE JAMES!

POW! POW!

LATER, ANOTHER GUNMAN APPEARED... AND HE TOO MADE A NAME OF TERROR FOR HIMSELF WITH A GUN...

WHEN YUH HEAR THIS-- YUH KNOW BILLY THE KID IS SIGNIN' HIS NAME IN LEAD!

BAM BAM BAM!

BUT SOONER OR LATER, JUSTICE CAUGHT UP WITH JESSE JAMES AND HIS GANG-- AND BILLY THE KID...

THAT'S WHERE THEY ALL END UP, SON! ON BOOT HILL!

THE YEARS GO BY--THE OLD WEST BECOMES THE MODERN WEST... AND THE GUNMEN WHO RODE THROUGHOUT THE LAND RUTHLESSLY...ARE NOW BUT CHARACTERS IN A BOOK...

Famous Outlaws Of The West

SSE JAMES

AND NOW IT IS THE PRESENT, AND AT MILITARY INTELLIGENCE, LT. DIANA PRINCE IS FOLLOWING THE PROGRESS OF HER FRIEND COL. STEVE TREVOR IN HIS PLANE ON HER AMAZON OMNI-RECEIVER WHEN...

ST-9 CALLING BASE! SOMETHING MUST BE WRONG WITH MY OXYGEN INTAKE! I'M HAVING HALLUCINATIONS!

GREAT HERA! STEVE'S IN TROUBLE!

2

EVEN AS DIANA CHANGES INTO HER SECRET IDENTITY OF **WONDER WOMAN**, THE CELEBRATED AMAZON, THE PILOT STAMMERS HIS REPORT...

I--I--DAREN'T REPORT WHAT I SEE--PERHAPS--IT WILL GO AWAY!

SUMMONING HER ROBOT PLANE, WHICH RESPONDS TO THE VIBRATIONS OF HER VOICE...

I'VE NEVER HEARD STEVE SO CONFUSED! HE MUST BE IN TERRIBLE PERIL! PLANE-- ZOOM AND HEAD DUE EAST AT MAXIMUM SPEED!

WITH FLASHING SPEED, THE UNIQUE PLANE HURLS **WONDER WOMAN** TOWARDS HER RENDEZVOUS WITH THE THREATENED PILOT'S PLANE...

STEVE'S STILL SENDING! AT LEAST HE'S STILL IN THE AIR! THANK HERA!

I WISH THERE WAS SOMEONE ELSE UP HERE TO--TO CONFIRM OR DENY-- WHAT I SEE!

AND THEN, THE AMAZON REACHES THE SPOT IN THE SKIES WHERE STEVE IS FLYING AND...

SHADES OF PLUTO! I SEE THE SAME THING THAT STEVE DOES! IT MAY BE IMPOSSIBLE! BUT--I CAN'T DENY WHAT'S IN FRONT OF MY EYES!

THE SPECTACLE THAT HAS STARTLED EVEN THE CALM **WONDER WOMAN** WHOSE CAREER IS STUDDED WITH INCREDIBLE HAPPENINGS...

ST-9 CALLING BASE! IT'S NO USE! THEY'RE STILL THERE! I'M BEING ATTACKED BY JESSE JAMES AND HIS GANG! FORTY-NINE THOUSAND FEET IN THE AIR! ON HORSEBACK!

3

LEAPING OUT ONTO A WING OF HER *ROBOT PLANE*, **WONDER WOMAN** DIRECTS IT AT THE OUTLAWS, WHILE SHE HURLS HER AMAZON LASSO AT THEM...

I'LL LASSO THESE SKY OUTLAWS--AND BRING THEM DOWN TO THE GROUND!

BUT, AS THE GOLDEN-LINKED LASSO NEARS HIM, JESSE JAMES LAUGHS SCORNFULLY AND...

THET AMAZON GIRL MUST BE LOCO-- THINKIN' SHE KIN CORNER US WITH THAT!

POW! POW!

PERPLEXED AT THE UNEXPECTED FAILURE OF HER UNIQUE LASSO--BUT STILL UNDAUNTED, *WONDER WOMAN* COMMANDS...

PLANE--EMERGENCY SPEED--FULL AHEAD! I'LL USE THE PLANE TO FORCE THOSE RIDERS DOWN!

BUT THE AMAZON IS DUE FOR ANOTHER SHOCK...

HO! HO! HO! HO!

THUNDERBOLTS OF JOVE! THEY'RE LEAVING ME BEHIND AS IF MY PLANE WERE PARKED!

AT THAT MOMENT, STEVE'S PLANE DIVES SHARPLY DOWNWARD...

SUFFERING SAPPHO! STEVE'S PLANE IS IN TROUBLE! SHOTS MUST HAVE DAMAGED IT! I'LL HAVE TO FORGET ABOUT PURSUING THOSE CLOUD GUNMEN FOR THE MOMENT! *PLANE DIVE!*

INSTANTLY, THE ROBOT PLANE WHICH COULDN'T OVERTAKE THE FLYING HORSES OF THE GUNMEN -- SURGES UNDER THE FALLING PLANE ...

I HOPE STEVE HASN'T BEEN HURT BY ANY OF THEIR BULLETS!

WITH STARTLING MIGHT, *WONDER WOMAN* CATCHES THE HURTLING PLANE AS IF IT WERE A MERE TOY...

STEVE-- STEVE--ARE YOU ALL RIGHT?

THE GRINNING FACE OF HER CELEBRATED SWEETHEART REASSURES THE LOVELY AMAZON MAID...

I WAS...AS SOON AS I SAW YOU ON THE SCENE, ANGEL!

TOSSING THE FLAMING PLANE A SAFE DISTANCE AWAY-- *WONDER WOMAN* LANDS...

NOW THAT WE'RE OUT OF THE AIR--DID YOU SEE WHAT *I* SAW? OR WAS I DREAMING?

IF YOU WERE DREAMING, STEVE-- SO WAS I! THE SAME DREAM! JESSE JAMES AND HIS GANG--ATTACKING YOU IN MID-AIR! ON HORSE-BACK!

5

SUDDENLY, WONDER WOMAN'S OMNI-RECEIVER IN HER PLANE, WHICH IS TUNED TO ALL WAVE LENGTHS, BUZZES AN ALERT...

HELP! THE MAIL CAR IS BEING ATTACKED!

AS THE FRANTIC CALLER'S FACE IS FLASHED ON THE SCREEN...

I--I-- MUST BE IMAGINING THINGS!... I CAN'T BE SEEING WHAT I THINK I AM! THIS ROBBER CAN'T BE--

THE URGENT APPEAL ENDS WITH...

GREAT HERA! BULLETS MUST HAVE CUT OFF THE CONNECTION!

THAT WAS THE SUPER-SPEEDSTER CALLING! THE CRACK TRANS-CONTINENTAL TRAIN! NOW WHO IN THE WORLD WOULD ATTACK A TRAIN NOWADAYS!

POW-- POW!

WONDER WOMAN AND STEVE IMMEDIATELY BOARD HER PLANE AND HURTLE AWAY AT DAZZLING SPEED...

WE'LL SOON SEE! THAT CALL DIDN'T COME FROM FAR AWAY!

VROOOOSH!

MOMENTS LATER, AS THE AMAZON PLANE FLASHES TOWARDS THE CRACK TRAIN-- ANOTHER BEWILDERING SIGHT...

POW! KPOW!

STEVE! LOOK! THE TRAIN IS BEING HELD UP BY A LONE GUNMAN! HOW CAN HE RIDE HIS HORSE OVER THE ROOF OF THE TRAIN?

DO YOU SEE WHO IT IS? IT'S BILLY THE KID!

INSTANTLY, THE INDOMITABLE AMAZON LEAPS TO- WARDS THE TRAIN...

BILLY THE KID! FIRST JESSE JAMES -- NOW **THIS** GUNMAN WHO TERRORIZED THE WEST MORE THAN HALF A CENTURY AGO!

WHIPPING HER TIARA FORWARD...

FIRST -- I'LL DISARM HIM! KNOCK HIS GUN OUT OF HIS HANDS WITH MY TIARA! THEN I'LL ASK HIM QUESTIONS AFTERWARDS!

BUT AS THE UNIQUE TIARA REACHES THE WESTERN OUTLAW...

SUN-STRUCK AMAZON!

POW!

HE SENDS IT BACK...

THINKIN' TUH STOP **ME**!

POW!

WITH A VOLLEY OF SHOTS...

BILLY THE KID!

POW! POW!

AS THE BOOMERANG QUALITY OF THE TIARA RETURNS IT TO THE STARTLED **WONDER WOMAN'S** HAND...

MY TIARA -- USELESS -- BUT AT LEAST -- I CAN USE IT -- TO DEFEND MYSELF!

WITH INCREDIBLE TIMING, THE FEARLESS AMAZON USES THE TIARA AS A SHIELD WHICH...

THE BULLETS ARE RICOCHETING RIGHT BACK AT THE GUNMAN!

VIIP! VIIP!

HE'S GOT TO SURRENDER!

VIIP! ZIING!

BUT, TO *WONDER WOMAN'S* AMAZEMENT...

THUNDERBOLTS OF JOVE! HIS CLOTHES MUST BE MADE OF SOME KIND OF METAL--JUST LIKE MY TIARA! THEY'RE RICOCHETING RIGHT OFF THEM!

SPLANG!

THE NEXT MOMENT... THE FIGHTING MAID HAS TO DODGE DESPERATELY AS...

OUT OF THUH WAY, AMAZON!

I'LL JUMP ON THE BACK OF HIS HORSE AS IT PASSES!

SWIFT AS SHE IS, *WONDER WOMAN* MISSES HER CHANCE BY THE TOTALLY UNEXPECTED MOVE OF THE OUTLAW...

HE FLEW RIGHT OUT OF THE WAY!

HO, HO, HO!

WHROOSH!

WITH DAZZLING AGILITY, THE AMAZON ALIGHTS ON HER ROBOT PLANE... BUT...

THAT FLYING HORSE-- HAS ALREADY TAKEN HIM OUT OF SIGHT!

BACK IN HER PLANE, THE AMAZON DISCUSSES THE STRANGE EVENTS WITH STEVE...

JESSE JAMES AND BILLY THE KID COULDN'T COME BACK! AND WHO SAW FLYING HORSES? AND GUNS AGAINST WHICH YOUR SUPER WEAPONS HAVE NO EFFECT?

WE'VE SEEN THEM IN ACTION, STEVE!

18

MEANWHILE, ON A STRANGE PLANET, A VILLAINOUS CREW WATCHES THE PROCEEDINGS ON EARTH WITH GREAT GLEE...

LOOK--NOW WONDER WOMAN-- CAN'T CATCH RONNKN!

HO! HO! HO!

YOU MEAN BILLY THE KID! THAT'S THE EARTH GUNMAN HE CHOSE TO IMPERSONATE!

SHE FAILED MISERABLY AGAINST ZUGGM-- I MEAN JESSE JAMES--TOO! HO! HO! HO!

THE LEADER SPEAKS... WHAT GREATER SPORT FOR US-- THAN TO ASSUME THE IDENTITIES OF NOTORIOUS CRIMINALS WHO USED TO PLAGUE EARTH! THEN RETURN TO CAUSE COMPLETE HAVOC WITH OUR ADVANCED WEAPONS AND INVENTIONS --WHICH WE CAN MAKE TO RESEMBLE ORDINARY GUNS AND HORSES!

WHEN RONNKN AND ZUGGM-- IN THE IMPERSONATIONS OF JESSE JAMES AND BILLY THE KID RETURN TRIUMPHANTLY-- WE SHALL INVADE THE EARTH IN WHATEVER CRIMINAL IDENTITY IT AMUSES US TO TAKE!

ON EARTH, THE CRIMINAL IMPERSONATORS GATHER...

WONDER WOMAN WAS SUPPOSED TO BE OUR NEMESIS! IF SHE DEFEATED US--THE INVASION BY THE REST OF OUR PEOPLE WOULD HAVE BEEN HALTED! THAT WAS THE AGREEMENT BEFORE WE LEFT!

WE'VE MADE A FOOL OF WONDER WOMAN ALREADY-- WITH OUR UNIQUE MECHANIZED HORSES AND SUPER GUNS! NOW--WE SHALL MAKE HER A COMPLETE LAUGHING STOCK--BY BRINGING HER BACK TO OUR PLANET-- A PRISONER!

MEANWHILE, *WONDER WOMAN* AND STEVE LAND AT THE NEAREST TOWN...

SO YOU THINK THESE GUNMEN ARE INVADERS FROM ANOTHER PLANET?

NO QUESTION OF IT! THEIR WEAPONS ARE SUPERIOR TO MINE! BUT MAYBE I CAN CAPTURE THEM BY A SIMPLE, ORDINARY TRICK!

WHAT'S YOUR PLAN?

THE BULLETS RICOCHETING OFF *BILLY THE KID'S* CLOTHES GAVE ME AN IDEA!... OH, SIR! DO YOU HAVE ANY MAGNETS?

THE PROPRIETOR LEADS THEM BACK INTO THE STORE WHERE—

THE MAN WHO OWNED THE STORE BEFORE ME BOUGHT THOUSANDS OF THESE, THINKIN' THIS WOULD BE A BOOM TOWN FILLED WITH KIDS—STEAD OF A GHOST TOWN!

WHAT CAN YOU HOPE TO ACCOMPLISH WITH THESE TINY MAGNETS, *WONDER WOMAN*?

WITH INCREDIBLE POWER, THE MIGHTY AMAZON BEGINS PUSHING THE SMALL MAGNETS TOGETHER...

FINALLY, WHEN ALL THE MAGNETS ARE FUSED TOGETHER, SHE FASHIONS THEM INTO ONE GIGANTIC ONE...

NOW WHAT ARE YOU GOING TO DO WITH THIS?

IT DEPENDS ON WHETHER I WAS RIGHT ABOUT WHAT SUBSTANCE *BILLY THE KID'S* CLOTHES ARE MADE OF!

SHORTLY, THE KEEN EYES OF THE INVADERS SPOT THE AMAZON MAID...

THERE'S *WONDER WOMAN*!

SHE'S AN EASY CAPTURE! SHE HAS NO WEAPONS TO MATCH OURS!

THE FEARLESS *WONDER WOMAN* GLANCES BACK...

I WONDERED HOW LONG IT WOULD BE-- BEFORE THEY CAME BACK LOOKING FOR ME?

THE MOMENT THE FLYING HORSEMEN NEAR THE TENSE AMAZON, SHE YANKS HER LASSO TRAILING BEHIND HER, AND BREAKING THROUGH THE EARTH WHERE IT HAD BEEN HIDDEN--*THE MAGNET!*

HERA HELP MY DEDUCTION TO BE CORRECT!

INSTANTLY, THE MASQUERADING INVADERS ARE CLAMPED TO THE TREMENDOUS MAGNET BY A FORCE THEY CANNOT EVADE...

THANK HERA! I WAS RIGHT! THEY'RE ALL WEARING METALLIC CLOTHES!-- WHICH IS MAGNETIZING THEM TO THE MAGNET! HAD THEY WORN ORDINARY ONES--MY PLAN WOULD HAVE FAILED!

WONDER WOMAN SPEAKS STERNLY TO THE CAPTIVES...

I'LL GIVE YOU YOUR CHOICE! TO SPEND THE REST OF YOUR LIVES IMPRISONED ON EARTH ON THAT MAGNET! OR DIRECT ME TO YOUR PLANET!

THE SPACE GUNSLINGERS HAVE BUT ONE ANSWER...

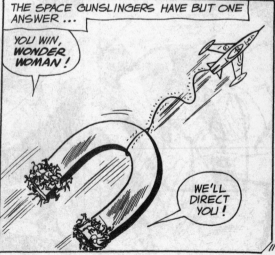

YOU WIN, WONDER WOMAN!

WE'LL DIRECT YOU!

AND SO, AN AMAZING CARGO IS DROPPED ON THE STUNNED PLANET!

IT'S NO USE! WE CAN'T INVADE EARTH!

NOT WITH *WONDER WOMAN* ON GUARD!

BACK TOWARDS HER HOME PLANET *WONDER WOMAN* FLASHES...

NOW THAT WE KNOW WHERE THEY COME FROM -- WE CAN ALWAYS KEEP OUR EYE ON THEM!

MIND IF *I* KEEP MY EYE ON YOU, BEAUTIFUL?

The End

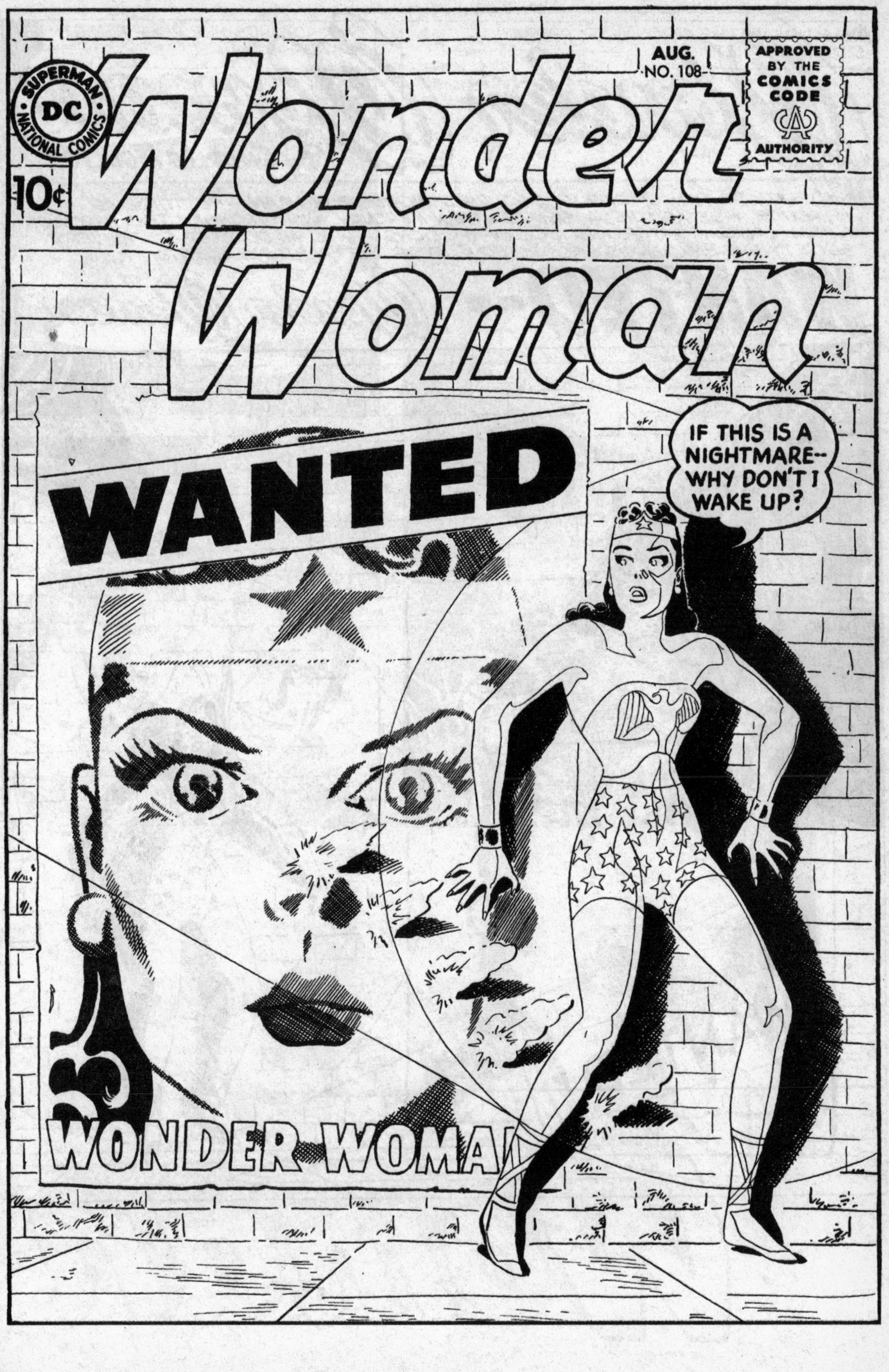
SUPERMAN DC NATIONAL COMICS
10¢
Wonder Woman
AUG. NO. 108
APPROVED BY THE COMICS CODE AUTHORITY
WANTED
IF THIS IS A NIGHTMARE-- WHY DON'T I WAKE UP?
WONDER WOMA

Wonder Woman
By Charles Moulton

WHAT FANTASTIC TURN OF EVENTS HAS TURNED *WONDER WOMAN*--BEAUTIFUL AS APHRODITE, WISE AS ATHENA, SWIFTER THAN MERCURY, AND STRONGER THAN HERCULES-- A REAL CRIME-FIGHTER AND IDOL OF MILLIONS--INTO AN OUTCAST OF THE VERY SOCIETY SHE HAS ALWAYS PROTECTED? READ THE STARTLING EVENTS IN...

WANTED-- Wonder Woman

WANTED!

AT MILITARY INTELLIGENCE, LT. DIANA PRINCE AND COL. STEVE TREVOR GLANCE AT THE TICKER TAPE IN THE DECODING ROOM...

REPORT OF A FLYING SAUCER AT COORDINATES THREE-SEVEN-TWO!

PROBABLY ANOTHER WILD-GOOSE CHASE! BUT I'LL DO A SWEEP IN THAT AREA! JUST IN CASE!

I HAD A DINNER DATE WITH WONDER WOMAN! TELL HER I MIGHT BE LATE, DI!

STEVE DOESN'T KNOW WHOM HE'S REALLY TALKING TO!

IN THE PRIVACY OF HER OFFICE, THE YOUNG OFFICER MAKES A LIGHTNING CHANGE INTO HER SECRET IDENTITY... OF WONDER WOMAN!

I'LL CALL MY PLANE AND MEET STEVE--SO WE CAN SPEND SOME TIME TOGETHER BEFORE DINNER!

A FEW MOMENTS LATER, THE CELEBRATED AMAZON FLASHES OVER THE AREA WHERE STEVE IS MAKING HIS SEARCH OF THE REPORTED "FLYING SAUCER"--AND WITH AN AGILE LEAP...

I'M SEEING THINGS! I BETTER CHECK MY VISION AGAIN! IT LOOKS LIKE MY ANGEL!

SCARCELY HAS THE BEAUTIFUL WONDER WOMAN DROPPED BESIDE THE FLIER THAN...

BY JOVE'S THUNDERBOLTS--!

THEN YOU SEE IT TOO! THE REPORT WASN'T A DELUSION! IT IS A FLYING SAUCER! I'M GOING TO CHASE IT!

THE DARING AMAZON LEAPS TO THE WING OF STEVE'S PLANE...

NO ONE HAS EVER EXAMINED A *FLYING SAUCER!*

AS IT PASSES, SHE HURLS HERSELF AT IT LIKE A HUMAN ARROW...

MAYBE I CAN BOARD IT!

BUT THE INCREDIBLE SPEED OF THE *FLYING SAUCER* CREATES SUCH TURBULENCE THAT BOTH THE DARING AMAZON AND STEVE'S PLANE ARE TOSSED ABOUT LIKE CORKS IN A STORMY SEA...

VROOOM!

SKILLFULLY, *WONDER WOMAN* "RIDES" THE AIR CURRENTS BACK TO STEVE'S PLANE...

GUESS THAT'S THE LAST OF THE *FLYING SAUCER!*

FATE, HOWEVER, HAS OTHER STARTLING PLANS--BECAUSE ON THE STRANGE OBJECT FROM OUTER SPACE... *WONDER WOMAN* IS BEING WATCHED...

THERE'S OUR GUINEA PIG! EARTH'S MOST IRON-WILLED-- STEELY-NERVED INHABITANT! *WONDER WOMAN!*

THE LEADER OF THE *FLYING SAUCER* UNFOLDS HIS PLAN...

IF WE CAN *FORCE HER* TO OBEY OUR EVERY LONG DISTANCE COMMAND - NO MATTER HOW *CONTRARY* TO HER *REAL* NATURE -- THEN EVERY OTHER EARTHLING WILL BE POWERLESS AGAINST US! AND OUR INVASION WILL EASILY SUCCEED!

WE WILL START WITH SIMPLE COMMANDS AND OBSERVE HER REACTIONS -- UNTIL WE FORCE HER, BY HER OWN ACTIONS -- TO BECOME AN OUTCAST FROM HER OWN WORLD!

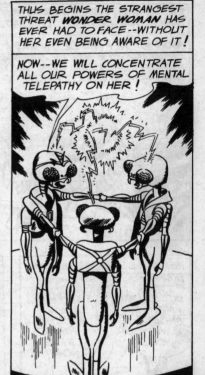

THUS BEGINS THE STRANGEST THREAT *WONDER WOMAN* HAS EVER HAD TO FACE -- WITHOUT HER EVEN BEING AWARE OF IT!

NOW -- WE WILL CONCENTRATE ALL OUR POWERS OF MENTAL TELEPATHY ON HER!

THE SPACE INVADERS' MENTAL RAYS PIERCE EVERY BARRIER UNTIL...THEY FOCUS ON *WONDER WOMAN* IN STEVE'S PLANE...

I WISH YOU'D CHANGE YOUR MIND ABOUT NOT MARRYING ME -- UNTIL YOUR SERVICES ARE NO LONGER REQUIRED TO COMBAT EVIL -

WHY -- OF COURSE I'LL MARRY YOU, STEVE!

ANGEL! YOU'VE MADE ME THE HAPPIEST MAN ON EARTH! WHAT MADE YOU CHANGE YOUR MIND SO SUDDENLY?

I -- I DON'T KNOW! S-S-SOMETHING JUST CAME OVER ME!

SOMETHING HAS TAKEN HOLD OF ME! I -- I FEEL LIKE A -- A -- *PUPPET!* I CAN'T MARRY STEVE! CONDITIONS HAVEN'T CHANGED! I'M STILL NEEDED TO FIGHT CRIME AND INJUSTICE ON A FULL-TIME BASIS!

IN THE *UFO* (UNIDENTIFIED FLYING OBJECT) THE SPACE INVADERS ARE JUBILANT...

THIS IS ONLY THE BEGINNING! WE WILL INCREASE OUR MENTAL PRESSURE--AND FORCE HER TO DO MORE AND MORE THINGS SHE WOULD NEVER DO!

AGAIN THE SPACE INVADERS PROJECT THEIR EXTRAORDINARY MENTAL POWERS OUT...

MEANWHILE, *WONDER WOMAN* STAMMERS TO STEVE...

BUT YOU **WILL** MARRY ME, ANGEL! YOU GAVE YOUR WORD!

I KN-KNOW, STEVE! B-BUT I HAVE TO LEAVE NOW!

LEAPING ONTO A WING OF STEVE'S PLANE, *WONDER WOMAN* SUMMONS HER ROBOT PLANE...

I--I CAN'T UNDERSTAND WHAT CAME OVER ME! I KNOW I GAVE MY WORD TO STEVE! BUT I CAN'T MARRY HIM! NOT YET! SOMEHOW, I'LL HAVE TO WORK MY WAY OUT OF THAT DILEMMA!

AS THE DARING AMAZON CATA-PULTS HERSELF TOWARDS HER UNIQUE PLANE IN WHAT WOULD BE AN ORDINARY FEAT FOR HER, SHE FINDS HERSELF COMMANDING...

PLANE ZOOM AT MAXIMUM SPEED!

AND THEN, FOR THE FIRST TIME!

SUFFERING SAPPHO! THE L-L-LAST THING IN THE WORLD I WANTED WAS TO ORDER THE P-P-PLANE OUT OF MY REACH!

ZZOOM!

NOWHERE CAN THE PLUNGING *WONDER WOMAN*.. FIND ANY AIR CURRENTS... TO SUPPORT HER!

BUT, HER FIGHTING HEART DOES NOT DESPAIR, AND AS SHE COMES WITHIN REACH OF TWO POWERFUL HAWKS...

I'VE HALTED MY FALL! I'LL USE THEM TO HELP ME DOWN!

UNTIL... TO HER BEWILDERMENT...

SHADES OF PLUTO! THEY'VE SHAKEN ME OFF! I COULDN'T HOLD ON! MY FINGERS FEEL LIKE BUTTER! WHAT HAS HAPPENED TO ME?

WHAT WILL HAPPEN TO WONDER WOMAN? THIS AMAZING TALE CONTINUES ON THE NEXT PAGE...

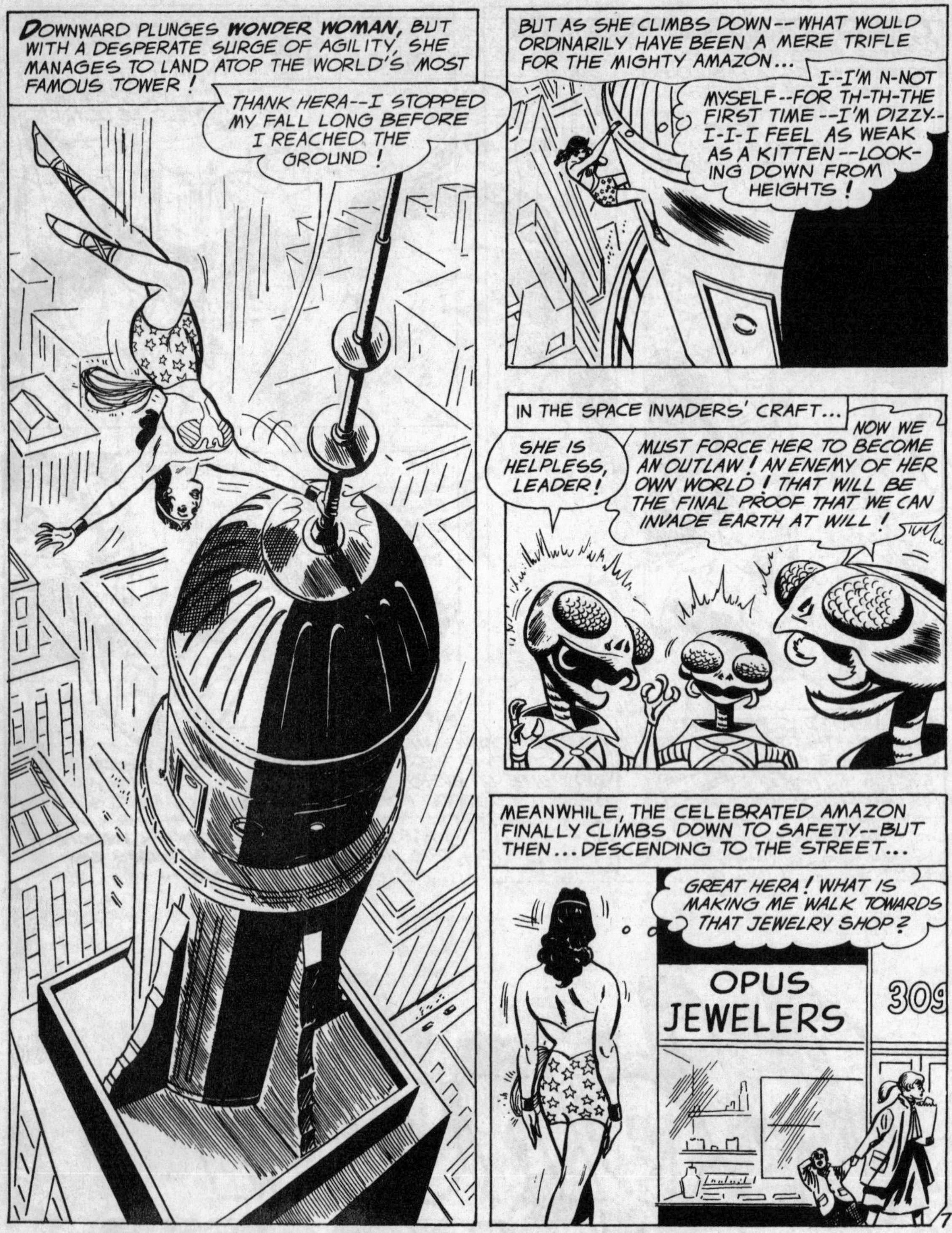
DOWNWARD PLUNGES WONDER WOMAN, BUT WITH A DESPERATE SURGE OF AGILITY, SHE MANAGES TO LAND ATOP THE WORLD'S MOST FAMOUS TOWER!
THANK HERA--I STOPPED MY FALL LONG BEFORE I REACHED THE GROUND!
BUT AS SHE CLIMBS DOWN--WHAT WOULD ORDINARILY HAVE BEEN A MERE TRIFLE FOR THE MIGHTY AMAZON...
I--I'M N-NOT MYSELF--FOR TH-TH-THE FIRST TIME--I'M DIZZY--I-I-I FEEL AS WEAK AS A KITTEN--LOOKING DOWN FROM HEIGHTS!
IN THE SPACE INVADERS' CRAFT...
SHE IS HELPLESS, LEADER!
NOW WE MUST FORCE HER TO BECOME AN OUTLAW! AN ENEMY OF HER OWN WORLD! THAT WILL BE THE FINAL PROOF THAT WE CAN INVADE EARTH AT WILL!
MEANWHILE, THE CELEBRATED AMAZON FINALLY CLIMBS DOWN TO SAFETY--BUT THEN...DESCENDING TO THE STREET...
GREAT HERA! WHAT IS MAKING ME WALK TOWARDS THAT JEWELRY SHOP?
OPUS JEWELERS
309
7

AS THE WORLD-FAMOUS CRIME-FIGHTER FINDS HER STEPS DRAWN TOWARDS A FABULOUS NECKLACE, SHE REALIZES TO HER DISMAY...

MERCIFUL MINERVA! WHAT AM I THINKING ABOUT?

WITH A FANTASTIC DISPLAY OF WILL POWER, SHE STRUGGLES ON A SILENT BATTLEGROUND INSIDE HER...

NO--NO--NO!

FINALLY, SHAKEN AS IF SHE HAD LITERALLY MOVED A MOUNTAIN...

I--I--DON'T KNOW--HOW--LONG--I WILL BE ABLE--TO RESIST!

SO UNNERVED IS WONDER WOMAN--THAT FOR THE FIRST TIME IN HER FABULOUS CAREER--IT IS HER LIFE THAT IS SAVED BY STEVE...

THANK HEAVENS I FOUND YOU! IT IS A GOOD THING YOU WEREN'T HARD TO TRACE! IT LOOKS LIKE I'VE JUST COME IN TIME! WHAT'S COME OVER YOU, SWEETHEART?

SWISH

HOW CAN I TELL HIM? AM I BECOMING AN ENEMY OF SOCIETY? THE OPPOSITE OF EVERY-THING I'VE STOOD FOR! HOW CAN I TELL HIM?

AND ON THE FLYING SAUCER, THE "HUMAN GUINEA PIG'S" ACTIONS ARE STUDIED...

WONDER WOMAN RESISTED STEALING THAT NECKLACE! BUT THERE IS NO DOUBT THAT SHE IS BREAKING! NOW--FOR THE FINAL TEST!

LATE THAT NIGHT, AN UNEXPECTED FIGURE IS SEEN TURNING THE BRICKS IN THE MAGNUS BANK TO POWDER--WITH A SINGLE BLOW OF HER MIGHTY FIST...

IT--IT CAN'T BE--! I--I-- MUST BE SEEING THINGS!

HASTENING TO THE HOLE MADE BY THE INTRUDER, THE WATCHMAN IS STARTLED TO SEE ...

ONLY ONE PERSON ON EARTH CAN CUT A HOLE IN THE STEEL OF THAT VAULT --WITH HER FINGER-NAILS !

BUT--BUT I STILL CAN'T BELIEVE IT !

A MOMENT LATER, THE WATCHMAN IS FACED WITH PROOF POSITIVE--BUT EVEN THEN...

MAYBE IT'S HER DOUBLE ! MAYBE--? STOP--STOP-- OR I'LL SHOOT !

THE BULLETS OF THE WATCHMAN SPEED AT THE CRIMINAL--BUT...

POW! POW!

ONLY ONE PERSON CAN FLIP BULLETS BACK WITH HER BRACELETS ! THERE'S NO MISTAKE ABOUT IT THIS TIME ! IT'S WONDER WOMAN !

SPANGG !

AND SHORTLY, OVER ALL ALARMS...

WONDER WOMAN WANTED ! AT ALL COSTS ! USE EXTREME CAUTION !

AT FIRST, WHEN *WONDER WOMAN* IS SPOTTED..

LET HER HAVE THE HOSE! WATER WILL STOP HER-- BUT NOT HURT HER!

BUT THE MIGHTY AMAZON EXHALES SUCH A TITANIC GUST OF AIR...

WHOOOSH!

THAT AN AMAZING TRANSFORMATION TAKES PLACE!

SHE'S TURNED THE WATER INTO SNOW!

POSTERS OF THE ONCE FAMOUS CRIME-FIGHTER ARE DISPLAYED EVERYWHERE...

WANTED!

WANTED!

WANTED!

AND IT IS AGAINST SUCH A DRAMATIC BACKDROP THAT SHE IS CORNERED!

BETTER DROP YOUR LOOT, WONDER WOMAN!

DO WHAT HE SAYS--YOU HAVEN'T A CHANCE!

COME AND GET ME!

10

AT THAT MOMENT, IN THE FLYING SAUCER...

IS THERE ANY DOUBT NOW, LEADER--THAT **WONDER WOMAN** IS HELPLESS? HAS SHE NOT BECOME A COMPLETE MENACE TO HER OWN WORLD?

AYE! NOW WE CAN INVADE EARTH WITHOUT ANY HESITATION BECAUSE IF SHE CANNOT STAND BEFORE OUR MENTAL BARRAGE--NO ONE CAN!

SCORNFULLY, THE SPACE INVADER WINGS TOWARD EARTH...

FIRST--WE WILL DESTROY THAT STATUE--THE STATUE SIGNIFYING LIBERTY!

BECAUSE THE LAST THING EARTHLINGS WILL HAVE FROM NOW ON--IS LIBERTY!

HEE--! HEE--!

AT THAT MOMENT, A TINY FIGURE HURLS HERSELF LIKE A THUNDERBOLT FROM THE WORLD'S HIGHEST TOWER...

MY PLAN HAS DECOYED THE DIABOLICAL POWER BEHIND ALL THIS--OUT INTO THE OPEN! AND IT IS--THE **FLYING SAUCER!**

DAUNTLESSLY, THE AMAZON ALIGHTS ON TOP OF THE STATUE SIGNIFYING LIBERTY TO THE WHOLE WORLD...

THERE'S NO DOUBT THAT THIS IS THE START OF THEIR INVASION! PRAY HERA I CAN STOP THEM!

AS **WONDER WOMAN'S** UNIQUE AMAZON LASSO ENCIRCLES THE SPACE INVADER, THE LEADER ORDERS...

REVERSE-- AND BREAK THIS CHAIN!

THEY ARE DOING EXACTLY WHAT I ANTICIPATED-- TIGHTENING MY LASSO!

WHAT DESPERATE PLAN DOES THE AMAZON DEPEND ON? WILL IT WORK?

THE NEXT MOMENT, *WONDER WOMAN'S* UN-BREAKABLE LASSO, WITH THE WORLD'S MIGHTIEST BUILDING ACTING AS A MASSIVE SLING, HURLS THE INVADING CRAFT INTO THE ATMOSPHERE WITH SUCH FORCE--THAT FRICTION DESTROYS IT...

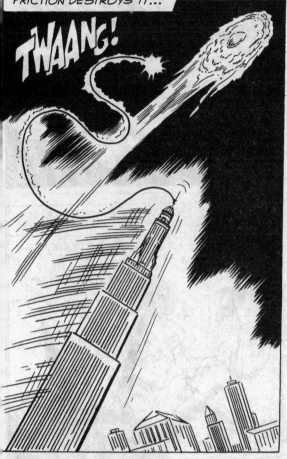

TWAANG!

THE STATUE SIGNIFYING LIBERTY STILL STANDS UNSCATHED AS THE AMAZON LIGHTLY LEAPS ONTO STEVE'S PLANE...

I WON'T HOLD YOU TO YOUR PROMISE, ANGEL! ABOUT MARRYING ME, I MEAN! I KNOW YOU WERE FIGHTING AN EVIL POWER THAT MEANT THE END OF OUR WORLD! IMAGINE! THEY THOUGHT YOU REALLY ROBBED A BANK!

THEY DIDN'T KNOW THE ONLY THING I TOOK WAS ALREADY PLANTED THERE! BLOTTERS-- PENS-- CALENDARS!

The End

12

Wonder Woman

By Charles Moulton

THEY WERE THREE ORDINARY POSTAGE STAMPS--STAMPS HONORING THE EXPLOITS OF *WONDER WOMAN!* THEY WERE JUST THREE BITS OF PAPER--YET, *WONDER WOMAN*--BEAUTIFUL AS APHRODITE, WISE AS ATHENA, SWIFTER THAN MERCURY, AND STRONGER THAN HERCULES-- NEEDED EVERY POWER AT HER COMMAND TO COMBAT THE DEADLY MENACE OF...

The STAMPS OF DOOM!

MERCIFUL MINERVA! I'M PINNED!-- AND THE STAMP IS ABOUT TO EXPLODE!

ONE HOT AFTERNOON, PAUSING FOR A SWIM AT A DESERTED BEACH, *WONDER WOMAN* SEES...

A TOY BOAT! SOME CHILD MUST HAVE LOST IT!

SUDDENLY, TO THE FAMOUS AMAZON'S AMAZEMENT...

GREAT HERA! THE TOY BOAT--IT'S STARTING TO *GROW*!

IN A FEW STARTLING MOMENTS...

IT'S GROWN TO THE SIZE OF A REAL MOTOR BOAT--AND IT'S *STILL GROWING*!

UPON REACHING ITS PEAK GROWTH, THE BOAT NOW BEGINS TO GLOW WEIRDLY...

SOMETHING HAS EXPANDED THE BOAT'S ATOMIC STRUCTURE! IT MAY EXPLODE! I'LL HURL IT WHERE IT WON'T CAUSE HARM TO ANY-ONE!

THEN, A TITANIC BLAST CHURNS THE SEA...

WHROOOM!

GREAT HERA! EXACTLY ONE MINUTE AFTER IT BEGAN TO GLOW--THE BOAT EXPLODED! WHAT CAUSED THIS? WHO WAS RE-SPONSIBLE FOR IT?

VILLAINOUS EYES WATCH THE BIZARRE EPISODE FROM A NEARBY HIDING PLACE...

WONDER WOMAN DOESN'T KNOW I ONLY USED THAT TOY BOAT TO TRY OUT MY NEW FORMULA! NOW THAT IT HAS PASSED THE TEST--I'M READY TO SET MY PLAN IN MOTION!

2

LATER... AT MILITARY INTELLIGENCE, GENERAL DARNELL DISPLAYS THREE STAMPS TO WONDER WOMAN--EACH ONE DEPICTING A GREAT FEAT SHE HAS PERFORMED...

THESE THREE STAMPS WILL BE ON PUBLIC EXHIBITION-- UNTIL TOMORROW WHEN THEY'LL BE CARRIED BY THREE PEOPLE ON SPECIAL GOVERNMENT MISSIONS!

SPECIAL ISSUE Wonder Woman 4¢ U.S. POSTAGE

SPECIAL ISSUE WONDER WO 9¢ U.S. POSTAGE

SPECIAL ISSUE 7¢ U.S. POSTAGE

WHO ARE THE *THREE* PEOPLE, GENERAL DARNELL?

TOMORROW, ONE STAMP WILL RIDE WITH COL. TREVOR AS HE PILOTS A SPACE-SHIP EQUIPPED TO RECOVER ONE OF OUR ARTIFICIAL SATELLITES ORBITING AROUND EARTH!

WONDERFUL! WHO'S THE SECOND CARRIER?

ANOTHER STAMP WILL GO WITH *YOU, WONDER WOMAN*--IN AN ATOMIC SUBMARINE ATTEMPTING TO SET A SPEED RECORD TO THE NORTH POLE!

I'M HONORED! AND WHO WILL BE CARRYING THE *THIRD STAMP?*

THE THIRD STAMP WILL RIDE WITH ME AND *LT. DIANA PRINCE* IN A DRIVERLESS, ROBOT-CONTROLLED CAR ON A TEST RUN! I'M GOING TO LT. PRINCE'S OFFICE TO TELL HER ABOUT IT NOW!

GREAT HERA! IN MY SECRET IDENTITY-- I AM DIANA PRINCE! I'D BETTER GET TO MY OFFICE AND CHANGE TO MY OTHER IDENTITY QUICKLY!

3

As THE TWO TURN TO LEAVE FOR *LT. PRINCE'S* OFFICE, *WONDER WOMAN* MAKES A LIGHTNING CHANGE NO HUMAN EYE CAN FOLLOW...

SWIFTER THAN A PUFF OF WIND--THE AMAZON WHIRLS PAST THEM UNOBSERVED...

IN THAT SAME FLASHING INSTANT...SHE REACHES HER OFFICE JUST AS...

LT. PRINCE! I HAVE A VERY PLEASANT SURPRISE FOR YOU! YOU ARE GOING TO BE THE THIRD CARRIER OF *WONDER WOMAN* STAMPS!

NOW I'VE GOT TO FIGURE OUT HOW TO BE IN TWO PLACES AT ONCE!

LATER, STEVE AND DIANA JOIN THE CROWDS FLOCKING TO THE EXHIBIT OF *WONDER WOMAN* STAMPS...

JUST THINK--TOMORROW YOU, I AND *WONDER WOMAN* WILL HELP THESE STAMPS MAKE HISTORY!

THEY WON'T--UNLESS I CAN FIGURE OUT HOW I CAN BE IN THE SUB AS WONDER WOMAN--AND THE CAR AS DIANA PRINCE!

NIGHTFALL...THE EXHIBIT CLOSES...AND THE UNIFORMED GUARD IS ALONE...

YES--COL. STEVE TREVOR--TOMORROW THESE STAMPS WILL MAKE HISTORY--BUT NOT IN THE WAY YOU THINK! TAKING THE REGULAR GUARD'S PLACE WAS THE FIRST STEP IN MY SCHEME!

TOMORROW--THE WONDER WOMAN STAMPS WILL BECOME STAMPS OF DOOM--AFTER I TREAT THEM WITH MY NEW EXPLOSIVES--THEY WILL REACT JUST LIKE THE TOY BOAT I TESTED!

THE VILLAIN REACHES FOR THE STAMPS...

TOMORROW, THE EXPLOSIONS WILL BE DRAMATIC PROOF OF THE POWER OF MY NEW EXPLOSIVE TO THE FOREIGN POWER WHO OFFERED ME A MILLION DOLLARS IF MY FORMULA WORKS! AND IT WILL WORK-- NOTHING--AND NO ONE CAN STOP ME!

THE NEXT DAY, AS THE FIRST STAMP IS PLACED INSIDE STEVE'S SHIP, *WONDER WOMAN* LOOKS ANXIOUSLY AT THE MAN SHE LOVES...

I'LL BE BACK AS SOON AS I RECOVER THE SPACE SATELLITE THAT'S DUE TO FALL FROM ITS ORBIT TODAY!

GOOD LUCK, DARLING!

SHORTLY, WITH A FLAMING ROAR, STEVE'S SHIP HURTLES TOWARD SPACE--CARRYING WITH IT A STAMP OF DOOM...

NOW I'D BETTER GET OVER TO THE DOCK WHERE THE SUBMARINE IS WAITING FOR ME!

IN HER CABIN ABOARD THE SUB, SOON AFTERWARDS...

THESE STAMPS CERTAINLY PUT ME IN THE GREATEST DILEMMA OF MY CAREER! HOW CAN I GO ON MY OTHER MISSION AS DIANA PRINCE WITH GENERAL DARNELL-- WHILE I'M ALSO HERE AS *WONDER WOMAN*?

AS THE ATOMIC SUBMARINE GETS UNDER WAY... THE AMAZON IS PASSING THROUGH THE TORPEDO ROOM ...

NO ONE HERE FOR THE MOMENT! THIS IS MY CHANCE TO EXIT--WHILE EVERYONE THINKS I'M ASLEEP IN MY CABIN!

SOON AFTER, A HUMAN PRO- JECTILE EXITS FROM THE SUB--THROUGH THE TORPEDO TUBE!

I'M OUT AT LAST! NOW I'LL SWIM BACK TO SHORE SWIFTLY--AND CHANGE TO MY *DIANA PRINCE* IDENTITY!

WHOOSH!

BUT--THE AMAZON IS UNAWARE OF THE EXPLOSIVE STAMP THE SUB IS CARRYING!

5

SUMMONING HER *ROBOT PLANE*, *WONDER WOMAN* LEAPS UPWARDS...

I'VE GOT TO CHANGE AND GET TO GENERAL DARNELL BEFORE HE BEGINS TO SUSPECT MY DUAL IDENTITY!

WROOOOSH!

LEAVING HER PLANE SHORTLY IN HER OTHER DISGUISE...

SORRY-- I'M LATE, GENERAL'!

YOU'RE HERE! THAT'S WHAT COUNTS! WE'RE TESTING THE CAR OF THE FUTURE, LT. PRINCE A ROBOT CAR THAT DRIVES AND STEERS ITSELF SAFELY BY ELECTRONIC CONTROLS!

NO DANGER **FROM** THE CAR--BUT THERE IS DOOM--DOOM WAITING IN THE CAR WITH THEM IN THE FORM OF A STAMP!

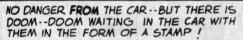

WHOOOOSH!

AS THE ROBOT CAR SPEEDS ALONG ITS TEST ROUTE, SUDDENLY DIANA IS AWARE OF A FANTASTIC OCCURRENCE...

THE STAMP--IT'S GROWING--LIKE THE TOY BOAT DID YESTERDAY! SUFFERING SAPPHO! NOW I UNDERSTAND! YESTERDAY'S EXPLOSION WAS ONLY A *TEST!* SOMEONE'S REAL OBJECTIVE IS THE DESTRUCTION OF THE THREE GOVERNMENT MISSIONS--BY MEANS OF THESE STAMPS!

SPECIAL ISSUE

I MUST BECOME WONDER WOMAN SWIFTLY-- AND GET AWAY TO PREVENT THE STAMPS FROM EXPLODING! BUT HOW CAN I-- WITHOUT GENERAL DARNELL NOTICING THAT I'M GONE!

THINKING AND ACTING SWIFTLY, THE YOUNG OFFICER SHAPES THE EXPANDING STAMP INTO A PROPELLOR--AND THEN POKES HER FINGER THROUGH ITS CENTER...

NOW A POWERFUL PUFF OF MY BREATH WILL START IT SPINNING!

WHAT DOES SHE HOPE TO ACCOMPLISH? |6.

LIKE A HUMAN HELICOPTER, THE ASTOUNDING MAID RISES UP--*UP*--OUT OF THE ROBOT CAR...

HE'S UNAWARE OF MY ABSENCE! BUT HE MIGHT BE--IF HE TURNS AROUND!

THE QUICK-THINKING AMAZON AIMS HER PROPELLER AT THE SANDY BEACH AND...

THE PROPELLOR'S BACKWASH IS STIRRING UP A SAND STORM! THE GENERAL WON'T NOTICE MY ABSENCE!

BUT THEN... MERCIFUL MINERVA! THE STAMP IS STARTING TO *GLOW*! IT WILL EXPLODE SHORTLY! I'VE GOT TO BURY IT SOMEPLACE--WHERE IT CAN DO NO HARM!

INSTANTLY, THE AMAZON HURLS IT DEEP INTO THE SAND...

IT EXPLODED HARMLESSLY! THAT WILL ADD TO THE SAND STORM I'VE ALREADY CREATED AND GIVE ME THE PRECIOUS TIME I NEED! NOW I MUST SUMMON MY ROBOT PLANE AND HURRY TO **STEVE'S** AID!

WHROOM!

AS SHE CHANGES BACK TO *WONDER WOMAN*--THE MAID IS TORN BY A DECISION...

THE *SUB* IS CARRYING A STAMP *TOO*! IT'S STEVE'S LIFE--AGAINST THAT OF ALL THE MEN IN THE SUB!

IN ANGUISH, *WONDER WOMAN* SUMMONS HER ROBOT PLANE AND SENDS IT FLASHING DOWNWARDS...

I'LL HAVE TO GET THE STAMP OUT OF THE SUB--AND PRAY THAT I'M IN TIME TO HELP STEVE!

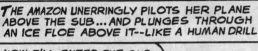

THE AMAZON UNERRINGLY PILOTS HER PLANE ABOVE THE SUB...AND PLUNGES THROUGH AN ICE FLOE ABOVE IT--LIKE A HUMAN DRILL..

NOW I'LL ENTER THE SUB THE SAME WAY I LEFT-- THROUGH THE TORPEDO TUBE!

INSTANTS LATER, UPON SNATCHING UP THE DEADLY STAMP FROM HER CABIN...

THERE'S ONLY ONE WAY I CAN GET THROUGH THE TORPEDO TUBE WITH THE STAMP THE SIZE IT IS NOW... AND THAT'S TO WRAP IT AROUND ME!

AGAIN, THE AMAZON EXITS THROUGH A TOR-PEDO TUBE--BUT TO HER HORROR...

VROOSH!

MERCIFUL MINERVA! I'M CAUGHT BY A GIANT SQUID--AND THE STAMP IS STARTING TO GLOW! THAT MEANS IT WILL EXPLODE IN A FEW MOMENTS!

EXERTING HER AMAZING AMAZON STRENGTH, *WONDER WOMAN* TURNS HER BODY INTO A PROPELLOR-LIKE SPIN...

HERA HELP ME IN MY PLAN TO ESCAPE BEFORE THE SUB IS THREATENED BY THE EXPLOSION!

LIKE A HUMAN PROPELLOR, *WONDER WOMAN* PULLS THE SQUID UP-UP-UP-'INTO THE SKY!

THE MONSTER HAS RELEASED ME

FURLING THE STAMP INTO A HARPOON...

THAT ICEBERG WILL ENDANGER SHIPS-- UNLESS I CAN DESTROY IT!

WHOOOSH!

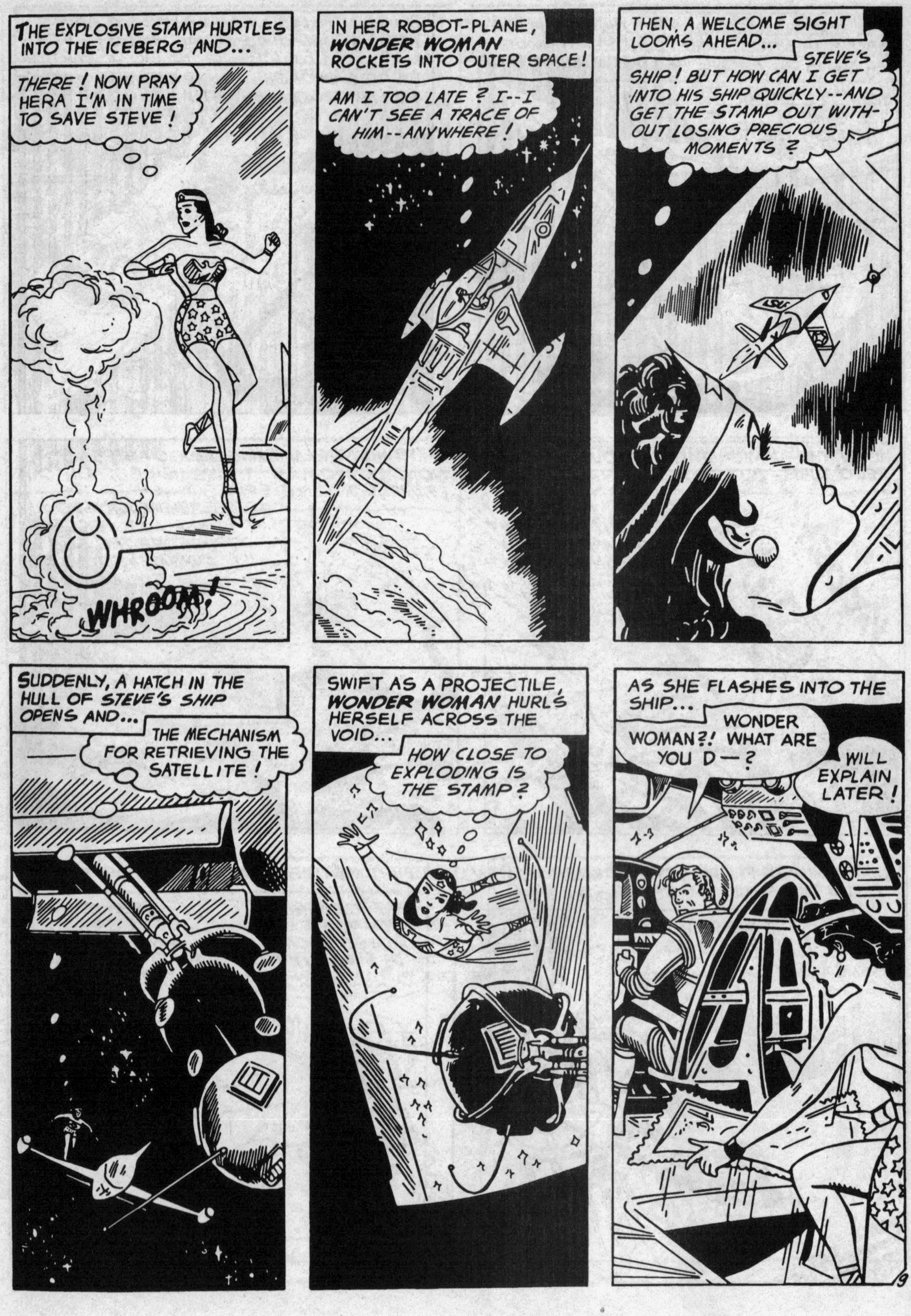
THE EXPLOSIVE STAMP HURTLES INTO THE ICEBERG AND...
THERE! NOW PRAY HERA I'M IN TIME TO SAVE STEVE!
WHROOM!
IN HER ROBOT-PLANE, WONDER WOMAN ROCKETS INTO OUTER SPACE!
AM I TOO LATE? I--I CAN'T SEE A TRACE OF HIM--ANYWHERE!
THEN, A WELCOME SIGHT LOOMS AHEAD...
STEVE'S SHIP! BUT HOW CAN I GET INTO HIS SHIP QUICKLY--AND GET THE STAMP OUT WITHOUT LOSING PRECIOUS MOMENTS?
SUDDENLY, A HATCH IN THE HULL OF STEVE'S SHIP OPENS AND...
THE MECHANISM FOR RETRIEVING THE SATELLITE!
SWIFT AS A PROJECTILE, WONDER WOMAN HURLS HERSELF ACROSS THE VOID...
HOW CLOSE TO EXPLODING IS THE STAMP?
AS SHE FLASHES INTO THE SHIP...
WONDER WOMAN?! WHAT ARE YOU D—?
WILL EXPLAIN LATER!

SEIZING THE STAMP—WONDER WOMAN FLASHES OUT AGAIN JUST AS THE HATCH CLOSES...

I DON'T KNOW HOW FAR I'LL HAVE TO GO WITH THE STAMP--SO ITS EXPLOSION WON'T AFFECT STEVE!

SPREADING THE DEADLY STAMP LIKE A GLIDER, WONDER WOMAN RIDES DOWN THROUGH SPACE-- FASTER--EVER FASTER--TO THE TUG OF EARTH'S GRAVITATIONAL PULL ...

THEN, AS THE STAMP ENTERS EARTH'S ATMOSPHERE--THE INEVITABLE HAPPENS...

THE FRICTION HEAT OF THE ATMOSPHERE HAS CAUSED IT TO BURN--LIKE A METEOR! IT WON'T EXPLODE NOW!

LEAPING ABOARD HER ROBOT PLANE...

NOW--TO CATCH THE VILLAIN RESPONSIBLE FOR THESE CRIMES! PLANE--DIVE AT MAXIMUM SPEED!

LATER... WONDER WOMAN RE-ENTERS THE EXHIBIT HALL...

WONDER WOMAN! B-BUT I READ THAT--THAT YOU'D BE ON THE SUBMARINE WITH A STAMP!

THE SUB NEEDED SOME LAST— MINUTE REPAIRS-- SO I'M RETURNING THIS STAMP TO THE EXHIBIT CASE UNTIL TOMORROW!

SUDDENLY, THE STAMP "FALLS" OUT OF ITS CASE...

I'VE DROPPED THE STAMP! PICK IT UP FOR ME, PLEASE!

I--I...

GREAT HERA! THE STAMP'S STARTING TO EXPAND!

L-LET ME OUT OF HERE-- BEFORE IT EXPLODES!

JUST AS I FIGURED--ONLY YOU--WHO WERE ALONE WITH THE STAMPS--HAD THE OPPORTUNITY TO TAMPER WITH THEM!

IT--IT'S NOT ONE OF MY STAMPS--!

NO! I FASHIONED IT OUT OF RUBBER THAT INFLATES-- LIKE AN INFLATABLE RUBBER RAFT!

SSSSSSSSS!

RACING TO MILITARY HEAD-QUARTERS *WONDER WOMAN* SWIFTLY DELIVERS HER CAPTIVE...

WONDER WOMAN! WHY AREN'T YOU IN THE SUBMARINE?

I WAS-- BUT I HAD SOME UN-FINISHED BUSINESS TO DO!... I'LL EXPLAIN LATER!

MILITA POLICE

AGAIN SUMMONING HER ROBOT PLANE...

NOW-- I HAVE TO GET BACK TO GENERAL DARNELL BE-FORE HE DISCOVERS I'M MISSING!

FLASHING BACK TO THE ROBOT CAR... THE AMAZON LEAPS DOWN ...

QUITE A SANDSTORM! CAN'T SEE!

Y-YES, GENERAL DARNELL!

LATER, WHEN THE MISSIONS ARE COMPLETED, IT IS AS *WONDER WOMAN* THAT THE AMAZON TELLS OF THE *STAMPS OF DOOM*..

Hmm! OBVIOUSLY, WHEN YOU SAW THE STAMP GROWING IN THE SUB, YOU REALIZED THE OTHER TWO STAMPS WERE EXPLOSIVES, TOO-- AND WENT AFTER THEM!

SO THAT ACCOUNTS FOR THE EXPLOSION I HEARD FROM THE CAR! YOU MUST HAVE TAKEN THE STAMP FROM THE CAR SO QUICKLY THAT LT. PRINCE DIDN'T EVEN SEE YOU!

THE NEXT DAY, AS *WONDER WOMAN* IS LED BY STEVE INTO A POST OFFICE....

FIRST DAY SALE OF WONDER WOMAN POSTAGE STAMPS!

WHY DID YOU COME IN HERE?

I'M GOING TO BUY SOME *WONDER WOMAN* STAMPS--ENOUGH STAMPS TO PAPER MY ROOM-- SO THAT WHEREVER I LOOK--I'LL SEE YOUR LOVELY FACE!

The End 12

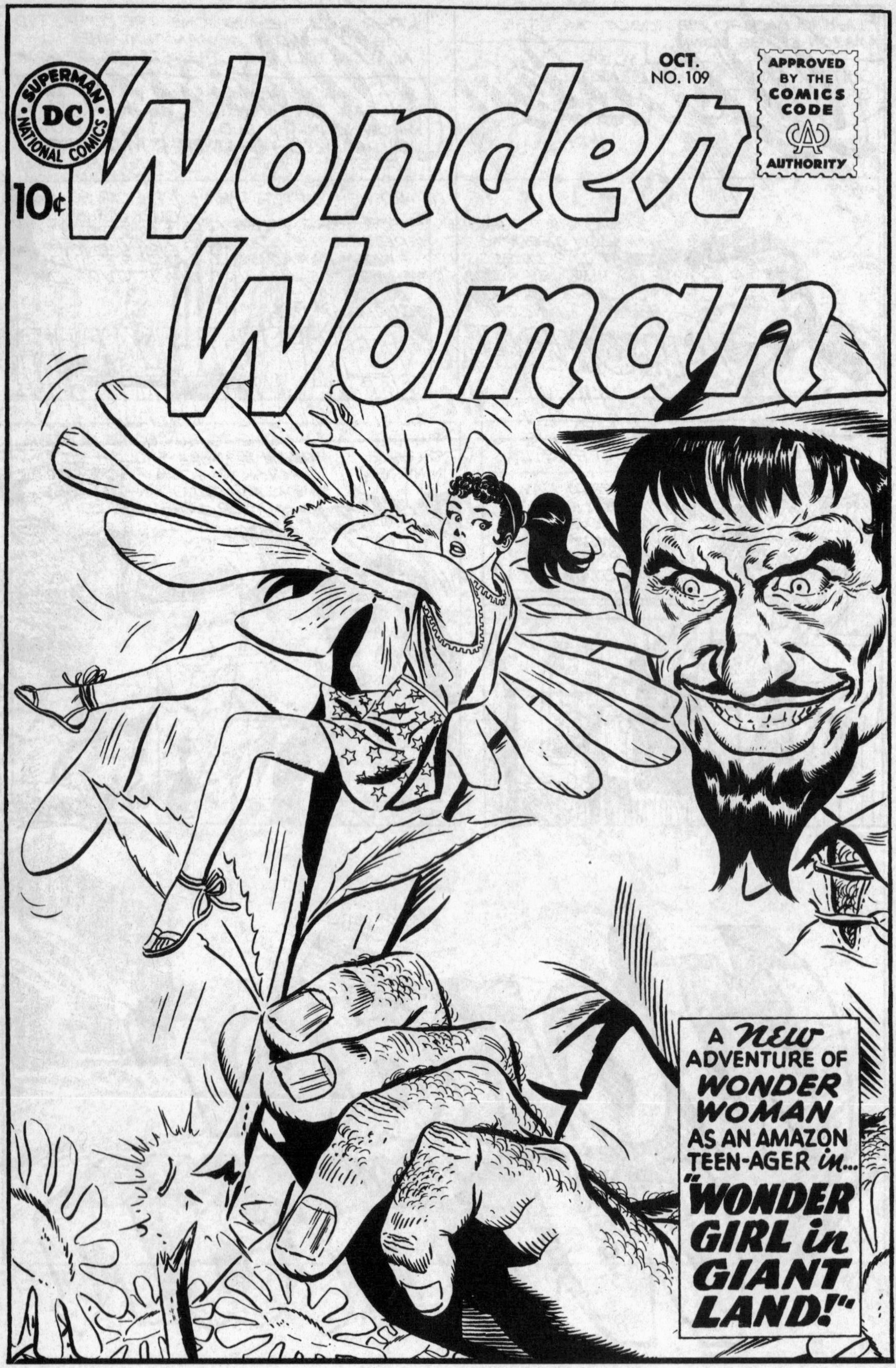
SUPERMAN DC NATIONAL COMICS
10¢
Wonder Woman
OCT. NO. 109
APPROVED BY THE COMICS CODE AUTHORITY
A NEW ADVENTURE OF WONDER WOMAN AS AN AMAZON TEEN-AGER in...
"WONDER GIRL in GIANT LAND!"

"IN ANSWER TO REQUESTS FOR MORE TALES ABOUT MYSELF AS AN AMAZON TEEN-AGER, HERE ARE THE STARTLING ADVENTURES THAT I PLUNGED INTO -- WHEN *PARADISE ISLAND* SEEMED DOOMED BY A TOWERING MENACE AGAINST WHICH NO DEFENSE SEEMED TO PREVAIL! BEGIN AN INCREDIBLE JOURNEY WITH..."

WONDER GIRL in GIANT LAND!

HERA HELP ME HANG ON -- OR ALL THE AMAZONS ARE LOST!

AT *PARADISE ISLAND*, SECRET HOME OF THE AMAZONS, *WONDER GIRL* IS DEVELOPING HER SKILLS FOR THE FUTURE, WHEN, AS THE GROWN *WONDER WOMAN*, SHE WILL BATTLE CRIME AND INJUSTICE EVERYWHERE..

OUR PRINCESS HAS BEEN HOLDING US UP FOR AN HOUR!

SHE IS TIRELESS!

SUDDENLY, THE INCREDIBLY KEEN HEARING OF THE AMAZON TEEN-AGER-LIKE SONAR DETECTS...

SOMETHING HUGE IS FALLING DOWN AT THE ISLAND FROM THE RIFT IN THE CLOUDS! BUT-- OUR AMAZON AIR RAID DEFENSES ARE SURE TO TURN IT AWAY BEFORE IT REACHES US!

FROM THE SKIES OVERHEAD A MONSTROUS MISSILE HURTLES THROUGH THE RIFT...

VREEEE!

INSTANTLY--THE ALERT *WONDER GIRL* HURLS THE HUMAN PYRAMID TOWARDS SAFETY JUST AS...

THUNDERBOLTS OF JOVE! IT'S PIERCED OUR MISSILE-SCREEN!

WHAM!

2

QUEEN HIPPOLYTA, *WONDER GIRL'S* MOTHER, RUSHES TO HER SIDE...

DIANA--! ARE YOU ALL RIGHT?

Y-Y-YES, MOTHER! JUST-- A LITTLE-- DAZED!

JUST THEN...TWO MORE OF THE GIGANTIC MISSILES HURTLE DOWN FROM SPACE... THROUGH THE RIFT IN THE CLOUDS...

VREEEEE!

TO THE AMAZEMENT OF THE QUEEN AND HER DAUGHTER...

WHAAM!

WHAAM!

SUFFERING SAPPHO! LOOK AT THE SKY! IT'S CLEAR OF A NETWORK OF FIRE THAT SHOULD STOP THESE ATTACKS AUTOMATICALLY!

MOTHER-- OUR DEFENSES AREN'T WORKING AGAINST THOSE MISSILES!

HERE COMES ANOTHER ONE THROUGH THAT RIFT IN THE CLOUDS! RUN, DIANA! I'LL TRY TO STOP IT!

MOTHER IS TRYING TO SACRIFICE HERSELF FOR ME!

INSTANTLY, WITH THE UNCANNY SKILL SHE IS RENOWNED FOR, *WONDER GIRL* HURLS HERSELF UP ON AN AIR CURRENT...

DIANA-- DAUGHTER!

3

AGILELY, *WONDER GIRL* ALIGHTS ON TOP OF THE HUGE MISSILE ...

HERA HELP ME TURN THIS SHELL AWAY OR *PARADISE ISLAND* WILL BE DESTROYED!

THE AMAZON TEEN-AGER LASSOES THE DEADLY MISSILE ...

CAN I TURN IT? WILL I BE ABLE TO DISTURB WHATEVER MECHANISM IS PROPELLING THIS --SO I CAN DIVERT IT AWAY FROM THE ISLAND?

AS IF SHE WERE RIDING A ROBOT STEED *WONDER GIRL* MANEUVERS IT WITH STARTLING SPEED STRAIGHT TOWARDS ...

ALL THE MISSILES CAME THROUGH THIS RIFT IN THE CLOUDS!

I'LL STEER THIS ONE RIGHT BACK THROUGH IT! PERHAPS THE ANSWER TO *WHERE* THEY CAME FROM-- WILL BE ON THE OTHER SIDE?

VROOSH!

NO SOONER DOES SHE PLUNGE THROUGH THE CLOUD-RIFT THAN ...

SHADES OF PLUTO! THIS IS NO ORDINARY OPENING IN THE CLOUDS!

SUDDENLY, WHAT TO *WONDER GIRL* HAD BEEN A HUGE MISSILE -- A MIGHTY ENGINE OF DESTRUCTION -- IS NO MORE THAN A TOY TO A GIGANTIC HAND!

THIS RIFT IN THE CLOUDS-- IS REALLY-- *A TIME WARP!* I'VE PASSED THROUGH IT --TO ANOTHER DIMENSION!

WHAT ARE *YOU* DOING ON THAT FIRE-CRACKER?

4

WONDER GIRL FINDS HERSELF UNDER THE GIGANTIC GAZE OF THE GIANTS -- BUT BRAVELY CONFRONTS THEM ...

DID YOU EVER SEE THE LIKES OF *THIS* ? IT'S TRYING TO INTERFERE WITH OUR FIREWORKS ENTERTAINMENT !

YOUR CELEBRATION THREATENS TO DESTROY OUR ISLAND ! PLEASE STOP IT !

THE LAUGHTER OF THE GIANTS IS DEAFENING ... AS ...

MERCIFUL MINERVA ! THEY'RE STARTING AGAIN ! I'VE GOT TO STOP THEM SOME WAY -- OR IT WILL BE THE END OF THE AMAZONS !

HO!

HO!

VROOSH!!

HO!

DAUNTLESSLY, THE AMAZON TEEN-AGER ISSUES A CHALLENGE ...

I'LL MEET *ANY OPPONENT* YOU SELECT -- IN *ANY KIND* OF COMPETITION YOU DEVISE ! IF I *WIN* -- YOU WILL STOP SENDING OFF THESE FIRE-WORKS ! WOULDN'T SUCH A CONTEST BE MORE ENTERTAINING THAN THE FIREWORKS ?

WAIT ! YOU HAVEN'T SAID WHAT WILL HAPPEN IF YOU LOSE ! WE WILL CONTINUE WITH OUR FIRE-WORKS -- AND SINCE YOU WILL BE THE LONE SURVIVOR OF YOUR ISLAND -- WE WILL KEEP YOU HERE ! AGREED ?

AT WONDER GIRL'S REPLY...

AGREED!

YOU DON'T KNOW IT ! BUT YOU CANNOT POSSIBLY WIN -- AS YOU SHALL SOON FIND OUT ! FOR -- WE ARE GOING TO ASK YOU TO PERFORM FEATS -- WHICH EVEN *WE CANNOT* ! HO ! HO ! HO !

WONDER GIRL IS TAKEN TO THE EDGE OF A VAST CHASM WHERE...

NONE OF US HAS EVER BEEN ABLE TO LEAP ACROSS THIS **WITHOUT** FALLING DOWN! IF YOUR OPPONENT SUCCEEDS -- AND YOU FAIL -- YOU LOSE THE CONTEST! USE ANY MEANS YOU CAN! IT WILL AVAIL YOU NOT!

I CAN'T JUST JUMP AND MAKE IT! AND-- THERE ARE NO AIR CURRENTS HERE I CAN USE TO "RIDE" ACROSS!

SUDDENLY, THE GROUND TREMBLES AS...

THERE GOES MY OPPONENT!

INSTANTLY, THE DARING AMAZON TEEN-AGER HURLS HERSELF ONTO THE GREAT BOOT OF THE GIANT!...

THEY SAID I COULD USE **ANY** MEANS! I'LL "RIDE" ACROSS ON HIS BOOT!

16

SWIFTLY, **WONDER GIRL** CLIMBS UP THE GIANT'S BOOT...

I'M TOO FAR AWAY HERE—FROM THE OTHER SIDE OF THE CHASM!

AGILELY, SHE RACES ALONG THE FLYING FORM...

I'VE GOT TO GET CLOSER!

OUT ALONG THE MASSIVE ARM SHE SPEEDS...

IF I CAN GET OUT ONTO HIS HANDS--MAYBE I CAN SPRING ONTO SOME AIR CURRENT AND "RIDE" THE REST OF THE WAY ACROSS!

FINALLY, PERCHED ON A GIANT HAND, **WONDER GIRL** IS DISMAYED TO LEARN...

THE AIR IS ABSOLUTELY STILL! THERE ARE NO AIR CURRENTS I CAN RIDE!

IT IS AT THAT MOMENT THAT THE GIANTS BREAK INTO THUNDEROUS LAUGHTER...

HE'S NOT GOING TO REACH THE OTHER SIDE! AND NEITHER WILL SHE! SHE HAS FAILED!

HO! HO! HO! HO!

THE ROARING LAUGHTER OF THE GIANTS TURNS INTO A BOON TO *WONDER GIRL* AS HER OPPONENT STARTS TO FALL ...

PRAISE HERA ! THE LAUGHTER HAS CREATED AIR CURRENTS WHICH I CAN "RIDE" !

HO! HO! HO! HO!

GRACEFULLY AS A FLOATING LEAF, THE AMAZON TEEN-AGER SOARS ALONG THE AIR CURRENTS ...

I HAVE THE GIANTS TO THANK FOR SUCCEEDING IN *THIS* CONTEST !

SPLASH!

THE INTREPID *WONDER GIRL* WAVES FROM THE FAR SIDE OF THE CHASM !

WAIT UNTIL SHE SEES THE SECOND FEAT-- WHICH NO ONE OF US HAS BEEN ABLE TO PERFORM ! WHICH WILL SURELY BE IMPOSSIBLE FOR HER !

THE GIANTS JOIN THE YOUNG AMAZON BY A BRIDGE ACROSS THE CHASM AND TAKE HER TO A HUGE FIELD WHERE...

IT'S A GIGANTIC *UNICORN* !

PERHAPS YOUR OPPONENT WILL BE ABLE TO RIDE HIM *THIS* TIME ! NONE OF US HAS UP UNTIL NOW ! BUT-- *YOU* WILL *HAVE* TO-- NOT TO LOSE !

UNEXPECTEDLY, AS THE GIANT RIDER IS SEATED...

YOU MIGHT AS WELL GET ON THIS HORSE *NOW!* IT WILL GIVE YOU MORE TIME TO THINK OF A PLAN TO RIDE HIM! HA! HA! HA!

THE NEXT MOMENT, THE AMAZON TEEN-AGER HOLDS ON FOR DEAR LIFE AS...

NO--EARTHQUAKE IS AS VIOLENT AS THIS!

IN A FEW MOMENTS, EVEN THE MASSIVE GRIP OF THE GIANT RIDER IS TORN LOOSE...

HE'S BEING TOSSED OFF--AND SO AM I!

DESPERATELY, THE AGILE *WONDER GIRL* SEIZES HOLD OF THE HUGE ANIMAL'S MANE

IF THERE WAS--ONLY SOME WAY--OF CONTROLLING-- THIS BEAST?

AGAIN THE GIANTS ROAR...

SHE IS INDEED PROVIDING US WITH ENTER- TAINMENT!

BUT SHE IS LOST! ANY MOMENT NOW--SHE WILL BE DRAGGED OFF BY THE VINES IN THOSE WOODS!

BUT, THE INGENUITY OF *WONDER GIRL* COMES TO HER AID--BECAUSE EVEN AS THE VINES WHIP AT HER...SHE SNATCHES AT THEM...

THE GIANTS TRIED TO RIDE THIS UNMANAGE- ABLE BEAST WITHOUT REINS! BUT--IF I CAN FASHION REINS OUT OF THOSE TOUGH VINES--PERHAPS--?

19

WITH DAUNTLESS COURAGE THE AMAZON TEEN-AGER SLIPS THE HUGE LOOP INTO THE PLUNGING UNICORN'S MOUTH...

THANK HERA I DON'T HAVE TO FIGURE OUT HOW TO OPEN HIS MOUTH!

ONTO THE RAGING ANIMAL'S BACK, *WONDER GIRL* LEAPS...

NOW--WE SHALL SEE HOW HE'LL ACT UNDER THE CONTROL OF REINS!

DESPITE THE BUCKING UNICORN'S STRUGGLE, THE YOUTHFUL AMAZON HANGS ON GRIMLY...

CAN'T LET--GO-- LIVES OF ALL-- THE AMAZONS-- AT STAKE!

IN FRONT OF THE GIGANTIC AUDIENCE--*WONDER GIRL* REINS HER MOUNTAINOUS STEED...

YOU ARE A GREAT BATTLER! BUT--YOU MUST FAIL IN THE LAST FEAT! JUST AS ALL OF US HAVE!

AT THE EDGE OF A FOAMING RIVER, *WONDER GIRL* WATCHES A GIANT PLUNGE IN... AND...

NONE OF US HAS BEEN ABLE TO SWIM UPSTREAM TO THAT ROCK--AS YOU CAN SEE!

WITHOUT WARNING, THE AMAZON *TEEN-AGER* IS TOSSED IN...

SWIM UPSTREAM TO THAT ROCK-- AND YOUR ISLAND WILL BE SAVED! FAIL--AND WE WILL CONTINUE 'ITH OUR FIREWORKS ENTERTAINMENT!

SPLASH!

INSTANTLY, THE RAGING CURRENT YANKS THE AMAZON BACK ...

THEY'RE RIGHT! THAT SUN-- NOW SETTING--WILL RISE AND SET A MILLION TIMES-- BEFORE I CAN SWIM UP- STREAM!

BELOW THE SURFACE *WONDER GIRL* IS HURLED BY THE CURRENT...

I'VE HAD NO TROUBLE--SWIMMING IN WORSE--WHIRLPOOLS THAN--THAN--? Hmm-- THAT GIVES ME AN IDEA!

WITH A STRENGTH BORN OF DESPERATION, THE AMAZON SCOOPS A DEEP HOLE IN THE RIVER BED...

ONLY WAY I CAN MANAGE TO SWIM UPSTREAM--IS TO--DIVERT--THE CURRENT!

FINALLY... WITH THE HOLE DUG...

THE HOLE--HAS CREATED A WHIRLPOOL--

NOW THAT WONDER GIRL IS IN THE GRIP OF A FIERCE CIRCULAR MOTION-- WHAT DOES SHE HOPE TO ACCOMPLISH?

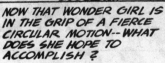

UP--*UP*--*UP*--WONDER GIRL FOLLOWS THE WHIRLPOOL UNTIL ...

THANK HERA! THE POSITION OF THE SUN--TELLS ME WHERE TO AIM MYSELF! BUT--I'LL ONLY HAVE AN INSTANT TO DO IT IN!

LIKE A CHIP IN A SPINNING ROULETTE TABLE THE AMAZON IS WHIRLED AROUND...

THE SUN IS AT MY RIGHT!

AT THE PRECISE MOMENT, THE DARING SWIMMER UTILIZES THE SPINNING VELOCITY OF THE OUTER EDGE OF THE WHIRLPOOL TO HURL HERSELF UPSTREAM...

THAT MEANS UP-STREAM...

IS...

STRAIGHT AHEAD!

LIKE A PEBBLE BOUNCING ON THE SURFACE OF THE WATER, THE INGENIOUS *WONDER GIRL* ALIGHTS ON THE ROCK...

SHE HAS WON!

HURRAY FOR THE LILLIPUTIAN!

AS THE AMAZON TEEN-AGER BIDS FAREWELL TO THE GIANTS...

IF A MERE CHILD CAN DO ALL YOU'VE DONE--WE WOULD BE OVERWHELMED BY YOUR ELDERS! SO--GO IN PEACE--AND FORGIVE US FOR UNWITTINGLY CAUSING YOU TROUBLE! YOU WON'T HEAR FROM US AGAIN! FAREWELL!

FAREWELL!

BACK THROUGH THE RIFT IN TIME *WONDER GIRL* RIDES A HARMLESS ROCKET BACK TO *PARADISE ISLAND*...

WE'LL HOLD A CELEBRATION ON *PARADISE*--WITHOUT FIREWORKS!

LOOK FOR MORE EXCITING *WONDER GIRL* ADVENTURES IN FUTURE ISSUES OF *WONDER WOMAN*!

/12

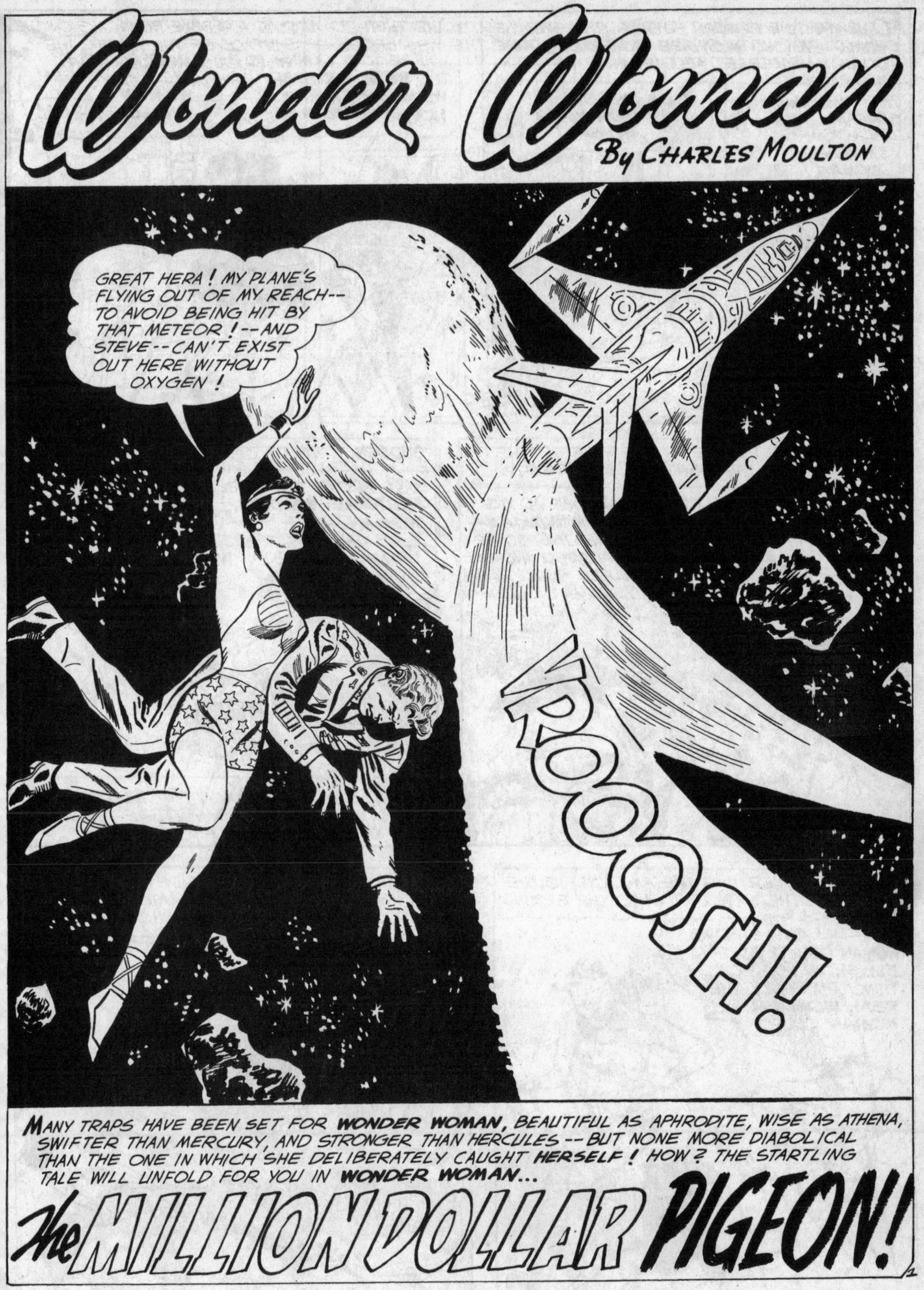
Wonder Woman
By Charles Moulton
GREAT HERA! MY PLANE'S FLYING OUT OF MY REACH-- TO AVOID BEING HIT BY THAT METEOR! --AND STEVE--CAN'T EXIST OUT HERE WITHOUT OXYGEN!
VROOOOSH!
MANY TRAPS HAVE BEEN SET FOR WONDER WOMAN, BEAUTIFUL AS APHRODITE, WISE AS ATHENA, SWIFTER THAN MERCURY, AND STRONGER THAN HERCULES--BUT NONE MORE DIABOLICAL THAN THE ONE IN WHICH SHE DELIBERATELY CAUGHT HERSELF! HOW? THE STARTLING TALE WILL UNFOLD FOR YOU IN WONDER WOMAN...
The MILLION DOLLAR PIGEON!
1

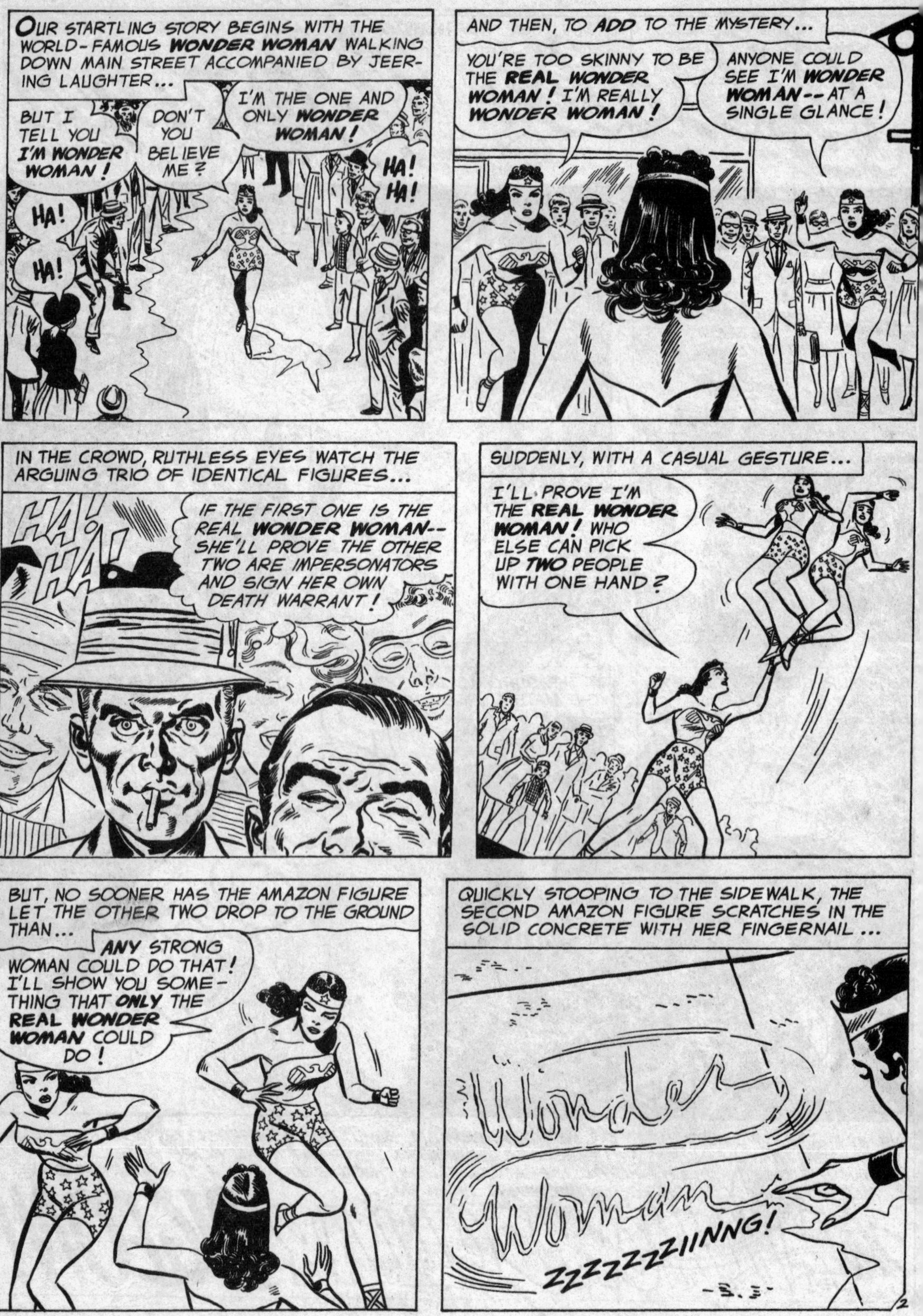
OUR STARTLING STORY BEGINS WITH THE WORLD-FAMOUS WONDER WOMAN WALKING DOWN MAIN STREET ACCOMPANIED BY JEERING LAUGHTER...
BUT I TELL YOU I'M WONDER WOMAN!
DON'T YOU BELIEVE ME?
I'M THE ONE AND ONLY WONDER WOMAN!
HA! HA!
HA! HA!
AND THEN, TO ADD TO THE MYSTERY...
YOU'RE TOO SKINNY TO BE THE REAL WONDER WOMAN! I'M REALLY WONDER WOMAN!
ANYONE COULD SEE I'M WONDER WOMAN--AT A SINGLE GLANCE!
IN THE CROWD, RUTHLESS EYES WATCH THE ARGUING TRIO OF IDENTICAL FIGURES...
HA! HA!
IF THE FIRST ONE IS THE REAL WONDER WOMAN--SHE'LL PROVE THE OTHER TWO ARE IMPERSONATORS AND SIGN HER OWN DEATH WARRANT!
SUDDENLY, WITH A CASUAL GESTURE...
I'LL PROVE I'M THE REAL WONDER WOMAN! WHO ELSE CAN PICK UP TWO PEOPLE WITH ONE HAND?
BUT, NO SOONER HAS THE AMAZON FIGURE LET THE OTHER TWO DROP TO THE GROUND THAN...
ANY STRONG WOMAN COULD DO THAT! I'LL SHOW YOU SOMETHING THAT ONLY THE REAL WONDER WOMAN COULD DO!
QUICKLY STOOPING TO THE SIDEWALK, THE SECOND AMAZON FIGURE SCRATCHES IN THE SOLID CONCRETE WITH HER FINGERNAIL...
Wonder Woman
ZZZZZZZIINNG!

AND WHEN SHE IS FINISHED, THE SAME PAIR OF COLD, CALCULATING EYES GAZE AT THE RESULT...

THAT'S AN EVEN MORE TYPICAL *WONDER WOMAN* STUNT THAN THE FIRST ONE!

BUT THEN, THE *WONDER WOMAN* WHO HAD FIRST APPEARED TO THE JEERING PEOPLE EXCLAIMED...

I'LL SHOW YOU SOMETHING THAT WILL PROVE BEYOND A SHADOW OF A DOUBT-- THAT I--AND I ALONE AM THE *REAL WONDER WOMAN!*

MEN AT WORK

BUT--HURLED FORWARD BY THE OILY SLICK ON THE STREET FROM THE TRAFFIC...

OHHH-- HELP!

IN THE SURGING DEPTHS OF THE WATER UNDERNEATH...

I'VE GOT TO SWIM OUT OF SIGHT OF EVERYONE--BEFORE I CAN SURFACE!

FROM THE SWIRLING CURRENTS FINALLY, THE SWIMMER EMERGES...

I'VE GOT TO WORK FAST-- AND GET BACK TO WHERE EVERYONE SAW ME FALL IN!

UNOBSERVED, THE AMAZON FIGURE REMOVES A LINK FROM HER GOLDEN LASSO...WHICH IMMEDIATELY EXPANDS WHEN EXPOSED TO THE ATMOSPHERE...UNTIL IT BECOMES THE FULL-LENGTH COSTUME OF LT. DIANA PRINCE!

ATTIRED IN THE COSTUME OF THE YOUNG MILITARY INTELLIGENCE OFFICER, SHE RACES IN A FEW INSTANTS BACK TO WHERE SHE HAS FALLEN...

IT'S LT. DIANA PRINCE!

WONDER WOMAN'S CLOSEST FRIEND! SHE CAN TELL US WHICH ONE IS REALLY WONDER WOMAN!

JUST THEN, BY AN IRONICAL TWIST OF FATE, NONE OTHER THAN COL. STEVE TREVOR, THE AMAZON'S SWEETHEART, IS STOPPED BY THE TRAFFIC...

COL. TREVOR! LT. PRINCE WON'T ANSWER US! BUT YOU SURELY CAN! YOU TELL US! WHICH ONE IS THE REAL WONDER WOMAN?

AGAIN, COLD MERCILESS EYES WATCH THE COLONEL STARE AT ONE AMAZON FIGURE AND THEN THE OTHER...

HE DOESN'T KNOW HE'LL SIGN THE DEATH WARRANT OF WHICH-EVER ONE HE PICKS!

AT THAT MOMENT, HIGH ABOVE THE TENSE CROWD, ON THE BUILDING BEING ERECTED ACROSS THE STREET...

CRACK!

CABLE SNAPPED!

NOTHING CAN SAVE US!

AND THEN, A GASP IS HEARD FROM THE CROWD AS...

IT'S LT. PRINCE!

I NEVER SAW DI MAKE SUCH A STUPENDOUS LEAP!

LIKE A HUMAN ARROW, LT. PRINCE FLASHES UNDER THE MASSIVE GIRDER--AND WITH OUT-STRETCHED ARMS HALTS ITS FALL!

SHIFTING THE IMMENSE WEIGHT ONTO ONE HAND--SHE AGILELY STEPS ONTO THE NEAREST CATWALK OF THE STEEL STRUCTURE...

SHE SAVED OUR LIVES!

SHE MUST BE WONDER WOMAN!

AS THE MEN SCRAMBLE TO SAFETY...

WILL MY PLAN WORK?

WHAT PLAN IS DIANA REFERRING TO? TO SHED SOME LIGHT ON ALL THIS MYSTERY WE MUST TURN BACK THE CLOCK TO A WEEK AGO...

THIS STARTLING TALE STARTED A WEEK AGO AT A SINISTER-LOOKING RETREAT IN THE NEARBY MOUNTAINS...

AS LONG AS WE DON'T KNOW WHO WONDER WOMAN IS IN HER SECRET IDENTITY--SHE CAN STRIKE AT OUR OPERATIONS FROM ANYWHERE AT ANY TIME!

IT'S NO USE TRYING TO LOCATE WONDER WOMAN OURSELVES! WE'D NEED AN ARMY!

AND AT THIS MEETING OF THE UNDERWORLD...

I'VE GOT A SCHEME TO FORCE WONDER WOMAN HERSELF--TO REVEAL HER OWN SECRET IDENTITY!

WE'LL START A PHONEY ORGANIZATION. WE'LL OFFER A MILLION DOLLARS TO *WONDER WOMAN*-- IF SHE REVEALS HER SECRET IDENTITY! HUNDREDS OF MIXED-UP PEOPLE WILL BE HURT--TRYING TO PROVE THEY'RE *WONDER WOMAN!*

YOU ALL KNOW *WONDER WOMAN!* TO SAVE ALL THOSE PEOPLE FROM HARM-- SHE'LL HAVE TO RISK REVEALING HER SECRET IDENTITY! *THEN*-- WE'LL NET HER LIKE A PIGEON!

HERE'S TO THE *MILLION DOLLAR PIGEON!*

TERRIFIC IDEA, SLICKER!

WE CAN'T MISS!

NEWS OF THE PRIZE MONEY SWEPT THE COUNTRY...

AT FIRST, LT. DIANA PRINCE AND COL. STEVE TREVOR HAD A GOOD LAUGH ABOUT IT...

THEY SHOULD ASK *ME* WHAT *WONDER WOMAN'S* SECRET IDENTITY IS! I SHOULD KNOW! WE'RE *ENGAGED!* AND THE MOMENT I EVER MEET HER IN HER *OTHER* IDENTITY--I WOULD SPOT HER INSTANTLY! BUT I *HAVEN'T* YET!

I WONDER WHAT STEVE WOULD SAY IF HE KNEW THAT HE WAS RIDING RIGHT NEXT TO *WONDER WOMAN* AT THIS VERY MOMENT!

CONTINUED ON THE PAGE FOLLOWING

JUST THEN...

WONDER WOMAN!

SHE'S JUST AN IMPERSONATOR! *I'M WONDER WOMAN!* BUT-- I CAN'T SAY ANYTHING WITHOUT REVEALING MY SECRET IDENTITY-- WHICH HAS ENABLED ME TO BATTLE CRIME AND INJUSTICE!

THE AMAZON FIGURE RACED UNHESITATINGLY INTO THE CAR'S PATH...

I'LL PROVE I'M THE REAL *WONDER WOMAN*-- BY LEAPING OVER THAT CAR!

AS STEVE DESPERATELY WRENCHED THE STEERING WHEEL TO AVOID HITTING THE ONRUSHING FIGURE..

I'M GOING INTO A SKID! WE'RE GOING TO GO OVER THE CLIFF!

SKREE!

THE CAR PLUNGED OVER-- OUT OF CONTROL ...

GREAT HERA! STEVE'S BEEN THROWN OUT OF THE CAR!

CRASH!

WITH SPEED NO HUMAN COULD MEASURE, DIANA CHANGED INTO *WONDER WOMAN* INSIDE THE HURTLING CAR...

WITH ANOTHER DAZZLING BURST OF MOTION, SHE DIVED TOWARDS THE PLUMMETING STEVE ...

WONDER WOMAN!

7

ALIGHTING ON THE BEACH BELOW WITH HER BURDEN, SHE THRUST UP A POWERFUL ARM JUST AS...

I THOUGHT I WAS A GONER--UNTIL YOU ARRIVED, ANGEL! I GUESS YOU ALREADY SAVED DI?

YES, DARLING!

WITH THE DISASTER AVERTED...

I HOPE NO ONE ELSE TRIES ANY MORE FOOL STUNTS LIKE THAT FOOL GIRL! IF YOU WEREN'T ON THE SCENE--WHO KNOWS HOW MANY PEOPLE WOULD HAVE BEEN HURT!

IT PROBABLY WON'T HAPPEN AGAIN!

SOON, **WONDER WOMAN** WAS SO BUSY RESCUING HER IMPERSONATORS...AROUND THE CLOCK...

THAT... I HAVE NO TIME ANYMORE TO BATTLE CRIME AND IN-JUSTICE! THERE'S ONLY ONE THING TO DO TO HALT THIS MADNESS--*REVEAL MY SECRET IDENTITY*--BEFORE *IMPOSSIBLE DAMAGE HAS BEEN DONE!*

AND SO, THE AMAZON DELIBERATELY REVEALS HER SECRET IDENTITY OF LT. DIANA PRINCE... AND AS SHE RETURNS FROM HER RESCUE OF THE MEN ON THE GIRDER--WE CONTINUE WITH THIS STARTLING TALE...

DI...WHAT A FOOL I'VE BEEN! CAN YOU EVER FORGIVE ME?

AND AS THE TWO DROVE AWAY TOGETHER-- RUTHLESS EYES WATCHED THEM...

THERE GOES OUR *MILLION DOLLAR PIGEON!* WONDER WOMAN IS FINISHED--NOW THAT WE KNOW HER SECRET IDENTITY!

AND IN THE CAR...

I HAVE SET MYSELF AN ALMOST IMPOSSIBLE TASK! TO FOOL BOTH STEVE--AND WHOEVER IS BEHIND THIS PLOT TO LEARN MY DUAL IDENTITY--THAT *I AM NOT WONDER WOMAN!*

CAN THE INGENIOUS AMAZON PERFORM THIS TWO-FOLD FEAT? WE SHALL SEE!

STEVE DROVE TO LOOKOUT POINT WHERE..

HONEY--NOW THAT YOUR SECRET IS OUT--AND YOUR EFFICIENCY AS A CRIME-FIGHTER HAS BEEN WEAKENED-- DON'T YOU THINK IT'S TIME WE WERE MARRIED?

STEVE IS SO POSITIVE-- IT WILL BE A TITANIC TASK TO CONVINCE HIM I'M NOT *WONDER WOMAN* --FOR THE BENEFIT OF MY WORK! STILL, I MUST DO IT... SOMEHOW!

SUDDENLY, A CONTAINER HURTLED DOWN AT STEVE'S JEEP FROM ABOVE...

DI--R-R-RUN BEFORE-- BE--!

SUFFERING SAPPHO!... I DIDN'T THINK...THE VILLAIN... BEHIND...TH-THIS...WOULD ST-STRIKE SO SOON....I DIDN'T F-F-FIGURE ON STEVE B-BEING WITH M...

THUD!

AND THEN, FROM THE VILLAIN'S GIANT HELI- COPTER WHICH HAD BEEN TRACKING STEVE'S JEEP, A MASSIVE CRANE IS LOWERED...

WE'VE GOT *WONDER WOMAN* --WHEN WE'VE GOT LT. DIANA PRINCE!

YOU SURE DID, SLICKER!

9

TO A DESERTED BEACH THE HELICOPTER DRONED AND THERE...

LOWER WONDER WOMAN INTO THE ROCKET!

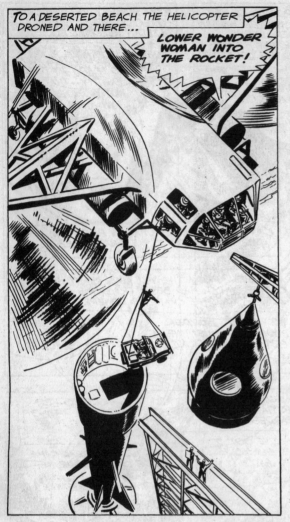

SHORTLY, THE GIANT ROCKET IS FIRED TO THE GREAT GLEE OF THE ASSEMBLED VILLAINS...

VROOOOOSH!

THERE'S THE END OF **WONDER WOMAN**! FROM NOW ON -- SHE'LL CIRCLE THE EARTH FOREVER -- IN A FLYING PRISON! AND WE CAN PLOT OUR BIGGEST CRIMES WITHOUT INTERFERENCE FROM HER!

HA! HA! HA!

IN THE ROCKET HURTLING INTO SPACE, THE INDOMITABLE WILL OF THE AMAZON BEGAN TO ASSERT ITSELF...

TH-THANK HERA -- STEVE'S ST-STILL UNCONSCIOUS... AT LEAST... I'LL HAVE A CHANCE TO TRY TO RESCUE HIM -- AND FOOL HIM INTO TH-THINKING DIANA PRINCE IS NOT **WONDER WOMAN**!

AGAIN AN EYE-BLURRING TRANSFORMATION IS MADE...

BUT CONVINCING STEVE HE IS MISTAKEN -- IS ONLY HALF THE BATTLE! I MUST ALSO CONVINCE THE VILLAIN BEHIND THIS PLOT!

CAN **WONDER WOMAN** ACCOMPLISH THIS IN A ROCKET SOARING INTO SPACE?

10

SUDDENLY, A SURGE SHOOK THE WHOLE ROCKET AS...

GREAT HERA! THE FIRST STAGE HAS ALREADY DROPPED OFF! I HAVE VERY LITTLE TIME LEFT!

VROOOSH!

WITH ALL THE POWER OF HER VOCAL CORDS *WONDER WOMAN* CALLED FOR HER UNIQUE AMAZON PLANE WHICH ONLY RESPONDED TO THE VIBRATIONS OF HER VOICE...

CALLING PLANE!... CALLING PLANE!...

AH--THERE IT IS!

FOR A MOMENT, RECOVERING CONSCIOUSNESS, STEVE DAZEDLY RECOGNIZED...

WONDER WOMAN'S PLANE!... H-H-HOW IS TH-THAT POSSIBLE-- IF--IF--?

EVEN AS THE PILOT LAPSED BACK INTO UNCONSCIOUSNESS AGAIN...

THE SECOND STAGE HAS FALLEN OFF THE ROCKET! IN A FEW MORE INSTANTS-- THE NOSE CONE WE'RE IN WILL BE ORBITING IN SPACE!

DESPERATELY, *WONDER WOMAN* TOOK OFF HER TIARA, MADE OF AMAZONIUM, HARDEST METAL KNOWN, AND...

I'VE GOT TO CUT AN ESCAPE HATCH!

SKRUNGG!

AND THEN, HOLDING HER SWEETHEART, THE DARING AMAZON LEAPED OUT OF THE ROCKET AS...

HERA HELP ME REACH THE INSIDE OF MY PLANE IN TIME--BEFORE THE LACK OF OXYGEN KILLS STEVE!

11

BUT, JUST AS THE TWO FLYING FIGURES NEARED THE PLANE--IT DARTED IN A DIFFERENT DIRECTION AS...

THUNDERBOLTS OF JOVE! MY PLANE AUTOMATICALLY DIVED OUT OF THE WAY OF THAT METEOR--AND OUT OF MY GRASP! STEVE CAN'T SURVIVE OUT HERE WITHOUT OXYGEN!

INSTANTLY, EVEN AS SHE HURLED HERSELF AFTER THE ROBOT PLANE, WONDER WOMAN ACTS LIKE AN INGENIOUS OXYGEN TANK!

GOT TO... BREATHE WHATEVER AIR... IS IN MY... LUNGS... INTO... STEVE'S... OR HE'S... FINISHED...!

WITH A DAZZLING BURST OF SPEED, THE AMAZON REACHED THE EMERGENCY ENTRANCE INTO HER PLANE WITH STEVE SAFELY...

THANK HERA! STEVE WILL BE ALL RIGHT! I'LL HEAD DOWN FOR THE LAUNCHING SITE FROM WHICH THE ROCKET WAS FIRED!

DOWN, WONDER WOMAN PILOTED HER FLASHING PLANE UNTIL...

WONDER WOMAN'S PLANE! HOW'S THAT POSSIBLE WHEN SHE'S INSIDE THE ROCKET, SLICKER?

MAYBE IT'S ANOTHER AMAZON! SHOOT DOWN THAT PLANE--WE'LL SEE!

POW! POW!

BUT, WONDER WOMAN LEAPED OUT ON A WING OF HER PLANE, AND WHIRLING HER LASSO AROUND AT TREMENDOUS SPEED...

SHE'S TURNING US OVER JUST BY WHIRLING HER LASSO AROUND--ONLY WONDER WOMAN CAN DO THAT STUNT!

VROOSH!

LIKE A GIANT CARTWHEEL, **WONDER WOMAN** DROPS THE STUNNED GANG AT POLICE HEAD-QUARTERS...

BLAST THAT **AMAZON**! WE STILL DON'T KNOW HER SECRET IDENTITY!

WELL, SLICKER! WE'VE BEEN LOOKING FOR YOU AND YOUR GANG FOR A LONG TIME!

CRASH!

SLOWLY, STEVE RECOVERED CONSCIOUSNESS...

I THOUGHT SO! IT **WAS** YOU... FLYING TO DIANA'S AND MY RESCUE... I SAW YOUR PLANE OUTSIDE THE ROCKET... GUESS SHE'S ALL RIGHT--OR YOU WOULDN'T BE HERE! FUNNY--ME THINKING ANY-ONE AS BEAUTIFUL AS YOU--COULD ALSO BE DI!

I DREAMED YOU KISSED ME!

DREAM'S OVER, STEVE!

The End 13

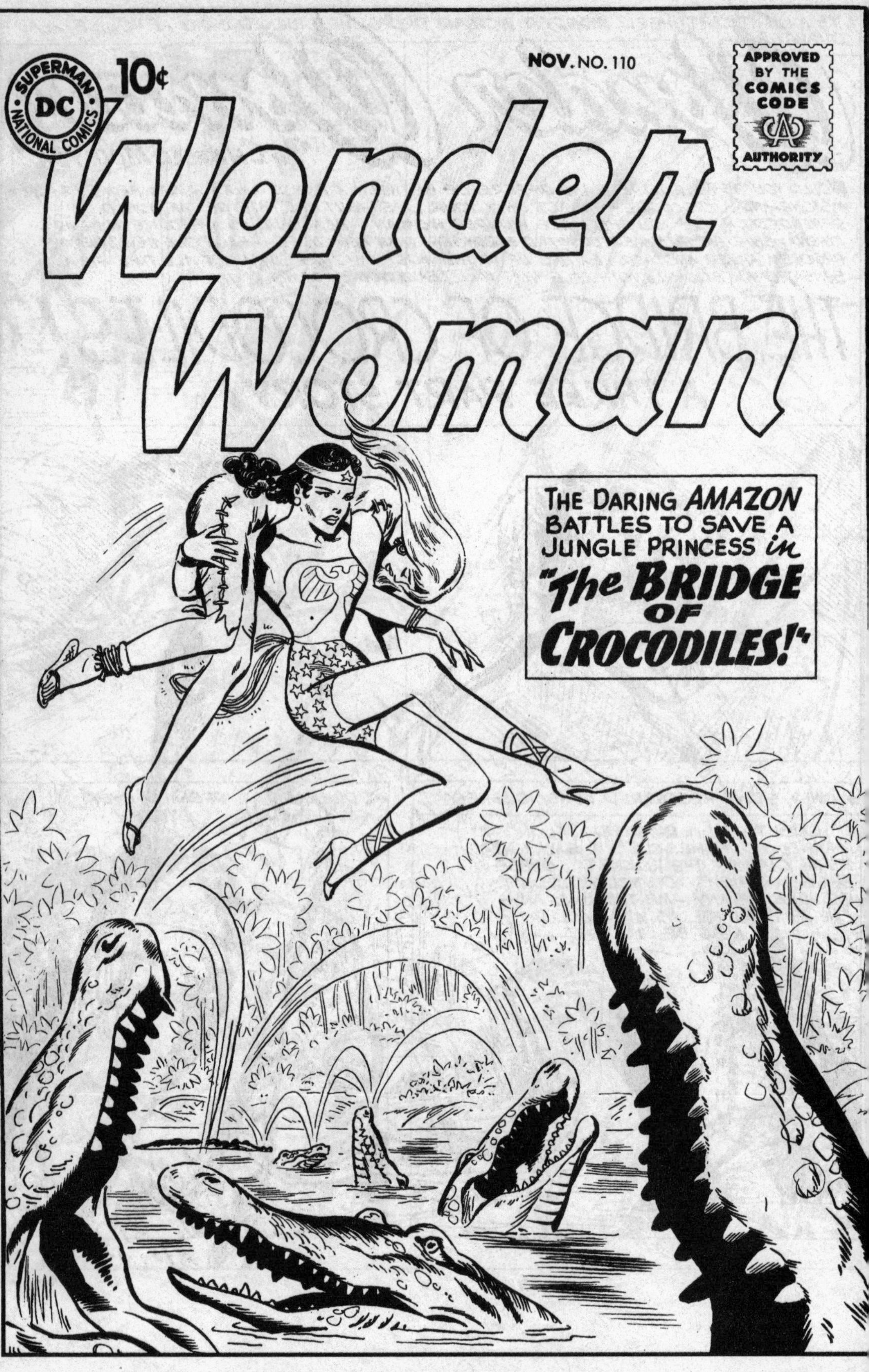
SUPERMAN DC NATIONAL COMICS
10¢
NOV. NO. 110
APPROVED BY THE COMICS CODE AUTHORITY
Wonder Woman
THE DARING AMAZON BATTLES TO SAVE A JUNGLE PRINCESS in "The BRIDGE OF CROCODILES!"

Wonder Woman

By Charles Moulton

WOULD YOU BE ABLE TO TELL THE DIFFERENCE BETWEEN A ROBOT AND A HUMAN BEING? --OR A STONE AND A CROCODILE-- IF NOT ONLY *YOUR* LIFE --BUT THE FATE OF THE WORLD DEPENDED ON IT? YOU SHALL SEE *WONDER WOMAN* --BEAUTIFUL AS APHRODITE, WISE AS ATHENA, SWIFTER THAN MERCURY, AND STRONGER THAN HERCULES--FACE ONE BEWILDERING PROBLEM AFTER ANOTHER LEADING UP TO THE MOST AMAZING CLIMAX OF ALL TIME--IN A SENSATIONAL BOOK-LENGTH TALE THAT WILL LEAVE YOU GASPING!

THE BRIDGE OF CROCODILES!
A THREE PART STORY!

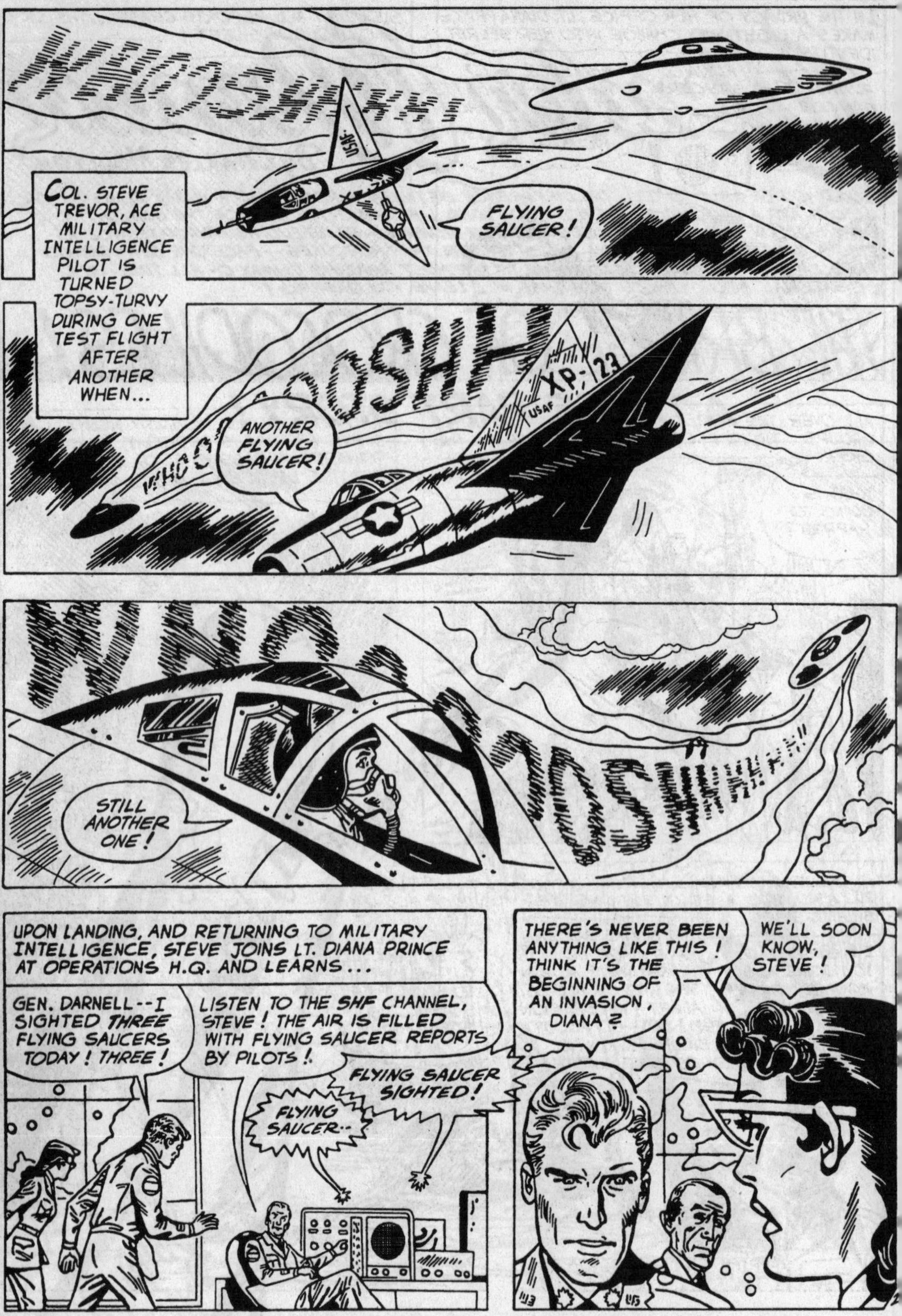
WHOOSHHH!
COL. STEVE TREVOR, ACE MILITARY INTELLIGENCE PILOT IS TURNED TOPSY-TURVY DURING ONE TEST FLIGHT AFTER ANOTHER WHEN...
FLYING SAUCER!
WHOOOOSHH
ANOTHER FLYING SAUCER!
WHOOOSHHHH!
STILL ANOTHER ONE!
UPON LANDING, AND RETURNING TO MILITARY INTELLIGENCE, STEVE JOINS LT. DIANA PRINCE AT OPERATIONS H.Q. AND LEARNS...
GEN. DARNELL--I SIGHTED THREE FLYING SAUCERS TODAY! THREE!
LISTEN TO THE SHF CHANNEL, STEVE! THE AIR IS FILLED WITH FLYING SAUCER REPORTS BY PILOTS!
FLYING SAUCER SIGHTED!
FLYING SAUCER--
THERE'S NEVER BEEN ANYTHING LIKE THIS! THINK IT'S THE BEGINNING OF AN INVASION, DIANA?
WE'LL SOON KNOW, STEVE!

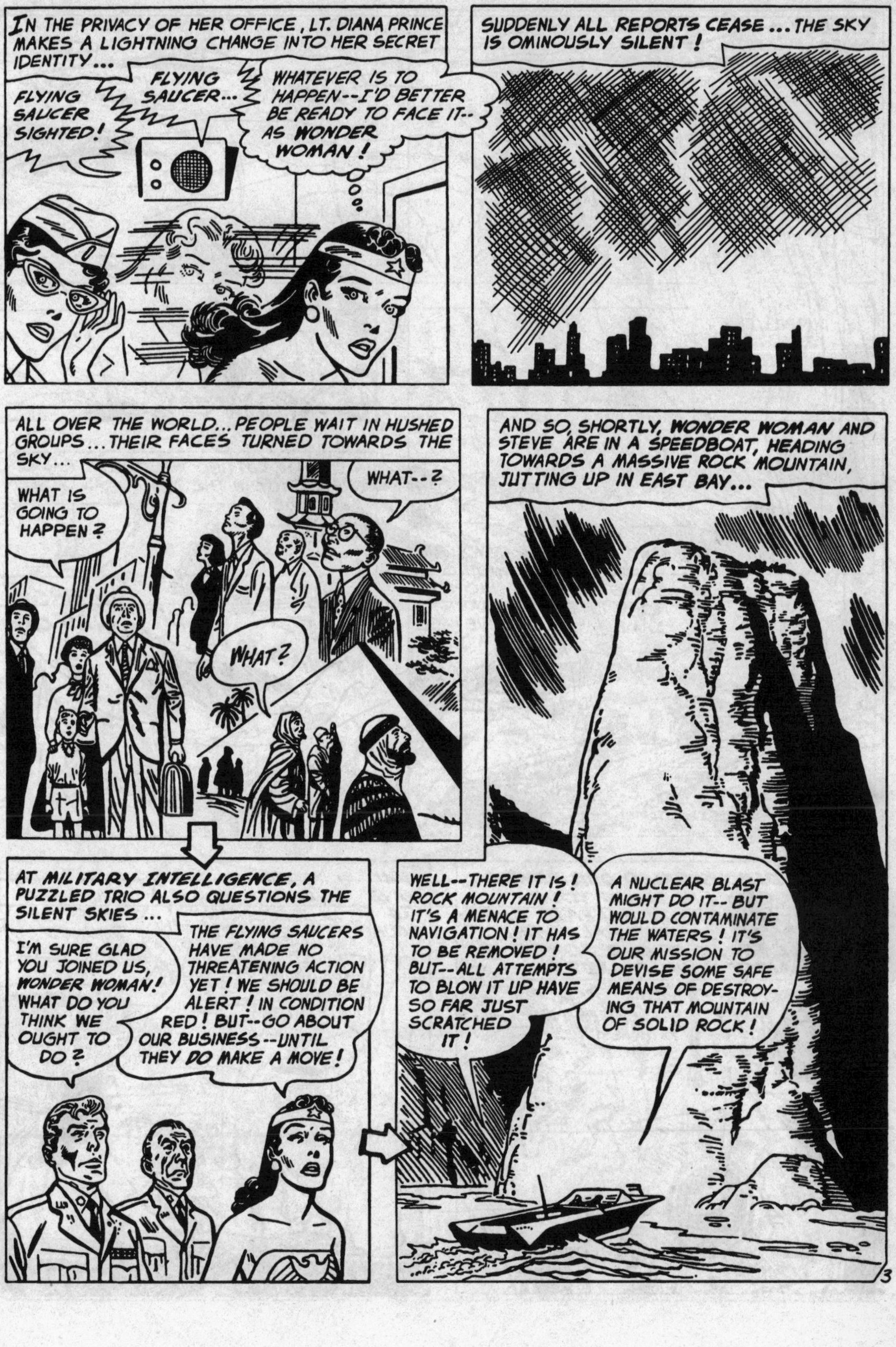
IN THE PRIVACY OF HER OFFICE, LT. DIANA PRINCE MAKES A LIGHTNING CHANGE INTO HER SECRET IDENTITY...
FLYING SAUCER SIGHTED!
FLYING SAUCER...
WHATEVER IS TO HAPPEN--I'D BETTER BE READY TO FACE IT--AS WONDER WOMAN!
SUDDENLY ALL REPORTS CEASE...THE SKY IS OMINOUSLY SILENT!
ALL OVER THE WORLD...PEOPLE WAIT IN HUSHED GROUPS...THEIR FACES TURNED TOWARDS THE SKY...
WHAT IS GOING TO HAPPEN?
WHAT--?
WHAT?
AND SO, SHORTLY, WONDER WOMAN AND STEVE ARE IN A SPEEDBOAT, HEADING TOWARDS A MASSIVE ROCK MOUNTAIN, JUTTING UP IN EAST BAY...
AT MILITARY INTELLIGENCE, A PUZZLED TRIO ALSO QUESTIONS THE SILENT SKIES...
I'M SURE GLAD YOU JOINED US, WONDER WOMAN! WHAT DO YOU THINK WE OUGHT TO DO?
THE FLYING SAUCERS HAVE MADE NO THREATENING ACTION YET! WE SHOULD BE ALERT! IN CONDITION RED! BUT--GO ABOUT OUR BUSINESS--UNTIL THEY DO MAKE A MOVE!
WELL--THERE IT IS! ROCK MOUNTAIN! IT'S A MENACE TO NAVIGATION! IT HAS TO BE REMOVED! BUT--ALL ATTEMPTS TO BLOW IT UP HAVE SO FAR JUST SCRATCHED IT!
A NUCLEAR BLAST MIGHT DO IT--BUT WOULD CONTAMINATE THE WATERS! IT'S OUR MISSION TO DEVISE SOME SAFE MEANS OF DESTROYING THAT MOUNTAIN OF SOLID ROCK!
3

SUDDENLY, A LIGHT RAY STREAKS THROUGH THE SKIES, AND WITH THE UNLEASHED FURY OF COUNTLESS THUNDERBOLTS...

I--I CAN'T BELIEVE IT--! THAT--THAT *THING* HAS TURNED THE ROCK INTO FLAME!

IF YOU'RE HAVING A NIGHTMARE, STEVE--SO AM I!

ABOVE THEM, THE STARTLED PAIR SEES A FAMILIAR SIGHT...

FLYING SAUCER!

THAT ANNIHILATING RAY CAME FROM IT!

AND THEN, CUTTING INTO EVERY RADIO FREQUENCY IN THE WORLD, AN OMINOUS MESSAGE...

WARNING TO EARTH! OUR FIRST-- AND LAST! WHOEVER HAS CAPTURED OUR PRINCESS-- FREE HER!

WE HAVE DEMONSTRATED OUR POWER ON ROCK ONLY! IN 24 OF YOUR HOURS--UNLESS YOU RELEASE OUR PRINCESS TO US--WE SHALL HURL THE FULL FORCE OF OUR POWER AGAINST YOUR PLANET!

YOU HAVE 24 HOURS!

SO THAT'S THE REASON FOR THEIR ACTIVITY! THEY WERE SEARCHING FOR THEIR PRINCESS!

AND WE'VE GOT TO FIND HER-- OR EARTH IS DOOMED!

IN *WONDER WOMAN'S* ROBOT PLANE, SHE AND STEVE SPEARHEAD SEARCH PARTIES ALL OVER THE WORLD...ON LAND, SEA, UNDER THE SEA AND IN THE AIR...

WE'LL START OUR ASSIGNED SEARCH SECTION NOW, STEVE!

ROGER!

IT JUST OCCURRED TO ME, ANGEL! WE DON'T KNOW *WHAT* A FLYING SAUCER PRINCESS WOULD LOOK LIKE! NO ONE HAS EVER SEEN THE FLYING SAUCER PEOPLE!

SHE COULD BE IN ANY SHAPE!

ANIMAL.

MINERAL.

VEGETABLE.

ROBOT.

FANTASTIC INDEED IS THE TASK BEFORE *WONDER WOMAN*—WITH THE FATE OF THE WORLD DEPENDING UPON HER SUCCESS!

THERE'S ONLY ONE PRINCESS IN THIS SOLAR SYSTEM I'M MAD ABOUT! AN AMAZON ONE! YOU, ANGEL! WHEN ARE YOU GOING TO MARRY ME?

I TOLD YOU A HUNDRED TIMES, STEVE! WHEN MY SERVICES ARE NO LONGER NEEDED TO BATTLE CRIME AND INJUSTICE!

SUDDENLY, THE ALERT AMAZON SPOTS BELOW..

GREAT HERA! A SHIP--BLINDED BY FOG--HEADING STRAIGHT FOR THAT HUGE ICEBERG!

INSTANTLY LEAPING OUT OF HER PLANE, THE DARING AMAZON LEAVES STEVE AT THE CONTROLS...

THE SHIP'S CONTROLS MUST BE JAMMED FOR IT NOT TO DETECT THAT GIGANTIC ICEBERG! IT'S TOO LATE FOR IT TO TURN OUT OF THE WAY NOW! IT'S ALL UP TO *WONDER WOMAN!*

THE SHIP IS ALMOST UPON THE ICEBERG!

SPLASH!

INTO THE INTENSELY FRIGID WATERS *WONDER WOMAN* HURTLES, AND AS SHE GRIMLY ATTEMPTS TO YANK THE HUGE ICE FLOE DOWN OUT OF THE WAY OF THE SHIP...

SUFFERING SAPPHO! TOO SLIPPERY-- FOR ME TO GRASP HOLD!

AND THEN, AS IF THE MIGHTY AMAZON IS NOT FACED WITH A FORMIDABLE TASK ALREADY-- A TERRIFYING SHAPE KNIFES TOWARDS HER ...

A GIGANTIC SWORDFISH! THE MOST GIGANTIC ONE I EVER SAW!

ONCE! TWICE--THRICE--THE AGILE AMAZON NARROWLY ESCAPES DESTRUCTION FROM THE STUPENDOUS BLADE...

--EVERY INSTANT OF DELAY HERE--

--SENDS THE SHIP ABOVE--

--CLOSER TO DOOM!

WITH A LIGHTNING TWIST OF HER GOLDEN LASSO, *WONDER WOMAN* CAPTURES THE SEA MONSTER...

I CAN KEEP IT FROM HARMING ME NOW--BUT THAT WON'T SAVE THE SHIP FROM DISASTER! IF THERE WAS ONLY SOME WAY OF WHITTLING THE ICEBERG DOWN--?

AGILELY, THE AMAZON HURLS HERSELF ABOARD THE ENRAGED FISH...

I HAVE AN IDEA-- MIGHTY NEPTUNE SMILE ON MY TASK!

WITH DAZZLING SKILL, *WONDER WOMAN* MANIPULATES HER MASSIVE LIVING SAW, SLASHING THE ICEBERG IN HALF...

THE ICEBERG IS SINKING--BUT HAS IT SUNK LOW ENOUGH TO BE OUT OF THE WAY OF THE SHIP?

CRACK!

UP TO THE SURFACE, THE FEARLESS AMAZON RIDES HER UNDERSEA STEED...

THANK HERA! THE SHIP IS SAFE!

RELEASING THE SEA MONSTER, *WONDER WOMAN* LEAPS UP TOWARDS HER PLANE WHEN...

STEVE! WHAT'S WRONG? WHY ARE YOU FLYING *AWAY* FROM ME? STEVE--? *STEVE!*

WHOOOSH!!

BUT, AT THE CONTROLS OF THE AMAZON PLANE, AN UTTERLY TRANSFORMED STEVE COMPLETELY IGNORES HIS SWEETHEART'S PLEAS...

STEVE!-- STEVE--! COME BACK!

WHAT EXTRAORDINARY EVENT COULD HAVE TURNED STEVE AGAINST THE GIRL HE LOVES--? WE SHALL SEE IN THE SECOND PART OF THIS STARTLING TALE ON NEXT PAGE FOLLOWING!

8

Wonder Woman

By Charles Moulton

PART TWO: THE BRIDGE OF CROCODILES!

WITH A DESPERATE CAST OF HER LASSO, WONDER WOMAN SNAPS HERSELF BACK ONTO HER PLANE AS IF SHE WERE A BALL AT THE END OF A RUBBER BAND!

STEVE BETTER HAVE SOME EXPLANATION FOR HIS MAD BEHAVIOR!

BUT, UPON RE-ENTERING HER PLANE, THE LOVELY AMAZON IS PUZZLED STILL FURTHER, WHEN..

LISTEN!... LISTEN--!

STEVE-- I DON'T HEAR A THING!

CAN'T RESIST-- CAN'T RESIST-- HEAR IT?

HEAR WHAT, DARLING--?

LISTEN!... LISTEN...!

WHAT DO YOU HEAR?

BUT THE PILOT STARES STRAIGHT AHEAD AS IF HE WERE ALONE...

HE ACTS AS IF HE'S SPELL-BOUND--HEARING SOUNDS EVEN MY AMAZON HEARING CANNOT DETECT! WHAT CAN THEY BE?

AND THEN... THUNDERBOLTS OF JOVE! NOW STEVE IS HEADING FOR A LANDING IN A DENSE JUNGLE!

AS STEVE UNERRINGLY LANDS THE PLANE IN A CLEARING IN THE JUNGLE, WHICH HAD NOT BEEN APPARENT FROM THE AIR... WONDER WOMAN IS STARTLED TO BEHOLD...

WHAT IS THAT BEAUTY DOING IN THE JUNGLE?

SKREEEE!

AND THEN, AS STEVE IMMEDIATELY STUMBLES OUT OF THE PLANE AS IF HE WERE IN A TRANCE...

THE FLUTE THAT GIRL IS PLAYING--I CAN'T HEAR IT--BUT STEVE CAN! LIKE SONAR--HE'S ATTUNED TO IT BUT NOT I!

EARTH MAN--HAVE YOU EVER LOVED ANYONE BEFORE?

NO ONE--ONLY YOU... ONLY YOU!

TEARS FILL THE LOVELY YOUNG AMAZON'S EYES AS...

STEVE -- *STEVE* -- YOU CAN'T HAVE FORGOTTEN ME! I...

I NEVER... SAW YOU... BEFORE... IN MY... LIFE!

MASKING HER HEARTACHE, THE AMAZON DEMANDS...

I DON'T KNOW WHO YOU ARE.. OR WHAT YOU'RE DOING HERE -- BUT I ORDER YOU TO RELEASE HIM FROM YOUR SPELL! I AM PRINCESS DIANA OF THE AMAZONS!

THE STRANGE SIREN LAUGHS AND MERELY POINTS HER FLUTE AT *WONDER WOMAN*...

THE RAY -- PARALYZED ME! THIS STRANGER -- WHOEVER SHE IS -- HAS MIGHTY POWERS!

HELPLESSLY, *WONDER WOMAN* WATCHES THE SPELL-BOUND STEVE... AS...

SUFFERING SAPPHO! NOT ONLY HAVE I FAILED TO FIND THE FLYING SAUCER PRINCESS -- BUT STEVE HAS BEEN CAPTURED BY A STRANGE JUNGLE SIREN!

MEANWHILE, ALL OVER THE WORLD, THE DESPERATE SEARCH CONTINUES...

NO SIGN OF FLYING SAUCER OR PRINCESS...!

SEARCH REVEALS NO TRACE OF FLYING SAUCER PRINCESS!

NO CONTACT MADE OF MISSING PRINCESS!

RESULTS NEGATIVE!

IN THE HARBOR, GRIM TESTIMONY TO THE MIGHT OF THE FLYING SAUCER PEOPLE, THE SOLID MOUNTAIN OF ROCK BURNS LIKE A FIERCE FLAME..

AND FROM THE FLYING SAUCERS, AN OMINOUS REMINDER INTERRUPTS ALL RADIO FREQUENCIES...

WARNING TO EARTH! 12 OF YOUR HOURS HAVE ALREADY PASSED WITHOUT YOUR RELEASING OUR MISSING PRINCESS! YOU HAVE BUT TWELVE HOURS MORE!

OVER THE WORLD'S MIGHTIEST SKY-SCRAPER A SAUCER HOVERS...

REMOVE EVERYONE FROM THIS BUILDING IMMEDIATELY!

A SINGLE BLAST FROM THE OBJECT FROM OUTER SPACE TURNS THE SKYSCRAPER INTO A LOFTY TURRET OF SOLID ICE!

THIS IS ANOTHER DEMONSTRATION OF THE FORCE WE WILL USE AGAINST EARTH-- IF YOU FAIL TO PRODUCE OUR PRINCESS!

ZZZZZT!

AT MILITARY INTELLIGENCE, GENERAL DARNELL RECEIVES ALL REPORTS...

ANYTHING NEW ON THE SEARCH, GENERAL?

ALL SEARCHING PARTIES EXCEPT **WONDER WOMAN** REPORT NEGATIVE! NO SIGN OF THE MISSING FLYING SAUCER PRINCESS!

WONDER WOMAN HASN'T REPORTED BACK IN A LONG TIME! SHE MIGHT BE ON THE TRAIL OF THE MISSING FLYING SAUCER PRINCESS! OUR HOPES TO AVERT A CATASTROPHE-- NOW REST ON THE AMAZON!

AND WHAT OF **WONDER WOMAN?**... AT THIS CRUCIAL MOMENT, SHE IS NUMB FROM THE PARALYZING EFFECTS OF THE RAY THE JUNGLE SIREN HAD BLASTED HER WITH!

IF I DIDN'T KNOW A FLYING SAUCER CREATURE COULDN'T RESEMBLE AN EARTH BEING--I WOULD THINK **THIS** POWERFUL GIRL WAS THE MISSING PRINCESS! BUT-- SHE ISN'T A ROBOT, VEGETABLE OR MINERAL!

FOOLISH EARTH GIRL! I WILL LEAVE YOU HERE TO FACE WHATEVER PERILS THE JUNGLE WILL HURL AT YOU! COME, EARTHMAN!

I GO WHEREVER YOU LEAD ME, BEAUTIFUL ONE!

IN THE DEPTHS OF DESPAIR **WONDER WOMAN** WATCHES HER SWEETHEART DEPART WITH THE SIREN...

STEVE... STEVE--DON'T LEAVE ME!

THEN--WITH AN INCREDIBLE EFFORT, THE ONCE AGILE AMAZON...HOPS...

I MUST... FOLLOW.. THEM...

...RESTORE STEVE TO HIS SENSES SOMEHOW--AND CONTINUE LOOKING FOR THE MISSING FLYING SAUCER PRINCESS!

LIKE A TOY JUMPING JACK WONDER WOMAN HOPS INTO THE JUNGLE...

IT'S SO DENSE IN HERE-- STEVE AND THAT--THAT STRANGE GIRL--ARE OUT OF SIGHT ALREADY! I MUST CATCH UP TO THEM!

THOSE SONAR-LIKE NOTES SHE PLAYS--AND THAT RAY SHE PARALYZED ME WITH--ARE OUTER SPACE INVENTIONS! I WONDER IF SHE FOUND THAT FLUTE-LIKE INSTRUMENT? IF SO-- IT MEANS--?

AT THAT MOMENT, WARNED BY THE ALMOST SILENT RUSH OF THE JUNGLE BEAST THROUGH THE AIR...

THE AMAZON LEAPS STIFFLY UP...

THUD!

BUT FALLS DOWN ON THE VERY BACK OF THE ANIMAL!

THUMP!

AS THE FROZEN *WONDER WOMAN* IS TOSSED OFF BY THE ENRAGED JUNGLE ANIMAL...

I'VE GOT TO CAGE HIM--BEFORE HE CHARGES AGAIN!

ROWR!

CALLING UPON INCREDIBLE INNER CONTROL OF HER MUSCLES, THE TIRELESS AMAZON SPINS LIKE A HUMAN TOP...DIGGING A HOLE IN THE JUNGLE FLOOR...

HERE HE COMES!

VOOOOOOM!

WITH DAZZLING TIMING *WONDER WOMAN* LEAPS OUT OF THE PIT SHE HAS DUG, ESCAPING SLASHING CLAWS BY INCHES!

THANK HERA! HE'LL BE OUT OF HARM'S WAY HERE! NOW I CAN CONTINUE LOOKING FOR STEVE!

BUT AS SHE ALIGHTS OUTSIDE THE PIT...SHE IS STARTLED BY...

JUNGLE NATIVES--! THEY MUST HAVE SEEN EVERYTHING!

YOU GREAT MAGIC! WE TAKE YOU TO MIGHTY CHIEF!

GOOD! PERHAPS I CAN PERSUADE THEM TO HELP ME LOOK FOR STEVE AND THE GIRL!

15.

THE NUMB *WONDER WOMAN* IS CARRIED TO A VILLAGE IN THE JUNGLE WHERE SHE BEHOLDS AN INCREDIBLE SIGHT...

THERE! OUR MIGHTY CHIEF ON FLYING THRONE! YOU SHOW HER YOUR MAGIC!

THUNDERBOLTS OF JOVE! THAT BLONDE LORELEI ON A FLYING SAUCER! WITH STEVE! REGARDLESS OF WHAT SHE LOOKS LIKE--SHE *MUST* BE THE MISSING PRINCESS!

WITH A TREMENDOUS EFFORT, THE INDOMITABLE AMAZON FORCES HER VOCAL CHORDS TO FUNCTION AGAIN...

YOU--ARE--THE--MISSING--FLYING--SAUCER--PRINCESS! YOU--MUST--RETURN--TO--YOUR--PLANET! YOUR--PEOPLE--THREATEN--TO--ATTACK--THE--EARTH--IF--YOU--DON'T!

I REFUSE! AND YOU *CAN'T* MAKE ME GO, EARTHLING!

NEVER HAS WONDER WOMAN BEEN SO HELPLESS--WHEN ALL HER MIGHTY POWERS ARE DESPERATELY NEEDED TO PREVENT THE EARTH'S DOOM! FOR THE AMAZING CONCLUSION TO THIS STORY, TURN TO PART THREE ON THE PAGE FOLLOWING!

116

PART THREE: The BRIDGE OF CROCODILES!

DESPERATELY, *WONDER WOMAN* APPEALS TO HER SWEETHEART...

STEVE--*STEVE*--TELL HER SHE IS ENDANGERING THE WORLD! TELL HER SHE MUST RETURN TO HER OWN PLANET!

BUT, TO THE AMAZON'S ANGUISH, STEVE IS DEAF TO HER PLEA...

IT'S NO USE! HE IS COMPLETELY UNDER HER SPELL!

WHEN *WONDER WOMAN* AGAIN APPEALS TO THE CREATURE FROM OUTER SPACE, SHE REPLIES IN A LANGUAGE ONLY THE AMAZON, VERSED IN ALL LANGUAGES, CAN UNDERSTAND...

I AM CONSIDERED A GODDESS HERE! DO YOU THINK I WILL RETURN TO MY PLANET, WHERE I AM MERELY ONE PRINCESS AMONG 2785 OTHERS?

"ON MY FLYING SAUCER PLANET, I WAS PRINCESS NO. 1003...WE WERE ALWAYS IN A GROUP... WHEN WE PLAYED..."

I MIGHT AS WELL BE IN AN ANT COLONY!

"OR MOVED FROM PLACE TO PLACE..."

WHAT'S THE USE OF BEING A PRINCESS-- IF NO ONE PAYS SPECIAL ATTENTION TO ME--BECAUSE THERE ARE *2785* OF US?

"ONE NIGHT I DECIDED TO LEAVE MY 2785 SISTER PRINCESSES!"

I'M GOING TO GO TO SOME OTHER PLANET--WHERE I'LL BE UNIQUE! AND EVERY-ONE WILL PAY ATTENTION ONLY TO ME!

"I PICKED OUT A COMPLETE DISGUISE--IN THE INTERPLANETARY WAREHOUSE!"

THIS LITTLE EARTH MODEL COMPLETE WITH RAY WAND IS JUST WHAT I NEED TO MAKE ME IRRESISTABLE TO ANY EARTH MAN!

"I BORROWED A SHIP FROM THE PALACE GARAGE WHEN NO ONE WAS ON GUARD... AND DEPARTED FOR EARTH!"

I NEVER THOUGHT THERE WOULD BE SO MANY CONTROLS!

"I HAD MORE TROUBLE THAN I EXPECTED MANIPULATING THE CONTROLS!"

OOOOH-- THAT WAS CLOSE!

VROOOSH!

"I NEVER DREAMED SPACE TRAVEL WOULD BE SO DIFFICULT-- EVEN WHEN I SET THE DESTINATION LEVER FOR EARTH!"

VROOOSH!

I'M OUT OF CONTROL! I'M GOING TO CRASH!

"BUT THERE WAS SOME SAFETY DEVICE THAT STOPPED THE SHIP FROM CRASHING!"

EARTH-- AT LAST!

WROOS...H!

"WHEN I GOT OUT, I WAS SURROUNDED BY EARTH MEN!"

ARE THEY WELCOMING ME--OR THREATENING ME?

"WITH ONE CIRCULAR BLAST OF MY RAY WAND--I TURNED THEIR WEAPONS INTO FLAME..."

THIS IS THE MIGHTIEST MAGIC OF ALL!

AIE! AIE!

SHE IS THE ONE...WISE MEN TELL ABOUT FOR MANY MANY MOONS!

AIE!

"THE LEADER HIMSELF LED THE OTHERS IN PRAISE OF ME!"

ALL HAIL GODDESS OF FLAME! DAUGHTER OF SUN!

ALL HAIL!

HAIL!

AIE!

"NO LONGER WAS I ONE AMONG 2785 OTHERS--HERE I RULED SUPREME....AND YET...I WANTED ONE THING MORE!"

A HANDSOME PRINCE! ON A WHITE STEED! MY MUSIC WILL SEEK HIM OUT--AND GUIDE HIM TO ME!

AS THE FLYING SAUCER PRINCESS FINISHES HER AMAZING STORY...

WITH THIS HANDSOME PRINCE AT MY SIDE--I NOW HAVE EVERYTHING I WANT! AND YOU WANT ME TO GIVE ALL THIS UP--AND BECOME PRINCESS 1003 AGAIN? NEVER! EVEN THOUGH YOUR WORLD IS DESTROYED! YOU'RE POWERLESS AGAINST ME HERE! I RULE! MY POWER IS MIGHTIEST!

SHE MEANS IT--AND EARTH IS DOOMED--UNLESS I CAN RETURN HER TO HER OWN PEOPLE! ONLY A FEW HOURS ARE LEFT BEFORE THE FLYING SAUCERS WILL STRIKE! THERE IS ONLY ONE THING LEFT FOR ME TO DO!

VERSED IN THE CUSTOMS OF ALL PEOPLES, PAST AND PRESENT, THE DESPERATE *WONDER WOMAN* UTTERS ...

I CHALLENGE YOU TO A CONTEST TO DECIDE WHICH ONE OF US HAS THE MIGHTIEST POWERS!

FOOL! I HAVE ALREADY PROVEN I AM MORE POWERFUL! I HAVE TAKEN AWAY YOUR PRINCE--AND MADE YOU AS STIFF AS A STICK! AND YOU--YOU CHALLENGE ME! HA! HA! HA! RIDICULOUS!

ALL AROUND HER, THE NUMB AMAZON IS RINGED BY MOCKING LAUGHTER ...BUT THERE IS ONLY ONE VOICE WHICH STABS HER LIKE A KNIFE...

OH, STEVE--STEVE DARLING-- I CAN BEAR ANYTHING--BUT YOU--RIDICULING ME--AS IF I--NEVER EXISTED...

HA! HA! HA! HA! HA! HA!

AT A SIGNAL FROM THE TRIBAL CHIEFTAIN...THE LAUGHTER CEASES...

CHALLENGE MUST BE ANSWERED! DUEL MUST BE FOUGHT! LOSER MUST PAY PENALTY-- IT IS CUSTOM!

WHAT IS THE PENALTY, O'CHIEF?

THROUGH A CLEARING IN THE TREES, *WONDER WOMAN* IS SHOWN A RIVER ...

PENALTY FOR LOSING DUEL IS *WALK ACROSS BLACK STONES!*

A HARMLESS PENALTY!

HARMLESS? THE AMAZON IS IN FOR THE GREATEST SHOCK OF HER LIFE WHEN SHE WILL DISCOVER WHAT THE BLACK STONES REALLY ARE

20

ON THE WRECKED FLYING SAUCER, THE TWO DUELISTS FACE EACH OTHER AS...

DAUGHTER OF SUN MUST HIT CHALLENGER WITH SUN RAYS! SHE HAS TWO CHANCES! CHALLENGER MUST REMAIN IN SAME SPOT! AND AVOID BEING STRUCK! LOSER MUST WALK ACROSS BLACK STONES! BEGIN!

WITH A JEERING LAUGH, THE FLYING SAUCER PRINCESS HURLS A BLASTING RAY AT HER AMAZON ANTAGONIST... AS THE SPELLBOUND STEVE WATCHES...

FOOLISH GIRL--TO CHALLENGE ME! WHY--SHE STILL CAN'T MOVE FROM THE EFFECTS OF MY FIRST BLAST AT HER!

THAT NO ONE IS AS... MIGHTY.. AS YOU!

ZZZZZT!

AS THE DAZZLING RAY HURTLES AT HER, WONDER WOMAN FORCES HER HEAD FORWARD AND CATCHES IT ON HER TIARA OF AMAZONIUM, HARDEST METAL KNOWN!

IF STEVE WEREN'T AT HER SIDE--I'D TRY TO SEND THE RAY BACK LIKE A BOOMERANG--THAT WOULD KNOCK THE RAY WAND OUT OF HER HAND-- BUT I'M AFRAID TO RISK HURTING HIM!

ZZZZT!

OUT OF THE DUELING GROUND, THE AMAZON'S PARRY HURLS THE RAY...

CHALLENGER ESCAPE BEING STRUCK BY RAY--WITHOUT LEAVING SPOT! DAUGHTER OF SUN HAS ONE MORE CHANCE TO HIT CHALLENGER! LOSER MUST WALK ON BLACK STONES!

SPLANG!

I DID NOT REALLY TRY HARD--BECAUSE I THOUGHT THE AMAZON WAS POWERLESS! BUT NOW, I SHALL SET A TRAP FOR HER SHE WILL NOT BE ABLE TO ESCAPE!

21

AT THE FLYING SAUCER PRINCESS' DEMAND, THE DUEL CONTINUES IN A NEW PLACE SHE HAS SELECTED...

IF DAUGHTER OF SUN MISS CHALLENGER WITH RAY-- SHE LOSE ! IF CHALLENGER MOVE FROM SPOT TO AVOID BEING STRUCK-- SHE LOSE ! LOSER MUST WALK ACROSS BLACK STONES !... BEGIN !

TOWARDS THE MOTIONLESS WONDER WOMAN, THE MASSIVE TREE TOPPLES !

CRRACK!

THAT WAS A DIABOLICAL STROKE! IF I LEAP OUT OF THE WAY--I LOSE-- AND THE WORLD WILL BE ATTACKED! IF I DON'T-- I'M RIGHT IN THE PATH OF THAT GIGANTIC TREE !

THIS TIME THE DUELIST FROM OUTER SPACE DOES NOT EVEN AIM AT HER OPPONENT...

I'M NOT GOING TO TAKE THE CHANCE OF MISSING THAT AGILE AMAZON AGAIN! INSTEAD--I'M GOING TO FORCE HER TO MOVE FROM HER SPOT--AND LOSE THAT WAY ! HA! HA!

ZZZT!

LIKE A LIGHTNING BOLT, THE RAY SLICES RIGHT THROUGH A HUGE TREE...

ZZZZT!

CAN THE AMAZON SOLVE THIS AMAZING DILEMMA?

22

STILL NUMB FROM THE EFFECTS OF THE RAY BLAST, WONDER WOMAN MANAGES TO SOMERSAULT LIKE A STICK...

I HAVEN'T MOVED FROM THIS SPOT! ONLY CHANGED MY POSITION!

WITH INCREDIBLE SKILL, SHE BALANCES HERSELF ON HER HEAD...

HERA HELP MY PLAN SUCCEED! IT IS NOT MERELY MY FATE--BUT THE WORLD'S-- WHICH DEPENDS ON IT!

THE AMAZON'S HEELS, MADE OF AMAZONIUM, ARE LIKE AN INDESTRUCTIBLE BLADE, AGAINST WHICH THE FALLING TREE SPLITS ITSELF IN TWO, LEAVING A SAFE SPACE IN WHICH WONDER WOMAN IS UNHARMED...

CR-R-ACK!!

THE AMAZON HAS WON! ESCAPED BEING STRUCK-- WITHOUT MOVING FROM SPOT! SHE IS OUR NEW GODDESS! LOSER MUST NOW WALK ACROSS BLACK STONES!

23

SHORTLY, AT THE RIVER BANK... THE LOSER PAYS HER PENALTY...

AS SOON AS THE FLYING SAUCER PRINCESS WALKS ACROSS THE BLACK STONES TO SATISFY A TRIBAL CUSTOM-- I'LL TAKE HER BACK TO HER PEOPLE! IT'S A HARMLESS ENOUGH PENALTY TO PAY FOR LOSING!

SUDDENLY, THE PRINCESS FREEZES, AS UNDER HER, ONE OF THE BLACK STEPPING STONES MOVES!

THE STONE IS--ALIVE! IT'S--A CROCODILE!

HORRIFIED AT HER COMPETITOR'S IMPENDING FATE, WONDER WOMAN LEAPS BESIDE HER ON THE SNOUT OF THE GIANT CROCODILE...

SHE'S FAINTED-- THANK HERA--THE EFFECT OF THE RAY HAS FINALLY WORN OFF ME!

WITH DAZZLING AGILITY, THE FEARLESS AMAZON LEAPS WITH HER UNCONSCIOUS BURDEN FROM ONE YAWNING BEAST AFTER ANOTHER...

HERA HELP ME KEEP MY BALANCE ON THIS BRIDGE OF CROCODILES!

AND THEN...

IT'S STEVE-- RESCUING US--WITH MY PLANE! PRAISE VENUS--HE HAS COME TO HIS SENSES!

BUT, WHEN WONDER WOMAN RE-ENTERS HER PLANE AGAIN, SHE RECEIVES A BITTER BLOW...

I WILL GO WITH YOU-- WHEREVER-- YOU LEAD ME!

YOU LOSE, AMAZON. I AM TAKING HIM BACK WITH ME TO MY PLANET!

AT THE LAST MOMENT, WONDER WOMAN WINGS UP TO THE FLYING SAUCER INVASION FLEET...

HERE IS YOUR MISSING PRINCESS! AN--AN-- EARTH MAN WISHES TO--TO ACCOMPANY HER--BACK TO YOUR WORLD!

FROM THE LEAD FLYING SAUCER A RAY ENVELOPS THE CREATURE STANDING BESIDE STEVE ...

NO ONE FROM OUR WORLD LOOKS LIKE THAT! THIS RAY WILL REMOVE ANY DISGUISE!

ZZZZZZZ

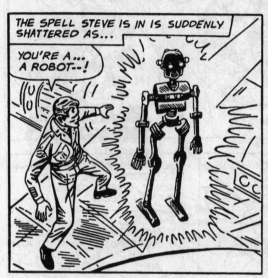

THE SPELL STEVE IS IN IS SUDDENLY SHATTERED AS...

YOU'RE A ... A ROBOT--!

ACROSS THE INTERVENING SPACE, THE RUNAWAY PRINCESS IS FERRIED BACK TO A FLYING SAUCER ...

HOW CAN WE EXPRESS OUR THANKS TO YOU, AMAZON? IT IS APPARENT YOUR WORLD IS INNOCENT!

REGARDLESS OF THE ANGUISH THE OUTER SPACE PRINCESS HAS CAUSED HER, WONDER WOMAN REPLIES CHARACTERISTICALLY...

TREAT THE PRINCESS AS IF SHE WERE AN INDIVIDUAL! A PERSON! SHOW HER LOVE AND AFFECTION--AND SHE WILL BE HAPPY--AND NEVER WANT TO RUN AWAY AGAIN!

ONCE MORE THE SKY IS EMPTY OF THE FLYING SAUCERS ...AS THE TWO CELEBRATED SWEET-HEARTS ARE RE-UNITED ...

WHAT ARE YOU THINKING ABOUT, ANGEL?

I'M GLAD THIS BRIDGE WON'T SUDDENLY START MOVING!

The End

25

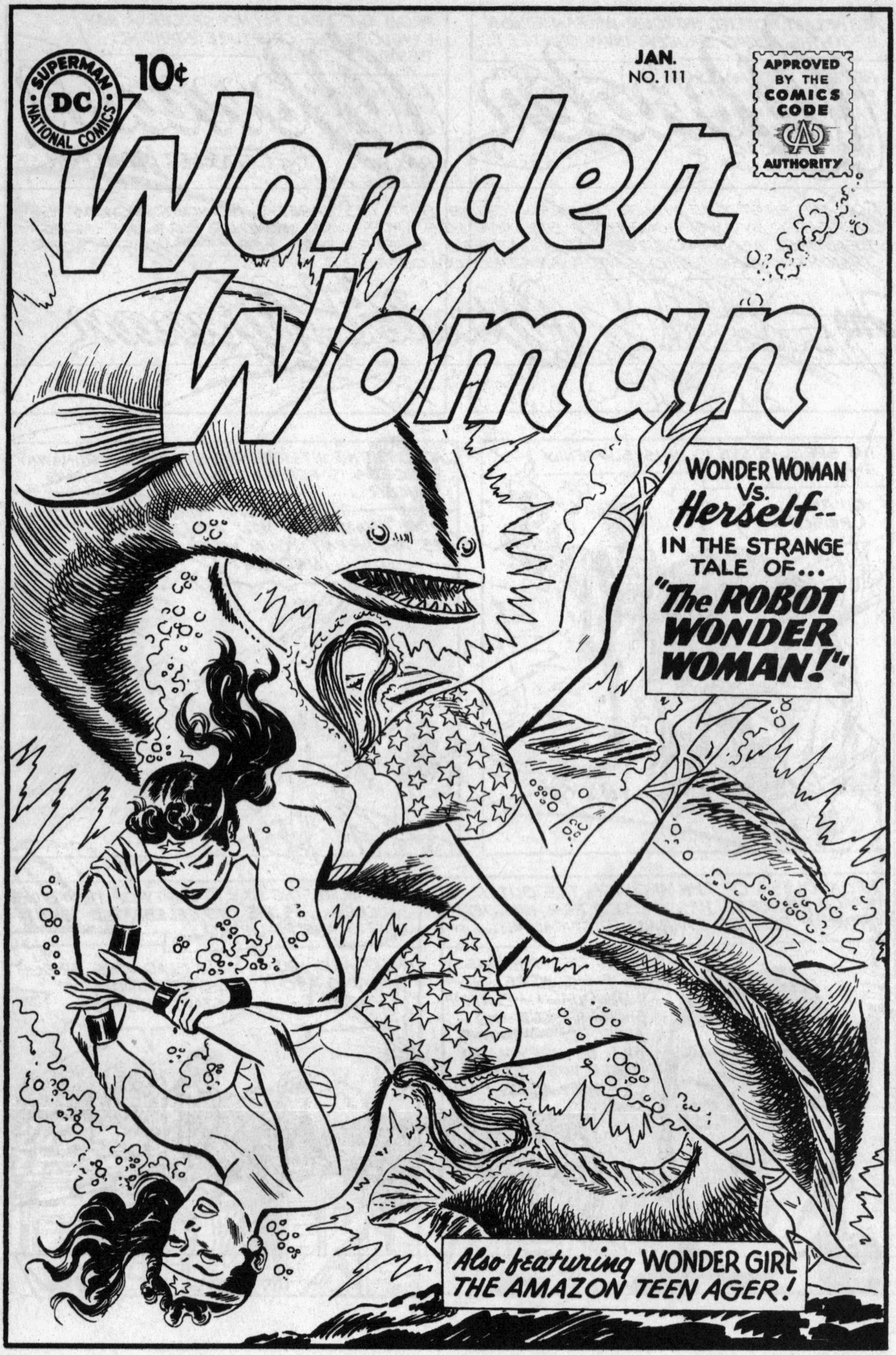
SUPERMAN DC NATIONAL COMICS
10¢
JAN.
NO. 111
APPROVED BY THE COMICS CODE AUTHORITY
Wonder Woman
WONDER WOMAN Vs. Herself-- IN THE STRANGE TALE OF... "The ROBOT WONDER WOMAN!"
Also featuring WONDER GIRL THE AMAZON TEEN AGER!

Wonder Woman
By Charles Moulton

FOR THE FIRST TIME IN HER COLORFUL CRIME-BATTLING CAREER, *WONDER WOMAN* IS DEFEATED BY AN OPPONENT! A STRANGE FOE WHO--LIKE *WONDER WOMAN*--IS AS BEAUTIFUL AS APHRODITE, WISE AS ATHENA, SWIFTER THAN MERCURY, AND STRONGER THAN HERCULES! WHO IS THIS AMAZING CONQUEROR? SHE IS...

The ROBOT Wonder Woman

I NEED AIR... BUT I CAN'T BREAK FREE-- AND WE'RE HEADING INTO THAT GIANT ELECTRIC EEL! I'M DOOMED... UNLESS...

AT AN EMERGENCY MEETING OF GANG-LAND'S CHIEFS...

OKAY, PROF. MENACE! WE GAVE YOU A MILLION BUCKS TO PRODUCE A SECRET WEAPON THAT WOULD FINISH *WONDER WOMAN* FOR GOOD!

WHERE IS IT?

BEHIND THIS CURTAIN! IN ONE MOMENT I SHALL DRAW THE CURTAIN... AND YOU SHALL SEE FOR YOURSELVES!

A GASP RISES FROM GANGSTER THROATS AS A CELEBRATED FIGURE IS REVEALED BEHIND THE CURTAIN...

WONDER WOMAN!

INSTANTLY, THE STARTLED GUNMEN LOOSE A HAIL OF FIRE AT THEIR HATED ENEMY...

WHAT A PRESENT!

DELIVERIN' *WONDER WOMAN* RIGHT INTO OUR HANDS!

PROF. MENACE-- YOU'LL GET A BONUS FOR THIS!

POW! POW! POW!

BUT TO THE DISMAY OF THE HOODLUM LEADERS, THEIR AMAZON TARGET PARRIES THEIR BULLETS WITH LIGHTNING SPEED!

BWEE! ZIING! ZING!

BWEE! ZIIP! ZIING!

ZIING! BWEE!

THE VILLAINOUS INVENTOR GRINS AT THE BEWILDERMENT OF THE GANGLAND CHIEFS...

THERE'S THE SECRET WEAPON THAT WILL FINISH WONDER WOMAN! A ROBOT AMAZON! PERFECT! TIRELESS! SUPERIOR IN EVERY WAY TO THE REAL WONDER WOMAN!

TERRIFIC, PROF. MENACE! HOW ARE YOU GOIN' TO USE THIS?

YOU SHALL SEE! BUT I CAN PROMISE YOU ONE THING-- NOT ONLY WILL THE ROBOT WONDER WOMAN COMMIT THE GREATEST ROBBERY IN HISTORY--BUT THE REAL WONDER WOMAN WILL BE HELPLESS TO PREVENT IT!

MEANWHILE, UNAWARE OF THE DIABOLICAL PLOT AGAINST HER, WONDER WOMAN, IN HER SECRET IDENTITY OF LT. DIANA PRINCE, IS LISTENING TO COL. STEVE TREVOR, AT MILITARY INTELLIGENCE...

I WISH YOU'D COME WITH ME TO MEET WONDER WOMAN, DI! AND HELP ME CONVINCE HER SHE OUGHT TO MARRY ME!

THREE'S A CROWD, STEVE! IF ANYONE CAN CONVINCE HER-- YOU CAN!

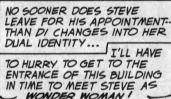

NO SOONER DOES STEVE LEAVE FOR HIS APPOINTMENT-- THAN DI CHANGES INTO HER DUAL IDENTITY...

I'LL HAVE TO HURRY TO GET TO THE ENTRANCE OF THIS BUILDING IN TIME TO MEET STEVE AS WONDER WOMAN!

LIGHTLY AS A TUMBLEWEED, THE LITHE AMAZON WHIRLS THROUGH THE AIR FROM HER OFFICE...

AND ALIGHTS GRACEFULLY AT HIS SIDE...

WONDER WOMAN-- WHEN ARE YOU GOING TO MARRY ME?

I'VE TOLD YOU A DOZEN TIMES, DARLING! WHEN I'M NO LONGER NEEDED TO BATTLE CRIME AND INJUSTICE!

AT A NEARBY SQUARE, THE TWO CELEBRATED SWEETHEARTS CONTINUE THEIR DISCUSSION AS A TRUCK TOWS A HOUSE PAST...

BUT I LOVE YOU, ANGEL! WHY WON'T YOU MARRY ME?

I LOVE YOU TOO, STEVE--BUT YOU'LL HAVE TO BE PATIENT!

SUDDENLY, THE CABLES HOLDING THE HOUSE FAST-- *SNAP...*

KRANG

LIKE A HUGE BATTERING RAM, THE RUNAWAY HOUSE HURTLES DOWN THE STREET...

RRRUMBLE!

HELP!

LOOK OUT!

RUN FOR YOUR LIVES!

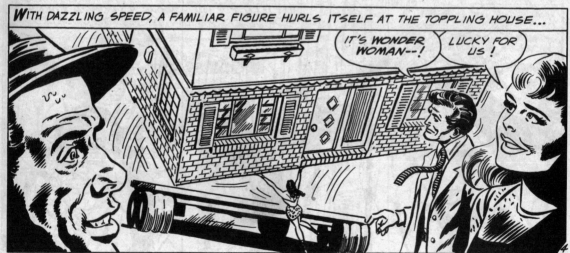

WITH DAZZLING SPEED, A FAMILIAR FIGURE HURLS ITSELF AT THE TOPPLING HOUSE...

IT'S WONDER WOMAN--!

LUCKY FOR US!

WITHOUT A BREAK IN ITS STRIDE, THE AMAZON FIGURE PICKS UP THE HOUSE AS IF IT WERE A MERE TOY AND...

SHE'S SAVED OUR LIVES!

NOW SHE'S CARRYING THE HOUSE OVER TO THE LOT!

A ROVING PHOTOGRAPHER SNAPS THE SCENE, AND THE CROWDS BREAK INTO CHEERS, AS THE CELEBRATED FIGURE PUTS THE HOUSE DOWN AS IF IT WERE A FEATHER!

HURRAY FOR WONDER WOMAN!

NO ONE ELSE IN THE WORLD COULD HAVE DONE THAT!

AND THEN, STARTLING THE PEOPLE WITH ITS STRANGENESS!

WHAT'S THE MATTER WITH WONDER WOMAN?

WHY DOESN'T SHE SAY SOMETHING?

WHY DOES SHE JUST STAND THERE--LIKE--LIKE A STATUE?

BECAUSE THIS IS A **ROBOT** WONDER WOMAN! A REALLY PERFECT AMAZON! SUPERIOR IN EVERY POSSIBLE WAY TO THE REAL AMAZON! IN FACT, I WILL PROVE MY ROBOT MAKES WONDER WOMAN **OBSOLETE!** USELESS!

BY THIS TIME, THE REAL **WONDER WOMAN** HAS RUN UP AND STARES AT HER ROBOT DUPLICATE...

WHILE *YOU* WERE CAUGHT NAPPING, WONDER WOMAN--MY ROBOT DID YOUR JOB FOR YOU--AS EVERYONE HERE WILL TESTIFY!

AN ACCIDENT! IT COULD NEVER HAPPEN AGAIN, COULD IT, STEVE?

TORN BY AN INNER STRUGGLE, STEVE IS SILENT...

I'M ALL FOR WONDER WOMAN OF COURSE!... BUT--IF THIS ROBOT CAN TAKE HER PLACE... BATTLING CRIME AND INJUSTICE... THERE'LL BE NO REASON STOPPING MY DARLING FROM MARRYING ME!

CONCEALING HER CHAGRIN AT STEVE'S SILENCE, THE DAUNTLESS AMAZON ANSWERS THE CUNNING STRANGER...

IF YOU STILL DON'T THINK MY ROBOT *WONDER WOMAN* MAKES YOU USELESS--THEN YOU CAN'T OBJECT TO COMPETING WITH IT! AND IF YOU LOSE--TO GO BACK WHERE YOU CAME FROM--THE SECRET ISLAND HOME OF THE AMAZONS--FOREVER!

YOU HAVE THE WORD OF AN AMAZON!

WONDER WOMAN DOESN'T REALIZE SHE HAS JUST SEALED HER OWN DOOM--HA-HA-HO!

YOUR FIRST TEST IS AN EASY ONE! LET'S SEE HOW LONG YOU AND THE ROBOT CAN GO *WITHOUT SLEEP!* WE'LL HOLD THE CONTEST AT THE CITY STADIUM! THE PROCEEDS TO GO TO CHARITY!

THE CHALLENGE STARTLES THE ASSEMBLED PEOPLE...

WONDER WOMAN IS BEATEN BEFORE SHE STARTS!

A ROBOT NEVER NEEDS SLEEP!

THE AMAZON MIGHT AS WELL GIVE UP NOW!

BUT, THE INTREPID WONDER WOMAN ANSWERS...

I ACCEPT!

HOW WILL THIS STRANGE CONTEST END?

TWENTY-THREE DAYS AND FOURTEEN HOURS LATER... AT CITY STADIUM...AN ENTHRALLED AUDIENCE STARES AT THE TWO IDENTICAL FIGURES...

IT'S A WONDER SHE'S LASTED THIS LONG!

KEEP IT UP MUCH LONGER-- EVEN IF SHE IS A WONDER WOMAN!

NEVER BEFORE HAS WONDER WOMAN EVER HAD SUCH A STRANGE OPPONENT-- OR WAGED SUCH AN UNUSUAL STRUGGLE...

GOT TO...KEEP MY...EYES OPEN...

IN THE REAL WONDER WOMAN'S CORNER, STEVE WATCHES WITH TREMENDOUSLY MIXED FEELINGS...

IT'S BREAKING MY HEART--TO SEE THE TERRIFIC FIGHT MY ANGEL'S PUTTING UP-- BUT--I DON'T SEE HOW SHE CAN POSSIBLY WIN AGAINST THE ROBOT!

AND IN THE OTHER CORNER, A GLEEFUL VILLAIN...

MY SCHEME IS WORKING PER- FECTLY! EACH DAY THAT PASSES-- SPELLS WONDER WOMAN'S DOOM! HA-HA-HO! IT'S ONLY A QUESTION OF TIME! HO-HO-HA!

DAY AND NIGHT WONDER WOMAN FIGHTS SLEEP...

MUSN'T CLOSE MY EYES!

SMASHING ALL RECORDS...

MUST...N'T... CLOSE...MY...

UNTIL FINALLY...

AT THAT MOMENT, HURTLING INTO THE CROWDED STADIUM ...

LOOK OUT-- THE PLANE'S GOING TO CRASH!

IT'LL BE A CATASTROPHE!

INSTANTLY, AN AMAZON FIGURE LEAPS UP TO MEET THE SMOKING PLANE ...

THE SHIP'S BEEN SAVED! BUT THE FIRE MIGHT STILL CAUSE AN EXPLOSION!

BUT, WITH UNCANNY SPEED, THE POWERFUL FIGURE WHIRLS THE PLANE AROUND WITH SUCH FORCE THAT...THE WIND SNUFFS THE FLAMES OUT!

VROOOSH!

PART TWO OF THIS STARTLING TALE CONTINUES ON THE PAGE FOLLOWING!

18

PART TWO

NOW--DO YOU NEED ANY *MORE* PROOF THAT MY ROBOT IS SUPERIOR TO *WONDER WOMAN?* IN THAT MOMENT WHEN *WONDER WOMAN'S* EYES CLOSED--MY ROBOT PREVENTED A CATASTROPHE!

I HAVE SHOWN THAT *WONDER WOMAN* IS OBSOLETE! I NOW CALL UPON HER TO KEEP HER *PROMISE!* TO LET MY ROBOT TAKE HER PLACE--WHILE SHE RETIRES FOREVER FROM PUBLIC SERVICE!

FOR THE FIRST TIME IN THE AMAZON'S COLORFUL CAREER OF BATTLING CRIME AND IN-JUSTICE EVERYWHERE... SHE BREAKS DOWN...

I... I... WILL... LEAVE...AND LET THE...THE ROBOT.. WONDER WOMAN... BATTLE CRIME.. AND INJUSTICE... IN MY...PLACE...

A HUSH FALLS UPON THE ASSEMBLED PEOPLE...AS STEVE LEADS THE WEEPING FIGURE AWAY...

THERE... THERE--ANGEL! DON'T CRY! LOOK HOW LONG YOU'VE DONE A WONDERFUL JOB! THERE *HAD* TO COME A TIME WHEN YOU'D BE FORCED TO RETIRE!

WITH SILENT GLEE, THE *ROBOT MASTER* WATCHES THE BEATEN AMAZON...

THE RUNAWAY HOUSE--THE SMOKING PLANE-- ALL PARTS OF MY SCHEME TO BEAT *WONDER WOMAN*-- HA, HA! I HAVE SUCCEEDED!

EXIT

NOW-- FOR THE SECOND PART OF MY MASTER PLAN! TO TURN MY ROBOT INTO AN INVINCIBLE CRIMINAL! FOR IT OPERATES ELECTRONICALLY ON MY BRAIN-WAVE IMPULSES! AND EVERY DIRECTION I'LL GIVE IT FROM NOW ON-- WILL BE FOR CRIME!

IN THE DIRECTOR'S OFFICE...WHILE THE IMMENSE CROWD IS STILL FILING OUT...

THERE ARE MILLIONS IN THIS SAFE FROM THE TICKET PROCEEDS, PROFESSOR! AND IT'S ALL GOING TO CHARITY! THANKS TO YOU--AND YOUR WONDERFUL ROBOT!

I WAS GLAD TO HELP, SIR!

SUDDENLY FELLED BY A TREACHEROUS BLOW...

ESPECIALLY SINCE ALL THIS LOOT WILL NOW GO TO ME! HA! HA!

WITH EASE, THE ROBOT PICKS UP THE MASSIVE SAFE...

YOU AND I WILL NOW BEGIN A CRIMINAL CAREER THAT WILL PLAY HAVOC WITH LAW AND ORDER EVERYWHERE! NOW BREAK THROUGH THAT WALL!

HOVERING OVER THE ROOF OF THE STADIUM BUILDING...

RESPONDING ELECTRONICALLY, THE CRIMINAL CREATION EASILY BOUNDS THROUGH THE STONE WALL...

THE GANG SHOULD BE WAITING FOR US!

THIS IS ONLY THE BEGINNING! NOTHING CAN STOP US!

CRA

MEANWHILE, PHOTOGRAPHERS AND BROADCASTERS RECORD *WONDER WOMAN'S* DEPARTURE AT MILITARY INTELLIGENCE AIRFIELD...

WHY CAN'T YOU MARRY ME NOW, HONEY? YOU'RE NOT NEEDED TO BATTLE CRIME AND INJUSTICE! THE ROBOT'S TAKING YOUR PLACE!

YOU FORGET I PROMISED TO RETURN TO THE AMAZON ISLAND FOREVER--IF I LOST, STEVE!

WHAT A FOOL I WAS! ALL I COULD THINK OF WAS THAT WE'D BE TOGETHER IF YOU LOST! FORGIVE ME!

THERE'S NOTHING... TO...FORGIVE...

THE CELEBRATED SWEETHEARTS EMBRACE FOR THE LAST TIME...

LIFE WON'T BE THE SAME WITHOUT YOU!

DON'T SPEAK--DON'T SAY ANYTHING MORE-- OR I'LL START-- CRYING!

NEARBY, IN THE ROBOT MASTER'S GIANT HELICOPTER, *WONDER WOMAN'S* DEPARTURE IS WATCHED ON A VIDEO-SCREEN!

AND THUS ENDS ONE OF THE MOST COLORFUL CAREERS IN HISTORY... AS *WONDER WOMAN* TAKES OFF FOR THE SECRET ISLAND HOME OF THE AMAZONS-- AN OBSOLETE CRIME-FIGHTER-- REPLACED BY A ROBOT!

AS LONG AS *WONDER WOMAN* LIVES-- SHE'S A MENACE TO THE UNDERWORLD! BUT SHE WON'T BE FOR LONG!

AND AS *WONDER WOMAN* FLIES OUT TO SEA, FROM THE TRAILING HELICOPTER LEAPS THE ROBOT...

WHAT STRANGE DEVELOPMENT WILL NOW TWIST THIS AMAZING TALE?

INTO THE AMAZON'S PLANE, THE ROBOT IS DIRECTED ELECTRONICALLY...

WHAT IS IT--? WHAT ARE YOU DOING HERE?

A UNIQUE STRUGGLE BEGINS AS WONDER WOMAN BATTLES HER ROBOT LIKENESS...

STOP IT-- YOU'RE TWISTING THE CONTROLS! THE PLANE'S STARTING TO SPIN--!

FROM HIS HELICOPTER, THE ROBOT MASTER AND HIS GANG LAUGH AS:..

LOOK--! MY ROBOT HAS SENT WONDER WOMAN'S PLANE CRASHING INTO THE SEA!

WHAT NEXT?

CRASH!

THE ROBOT WILL KEEP HER DOWN--UNTIL SHE'S FINISHED! THEN IT WILL COME BACK HERE TO THE HELICOPTER-- FOR A CRIME SPREE THAT NO ONE CAN STOP--NOW THAT WONDER WOMAN IS FINISHED!

AS HER PLANE DIVES INTO THE SEA, THE IMPACT HURLS WONDER WOMAN AND THE ROBOT OUT...

MERCIFUL MINERVA! HELP ME TO ESCAPE THIS MECHANICAL MONSTER!

DESPITE ALL HER STRENGTH THE AMAZON FINDS HERSELF UNABLE TO ELUDE THE ROBOT'S CLUTCHES...

UNLESS I BREAK ITS HOLD... IT'S ONLY A MATTER OF TIME... BEFORE... I--I--!

12

SUDDENLY, IN THE MIDST OF HER DESPERATE STRUGGLE, WONDER WOMAN SEES WITH DIMMING EYES...

A GIANT... ELECTRIC... EEL--!

SUMMONING EVERY FRACTION OF HER WANING STRENGTH, THE FEARLESS AMAZON HURLS HERSELF TOWARD THE UNDERSEA BEAST...

ROBOT... IS.... UNDOUBTEDLY... ELECTRONICALLY GUIDED... NOW IF... I CAN... ONLY... REACH... THAT... ELECTRIC EEL--?

ONLY HER FIGHTING HEART ENABLES WONDER WOMAN TO TUMBLE THE ROBOT AND HERSELF INTO THE GIANT ELECTRIC EEL--WHOSE CONTACT TURNS THE WATER INTO FROTH...

HERA HELP ME-- HERA HELP ME--!

ABOVE, THE ROBOT-MASTER SUDDENLY CLUTCHES HIS HEAD...

YEEOOOWW!-- MY HEAD--! I FEEL AS IF--I'VE BEEN HIT BY A THIRD RAIL!

A FEW MOMENTS LATER...

RIGHT NOW! THERE'S THE ROBOT! THIS ROBOT IS MY GREATEST CREATION! YOU HAVE ALL SEEN IT ROB THE CHARITY FUNDS--AND DISPOSE OF WONDER WOMAN! BUT THAT'S ONLY THE BEGINNING!

EVERYTHING'S ALL

13

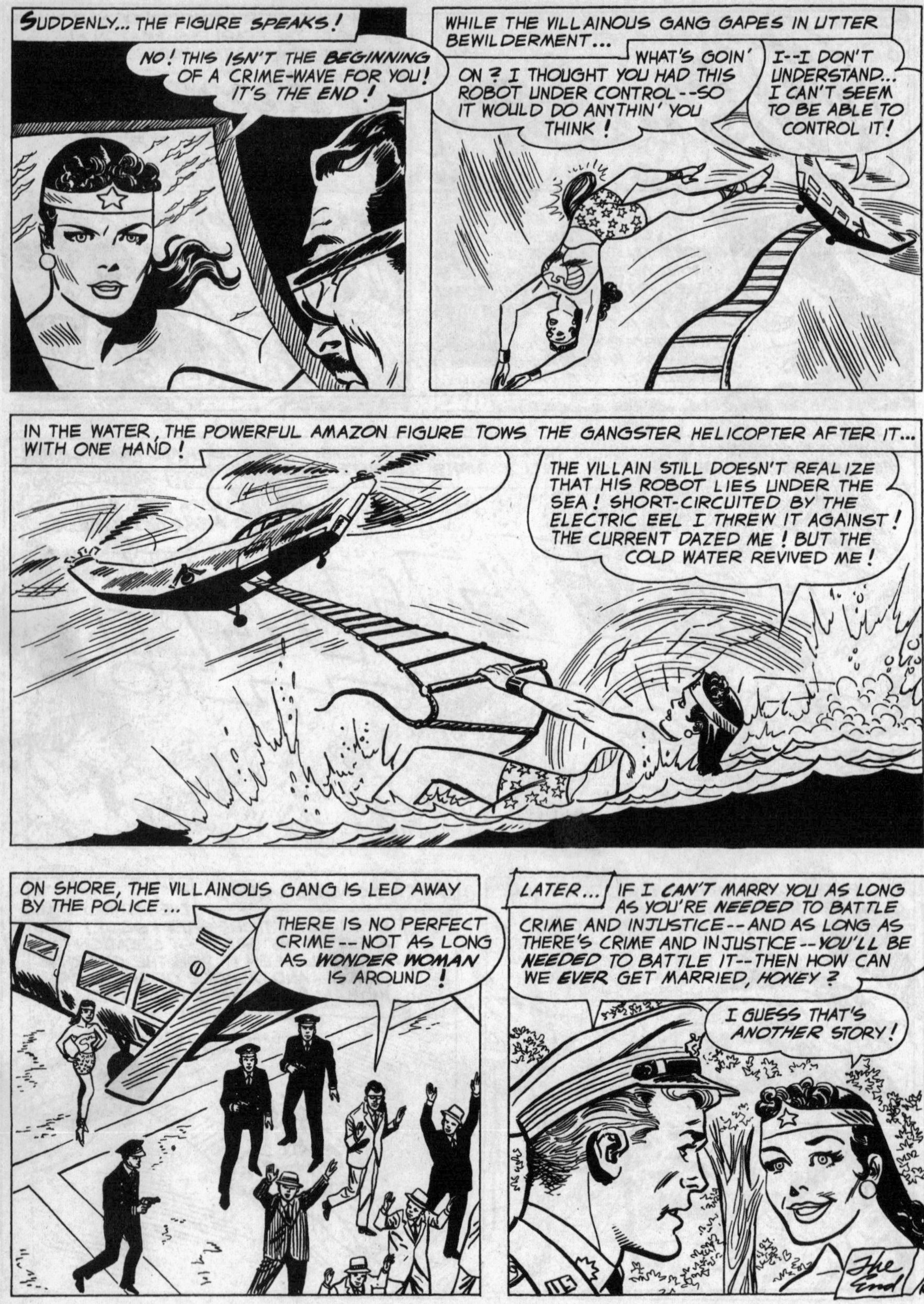
SUDDENLY... THE FIGURE SPEAKS!
NO! THIS ISN'T THE BEGINNING OF A CRIME-WAVE FOR YOU! IT'S THE END!
WHILE THE VILLAINOUS GANG GAPES IN UTTER BEWILDERMENT...
WHAT'S GOIN' ON? I THOUGHT YOU HAD THIS ROBOT UNDER CONTROL--SO IT WOULD DO ANYTHIN' YOU THINK!
I--I DON'T UNDERSTAND... I CAN'T SEEM TO BE ABLE TO CONTROL IT!
IN THE WATER, THE POWERFUL AMAZON FIGURE TOWS THE GANGSTER HELICOPTER AFTER IT... WITH ONE HAND!
THE VILLAIN STILL DOESN'T REALIZE THAT HIS ROBOT LIES UNDER THE SEA! SHORT-CIRCUITED BY THE ELECTRIC EEL I THREW IT AGAINST! THE CURRENT DAZED ME! BUT THE COLD WATER REVIVED ME!
ON SHORE, THE VILLAINOUS GANG IS LED AWAY BY THE POLICE...
THERE IS NO PERFECT CRIME--NOT AS LONG AS WONDER WOMAN IS AROUND!
LATER...
IF I CAN'T MARRY YOU AS LONG AS YOU'RE NEEDED TO BATTLE CRIME AND INJUSTICE--AND AS LONG AS THERE'S CRIME AND INJUSTICE--YOU'LL BE NEEDED TO BATTLE IT--THEN HOW CAN WE EVER GET MARRIED, HONEY?
I GUESS THAT'S ANOTHER STORY!
The End
14

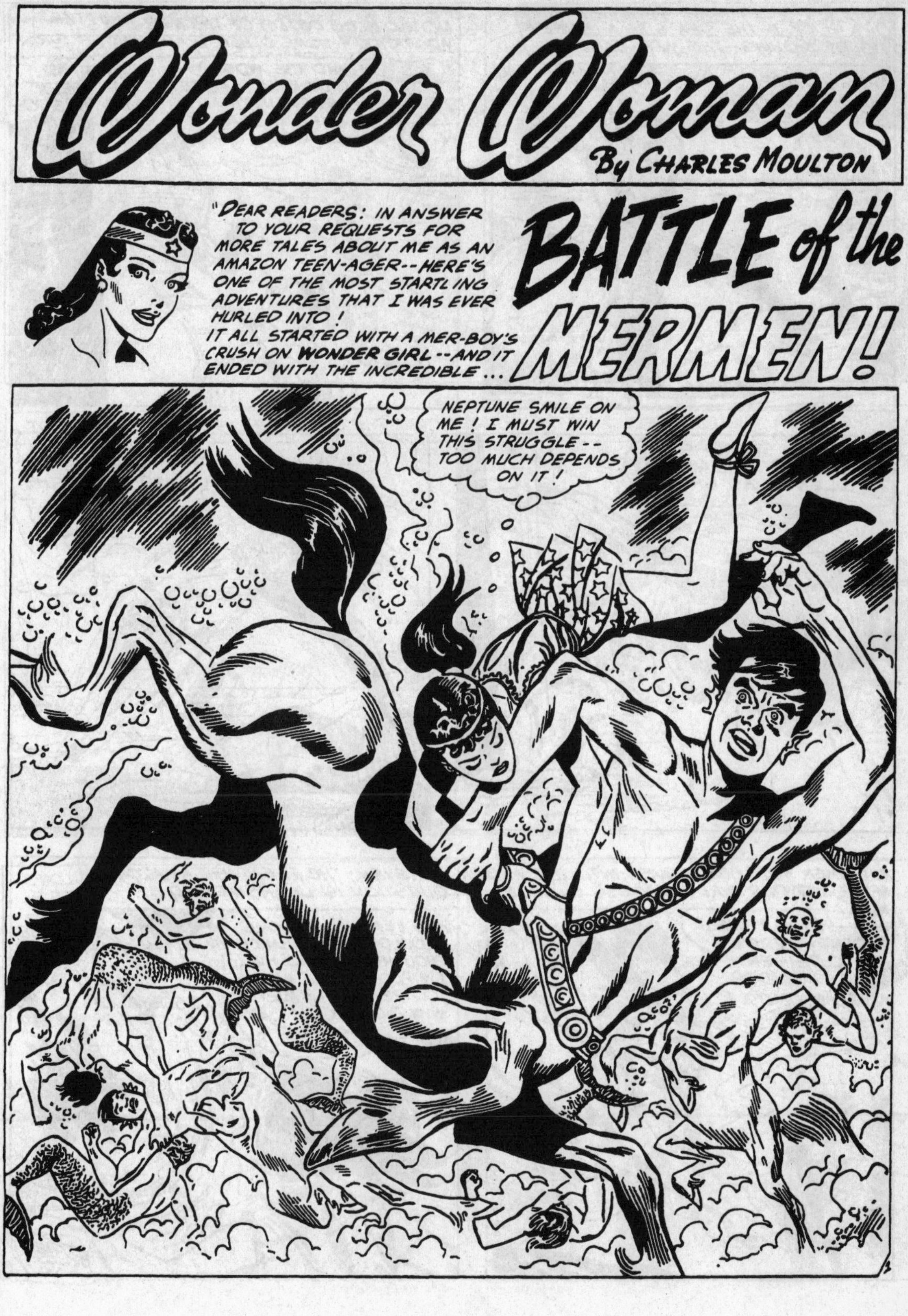
Wonder Woman
By CHARLES MOULTON
"DEAR READERS: IN ANSWER TO YOUR REQUESTS FOR MORE TALES ABOUT ME AS AN AMAZON TEEN-AGER--HERE'S ONE OF THE MOST STARTLING ADVENTURES THAT I WAS EVER HURLED INTO! IT ALL STARTED WITH A MER-BOY'S CRUSH ON WONDER GIRL--AND IT ENDED WITH THE INCREDIBLE...
BATTLE of the MERMEN!
NEPTUNE SMILE ON ME! I MUST WIN THIS STRUGGLE--TOO MUCH DEPENDS ON IT!

ON A ROCK IN THE SEA SITS A LONELY FIGURE SIGHING--THE MER-BOY...

SHE'S BEAUTIFUL-- THE MOST BEAUTIFUL GIRL I'VE EVER SEEN!

AND WHO IS THE OBJECT OF THE MER-BOY'S ADORATION? NONE OTHER THAN WONDER GIRL!

AND THE MOST GRACEFUL-- MORE GRACEFUL THAN EVEN A SEA-GULL!

NOT EVEN A SWORDFISH CAN SLIP INTO THE WATER AS SILENTLY AS SHE!

I MUST SPEAK TO HER--TELL HER ABOUT THE BIG AFFAIR NEXT WEEK!

BUT WHEN MER-BOY CURVES INTO THE WATER AFTER WONDER GIRL...SHYNESS SILENCES HIM...

BY NEPTUNE'S TRIDENT! THERE'S THAT CUTE MER-BOY! I WONDER WHAT HE WANTS!

HOWEVER, THE TEEN-AGE AMAZON'S QUESTION IS UNANSWERED...

HE'S LEAVING--BEFORE I COULD HAVE A CHANCE TO THOUGHT-SPEAK TO HIM! I'M POSITIVE HE WANTED TO SPEAK WITH ME! WHY DID HE CHANGE HIS MIND?

WITH INCREDIBLE SPEED, WONDER GIRL KEEPS THE MER-BOY IN VIEW AS...

HE'S ENTERING THAT GIGANTIC SEA-SHELL!

BY THE TIME THE AMAZON TEEN-AGER REACHES THE GIANT SEASHELL...

BY THE WINDS OF AEOLUS--THE MER-BOY'S GONE BACK TO THE MERMEN WORLD! IF THE MER-BOY'S IN TROUBLE--I'D LIKE TO HELP HIM! BUT I CAN'T DO A THING UNLESS HE TELLS ME WHAT'S BOTHERING HIM!

THUMP

MEANWHILE, THE MER-BOY EMERGES FROM A SECRET PASSAGE IN THE GIANT SEASHELL INTO THE MERMEN WORLD UNDERNEATH THE BOTTOM OF THE SEA...

HO--RONNO--! WHOM ARE YOU TAKING TO OUR ANNUAL SEA DANCE?

YOU HAD BETTER PICK A FINE MER-GIRL DANCER, RENNO--OR YOU WILL NEVER WIN THE PRIZE!

THE LOVE-SICK MER-BOY GLANCES AT THE PRIZE--A TIARA OF PEARLS...

THAT TIARA BELONGS ON WONDER GIRL'S HEAD! I WOULD LOVE TO WIN IT FOR HER! BUT WHAT CHANCE DO I HAVE OF EVER INVITING HER TO COME TO THE DANCE WITH ME?

ON THE DAY OF THE GREAT SEA-DANCE, THERE IS ONLY *ONE* SAD FACE IN THE WORLD OF THE MERMEN AND MERMAIDS...

WHERE IS YOUR DATE, RENNO? THE DANCE IS STARTING!

ARE YOU KEEPING IT A SECRET UNTIL THE LAST MOMENT, RENNO? WHERE IS SHE?

WITHOUT ANSWERING, THE MER-BOY FLIPPERS AWAY...

I FEEL LIKE A GHOST FISH AT A FEAST! I'LL SWIM OUTSIDE--WHERE I MIGHT CATCH A GLIMPSE OF *WONDER GIRL!*

AS THE MELANCHOLY RENNO EXITS FROM THE SEA-SHELL PASSAGE, HE IS UNAWARE THAT HE IS BEING WATCHED BY STRANGE HOSTILE EYES...

I TOLD YOU WE WOULD FIND THE SECRET ENTRANCE TO THE MERMEN'S WORLD IF WE WATCHED LONG ENOUGH! THERE'S A MER-BOY EXITING NOW!

QUEER-LOOKING THING, ISN'T HE? AND CLUMSY! NOT GRACEFUL LIKE US SEA-CENTAURS!

WHAT DO YOU EXPECT? NO HOOFS! NOT A SINGLE ONE!

WE'LL WAIT UNTIL THE RIGHT MOMENT.. THEN CRASH THEIR DANCE--AND STEAL THE PEARL CROWN PRIZE!

MEANWHILE, AS THE MER-BOY SWIMS TO THE SURFACE...

GREAT NEPTUNE! WONDER GIRL FLOATING--ASLEEP! AND A SHARK'S COMING TOWARD HER!

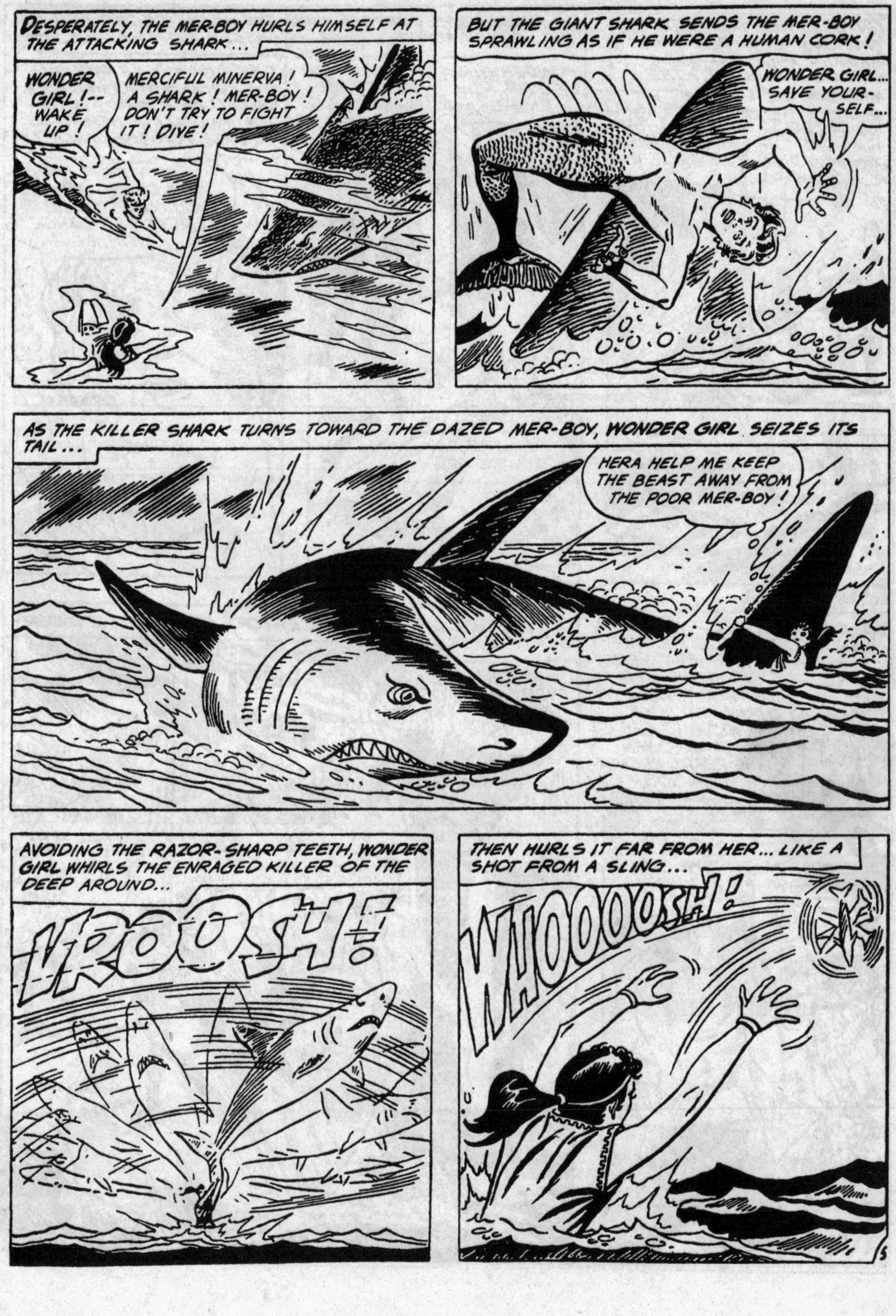
DESPERATELY, THE MER-BOY HURLS HIMSELF AT THE ATTACKING SHARK...
WONDER GIRL!-- WAKE UP!
MERCIFUL MINERVA! A SHARK! MER-BOY! DON'T TRY TO FIGHT IT! DIVE!
BUT THE GIANT SHARK SENDS THE MER-BOY SPRAWLING AS IF HE WERE A HUMAN CORK!
WONDER GIRL... SAVE YOURSELF...
AS THE KILLER SHARK TURNS TOWARD THE DAZED MER-BOY, WONDER GIRL SEIZES ITS TAIL...
HERA HELP ME KEEP THE BEAST AWAY FROM THE POOR MER-BOY!
AVOIDING THE RAZOR-SHARP TEETH, WONDER GIRL WHIRLS THE ENRAGED KILLER OF THE DEEP AROUND...
VROOSH!
THEN HURLS IT FAR FROM HER... LIKE A SHOT FROM A SLING...
WHOOOOSH!

TENDERLY, THE AMAZON TEEN-AGER TOWS THE MER-BOY DOWN TOWARD THE SEA-SHELL ENTRANCE TO THE MERMEN WORLD...

HE'S STILL TOO DAZED TO SWIM! I'LL TAKE HIM HOME! HE WAS VERY BRAVE-- TRYING TO SAVE ME FROM THAT SHARK!

AS WONDER GIRL EMERGES INTO THE MERMEN WORLD...

WONDER GIRL! YOU'RE ALL RIGHT?

THANKS TO YOU! YOU WERE VERY BRAVE! A REAL HERO!

THE HEART OF THE MER-BOY SWELLS WITH PRIDE...

I MUST HAVE BEEN KNOCKED SENSELESS SAVING HER! SHE CALLED ME A HERO! NOW IS THE TIME TO ASK HER TO BE MY DATE FOR THE DANCE!

WONDER GIRL-- WOULD YOU--WOULD YOU COME TO THE GREAT SEA-DANCE WITH ME?

I WOULD BE HONORED, MER-BOY!

YOU--YOU'VE MADE ME THE HAPPIEST MER-BOY IN THE MER-MEN WORLD, *WONDER GIRL!* AND JUST YOU WAIT AND SEE! I'M GOING TO WIN THE PEARL CROWN FOR YOU!

AS WONDER GIRL AND HER ESCORT APPROACH THE UNDER-SEA DANCE FLOOR..

WH-WHY HAS EVERYONE STOPPED DANCING?

I--I DON'T KNOW!

6

AS WONDER GIRL TAKES HER PLACE WITH THE DANCERS...

SO THAT'S WHY YOU DIDN'T TELL US WHOM YOU WERE TAKING TO THE DANCE, RENNO! AN AMAZON GIRL!

Hmph! YOU MUST BE PRETTY BLIND, RENNO-- NOT TO PREFER A MERMAID!

SLOWLY THE DANCE CONTINUES...

PERHAPS...I SHOULD GO...IF MY PRESENCE HERE...EMBARRASSES YOU...RENNO?

NO--NO, WONDER GIRL! DON'T LISTEN TO THEM! JUST LOOK AT THE CROWN ATOP THERE--THAT I'M GOING TO WIN FOR YOU-- SO YOU'LL BE CROWNED QUEEN OF THE SEA-DANCE!

BUT THE REMARKS DO NOT STOP...

LOOK AT HOW CLUMSY SHE IS!

WHAT DO YOU EXPECT?--NO TAIL!

WHAT TERRIBLE SKIN!

NATURALLY.. NO SCALES!

LOOK AT THOSE BIG FEET!

AREN'T WE LUCKY NOT TO HAVE ANY!

SUDDENLY, LIKE A STAMPEDING HERD, THE UNDERSEA CENTAURS GALLOP INTO THE MERMEN WORLD...

DON'T BE FRIGHTENED, WONDER GIRL, I WILL PROTECT YOU!

ANXIOUSLY, THE AMAZON TEEN-AGER WATCHES HER MER-BOY ESCORT VALIANTLY HURL HIMSELF ON THE UNDERSEA PARTY CRASHERS...

GREAT HERA! THE CENTAUR LEADER HAS STOLEN THE CROWN! AND RENNO IS TRYING TO GET IT BACK! BUT, I MUSN'T INTER-FERE--IT WOULD HURT HIS FEELINGS!

BUT, IN THE RIOT, WONDER GIRL SEES...

THOSE CENTAURS HAVE KNOCKED OVER THE DANCE POLE! IT'S GOING TO CRASH ON THOSE POOR MER-MEN AND MERMAIDS!

LIKE AN UNDERSEA BOLT OF LIGHTNING, THE MIGHTY TEEN-AGE AMAZON HURLS HERSELF AT THE MASSIVE POLE...

DID YOU SEE HOW FAST WONDER GIRL SWAM? EVEN WITH-OUT FLIPPERS!

AND SHE SAVED US FROM HARM!

AT THAT MOMENT, SEVERAL UNDERSEA CEN-TAURS GALLOP AGAINST WONDER GIRL...

WE'LL PLAY WATER POLO WITH HER!

SHE'LL BE THE BALL!

THE VIBRATIONS IN THE WATER WARN THE AMAZON TEEN-AGER OF HER DANGER...

TOO LATE TO SWIM OUT OF THEIR WAY!

WITH INCREDIBLE AGILITY, WONDER GIRL USES THE DANCE POLE AS A POLE VAULT AND...

WHAT HAPPENED TO HER?

SHE DISAPPEARED LIKE MAGIC!

LIGHTLY, THE TEEN-AGE AMAZON ALIGHTS ON THE STARTLED UNDERSEA CENTAURS...

RENNO'S STILL FIGHTING FOR THE CROWN -- AND HE'S BEING CARRIED AWAY!

WITH AN EXPERT TOSS, WONDER GIRL LASSOES HER MOUNTS...

WHO KNOWS WHAT WILL HAPPEN TO HIM?

NEVER BEFORE HAS THE MERMEN WORLD SEEN SUCH DAZZLING SKILL AS THE AMAZON TEEN-AGER RIDES HER PLUNGING STEEDS IN PURSUIT OF THEIR RUNAWAY LEADER!

I PRAY HERA I'M NOT TOO LATE TO HELP THE BRAVE MER-BOY!

THROUGH THE SEASHELL EXIT FROM THE MERMEN WORLD *WONDER GIRL* RIDES TO SEE AN AWESOME SPECTACLE...

THEY'VE BEEN ATTACKED BY A WHALE!

SUDDENLY, THE AMAZON TEEN-AGER FINDS HER-SELF TUMBLING AS...

THEY'VE RUN AWAY IN TERROR! AND THEY'RE CARRYING MY LASSO WITH THEM! HOW CAN I BATTLE THE WHALE?

FINDING HERSELF ON A HUGE BED OF CORAL, *WONDER GIRL* RUBS A GREAT FRAGMENT WITH INCREDIBLE SPEED UNTIL...

THERE!-- IT'S SHINY AS A MIRROR!

SEIZING THE GREAT CORAL MIRROR, THE DAUNTLESS AMAZON LEAPS UP WITH IT--IN FRONT OF THE WHALE...

A KILLER WHALE WILL ATTACK EVERYTHING IN SIGHT! WILL *THIS* ONE DO THE SAME?

AS THE WHALE SIGHTS ITS IMAGE--AN IMAGE IT HAD NEVER SEEN BEFORE--IT MISTAKES ITSELF FOR ANOTHER FISH--AND IN A FIT OF RAGE--CHARGES THE CORAL MIRROR WITH THUNDEROUS FORCE...

AGAIN AND AGAIN THE WHALE HURLS ITSELF AGAINST THE MASSIVE CORAL MIRROR HELD UP BY WONDER GIRL UNTIL...

THUD!

THUD! THUD!

THUD

THANK HERA! IT'S KNOCKED ITSELF SENSELESS!

A MOMENT LATER...

YOU SAVED OUR LIVES, WONDER GIRL!

IF THERE'S ANYTHING YOU WANT--ANYTHING-- JUST NAME IT!

I WANT YOU TWO TO SHAKE HANDS! THERE-- SEE? THERE'S NO REASON FOR YOU NOT TO BE FRIENDS--JUST BECAUSE ONE OF YOU HAS HOOFS--OR FLIPPERS--DOESN'T MEAN YOU SHOULD BE ENEMIES!

LATER AT THE GREAT SEA-DANCE...

LOOK HOW HAPPY EVERYONE IS, WONDER GIRL--THANKS TO YOUR SHOWING US THERE'S NO REAL DIFFERENCE BETWEEN PEOPLE--AS LONG AS THERE IS FRIENDSHIP IN THEIR HEARTS!

WE AMAZONS HAVE ALWAYS BE- LIEVED IN THIS, RENNO! WE HOPE THE REST OF THE WORLD WILL FIND THIS OUT TOO!

The End

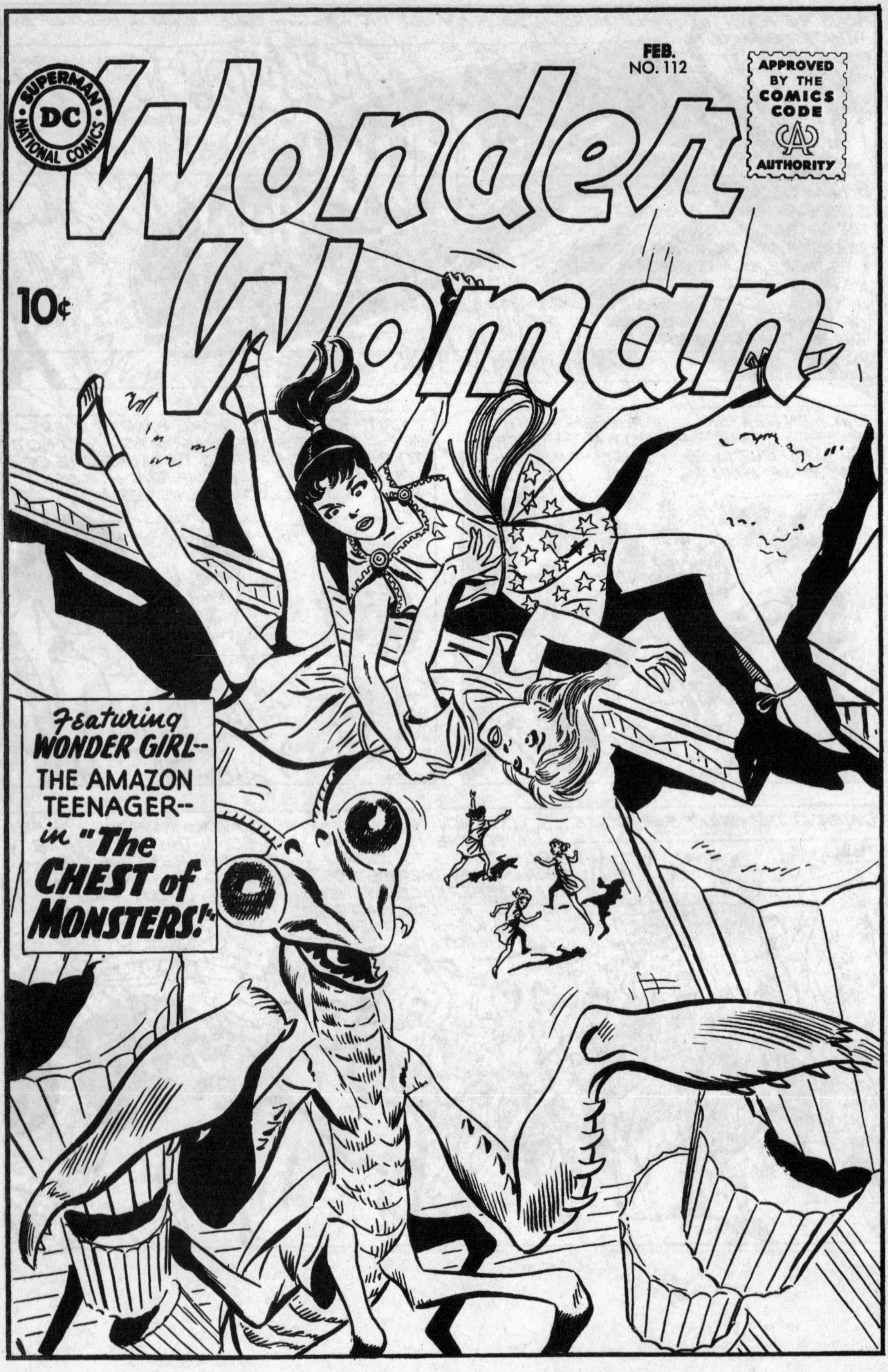
SUPERMAN DC NATIONAL COMICS
Wonder Woman
FEB. NO. 112
APPROVED BY THE COMICS CODE AUTHORITY
10¢
Featuring WONDER GIRL-- THE AMAZON TEENAGER-- in "The CHEST of MONSTERS!"

Wonder Woman

By Charles Moulton

SO MANY READERS HAVE ASKED QUESTIONS ABOUT *PARADISE ISLAND*, THE SECRET ISLAND HOME OF THE AMAZONS, AND **WONDER WOMAN'S** LIFE THERE AS A TEENAGER, THAT WE WILL ANSWER THESE QUESTIONS IN A WAY WHICH WILL STARTLE EVERYONE OF YOU! AS YOU SHALL SEE IN THE THREE-PART ADVENTURE!

WONDER GIRL in The CHEST of MONSTERS!

AT MILITARY INTELLIGENCE, COL. STEVE TREVOR CALLS ON LT. DIANA PRINCE...

TIME TO HEAR *WONDER WOMAN'S* BROADCAST, DI! YOU CAN GO BACK TO YOUR WORK AS SOON AS IT'S OVER!

B-B-BUT, STEVE--? I CAN'T LEAVE JUST YET--!

OUTSIDE, IN THE CORRIDOR, THE LOVELY GIRL FACES A STARTLING DILEMMA!

GREAT HERA! I DIDN'T EXPECT STEVE TO DROP IN ON ME UNEXPECTEDLY! I'VE GOT TO "ESCAPE" HIM SOMEHOW! OR *WONDER WOMAN* WILL *NEVER APPEAR* FOR THAT SPECIAL BROADCAST!

WITH SUPER-SONIC SPEED, DIANA VIBRATES OUT OF STEVE'S GRASP, WITHOUT HIS BEING AWARE THAT SHE HAS LEFT...

I WONDER WHAT *WONDER WOMAN'S* BROADCAST WILL BE ABOUT? SOMETHING VERY SPECIAL...

STILL WHIRLING AT A SPEED NO HUMAN EYE CAN DISCERN, DIANA HURTLES THROUGH THE OFFICE IN WHICH SHE HAS TAKEN REFUGE...

I MUST REJOIN STEVE BEFORE HE REACHES THE END OF THE CORRIDOR--OR HE'LL DISCOVER MY SECRET!

OUT OF THE WINDOW AND ALONG THE LEDGE TOWARD ANOTHER WINDOW, THE DARING GIRL CONTINUES AT UNBELIEVABLE SPEED, CHANGING INTO HER SECRET IDENTITY...

IN A FRACTION OF A SECOND STEVE WILL REALIZE HE IS HOLDING ON TO EMPTY SPACE!

BUT, SO SWIFT THAT STEVE CANNOT DETECT THE SUBSTITUTION OF ONE GIRL FOR ANOTHER.

...DON'T YOU THINK, DI?.. *WONDER WOMAN!*-- WHAT HAPPENED TO DIANA?

I GUESS YOU WERE SO BUSY SPEAKING, STEVE, YOU DIDN'T NOTICE THAT SHE DROPPED INTO THE SECRETARIAL OFFICE! SHE'LL JOIN YOU AGAIN LATER!

SWISH

2

WONDER WOMAN'S SPECIAL BROADCAST IS HEARD ALL OVER THE COUNTRY...

...AND SO THIS EMINENT JURY OF THREE HERE WITH ME... WILL PICK THE BOY OR GIRL WHOSE DEEDS **MOST** REFLECT CREDIT TO AMERICA DURING THE NEXT MONTH!

THE WINNER'S PRIZE IS A SECRET! BUT--I GUARANTEE ON THE WORD OF AN AMAZON-- THAT IT WILL BE THE MOST EXTRAORDINARY EVER PRESENTED!

THE COUNTRY BUZZES WITH SPECULATION...

THINK THE PRIZE IS MONEY?

AN AMAZON LASSO?

A TRIP AROUND THE WORLD?

AND FROM EVERYWHERE... THE NAMES OF ENTRANTS ARE SENT IN...

Math Genius

World's Youngest Pilot

Musical Prodigy

WITH ONE DAY LEFT BEFORE THE END OF THE CONTEST, BONNIE BATES, A YOUNG COUNTRY GIRL, HERDS HER PARENTS' FLOCK TO SHELTER...

I WONDER WHO'S GOING TO WIN THE **WONDER WOMAN** CONTEST? GOSH! IMAGINE BEING ABLE TO SEE HER IN PERSON? IT WOULD BE LIKE AN IMPOSSIBLE DREAM COME TRUE!

FROM THE RIVER, SWOLLEN BY THE UNEXPECTED CLOUD-BURST...

WAS THAT... A CRY... FOR HELP?

SWEPT ALONG THE RAGING CURRENTS TOWARDS HER, BONNIE IS HORRIFIED TO SEE...

IT'S EDIE-- AND MAL--!

WITHOUT HESITATION, THE YOUNG SHEPHERDESS HURLS HERSELF INTO THE TUMBLING WATERS...

DURING THE MOMENT THE CAPSIZED BOAT IS ABOUT TO PASS HER...

IT'S ALL RIGHT, KIDS--I'VE GOT YOU!

FIFTY FEET FURTHER DOWN THE RIVER, WHERE IT PLUNGES OVER SNAKETAIL FALLS, A NATURE PHOTOGRAPHER, ALSO CAUGHT BY THE STORM...

CAPSIZED BOAT--! WHAT HAPPENED TO THE OCCUPANTS--? IF THEY'RE IN THESE WATERS-- THEY'RE DOOMED!

IN THE FROTHING CURRENT, THE YOUNG COUNTRY GIRL BATTLES AGAINST DEATH WITH BLIND COURAGE...

BONNIE! BONNIE!

DON'T BE AFRAID!

I'M...SO... TIRED...

I WON'T LET YOU GO...

...NO MATTER WHAT HAPPENS!

BONNIE COULD HAVE SAVED HER OWN LIFE... HAD SHE LET GO OF HER TERRIFIED CHARGES...

WONDER WOMAN... WOULD... NEVER... LET... GO...

AN AGONIZING ETERNITY LATER...

WE'RE OUT... OF THE... WATER! WE'RE SAFE-- SAFE!

BUT THE YOUNG COUNTRY GIRL FINDS HERSELF GREETED BY AN OMINOUS SILENCE...

THEY'RE NOT... BREATHING--!

FROM HER READING, BONNIE RECALLS...

GOT TO... START EDIE... BREATHING AGAIN --

AND WHENEVER HER STRENGTH FALTERS, THE EXHAUSTED COUNTRY GIRL SOMEHOW SUMMONS UP ANOTHER LAST EFFORT...

WONDER WOMAN... WOULDN'T... GIVE UP--!

STUMBLING TOWARD THE LITTLE TRIO -- THE PHOTOGRAPHER...

MY TELEPHOTO LENS GOT IT ALL --!

5

AND SO IT IS THAT A WEEK LATER...THE BLUSHING BONNIE STANDS BEFORE HER IDOL...

...BASED ON THE ACTUAL PICTURES OF THE DEED, AND THE EYE-WITNESS TESTIMONY OF THE PHOTOGRAPHER--THE JURY CHOSE BONNIE BATES--AS A YOUNG AMERICAN EVERYONE CAN BE PROUD OF!

YOU'RE **WONDER WOMAN'S** SWEETHEART, COL. TREVOR! HAS **SHE** TOLD YOU WHAT THE PRIZE WILL BE?

NO--I'M AS ANXIOUS TO HEAR WHAT IT IS--AS YOU ARE!

AND THEN, LIKE A THUNDERBOLT, THE UNIQUE PRIZE--STARTLING THE YOUTHFUL WINNER!

YOUR PRIZE, BONNIE--IS THREE WISHES! **ASK THREE WISHES OF ME!** THERE IS NO LIMIT TO WHAT YOU MAY ASK!

IT SEEMS AS IF THE WHOLE COUNTRY WAITS WITH BATED BREATH FOR THE YOUNG COUNTRY GIRL'S ANSWER....AS SHE PONDERS SILENTLY... IF YOU WERE IN THE SAME PLACE, READER-- WHAT WOULD **YOUR THREE WISHES BE?**

AND THEN--HER ANSWER--STARTLING **WONDER WOMAN** IN TURN!

I--I WOULD LOVE TO GO TO THE SECRET ISLAND HOME OF THE AMAZONS WITH YOU, **WONDER WOMAN!** I'VE OFTEN READ ABOUT IT... IT'S BEEN MY DREAM ... COULD YOU TAKE ME?

AND THUS STARTS ONE OF THE MOST IN- CREDIBLE ADVENTURES OF ALL TIME... WITH WHAT STAGGERING SCENES YOU SHALL SEE...WHEN **WONDER WOMAN** SUMMONS HER ROBOT PLANE AND WITH AN ELECTRIFYING LEAP...

BON VOYAGE!

PARADISE ISLAND-- NEXT STOP!

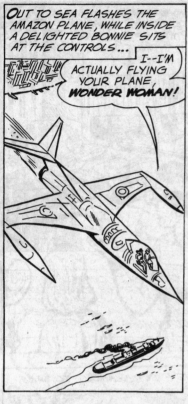

OUT TO SEA FLASHES THE AMAZON PLANE, WHILE INSIDE A DELIGHTED BONNIE SITS AT THE CONTROLS...

I--I'M ACTUALLY FLYING YOUR PLANE, *WONDER WOMAN!*

HURTLING AT BLAZING SPEED ON A SECRET COURSE, THE UNIQUE PLANE SOON CIRCLES OVER...

PARADISE ISLAND-- SECRET ISLAND HOME OF THE AMAZONS!

I'LL TAKE OVER FOR THE LANDING NOW, BONNIE!

ASSEMBLED TO GREET THE VISITOR IS *WONDER WOMAN'S* MOTHER, QUEEN HIPPOLYTA AND...

WELCOME TO *PARADISE ISLAND!*

HOLA, BONNIE!

IN *WONDER WOMAN'S* CHAMBERS SHORTLY...

AN AMAZON COSTUME-- JUST FOR ME? B-B-BUT WHY?

FOR THE CEREMONY, BONNIE!

AFTERWARDS IN THE GREAT BANQUET HALL...

...AND FOR HER UNSELFISH HEROISM DEMONSTRATING TO THE WORLD WHAT A YOUNG AMERICAN IS REALLY LIKE-- I PROCLAIM BONNIE BATES-- AN *HONORARY AMAZON!*

TEARS OF JOY FILL THE YOUNG HONORARY AMAZON'S EYES AS...

AND NOW, BONNIE, MY SISTER AMAZON-- WHAT IS YOUR *SECOND* WISH?

ALL KEEN AMAZON EYES ARE FIXED ON BONNIE, AS SHE PONDERS WHAT THE NEXT WISH IS TO BE...

WHAT IS YOUR SECOND WISH, BONNIE?

I-I CAN'T THINK OF ANYTHING JUST NOW, **WONDER WOMAN!** COULD I-- HAVE A LITTLE MORE TIME?

WHILE BONNIE IS TRYING TO THINK OF A SECOND WISH, SHE IS TAKEN ON A TOUR OF THE VAST AMAZON CHAMBERS...

HERE IS WHERE WE "FIX" EVERY **SOS** HEARD IN OUR SOLAR SYSTEM! AND WE ANSWER EVERY APPEAL--IF NO OTHER HELP IS AVAILABLE!

OUR STUDIES DO NOT END WITH SLEEP! TAPE RECORDERS CONTINUE THE PROCESS!

THE TOUR CONTINUES TO THE **FIELD OF SKILL** WHERE A UNIQUE EVENT IS ABOUT TO TAKE PLACE...

THIS NEW GAME HAS JUST BEEN INVENTED! NO ONE CAN HURTLE THROUGH **ALL** THE RINGS! BUT THE AMAZON WHO CAN PASS THROUGH **MORE** OF THEM THAN ANY OTHER--IS THE WINNER!

KLUNG!

KLUNG!

END OF **PART ONE** OF THE SUSPENSE-LADEN TALE OF THE **"CHEST OF MONSTERS!"** **PART TWO** CONTINUES ON THE PAGE FOLLOWING!

8

WONDER GIRL CHEST of MONSTERS PART TWO

ONE AFTER THE OTHER, **PARADISE ISLAND'S** FINEST AMAZON ATHLETES COLLIDE AGAINST ONE OF THE RINGS...

CLANG! CLANG! CLANG! CLANK!

AND THEN...

DON'T YOU HOPE **YOUR** DAUGHTER WILL **WIN**, QUEEN?

IT WOULD NOT BE FAIR FOR ME TO BE PREJUDICED IN FAVOR OF ANYONE, BONNIE! EVEN MY DAUGHTER! I JUST HOPE THE **BEST** AMAZON WILL WIN! WHOEVER SHE WILL BE!

AS THE AMAZON PRINCESS HURLS HERSELF LIKE A HUMAN LIGHTNING BOLT INTO THE GAME OF RINGS...

I CAN'T HELP WISHING **WONDER WOMAN** WILL WIN! I WISH SHE **DOES**!

AS IF MADE LIGHT AS A FEATHER BY BONNIE'S WISH, **WONDER WOMAN** SOARS THROUGH ONE RING AFTER ANOTHER IN A DAZZLING DISPLAY OF AGILITY UNTIL...

WHOOSH! WHOOOOSH! WHOOOOOSH!

ELATEDLY, BONNIE GREETS **WONDER WOMAN** AT THE CONCLUSION OF HER SENSATIONAL FEAT...

I **WISHED** THAT YOU WOULD WIN, **WONDER WOMAN**! I **WISHED** IT--AND ??¿!!

A STARTLED GASP ARISES FROM THE ASSEMBLED AMAZONS, AS BONNIE REALIZES..

THE SECOND WISH !... I--I **ALREADY** MADE IT--WISHING YOU WOULD WIN, **WONDER WOMAN**!... GUESS I'VE ONLY GOT ONE WISH MORE !

ALL THE AMAZONS HOLD THEIR BREATH IN SUSPENSE AS...

BE **VERY** CAREFUL NOW, BONNIE ! DON'T UTTER IT UNLESS IT'S EXACTLY WHAT YOU WANT ! NOW-- WHAT IS YOUR THIRD AND **LAST** WISH !

THOUGHTS TUMBLE THROUGH BONNIE'S MIND LIKE HUNDREDS OF CARDS FALLING DOWN...

BEFORE SHE FINALLY ANSWERS...

I NEED MORE TIME, **WONDER WOMAN**!-- I CAN'T THINK--!

ALL RIGHT, BONNIE ! I UNDERSTAND ! BUT--YOU ONLY HAVE UNTIL NIGHTFALL !

BECAUSE WHEN THE SUN BEGINS TO SET, I MUST TAKE YOU BACK TO YOUR WORLD, BONNIE ! SO THINK ...THINK ABOUT WHAT YOU WANT TO **HAVE** ! OR **SEE** ! OR **DO** ! AND LET ME KNOW YOUR LAST WISH !

WHAT WOULD **YOU** WISH FOR IF **YOU** WERE IN BONNIE'S PLACE, READER ?

10

TO ENABLE HER TO CONCENTRATE ON HER LAST WISH, THE HONORARY YOUNG AMAZON IS ALLOWED TO WANDER AS SHE WILL ON *PARADISE ISLAND*... IN THE THEATRE OF LANGUAGES...

EVERY LANGUAGE THAT WAS EVER SPOKEN CAN BE LEARNED HERE, BONNIE! FROM CAVEMAN TO MARTIAN!

UG-- UPNN... NGHH!

KKKEEE TTTOOO..

OUT TO THE BEACH WANDERS THE REFLECTIVE YOUNG GIRL...

CAN I GO FOR A SWIM, *WONDER WOMAN?* IT'S PRETTY WARM!

GO RIGHT AHEAD, BONNIE! I'LL KEEP MY EYE ON YOU FROM HERE!

INTO THE WATER PLUNGES BONNIE, AN EXPERT SWIMMER...

THERE ARE SO *MANY* THINGS I'D LIKE TO *WISH* FOR--THAT I CAN'T THINK OF ANY *ONE* THING!

SUDDENLY, WITH A TERRIFYING ROAR...

S-S-SOMETHING L-L-LIFTING ME RIGHT UP OUT OF THE WATER!

RRUMBLE

THE NEXT INSTANT, WHIRLING UP FROM THE VERY DEPTHS OF THE SEA, AND ENGULFING THE YOUNG SWIMMER...

BY NEPTUNE'S TRIDENT! BONNIE'S IN THE GRIP OF A GIGANTIC WATERSPOUT!

VROOOSH!

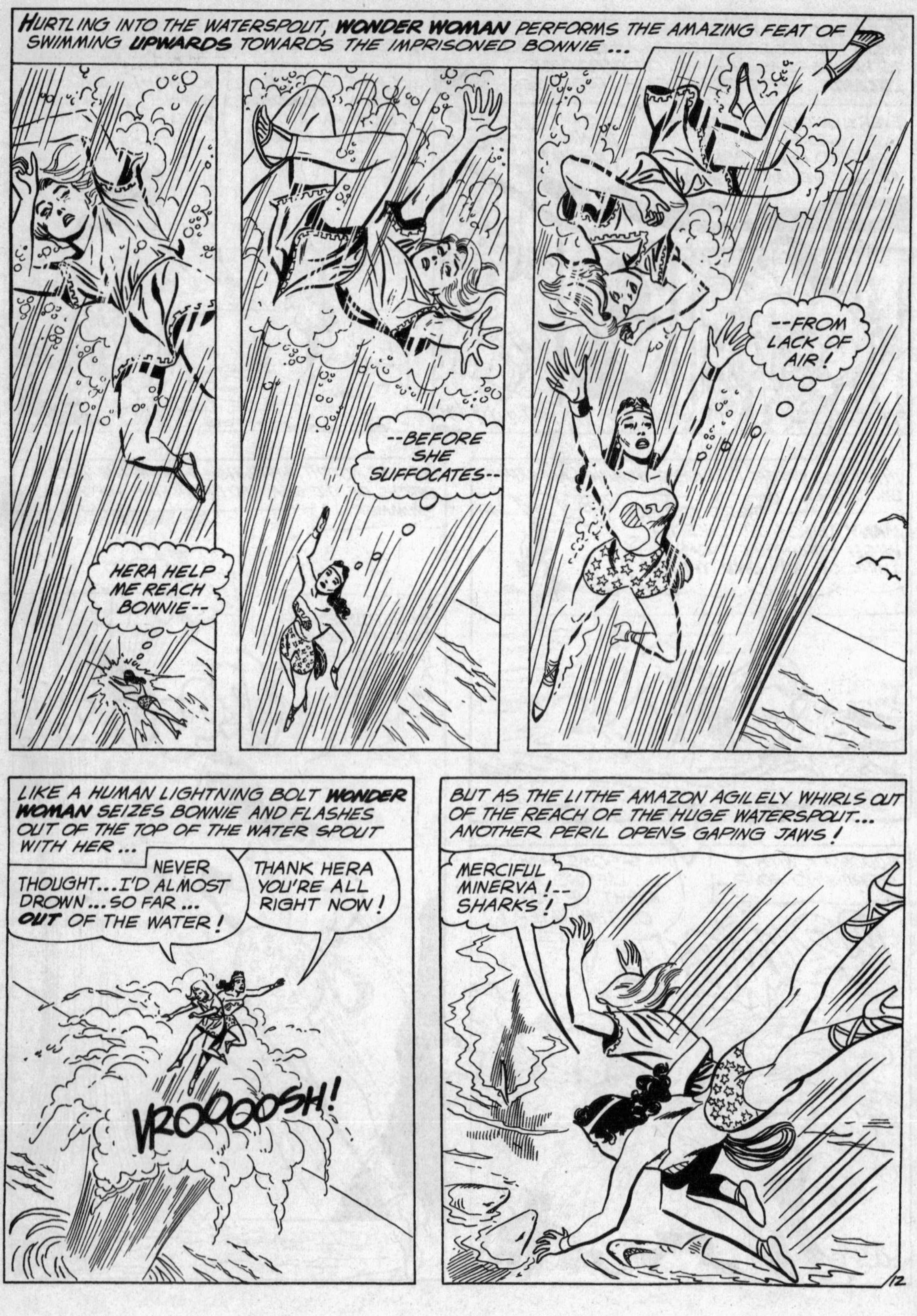
HURTLING INTO THE WATERSPOUT, WONDER WOMAN PERFORMS THE AMAZING FEAT OF SWIMMING UPWARDS TOWARDS THE IMPRISONED BONNIE ...
HERA HELP ME REACH BONNIE--
--BEFORE SHE SUFFOCATES--
--FROM LACK OF AIR!
LIKE A HUMAN LIGHTNING BOLT WONDER WOMAN SEIZES BONNIE AND FLASHES OUT OF THE TOP OF THE WATER SPOUT WITH HER ...
NEVER THOUGHT...I'D ALMOST DROWN...SO FAR... OUT OF THE WATER!
THANK HERA YOU'RE ALL RIGHT NOW!
VROOOOOSH!
BUT AS THE LITHE AMAZON AGILELY WHIRLS OUT OF THE REACH OF THE HUGE WATERSPOUT... ANOTHER PERIL OPENS GAPING JAWS!
MERCIFUL MINERVA!-- SHARKS!
12

EVEN AS SHE HURTLES DOWNWARDS TOWARDS THE AWAITING SCHOOL OF SHARKS, *WONDER WOMAN* WHIPS HER AMAZON LASSO AT THEM WITH HER FREE HAND...

HERA HELP MY AIM TO BE TRUE!

WHIIIIIIP!

INSTANTLY, THE UNBREAKABLE LASSO CLAMPS THE YAWNING JAWS OF THE SHARKS TIGHT...

WHUMMMP!

AND WITH HER INCREDIBLE SENSE OF BALANCE, THE MIGHTY AMAZON ALIGHTS ON THE BACKS OF THE SHARKS... AND...

YOU'RE DRIVING THE SHARKS AS IF--AS IF THEY'RE HORSES, *WONDER WOMAN!*

RELEASING HER GOLDEN LASSO, *WONDER WOMAN* LEAPS TO SAFETY WITH HER YOUNG CHARGE...

I'M GOING TO LEAVE YOU IN A NICE QUIET PLACE, BONNIE-- WHERE YOU CAN THINK UNDISTURBED UNTIL YOU DECIDE ON YOUR THIRD WISH!

WHIT!

A FEW MOMENTS LATER, IN THE AMAZON LIBRARY, THE YOUNG CONTEST WINNER LEAFS THROUGH A BOOK...

I'VE GOT IT--*I'VE GOT IT*--THIS SCRAP BOOK GAVE ME THE IDEA FOR MY THIRD WISH!

13

As **WONDER WOMAN** RUSHES TO THE EXCITED BONNIE'S SIDE...

MY THIRD WISH IS TO SPEND A FEW HOURS WITH YOU--WHEN YOU WERE **MY** AGE, **WONDER WOMAN!** WHEN YOU WERE **WONDER GIRL!**

THE STARTLED AMAZON TAKES BONNIE TO THE AMAZON HALL OF TIME AND SPACE...

YOU MAY HAVE YOUR THIRD WISH, BONNIE! BUT THE ONLY WAY IT CAN BE GRANTED-- IS FOR YOU TO TRAVEL BACK INTO THE PAST--IN THE TIME MACHINE!

I...I AM READY!

INSIDE THE TIME AND SPACE MACHINE, THE TEENAGE CONTEST WINNER STARES AT **WONDER WOMAN**...

WILL IT REALLY HAPPEN?...WILL I--?

THE SWITCH IS THROWN... TIME AND SPACE WHIRL BY..

ZZZZT!

AND THEN, AS IF NO MORE THAN A BREATH HAS PASSED.

WONDER GIRL! WONDER GIRL! IS IT REALLY YOU? AM I DREAMING ALL THIS?

CAN YOU TOUCH A DREAM?

YOU'RE REAL-- REAL--I CAN FEEL YOUR HAND!

WHAT NEW ADVENTURES WILL BE- FALL THE TEENAGE TIME TRAVELER AS SHE SPENDS A FEW HOURS IN THE PAST WITH **WONDER GIRL**, THE TEENAGE AMAZON? END OF PART TWO OF **WONDER GIRL** IN THE "CHEST OF MONSTERS!" PART THREE OF THIS ADVENTURE CONTINUES ON THE PAGE FOLLOWING! ⑭

WONDER GIRL in The CHEST OF MONSTERS!

THE LAST WISH IS GRANTED...AS BONNIE TRAVELS BACK THROUGH TIME AND MEETS WONDER WOMAN WHEN SHE IS A TEENAGE AMAZON-- *WONDER GIRL* !

WAIT UNTIL I TELL THE KIDS ON THE BLOCK THAT I'VE ACTUALLY VISITED YOU, *WONDER GIRL* !-- WHAT AM I TALKING ABOUT ? I'VE GONE BACK TO THE PAST ! AND THE *PAST* IS THE *PRESENT* ! AND *I'M* WITH *YOU* RIGHT *NOW* ! OH-- IT'S SO EXCITING ! SO WONDERFUL ! I HARDLY KNOW WHAT I'M SAYING !

SHORTLY, ON A NEARBY FIELD, BONNIE WATCHES THE AGILITY OF THE AMAZON TEENAGER WITH AWE AS...

GOSH, WONDER GIRL ! IT--IT'S SIMPLY AMAZING-- THE WAY YOU CAN FLY !

I *CAN'T* FLY, BONNIE ! I'M RIDING THE UP AND DOWN DRAFTS--THE AIR CURRENTS ! I'LL SHOW YOU HOW I DO IT !

LIFTING BONNIE, *WONDER GIRL* SOARS WITH HER EFFORTLESSLY...

IT'S LIKE--LIKE YOU'RE FLOAT-ING IN THE AIR !

AS IF YOU'RE A FEATHER !

DO YOU THINK *I* COULD EVER LEARN TO DO THIS, *WONDER GIRL* ?

YOU COULD-- IF YOU WERE AN AMAZON !

WONDER GIRL LEADS BONNIE TO THE AMAZON TESTING LABORATORY WHERE...

TO BE A GOOD AMAZON YOU MUST ALWAYS BE STUDYING! TAKE THE SUBJECT OF TEMPERATURE FOR INSTANCE! COLD! HOW MUCH DO YOU KNOW ABOUT THE EFFECTS OF COLD?

TEMPERATURE CHAMBER

THE TEMPERATURE IN THIS CHAMBER IS MAINTAINED AT ABSOLUTE ZERO! HAVE YOU ANY IDEA WHAT WOULD HAPPEN TO METAL IF PLACED INSIDE HERE?

I HAVE A FIVE AND DIME RING, **WONDER GIRL**! COULD WE USE IT FOR THE EXPERIMENT?

THE TEENAGER'S METAL RING ROLLS THROUGH A SLOT PAST THE "WEATHERIZED" WALLS OF THE CHAMBER... AND DROPS ONTO THE FLOOR... WHERE THE EXTREME COLD ACTUALLY SHRINKS IT... UNTIL IT CAN ONLY BE DETECTED BY A MICROSCOPE!

KLANK!

WHY--THE WAY THAT METAL RING OF MINE DISAPPEARED-- WAS LIKE--LIKE MAGIC!

SCIENCE **SEEMS** TO WORK LIKE MAGIC SOMETIMES, BONNIE! BUT, THE DIFFERENCE IS THAT SCIENCE HAS AN **EXPLANATION** FOR ITS "MAGIC"! NOW--IS THERE ANYTHING YOU'D LIKE TO HAVE ME DO? OR ANYTHING YOU'D LIKE TO SEE?

I'VE READ ABOUT YOUR FRIEND, THE **MER-BOY, WONDER GIRL**! THE BOY WHO LIVES AT THE BOTTOM OF THE SEA! I'D LOVE TO VISIT HIS HOME! BUT--IT'S IMPOSSIBLE! I CAN'T BREATHE UNDERWATER THE WAY YOU DO!

BUT I CAN'T BREATHE UNDERWATER, BONNIE! I THOUGHT YOU KNEW THAT!

AT THE AMAZON EQUIPMENT LABORATORY SHORTLY... WHERE **WONDER GIRL** HAS LED BONNIE...

HERE ARE SPECIAL SUITS DEVISED TO MEET ANY CONDITIONS!

WHERE? I DON'T SEE THEM!

SPACE SUITS

ARCTIC SUITS

TROPICAL SUITS

SKIN-DIVING SUITS

LAUGHING AT HER GUEST'S BEWILDERMENT, THE AMAZON TEENAGER DEMONSTRATES...

I CAN STAY UNDERWATER INDEFINITELY IN THIS SKIN-DIVING OUTFIT, BONNIE! TRY THIS ONE ON FOR SIZE!

NO WONDER I COULDN'T SEE IT! IT'S TRANSPARENT!

SHORTLY... EQUIPPED WITH THE SPECIAL SUITS...

WE'LL HAVE TO MAKE HAND SIGNALS TO UNDERSTAND EACH OTHER--ONCE WE'RE UNDERWATER?

NO, BONNIE! THAT WON'T BE NECESSARY! WE'LL BE ABLE TO SPEAK TO EACH OTHER!

THE TEENAGE VISITOR IS PUZZLED BY THE YOUNG AMAZON'S REPLY...

I DON'T UNDERSTAND WHAT **WONDER GIRL** MEANS! YOU CAN'T OPEN YOUR MOUTH TO SPEAK UNDERWATER! SO HOW ELSE CAN YOU COMMUNICATE-- EXCEPT BY HAND SIGNALS?

YOU CAN **THINK** WHAT YOU'RE GOING TO SAY, CAN'T YOU, BONNIE?

WITHOUT REALIZING IT, BONNIE REPLIES TO **WONDER GIRL'S** UNSPOKEN THOUGHT...

OF COURSE I CAN--?? **WONDER GIRL**--!! I HEARD EXACTLY WHAT YOU SAID!!

YOU "HEARD" MY THOUGHTS! THAT'S HOW AN AMAZON COMMUNICATES UNDERWATER! OUR SUITS HAVE A UNIQUE THOUGHT-WAVE TRANSMITTER BUILT IN!

DEEPER AND DEEPER INTO THE OCEAN'S DEPTHS THE TWO TEEN-AGERS GLIDE...

I WONDER WHEN WE'RE GOING TO MEET THE MER-BOY?

SOONER THAN YOU THINK, BONNIE! HE LIKES TO APPEAR UNEXPECTEDLY! IF HE CAN APPEAR FROM A HIDING PLACE **BEFORE** I CAN SEE HIM-- HE WINS! IF I CAN FIND HIM **FIRST**--I WIN!

17

WITH A LIGHTNING-LIKE TWIST OF HER POWERFUL WRIST, **WONDER GIRL** HURLS OPEN THE GIANT SEA-SHELL AND...

BY NEPTUNE'S BEARD! HOW DID YOU DETECT ME?

I THOUGHT IT **ODD** TO HEAR A **SHELL BREATHING!** BY THE WAY, THIS IS MY FRIEND FROM MAN'S WORLD! BONNIE--THIS IS THE **MER-BOY!**

I'VE READ ALL ABOUT YOU IN THE **WONDER WOMAN** MAGAZINE, MER-BOY! BUT I NEVER IMAGINED THAT I WOULD EVER MEET YOU! IT'S ALL LIKE A WONDERFUL DREAM!

YOU HAVEN'T SEEN ANYTHING YET, BONNIE! YOU AND **WONDER GIRL** TAKE HOLD OF MY TAIL--AND I'LL SHOW YOU SOMETHING I'VE JUST FOUND!

TOWED BY THE FROLICSOME **MER-BOY**, THE TWO TEENAGERS ARE LED THROUGH THE FANTASTIC UNDERSEA WORLD TOWARDS A WRECKED SPANISH GALLEON SHIP...

AN ANCIENT SUNKEN SHIP!

I HAVEN'T HAD A CHANCE TO EXPLORE IT YET!

CAN'T I GO INSIDE WITH YOU TO EXPLORE THE SHIP, **WONDER GIRL**?

NO, BONNIE! YOU'LL BE SAFER ON DECK! THERE'S NO TELLING WHEN A CURRENT MIGHT CAPSIZE THE SHIP--PERHAPS IMPRISONING YOU INSIDE!

INTO THE MYSTERIOUS INTERIOR OF THE SUNKEN SHIP, THE YOUNG AMAZON AND THE **MER-BOY** MAKE THEIR WAY...

WE'LL SEPARATE AND MEET BACK UP ON DECK! PERHAPS ONE OF US WILL FIND A TREASURE CHEST--OR SOMETHING?

PERHAPS!

WONDER GIRL SEARCHES CABIN AFTER CABIN-- AND THEN!

HELP--!

BY NEPTUNE'S TRIDENT--**MER-BOY'S** IN TROUBLE!

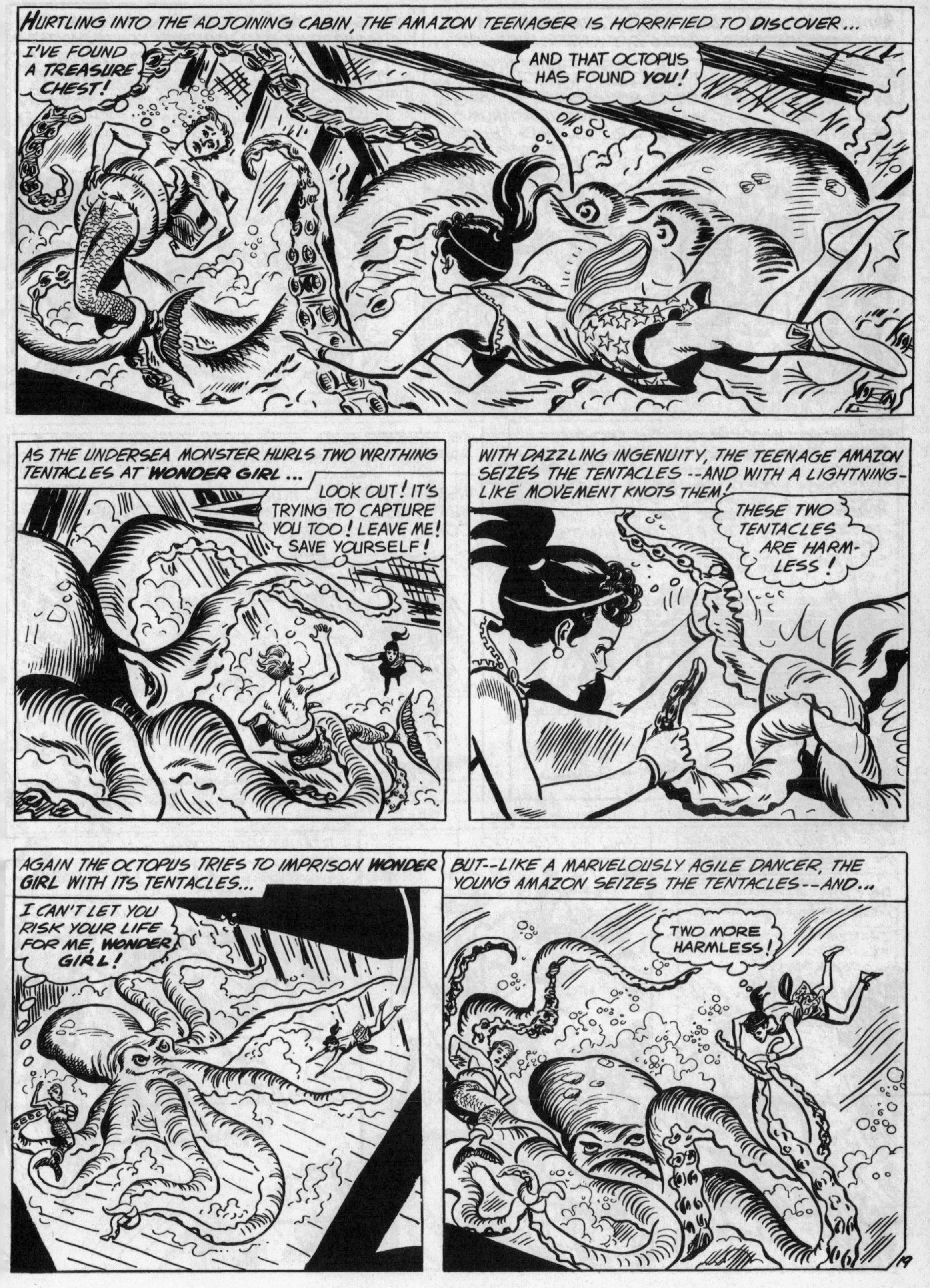
HURTLING INTO THE ADJOINING CABIN, THE AMAZON TEENAGER IS HORRIFIED TO DISCOVER...
I'VE FOUND A TREASURE CHEST!
AND THAT OCTOPUS HAS FOUND YOU!
AS THE UNDERSEA MONSTER HURLS TWO WRITHING TENTACLES AT WONDER GIRL...
LOOK OUT! IT'S TRYING TO CAPTURE YOU TOO! LEAVE ME! SAVE YOURSELF!
WITH DAZZLING INGENUITY, THE TEENAGE AMAZON SEIZES THE TENTACLES --AND WITH A LIGHTNING-LIKE MOVEMENT KNOTS THEM!
THESE TWO TENTACLES ARE HARM-LESS!
AGAIN THE OCTOPUS TRIES TO IMPRISON WONDER GIRL WITH ITS TENTACLES...
I CAN'T LET YOU RISK YOUR LIFE FOR ME, WONDER GIRL!
BUT--LIKE A MARVELOUSLY AGILE DANCER, THE YOUNG AMAZON SEIZES THE TENTACLES--AND...
TWO MORE HARMLESS!
19

AGAIN AND AGAIN THE OCTOPUS FURIOUSLY ATTACKS--BUT WONDER GIRL FEARLESSLY KNOTS THEM UNTIL...

I'M FREE--I'M FREE! THE OCTOPUS RELEASED ME TRYING TO SEIZE YOU!

IT'S A GOOD THING AN OCTOPUS ONLY HAS EIGHT TENTACLES-- I DON'T KNOW HOW LONG I COULD HAVE CONTINUED THIS!

AS THE MER-BOY AND THE AMAZON TEEN-AGER SWIM BACK ON DECK TOWARDS THE AWAITING BONNIE...

YOU MUST TAKE THE TREASURE CHEST, WONDER GIRL! I INSIST! IT'S THE CUSTOM OF THE MERMEN TO REPAY THE ONE WHO SAVES YOUR LIFE! OTHERWISE I'LL BE IN DEBT TO YOU FOR THE REST OF MY LIFE!

THE MER-BOY ACCOMPANIES THE TWO GIRLS BACK TO PARADISE ISLAND...

FAREWELL, BONNIE! FAREWELL, WONDER GIRL!

AREN'T YOU GOING TO OPEN THE TREASURE CHEST RIGHT AWAY, WONDER GIRL? I'M DYING TO FIND OUT WHAT'S IN IT!

GOODBY, MER-BOY!

GOODBY, MER-BOY!

AS WONDER GIRL FLIPS OPEN THE CHEST WITH A POWERFUL TUG--STARTLING ARE THE CONTENTS...

INSECTS! METALLIC INSECTS! WHAT WOULD INSECTS BE DOING IN THIS CHEST?

LIKE A LIVING NIGHTMARE THE INSECTS HOP AWAY...

THEY'RE GROWING!

AND AS THEY DO...

BY LEAPS--

A TITANIC TRANSFORMATION TAKES PLACE...

--AND BOUNDS!!

20

GRIMLY, **WONDER GIRL** RACES AFTER THE STRANGE MONSTERS!

STAY OUT OF HARM'S WAY, BONNIE--UNTIL I COME BACK FOR YOU! ALTHOUGH MY SISTER AMAZONS WILL PUT THESE MONSTROUS CREATURES TO ROUT!

BUT, AS THE AMAZON TEENAGER NEARS THE AMAZON BUILDINGS...

WHAT IS HAPPENING?

THE VALIANT AMAZONS REEL AND TOPPLE BEFORE THEY EVEN GET NEAR ENOUGH TO GRAPPLE WITH THE INVADERS...

THESE MONSTERS...EXHALE...A CHOKING GAS--ONLY...YOU...DAUGHTER...SEEM...UNAFFECTED...THE FUTURE...OF THE...AMAZONS...DEPENDS ON...YOU...

MOTHER...MOTHER!

SUDDENLY...

WONDER GIRL--!

MERCIFUL MINERVA!--IT'S BONNIE! FALLEN INTO THE CLUTCHES OF ONE OF THESE MONSTERS! BUT THE FUMES--THEY DON'T SEEM TO AFFECT HER EITHER!

LIKE A CATAPULT, **WONDER GIRL** BOUNDS ONTO THE HEAD OF THE GIANT METALLIC INSECT...

HERA HELP ME ENRAGE THIS MONSTER ENOUGH TO DROP BONNIE--AND GO AFTER ME!

21

WONDER GIRL DODGES THE GARGANTUAN INSECT'S FEELERS -- WAVING IN SEARCH OF HER ... UNHESITATINGLY, THE YOUNG AMAZON HURLS HERSELF AT HER FRIEND AND SO UNEXPECTED IS THIS FEARLESS ACTION THAT...

Y-Y-YOU MADE IT LET ME GO!

THUD!

KLINK-CLINK!

EVEN AS THE TWO YOUNG TEENAGERS TUMBLE ONTO THE ROOF OF THE AMAZON BUILDING NEARBY ... THE ENRAGED CREATURE TEARS AT THE PILLARS!

DID YOU EARTHLINGS THINK TO ESCAPE ME?

HE'S SPEAKING! I--UNDERSTAND IT! HOW--?

IT'S THE THOUGHT-WAVE TRANSMITTER IN OUR SKIN-DIVING SUITS CONVEYING ITS LANGUAGE TO US--! JOVE'S THUNDERBOLTS! NOW I UNDERSTAND WHY WE TWO ARE THE ONLY ONES UNAFFECTED BY THEIR FUMES!

RRRRRRIP!

THIS WAY, INSEKTTEES! ONLY THESE TWO DEFY OUR SUFFOCATING FUMES! OVERCOME THEM -- AND VICTORY IS OURS!

CRASH!

SUDDENLY, WONDER GIRL SEEMS TO LOSE HER HOLD BUT EVEN AS SHE DOES, SHE HURLS BONNIE BACK TO SAFETY...

THIS ONE IS FALLING INTO OUR ANTENNAS!

22

BUT JUST AS THE INSECT HORDE THINKS TO CAPTURE **WONDER GIRL**, SHE USES AN AIR CURRENT TO SLIP OUT OF THEIR REACH..

THIS EARTHLING WILL NOT ESCAPE US! AND TO THINK IT WAS **SHE** WHO FREED US AFTER OUR SPACESHIP FELL INTO THE SEA! AND OUR EXIT HATCH LOCKS JAMMED BECAUSE OF THE EFFECT OF THE WATER!

HREEEE!

LAB

LIKE A FALLING LEAF, THE AGILE AMAZON TEEN-AGER SLIPS AND TWISTS OUT OF THE WAY OF THE METALLIC CREATURES...

ONCE WE COMMUNICATE TO OUR PLANET THAT THE **OXYGEN** WE BREATHE ON EARTH **EXPANDS** US, AND THE FUMES WE **EXHALE SUFFOCATE** EARTHLINGS--WAVES OF OUR METALLIC PEOPLE WILL INVADE EARTH--AND EASILY CONQUER IT!

KLINK! KLINK!

INTO THE CHAMBER OF ABSOLUTE ZERO COLD RACES THE AMAZON TEENAGER...

HREEEE!

KLINK. KLINK!

AND AS THE METALLIC INSECTS RACE AFTER HER...

THIS WILL CLOSE THE DOOR ON US! HERA HELP MY PLAN SUCCEED! OR ALL MAY BE LOST!

CLICK!

ON

OFF

/23

AND NOW, ANOTHER INCREDIBLE TRANSFORMATION TAKES PLACE... AS THE TEMPERATURE OF ABSOLUTE ZERO SHRINKS THE METALLIC MONSTERS, EVEN AS THEY ADVANCE TOWARDS THE RESOLUTE **WONDER GIRL**...

I'VE TRAINED TO WITHSTAND TEMPERATURE AS LOW AS THIS...

KLINK-KLINK!

BUT HERA HELP ME TO HOLD OUT!

UNTIL... THEY'RE...

...GONE!!

THE TEENAGERS ALONE ARE CONSCIOUS ON THE ISLAND...

BUT, **WONDER GIRL**? WHY DIDN'T WE FALL BEFORE THE SUFFOCATING FUMES?

WE HAD ON SKIN-DIVING SUITS CARRYING OUR OWN OXYGEN SUPPLY OR WE WOULD HAVE BEEN AFFECTED TOO!

WITH THE INVASION OF THE METALLIC INSECTS DEFEATED, AND THE AMAZONS RECOVERED...

THANKS FOR THE MOST WONDERFUL TIME OF MY LIFE, **WONDER GIRL**! GOODBY, QUEEN HIPPOLYTA!

GOODBY, BONNIE! I'M GOING TO TURN ON THE TIME MACHINE! HOLD YOUR BREATH! BY THE TIME YOU LET IT GO--YOU'LL BE IN THE FUTURE AGAIN AND...

24

AGAIN TIME AND SPACE REELS BEFORE THE TEEN-AGE TIME TRAVELER...

AND AS IN THE SPACE IT TAKES FOR A SINGLE BREATH...

WELCOME BACK TO THE PRESENT, BONNIE!

WONDER WOMAN!!

AMIDST THE CHEERS OF THE AMAZONS, THE YOUNG CONTEST WINNER TAKES OFF FOR HER HOME, WITH WONDER WOMAN...

IT WAS SO WONDER-FUL! YET--IT'S BEGINNING TO SEEM LIKE A DREAM!

PERHAPS! BUT--AREN'T YOU WEARING PROOF THAT IT WASN'T A DREAM?

MY AMAZON COSTUME! OH, WONDER WOMAN! I'VE HAD SUCH A WONDERFUL TIME! CAN'T YOU CONDUCT MORE CONTESTS--SO OTHER WINNERS CAN BE WITH YOU?

I'D LIKE TO HEAR FROM THE READERS ABOUT IT FIRST, BONNIE! I CAN BE REACHED CARE OF WONDER WOMAN, NATIONAL COMICS.

The End

25

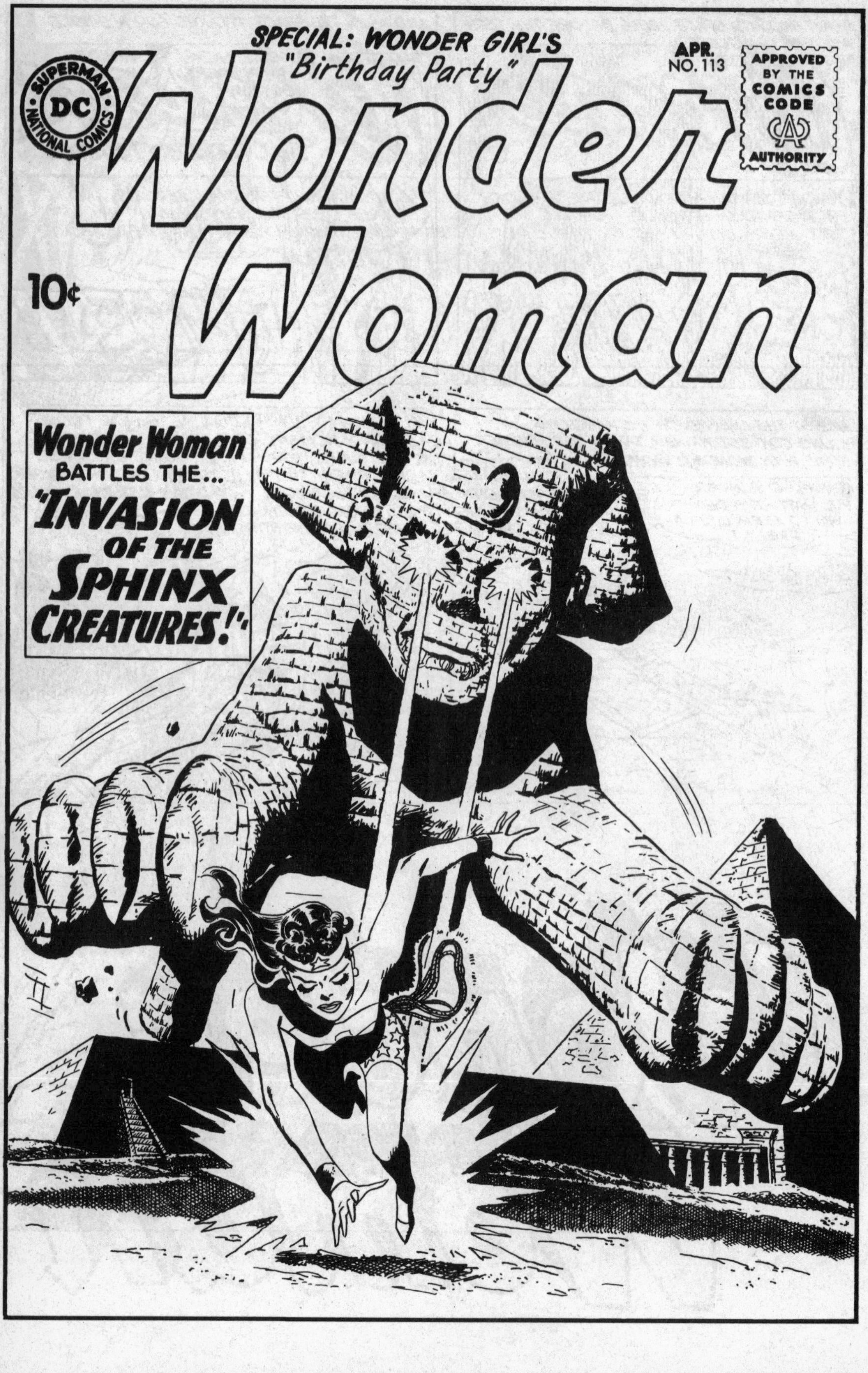
SPECIAL: WONDER GIRL'S
"Birthday Party"
APR.
NO. 113
SUPERMAN
DC
NATIONAL COMICS
APPROVED BY THE COMICS CODE AUTHORITY
Wonder Woman
10¢
Wonder Woman BATTLES THE... "INVASION OF THE SPHINX CREATURES!"

Wonder Woman

By Charles Moulton

WONDER WOMAN--BEAUTIFUL AS APHRODITE, WISE AS ATHENA, SWIFTER THAN MERCURY, AND STRONGER THAN HERCULES, BATTLES NOT ONLY CREATURES OF STONE, BUT AN EVIL TWIN, 7000 YEARS OLD, IN THE FANTASTIC ADVENTURE WHICH CAN ONLY BE **WHISPERED** ABOUT!

PART ONE — THE INVASION OF THE SPHINX CREATURES!

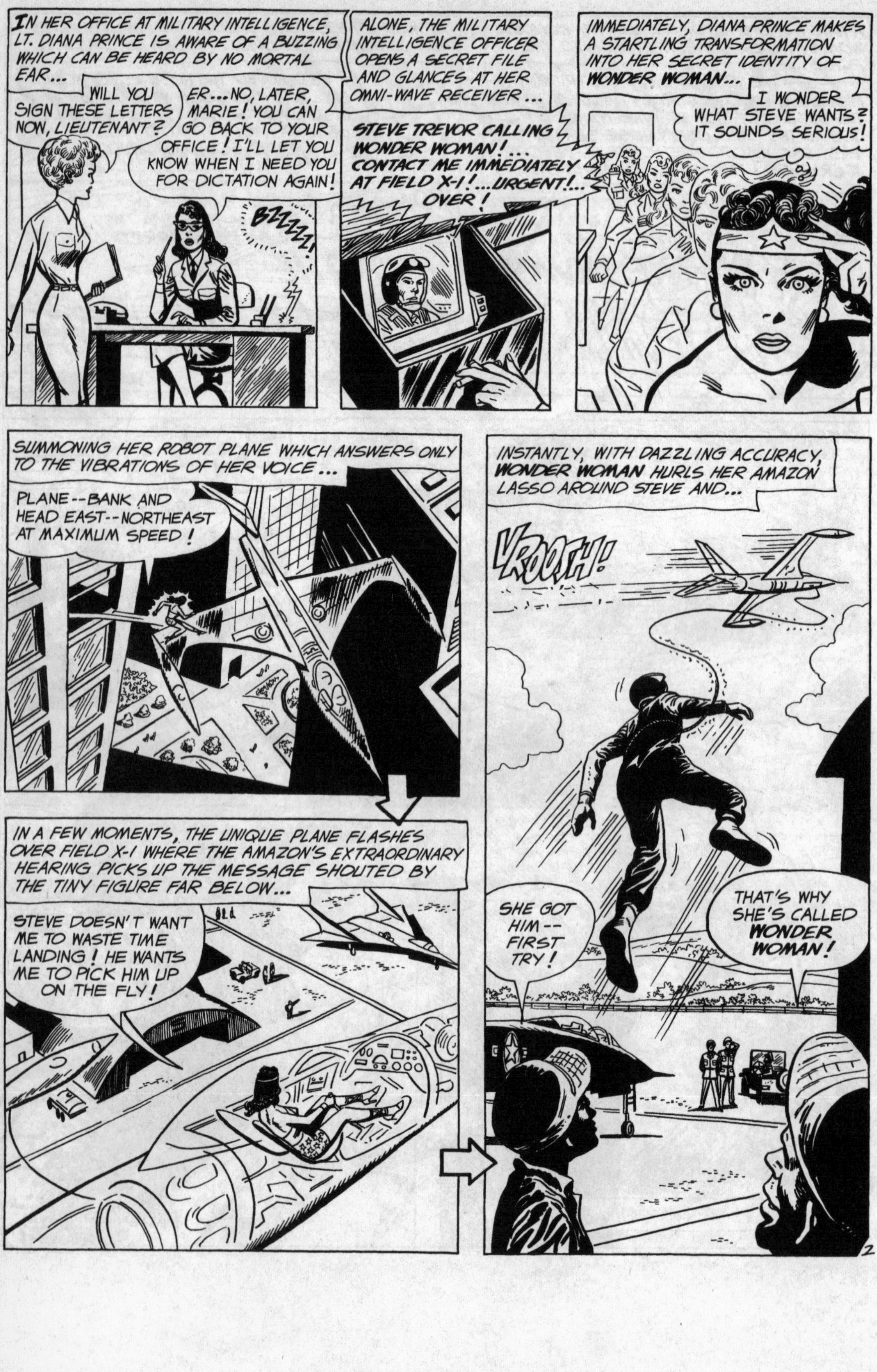
IN HER OFFICE AT MILITARY INTELLIGENCE, LT. DIANA PRINCE IS AWARE OF A BUZZING WHICH CAN BE HEARD BY NO MORTAL EAR...
WILL YOU SIGN THESE LETTERS NOW, LIEUTENANT?
ER...NO, LATER, MARIE! YOU CAN GO BACK TO YOUR OFFICE! I'LL LET YOU KNOW WHEN I NEED YOU FOR DICTATION AGAIN!
BZZZZZZ!
ALONE, THE MILITARY INTELLIGENCE OFFICER OPENS A SECRET FILE AND GLANCES AT HER OMNI-WAVE RECEIVER...
STEVE TREVOR CALLING WONDER WOMAN!... CONTACT ME IMMEDIATELY AT FIELD X-1!...URGENT!... OVER!
IMMEDIATELY, DIANA PRINCE MAKES A STARTLING TRANSFORMATION INTO HER SECRET IDENTITY OF WONDER WOMAN...
I WONDER WHAT STEVE WANTS? IT SOUNDS SERIOUS!
SUMMONING HER ROBOT PLANE WHICH ANSWERS ONLY TO THE VIBRATIONS OF HER VOICE...
PLANE--BANK AND HEAD EAST--NORTHEAST AT MAXIMUM SPEED!
IN A FEW MOMENTS, THE UNIQUE PLANE FLASHES OVER FIELD X-1 WHERE THE AMAZON'S EXTRAORDINARY HEARING PICKS UP THE MESSAGE SHOUTED BY THE TINY FIGURE FAR BELOW...
STEVE DOESN'T WANT ME TO WASTE TIME LANDING! HE WANTS ME TO PICK HIM UP ON THE FLY!
INSTANTLY, WITH DAZZLING ACCURACY, WONDER WOMAN HURLS HER AMAZON LASSO AROUND STEVE AND...
VROOSH!
SHE GOT HIM--FIRST TRY!
THAT'S WHY SHE'S CALLED WONDER WOMAN!
2

A HATCH OPENS AUTOMATICALLY AS **WONDER WOMAN** HAULS STEVE TREVOR INTO THE PLANE...

THE NOSE CONE OF THE TRIDENT MISSILE IS **UNEXPECTEDLY** FALLING TOWARD THE DESERT OF THE SPHINXES, ANGEL! YOU'RE THE ONLY ONE WHOSE SHIP IS FAST ENOUGH TO INTERCEPT IT--BEFORE IT CRASHES! THAT'S WHY I CALLED YOU!

AT MIND-STAGGERING SPEED, THE AMAZON FLIES HER UNIQUE PLANE OVER THE SEA OF SAILS...

WE'D HOPED THE NOSE CONE WOULD FALL INTO THE SEA-- WHERE THE INSTRUMENTS WOULD MORE LIKELY BE UNDAMAGED THAN CRASHING ONTO SOLID GROUND!

VROOOSH!

OVER THE DESERT OF THE SPHINXES THE ROBOT PLANE FLASHES... A MODERN INVENTION CONTRASTING DRAMATICALLY WITH THE STRANGE FIGURE THOUSANDS OF YEARS OLD...

VROOOSH!

WHAT AN EERIE FACE THAT SPHINX HAS!

LITTLE DOES **WONDER WOMAN** KNOW THAT THIS INSCRUTABLE FACE WILL HURL HER INTO AN ADVENTURE WHICH WILL STUN THE HUMAN MIND...

MORE OF THAT LATER...

MEANWHILE, AHEAD, HURTLING OUT OF THE BLAZING SUN...

THE NOSE CONE!

THUNDER-BOLTS OF JOVE! IT'S GOING TO CRASH INTO US!

3

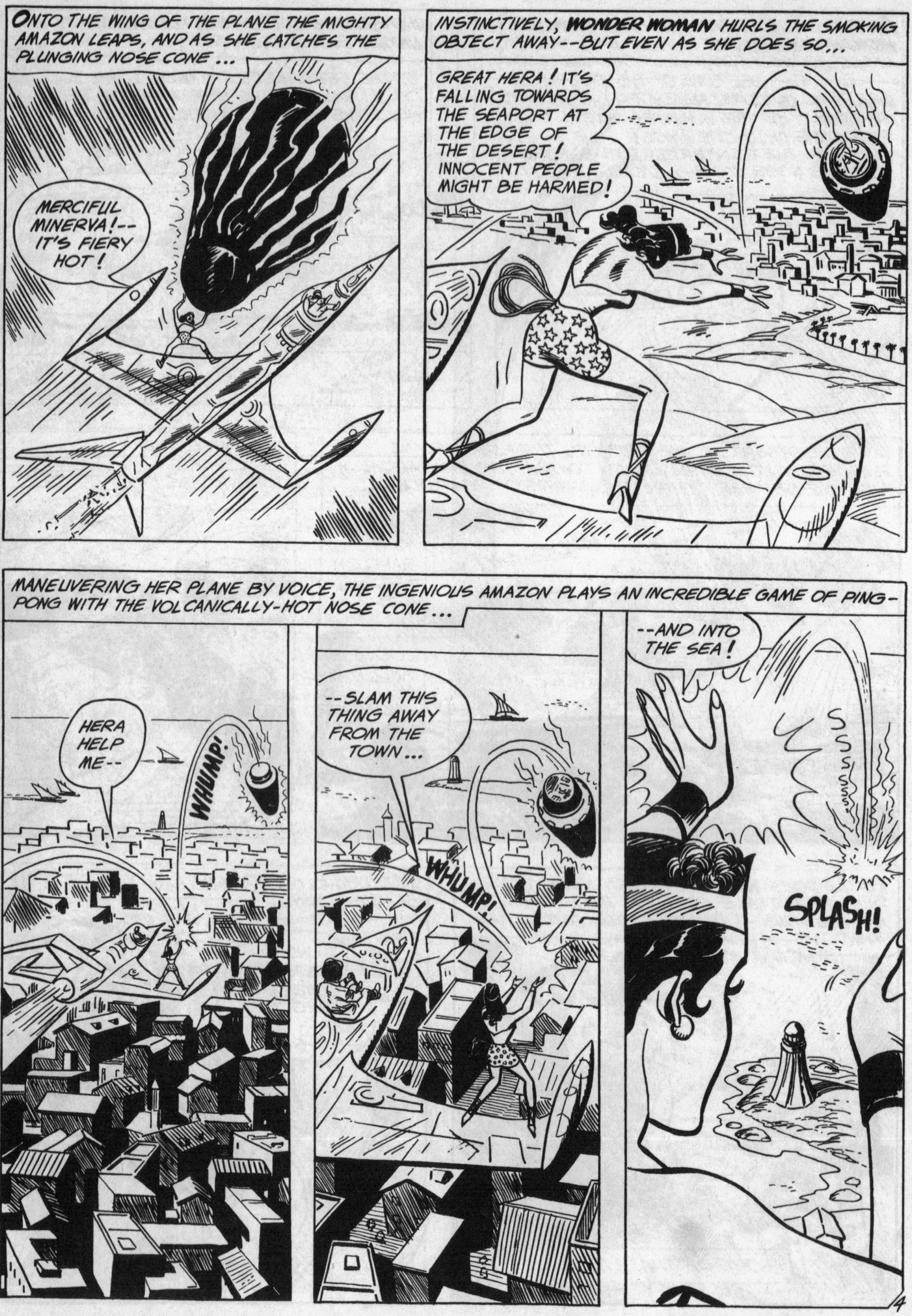

ONTO THE WING OF THE PLANE THE MIGHTY AMAZON LEAPS, AND AS SHE CATCHES THE PLUNGING NOSE CONE ...
MERCIFUL MINERVA!-- IT'S FIERY HOT!
INSTINCTIVELY, WONDER WOMAN HURLS THE SMOKING OBJECT AWAY--BUT EVEN AS SHE DOES SO...
GREAT HERA! IT'S FALLING TOWARDS THE SEAPORT AT THE EDGE OF THE DESERT! INNOCENT PEOPLE MIGHT BE HARMED!
MANEUVERING HER PLANE BY VOICE, THE INGENIOUS AMAZON PLAYS AN INCREDIBLE GAME OF PING-PONG WITH THE VOLCANICALLY-HOT NOSE CONE ...
HERA HELP ME--
WHUMP!
--SLAM THIS THING AWAY FROM THE TOWN...
WHUMP!
--AND INTO THE SEA!
SPLASH!
4

AS THE SEA COOLS OFF THE FLAMING NOSE CONE, *WONDER WOMAN* REELS IT UP WITH HER GOLDEN LASSO FORGED FROM UNBREAKABLE LINKS...

GREAT WORK! I'VE ALREADY RADIOED THE NEWS! A PICK-UP SHIP IS ON ITS WAY FOR THE CONTENTS OF THE NOSE CONE!

LATER...THE CELEBRATED COUPLE VISITS A NATIVE BAZAAR...

BY THE SEVEN MOONS OF MIKRA, LADY-- WHO ARE YOU?

WHY--EVERYONE KNOWS SHE'S *WONDER WOMAN--* THE AMAZON!

THE SELLER OF ANTIQUES DISPLAYS AN ASTONISHING PIECE OF SCULPTURE...

LOOK YOU! AS ALIKE AS TWO GRAINS OF SAND ON THE DESERT IS QUEEN MIKRA, WHO RULED OVER THE DESERT KINGDOM OF MIKRA *7000* YEARS AGO-- AND THIS LADY YOU CALL *WONDER WOMAN!*

AND THIS IS A REPLICA OF THE GREAT SPHINX OF MIKRA--STILL TO BE SEEN ON THE DESERT! THE LEGEND SAYS THAT THE SPHINX WILL COME ALIVE WHEN IT SEES ITS QUEEN AGAIN!

IT'S A COINCIDENCE, OF COURSE! BUT THE RESEMBLANCE IS UNCANNY! AS IF YOU REALLY WERE THE REINCARNATION OF QUEEN MIKRA, WHO LIVED *7000* YEARS AGO!

5

STUNG BY CURIOSITY, *WONDER WOMAN* ASKS...

I'D LIKE TO SEE THE TOMB OF QUEEN MIKRA! WHAT MUSEUM IS SHE IN?

THE TOMB OF QUEEN MIKRA IS *YET* TO BE DISCOVERED, LADY! EVEN NOW, SCIENTISTS ARE IN THE DESERT SEARCHING FOR HER! BUT NONE HAVE FOUND HER!

THE NEXT DAY, THE CELEBRATED COUPLE VISITS THE DESERT...

I JUST *HAD* TO SEE THE SPHINX OF MIKRA, STEVE!

YOU WOMEN ARE ALL ALIKE! CURIOUS AS CATS!

BEFORE THE GREAT SPHINX OF MIKRA THE TWO HALT...

SO THAT THING IS SUPPOSED TO COME ALIVE WHEN IT SEES QUEEN MIKRA AGAIN!

IT'S JUST A MYTH! LET'S GO, STEVE!

THE TWO RIDERS START TO LEAVE... WHEN THEIR STEEDS BOLT TERRIFIEDLY AS, WITH A GREAT RENDING SOUND...

RRUMBLE!

RROAR!

THE SPHINX--?

SHADES OF PLUTO! IT'S MOVING--! COMING TO LIFE!

END OF PART ONE! PART TWO CONTINUES ON THE PAGE FOLLOWING...

Wonder Woman

PART The INVASION OF THE TWO SPHINX CREATURES!

HURLED VIOLENTLY TO THE GROUND BY HIS BOLTING CAMEL, STEVE LIES STILL...

STEVE--?!

BUT BEFORE **WONDER WOMAN** CAN REACH HIM, TWIN BEAMS OF BALEFUL LIGHT SHOOT OUT FROM THE SPHINX'S STONY ORBS...

AND AS THE EERIE LIGHT ENVELOPS THE LOVELY AMAZON...

TH-THUNDERBOLTS OF J-J-JOVE...I...I FEEL NUMB...!

INCREDULOUSLY, THE FROZEN **WONDER WOMAN** STARES UPWARD AS A HUGE PAW DESCENDS TOWARDS HER...

QUEEN MIKRA-- AT LAST YOU HAVE RETURNED!

IT--IT'S A NIGHTMARE--! I--I'M GOING TO WAKE UP--ANY MOMENT!

INSTEAD, THE NIGHTMARE BECOMES A REALITY, AS THE BEWILDERED AMAZON IS CAREFULLY CARRIED BY THE HUGE CREATURE OF THE DESERT...

THE SIGHT OF YOU HAS BROUGHT ME BACK TO LIFE AGAIN, O QUEEN MIKRA! NOW SHALL WE BEGIN THE CONQUEST OF ALL THE LANDS BEYOND THE DESERT!

I STILL CAN'T BELIEVE THE SPHINX HAS COME TO LIFE! IT MUST BE A NIGHTMARE!

AS THE SPHINX OF MIKRA BEGINS ITS MARCH ACROSS THE DESERT, A FANTASTIC SPECTACLE STARTLES THE HELPLESS *WONDER WOMAN*...

HAIL, QUEEN MIKRA!

SHADES OF PLUTO! THESE SPHINX CREATURES--

HAIL!

--ARE MASSING TOGETHER--

HAIL!

--FOR AN INVASION!

AT THAT MOMENT...

PLANES FROM THE DESERT PATROL! PRAY HERA THEY WILL ATTACK THESE SPHINX CREATURES--REGARDLESS OF WHAT WILL HAPPEN TO ME!

THE PILOT OF THE LEAD PLANE STARES IN BEWILDERMENT...

BY MIKRA'S BLAZING SUN! EITHER THAT IS A MIRAGE BELOW! OR--OR--SPHINXES WALKING! LET US FLY LOW TO INVESTIGATE!

AYE--!

AS THE LEAD PILOT SWOOPS PAST THE GREAT SPHINX OF MIKRA, IT THRUSTS A MASSIVE STONE PAW AGAINST THE PLANE WHICH...

WHAM!

THUNDERBOLTS OF JOVE! ONE SHIP IS SMASHED! BUT THE OTHER GOT AWAY! AT LEAST--HE CAN WARN THE AUTHORITIES!

BUT, THE NEXT MOMENT...

HE'S TURNED-- HE'S ATTACKING!

RAT-A-TAT!

A TORRENT OF FIRE POURS FROM THE PLANE'S MACHINE GUNS DOWN AT THE EERIE STONE FIGURE...

BY THE SANDS OF THE DESERT! MY BULLETS MERELY REBOUND OFF THE SPHINX!

RATATATAT!

AND THEN, EVEN AS THE PILOT DESPERATELY ATTEMPTS TO ZOOM OUT OF THE WAY...

BLAM!

MERCIFUL MINERVA! THE SECOND PLANE IS DESTROYED!

AS THE MASSIVE MARCHERS CONTINUE ON THEIR WAY THROUGH THE DESERT...

I MUST FIND OUT IF THESE SPHINX CREATURES HAVE ANY WEAKNESSES THAT I CAN USE AGAINST THEM-- TO HALT THEIR INVASION-- WHEN THE NUMBING EFFECT OF THE RAY WEARS OFF!

WITH DISARMING GUILE, **WONDER WOMAN** ASKS...

IF I AM YOUR QUEEN, O SPHINX, WHY SEEK TO HARM ME WITH YOUR RAY?

NOT TO HARM YOU, GREAT QUEEN! BUT TO HALT YOU FROM REACHING YOUR COMPANION! FOR THERE CAN BE ROOM FOR ONLY **ONE** ON YOUR THRONE! YOU--AND NO OTHER!

WHAT QUEEN HAD SO INVINCIBLE A GUARDIAN OF HER THRONE, O SPHINX? YOU **ARE** INVINCIBLE, ARE YOU NOT?

INVINCIBLE ENOUGH, GREAT QUEEN! FOR **ONLY** BY A **SPHINX** CAN A **SPHINX** BE DEFEATED! AND NO SPHINX CAN DEFEAT ME!

SUDDENLY, ANOTHER EARIE VOICE IS HEARD..

TOO LONG HAVE I HEARD YOU BOAST! I CHALLENGE YOU FOR THE HONOR TO BE THE QUEEN'S CHAMPION!

A GREAT STONE PAW LOWERS THE CAPTIVE AMAZON TO THE DESERT SANDS AS...

IF YOU YEARN FOR MY GLORY--YOU MUST EARN IT--OR BE DESTROYED! KNOWING THAT ONCE A SPHINX HAS CRUMBLED--IT CAN NEVER TAKE SHAPE AGAIN!

THAT FATE WILL BE YOURS!

10

AND BEFORE THE EYES OF **WONDER WOMAN**...

KRAACK!

SURELY THE MOST FANTASTIC BATTLE OF ALL TIMES ERUPTS...

KRAK!

AS SPHINX CRASHES AGAINST SPHINX WITH MASSIVE BLOWS, UNTIL...

KRUMMBLE

THUNDERBOLTS OF JOVE! IT *IS* AS THE SPHINX OF MIKRA FORETOLD! ONLY SPHINX CAN SPHINX DESTROY!

AS THE TITANIC PAW AGAIN LIFTS THE NUMB AMAZON...

I MUST FIND **SOME** MEANS OF HALTING THIS DREAD INVASION -- NO MATTER WHAT HAPPENS TO ME!

GREAT SPHINX! THERE IS NO NEED TO INVADE THE LANDS BEYOND THE DESERT! LET US RETURN TO THE SILENT SANDS! THERE IS MY TRUE KINGDOM! I WILL BE CONTENT THERE!

BEFORE YOUR LONG SLEEP, O QUEEN, YOU VOWED TO INVADE! NOTHING CAN STOP US! NOT EVEN YOU!

NEARBY, ON THE DESERT, ARCHEOLOGISTS MAKE AN EXCITING DISCOVERY...

AFTER YEARS OF FAILURE-- WE HAVE FOUND THE TOMB OF QUEEN MIKRA HERSELF!

JUST THEN, THE SCIENTISTS STARE AT A FANTASTIC SPECTACLE APPROACHING THEM...

L-L-LOOK! TH-THE GREAT SPHINX OF MIKRA-- LEADING OTHERS!

THE INSCRUTABLE FACE TURNS IN THE DIRECTION OF THE UN-COVERED MUMMY... TWIN LIGHTS BEAM FROM ITS EYES... TOWARDS THE CAMP...

...ALL ABOUT THE EXCAVATION... MEN CRUMBLE FROM THE AWFUL GLARE...

...UNTIL BUT A SINGLE FIGURE IS LEFT STANDING... FROM WHOSE FORM ANCIENT WRAPPINGS DROP... UNTIL THERE IS REVEALED...

HOW LONG WAS MY SLEEP?

BUT--NOW IT IS ENDED-- THANKS TO YOU, O SPHINX! AND WE CAN BEGIN OUR INVASION!

12

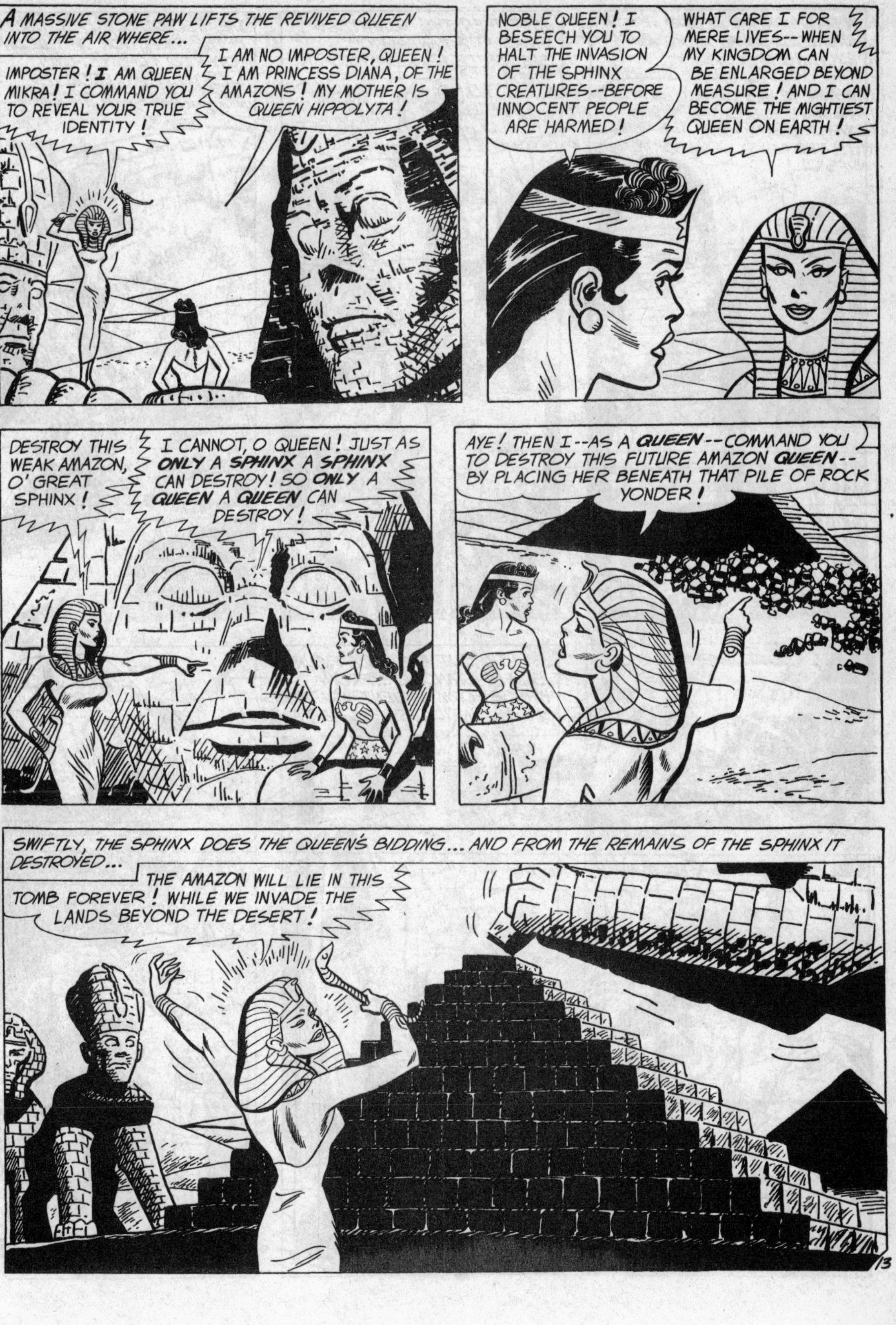
A MASSIVE STONE PAW LIFTS THE REVIVED QUEEN INTO THE AIR WHERE...
IMPOSTER! I AM QUEEN MIKRA! I COMMAND YOU TO REVEAL YOUR TRUE IDENTITY!
I AM NO IMPOSTER, QUEEN! I AM PRINCESS DIANA, OF THE AMAZONS! MY MOTHER IS QUEEN HIPPOLYTA!
NOBLE QUEEN! I BESEECH YOU TO HALT THE INVASION OF THE SPHINX CREATURES--BEFORE INNOCENT PEOPLE ARE HARMED!
WHAT CARE I FOR MERE LIVES--WHEN MY KINGDOM CAN BE ENLARGED BEYOND MEASURE! AND I CAN BECOME THE MIGHTIEST QUEEN ON EARTH!
DESTROY THIS WEAK AMAZON, O' GREAT SPHINX!
I CANNOT, O QUEEN! JUST AS ONLY A SPHINX A SPHINX CAN DESTROY! SO ONLY A QUEEN A QUEEN CAN DESTROY!
AYE! THEN I--AS A QUEEN--COMMAND YOU TO DESTROY THIS FUTURE AMAZON QUEEN--BY PLACING HER BENEATH THAT PILE OF ROCK YONDER!
SWIFTLY, THE SPHINX DOES THE QUEEN'S BIDDING... AND FROM THE REMAINS OF THE SPHINX IT DESTROYED...
THE AMAZON WILL LIE IN THIS TOMB FOREVER! WHILE WE INVADE THE LANDS BEYOND THE DESERT!
13

A NEW TOMB RISES FROM THE DESERT, WHILE THE DREAD FIGURES OF THE SPHINX CREATURES MARCH ON...

THE AMAZON IS FINISHED! NOW--ONWARD WITH THE INVASION!

AYE, O QUEEN! NOTHING CAN STOP US! FOR THE *SPHINX* THAT WOULD DESTROY *ME* IS *ITSELF* DESTROYED! AND THE *QUEEN* THAT WOULD HALT YOU--IS *HERSELF* DESTROYED!

INSIDE THE TOMB, **WONDER WOMAN** GRIMLY BATTLES TO OVERCOME HER NUMBNESS, BEFORE ALL THE OXYGEN IS EXHAUSTED!..

HERA HELP ME... FOR EVEN IF I DON'T KNOW *HOW* TO HALT THE INVASION OF THE SPHINX CREATURES... I MUST TRY SOMEHOW... FOR THE SAKE OF HUMANITY!

WITH TREMENDOUS EFFORT, THE PRISONER STANDS UP BETWEEN TWO HUGE ROCKS...

THESE ROCKS... SEEM TO SUPPORT THE WHOLE STRUCTURE... PERHAPS...?

CRAACK!

WITH A DESPERATE SURGE OF AMAZON STRENGTH, DIANA SENDS THE PILLAR-LIKE ROCKS FLYING... AND AS SHE DOES...

THANK HERA! I'M FREE OF THE TOMB! BUT--HOW CAN I BATTLE *SPHINXES*--WHO ONLY BY *SPHINXES*--CAN BE DESTROYED?

RRUMBLE!

SUDDENLY, **WONDER WOMAN** BEGINS RE-FORMING THE ROCKY RUINS, WITH URGENT SPEED...

THE EVIL SPHINX OF MIKRA--

--HAS GIVEN ME--

--THE SOLUTION TO ITS OWN RIDDLE!

/14

SHORTLY, THE PONDEROUS MARCH OF THE SPHINX INVADERS IS HALTED BY AN INCREDIBLE SIGHT!

SPHINXES OF THE DESERT! TURN BACK FROM YOUR INVASION!

THE SPHINX I DESTROYED RISES TO CHALLENGE ME AGAIN-- WITH A STRANGE VOICE! THIS TIME--ALL OF US WILL BATTLE IT--UNTIL IT IS TURNED TO DUST!

NOT SINCE THE SANDS OF THE DESERT WERE FIRST FORMED...

CRAAAACK!

ONLY A SPHINX A SPHINX CAN DESTROY--!

DID A BATTLE EXPLODE WITH SUCH FURY...

CRAAAACK!

AND THIS STRANGE SPHINX IN DESTROY-ING THE OTHERS...

AS MASSIVE CREATURES OF STONE, CRUMPLED INTO FRAGMENTS...

CRAACK!

--IS ITSELF DESTROYED!

/15

FROM THE RUINS OF THE SPHINX WHICH SHE HAD RE-FASHIONED, AND WHICH SHE HAD MANIPULATED FROM INSIDE, THE WEARY *WONDER WOMAN* EMERGES...

IT IS *HER* WORK! THE ROYAL AMAZON'S--WHO HAS THWARTED ME!

INSTANTLY, THE EVIL QUEEN LEAPS AT THE STARTLED AMAZON...

IF *ONLY* A *QUEEN* A *QUEEN* CAN DESTROY-- THEN *I* WILL METE OUT YOUR DOOM!

A FANTASTIC TRANSFORMATION TAKES PLACE... AS *WONDER WOMAN* GRIMLY STRUGGLES WITH A CREATURE OF EVIL THOUSANDS OF YEARS OLD... UNTIL...

SHADES OF PLUTO--

--SHE'S TURNING BACK INTO A MUMMY--

--INTO DUST!

JUSTICE TRIUMPHS, AS THE ROYAL AMAZON LEAVES THE SCENE OF THE MOST SENSATIONAL INVASION OF ALL TIMES!

NOTHING IS LEFT OF THE EVIL HERE... EXCEPT A HANDFUL OF DUST... AND FRAGMENTS OF ROCK...

LATER, WITH A RECOVERED STEVE, *WONDER WOMAN* LEAVES FOR HOME...

I THOUGHT THE PLANETS HELD MYSTERIES!

THERE IS MYSTERY ENOUGH HERE ON EARTH! AND WHO KNOWS WHEN ANOTHER WILL ASTOUND US!

The End

YOU WILL ALWAYS FIND FANTASTIC ADVENTURES IN EVERY ISSUE OF *WONDER WOMAN*!

116

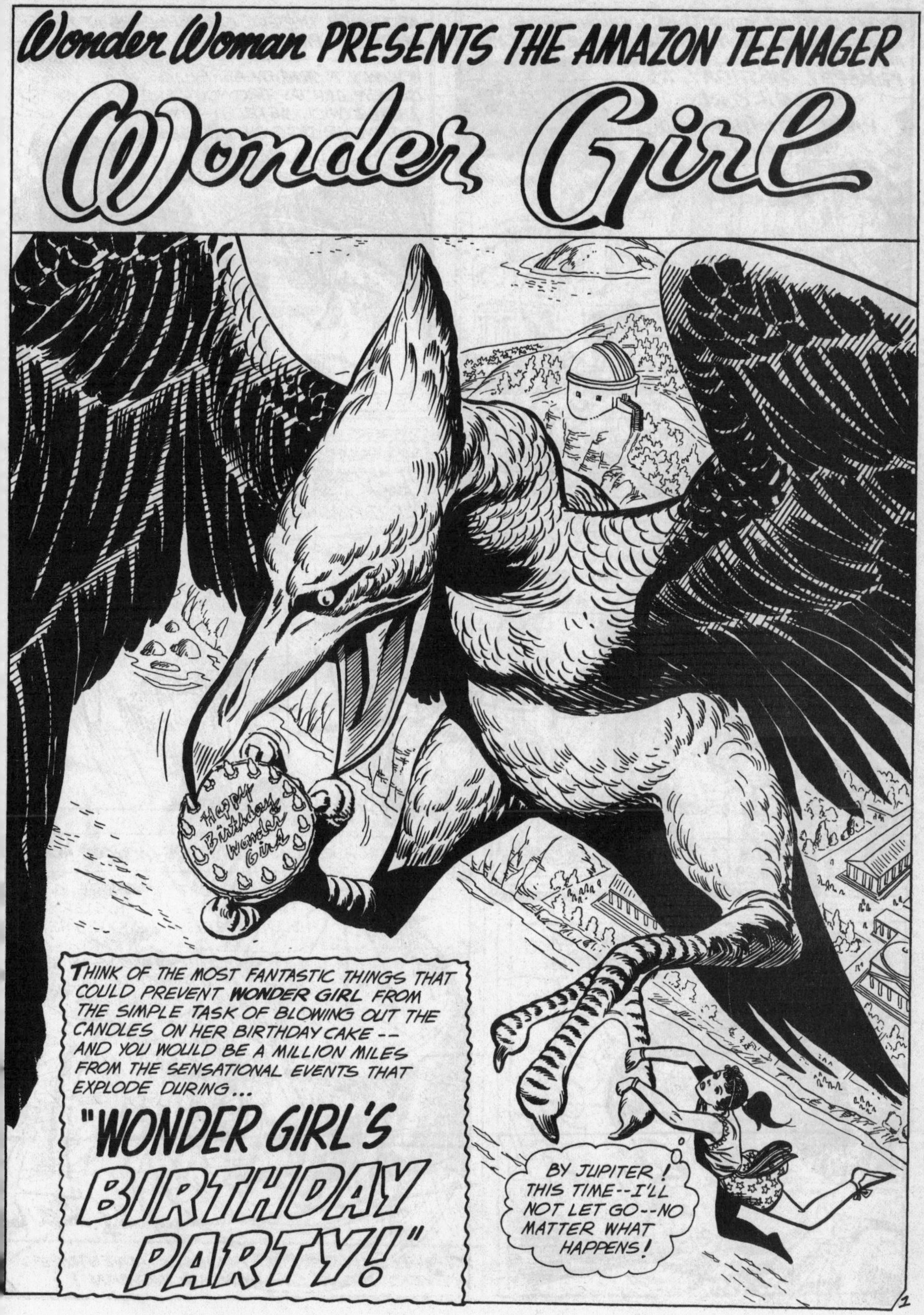
Wonder Woman PRESENTS THE AMAZON TEENAGER
Wonder Girl
Happy Birthday Wonder Girl
THINK OF THE MOST FANTASTIC THINGS THAT COULD PREVENT WONDER GIRL FROM THE SIMPLE TASK OF BLOWING OUT THE CANDLES ON HER BIRTHDAY CAKE -- AND YOU WOULD BE A MILLION MILES FROM THE SENSATIONAL EVENTS THAT EXPLODE DURING...
"WONDER GIRL'S BIRTHDAY PARTY!"
BY JUPITER! THIS TIME--I'LL NOT LET GO--NO MATTER WHAT HAPPENS!
1

AT THE OPEN AIR BANQUET HALL ON PARADISE ISLAND, SECRET ISLAND HOME OF THE AMAZONS...

♪ HAPPY BIRTHDAY TO WONDER GIRL-- HAPPY BIRTHDAY TO WONDER GIRL! ♪

AS QUEEN HIPPOLYTA GAZES FONDLY AT HER DAUGHTER, PRINCESS DIANA...

HOW TIME FLIES! IT SEEMS LIKE ONLY YESTERDAY THAT YOU WERE A BABE OF TWO--ABOUT TO BLOW OUT THE CANDLES ON YOUR SECOND BIRTHDAY!

WHAT WAS I LIKE, MOTHER?

"YOU WERE STANDING THERE, JUST LIKE YOU ARE NOW, YOUR LITTLE CHEEKS ALL PUFFED OUT, READY TO BLOW OUT THE TWO CANDLES FOR YOUR AGE, AND THE EXTRA ONE FOR GOOD LUCK ..."

BLOW HARD, DARLING!

"YOU SENT THE CAKE UP INTO THE AIR AS IF IT HAD BEEN CATAPULTED INTO SPACE FROM A ROCKET-LAUNCHING PLATFORM... UP IT FLASHED ...UP... UP... UP ..."

"YOU WERE ONLY TWO--BUT EVEN THEN-- YOUR STRENGTH WAS REMARKABLE ..."

VROOSH!

"WHEN THE BIRTHDAY CAKE VANISHED FROM SIGHT, IT WAS TRACKED BY THE AMAZON SPACE LABORATORIES..."

THERE IS THE CAKE, QUEEN HIPPOLYTA!

AMAZING!

MY CAKE! MY CAKE!

LOOK THROUGH HERE, DARLING--AND YOU SHALL SEE YOUR CAKE!

"YES--LONG BEFORE MAN LAUNCHED THE FIRST SATELLITE IN SPACE CONTAINING SCIENTIFIC INSTRUMENTS.. YOU, *WONDER GIRL*, HAD SENT UP THE ONLY BIRTHDAY CAKE IN HISTORY..."

AS THE AMAZON QUEEN FINISHES HER TALE, *WONDER GIRL* EXCITEDLY ASKS...

DID ANYTHING AS INTERESTING HAPPEN ON MY THIRD BIRTH-DAY, MOTHER?

SOMETHING REMARKABLE HAPPENED ON *ALL* YOUR BIRTHDAYS, *WONDER GIRL*! LET ME SEE....I CAN'T REMEMBER THE THIRD TOO CLEARLY...BUT--THE FOURTH...

"ON YOUR FOURTH BIRTHDAY, IT SEEMED AS IF NOTHING UNUSUAL WOULD HAPPEN..."

HAPPY BIRTHDAY TO WONDER GIRL...

BLOW OUT THE CANDLES, DARLING!

3

"BUT, BEFORE YOU COULD BLOW OUT THE CANDLES ON YOUR FOURTH BIRTHDAY CAKE, WONDER GIRL, THERE WAS AN OMINOUS, UNDERGROUND ROAR AND..."

CRAAACK!

EARTHQUAKE! EVERYONE OUT INTO THE OPEN-- BEFORE THE ROOF CAVES IN!

RRRRRUMBLE!

"I WAS ONE OF THE MANY AMAZONS STRUCK UNCONSCIOUS BY FALLING CHUNKS OF MARBLE... FALLING FROM THE CENTER OF THE CEILING..."

MOTHER--!

"I WAS TOLD BY EYE-WITNESSES THAT YOU UNHESITATINGLY CAUGHT A TOPPLING MARBLE PILLAR!"

R-RR-RRUMBLE!

"AND THAT WITH ASTONISHING INGENUITY, YOU USED IT TO SUPPORT THE MASSIVE CRACKING CEILING ...WHILE... "

CARRY OUT THE INJURED! HURRY!-- HURRY!

R-RRR RUMBLE

RRUMBLE!

THUNDERBOLTS OF JOVE! WONDER GIRL IS SACRIFICING HERSELF FOR US! HOW WILL SHE ESCAPE HERSELF-- WHEN SHE HAS TO LET GO OF THE PILLAR?

"BY THE TIME ALL THE INJURED AMAZONS HAD BEEN CARRIED TO SAFETY, I HAD REVIVED, AND SAW WITH MY OWN EYES HOW..."

"RRRR-RRRRUMBLE!"

SHADES OF PLUTO! *WONDER GIRL* IS PROTECTING HERSELF AGAINST THE COLLAPSING HALL WITH THE MASSIVE PILLAR AS A SHIELD!

"BUT, DESPITE YOUR STAGGERING FEAT, YOU WERE STILL A LITTLE GIRL..."

MY BIRTHDAY CAKE... MOTHER...IT...IT'S.. C-CRUSHED...I...I... C-COULDN'T S-SAVE IT--!

DON'T CRY, DIANA! WE'LL BAKE YOU ANOTHER!

"ON YOUR SIXTH BIRTHDAY, ONCE AGAIN YOU WERE ABOUT TO BLOW OUT THE CANDLES ON YOUR BIRTHDAY CAKE..."

I WONDER IF I'LL EVER BE ABLE TO BLOW OUT THE CANDLES ON MY BIRTHDAY CAKE WITHOUT SOMETHING HAPPENING, MOTHER?

WHAT CAN HAPPEN NOW, DIANA? GO RIGHT AHEAD, DARLING!

"I REMEMBER THE WAY YOU PUFFED OUT YOUR CHEEKS..."

MOTHER'S RIGHT! WHAT COULD HAPPEN NOW?

HAPPY BIRTHDAY TO *WONDER GIRL* ... HAPPY BIRTHDAY TO... ♫

"AND THEN, WITH AN EERIE WAILING..."

MY CANDLES--! WHAT BLEW THEM OUT?

WHOOOOOOOOOOOOOOOOOOO

5

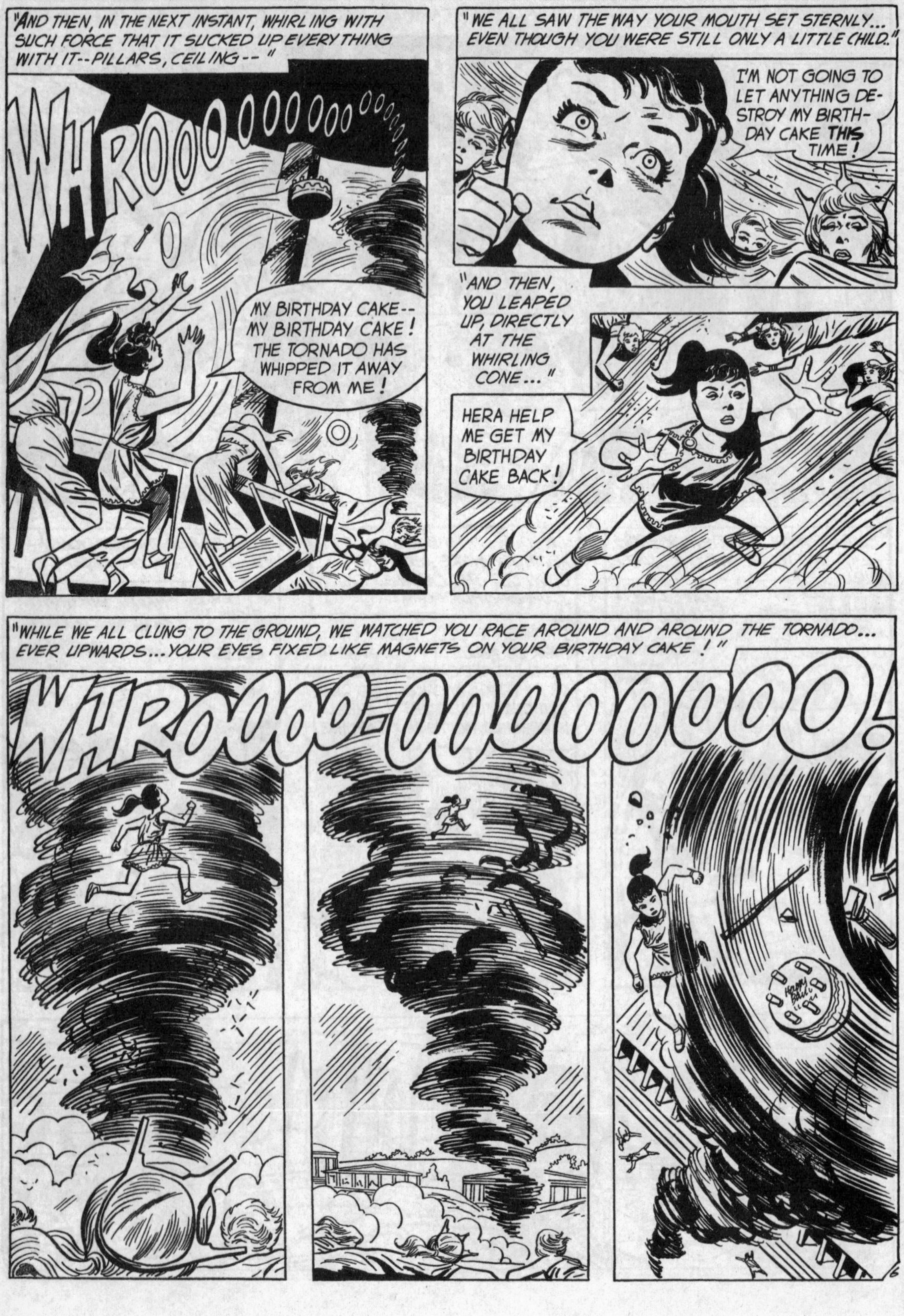
"AND THEN, IN THE NEXT INSTANT, WHIRLING WITH SUCH FORCE THAT IT SUCKED UP EVERYTHING WITH IT--PILLARS, CEILING--"
WHROOOOOOOOOOOOOOO
MY BIRTHDAY CAKE--MY BIRTHDAY CAKE! THE TORNADO HAS WHIPPED IT AWAY FROM ME!
"WE ALL SAW THE WAY YOUR MOUTH SET STERNLY... EVEN THOUGH YOU WERE STILL ONLY A LITTLE CHILD."
I'M NOT GOING TO LET ANYTHING DESTROY MY BIRTHDAY CAKE THIS TIME!
"AND THEN, YOU LEAPED UP, DIRECTLY AT THE WHIRLING CONE..."
HERA HELP ME GET MY BIRTHDAY CAKE BACK!
"WHILE WE ALL CLUNG TO THE GROUND, WE WATCHED YOU RACE AROUND AND AROUND THE TORNADO... EVER UPWARDS... YOUR EYES FIXED LIKE MAGNETS ON YOUR BIRTHDAY CAKE!"
WHROOOO-OOOOOOOOO!
6

"*ONLY* **YOU** *COULD HAVE SNATCHED YOUR BIRTHDAY CAKE FROM THE VERY GRIP OF THE TORNADO!...*"

THANK HERA-- I'VE GOT IT!

"*ONLY* **YOU** *COULD HAVE CAREFULLY RIDDEN THE AIR CURRENTS DOWN CLUTCHING YOUR PRECIOUS CAKE...*"

THE CAKE IS IN GOOD CONDITION! THE PARTY CAN GO ON NOW!

"*AND ONLY* **YOU**, *DARLING, AFTER SUCH A TREMENDOUS FEAT COULD HAVE STUMBLED INTO THE CAKE, AS YOU TOUCHED THE GROUND...*"

OH, MOTHER--LOOK WHAT I DID!

NEVER MIND, DIANA! WE'LL NEVER FORGET WHAT YOU DID DO TO WREST THE CAKE BACK FROM A TORNADO!

SQUISH!

AS THE QUEEN FINISHES HER TALE..

BUT NOTHING CAN STOP YOU NOW, **WONDER GIRL!** NO TORNADO -- NO EARTHQUAKE -- AND YOU'RE NOT GOING TO BLOW HARD ENOUGH TO SEND THE CAKE INTO ORBIT!

AT LAST!

BUT, AT THAT VERY MOMENT--A GIGANTIC TALON REACHES IN AND...

MY CAKE!

A GIANT ROC HAS STOLEN MY CAKE!

AS THE GARGANTUAN BIRD STARTS TO FLY AWAY, **WONDER GIRL** UNHESITATINGLY HURLS HERSELF UPWARD...

NO MATTER WHAT HAPPENS **THIS** TIME, I'M NOT GOING TO LET ANYTHING DESTROY MY BIRTHDAY CAKE!

BUT TO THE *TEEN-AGE AMAZON'S* DISMAY...

SUFFERING SAPPHO! THIS BEAST'S GOING TO EAT MY CAKE!

WITH ALL HER STRENGTH, **WONDER GIRL** HAULS DOWN SHARPLY ON THE GREAT ROC'S TALON...

I'VE GOT TO KEEP IT OFF BALANCE -- PREVENT IT FROM GOBBLING UP MY CAKE!

THE AMAZON TEEN-AGER TURNS THE HUGE BIRD TOPSY-TURVY BY HER DARING FEAT BUT...

GREAT HERA! IT DROPPED THE CAKE -- BEFORE I COULD CATCH IT! AND IT'S FALLING TOWARDS THE SEA!

8

GRIMLY, *WONDER GIRL* HURTLES AFTER THE CAKE, ONLY TO SEE IT PLUNGE STRAIGHT FOR A TUNNEL-LIKE MOUTH...

BY NEPTUNE'S TRIDENT! MY CAKE IS GOING TO DISAPPEAR INTO THAT WHALE'S MOUTH!

BY A DAZZLING SUMMERSAULT, THE TENACIOUS AMAZON TEEN-AGER MANAGES TO SEIZE HOLD OF THE WHALE'S HIGH TAIL...

HERA HELP ME YANK IT BACK-- BEFORE IT SWALLOWS MY CAKE!

AGAIN, BY A TREMENDOUS SURGE OF STRENGTH, *WONDER GIRL* USES A JUI-JITSU HOLD ON THE MONSTER OF THE DEEP AND...

WHERE'S THE CAKE?-- I DON'T SEE IT! PERHAPS--THE WHALE DROPPED IT--BEFORE IT HAD A CHANCE TO EAT IT!

BUT, AS THE YOUTHFUL AMAZON SEARCHES THE DEEP FOR IT, THE WHALE PLUNGES PAST...

SUFFERING SAPPHO! THERE'S THE MONSTER--WITH WHIP CREAM SMEARED ALL OVER ITS MOUTH! THERE'S NO GUESS-ING WHERE *THAT* CAME FROM!

LATER, *WONDER GIRL* RETURNS TO THE ISLAND OF THE AMAZONS, WHERE...

THIS IS ALL I COULD FIND THAT WAS LEFT OF MY BIRTHDAY CAKE, MOTHER!

NEVER MIND-- DARLING! THE FABULOUS FEATS YOU PERFORMED TO RESCUE YOUR CAKE WILL GO DOWN IN THE ANNALS OF THE AMAZONS!

The End

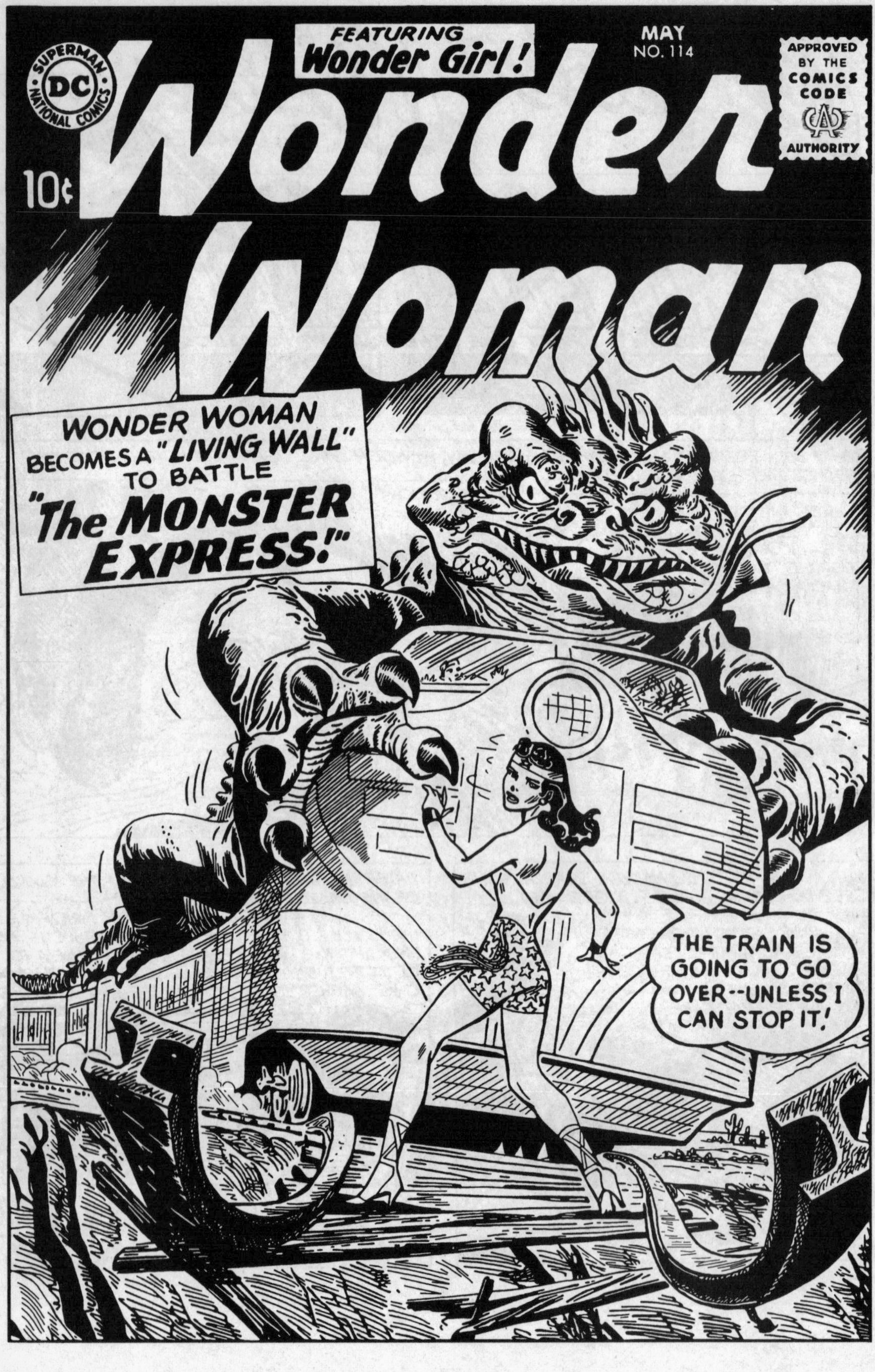
FEATURING
Wonder Girl!
MAY
NO. 114
SUPERMAN DC NATIONAL COMICS
APPROVED BY THE COMICS CODE AUTHORITY
10¢
Wonder Woman
WONDER WOMAN BECOMES A "LIVING WALL" TO BATTLE "The MONSTER EXPRESS!"
THE TRAIN IS GOING TO GO OVER--UNLESS I CAN STOP IT!

Wonder Woman

By Charles Moulton

WHAT IS REAL? AND WHAT ISN'T? ARE YOU SURE *YOU* CAN TELL? THEN JOIN *WONDER WOMAN*-- BEAUTIFUL AS APHRODITE--WISE AS ATHENA--STRONG AS HERCULES AND SWIFT AS MERCURY-- WHO BATTLES THE MOST FANTASTIC INVASION OF THE EARTH, IN THE SENSATIONAL *TWO-PART* ADVENTURE...

The MONSTER EXPRESS!

A TWO PART STORY! PART ONE · THE RUNAWAY BALLOONS!

HERA HELP ME STOP THIS TRAIN-- *BEFORE* IT PLUNGES TO DESTRUCTION!

AT A TOP SECRET MEETING AT MILITARY INTELLIGENCE... GEN. DARNELL SPEAKS TO HIS STAFF...

IT LOOKS LIKE OUR LISTENING POSTS-- ON 24 HOUR ALERT--ARE KEEPING ALL INTER-PLANETARY INVADERS AT A DISTANCE -- INCLUDING THAT WELL-KNOWN PHENOMENA -- THE FLYING SAUCERS!

COL. STEVE TREVOR AND LT. DIANA PRINCE DISCUSS THE MEETING...

AS THE GENERAL SAID-- WE CAN'T MAKE A MOVE-- UNLESS THEY DO!

LET'S HOPE THEY WON'T!

AN UNEVENTFUL MONTH PASSES--THEN...IN FRONT OF MILITARY INTELLIGENCE...

B-B-BUT I HAVE SOME WORK TO DO IN MY OFFICE, STEVE--!

IT CAN WAIT, DI! HOP IN! YOU DON'T WANT TO MISS WONDER WOMAN IN THE TRACY DAY PARADE, DO YOU?

AS THE COLONEL DRIVES OFF WITH HIS RELUCTANT PASSENGER...

I WONDER WHAT KIND OF GIANT BALLOONS THEY'RE GOING TO HAVE IN THE PARADE THIS TIME?

WONDER WOMAN WON'T BE IN THE PARADE, UNLESS I CAN SOMEHOW ESCAPE FROM STEVE-- BECAUSE I AM REALLY WONDER WOMAN-- IN MY SECRET IDENTITY!

AS THE TWO PAUSE FOR A TRAFFIC LIGHT...

LOOK AT THAT SCAFFOLD UP THERE-- IT'S ABOUT TO FALL!

THOSE TWO MEN CLINGING TO IT-- WILL PLUNGE TO THEIR DEATHS-- UNLESS SOMETHING WILL STOP THEM!

SUDDENLY...

YOU ARE, DI--I'M GOING TO TRY TO BREAK THOSE MEN'S FALL!

STAY WHERE

YOU CAN'T DO IT, STEVE! YOU'LL BE KILLED YOURSELF!

SWIFTER THAN THE HUMAN EYE CAN PERCEIVE, DI CHANGES INTO HER DUAL IDENTITY...

I CAN'T DO A THING AS DIANA PRINCE WITHOUT REVEALING THE SECRET OF MY DUAL IDENTITY!

SWIFTLY, THE AMAZON HURTLES OUT OF THE CAR JUST AS...

MERCIFUL MINERVA! STEVE'S BRAVERY WILL COST HIM HIS LIFE--UNLESS I CAN REACH HIM IN TIME!

AT THE EXACT MOMENT THAT STEVE IS GRAZED BY A TIP OF THE SCAFFOLD, *WONDER WOMAN* LEAPS UNDER IT AND...

IT'S WONDER WOMAN!

SHE SAVED OUR LIVES!

B-BUT STEVE'S BEEN HURT!

SWISH

ANXIOUSLY HURRYING TO STEVE'S SIDE...

ANGEL--IF I'M DREAMING-- DON'T LET ME WAKE UP!

YOU'RE ALL RIGHT...BUT YOU GAVE ME SUCH A SCARE!

THE CELEBRATED COUPLE CONTINUES A FEW MOMENTS LATER...

I GUESS DI WENT BACK TO THE OFFICE--WHEN SHE SAW YOU ON THE SCENE! SHE'S A NICE GIRL-- BUT I'D RATHER BE ALONE WITH YOU-- THAN TO HAVE HER TAGGING ALONG!

Hmm--SOME DAY I'LL TAKE THAT MATTER UP WITH YOU, MR. SMARTIE! WHEN I CAN REVEAL MY DUAL IDENTITY!

3

THE FAMOUS TOY PARADE THRILLS COUNTLESS WATCHERS WITH ITS GIGANTIC BALLOONS...

THESE TOY MONSTERS CERTAINLY LOOK REAL!

I'D SURE HATE TO RUN AGAINST THEM--EVEN IN A JET!

THE SENSATIONAL PROCESSION COMES TO A THUNDEROUS CLIMAX WITH THE QUEEN OF THE PARADE--THE MIGHTY AMAZON!

IN THIS WIND-- THEY NEED CARS TO HOLD THE OTHER GIANT BALLOONS STEADY! BUT-- WONDER WOMAN IS DOING IT ALL BY HERSELF!

THEY DON'T CALL HER WONDER WOMAN FOR NOTHING!

SUDDENLY...

VROOOOOO!

GREAT HERA! WHERE DID THIS WIND COME FROM?

THE NEXT MOMENT AS IF PROJECTED FROM A CATAPULT...

MERCIFUL MINERVA-- THIS HUGE BALLOON IS BEING DRAWN UPWARDS BY THE WIND--AS IF IT WERE A MERE STRAW--!

4

THE PARADE TURNS INTO AN AWESOME SPECTACLE OF CHAOS AS ONE GIGANTIC BALLOON AFTER ANOTHER WHIRLS SKYWARD...

WHOOOOOOOOOOOOOOOOOOOO

HELP!

HELP!

HELP!

WITHOUT HESITATION, THE HEROIC **WONDER WOMAN** INSTANTLY LETS GO OF THE ROPES HOLDING HER BALLOON EFFIGY AND...

SUFFERING SAPPHO! THAT TRUCKLOAD OF PEOPLE IS TEARING LOOSE TO ITS DOOM!

IN MID-AIR, THE MIGHTY AMAZON CATCHES THE FALLING TRUCK...

I'VE SAVED **ONE** TRUCK-- LOAD--BUT THERE ARE OTHERS!

HURRAY FOR **WONDER WOMAN**!

HOW CAN **WONDER WOMAN** SOLVE THIS DILEMMA?

END OF PART ONE OF THE **MONSTER EXPRESS**! THE EVEN MORE SENSATIONAL **PART TWO** CONTINUES ON THE PAGE FOLLOWING!

Wonder Woman

The MONSTER EXPRESS — PART TWO

As Wonder Woman's unique plane gently touches the ground, the incredible Amazon places *each* truckload of people down as lightly as if they were feathers...

THIS IS THE REAL CLIMAX OF THE PARADE!

NO ONE CAN EVER TOP *THIS* STUNT...

NOT EVEN WONDER WOMAN HERSELF!

STEVE HURRIES TO THE AMAZON'S SIDE AS SHE BOARDS HER PLANE AGAIN, AND AS IT ZOOMS UPWARDS...

YOU'VE SAVED EVERYONE! WHAT ARE YOU LOOKING FOR NOW, *WONDER WOMAN?*

THE RUNAWAY BALLOONS!

BUT, DESPITE AN EXHAUSTIVE SEARCH...

NOT A SINGLE TRACE OF THEM! I CAN'T UNDERSTAND IT!

WHY NOT? THAT TERRIFIC WIND MUST HAVE SCATTERED THEM OVER THE OCEAN-- OR SOMETHING!

THE NEXT FEW DAYS, WONDER WOMAN'S UNEASINESS CAUSES HER TO PATROL THE SKIES...UNTIL...

STEVE--DO YOU SEE WHAT I SEE?

IT'S ONE OF THE BALLOONS!

BUT, STEVE--IT'S BEEN MISSING FOR THREE WHOLE DAYS! WHAT COULD HAVE KEPT IT UP IN THE AIR FOR SO LONG?

IT'S NOT IMPOSSIBLE THAT IT'S BEEN DRIFTING ON ONE AIR CURRENT AFTER ANOTHER! AFTER ALL--IT *IS* A BALLOON--LIGHTER THAN AIR!

SUDDENLY, THE PLANE IS SEIZED IN A GIGANTIC BEAK!

STEVE--IS THIS A NIGHTMARE? OR--HAS THE BALLOON MONSTER COME ALIVE?

WE--WE MUST BE DREAMING! THIS CAN'T BE REAL--IT CAN'T BE!

IF THIS IS A DREAM--WHEN WILL IT END? THIS CREATURE IS FLYING AWAY WITH US!

I'M AFRAID--IT'S NO DREAM, *WONDER WOMAN!* THIS IS REALLY HAPPENING! HOW WILL WE EVER GET OUT OF ITS CLUTCHES! IT'S AS BIG AS A HOUSE!

THERE'S ONE CHANCE! PRAY HERA--IT WILL WORK! *PLANE--DIVE AT MAXIMUM SPEED!*

8

THOUGH THE ROBOT PLANE TWISTS AND TURNS AT **WONDER WOMAN'S** FRANTIC COMMANDS...

FASTER-- FASTER!

THIS CREATURE WON'T LET GO!

VROOSH!

I'LL HAVE TO TRY SOMETHING ELSE!

THIS TIME THE GRIM AMAZON SENDS HER PLANE INTO A HURTLING DIVE INTO A GORGE IN THE ROCKY MOUNTAIN BELOW HER ...

WHOOSH!

THE GORGE IS NARROWING! THERE WON'T BE ENOUGH ROOM FOR BOTH OF US!

WITH ANNIHILATING FORCE THE NARROWING WALLS OF THE GORGE DESTROYS THE STRANGE MONSTER AS ...

THAT'S WHAT I WAS HOPING BEFORE WE REACHED THE BOTTOM-- WHERE THE GORGE WIDENS OUT OVER THAT RIVER!

BLAAM

As WONDER WOMAN PILOTS HER PLANE OVER THE RIVER... TOWARDS THE GREAT DAM HOLDING ITS FROTHING WATERS BACK...

WHAT WAS THAT, ANGEL? IT DEFINITELY WAS ONE OF THE RUN-AWAY BALLOONS FROM THE PARADE! I KNOW-- I RECOGNIZED IT!

SO DID I, STEVE! BUT IT WAS A BALLOON WHICH BECAME ALIVE!

IT'S TOO FANTASTIC FOR WORDS! MAYBE IT'S ONE OF THOSE THINGS THAT HAPPENS IN A MILLION YEARS! FOR WHICH THERE IS REALLY **NO** EXPLANATION! ANYWAY-- IT'S OVER!

IS IT?

AS THE PERTURBED AMAZON SENDS HER PLANE SOARING OVER THE GREAT WALL OF THE DAM, A FANTASTIC SIGHT IS REVEALED...

SHADES OF PLUTO, ANOTHER MONSTER BALLOON ALIVE!

IT'S RIPPING THE WALL OF THAT DAM APART!

CRAACK!

INSTANTLY, WONDER WOMAN LEAPS ONTO THE WING OF HER PLANE, AND HURLS HER UNBREAKABLE LASSO AT THE CREATURE...

HERA HELP ME DRAG THAT BEAST AWAY--BEFORE IT DESTROYS THE DAM WALL!

THE MIGHTY AMAZON SUCCEEDS--BUT...

MERCIFUL MINERVA! IT'S TOO LATE! THE DAM'S BURST!

RRUMBLE!

AS A MIGHTY WAVE OF WATER ENGULFS THE CREATURE...

THE BEAST DOOMED ITSELF--BUT ALSO ALL THE TOWNS IN THE PATH OF THIS TERRIBLE WALL OF WATER!

VROOOOSH!

AT FLASHING SPEED, WONDER WOMAN HURLS HER PLANE TO A LANDING IN FRONT OF THE FIRST OF MANY VALLEY TOWNS...

EVACUATE THE TOWN, STEVE! ALERT EVERY-ONE!

THE WATER WILL BE HERE LONG BEFORE THE PEOPLE CAN FLEE! THERE'S NO GROUND HIGH ENOUGH AROUND HERE TO SAVE THEM!

YOU'RE NOT GOING TO STAY HERE--DIRECTLY IN THE PATH OF THE FLOOD? I WON'T LET YOU!

THERE'S A CHANCE-- A CHANCE--BUT I'VE GOT TO DO IT ALONE! PLEASE, STEVE! HURRY-- AND WARN THE PEOPLE!

AS MILLIONS OF TONS OF RELEASED WATER ROARS TOWARDS THE LONE AMAZON LIKE A GIGANTIC MOVING WALL--SHE BORES INTO THE GROUND AT INCONCEIVABLE SPEED!

PRAY HERA--

I'M--

--IN TIME!

AFTER ALERTING THE TOWNSPEOPLE, STEVE RUSHES BACK TO *WONDER WOMAN*, WHO WATCHES THE TORRENT POUR INTO THE ALMOST BOTTOMLESS WELL SHE HAS DUG...

NOW, *WONDER WOMAN!* THESE RUNAWAY MONSTER BALLOONS HAVE BEEN ANIMATED-- MADE CAPABLE OF DESTRUCTION! BUT WHO IS MASTER OF SUCH DIABOLICAL INVENTION?

NO QUESTION *THAT'S* WHAT WE HAVE TO FIND OUT, STEVE!

SHORTLY, FLASHING OVER THE DESERT, *WONDER WOMAN* IS HORRIFIED TO SEE...

LOOK!--ANOTHER BALLOON MONSTER TEARING UP THE TRACKS ACROSS THE CHASM!

AND THEN... ATTRACTED BY A FRANTIC TRAIN WHISTLE...

GREAT HERA! THERE COMES THE DESERT EXPRESS--WITH ANOTHER GIANT CREATURE ON ITS ROOF!

SENDING HER ROBOT PLANE WHIRLING OUT OF THE WAY, THE DAUNTLESS AMAZON LEAPS TOWARDS THE TWISTED TRACKS...

WONDER WOMAN-- WONDER WOMAN!

I'VE GOT TO TRY TO STOP THE EXPRESS-- BEFORE IT PLUNGES INTO THE CHASM!

SUMMONING POWER FAR BEYOND THE HUMAN MIND...

SCREEE!

WHILE HURLED OFF BY THE SUDDEN STOP...

THE MONSTER THAT WAS ON THE TRAIN--IS CATAPULTING INTO THE ONE TEARING UP THE TRACKS!

THE TWO GIGANTIC CREATURES MAUL EACH OTHER AS THEY HURTLE DOWN...

SHADES OF PLUTO! IT'S--IT'S A BATTLE TO THE DEATH--

WITH THE TRAIN PASSENGERS RESCUED FROM CERTAIN DEATH, WONDER WOMAN AGAIN CONTINUES HER SEARCH IN HER PLANE...

MERCIFUL MINERVA, STEVE! LISTEN TO THE REPORTS COMING IN OVER THE OMNI-WAVE SET!

THE THREAT OF THE MONSTER BALLOONS IS NATION-WIDE!

MONSTERS THREATEN CITIES... PLANES ATTACK FLYING CREATURES, SHIPS RAMMED BY GIGANTIC CREATURES!

AND THEN--MOST STRANGE OF ALL!

S-BOMB STOLEN FROM GREAT MESA LAB BY GIANT FIGURE WHICH NOW HAS THE POWER TO THREATEN THE WORLD! THIS CREATURE IS NONE OTHER THAN-- TZZZZ--NNNGGGG--!

13

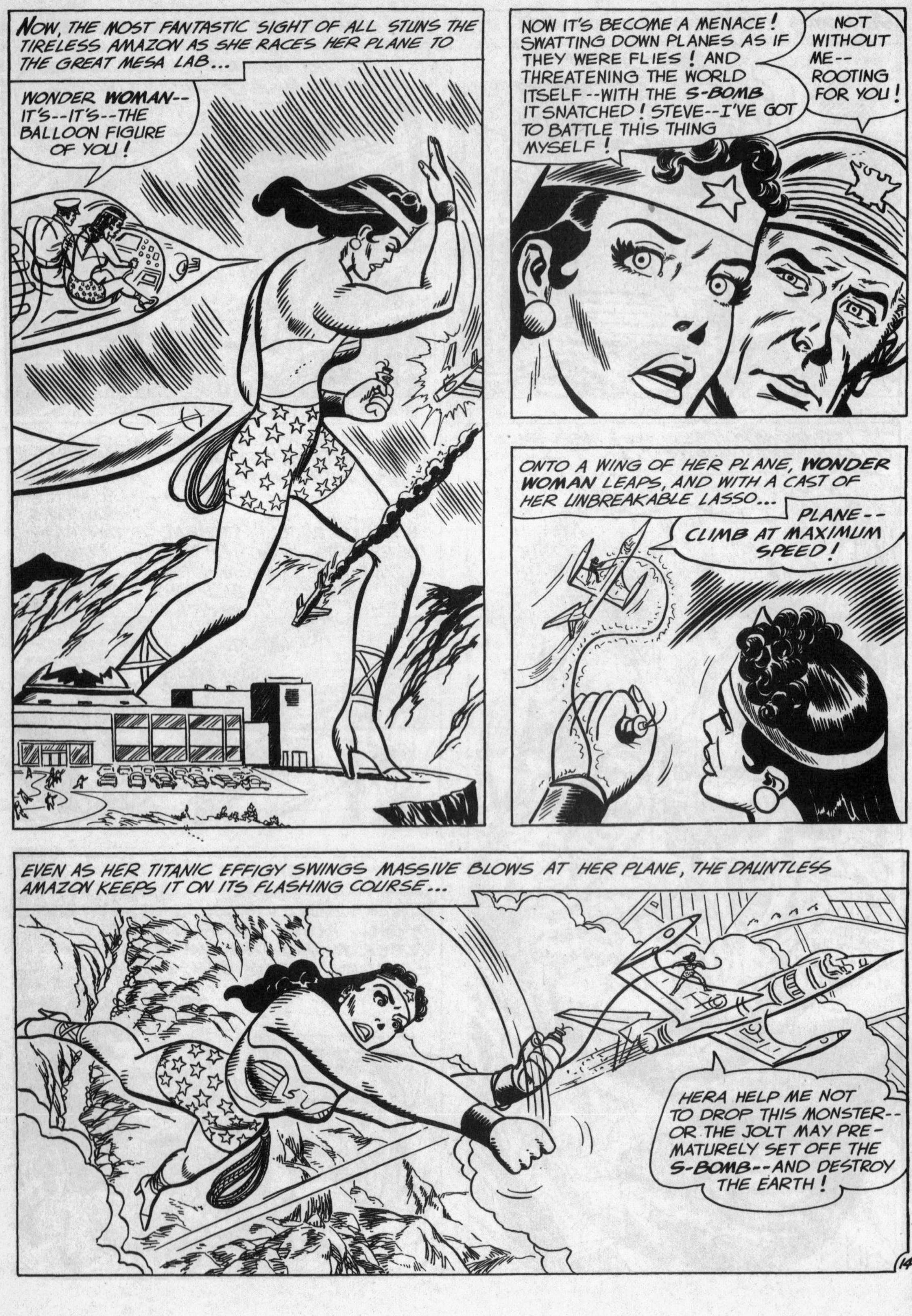
NOW, THE MOST FANTASTIC SIGHT OF ALL STUNS THE TIRELESS AMAZON AS SHE RACES HER PLANE TO THE GREAT MESA LAB...
WONDER WOMAN--IT'S--IT'S--THE BALLOON FIGURE OF YOU!
NOW IT'S BECOME A MENACE! SWATTING DOWN PLANES AS IF THEY WERE FLIES! AND THREATENING THE WORLD ITSELF--WITH THE S-BOMB IT SNATCHED! STEVE--I'VE GOT TO BATTLE THIS THING MYSELF!
NOT WITHOUT ME--ROOTING FOR YOU!
ONTO A WING OF HER PLANE, WONDER WOMAN LEAPS, AND WITH A CAST OF HER UNBREAKABLE LASSO...
PLANE--CLIMB AT MAXIMUM SPEED!
EVEN AS HER TITANIC EFFIGY SWINGS MASSIVE BLOWS AT HER PLANE, THE DAUNTLESS AMAZON KEEPS IT ON ITS FLASHING COURSE...
HERA HELP ME NOT TO DROP THIS MONSTER--OR THE JOLT MAY PREMATURELY SET OFF THE S-BOMB--AND DESTROY THE EARTH!
14

As WONDER WOMAN TOWS THE GIGANTIC CREATURE FAR ABOVE THE EARTH, SHE NEARS AN OMINOUS CIRCLE OF SPACE SHIPS...

IT'S THAT INFERNAL AMAZON! TRYING TO STOP OUR INVASION OF THE EARTH!

GREAT HERA-- THE FLYING SAUCERS ARE BEHIND ALL THIS!

MY PLAN TO FREE THE BALLOON CREATURES AND ANIMATE THEM TO DESTROY WILL SUCCEED-- ONCE WE ANNIHILATE WONDER WOMAN-- ALL SHIPS-- OPEN FIRE!

NEVER BEFORE HAS WONDER WOMAN BEEN SUCH AN EASY TARGET-- FIRE!!

BUT, THE GRIM AMAZON SENDS THE MASSIVE CREATURE HURTLING AHEAD OF HER LIKE A ROCKET FROM A LAUNCHING PLATFORM...

REGARDLESS OF WHAT HAPPENS TO US-- EARTH MUST BE SAVED FROM THOSE INVASION SHIPS! PLANE-- DIVE AT MAXIMUM SPEED! DIVE-- DIVE-- DIVE!

A TITANIC FLASH LIGHTS UP SPACE -- AS THE *S-BOMB* - CARRYING MONSTER CRASHES INTO THE INVADING FLYING SAUCERS WITH AN IMPACT WHICH SETS OFF THE BOMB...

WHRGOOM

EVEN THOUGH **WONDER WOMAN** HAS HURLED HER ROBOT PLANE DOWN AT INCREDIBLE SPEED, THE EFFECTS OF THE EXPLOSION SENDS IT OUT OF CONTROL...

HERA HELP ME REACH THE CONTROLS--

BEFORE--

WE CRASH!

FINALLY, HER INDOMITABLE WILL CARRIES THE MIGHTY AMAZON BACK INTO HER PLANE WHERE...

THAT EXPLOSION KNOCKED ME OUT--IF YOU HADN'T GOTTEN TO THE CONTROLS--?

IT'S ALL RIGHT NOW--EVERY-THING'S ALL RIGHT NOW!

VROOO

OOM!

DAYS LATER...

ISN'T THAT CUTE! LIKE ONE?

NO THANKS! I'VE HAD ENOUGH **BALLOONS** FOR A WHILE!

The End 16

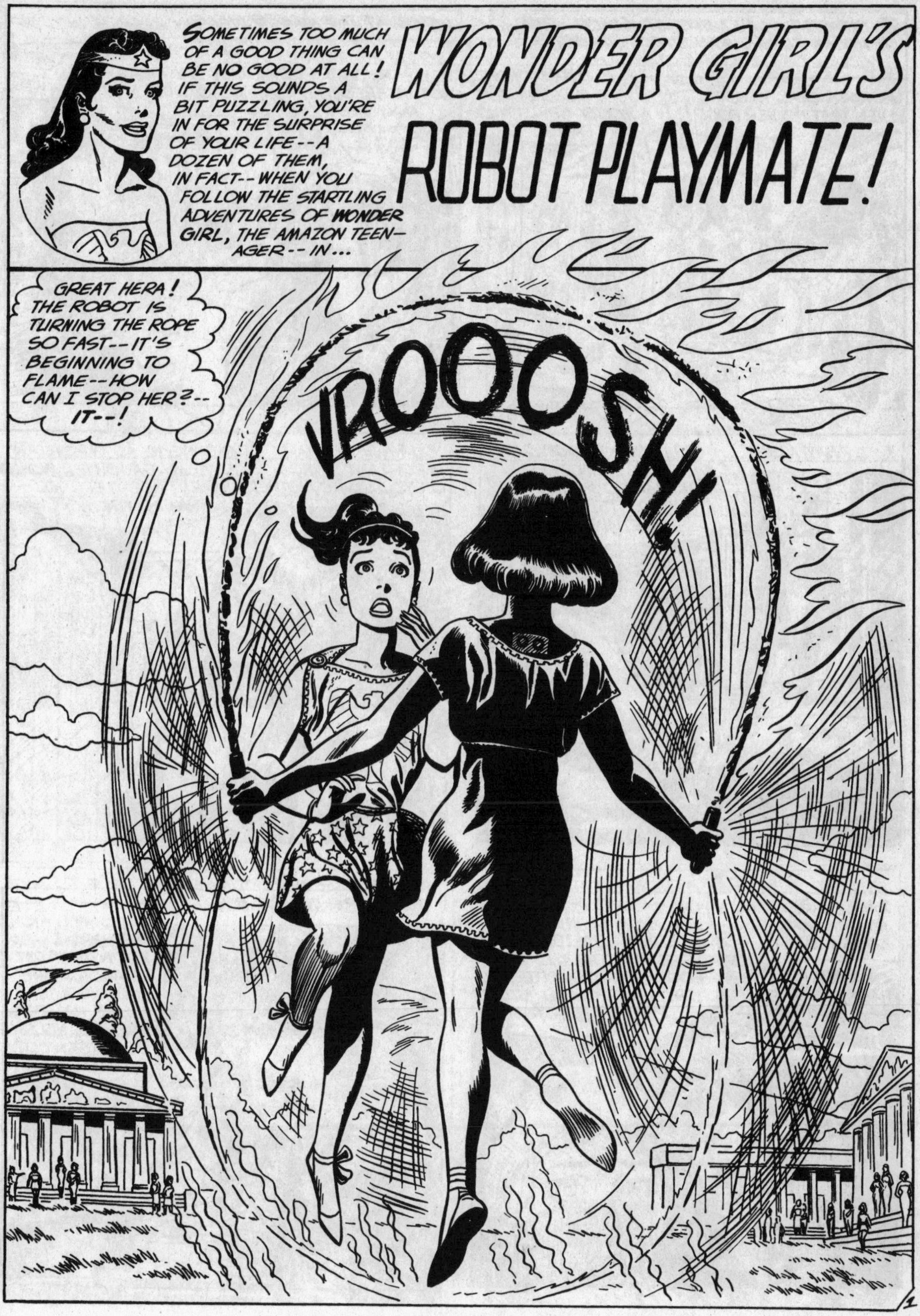
SOMETIMES TOO MUCH OF A GOOD THING CAN BE NO GOOD AT ALL! IF THIS SOUNDS A BIT PUZZLING, YOU'RE IN FOR THE SURPRISE OF YOUR LIFE--A DOZEN OF THEM, IN FACT--WHEN YOU FOLLOW THE STARTLING ADVENTURES OF WONDER GIRL, THE AMAZON TEEN-AGER--IN...
WONDER GIRL'S ROBOT PLAYMATE!
GREAT HERA! THE ROBOT IS TURNING THE ROPE SO FAST--IT'S BEGINNING TO FLAME--HOW CAN I STOP HER?--IT--!
VROOOSH!
1

ON PARADISE ISLAND, SECRET ISLAND HOME OF THE AMAZONS, QUEEN HIPPOLYTA GAZES ANXIOUSLY AT HER DAUGHTER...

WONDER GIRL IS NOT EVEN TASTING HER FOOD!

DO NOT WORRY, NOBLE QUEEN! IT IS A MOOD WHICH WILL PASS!

LATER, AT THE GAMES FIELD...

LOOK AT MY DAUGHTER NOW! THE GAMES DO NOT INTEREST HER ANYMORE!

PERHAPS SHE IS JUST DAYDREAM-ING, O'QUEEN!

LATE THAT NIGHT... STILL AWAKE, WONDER GIRL? TELL MOTHER WHAT IS TROUBLING YOU! MY HEART TELLS ME SOMETHING IS!

YOU HAVE SO MANY IMPORTANT THINGS ON YOUR MIND, MOTHER!

NOTHING IS AS IMPORTANT AS MY DAUGHTER, WONDER GIRL! NOW, TELL ME-- WHAT IS WRONG?

WELL...I...I WISH I HAD SOMEONE MY OWN AGE TO PLAY WITH!

BY HERA! YOU ARE THE ONLY CHILD IN THE KINGDOM OF THE AMAZONS! I DIDN'T REALIZE HOW LONELY IT MIGHT BE FOR YOU--DESPITE ALL THE GAMES AND STUDY PROVIDED FOR YOU!

AS WONDER GIRL TURNS HER FACE TO HIDE THE TEARS IN HER EYES...

IT--IT'S ALL RIGHT, MOTHER...I--I KNOW THAT ONLY AMAZONS ARE ALLOWED TO L-LIVE ON THIS ISLAND..NO ONE ELSE CAN COME HERE...EXCEPT FOR A VISIT... I--I KNOW TH--TH--THERE'S NOTHING YOU CAN DO ABOUT IT!

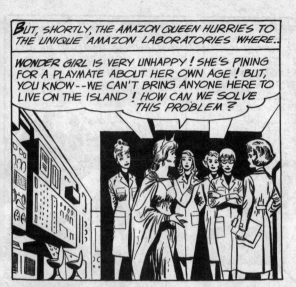

BUT, SHORTLY, THE AMAZON QUEEN HURRIES TO THE UNIQUE AMAZON LABORATORIES WHERE...

WONDER GIRL IS VERY UNHAPPY! SHE'S PINING FOR A PLAYMATE ABOUT HER OWN AGE! BUT, YOU KNOW--WE CAN'T BRING ANYONE HERE TO LIVE ON THE ISLAND! HOW CAN WE SOLVE THIS PROBLEM?

JUST LEAVE IT TO US, NOBLE QUEEN! WE HAVE SOLVED EVERYTHING FROM TIME-TRAVEL-- TO DECIPHERING THE LANGUAGE OF THE CAVEMEN! WE WILL CONCENTRATE ALL OUR EFFORTS ON HELPING WONDER GIRL TO BE HAPPY!

SOON, THE AMAZON PLANNING BOARD IS FILLED WITH THE MOST INTRICATE CAL- CULATIONS...

WHAT DO YOU THINK?

I THINK WE'VE GOT IT!

THEN--LET'S GET TO WORK!

NIGHT AND DAY LIGHTS BURN STEADILY IN THE AMAZON LABORATORIES WHERE THE MOST COM- PLEX PROBLEMS HAVE BEEN SOLVED...FINALLY...

WHAT'S IN THIS BOX, MOTHER?!

I DON'T KNOW, DARLING! IT WAS KEPT SECRET FROM ME, TOO!

JUST SAY-- "OPEN"-- PRINCESS DIANA!

AT THE TEEN-AGER AMAZON'S WORDS...

OPEN!

GREAT HERA-- LOOK, MOTHER!

A ROBOT GIRL!

SHE'LL MAKE A PERFECT PLAY- MATE FOR THE PRINCESS, NOBLE QUEEN! JUST AS IF SHE WERE A TWIN SISTER!

3

AS THE HAPPY WONDER GIRL LEAVES WITH HER ROBOT PLAYMATE...

YOU HAVE DONE WELL! MY WORRIES ABOUT MY DAUGHTER'S TROUBLES ARE OVER! ROBOT GIRL IS THE ANSWER TO OUR PROBLEM OF PROVIDING THE PERFECT PLAYMATE FOR HER!

IS SHE? WE SHALL SEE!

SHORTLY--ON THE GAME FIELD...

THIS IS THE GOLDEN BALL I GOT FOR A BIRTHDAY PRESENT, ROBOT GIRL! IT IS THE ONLY ONE OF ITS KIND! LET US PLAY WITH IT! HERE--CATCH!

CATCH!

VERY GOOD, ROBOT GIRL! NOW THROW IT BACK--AS HARD AND AS HIGH--AS YOU CAN!

HARD AND HIGH-- AS I CAN?

INSTANTLY, THE ROBOT GIRL RESPONDS WITH SUCH A TRE- MENDOUS TOSS THAT...

THUNDERBOLTS OF JOVE! SHE HAS THROWN THE GOLDEN BALL WITH SUCH FORCE-- THAT UNLESS I CAN STOP IT--IT WILL VANISH!

WHOOSH!

BUT EVEN THOUGH WONDER GIRL'S INCREDIBLE USE OF AIR CURRENTS HURLS HER LIKE A ROCKET--WITHIN REACH OF THE GOLDEN BALL...

SSSSSS!

GREAT HERA! ROBOT GIRL THREW THE BALL WITH SUCH FORCE--THAT FRICTION IS MELTING IT!

RUEFULLY, THE AMAZON TEEN- AGER RETURNS TO THE WAIT- ING ROBOT...

CATCH?

ER--NO--WE DON'T HAVE A BALL ANYMORE! BUT WE'LL FIND SOMETHING ELSE TO PLAY WITH!

④

SHORTLY, ALL SEEMS WELL AS WONDER GIRL AND ROBOT GIRL JUMP ROPE TOGETHER...

ISN'T THIS A BEAUTIFUL ROPE, ROBOT GIRL? IT IS WOVEN OUT OF THE HAIR OF AMAZONS! IT IS THE ONLY ONE OF ITS KIND! IT IS ANOTHER BIRTHDAY GIFT TO ME! LIKE IT?

LIKE IT!

YOU JUMP VERY WELL, ROBOT GIRL! NOW--IT IS YOUR TURN TO TURN THE ROPE!

TURN THE ROPE!

FASTER AND FASTER, ROBOT GIRL TURNS THE UNIQUE ROPE...

SHADES OF PLUTO!

SWIIIIISH!

UNTIL IT BEGINS TO SMOKE...

THE ROPE'S BURNING--!

VROOSH!

AND BEFORE WONDER GIRL CAN HALT ITS SCORCHING REVOLUTIONS THROUGH THE AIR..

TURNING TO CINDERS!

AND SO A SECOND GAME WITH THE ROBOT GIRL UNEXPECTEDLY ENDS IN DISASTER...

THE ROPE?

IT--IT'S GONE...BUT...DON'T WORRY.. I--I'LL FIND SOMETHING ELSE.... FOR US TO PLAY WITH!

A FEW MOMENTS LATER...

TELL YOU WHAT, ROBOT GIRL! JUMPING ROPE WAS--ER--"HOT" WORK! LET'S GO FOR A SWIM! WE CAN DIVE OFF THAT CLIFF THERE!

DIVE OFF THE CLIFF!

IS THIS THE END OF WONDER GIRL'S TROUBLES WITH HER NEWLY-MADE PLAYMATE? WE SHALL SEE!

LIKE BIRDS, THE TEEN-AGE AMAZON AND HER ROBOT PAL SOAR OFF THE CLIFF...

HOW GRACEFULLY YOU DIVE, *ROBOT* GIRL!

YOU DIVE GRACEFULLY, *WONDER* GIRL!

SILENTLY, THE TWO PLAYMATES SLIP BELOW THE GREEN WAVES...

ROBOT GIRL RESPONDS TO MY SPOKEN WORDS! BUT I DON'T KNOW WHETHER SHE CAN RESPOND TO MY THOUGHTS TOO WELL, THERE'S ONLY ONE WAY TO FIND OUT!

SWIFTLY AS A PORPOISE, *WONDER GIRL* DARTS AWAY FROM THE ROBOT...

LET'S PLAY "FOLLOW THE LEADER!" FOLLOW ME, ROBOT GIRL! FOLLOW ME!

AS WONDER GIRL CIRCLES A GIANT SEASHELL, SHE GLANCES BEHIND...

SUFFERING SAPPHO! A GIANT OCTOPUS IS GOING TO SEIZE ROBOT GIRL! LOOK OUT, ROBOT GIRL--LOOK OUT!

UNHESITATINGLY, THE VALIANT AMAZON TEEN-AGER HURLS HERSELF AT THE UNDERSEA BEAST...

I CAN'T COMMUNICATE WITH ROBOT GIRL UNDERWATER AS SHE RESPONDS ONLY TO THE VIBRATIONS OF MY VOICE! HERA HELP ME RESCUE HER!

GIANT TENTACLES WHIP AROUND *WONDER GIRL* AS SHE HURLS HERSELF AT THE EIGHT-ARMED CREATURE...

I CAN'T TELL ROBOT GIRL WHAT TO DO TO HELP -- I'LL HAVE TO FREE HER-- WITHOUT ANY HELP!

LIKE A HUMAN DRILL, THE YOUTHFUL AMAZON INSTANTLY BORES THROUGH THE BOTTOM OF THE SEA...

EVERYTHING DEPENDS ON THE OCTOPUS *NOT* LETTING GO OF ME!

WHAT IS *WONDER GIRL'S* DESPERATE PLAN? WE SHALL SEE!

6

WITH AN IRRESISTIBLE LUNGE, *WONDER GIRL* LEAVES THE GRIP OF THE TENTACLES AND.

THANK HERA-- IT WORKED! THE OCTOPUS' TENTACLES ARE STUCK INSIDE THE ROCKY SEA-BED!

AS THE AMAZON TEEN-AGER BORES THROUGH THE BOTTOM AGAIN...SHE IS SEIZED BY ANOTHER TENTACLE...

THE OCTOPUS MUST BE ENRAGED! IT'S USING THREE TENTACLES NOW TO CAPTURE ME!

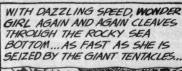

WITH DAZZLING SPEED, *WONDER GIRL* AGAIN AND AGAIN CLEAVES THROUGH THE ROCKY SEA BOTTOM...AS FAST AS SHE IS SEIZED BY THE GIANT TENTACLES...

AND SHE EMERGES WITH EQUAL RAPIDITY, LEAVING BEHIND HER...

SEVEN OF THE EIGHT TENTACLES HELD FAST-- ONE MORE TO GO!

AS THE INFURIATED MONSTER LASHES OUT AT THE AGILE AMAZON TEEN-AGER...

PRAISE BE TO NEPTUNE! THE OCTOPUS HAS LET GO OF THE ROBOT GIRL TO TRY TO CATCH ME!

LEAVING THE CREATURE STRUGGLING TO FREE ITSELF FROM HER INGENIOUS TRAP, *WONDER GIRL* ROCKETS UPWARDS WITH HER ROBOT PAL...

WHEW! THAT WAS A NARROW ESCAPE! I'M GOING RIGHT BACK TO PARADISE ISLAND WITH ROBOT GIRL BEFORE SOMETHING ELSE HAPPENS!

HAS WONDER GIRL SEEN THE LAST OF THE SURPRISES BROUGHT ABOUT BY HER UNIQUE PLAYMATE -- WHAT DO YOU THINK?

(7)

As WONDER GIRL emerges from the water with her robot playmate...

WHAT A RARE SPECIES OF BUTTERFLY! JUST WHAT I'VE BEEN LOOKING FOR--FOR MY COLLECTION!...STAY HERE--ROBOT GIRL--WHILE I GO AFTER IT!

AGAIN SKILLFULLY "RIDING" THE AIR CURRENTS, WONDER GIRL IS ALMOST WITHIN REACH OF HER BRILLIANTLY--COLORED PRIZE, WHEN...

SUFFERING SAPPHO! ROBOT GIRL'S DIVING BACK INTO THE SEA!

INSTANTLY, ABANDONING THE CHASE, THE AMAZON TEEN-AGER PLUMMETS DOWNWARD...

HERA ALONE KNOWS WHAT TROUBLE SHE IS HEADING FOR NOW!

BUT, AS WONDER GIRL DIVES BENEATH THE WAVES, SHE IS STARTLED TO SEE...

WHY--IT--IT'S THE MERBOY! HE--HE HAS HIS ARM AROUND ROBOT GIRL! IT WAS HE WHO MUST HAVE CALLED HER!

SADLY, THE TEEN-AGE AMAZON NOTES...

THEY'RE SOARING OUT OF THE WATER! WHAT A BEAUTIFUL COUPLE THEY MAKE--HOW GRACEFUL!

AND WHEN WONDER GIRL EMERGES FROM THE WATER, A STILL GREATER BLOW AWAITS HER!

HE--HE'S KISSING HER!

8

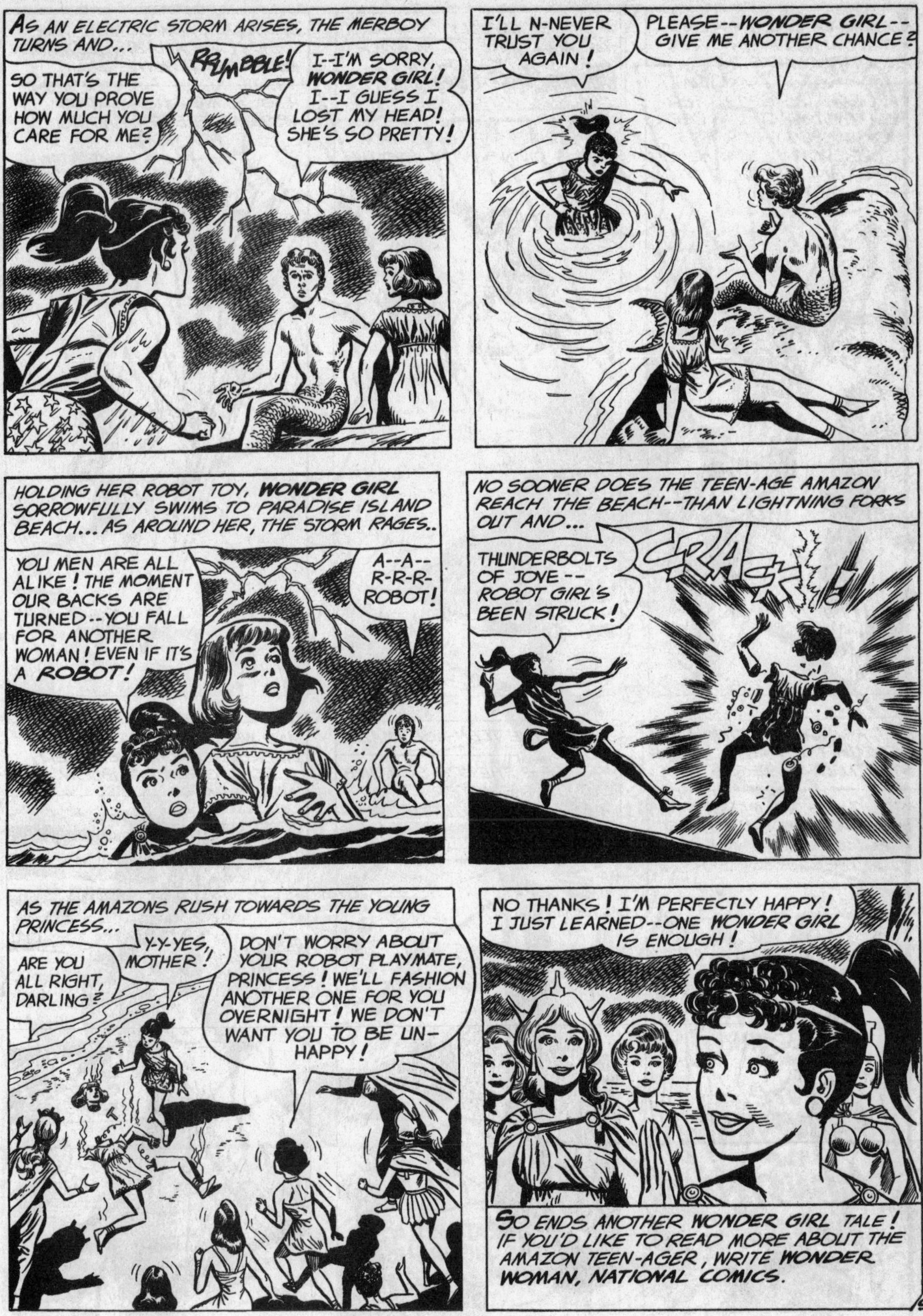
AS AN ELECTRIC STORM ARISES, THE MERBOY TURNS AND...
RRUMBBLE!
SO THAT'S THE WAY YOU PROVE HOW MUCH YOU CARE FOR ME?
I--I'M SORRY, WONDER GIRL! I--I GUESS I LOST MY HEAD! SHE'S SO PRETTY!
I'LL N-NEVER TRUST YOU AGAIN!
PLEASE--WONDER GIRL--GIVE ME ANOTHER CHANCE?
HOLDING HER ROBOT TOY, WONDER GIRL SORROWFULLY SWIMS TO PARADISE ISLAND BEACH... AS AROUND HER, THE STORM RAGES..
YOU MEN ARE ALL ALIKE! THE MOMENT OUR BACKS ARE TURNED--YOU FALL FOR ANOTHER WOMAN! EVEN IF IT'S A ROBOT!
A--A--R-R-R-ROBOT!
NO SOONER DOES THE TEEN-AGE AMAZON REACH THE BEACH--THAN LIGHTNING FORKS OUT AND...
THUNDERBOLTS OF JOVE--ROBOT GIRL'S BEEN STRUCK!
CRACK!
AS THE AMAZONS RUSH TOWARDS THE YOUNG PRINCESS...
ARE YOU ALL RIGHT, DARLING?
Y-Y-YES, MOTHER!
DON'T WORRY ABOUT YOUR ROBOT PLAYMATE, PRINCESS! WE'LL FASHION ANOTHER ONE FOR YOU OVERNIGHT! WE DON'T WANT YOU TO BE UN-HAPPY!
NO THANKS! I'M PERFECTLY HAPPY! I JUST LEARNED--ONE WONDER GIRL IS ENOUGH!
SO ENDS ANOTHER WONDER GIRL TALE! IF YOU'D LIKE TO READ MORE ABOUT THE AMAZON TEEN-AGER, WRITE WONDER WOMAN, NATIONAL COMICS.
9

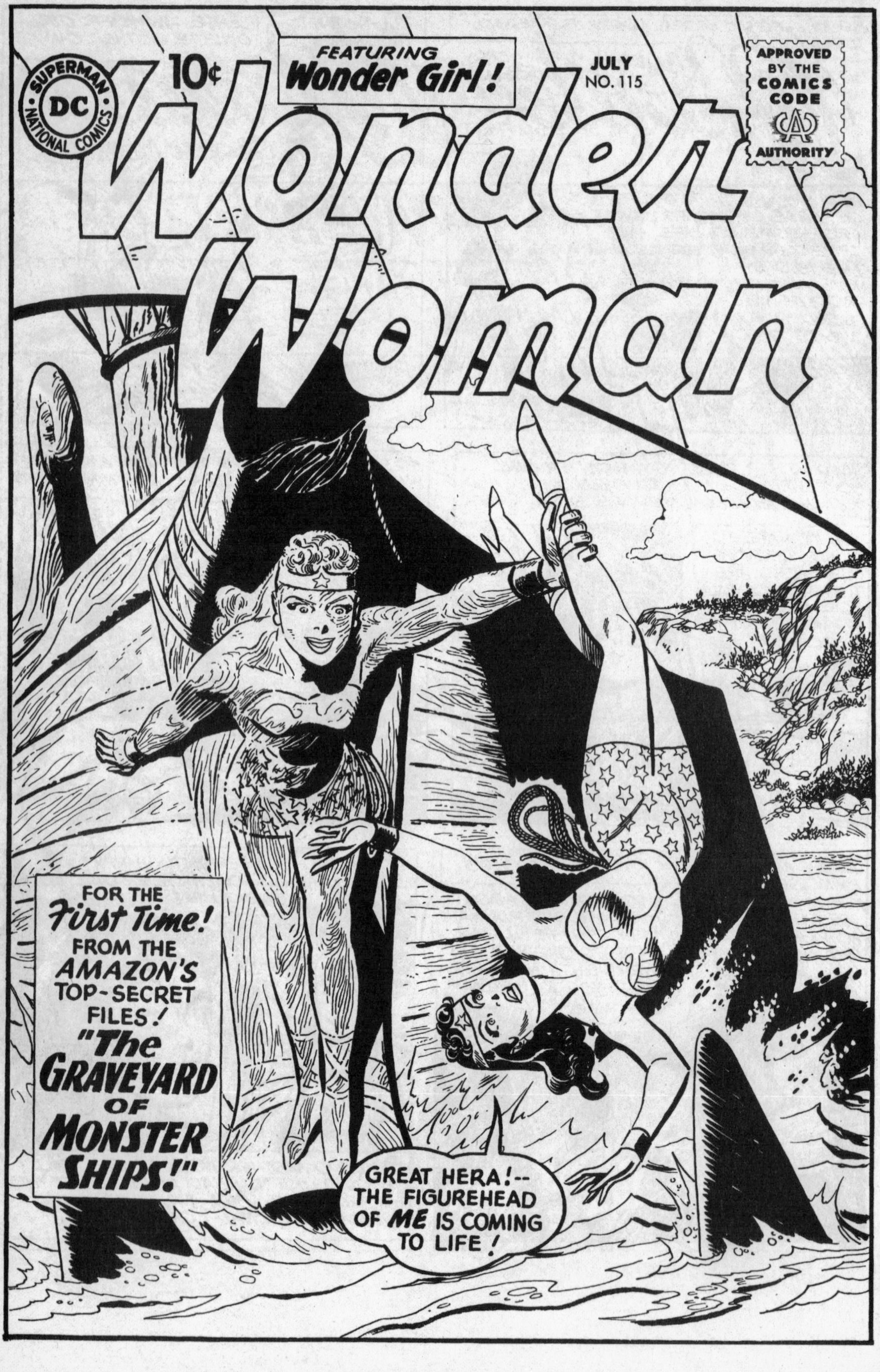
SUPERMAN DC NATIONAL COMICS
10¢
FEATURING Wonder Girl!
JULY NO. 115
APPROVED BY THE COMICS CODE AUTHORITY
Wonder Woman
FOR THE First Time! FROM THE AMAZON'S TOP-SECRET FILES! "The GRAVEYARD OF MONSTER SHIPS!"
GREAT HERA!-- THE FIGUREHEAD OF ME IS COMING TO LIFE!

Wonder Woman

By Charles Moulton

HOW CAN A WOODEN FIGUREHEAD OF HERSELF--CARVED CENTURIES AGO--COME TO LIFE AND THREATEN WONDER WOMAN? THIS IS ONLY THE FIRST OF MANY BAFFLING RIDDLES WHICH CONFRONT WONDER WOMAN WHEN SHE VISITS THE ...

GRAVEYARD OF MONSTER SHIPS!

IN A TRENCH AT THE BOTTOM OF ONE OF THE SEVEN SEAS, LIE MANY SHIPS WHICH HAVE SUNK THERE OVER THE CENTURIES...

SUDDENLY, A SHIFTING OF THE UNDERSEA CURRENT SENDS THESE GHOST SHIPS FROM MANY LANDS, FROM ANCIENT EGYPT, TO COLONIAL NEW ENGLAND, TO THE SURFACE...

AND *THERE* THEY ARE HELD FAST BY IMPRISONING SEAWEED, THEIR FANTASTIC FIGURE-HEADS STARING SIGHTLESSLY AT THE LIGHT OF DAY-- SEA SERPENTS, DRAGONS, EVEN ONE OF *WONDER WOMAN* HERSELF !

WHAT EFFECT WILL THIS STRANGE EVENT HAVE ON THE LIFE OF *WONDER WOMAN?* WE SHALL SEE !

MEANWHILE, AT A MOUNTAIN HIDEOUT, GANG-LAND CHIEFS STARE AT THE HUGE ROBOT THAT *ANGLE MAN,* THE CRIMINAL MASTER-MIND DISPLAYS ...

SO THAT'S WHAT YUH DID WITH THUH MILLION BUCKS WE GAVE YUH TO BEAT *WONDER WOMAN* WITH ? YUH BUILT A DOLL TUH PLAY WITH !

THIS "DOLL" IS A MECHANICAL BRAIN ! IT CAN *ANIMATE* ANY INANIMATE OBJECT ! IT WILL BEAT *WONDER WOMAN !* BECAUSE ONCE YOU GIVE IT AN ORDER-- *NOTHING* CAN STOP IT FROM CARRYING IT OUT !

THE ANGRY GANGLAND CHIEFS CHALLENGE *ANGLE MAN'S* STATEMENT...

YEAH? IF YOUR MECHANICAL BRAIN CAN ANIMATE *ANYTHIN'*--LET'S SEE IT MAKE A *CLUB* OUT'VE THIS *CIGAR* THAT'LL BEAT US OVER OUR HEADS!

--ALL BY ITSELF!

THE CRIMINALS MOCK THE INFAMOUS INVENTOR AS...

ALL YOU HAVE TO DO IS PUNCH THE COMMAND ON THIS MASTER CONTROL BOARD -- AND NOTHING CAN STOP IT--

HA! HA! HA!

LIGHTS FLASH--FROM INSIDE THE MAZE OF ELECTRONIC WIRES A HUMMING IS HEARD...

MMM MMM MMM M!

I BETTER SMOKE MY CIGAR BEFORE THAT PUNCH-DRUNK DOLL UP THERE GRABS IT AWAY FROM ME--! HA! HA! THAT THING MAY NOT WORK AGAINST *WONDER WOMAN*-- BUT IT'S GOOD FOR A MILLION BUCKS WORTH O' LAUGHS!

HA! HA! HA!

SUDDENLY, A STRANGE BEAM OF LIGHT FROM THE MECHANICAL BRAIN SEEMS TO TURN THE GANGSTER'S CIGAR INTO...

LOOK OUT--MY CIGAR'S GONE CRAZY!

THUD!

IT'S BECOME A FLYIN' CLUB!

STOP THAT THING, *ANGLE MAN*-- STOP THAT THING!

THUD!

THE DIABOLICAL CRIMINAL INVENTOR PRESSES "STOP" ON THE MECHANICAL BRAIN AND...

OKAY--OKAY--YUH CONVINCED US, ANGLE MAN! HOW'RE YUH GONNA BEAT WONDER WOMAN--SO SHE WON'T BE IN OUR WAY--EVERYTIME WE TRY TUH START A CRIME WAVE?

THE ARCH-SCHEMER HOLDS OUT A NEWSPAPER CLIPPING...

THIS STORY GIVES ME AN IDEA!

WONDER WOMAN TO EXPLORE GRAVEYARD OF ANCIENT SHIPS!

YEAH--MY LITTLE PAL, ANIMOX, AND I, ARE GOING TO PLAY A LITTLE JOKE ON WONDER WOMAN--A LAST LAUGH ON THAT BLASTED AMAZON!

SHORTLY, ANGLE MAN TAKES OFF IN HIS PRIVATE PLANE WITH HIS OMINOUS COMPANION...

WONDER WOMAN DOESN'T KNOW IT-- BUT HER MOMENTS ARE NUMBERED!

WHAT EFFECT WILL THIS STRANGE EVENT HAVE ON THE LIFE OF THE AMAZON? WE WILL SEE!

MEANWHILE, AT MILITARY INTELLIGENCE, LT. DIANA PRINCE MAKES A LIGHTNING CHANGE INTO HER SECRET IDENTITY OF WONDER WOMAN...

TIME TO FLY OVER TO THE GRAVEYARD OF SHIPS --AND GATHER DATA ON THEM FOR OUR RECORDS!

ON THE ROOF OF THE BUILDING, AS THE AMAZON PRINCESS SUMMONS HER ROBOT PLANE...

HOLD IT, ANGEL! I'VE BEEN ORDERED TO GO WITH YOU! NICEST ORDER I EVER "VOLUNTEERED" FOR! I'VE GOT FULL FROGMAN EQUIPMENT FROM EXPLOSIVES TO OXYGEN!

OH, STEVE-- YOU'RE-- YOU'RE IM-POSSIBLE!

④

WITH AN EFFORTLESS LEAP, *WONDER WOMAN* BOARDS THE AMAZON PLANE THAT RESPONDS ONLY TO THE VIBRATIONS OF HER OWN VOICE...

YOU CERTAINLY DON'T WASTE TIME ON A TAKE-OFF, SWEETHEART!

I WANT TO INVESTIGATE THE GRAVEYARD OF SHIPS, AND RETURN AS SOON AS POSSIBLE, STEVE! I'VE A LOT OF FAN MAIL TO ANSWER!

AS THE AGILE AMAZON TAKES OVER THE CONTROLS...

SO MANY READERS HAVE ASKED ME TO START A CLUB WHERE THEY CAN SEND LETTERS TO, THAT FROM NOW ON, I WILL ANSWER ALL LETTERS, AS SOON AS I CAN, IF THEY ARE SENT TO

Wonder Woman's Clubhouse, % National Comics.

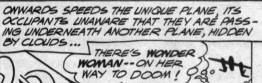

ONWARDS SPEEDS THE UNIQUE PLANE, ITS OCCUPANTS UNAWARE THAT THEY ARE PASSING UNDERNEATH ANOTHER PLANE, HIDDEN BY CLOUDS...

THERE'S *WONDER WOMAN*--ON HER WAY TO DOOM!

REMAINING FAR ABOVE, AND OUT OF SIGHT, ANGLE MAN GLOATS...

I DIDN'T HAVE TO LOOK FOR HER! ALL I HAD TO DO WAS WAIT ABOVE THE GRAVEYARD OF SHIPS SHE WAS GOING TO INVESTIGATE!.. SHE'S STARTING TO LAND RIGHT NOW!

SETTING HIS PLANE ON AUTOMATIC PILOT, THE CRIMINAL SETS THE MAZE OF ELECTRONIC WIRES IN THE MECHANICAL BRAIN IN MOTION.

D-E-S-T-R-O-Y W-O-M-A-N B-Y A-N-I-M-A-T-I-N-G...

CLICK! CLICK! CLICK!

BACK IN HIS SEAT, ANGLE MAN OPENS AN EXIT PANEL ...

OUT YOU GO, ANIMOX! TO DESTROY WONDER WOMAN BY A METHOD WHICH WILL BE A NIGHTMARE TO HER--HER LAST!

THROUGH THE AIR HURTLES THE SINISTER MECHANICAL BRAIN...

INTO THE SEA...

SPLASH!

AND DOWN TO THE DEPTHS...

THUD!

ONLY FISH ARE STARTLED BY THE FAINT HUMMING OF THE FOREST OF WIRES INSIDE **ANIMOX**, AND THE BALEFUL LIGHTS FLASHING ON AND OFF IT...

MMMMMM   MMMM

HOW CAN THIS SINISTER MECHANICAL BRAIN LYING AT THE BOTTOM OF THE SEA DESTROY WONDER WOMAN? WE SHALL SEE!

MEANWHILE, **WONDER WOMAN** HAS LANDED HER PLANE NEAR THE GRAVEYARD OF SHIPS AND...

I'LL GO AHEAD WHILE YOU FINISH PUTTING ON YOUR SKIN-DIVING GEAR!

OKAY, ANGEL! I'LL CATCH UP TO YOU IN A MINUTE!

AS THE AMAZON NEARS THE FLOTILLA OF SHIPS THAT HAD BEEN RAISED FROM THE BOTTOM BY A QUIRK OF SEA CURRENTS...

SHADES OF PLUTO! THERE'S THE AMAZON SHIP WITH A FIGUREHEAD OF ME ON IT! THE ONE MOTHER SAID SHE AND OTHER AMAZONS HAD TO ABANDON DURING A STORM!

AS **WONDER WOMAN** GLANCES TOWARD HER COMPANION...

STEVE!--STEVE!--THIS WAY! LOOK WHAT I'VE FOUND!

SUDDENLY, THE STARTLED AMAZON FINDS HER ANKLE SEIZED...

WH-WHAT'S HAPPENING TO ME?

THE NEXT MOMENT, AS IF SHE WERE IN A NIGHTMARE, **WONDER WOMAN** FINDS HERSELF DANGLED IN THE AIR BY...

MERCIFUL MINERVA! SOMETHING HAS ANIMATED THE FIGUREHEAD-- BROUGHT IT TO LIFE!

INCREDIBLE INDEED IS THE FANTASTIC SPECTACLE WHICH HORRIFIES THE CAPTIVE AMAZON...

ALL THE FIGURE- HEADS HAVE COME TO LIFE! ONE IS MENACING STEVE! STEVE-- STEVE-- LOOK OUT!

BUT, WONDER WOMAN'S WARNING COMES TOO LATE AS...

FLAP- FLAP- FLAP!

SUFFERING SAPPHO! STEVE HAS BEEN CAPTURED BY THAT FLYING FIGURE- HEAD!

DROPPED MY TNT! CAN'T FIGHT THIS THING!

WITH A POWER BORN OUT OF ANGUISH, THE AMAZON HURLS HERSELF DOWNWARD...

I'VE GOT TO SHAKE THIS THING'S GRIP!

CRACK!

SPLASH!

INTO THE DEPTHS THE EERIE STRUGGLE CONTINUES, WITH THE ANIMATED FIGURE- HEAD RETAINING ITS DEATH GRIP ON WONDER WOMAN...

THAT LOOKS LIKE A MECHANICAL BRAIN ON THE BOTTOM! IT'S OPERATING STILL! I HEAR IT! THAT LIGHT FLASH- ING FROM IT-- STRAIGHT TOWARD THE FIGUREHEAD --MUST BE ANIMATING IT!

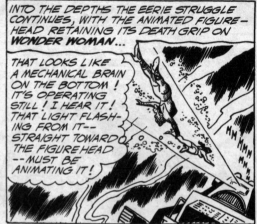

DESPERATELY THE AGILE AMAZON HURLS HER WOODEN NEMESIS AT THE SINISTER MACHINE WITH ALL HER STRENGTH...

HERA HELP ME SMASH THE FIGUREHEAD AND THE ROBOT BRAIN AT THE SAME TIME-- SO I CAN FIND OUT WHO'S BEHIND ALL THIS!

TO WONDER WOMAN'S DISMAY...

THE FIGUREHEAD'S SMASHED TO BITS! BUT, THIS ELECTRONIC VILLAIN ISN'T EVEN SCRATCHED!

BANG!

6

REMOVING HER BRACELETS, MADE OF AMAZONIUM, HARDEST METAL KNOWN...

THE ONLY WAY I CAN DE-ANIMATE THOSE FIGURE-HEADS AND SAVE STEVE--IS TO DEMOLISH THIS FIENDISH MACHINE WHICH IS ANIMATING THEM!

VIBRATING HER BRACELETS AGAINST THE ELECTRONIC BRAIN WITH A FORCE GREATER THAN ANY DRILL...

MY BRACELETS ARE SMOKING WITH THE TREMENDOUS HEAT THEY'RE EXERTING! THIS MACHINE SHOULD MELT SOON!

BRRRANG!

BUT, TO WONDER WOMAN'S DISMAY...

IT DIDN'T WORK! IT'S A CASE OF THE IRRESISTIBLE FORCE MEETING THE IMMOVABLE OBJECT! A STALEMATE! THE METAL DEFIES HEAT! I'LL HAVE TO TRY SOMETHING ELSE!

MMM!

AS A SINKING SHAPE CATCHES THE ANXIOUS AMAZON'S EYE..

STEVE'S FROGMAN GEAR! HE MUST HAVE DROPPED IT IN HIS EFFORTS TO FREE HIMSELF FROM THE FIGURE-HEAD WHICH CAPTURED HIM! STEVE MAY HAVE PROVIDED ME WITH THE MEANS OF DISMANTLING THIS MECHANICAL MONSTER!

A FEW MOMENTS LATER... WONDER WOMAN ATTACHES A TIME FUSE TO...

THE POWERFUL EXPLOSIVES IN STEVE'S EQUIPMENT SHOULD DESTROY THIS BALEFUL THING!

AT TOP SPEED THE MIGHTY AMAZON SPEEDS AWAY, WHILE BEHIND HER, WITH A RENDERING ROAR...

WHAAAM

THUNDER-BOLTS OF JOVE! THAT BLAST SHOULD MEAN THE END OF THAT MECHANICAL BRAIN!

HAS WONDER WOMAN FINALLY WON? WE SHALL SEE! 9

WONDER WOMAN'S DISMAY MOUNTS AS AFTER THE TITANIC EXPLOSION...

MERCIFUL MINERVA! NOT ONLY IS THAT ROBOT BRAIN ABSOLUTELY INTACT-- BUT IT'S ANIMATING ALL THE FIGURE-HEADS AFTER ME!

PLUNGING TOWARDS THE METAL MONSTER, THE PERPLEXED AMAZON SCOOPS IT UP...

I NEED TIME--TIME-- TO TRY TO FIGURE OUT HOW TO COMBAT THIS MENACE! BUT I DON'T HAVE TIME-- WITH THOSE WOODEN CREATURES PURSUING ME!

OUT OF THE WATER WONDER WOMAN LEAPS, CLUTCHING HER NEMESIS TO HER...

I'LL TAKE IT UP IN MY PLANE WITH ME--OUT OF THE REACH OF THOSE NIGHT-MARISH FIGURES--!

BUT EVEN AS THE ROBOT PLANE ZOOMS UPWARD AT HER COMMAND...

THEY'RE STILL FOLLOWING ME --TO DESTROY ME--AND THEY WILL --AS LONG AS THIS ELECTRONIC ANIMATOR ISN'T DESTROYED!

DESPERATELY, WONDER WOMAN EXAMINES THE INSTRUMENT PANEL...

THERE'S NO DOUBT THAT WHOEVER BUILT THIS MECHANICAL BRAIN--GAVE IT A COMMAND WHICH IT WILL CARRY OUT UNTIL--UNTIL WHAT? WHAT?

10

FROM HIS PLANE IN THE CLOUDS HIGH ABOVE, THE RUTHLESS ANGLE MAN SEES WONDER WOMAN'S DILEMMA...

I FIGURED EVERY ANGLE! THE AMAZON IS FINISHED! AND WITH HER FINISH-- A GREAT NEW CRIME WAVE WILL START!

BUT, THE MASTER CRIMINAL DOES NOT SEE THE AMAZON'S SUDDEN MOVE...AS SHE WORKS THE MECHANICAL BRAIN'S INSTRUMENT PANEL..

CLICK! CLICK! CLICK! CLICK! CLICK!

PRAY HERA I AM RIGHT--OR...

THE NEXT MOMENT, THE MAZE OF MACHINERY HUMS, LIGHTS FLASH ON AND OFF... AND WITH A SUDDEN SURGE...

IT WORKED--IT WORKED! I GAVE A NEW ORDER TO THE MECHANICAL BRAIN! TO ANIMATE ITSELF AND THE FIGUREHEADS INTO MISSILES--AND FLY INTO SPACE! MY NEW ORDER COUNTER-MANDED THE ORIGINAL ORDER! NOW TO LOOK FOR STEVE--AND THE VILLAIN WHO PLANNED ALL THIS!

WHIRROOOSH!

AS THE AMAZON STARES IN AMAZEMENT, THE ANIMATED MECHANICAL BRAIN AND THE FIGUREHEADS, HURTLE THROUGH THE CLOUDS AND...

CRASH!

THUNDERBOLTS OF JOVE! THEY'VE STRUCK A PLANE IN THOSE CLOUDS! A FIGURE IS TUMBLING OUT OF IT! PRAY HERA I CAN CATCH IT!

AND SO, AN IRONIC FATE TUMBLES THE DAZED CRIMINAL INTO THE ARMS OF HIS INTENDED VICTIM!

ANGLE MAN! SO YOU'RE BEHIND THIS PLOT!

YOU'VE BEATEN ME, WONDER WOMAN! MY INVENTION-- MY ANIMOX-- WILL BE LOST IN SPACE--AND EVEN NOW, THE FIGURE-HEADS IT ANIMATED ARE TURNING TO FLAME FROM THE FRICTION!

NO SOONER DOES *WONDER WOMAN* PLACE THE PRISONER ABOARD THAN ANOTHER HURTLING OBJECT ATTRACTS HER GAZE...

MERCIFUL MINERVA! IT'S STEVE! THE FIGUREHEAD WHICH SEIZED HIM-- MUST HAVE DROPPED HIM FROM A GREAT HEIGHT--WHEN IT CEASED TO BE ANIMATED! PRAY HERA-- TO GUIDE MY THROW!

THE AMAZON'S CAST UNERRINGLY BRINGS STEVE TO HER...

THANK HERA FOR HIS OXYGEN MASK! IF IT WEREN'T FOR THAT-- HE MIGHT NOT HAVE REACHED ME ALIVE!

INSIDE THE PLANE, THE LOVELY AMAZON REVIVES STEVE...

IF THIS IS A DREAM... DON'T LET ME... WAKE UP...

THE END.

Wonder Woman
By Charles Moulton

Dear Readers! THIS IS **WONDER WOMAN** SPEAKING! IN ANSWER TO AN AVALANCHE OF MAIL, HERE'S ANOTHER STORY OF MY ADVENTURES AS **WONDER GIRL**, THE AMAZON TEENAGER--WITH MY FRIEND, THE **MER-BOY**! IT ALL STARTED WHEN HE ASKED ME TO A PARTY, AND I REFUSED! FOR THE STARTLING REASON WHY, AND THE EVEN MORE STARTLING ADVENTURES THAT FOLLOWED, HERE IS THE ASTONISHING TALE OF...

MER-BOY'S UNDERSEA PARTY!

HERA HELP ME OVERTURN THIS GIGANTIC SEA TURTLE--AND MAKE IT RELEASE THE MER-BOY--OR HE'LL NEVER REACH HIS PARTY!

ON PARADISE ISLAND, SECRET ISLAND HOME OF THE AMAZONS, QUEEN HIPPOLYTA SMILES FONDLY AT HER DAUGHTER AS...

I CAN HARDLY WAIT UNTIL I GROW UP TO BE A WONDER WOMAN, MOTHER-- AND PERFORM GREAT FEATS TO HELP PEOPLE IN PERIL!

ONE CANNOT BECOME A WONDER WOMAN JUST BY GROWING OLDER, WONDER GIRL! YOU MUST FIRST MAKE YOURSELF FIT--WITH STUDY--AND EXERCISE! ISN'T IT TIME FOR YOUR FIRST LESSON OF THE DAY?

SHORTLY, IN THE AMAZON LANGUAGE CLASS-ROOM, WHERE ALL LANGUAGES PAST AND FUTURE ARE TAUGHT...

HOW DO YOU SAY "HELLO" IN CAVEMAN?

IN FRENCH?

IN SPANISH?

IN MARTIAN?

OGGNNG UNH!

BON JOUR!

BUENOS DIAS!

BEEPEREEPERUU!

IN THE MIDDLE OF THE DAY ON A CLIFF OVER-LOOKING THE SEA...

TODAY, WONDER GIRL, I'M TESTING YOU FOR THE LENGTH OF TIME YOU'RE ABLE TO REMAIN IN THE AIR, BY GLIDING ON THE UP AND DOWN AIR CURRENTS! YOU MUST STAY UP AT LEAST THIRTY MINUTES TO PASS! GO!

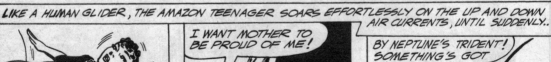

LIKE A HUMAN GLIDER, THE AMAZON TEENAGER SOARS EFFORTLESSLY ON THE UP AND DOWN AIR CURRENTS, UNTIL SUDDENLY..

I'VE GOT TO PASS THIS TEST!

I WANT MOTHER TO BE PROUD OF ME!

BY NEPTUNE'S TRIDENT! SOMETHING'S GOT HOLD OF MY ANKLE!

THE UNEXPECTED WEIGHT ON HER ANKLE SURPRISES HER SO, THAT THE AMAZON TEEN-AGER TOPPLES INTO THE SEA...

Ohhh--! WHATEVER PULLED ME DOWN-- MADE ME FAIL THE TEST!

SPLASH!

BELOW THE WAVES, **WONDER GIRL** GLARES AT A SMILING FACE...

GREETINGS, WONDER GIRL! I WAS LOOKING ALL OVER FOR YOU! I HAVE SOMETHING VERY IMPORTANT TO ASK YOU!

ANGRILY, THE TEENAGE AMAZON SLIPS OUT OF THE **MER-BOY'S** GRASP...

I WANTED TO ASK YOU--?

I DON'T CARE WHAT YOU WANTED TO ASK ME! YOU MADE ME FAIL THE TEST!

WONDER GIRL'S POWERFUL KICK CREATES AN UNDER-WATER WAKE WHICH ENGULFS THE **MER-BOY**...

*I CAN'T WASTE TIME PLAYING GAMES WITH YOU, MER-BOY! I HAVE TO SPEND EVERY MOMENT TRAIN-ING TO BECOME A **WONDER WOMAN**--IF I'M TO HELP PEOPLE IN PERIL! NO MATTER WHAT THE THREAT! OR WHERE IT COMES FROM!*

BUT I'M UGG--ULP--?!

MOMENTS LATER, AS THE YOUNG AMAZON GLANCES BACK...

GREAT HERA! A GIANT SHARK'S RACING TOWARD MER-BOY!

AS WONDER GIRL RACES BACK TOWARDS THE RAZOR-TOOTHED KILLER OF THE DEEP, SHE SNATCHES HER AMAZON LASSO FREE...

SUFFERING SAPPHO! THE MONSTER JUST STRUCK MER-BOY! ANOTHER BLOW MIGHT FINISH HIM! AND I'M STILL TOO FAR AWAY TO HELP HIM!

AT LIGHTNING SPEED, *WONDER GIRL* HURLS HER LASSO AT THE ATTACKING SHARK ... JUST AS IT SURGES TOWARDS THE *MER-BOY* AGAIN...

THANK HERA--I'VE STOPPED THE CREATURE IN TIME!

JUST THEN, THE TEENAGE AMAZON BECOMES AWARE OF AN OMINOUS SHAPE BEHIND HER...

SUFFERING SAPPHO! A GIANT OCTOPUS! IF I WASTE TIME TRYING TO ESCAPE ITS CLUTCHES-- THE SHARK WILL ATTACK THE UNCONSCIOUS *MER-BOY* AGAIN! IF I DON'T--THE OCTOPUS WILL SEIZE ME! HOW CAN I SOLVE *BOTH* THREATS AT THE SAME TIME?

WITH SPLIT-SECOND TIMING, THE QUICK-THINKING *WONDER GIRL* CATAPULTS THE SHARK INTO THE HOVERING OCTOPUS...

WHILE THESE TWO SEA BEASTS ARE OCCUPIED WITH EACH OTHER--

THUD!

--I'LL BRING *MER-BOY* TO THE SURFACE AND SEE HOW BADLY HURT HE IS!

ONTO A NEARBY HULK OF CORAL JUTTING OUT OF THE WATER, THE YOUNG AMAZON CARRIES *MER-BOY*...

MER-BOY--SPEAK TO ME, PLEASE? I DIDN'T MEAN TO HURT YOUR FEELINGS BY NOT LISTENING TO YOU! BUT--I WAS ANGRY BECAUSE YOU ACCIDENTALLY MADE ME FAIL MY TEST! *MER-BOY-- SPEAK TO ME?*

JUST THEN, THE KEEN-EYED *WONDER GIRL* PERCEIVES...

WHY YOU--YOU UNDERSEA FAKER! YOU WERE MAKING BELIEVE YOU WERE UNCONSCIOUS!

HOW ELSE CAN I GET YOU TO HOLD ME IN YOUR ARMS?

INSTANTLY, THE IRATE YOUNG AMAZON HURLS HERSELF ON AN UPWARD DRAFT...

WONDER GIRL! STOP! YOU KNOW I CAN'T "FLY" THE WAY YOU DO! LOOK! I WANT YOU TO WEAR MY SEASHELL FRATERNITY PIN--AND GO TO AN UNDERWATER PARTY WITH ME NEXT WEEK! *WONDER GIRL--PLEASE--* COME BACK!

I NEVER WANT TO SEE YOU AGAIN!

BUT, *WONDER GIRL* DOESN'T STOP UNTIL SHE ALIGHTS ON THE CLIFF SHE HAD TAKEN OFF FROM...

YOU'LL NEVER GROW UP TO BE A WONDER WOMAN, PRINCESS--UNLESS YOU STOP WASTING TIME PLAYING GAMES WITH THE MER-BOY!

I WASN'T PLAYING GAMES! OH-- WHAT'S THE USE OF EXPLAINING!

ALL THAT DAY, AND EVEN IN HER ROYAL CHAMBER, *WONDER GIRL* VOWS...

I WON'T LET MER-BOY DISTRACT ME FROM MY TRAINING --NO MATTER WHAT HE DOES!

MEANWHILE, IN THE MERMEN WORLD BELOW THE SEA...

WHY DON'T YOU CALL FOR YOUR GIRL FRIEND *WONDER GIRL*--AND JOIN US FOR A RIDE AND A SHRIMP-BURGER?

SOME OTHER TIME! I'VE GOT A LOT OF THINKING TO DO!

NEPTUNE HELP ME FIGURE OUT A WAY TO MAKE *WONDER GIRL* MY FRIEND AGAIN--OR SHE WON'T GO TO THE PARTY WITH ME!

AS DAY AFTER DAY WENT BY, MER-BOY'S FRIENDS TEASE HIM...

I THOUGHT YOU SAID WONDER GIRL WAS GOING TO WEAR YOUR FRATERNITY PIN?

SHE **WILL** WEAR MY PIN--AND SHE **WILL** GO TO THE PARTY WITH ME! NOW, LEAVE ME ALONE-- I TOLD YOU I'VE GOT A LOT OF THINKING TO DO!

TO THE SURFACE THE **MER-BOY** SWIMS...

WISH I WERE A FLYING FISH--SO I COULD FLY OVER **PARADISE ISLAND** AND PERSUADE **WONDER GIRL** TO GO WITH ME TO THE PARTY! BUT I'M NOT A FLYING FISH-- AND BY AMAZON LAW-- NO MAN IS ALLOWED TO SET FOOT ON THE ISLAND AND THAT INCLUDES ME!

AND ON THE ISLAND, THE TEENAGE AMAZON SMILES AS SHE TRAINS TO EVENTUALLY BECOME A **WONDER WOMAN**...

MER-BOY'S CUTE--BUT AS LONG AS I REMAIN **ON PARADISE ISLAND**--HE CAN'T BOTHER ME! HA! HA!

BUT, THE NEXT DAY, AS WONDER GIRL AND HER MOTHER DINE OUTSIDE THE PALACE...

MOTHER--WHY IS EVERYONE GIGGLING?

RANA-- WHAT IS THE JEST?

LOOK UP IN THE SKY, NOBLE QUEEN!

EVEN THE QUEEN BREAKS OUT INTO LAUGHTER AS...

HOW CLEVER OF MER-BOY TO STRING FLYING FISH TOGETHER INTO A MESSAGE FOR YOU!

HE--HE'S MAKING A LAUGHING STOCK OF ME! I'VE GOT TO STOP HIM!

WONDER GIRL UNFAIR TO MER-BOY! SHE'S BREAKING HIS HEART BY REFUSING TO WEAR HIS PIN AND GO TO THE DANCE WITH HIM

6

ONTO AN UPDRAFT *WONDER GIRL* LEAPS INDIGNANTLY...

EVERYONE'S LAUGHING AT ME! I'VE GOT TO STOP MER-BOY!

CATCHING THE STRING WHICH GUIDES THE FLYING FISH, THE AGILE AMAZON TEEN-AGER SLIDES ALONG IT...

I THOUGHT THE STRING WOULD LEAD TO THE *MER-BOY!* THERE HE IS! FLYING THE FISH FROM THAT NEST ON THE CLIFF!

AT *WONDER GIRL'S* IRATE APPROACH, THE MER-BOY DIVES TOWARDS THE SEA FAR BELOW...

HERE COMES WONDER GIRL! SHE LOOKS ANGRY! I'LL DIVE INTO THE SEA! SHE'LL FOLLOW ME--AND WHILE SHE "COOLS" OFF--I'LL SPEAK TO HER WHILE SHE'S CALM!

THE YOUNG AMAZON IS MADE STILL MORE ANGRY AS SHE NEARS THE NEST AND SEES...

OHH-- THE NERVE OF HIM-- NOW HE'S WRITING NOTES ON THE ROC'S EGG!

WONDER GIRL UNFAIR TO MER-BOY! SHE'S BREAKING HIS HEART BY REFUSING TO WEAR HIS PIN AND TO GO TO THE DANCE WITH HIM!

WONDER GIRL STARTS TO WIPE OFF THE LETTERING WHEN SHE IS AROUSED BY...

SHADES OF PLUTO! THE MER-BOY HAS FALLEN INTO THE CLUTCHES OF A GIANT ROC!

SKREE

...ING TO PIN AND TO THE DANCE WITH HIM!

INSTANTLY, THE TEENAGE AMAZON HURLS HER LASSO AT THE WINGED MONSTER...

HERA HELP ME LASSO THE MER-BOY OUT OF THAT CREATURE'S GRASP!

BUT, WITH A MIGHTY CUFF OF ITS GIGANTIC WING...

WHAAP!

SHADES OF PLUTO! THE ROC SLAPPED THE LASSO AWAY BEFORE IT COULD REACH ME!

SEIZING THE MASSIVE MONSTER'S EGG, THE DESPERATE WONDER GIRL LEAPS WITH IT INTO SPACE...

THE LASSO DIDN'T FREE THE MER-BOY! PRAY HERA MY PLAN SUCCEEDS THIS TIME!

WONDER GIRL UNFAIR TO MERBOY

ABOVE THE MIGHTY CREATURE, THE DARING YOUNG AMAZON LETS THE HUGE EGG FALL...

WILL THE ROC RELEASE THE MER-BOY TO CATCH ITS EGG?

SCREAMING WITH FURY LIKE A FACTORY WHISTLE, THE GIGANTIC BIRD LUNGES UPWARDS...

THANK HERA! IT DROPPED THE MER-BOY! BUT -- NOW THAT THE MONSTER HAS CAUGHT ITS EGG -- IT'S COMING AFTER ME!

SKREEEEEEE

8

PART TWO

Wonder Girl in
MER-BOY'S UNDERSEA PARTY!

AS WONDER GIRL DESPERATELY TRIES TO ESCAPE THE GIANT BIRD'S CLAWS...

MERCIFUL MINERVA!-- NOTHING--

--BUT--

--UP DRAFTS!

SKREEEEEEEEE EEE EEEE EEE

LUCKILY, THE AMAZON TEEN-AGER'S GRIM SEARCH SUDDENLY ENDS WHEN...

THANK AEOLUS, KEEPER OF THE WINDS! FOR THE **DOWN** DRAFT OF AIR THAT IS DROPPING ME LIKE A STONE-- OUT OF THIS CREATURE'S REACH!

INTO THE GREEN DEPTHS HURTLES THE ANGRY **WONDER GIRL** --RECOVERING HER LASSO ON THE WAY...

BY NEPTUNE'S TRIDENT! THERE'S THE **MER-BOY** ON A GIANT TURTLE! STILL SCRAWLING MESSAGES! HE'LL NEVER GET ME TO WEAR HIS PIN OR GO TO HIS PARTY ACTING THIS WAY!

9

BUT THE MER-BOY THINKS DIFFERENTLY...

WONDER GIRL MUST LOVE ME--OR SHE WOULDN'T BE SAVING MY LIFE ALL THE TIME! NO CHANCE OF ANYTHING HAPPENING *THIS* TIME--THIS TURTLE CAN'T REACH ME WHILE I'M ON ITS BACK!

BENEATH THE SEA, HOWEVER, WHERE GIANT CREATURES ARE ALWAYS ON THE PROWL, EVENTS CAN SWIFTLY CHANGE...

SUFFERING SAPPHO! THE *MER-BOY'S* IN DEADLY PERIL AGAIN!

INSTANTLY, THE DARING AMAZON TEENAGER HURLS BOTH HERSELF--AND HER UNIQUE LASSO--AT THE HUGE SEA-CREATURE THAT HAD CAPTURED THE MER-BOY...

THAT *MER-BOY!* NOW HE'S IN THE CLUTCHES OF A TREMENDOUS SEA TURTLE!

ALIGHTING ON THE HUGE BEAST'S BACK, *WONDER GIRL* SUMMONS ALL HER STRENGTH INTO A POWERFUL TUG BACKWARDS WHICH...

BY THE SEVEN SEAS! *WONDER GIRL* HAS TURNED THE GIANT TURTLE OVER--! MAKING IT LET ME GO! SHE'S SAVED ME AGAIN! ONE MORE MESSAGE--AND I'M SURE SHE'LL TAKE MY PIN AND GO WITH ME TO THE PARTY!

LEAPING OFF THE UNDERSEA BEAST'S BACK, THE IRATE WONDER GIRL LOOKS FOR THE MER-BOY...

THANK HERA THIS GIANT ELECTRIC EEL DOESN'T SEE THE MER-BOY! I'VE GOT TO STOP HIM FROM SCRAWLING MESSAGES ABOUT ME ON EVERYTHING HE CAN--UNDER THE SEA! THEN--I'LL NEVER SPEAK TO HIM AGAIN--EVER!

BUT, THE MER-BOY IS STILL BUSY WITH HIS SPECIAL UNDERWATER CRAYON...

THIS IS THE BEST PLACE YET FOR MY MESSAGE! THE BIGGEST, SMOOTHEST PART OF THE SEA'S BED I'VE SEEN YET! WONDER GIRL'S HEART WILL MELT WHEN SHE SEES IT!

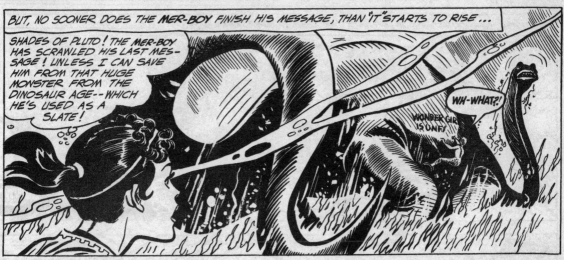

BUT, NO SOONER DOES THE MER-BOY FINISH HIS MESSAGE, THAN "IT" STARTS TO RISE...

SHADES OF PLUTO! THE MER-BOY HAS SCRAWLED HIS LAST MESSAGE! UNLESS I CAN SAVE HIM FROM THAT HUGE MONSTER FROM THE DINOSAUR AGE--WHICH HE'S USED AS A SLATE!

WH-WHAT?!

WONDER GIRL IS UNF!

THE TEENAGE AMAZON'S RESCUE ATTEMPT ENDS IN DISASTER AS...

MERCIFUL NEPTUNE! WONDER GIRL'S BEEN KNOCKED UNCONSCIOUS BY THIS MONSTER'S TAIL!

WHUMP!

WHILE WONDER GIRL LIES MOTIONLESS, THE MER-BOY HURLS HIMSELF IN FRONT OF THE AWESOME UNDERSEA CREATURE...

NEPTUNE HELP ME LEAD THIS BEAST AWAY FROM MY DARLING!

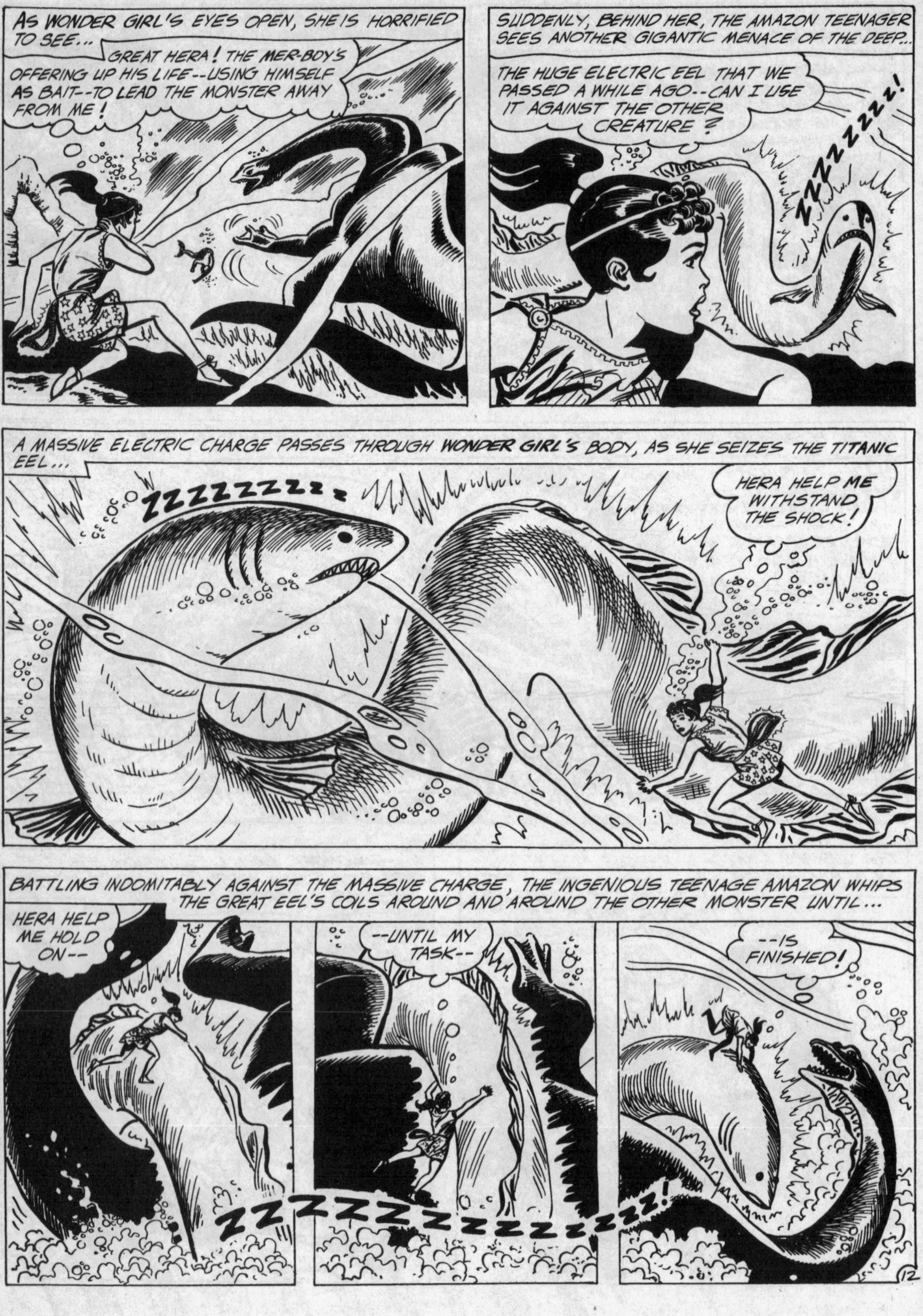
AS WONDER GIRL'S EYES OPEN, SHE IS HORRIFIED TO SEE...
GREAT HERA! THE MER-BOY'S OFFERING UP HIS LIFE--USING HIMSELF AS BAIT--TO LEAD THE MONSTER AWAY FROM ME!
SUDDENLY, BEHIND HER, THE AMAZON TEENAGER SEES ANOTHER GIGANTIC MENACE OF THE DEEP...
THE HUGE ELECTRIC EEL THAT WE PASSED A WHILE AGO--CAN I USE IT AGAINST THE OTHER CREATURE?
ZZZZZZZZZ!
A MASSIVE ELECTRIC CHARGE PASSES THROUGH WONDER GIRL'S BODY, AS SHE SEIZES THE TITANIC EEL...
ZZZZZZZZZ
HERA HELP ME WITHSTAND THE SHOCK!
BATTLING INDOMITABLY AGAINST THE MASSIVE CHARGE, THE INGENIOUS TEENAGE AMAZON WHIPS THE GREAT EEL'S COILS AROUND AND AROUND THE OTHER MONSTER UNTIL...
HERA HELP ME HOLD ON--
--UNTIL MY TASK--
--IS FINISHED!
ZZZZZZZZZZZZZZ!
12

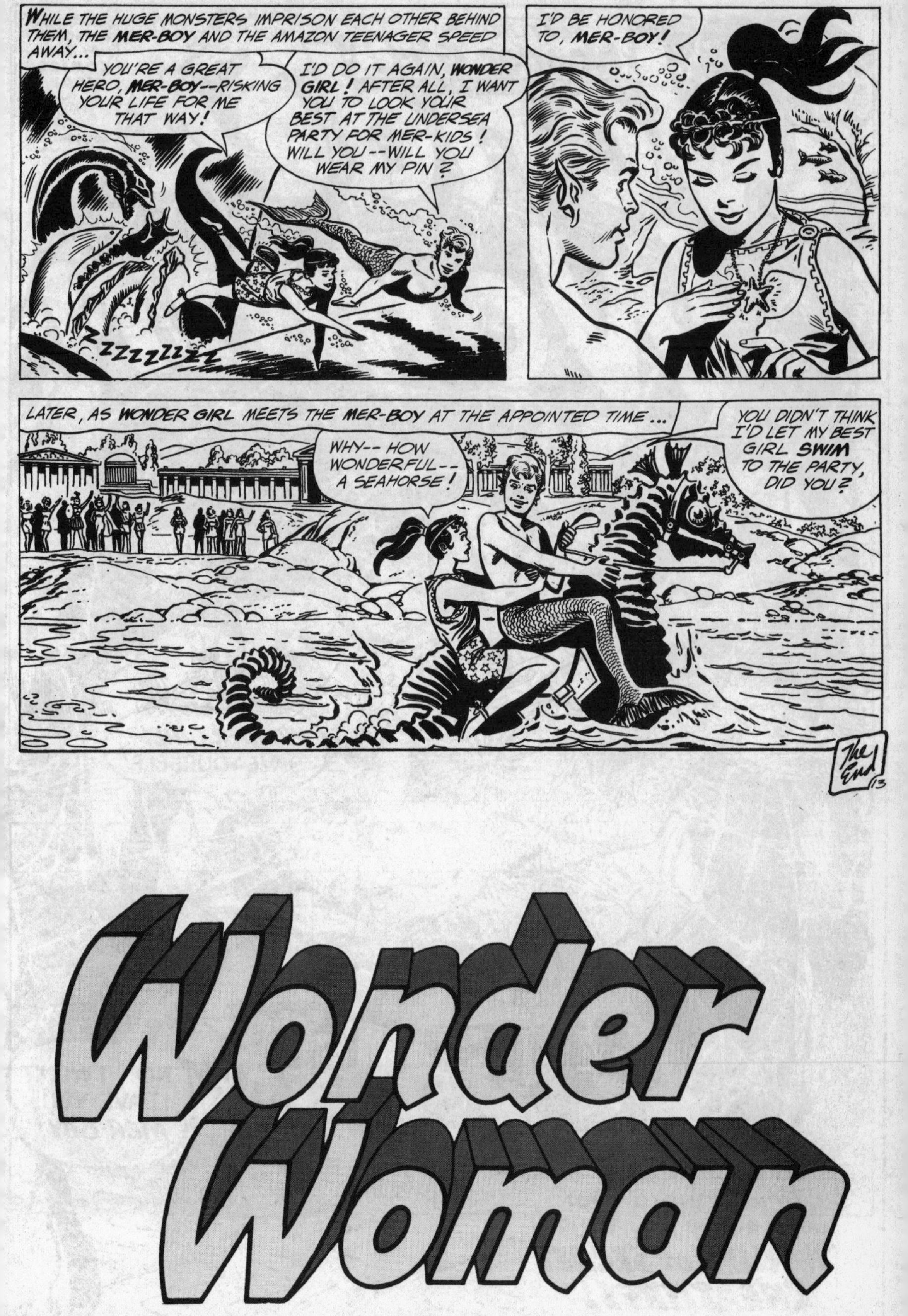
WHILE THE HUGE MONSTERS IMPRISON EACH OTHER BEHIND THEM, THE MER-BOY AND THE AMAZON TEENAGER SPEED AWAY...
YOU'RE A GREAT HERO, MER-BOY--RISKING YOUR LIFE FOR ME THAT WAY!
I'D DO IT AGAIN, WONDER GIRL! AFTER ALL, I WANT YOU TO LOOK YOUR BEST AT THE UNDERSEA PARTY FOR MER-KIDS! WILL YOU--WILL YOU WEAR MY PIN?
ZZZZZZZZZ
I'D BE HONORED TO, MER-BOY!
LATER, AS WONDER GIRL MEETS THE MER-BOY AT THE APPOINTED TIME...
WHY-- HOW WONDERFUL-- A SEAHORSE!
YOU DIDN'T THINK I'D LET MY BEST GIRL SWIM TO THE PARTY, DID YOU?
The End
13

Wonder Woman

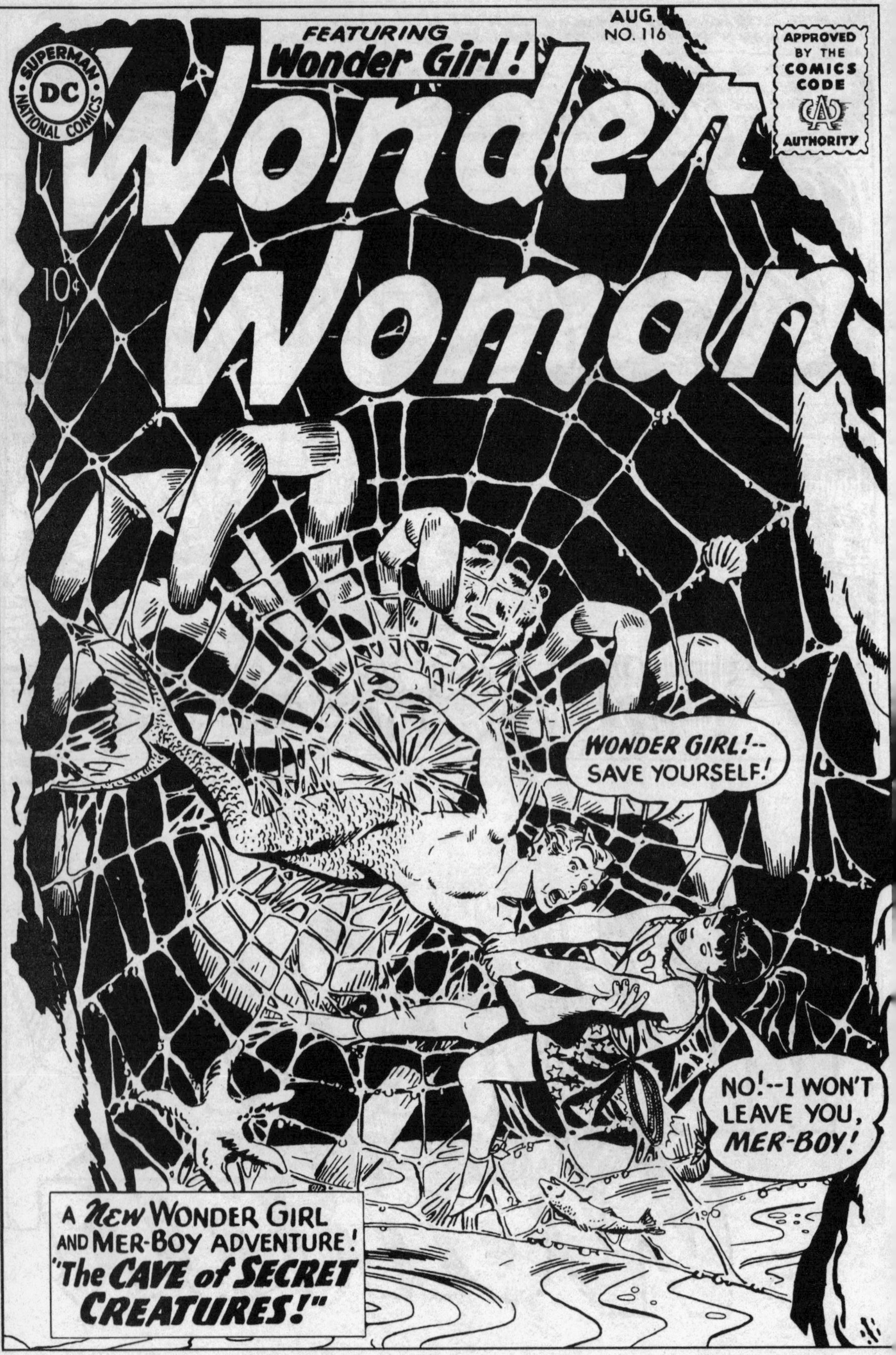
FEATURING
Wonder Girl!
AUG.
NO. 116
SUPERMAN
DC
NATIONAL COMICS
APPROVED
BY THE
COMICS
CODE
AUTHORITY
Wonder Woman
10¢
WONDER GIRL!--
SAVE YOURSELF!
NO!--I WON'T
LEAVE YOU,
MER-BOY!
A NEW WONDER GIRL
AND MER-BOY ADVENTURE!
"The CAVE of SECRET
CREATURES!"

Wonder Woman PRESENTS THE AMAZON TEENAGER
Wonder Girl

DEAR READERS:
IN ANSWER TO YOUR CONTINUED REQUESTS TO SEE WONDER GIRL AND HER UNIQUE FRIEND, THE MER-BOY IN ANOTHER ADVENTURE -- HERE IS A STARTLING TALE OF MYSELF AS AN AMAZON TEEN-AGER AND THE TROUBLE I HAVE TO RESCUE MY IMPULSIVE FRIEND FROM...

The CAVE OF SECRET CREATURES!

IN THE UNIQUE MER-WORLD BENEATH THE SEA, ALL THE MERMEN AND MERMAIDS ARE HAPPY, ALL EXCEPT-- MER-BOY...

WHY ARE YOU SO SAD, MER-BOY? WHAT COULD YOUR HEART DESIRE WHICH WE DO NOT HAVE HERE?

WONDER GIRL!-- THAT AMAZON TEENAGER MAKES MY HEART TURN SOMERSAULTS LIKE A PORPOISE! BUT--SHE DOESN'T FEEL THE SAME WAY ABOUT ME!

WHY NOT TRY AROUSING HER SYMPATHY? ALL GIRLS, WHETHER THEY LIVE *ABOVE* THE SEA OR *UNDER* IT ARE THE SAME! THEIR HEARTS CAN'T HELP BEING TOUCHED BY SOMEONE WHO SIGHS FOR THEM!

Hmmm--! I'LL TRY IT! EVEN THOUGH I HAVE THE PROBLEM OF NOT BEING ABLE TO SET FOOT ON HER ISLAND--BY AMAZON LAW!

THE NEXT DAY, WONDER GIRL IN HER TIRELESS TRAINING TO BECOME A WONDER WOMAN, HURTLES LIKE A ROCKET INTO THE AIR AS..

YOUR DAUGHTER'S TIMING IS PERFECT, O'QUEEN! OBSERVE HOW SHE CAUGHT THAT HUGE BIRD'S WING-TIP IN FULL FLIGHT!

AYE, NOLLA! BUT YOU AND HER OTHER INSTRUCTORS ARE NOT TO RELAX YOUR TESTS EVEN FOR A MOMENT!

REMEMBER! HER MISSION IN LIFE IS TO BECOME A WONDER WOMAN WHO WILL BE ABLE TO HELP PEOPLE IN DISTRESS NO MATTER WHAT THE ODDS AGAINST SUCCESS WILL BE!

2

MEANWHILE, WONDER GIRL'S AMAZON VISION DETECTS...

MERCIFUL MINERVA! MER-BOY'S LYING STILL AS A PIECE OF DRIFTWOOD BELOW!

LIKE A HUMAN ARROW, THE AMAZON TEENAGER HURTLES TO THE SILENT MER-BOY'S SIDE...

MER-BOY--! MER-BOY! WHAT HAS HAPPENED TO YOU?

GENTLY, WONDER GIRL PILLOWS THE MER-BOY'S HEAD IN HER LAP...

BY APHRODITE'S LAW, I CAN'T BRING HIM ONTO OUR ISLAND! I'LL HAVE TO ADMINISTER FIRST-AID TO HIM HERE, THEN BRING HIM TO HIS MER-WORLD!

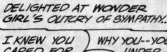

DELIGHTED AT WONDER GIRL'S OUTCRY OF SYMPATHY..

I KNEW YOU CARED FOR ME, WONDER GIRL! BUT--IT TOOK AN "ACCIDENT"! TO ME TO MAKE YOU REALIZE IT!

WHY YOU--YOU UNDER-WATER FAKIR-- YOU WERE SHAMMING!

AS IF IT WERE AN AERIAL LADDER, THE AMAZON TEENAGER LEAPS UP AN ASCENDING CURRENT OF AIR...

HOW ELSE CAN I EVER GET TO SEE YOU, EXCEPT BY ATTRACTING YOUR ATTENTION? YOU KNOW NO MAN CAN SET FOOT ON PARADISE ISLAND--WONDER GIRL--DON'T LEAVE ME!

BEYOND MER-BOY'S REACH SOARS WONDER GIRL ...

THERE GOES MY DREAM GIRL! I HAVEN'T A CHANCE WITH HER!

When Wonder Girl returns, and tells her mother, Queen Hippolyta, what happened...

Romantic young boys do foolish things, dear! But--you should show him more sympathy! After all, it's you who are having this effect on him!

You're right, mother, as usual! I will be nice to Mer-boy--no matter how foolish he acts!

Meanwhile, Mer-boy's "romance counselor" listens to his sad tale...

ROCK ROCK ROCK

It's no use, Firra! I don't stand a chance with Wonder Girl!

You Mer-boys! You always give up too easily! There's more than one channel to a girl's heart! We'll just have to try something else! And I know exactly what!

Two days later a seashell is hurled toward the beach of Paradise Island...

THUD!

An Amazon removes the note contained in the seashell...

It's for you, Princess, from Mer-boy!

Thank you, Leena!

THE NEXT DAY, WONDER GIRL BATHES IN THE UNIQUE AMAZON PERFUME GEYSER...

PONDERS OVER WHICH COSTUME TO WEAR...

BRUSHES HER HAIR A THOUSAND STROKES...

FINALLY... IT **WAS** SWEET OF MER-BOY TO INVITE ME TO A **PARTY**! ESPECIALLY SINCE I WAS SO RUDE TO HIM! HOW DO I LOOK, MOTHER?

LOVELY! I'LL BET HE WON'T LET YOU DANCE A SINGLE DANCE WITH ANYONE ELSE!

SHORTLY, THE AMAZON TEENAGER ARROWS INTO THE DEEP GREEN DEPTHS OF THE SEA OFF **PARADISE ISLAND**, SECRET HOME OF THE AMAZONS...

THERE'S THE ENTRANCE TO THE MER-WORLD!

THROUGH THE MER-WORLD'S SECRET PASSAGE WONDER GIRL GLIDES, TO BE MET BY HER ESCORT...

IT WAS SWEET OF YOU TO INVITE ME TO YOUR PARTY, MER-BOY!

MY PLEASURE, WONDER GIRL!

BUT, BEFORE THEIR FIRST DANCE...

DON'T FORGET, MER-BOY! YOU PROMISED **THIS** DANCE TO ME!

IF IT'S ALL RIGHT WITH **WONDER GIRL?** AFTER ALL, SHE'S MY DATE... DO YOU MIND, WONDER GIRL?

WHY... ER-- OF COURSE NOT!

I REALLY DON'T MIND MER-BOY DANCING THIS DANCE WITH HER--IF HE PROMISED! BUT-- THE LEAST HE COULD DO IS WAVE OR SMILE AT ME--TO SHOW THAT HE'S AWARE THAT I'M WAITING ...!

BUT, DANCE AFTER DANCE GOES BY...

BY HERA!

THAT PRETTY LITTLE MERMAID HAS TURNED MER-BOY'S HEAD!

HE'S FORGOTTEN I'M HERE!

FINALLY...

I'VE HAD ENOUGH! AND TO THINK OF ALL THE TIME I SPENT MAKING MYSELF PRETTY FOR THAT UN-GRATEFUL WRETCH!

WONDER GIRL'S LEAVING! OH--I HOPE I HAVEN'T HURT HER FEELINGS!

SHE'S JEALOUS! JUST AS I EXPECTED TO MAKE HER! NOW--SWIM AFTER HER--AND YOU'LL SEE SHE'LL PRACTICALLY FALL INTO YOUR ARMS!

6

AFTER WONDER GIRL, THE WORRIED MER-BOY DARTS...

WONDER GIRL!--WAIT FOR ME!

LET ME EXPLAIN!

WHAT IS THERE TO EXPLAIN? THE MOMENT YOU SEE A PRETTY GIRL--YOUR HEAD IS TURNED!

ANGRILY PICKING UP THE GIGANTIC SEA-SHELL...

AND TO THINK I BATHED MYSELF IN THE GEYSER PERFUME-- WORE MY PRETTIEST UNIFORM-- AND BRUSHED MY HAIR UNTIL MY HEAD HURT--JUST FOR YOU!

THUD

BNFF MMFFFF!!

WELL, I'VE LEARNED MY LESSON! I'LL NEVER SPEAK TO THAT--THAT-- THAT "UNDERSEA BUTTERFLY" AGAIN!

BY THE TIME MER-BOY EMERGES FROM THE HUGE SEASHELL...

I--I'VE FAILED... I--I'VE LOST HER...!

BUT, MER-BOY'S FEELING OF DEFEAT IS NOT SHARED BY HIS FRIEND FIRRA, THE MERMAID WHEN...

IT'S NO USE-- I'VE LOST HER FOR GOOD!

DON'T BE SILLY! IF SHE DIDN'T CARE FOR YOU--SHE WOULDN'T BE JEALOUS OF ANYTHING YOU DID!

GIRLS ARE ALL ALIKE ON LAND, SEA, OR IN THE AIR! THE BEST WAY TO A GIRL'S HEART IS TO GIVE HER A TOKEN OF YOUR ESTEEM! A LITTLE GIFT THAT NO ONE ELSE HAS! THE RARER THE BETTER! IF IT'S THE **ONLY** ONE OF ITS KIND--SHE CAN'T HELP FALLING IN LOVE WITH YOU FOR YOUR THOUGHTFULNESS!

MMMM--?? THAT'S AN IDEA!

NOW WHAT CAN I GIVE WONDER GIRL THAT NO ONE ELSE HAS?... WHAT IS THE ONLY ONE OF ITS KIND...IN THE WHOLE WIDE WORLD...?

MEANWHILE, ON PARADISE ISLAND, AS WONDER GIRL CONTINUES HER INCESSANT TRAINING FOR HER FUTURE ROLE OF A WONDER WOMAN...

BUT, DIANA--MAYBE MER-BOY ONLY ACTED THAT WAY TO ATTRACT YOUR ATTENTION?

I DON'T CARE! IT WAS HORRID!

TWO DAYS LATER, AS THE AMAZON TEENAGER IS PERFORMING GYMNASTICS ON THE BEACH...

LOOK-- A MERMAID!

WONDER GIRL! I MUST SEE YOU! IT'S ABOUT MER-BOY!

I DON'T CARE IF I NEVER SEE OR HEAR FROM HIM AGAIN AS LONG AS I LIVE! YOU CAN TELL HIM THAT!

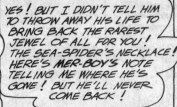

AS **WONDER GIRL** EASES HER SISTER GYMNASTS TO THE GROUND...

YOU DON'T UNDERSTAND! MER-BOY'S MADLY IN LOVE WITH YOU! EVERYTHING HE DID, HE DID TO AROUSE YOUR ATTENTION, ON MY ADVICE!

I SUPPOSE THAT INCLUDED NEGLECTING ME, WHILE HE DANCED EVERY DANCE WITH YOU?

YES! BUT I DIDN'T TELL HIM TO THROW AWAY HIS LIFE TO BRING BACK THE RAREST JEWEL OF ALL FOR YOU! THE SEA-SPIDER'S NECKLACE! HERE'S MER-BOY'S NOTE TELLING ME WHERE HE'S GONE! BUT HE'LL NEVER COME BACK!

HE--HE'LL NEVER--RETURN--ALIVE--FROM--FROM THE CAVE OF SECRET CREATURES!

NOT IF I CAN HELP IT!

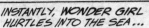

INSTANTLY, WONDER GIRL HURTLES INTO THE SEA...

I'LL GO WITH YOU AS FAR... AS FAR AS I DARE!

LIKE TWO GRACEFUL SHADOWS THE MERMAID AND THE AMAZON TEENAGER GLIDE INTO THE GREEN DEPTHS...

I--I HOPE IT ISN'T TOO LATE ALREADY!

PRAY HERA IT'S NOT!

SUDDENLY, A BOILING WALL OF WATER AHEAD!

TH-THIS IS THE F-F-FIRST OBSTACLE TO THE SEA SPIDER'S CAVE! I--I CAN'T SWIM TH-TH-THROUGH IT--!

GO BACK!--I'LL GO ON FROM HERE ALONE!

THROUGH THE FROTHING, CHURNING, RAGING WATERS...

WONDER GIRL HURLS HERSELF STEADILY ONWARDS...

UNTIL...

THANK HERA-- I'M THROUGH!

AHEAD LIES AN UNDERSEA THICKET INTO WHICH THE AMAZON TEENAGER PLUNGES...

THRESHING THROUGH THE GNARLED FRONDS...

WHICH SEEK TO TRAP HER...

PRAISE HERA-- I'M OUT OF THIS--TOO!

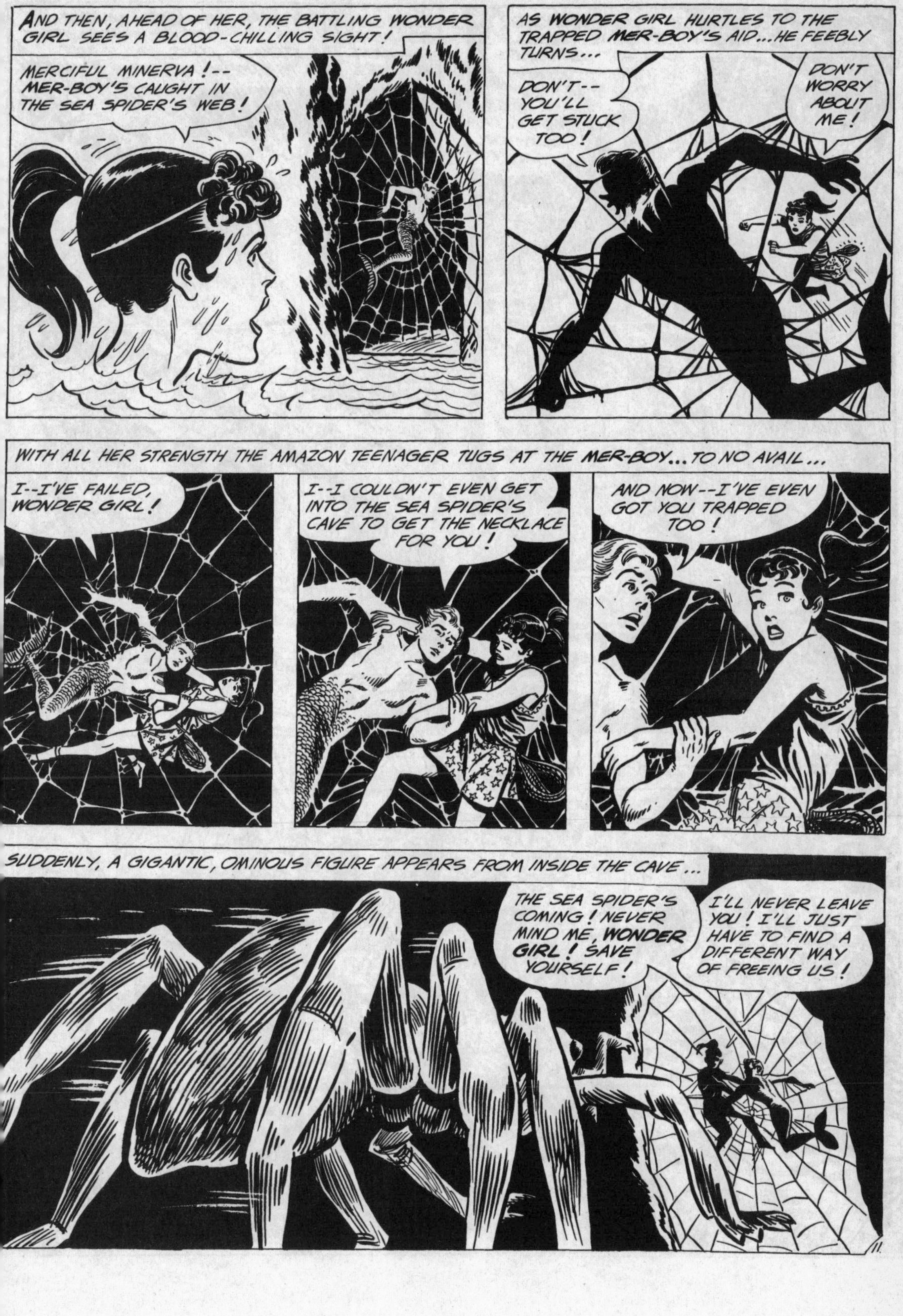
AND THEN, AHEAD OF HER, THE BATTLING WONDER GIRL SEES A BLOOD-CHILLING SIGHT!
MERCIFUL MINERVA!-- MER-BOY'S CAUGHT IN THE SEA SPIDER'S WEB!
AS WONDER GIRL HURTLES TO THE TRAPPED MER-BOY'S AID...HE FEEBLY TURNS...
DON'T-- YOU'LL GET STUCK TOO!
DON'T WORRY ABOUT ME!
WITH ALL HER STRENGTH THE AMAZON TEENAGER TUGS AT THE MER-BOY...TO NO AVAIL...
I--I'VE FAILED, WONDER GIRL!
I--I COULDN'T EVEN GET INTO THE SEA SPIDER'S CAVE TO GET THE NECKLACE FOR YOU!
AND NOW--I'VE EVEN GOT YOU TRAPPED TOO!
SUDDENLY, A GIGANTIC, OMINOUS FIGURE APPEARS FROM INSIDE THE CAVE...
THE SEA SPIDER'S COMING! NEVER MIND ME, WONDER GIRL! SAVE YOURSELF!
I'LL NEVER LEAVE YOU! I'LL JUST HAVE TO FIND A DIFFERENT WAY OF FREEING US!
11.

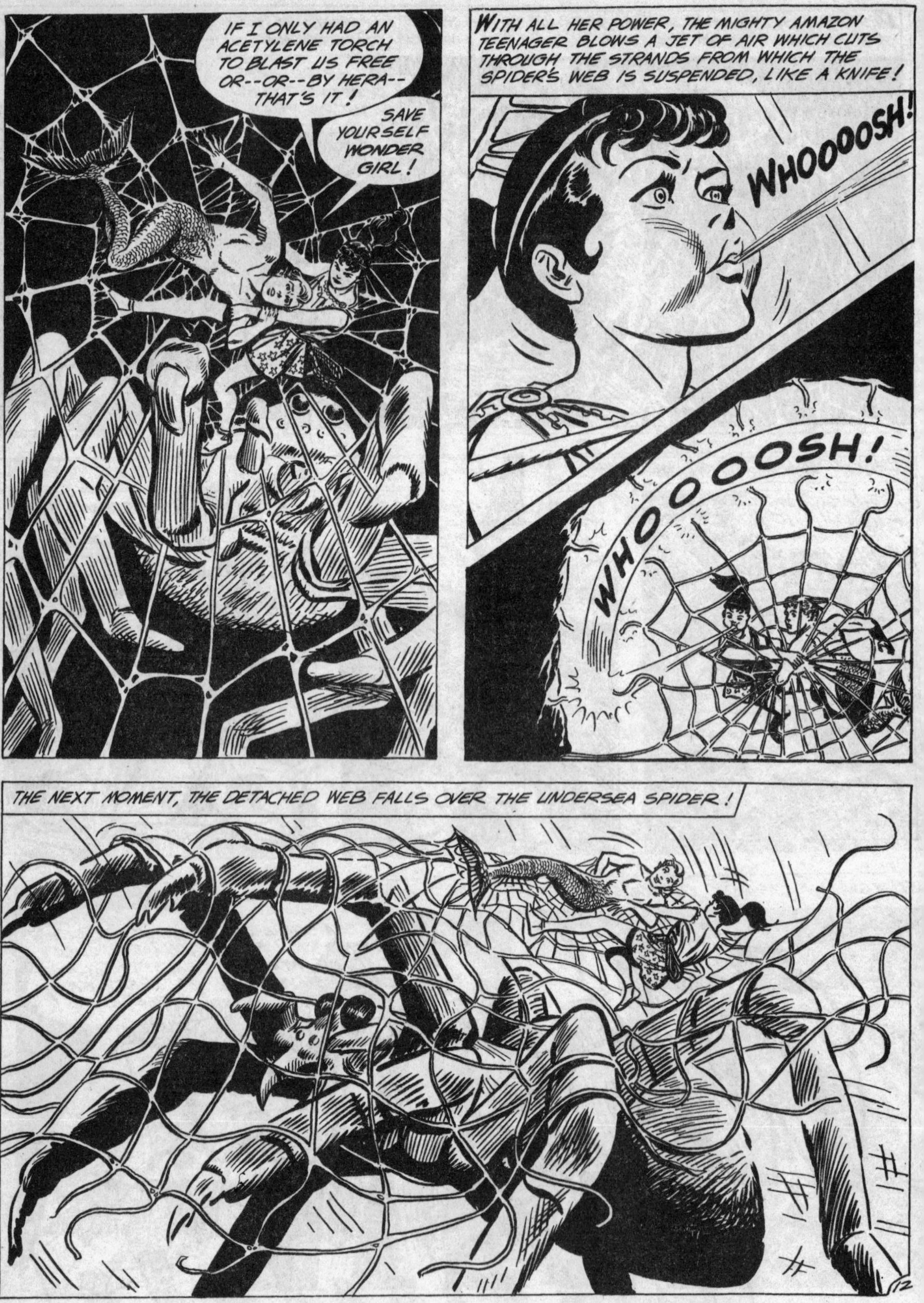
IF I ONLY HAD AN ACETYLENE TORCH TO BLAST US FREE OR--OR--BY HERA-- THAT'S IT!
SAVE YOURSELF WONDER GIRL!
WITH ALL HER POWER, THE MIGHTY AMAZON TEENAGER BLOWS A JET OF AIR WHICH CUTS THROUGH THE STRANDS FROM WHICH THE SPIDER'S WEB IS SUSPENDED, LIKE A KNIFE!
WHOOOOSH!
WHOOOOOOSH!
THE NEXT MOMENT, THE DETACHED WEB FALLS OVER THE UNDERSEA SPIDER!
12

DESPERATELY, THE AMAZON TEENAGER USES THE SAME BLASTING JETS OF AIR TO FREE MER-BOY AND HERSELF FROM THE CLUTCHES OF THE ENRAGED SEA SPIDER...

WE'RE FREE, WONDER GIRL! WE'RE FREE!

BACK, MER-BOY. OUT OF HERE BEFORE THE MONSTER GETS FREE!

WHOO-OOSH!

BACK TO SAFETY, THE TWO SWIM...

I'VE FAILED, WONDER GIRL! I THOUGHT TO WIN THE RAREST THING IN THE WORLD FOR YOU-- BUT I'VE FAILED!

NO, YOU HAVEN'T-- MER-BOY! IT'S NOT WHAT A BOY GIVES A GIRL BUT THE THOUGHT BEHIND IT--THAT'S THE RAREST SWEETEST THING IN THE WHOLE WORLD!

The End /3

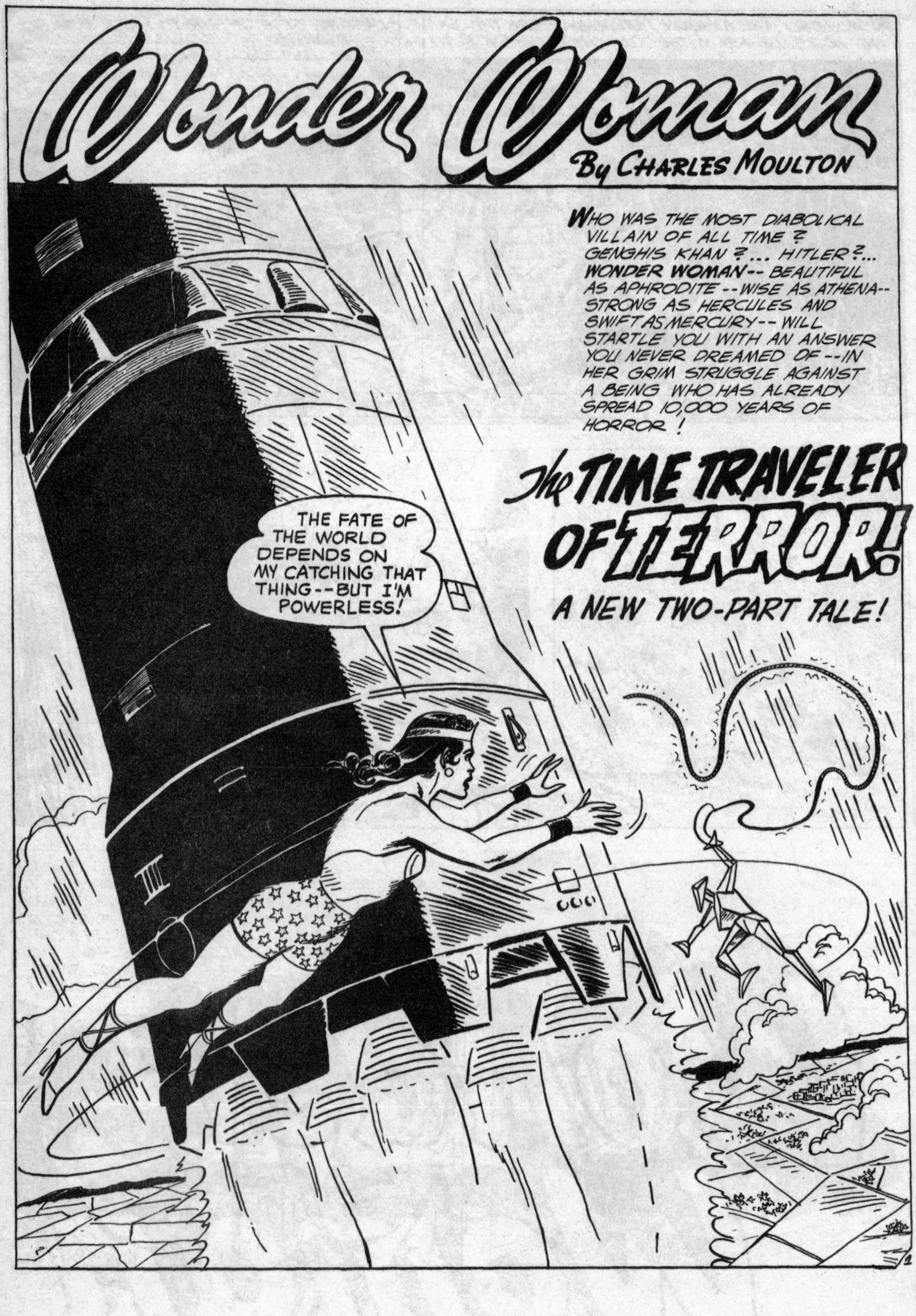
Wonder Woman
By Charles Moulton
WHO WAS THE MOST DIABOLICAL VILLAIN OF ALL TIME? GENGHIS KHAN?... HITLER?... WONDER WOMAN-- BEAUTIFUL AS APHRODITE--WISE AS ATHENA--STRONG AS HERCULES AND SWIFT AS MERCURY-- WILL STARTLE YOU WITH AN ANSWER YOU NEVER DREAMED OF--IN HER GRIM STRUGGLE AGAINST A BEING WHO HAS ALREADY SPREAD 10,000 YEARS OF HORROR!
The TIME TRAVELER OF TERROR!
A NEW TWO-PART TALE!
THE FATE OF THE WORLD DEPENDS ON MY CATCHING THAT THING--BUT I'M POWERLESS!

AT MILITARY INTELLIGENCE, LT. DIANA PRINCE IS IN THE VAST LIBRARY WITH COL. STEVE TREVOR...

EVER SEE THIS BOOK, DI? IT'S FASCINATING! IT CONTAINS PICTURES OF THE WORLD'S GREAT DISASTERS!

HERE'S ONE OF THE LOST CONTINENT OF *ATLANTIS!* SUPPOSEDLY FLOURISHING MORE THAN 10,000 YEARS AGO IN THE ATLANTIC OCEAN!

LEGEND RELATES THAT THE SEA ENGULFED THE UNLUCKY *ATLANTIS!*

AND HERE'S ONE OF A CROWD STANDING WHERE *ATLANTIS* IS SUPPOSED TO HAVE BEEN!

YES, DI! THEY SAY *ATLANTIS* WAS CUT OFF FROM THE MAINLAND-- BY THIS GREAT NATURAL DISASTER-- AND SUNK SOMEWHERE IN THE SEA!

THAT'S THE LEGEND, STEVE! BUT IT'S NEVER BEEN PROVEN! FOR THE SIMPLE REASON THAT *WITHOUT* THE *REDISCOVERY OF ATLANTIS*--WE HAVE NO WAY OF PROVING WHAT *ACTUALLY HAPPENED!*

HERE'S ONE OF *POMPEII,* AN ANCIENT TOWN IN ITALY, AT THE FOOT OF MT. VESUVIUS, AS IT LOOKED IN 63 A.D. !

Site of the ill-fated P...
in 63...

AND THE DESTRUCTION THAT HAPPENED WHEN MT. VESUVIUS ERUPTED--

--YES--IT RAINED FIRE ON THE ANCIENT CITY !

Resident

AS DIANA AND STEVE CONTINUE LOOKING THROUGH THE PAGES OF THE WORLD'S GREATEST DISASTERS...

HERE ARE ANCIENT ROMANS LOOKING AT THE DISASTER !

THERE ARE ALWAYS SPECTATORS AFTER A CATASTROPHE ! DRAWN BY CURIOSITY--NO MATTER WHAT THE AGE !

After th...

HERE'S ONE CLOSER TO OUR TIME, DI !

THE *CHICAGO* FIRE OF 1871 !

AS YOU CAN SEE-- IT PRACTICALLY DESTROYED *CHICAGO* !

HERE ARE THE PEOPLE DIGGING THEMSELVES OUT OF THE RUBBLE !

Rescue workers
aid the inj...
3

PAGE AFTER PAGE OF DISASTERS ARE NOTED BY DI AND STEVE AT THE MILITARY INTELLIGENCE LIBRARY...

THE **JOHNSTOWN** FLOOD OF 1889 RATES AS ONE OF THE WORLD'S GREAT DISASTERS! IT HAPPENED WHEN A NEARBY DAM BROKE, HURLING A MASS OF WATER 60 TO 70 FEET DEEP AT THIS PENNSYLVANIA TOWN!

AMAZING HOW **SOME** PEOPLE MANAGE TO SURVIVE!

WELL, DI! I HAVE TO LEAVE YOU NOW, TO MEET **WONDER WOMAN**!

Survivors of the flood gather in

BACK IN THE PRIVACY OF HER OWN OFFICE, DI MAKES A LIGHTNING CHANGE INTO HER SECRET IDENTITY OF **WONDER WOMAN**...

SOMETHING ODD... ABOUT THOSE PICTURES OF THE WORLD'S GREAT DISASTERS... BUT...I DON'T KNOW WHAT??

SHORTLY, WONDER WOMAN IS SPEEDING WITH STEVE IN HER UNIQUE AMAZON PLANE TOWARDS A ROCKET LAUNCHING SITE ON THE WEST COAST...

WHEN ARE YOU GOING TO BREAK DOWN AND MARRY ME, ANGEL?... ANGEL?...WONDER WOMAN!... AREN'T YOU WITH ME?

S-S-SORRY, STEVE! I--I GUESS MY THOUGHTS WERE ELSEWHERE! PLEASE FORGIVE ME! AS FOR MARRYING YOU-- I'D BE GLAD TO--WHEN I'M NO LONGER NEEDED TO COMBAT EVIL!

MOMENTS LATER, THE FLASHING ROBOT PLANE HEADS DOWN FOR A LANDING AT THE COUNTRY'S VITAL EXPERIMENTAL BASE...

THAT'S OUR BIGGEST ROCKET YET, ISN'T IT, STEVE?

IT **HAS** TO BE! TO CARRY A PAYLOAD THAT WILL ENABLE US TO PROBE OUTER SPACE--AND SEND US BACK INFORMATION WHICH WILL BE INVALUABLE TO SCIENCE ALL OVER THE WORLD!

4

ON THE FIELD, THE TWO ARRIVALS ARE INTRODUCED TO VISITING DIGNITARIES FROM ALL OVER THE WORLD...

AND THIS IS THE FAMOUS PROF. ANDRO! PROF. ANDRO--MEET WONDER WOMAN AND COL. STEVE TREVOR!

I'VE READ YOUR THEORIES OF OUTER SPACE, PROF. ANDRO!

THANK YOU, COLONEL!

SO THIS IS THE FAMOUS WONDER WOMAN! YOUR FACE IS FAMILIAR TO ME THROUGH PICTURES, OF COURSE!

STRANGE--THERE'S SOMETHING FAMILIAR ABOUT PROF. ANDRO'S FACE TOO...BUT...I DON'T KNOW WHAT IT IS?

LED ON BY AN INSTINCT, THE PUZZLED AMAZON FETCHES A CAMERA FROM HER PLANE AND...

I'D LIKE A PHOTO OF YOU FOR OUR AMAZON REFERENCE LIBRARY OF FAMOUS SCIENTISTS!

YOU FLATTER ME, WONDER WOMAN!

CLICK!

BACK TO HER PLANE WONDER WOMAN HURRIES...

WHAT'S THE MYSTERY, WONDER WOMAN?

I WON'T KNOW UNTIL I DEVELOP THE PICTURE AND RETURN TO THE LIBRARY AT MILITARY INTELLIGENCE!

MOMENTS LATER, WONDER WOMAN REOPENS THE BOOK OF THE WORLD'S GREAT DISASTERS...

SOME TIME AGO, STEVE, I GLANCED THROUGH THIS BOOK! MY PHOTOGRAPHIC MEMORY RETAINED EVERYTHING AS USUAL! WHEN I MET PROF. ANDRO-- WELL--SEE FOR YOURSELF!

THIS IS A PICTURE OF THE CROWD ON THE SPOT WHERE ATLANTIS SUNK MORE THAN 10,000 YEARS AGO DRAWN BY AN ARTIST ON THE SPOT!

As **WONDER WOMAN** PLACES PROF. ANDRO'S PHOTO UNDER A MAGNIFYING GLASS ALONGSIDE A MAN IN THE CROWD ON THE SITE OF THE LOST ISLAND OF **ATLANTIS...**

HERE'S THE PHOTO I JUST TOOK OF PROF. ANDRO!

GREAT SCOTT! HE BEARS A RESEMBLANCE TO THAT MAN IN THE CROWD THE ARTIST MUST HAVE DRAWN!

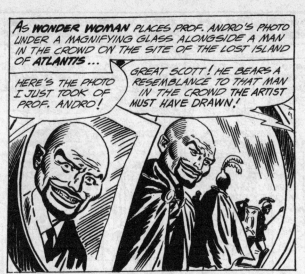

IT'S PURELY A COINCIDENCE OF COURSE! REMARKABLE HOW YOU REMEMBERED IT, THOUGH! SHALL WE GO BACK TO THE ROCKET LAUNCHING GROUNDS?

NOT YET!

HERE'S THE PICTURE OF THE CROWD AROUND THE RUBBLE OF **POMPEII!**

JUMPING JUDAS! ANOTHER CO-INCIDENCE! PROF. ANDRO LOOKS JUST LIKE THAT MAN OF 63 A.D.!

IMAGINE HIM BEING THE EXACT DUPLICATE OF A MAN WHO LIVED MORE THAN 10,000 YEARS AGO, AND ONE 1897 YEARS AGO! IT COULDN'T POSSIBLY HAPPEN AGAIN!

NO, STEVE! IT COULDN'T! BUT-- NOW LET'S EXAMINE THE PICTURE OF THE CROWD ON THE SCENE AFTER THE **CHICAGO** FIRE OF **1871!**

NO--NO! IT COULDN'T BE --IT COULDN'T!

BUT IT IS--STEVE! PROF. ANDRO AGAIN! NOW LET'S PLACE HIS PHOTO IN THE CROWD AFTER THE **JOHNSTOWN** FLOOD OF **1889!**

IT--IT CAN'T BE A COINCIDENCE ANY LONGER! HE CAN'T POSSIBLY MERELY **RESEMBLE** A MAN IN THE CROWD AFTER **EACH** OF THOSE **DISASTERS!**

INCREDIBLE AS IT MAY SEEM, STEVE-- WE CAN'T DENY THE EVIDENCE! IN EACH CASE-- THE SPECTATOR **WAS** PROF. ANDRO!

6

STUNNED BY THEIR DISCOVERY...

BUT **WONDER WOMAN** -- PROF. ANDRO COULDN'T BE A WITNESS AT THE DISASTER TO **ATLANTIS**, AND POSE FOR A PICTURE **TODAY**? THAT WOULD MAKE HIM MORE THAN 10,000 YEARS OLD! HOW COULD HE POSSIBLY SPAN ALL THOSE CENTURIES?

ONLY **ONE** WAY -- **TIME TRAVEL!**

SUMMONING HER ROBOT PLANE, WONDER WOMAN BOARDS IT IN FULL FLIGHT WITH STEVE...

PERHAPS HE WASN'T JUST A **SPECTATOR** AT THOSE DISASTERS! AFTER ALL, IF HE'S SO SCIENTIFICALLY ADVANCED AS TO TIME TRAVEL, HE **COULD** BE RESPONSIBLE FOR ALL THOSE TERRIBLE DISASTERS!

EXACTLY! AND NOW, HE'S HERE TODAY -- TO WITNESS THE LAUNCHING OF THE MIGHTIEST ROCKET SPACE PROBE THE WORLD HAS EVER SEEN! HERA ALONE KNOWS WHAT HORRIBLE DISASTER HE PLANS!

AT THE ROCKET FIELD **WONDER WOMAN** DISPLAYS HER EVIDENCE TO GEN. DARNELL...

GENERAL! HE IS A **TIME TRAVELER OF TERROR!** HE MUST BE STOPPED -- BEFORE HE IS RESPONSIBLE FOR ANOTHER GREAT DISASTER!

BE REASONABLE, **WONDER WOMAN!** DESPITE THESE AMAZING COINCIDENCES -- THERE IS NO REAL PROOF! I CAN'T POSSIBLY HOLD A WORLD-FAMOUS SCIENTIST LIKE PROF. ANDRO ON CHARGES YOU CANNOT PROVE!

JUST THEN...

PARDON ME! I OVERHEARD **WONDER WOMAN'S** CHARGE AGAINST ME! HER ZEAL IS COMMENDABLE! I DEMAND YOU INVESTIGATE ME THOROUGHLY!

THANK YOU, PROF. ANDRO!

WONDER WOMAN AND STEVE WAIT IMPATIENTLY UNTIL HOURS LATER...

FOR PROF. ANDRO TO BE **ALLOWED** TO WITNESS THE ROCKET BLAST-OFF IN THE **FIRST** PLACE, MEANT THAT HE HAD BEEN EXHAUSTIVELY INVESTIGATED BY SECURITY! **ANOTHER** CHECK REVEALED **NOTHING!** I CANNOT HOLD HIM! SORRY! BETTER FORGET ABOUT THE WHOLE THING!

AS THE DEJECTED TWO EXIT FROM THE GENERAL'S OFFICE...

NATURALLY, A SUPER-BEING ADVANCED ENOUGH TO TIME-TRAVEL, COULD BEAR ANY INVESTIGATION! LOOK AT HIM SMILE AT US!

HE KNOWS WE'RE POWERLESS TO PREVENT WHATEVER TERRIBLE DISASTER HE'S PLANNING!

UNEXPECTEDLY, THE PROFESSOR APPROACHES THE STARTLED PAIR...

YOU *WERE* RIGHT, WONDER WOMAN! BUT, YOU CANNOT PROVE IT! YOU ARE POWERLESS AGAINST ME! FOR I COME FROM A WORLD FAR SUPERIOR TO YOURS! HA! HA!

AS THE TWO TRY TO SEIZE THE DIABOLICAL VILLAIN...

YOU CAN'T TOUCH ME! MY SUPER-WILL PREVENTS YOU! JUST AS IT ENABLES ME TO TRAVEL THROUGH TIME OR SPACE BY *MENTOTRAVEL*! OR CAUSE VOLCANOES, EARTHQUAKES, FIRE OR FLOOD BY *MENTOFORCE*! HA HA!

STILL LAUGHING, THE VILLAIN FROM ANOTHER WORLD LEAVES...

THE PARALYSIS I HAVE WILLED YOU INTO WILL VANISH IN A FEW MOMENTS! SO YOU CAN WATCH THE ROCKET LAUNCHING WHICH THE AUTHORITIES *THINK* WILL PROBE OUTER SPACE! HA! HA!

AS *WONDER WOMAN* AND STEVE FEEL THE GRIP OF THE FANTASTIC WILL LOOSEN ON THEM...

THAT--THAT THING--WILL STOP US-- AT THE FIRST SUSPICIOUS MOVE WE MAKE!

OUR ONLY CHANCE IS TO *OUTWIT* IT, SOMEHOW! BY SOMETHING THAT *WON'T* MAKE IT *SUSPICIOUS*!

JUST THEN... WONDER WOMAN-- OUR OFFICIAL PHOTOGRAPHER WAS TAKEN ILL! YOU'RE AN EXPERT! WOULD YOU MIND TAKING PICTURES OF THE VISITING SPECTATORS AFTER THE LAUNCHING-- FOR THE NEWSPAPERS?

OF...COURSE... NOT...GEN. DARNELL!

TO THAT AMAZON PLANE *WONDER WOMAN* HURRIES WITH STEVE...

HOW MOCKING CAN FATE BE--FORCING YOU TO TAKE A PICTURE OF THAT VILLAIN WHO'S THREATENING OUR WORLD?

BY FORCING ME TO TAKE THIS PICTURE-- FATE MAY ALSO BE GIVING ME AN OPPORTUNITY OF STOPPING THIS VILLAIN!

WHAT DOES WONDER WOMAN MEAN? WE SHALL SEE...END OF PART ONE! PART TWO CONTINUES ON THE PAGE FOLLOWING!

BEFORE THE ASSEMBLED WITNESSES, EARTH'S MIGHTIEST ROCKET ROARS UPWARDS...

PART TWO...

THERE IT GOES! AS SOON AS IT'S SAFE, WE'LL STEP OUTSIDE AND HAVE OUR PHOTO-GRAPHS TAKEN FOR THE NEWS-PAPERS!

KROOSH!

IT SEEMS AS IF A MOCKING FATE COMPELS WONDER WOMAN TO BE THE INSTRUMENT IN WHICH THE TIME TRAVELER OF TERROR IS ONCE AGAIN RECORDED FOR POSTERITY...

HOLD STEADY, PLEASE ...THAT'S IT!

CLICK

FOR A SECOND EVERYONE IN THE GROUP IS FROZEN BY THE STRANGE LIGHT OF THE AMAZON FLASHLIGHT!

CLICK!

THEN, TO WONDER WOMAN'S DISMAY, A SINGLE MEMBER OF THE GROUP STEPS FORWARD...

I DID NOT THINK YOU WERE CLEVER ENOUGH TO TRY TO CAPTURE ME WITH A FLASHLIGHT PARALYSIS RAY, AMAZON! ANYWAY, IT DID NOT WORK!

MERCIFUL MINERVA! THE VILLAIN IS A CRYSTAL BEING!

AS RAIN STARTS TO FALL, THE CREATURE FROM ANOTHER WORLD SURGES UPWARDS...

GREAT HERA! THE ROCKET--IT--IT'S STOPPED--HOVERING IN MID-AIR! YOU DID THIS!

AIE, WONDER WOMAN! I HAVE SECRETLY PLACED AN S-TIME BOMB IN IT! IT WILL EXPLODE JUST ABOVE THE EARTH AND PRODUCE THE GREATEST CATASTROPHE SINCE YOUR TIME BEGAN! HA! HA! HA!

9

INTO THE ELECTRICAL STORM BREWING OVERHEAD, WONDER WOMAN CATAPULTS ON AN UPDRAFT...

HERA GUIDE MY LASSO--SO I CAN CAPTURE THIS SUPER VILLAIN!

BUT, THE AMAZON LASSO WHICH HAS HITHERTO NEVER BEFORE FAILED WONDER WOMAN...

HA! HA! HA! FOOLISH WONDER WOMAN! YOU ARE POWERLESS AGAINST ME!

SUFFERING SAPPHO! THAT CRYSTAL CREATURE RIPPED MY LASSO FROM ME!

DESPERATELY, WONDER WOMAN HURLS HER TIARA AT THE VILLAIN, MADE OF AMAZONIUM, HARDEST METAL KNOWN...

IF I COULD ONLY STUN HIM LONG ENOUGH TO WEAKEN HIS WILL POWER-- SO THE ROCKET CAN CONTINUE ON ITS TRIP TO OUTER SPACE!

ONCE AGAIN THE SHEER WILL POWER OF THE SUPER CRYSTAL CREATURE DIVERTS THE AMAZON'S DESPERATE CAST...

YOU FAILED AGAIN, WONDER WOMAN! HA! HA! HA!

OF HER LAST TWO WEAPONS WONDER WOMAN GRIMLY DIVESTS HERSELF...

HERA HELP MY AIM--SO ONE OF MY BRACELETS CAN DAZE THIS VILLAIN LONG ENOUGH FOR THE ROCKET TO RESUME ITS FLIGHT AND EXPLODE HARMLESSLY IN SPACE!

AND A THIRD TIME, THE UNIQUE VILLAIN LAUGHS AT THE NOW COMPLETELY DISARMED AMAZON...

I WILL SHOW YOU HOW HELP-LESS YOU ARE AGAINST ME BY CAPTURING YOU WITHOUT USING MY SUPER-WILL POWER! HA! HA!

CRACK!

10

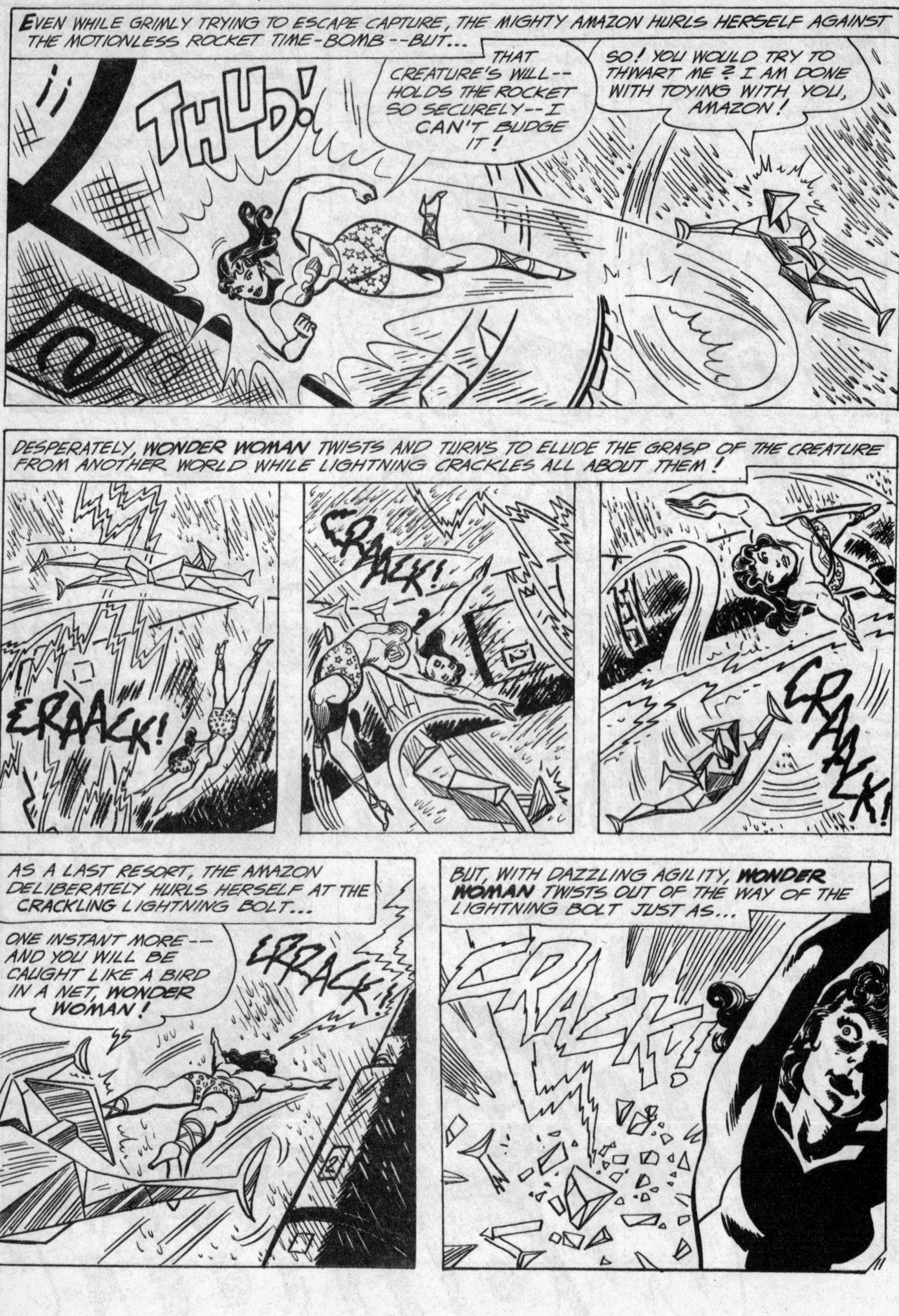
EVEN WHILE GRIMLY TRYING TO ESCAPE CAPTURE, THE MIGHTY AMAZON HURLS HERSELF AGAINST THE MOTIONLESS ROCKET TIME-BOMB--BUT...
THUD!
THAT CREATURE'S WILL--HOLDS THE ROCKET SO SECURELY--I CAN'T BUDGE IT!
SO! YOU WOULD TRY TO THWART ME? I AM DONE WITH TOYING WITH YOU, AMAZON!
DESPERATELY, WONDER WOMAN TWISTS AND TURNS TO ELUDE THE GRASP OF THE CREATURE FROM ANOTHER WORLD WHILE LIGHTNING CRACKLES ALL ABOUT THEM!
ERAACK!
CRAACK!
CRAAACK!
AS A LAST RESORT, THE AMAZON DELIBERATELY HURLS HERSELF AT THE CRACKLING LIGHTNING BOLT...
ONE INSTANT MORE--AND YOU WILL BE CAUGHT LIKE A BIRD IN A NET, WONDER WOMAN!
ERRACK!
BUT, WITH DAZZLING AGILITY, WONDER WOMAN TWISTS OUT OF THE WAY OF THE LIGHTNING BOLT JUST AS...
CRACK!

WITH THE CRYSTAL VILLAIN'S WILL POWER SHATTERED, AND HIS HOLD ON THE ROCKET'S FLIGHT BROKEN...

PRAY HERA-- THE ROCKET WILL ATTAIN ENOUGH DISTANCE--

FROM THE EARTH--

--TO EXPLODE HARMLESSLY IN SPACE!

WHOOSH

UNTIL...

WHROOOOOOOOM!

YOU DID IT AGAIN, ANGEL--SAVED THE EARTH!

DOWN TO THE GROUND WONDER WOMAN DROPS, AND WITH THE OTHERS RE- COVERING FROM HER NUMBING RAY, WAITS TENSELY...

The End

12

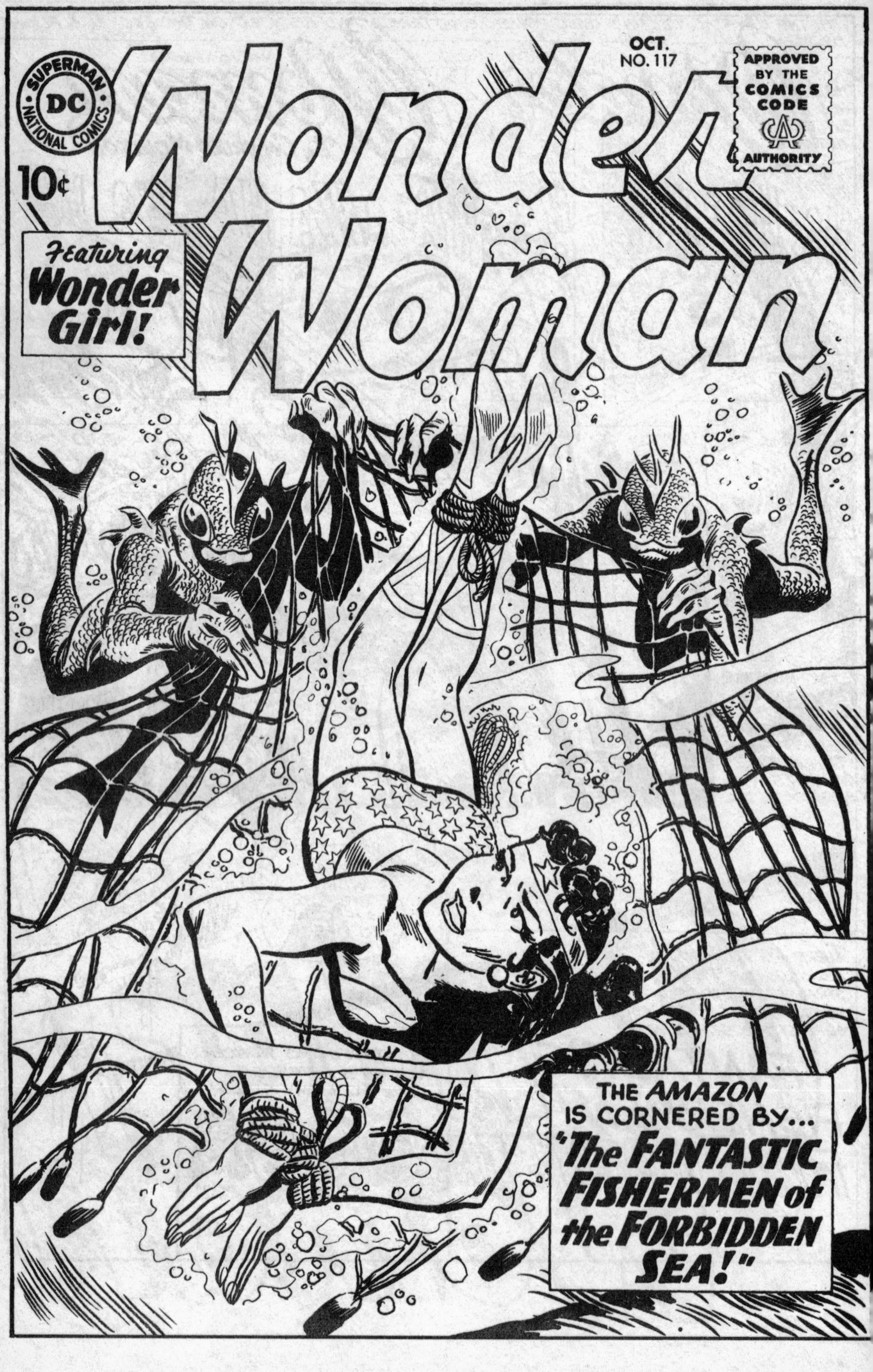
SUPERMAN DC NATIONAL COMICS
10¢
OCT.
NO. 117
APPROVED BY THE COMICS CODE AUTHORITY
Wonder Woman
Featuring Wonder Girl!
THE AMAZON IS CORNERED BY...
"The FANTASTIC FISHERMEN of the FORBIDDEN SEA!"

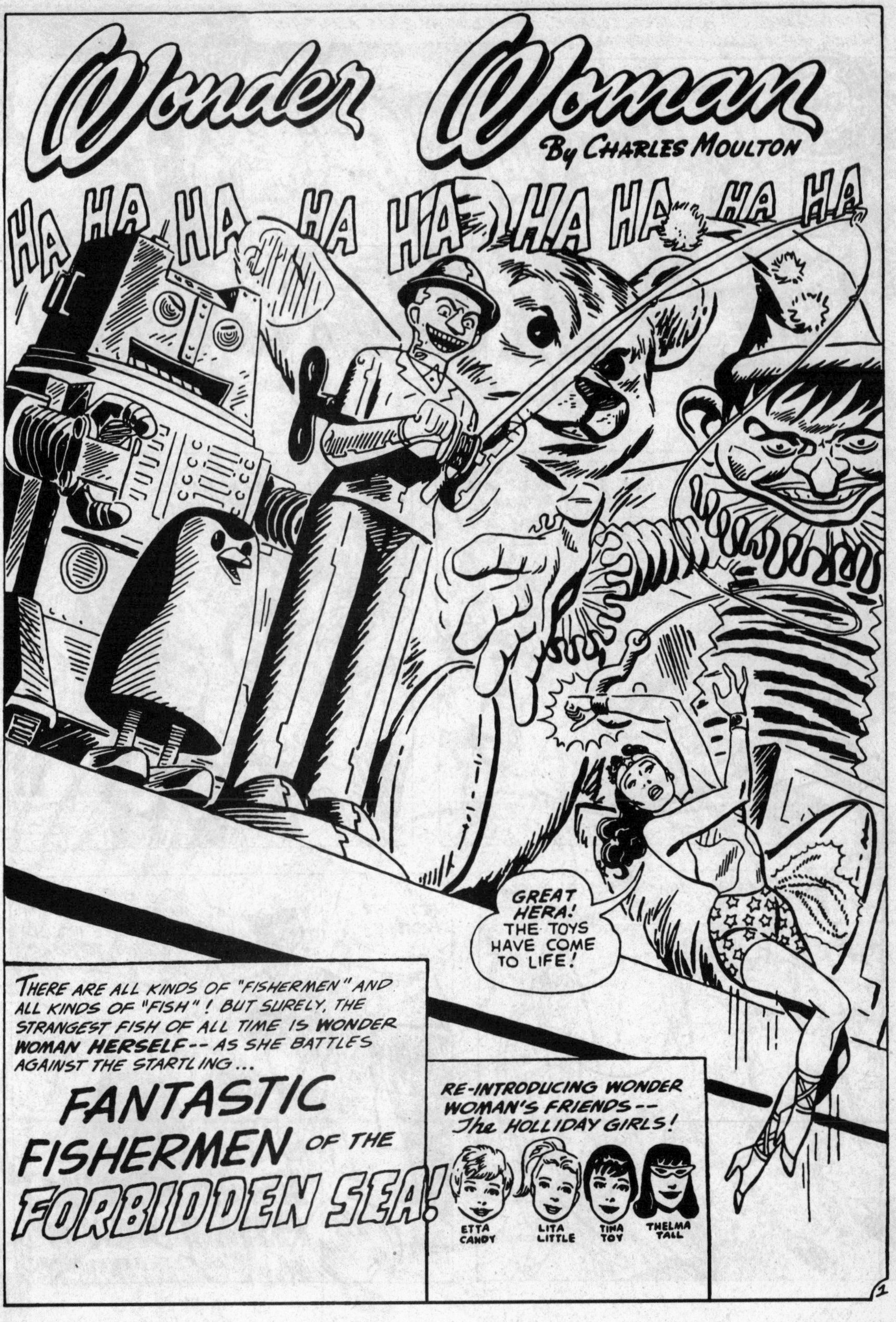
Wonder Woman
By Charles Moulton
HA HA HA HA HA HA HA HA HA HA HA
GREAT HERA! THE TOYS HAVE COME TO LIFE!
THERE ARE ALL KINDS OF "FISHERMEN" AND ALL KINDS OF "FISH"! BUT SURELY, THE STRANGEST FISH OF ALL TIME IS WONDER WOMAN HERSELF-- AS SHE BATTLES AGAINST THE STARTLING...
FANTASTIC FISHERMEN OF THE FORBIDDEN SEA!
RE-INTRODUCING WONDER WOMAN'S FRIENDS-- The HOLLIDAY GIRLS!
ETTA CANDY
LITA LITTLE
TINA TOY
THELMA TALL
1

ON THE CAMPUS OF HOLLIDAY COLLEGE, THE HOLLIDAY GIRLS AWAIT THE ARRIVAL OF A FAMOUS STORY TELLER...

I JUST LOVE CANDY SURE AS MY NAME IS *ETTA CANDY!*

I JUST LOVE TOYS! AND *TOY* IS MY SECOND NAME!

I'M AS *LITTLE* AS MY *NAME!* I WISH I WAS *TALLER.*

MY NAME'S *TALL!* BUT I WISH I WAS *LITTLE..!*

DOESN'T THAT LOOK LIKE A *REAL* FLYING SAUCER, GIRLS?

YOU COULDN'T FOOL *ME,* TINA! *Woo! Woo!*

WHoooSH!

WHEN ARE YOU GOING TO STOP EATING CANDY, ETTA?

WHEN MY SWEET TOOTH TURNS *SOUR! Woo! Woo!*

HA! HA!

JUST THEN, A FAMOUS TRANSPARENT PLANE GLIDES TOWARDS THE CAMPUS...

HERE SHE IS AT LAST!

HI, WONDER WOMAN!

HOLA, GIRLS! NOW, WHAT AMAZON ADVENTURE WOULD YOU LIKE TO HEAR ABOUT FOR THIS STORY HOUR?

HOW ABOUT A STORY ABOUT CANDY?

I'D LIKE ONE ABOUT TOYS!

DO YOU KNOW ONE ABOUT A **SHORT** GIRL WHO GREW **TALLER?**

OR ABOUT A TALL GIRL WHO GREW **SHORTER?**

I WAS THINKING OF ONE ABOUT "FISHING"!

WHAT'S SO INTERESTING ABOUT "FISHING", **WONDER WOMAN?** UNLESS IT'S ABOUT **CANDY** FISH?

SUPPOSE I TELL YOU ONE STORY ABOUT "FISHING" AND IF YOU DON'T LIKE IT--I'LL STOP AND TELL YOU ONE ABOUT SOMETHING ELSE!

AGREED!

"IT ALL STARTED ON **PARADISE ISLAND,** SECRET HOME OF THE AMAZONS; I WAS IN THE ROYAL CHAMBERS WITH MY MOTHER, QUEEN HIPPOLYTA, WHEN..."

NOBLE QUEEN! AMAZON PATROL NO. 11 IS MISSING!

MERCIFUL MINERVA!

"MY MOTHER IMMEDIATELY COMMUNICATED WITH OUR CONTROL TOWER BY HER WRIST TV TUNER..."

PATROL NO. 11's LAST REPORT CAME FROM THE VICINITY OF THE **FORBIDDEN SEA!**

I WILL SEARCH FOR PATROL NO. 11, MOTHER!

SPOKEN LIKE AN AMAZON, DAUGHTER! HERA KEEP YOU SAFE!

3

"AND AS I HURTLED TOWARDS THE SEA AROUND PARADISE ISLAND..."

FATHER NEPTUNE SMILES ON MY MISSION!

A PORPOISE!

"I FLATTENED MY HANDS TO BRAKE MY SPEED, AND LANDED LIGHTLY ON THE PORPOISE!"

HE HAS SENT ME "TRANSPORTATION"!

"THE FRISKY PORPOISE OBEYED MY TOUCH LIKE A SEA-GOING STEED..."

SPLASH!

SPLASH!

SPLASH!

"SUDDENLY, THE PORPOISE STOPPED AS IF IT WERE CONFRONTED BY AN INVISIBLE, MENACING WALL.."

THE BOUNDARY OF THE FORBIDDEN SEA! EVEN FISH DARE GO NO FURTHER!

"SUDDENLY, WITHOUT WARNING-- I WAS SEIZED BY A POWERFUL TIDE!"

HERA HELP ME-- ESCAPE THE GRIP-- OF THIS--TIDE!... IT...IT...HAS... OVERPOWERING CHEMICALS IN IT... I...I'M...LOSING... CON...!

"WHEN I AWOKE..."

SHADES OF PLUTO! I--I'M BOUND-- HAND AND FOOT!

"AND THEN I SAW..."

THESE MUST BE-- THE FANTASTIC FISHERMEN OF THE FORBIDDEN SEA!

"AT THE SIDE WERE FAMILIAR FIGURES..."

MY SISTER AMAZONS OF PATROL 11-- ALSO TAKEN PRISONER! PROBABLY BY EXACTLY THE SAME METHOD!

"VERSED IN ALL LANGUAGES, THE LEADER OF THE FANTASTIC FISHERMEN ISSUED A STRANGE CHALLENGE!...

WE KNEW THE DIS- APPEARANCE OF YOUR SISTER AMAZONS WOULD BRING YOU TO THE RESCUE, WONDER WOMAN! IT IS YOU WE WISH TO FISH FOR! ESCAPE US-- AND ALL OF YOU ARE FREE! IF YOU ARE CAUGHT--THE DOOM OF ALL IS SEALED!

"I COULD HAVE BUT ONE ANSWER! USING THE WRIGGLING MOTION OF AN EEL--I DESPERATELY FOUGHT TO KEEP OUT OF THE NET OF THE FANTASTIC FISHERMEN OF THE FORBIDDEN SEA!"

IT IS ONLY A MATTER OF TIME UNTIL THEY CATCH UP WITH ME! UNLESS--?

5

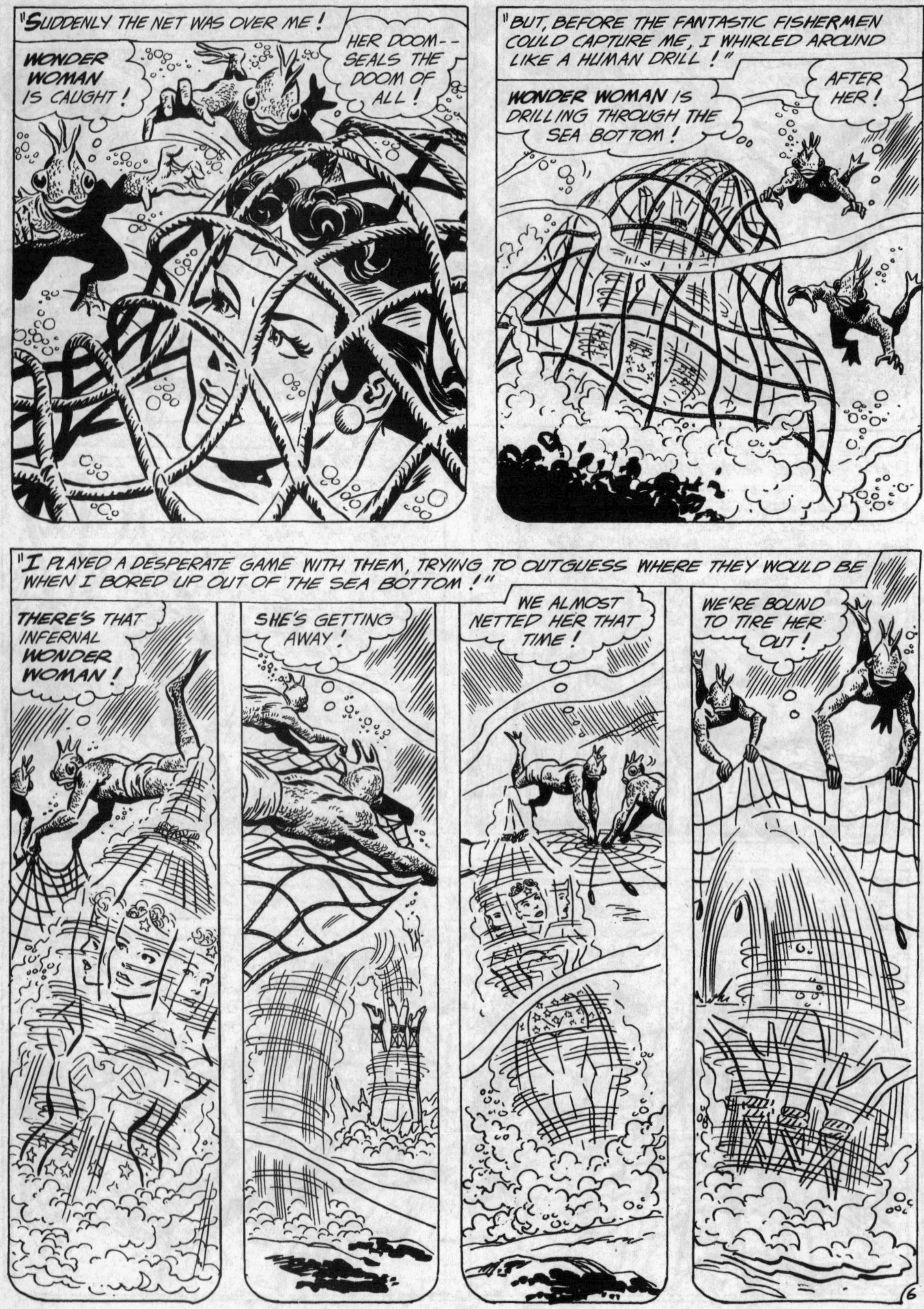
"SUDDENLY THE NET WAS OVER ME!
WONDER WOMAN IS CAUGHT!
HER DOOM-- SEALS THE DOOM OF ALL!
"BUT, BEFORE THE FANTASTIC FISHERMEN COULD CAPTURE ME, I WHIRLED AROUND LIKE A HUMAN DRILL!"
WONDER WOMAN IS DRILLING THROUGH THE SEA BOTTOM!
AFTER HER!
"I PLAYED A DESPERATE GAME WITH THEM, TRYING TO OUTGUESS WHERE THEY WOULD BE WHEN I BORED UP OUT OF THE SEA BOTTOM!"
THERE'S THAT INFERNAL WONDER WOMAN!
SHE'S GETTING AWAY!
WE ALMOST NETTED HER THAT TIME!
WE'RE BOUND TO TIRE HER OUT!
6

"WHEN I HAD LED THEM AS FAR FROM THE CAPTIVE AMAZONS AS I COULD..."

IT'S WONDER WOMAN!

"CLENCHING THE END OF THE ROPE WHICH TIED ALL THE CAPTIVES TOGETHER, I STARTED OFF BACKWARDS..."

WONDER WOMAN'S ESCAPING!

"BEFORE THE FANTASTIC FISHERMEN OF THE FORBIDDEN SEA COULD RECOVER FROM THEIR SURPRISE I HAD TOWED MY SISTER AMAZONS TO THE SAFETY OF OUR OWN WATERS!"

HOLA, DIANA! YOU DID WELL! AND OUR FORCE FIELD WILL PUT UP A WALL TO STOP THE FANTASTIC FISHERMEN FROM FURTHER PURSUIT!

AS WONDER WOMAN FINISHES HER TALE...

Woo! Woo! THAT STORY WAS SO EXCITING, I FORGOT TO EAT CANDY!

HAVE YOU ANOTHER STRANGE TALE OF FISHING, WONDER WOMAN?

MAYBE, ABOUT A TOY LIKE MY MINIATURE FLYING SAUCER?

NOT EXACTLY, TINA! LET'S SEE WHAT YOU THINK? IT ALL STARTED WHEN...

WHOOOSH!

"I WAS SHOPPING FOR PRESENTS IN THE TOY DEPARTMENT OF A STORE NEAR CLOSING TIME ONE DAY WHEN..."

ZZZZZZZZZZZZZZZ!

STRANGE--I SUDDENLY FEEL... SO... SLEEPY...!

"SUDDENLY, TO MY HORROR, I DISCOVERED..."

SHADES OF PLUTO-- I--I'M SHRINKING!

RAYS FROM THAT--THAT ELECTRONIC BRAIN-- ARE CAUSING THIS!

MERCIFUL MINERVA! I'VE BEEN REDUCED-- TO THE SIZE--OF A TOY!

"AND THEN, I HEARD THE ELECTRONIC BRAIN ROBOT LAUGH..."

AN EVIL INVENTOR BUILT ME-- BEFORE HE WAS JAILED! NO ONE KNOWS OF THE POWERS HE INSTALLED IN ME! ONE, TO SHRINK HUMANS! ANOTHER-- TO ANIMATE TOYS! HO! HO!

"THE NEXT MOMENT, I FELT A HOOK SEIZE MY BRACELET AND..."

YOU ALWAYS WANTED TO FISH FOR A HUMAN, FISHERMAN! HERE IS ONE!

SHADES OF PLUTO! THIS EVIL ELECTRONIC BRAIN ROBOT HAS ANIMATED THE TOY FISHERMAN! AND, I'M HIS "FISH"!

Ho! Ho! Ho!

PART TWO FANTASTIC FISHERMEN of the FORBIDDEN SEA!

"IT WAS LIKE A NIGHTMARE, AS THE ANIMATED TOY FISHERMAN REELED ME IN... IN PROBABLY THE STRANGEST 'FISHING' OF ALL TIME!"

HOW CAN I ESCAPE HIM?

I'M OFF BALANCE!

WHAT WILL MY FATE BE IF HE DOES NET ME?

"AS I REACHED THE COUNTER ON WHICH THE TOY FISHERMAN STOOD, I HURLED MYSELF AWAY FROM HIM AS FAR AS I COULD..."

DO YOU ANY GOOD, EARTHLING! THIS REEL IS MAGNETIC --TO HOLD ANY OBJECT FAST!

HO! HO!

"BUT MY FRANTIC BACKWARDS LEAP HAD PLACED ME NEAR TO..."

A TOY!

"IT WAS ALREADY LOADED...DESPERATELY I AIMED IT...FIRED..."

THERE'S ONLY ONE FORCE BEHIND ALL OF THIS ANIMATION --THE ROBOT!

BAM!

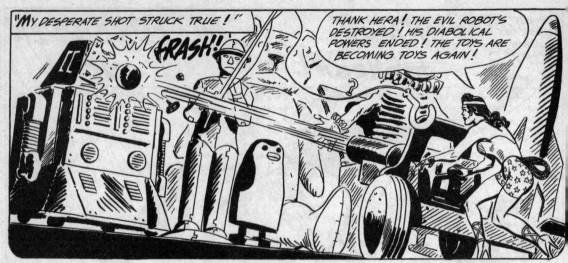

"MY DESPERATE SHOT STRUCK TRUE!"

CRASH!

THANK HERA! THE EVIL ROBOT'S DESTROYED! HIS DIABOLICAL POWERS ENDED! THE TOYS ARE BECOMING TOYS AGAIN!

"AND I MYSELF, RETURNING TO MY NORMAL SIZE, EVADED STILL ANOTHER "FISHERMAN"!

I HOPE THAT'S THE LAST TIME ANYONE EVER "FISHES" FOR ME!

AS WONDER WOMAN FINISHED HER SECOND TALE...

NOTHING EXCITING LIKE THAT COULD EVER HAPPEN TO US!

ANYWAY, HERE'S ONE TOY THAT WILL ALWAYS REMAIN A MINIATURE FLYING SAUCER!

WHOOSH!

BUT, AS THE LITTLE GROUP STARES AT THE TOY FLYING SAUCER, IT SEEMS TO GROW LARGER AND LARGER, UNTIL...

MMZZZZZZZZZZZZZ

THUNDERBOLTS OF JOVE!

ZZZZ

IT'S A REAL FLYING SAUCER!

ZZZZ

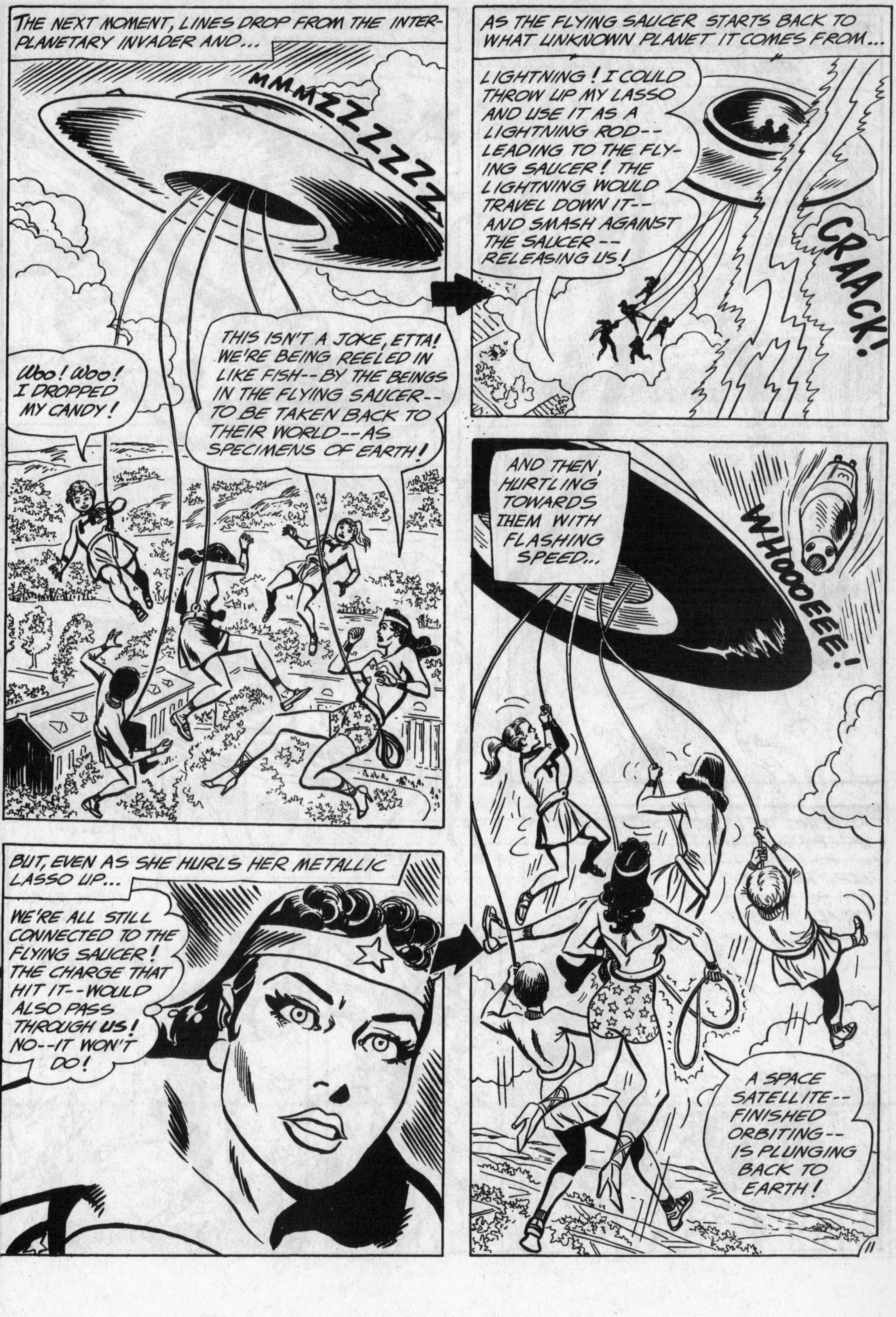
THE NEXT MOMENT, LINES DROP FROM THE INTER-PLANETARY INVADER AND...
MMMZZZZZZZ
WOO! WOO! I DROPPED MY CANDY!
THIS ISN'T A JOKE, ETTA! WE'RE BEING REELED IN LIKE FISH--BY THE BEINGS IN THE FLYING SAUCER--TO BE TAKEN BACK TO THEIR WORLD--AS SPECIMENS OF EARTH!
AS THE FLYING SAUCER STARTS BACK TO WHAT UNKNOWN PLANET IT COMES FROM...
LIGHTNING! I COULD THROW UP MY LASSO AND USE IT AS A LIGHTNING ROD--LEADING TO THE FLY-ING SAUCER! THE LIGHTNING WOULD TRAVEL DOWN IT--AND SMASH AGAINST THE SAUCER--RELEASING US!
CRAACK!
BUT, EVEN AS SHE HURLS HER METALLIC LASSO UP...
WE'RE ALL STILL CONNECTED TO THE FLYING SAUCER! THE CHARGE THAT HIT IT--WOULD ALSO PASS THROUGH US! NO--IT WON'T DO!
AND THEN, HURTLING TOWARDS THEM WITH FLASHING SPEED...
WHOOOOEEE!
A SPACE SATELLITE--FINISHED ORBITING--IS PLUNGING BACK TO EARTH!
11

THE FLYING SAUCER EASILY FLASHES OUT OF THE WAY OF THE ONCOMING FALLING SPACE SATELLITE...

THERE GOES OUR CHANCE OF GETTING FREE FROM THESE INTERPLANETARY FISHERMEN-- BY THE IMPACT OF THIS SATELLITE HITTING THE SAUCER!

WHOOEEE!

BUT, THE NEXT INSTANT, WONDER WOMAN HURLS HER AMAZON LASSO AT THE HUGE FALLING OBJECT...

THERE'S STILL A CHANCE TO FREE US ALL!

THE MIGHTY AMAZON SENDS THE SATELLITE HURTLING INTO THE FLYING SAUCER WITH SUCH TREMENDOUS FORCE THAT...

CRACK!

WE'RE FREE!

BUT-- A LONG WAY FROM CANDY!

WHIRLING THE LASSOED SATELLITE LIKE A MISSILE IN A CATAPULT...

HERA HELP MY AIM BE TRUE-- OR ALL IS LOST!

12

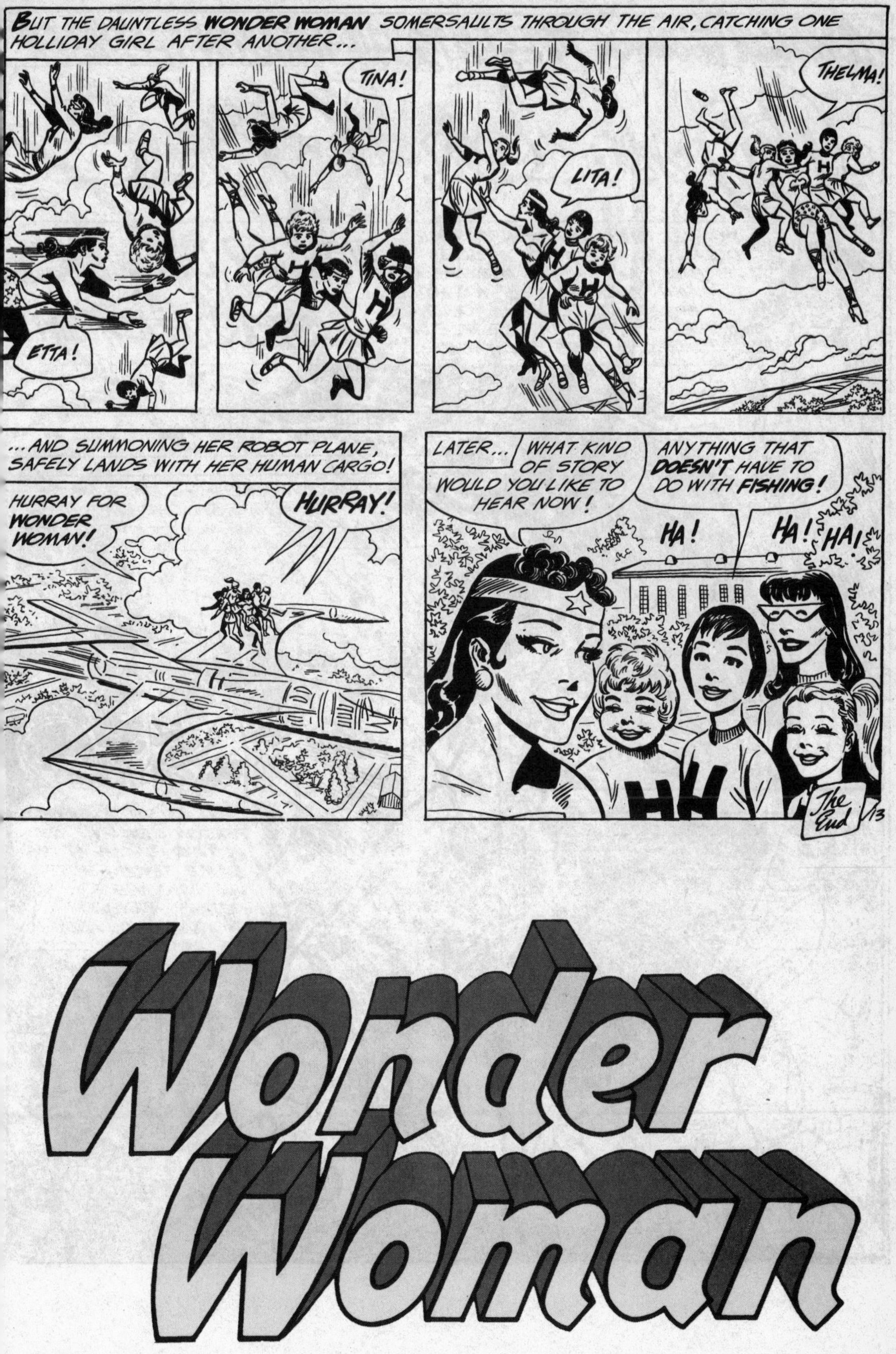
BUT THE DAUNTLESS WONDER WOMAN SOMERSAULTS THROUGH THE AIR, CATCHING ONE HOLLIDAY GIRL AFTER ANOTHER...
ETTA!
TINA!
LITA!
THELMA!
...AND SUMMONING HER ROBOT PLANE, SAFELY LANDS WITH HER HUMAN CARGO!
HURRAY FOR WONDER WOMAN!
HURRAY!
LATER...
WHAT KIND OF STORY WOULD YOU LIKE TO HEAR NOW!
ANYTHING THAT DOESN'T HAVE TO DO WITH FISHING!
HA!
HA!
HA!
The End
13

Wonder Woman

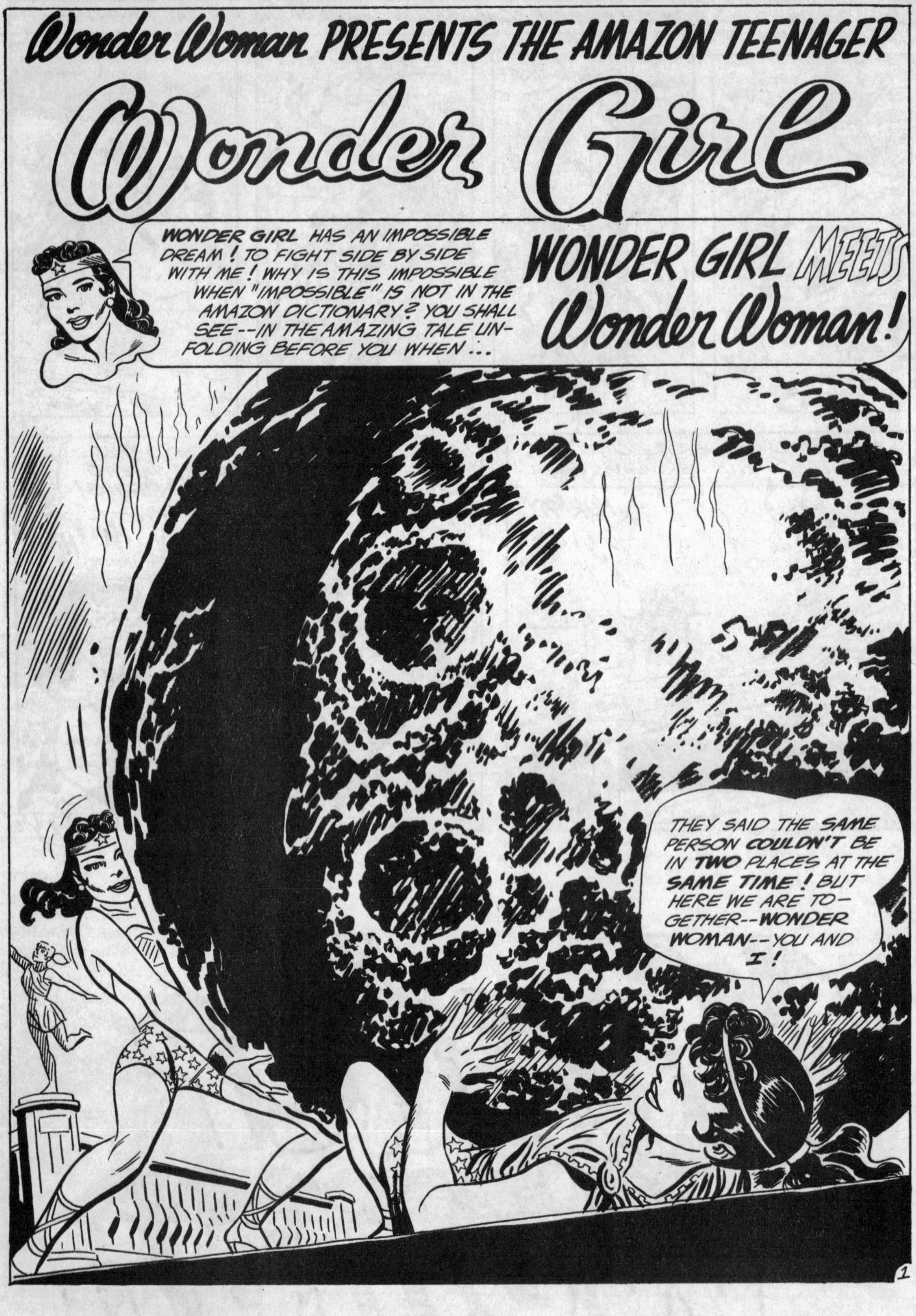
Wonder Woman PRESENTS THE AMAZON TEENAGER
Wonder Girl
WONDER GIRL HAS AN IMPOSSIBLE DREAM! TO FIGHT SIDE BY SIDE WITH ME! WHY IS THIS IMPOSSIBLE WHEN "IMPOSSIBLE" IS NOT IN THE AMAZON DICTIONARY? YOU SHALL SEE--IN THE AMAZING TALE UNFOLDING BEFORE YOU WHEN...
WONDER GIRL MEETS Wonder Woman!
THEY SAID THE SAME PERSON COULDN'T BE IN TWO PLACES AT THE SAME TIME! BUT HERE WE ARE TOGETHER--WONDER WOMAN--YOU AND I!
1

AT THE UNIQUE TIME AND SPACE THEATER ON *PARADISE ISLAND*...

WONDER GIRL INDULGES IN THE STARTLING EXPERIENCE OF WATCHING HERSELF IN THE FUTURE...

AS *WONDER WOMAN,* THE CELEBRATED AMAZON!

AT THE AMAZON EXPERIMENTAL LAB LATER, THE AMAZON TEENAGER SPEAKS TO HER MOTHER, QUEEN HIPPOLYTA...

MOTHER--I'D GIVE ANYTHING TO BATTLE INJUSTICE ALONGSIDE WONDER WOMAN!

YOU'VE ASKED ME THAT A THOUSAND TIMES, DIANA! AND FOR THE THOUSANDTH TIME I HAVE TO SAY: IT'S IMPOSSIBLE FOR ANYONE TO BE IN *TWO* PLACES AT EXACTLY THE *SAME* TIME!

BUT, THE WISTFUL AMAZON MAIDEN CAN'T GIVE UP HER DREAM...

THERE MUST BE SOME WAY!... AND WHAT A SENSATION TO SEE *WONDER GIRL* AND *WONDER WOMAN* TOGETHER!

TO THE AMAZON SCIENTISTS, THE TEENAGE PRINCESS MAKES A STARTLING REQUEST...

I'D LIKE YOU TO BUILD ME A TIME-AND-SPACE MACHINE WITH SCREEN--SMALL ENOUGH TO FIT ON MY WRIST! IS IT POSSIBLE?

TO AMAZON SCIENTISTS-- NOTHING IS IMPOSSIBLE!

AS *WONDER GIRL* WATCHES THE "CRASH" PROGRAM...

IF NOTHING IS IMPOSSIBLE, THEN I'LL REALIZE MY WISH OF BATTLING CRIME AND INJUSTICE SIDE BY SIDE WITH *WONDER WOMAN!*

FINALLY, THE AMAZING, MINIATURE TIME-AND-SPACE PROJECTOR IS COMPLETED...

I'LL "DIAL" THE FUTURE UNTIL I SEE MY-SELF AS *WONDER WOMAN*--DOING SOMETHING SENSATIONAL--THEN I'LL "PROJECT" MYSELF TO THE SAME TIME AND SPACE AND JOIN MYSELF!

BZZT!

WONDER GIRL "DIALS" THE FUTURE UNTIL SHE SEES HERSELF AS *WONDER WOMAN* APPEAR ON THE MINIATURE SCREEN...

WONDER WOMAN'S SURROUNDED BY GUNMEN!

WONDER GIRL "DIALS" HERSELF...

HERA HAS BEEN KINDER TO ME THAN I THOUGHT POSSIBLE!

INTO THE FUTURE...

I'LL NOT ONLY JOIN *WONDER WOMAN!*

UNTIL SHE REAPPEARS AT THE SAME PLACE SHE SAW WONDER WOMAN!

BUT ALSO HELP HER OUT OF HER PERIL!

3

BUT, EVEN AS *WONDER GIRL* APPEARS AT THE SCENE OF *WONDER WOMAN'S* DEADLY PERIL...

SHADES OF PLUTO! *WONDER WOMAN* HAS *ALREADY* OVERCOME THESE GUNMEN! AND HAS THEM READY FOR JAIL!

BUT SHE *JUST* LEFT! I SHOULD BE ABLE TO CATCH UP TO HER! SHE MUST BE OUTSIDE IN THE STREET!

OUTSIDE, *WONDER GIRL* BEHOLDS A HEART-RENDING SPECTACLE...

THAT WOMAN UP THERE HOLDING THE CHILD IS PANIC-STRICKEN! THE SMOKE IS GOING TO MAKE HER JUMP!

NO--NO! WAIT!

INSTANTLY, THE TEENAGE AMAZON HURLS A MIGHTY BREATH...

WHOOSH!

LIKE THE PRESSURE OF COMPRESSED AIR SUDDENLY RELEASED -- *WONDER GIRL'S* BREATH HURLS THE FIRE AND SMOKE BACKWARDS, AWAY FROM THE TREMBLING WOMAN...

VROOSH!

4

IN THAT SAME INSTANT, **WONDER GIRL** HURLS HERSELF UPWARDS ON A CURRENT OF AIR...

DON'T JUMP! I'LL TAKE YOU DOWN JUST THE WAY I CAME UP!

GENTLY AS A FEATHER, THE TEENAGE AMAZON DRIFTS DOWN WITH HER HUMAN CARGO...

YOU'VE SAVED OUR LIVES!

THE MOMENT SHE ALIGHTS ON THE GROUND, THE AMAZON MAIDEN RACES OFF...

WONDER WOMAN MUST BE WITHIN ARM'S REACH OF ME!

BUT SOON... THE PANTING **WONDER GIRL** REALIZES THAT...

WONDER WOMAN TRAVELS SO FAST--THE ONLY WAY I'LL BE ABLE TO FIND HER--IS BY "TUNING" IN ON HER-- WITH MY TIME-AND-SPACE PROJECTOR!

AGAIN, THE FLEET **WONDER WOMAN** APPEARS ON THE TIME-AND-SPACE SCREEN...

BY NEPTUNE'S TRIDENT! **WONDER WOMAN'S** IN REAL TROUBLE THIS TIME! SHE'S IN THE WAY OF A MISSILE BEING FIRED BY AN ENEMY SUB!

5

SWIFTLY, WONDER GIRL PROJECTS HERSELF TO WONDER WOMAN'S SIDE...

IT ISN'T MERE GUN-MEN SHE'S FACING! **WONDER WOMAN** WILL CERTAINLY NEED MY HELP **THIS** TIME!

BUT, IN THE TIME IT TAKES TO REACH THE SPACE OCCUPIED BY **WONDER WOMAN**...

AN EXPLOSION--? WH-WHAT'S HAP-HAPPENED?

WHROOM!

THUNDERBOLTS OF JOVE! WONDER WOMAN HAS ALREADY MADE THE ENEMY SUB'S ATTACK BOOMERANG ON ITSELF--AND HAS GONE ON TO OTHER MISSIONS!

OOOOM!

WHIRLED AWAY BY THE WAVES OF CON-CUSSION...

I KNOW BETTER THIS TIME--THAN TO TRY TO **CATCH UP TO WONDER WOMAN!** I'LL "TUNE" IN ON HER AND FIND OUT **EXACTLY** WHERE SHE IS--

THE TEENAGE AMAZON'S ATTENTION IS ATTRACTED HOWEVER TO...

A SKIN DIVER--WITH **RIPPED** EQUIPMENT!

6

As **WONDER GIRL** HASTENS TO THE SKIN DIVER'S SIDE...

HE'S SIGNALLING THAT **HE'S** ALL RIGHT--BUT THAT SOMEONE **ELSE** IS IN DANGER **BELOW!**

AS THE DIVER HEADS FOR THE SURFACE...

HE CAN'T STAY BELOW WITH HIS RIPPED EQUIPMENT! SO HE'S SWIMMING TO THE SURFACE FOR HELP! BUT, EVERY MOMENT COUNTS UNDERWATER WHEN DANGER STRIKES! I'LL SEE WHAT I CAN DO TO HELP!

PLUNGING EVER DEEPER, THE TEENAGE AMAZON AVOIDS...

GIANT ELECTRIC EEL!--IT CAN GIVE A NASTY SHOCK!--I'LL KEEP OUT OF ITS WAY!

AND THEN AHEAD OF HER, **WONDER GIRL** SEES A FANTASTIC SIGHT!

SHADES OF PLUTO! A HUGE CRAB OF DINOSAUR SIZE! PULLING A DIVING BELL TO ITS LAIR! THAT MUST BE WHERE THE SKIN DIVER ESCAPED FROM FOR AID-- FOR THE PEOPLE STILL TRAPPED INSIDE!

ACK FLASHES **WONDER GIRL** THROUGH THE ATER..

THERE'S ONLY ONE AY TO MAKE THAT CRAB ELEASE THE DIVING BELL!

ZZZZZZZ!

SHOCK WAVES WHICH WOULD PARALYZE THE ORDINARY HUMAN SHAKE THE AMAZON TEENAGER AS SHE SEIZES HOLD OF THE GIANT ELECTRICAL EEL!

HERA-HELP-- ME--HOLD-- ON!

ZZZZT!

KE A GREAT ELECTRICAL FLAIL, **WONDER GIRL** SLAMS THE HUGE EEL AGAINST THE STARTLED IGHTMARISH CRAB, WHICH.

HURRAY! WE'RE FREE! THANKS TO THAT GIRL OUT- SIDE!

SIDE THE BELL...PUZZLED EYES STARE ..

E'S SAVED OUR ES--AND WE ON'T EVEN OW WHO HE IS!

WONDER WHY SHE ISN'T STAYING AROUND EVEN FOR OUR THANKS!

THE ANSWER IS SIMPLE...

I'VE LOST **WONDER WOMAN** AGAIN!

8

AGAIN THE WEARY *WONDER GIRL* "TUNES" IN ON *WONDER WOMAN*...

WONDER WOMAN'S JUDGING A BATHING BEAUTY CONTEST! SHE'S NOT IN PERIL! ALL IS PERFECT!

INSTANTLY, SHE "PROJECTS" HERSELF...

THERE'S NOTHING TO PREVENT ME FROM MEETING HER--

THIS TIME!

BUT, IN THE TIME IT TAKES *WONDER GIRL* TO REACH THE TIME AND PLACE OCCUPIED BY THE TIRELESS *WONDER WOMAN*...

KLUNNG!

EEEE-

SHE'S ON HER WAY ALREADY TO HER NEXT MISSION! AND...SUFFERING SAPPHO!--THAT ROLLER COASTER IS PLUNGING OFF THE TRACKS!

INSTANTLY THE POWERFUL AMAZON TEENAGER HURLS HERSELF ON AN UPDRAFT AND AS SHE LOWERS THE RUNAWAY ROLLER COASTER BACK ON ITS RAILS...

WE'VE BEEN SAVED BY THAT GIRL!

SHE LOOKS LIKE *WONDER WOMAN*!

WHO IS SHE?

WHO ARE YOU?

WONDER GIRL! WONDER WOMAN AS A GIRL -- OF COURSE!

IMPOSSIBLE! HA! HA! HA!

WE JUST SAW WONDER WOMAN!

ONE PERSON CANNOT BE IN TWO PLACES AT **ONCE!**

EVEN WITH THE LAUGHTER OF THE PEOPLE RINGING IN HER EARS, THE TIRED **WONDER GIRL** AGAIN "TUNES" IN ON THE ELUSIVE WONDER WOMAN...

PRAISE HERA! EVEN WONDER WOMAN HAS TO REST ONCE IN A WHILE! SHE'S SUNNING HERSELF ON THE SUN DECK BACK AT PARADISE ISLAND!

BUT, AS **WONDER GIRL** REASSEMBLES ON THE **PARADISE ISLAND** SUN DECK, SHE SEES NOTHING BUT A GIGANTIC SHAPE HURTLING AT HER, WHICH SHUTS OUT EVERYTHING ELSE!...

WHOOH!

METEOR--!! IF I LET IT GO THROUGH THE ROOF -- IT WILL PLUMMET INTO ALL THE AMAZONS INSIDE THE BUILDING!

EAGERLY, THE AMAZON TEEN-AGER "PROJECTS" HERSELF ACROSS TIME AND SPACE...

THE NEXT MOMENT-- WONDER WOMAN AND I WILL BE TOGETHER!

10

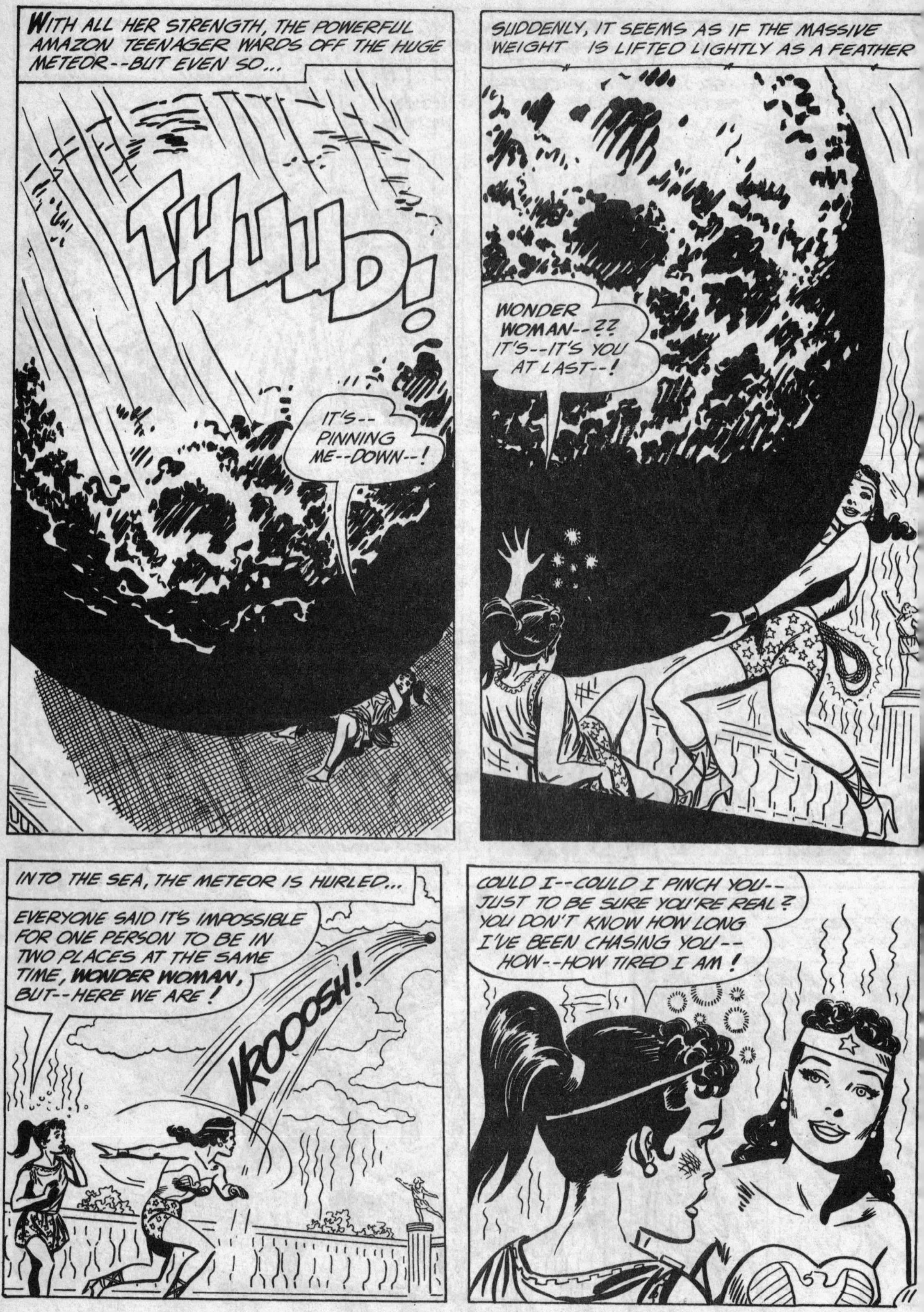
WITH ALL HER STRENGTH, THE POWERFUL AMAZON TEENAGER WARDS OFF THE HUGE METEOR--BUT EVEN SO...
THUD!
IT'S-- PINNING ME--DOWN--!
SUDDENLY, IT SEEMS AS IF THE MASSIVE WEIGHT IS LIFTED LIGHTLY AS A FEATHER
WONDER WOMAN--?? IT'S--IT'S YOU AT LAST--!
INTO THE SEA, THE METEOR IS HURLED...
EVERYONE SAID IT'S IMPOSSIBLE FOR ONE PERSON TO BE IN TWO PLACES AT THE SAME TIME, WONDER WOMAN, BUT--HERE WE ARE!
VROOOSH!
COULD I--COULD I PINCH YOU-- JUST TO BE SURE YOU'RE REAL? YOU DON'T KNOW HOW LONG I'VE BEEN CHASING YOU-- HOW--HOW TIRED I AM!

TREMBLING WITH EXCITEMENT, *WONDER GIRL* REACHES OUT AND...

I FEEL YOU--I FEEL YOU! THIS IS THE PROOF--THE PROOF THAT ONE PERSON COULD BE IN TWO PLACES AT ONCE!

BUT, THE NEXT MOMENT...

MOTHER--??!! IT--IT'S YOU--NOT *WONDER WOMAN*??

YOU MUST HAVE BEEN DAZED FROM THE IMPACT OF CATCHING THAT METEOR, DEAR, AND IMAGINED YOU SAW *WONDER WOMAN* IN PLACE OF ME!

I HOPE YOU'VE REALIZED BY THIS TIME THAT YOU CAN'T EVER MEET *WONDER WOMAN* FACE TO FACE! DIANA -- SO FAR, IT'S A SCIENTIFIC IMPOSSIBILITY!

I CAN DREAM, CAN'T I? AND MAYBE SOME-DAY, SOMEWHERE, SOMEHOW, I WILL!

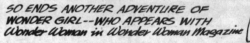

SO ENDS ANOTHER ADVENTURE OF *WONDER GIRL*--WHO APPEARS WITH *Wonder Woman in Wonder Woman Magazine*

The End

SHOWCASE
PRESENTS

OVER 500 PAGES OF DC'S CLASSIC HEROES AND STORIES PRESENTED IN EACH VOLUME!

**GREEN LANTERN
VOL. 1**

**SUPERMAN
VOL. 1**

**SUPERMAN
VOL. 2**

**SUPERMAN FAMILY
VOL. 1**

**JONAH HEX
VOL. 1**

**METAMORPHO
VOL. 1**

SEARCH THE GRAPHIC NOVELS SECTION OF
www.DCCOMICS.com
FOR ART AND INFORMATION ON ALL OF OUR BOOKS